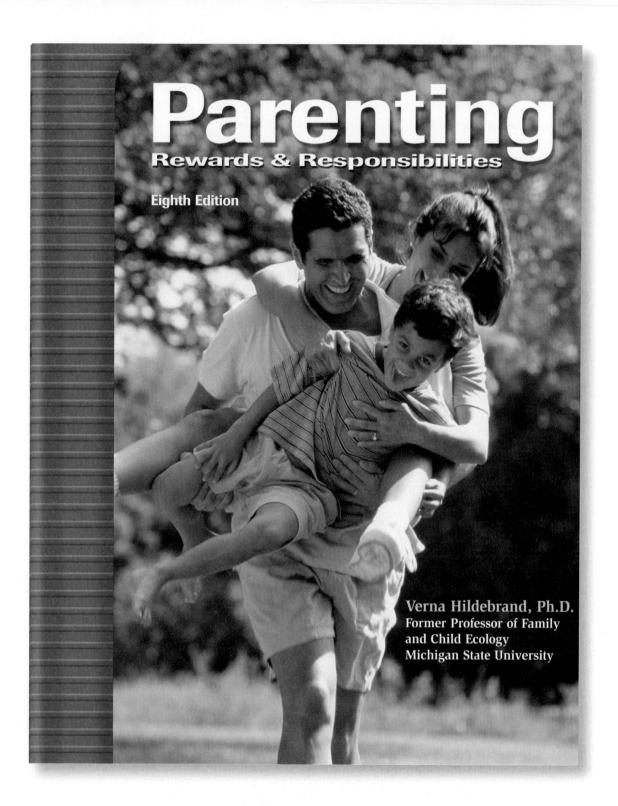

Parenting
Rewards & Responsibilities

Eighth Edition

Verna Hildebrand, Ph.D.
**Former Professor of Family
and Child Ecology
Michigan State University**

Glencoe

New York, New York   Columbus, Ohio   Chicago, Illinois   Peoria, Illinois   Woodland Hills, California

Safety Notice

The reader is expressly advised to consider and use all safety precautions described in this textbook or that might also be indicated by undertaking the activities described herein. In addition, common sense should be exercised to help avoid all potential hazards and, in particular, to take relevant safety precautions concerning any known or likely hazards involved in using the procedures described in *Parenting: Rewards & Responsibilities*.

Publisher and Author assume no responsibility for the activities of the reader or for the subject matter experts who prepared this book. Publisher and Author make no representation or warranties of any kind, including but not limited to the warranties of fitness for particular purpose or merchantability, nor for any implied warranties related thereto, or otherwise. Publisher and Author will not be liable for damages of any type, including any consequential, special or exemplary damages resulting, in whole or in part, from reader's use or reliance upon the information, instructions, warnings or other matter contained in this textbook.

Brand Name Disclaimer

Glencoe/McGraw-Hill does not necessarily recommend or endorse any particular company or brand name product that may be discussed or pictured in this textbook. Brand name products are used because they are readily available, they are likely to be known to the reader, and their use may aid in the understanding of the text. The publisher recognizes that other brand name or generic products may be substituted and work as well as or better than those featured in the text.

The McGraw-Hill Companies

Send all inquiries to:
Glencoe/McGraw-Hill
3008 W. Willow Knolls Drive
Peoria, Illinois 61614-1083

13-digit ISBN 978-0-07-869057-0
10-digit ISBN 0-07-869057-9

Printed in the United States of America

6 7 8 9 10 WVR 10

Reviewers

Technical Reviewer

Marsha Markle, M.A., M.A., Ed.S.
Former School Psychologist
Coronado Unified School District
Coronado, California

Teacher Reviewers

Lynnette R. Abbott, M.S.
FACS Department Chairperson
Oskaloosa High School
Oskaloosa, Kansas

Rosemary Bailey
FACS Instructor
Newport Middle High School
Newport, New Hampshire

Renee Becker
FACS Instructor
Bismarck High School
Bismarck, North Dakota

Beverly Card, CFCS, NBCT
FACS Teacher
Mount Vernon High School
Alexandria, Virginia

Martha Jo S. Cook
FACS Instructor
Northwest Whitfield High School
Tunnel Hill, Georgia

Laurie M. Dean
FACS Teacher
Culpeper County High School
Culpeper, Virginia

Linda L. Valentine, CFCS
Master Teacher
University Schools
Greeley, Colorado

Pamela J. Vukelic, M.S.
FACS Teacher
Bismarck High School
Bismarck, North Dakota

Contents in Brief

Unit 4　Nurturing Children

Unit 5　Guiding Children

Unit 6　Parenting Concerns

Career Guide　606

Contents

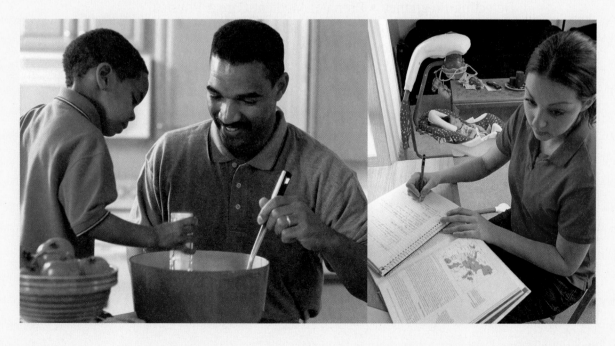

Unit 2   Becoming a Parent

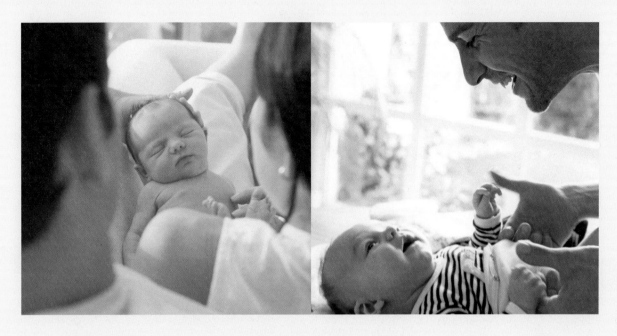

Unit 3   Caring for Children

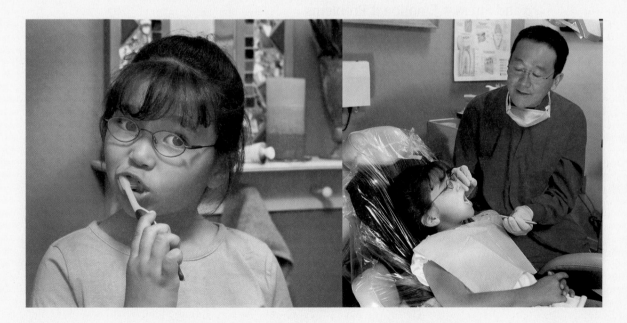

Unit 4 Nurturing Children

Unit 5   Guiding Children

Unit 6   Parenting Concerns

Career Guide   606

Career Planning • Career Preparation • Looking for a
Job • Interviewing • Success on the Job • Leaving a Job
• Lifelong Learning

THE DEVELOPING BRAIN

Brief highlights of brain development research findings are found throughout this textbook.

Modeling CHARACTER

Parenting Pointers

Health & Safety

Child & Family Services
CAREERS

Understanding Parenting

CHAPTER 1

Parenting and Families

CHAPTER OBJECTIVES

- Assess the impact of parenting on individuals, families, and society.
- Identify reasons for learning about parenting.
- Examine issues that impact parenting.
- Describe family functions, family structures, and the stages of the family life cycle.
- Analyze factors that build strong families.

PARENTING TERMS

- parenting
- biological parents
- stepparent
- adoptive parents
- foster parents
- caregivers
- values
- nuclear family
- extended family
- single-parent family
- blended family
- culture
- family life cycle

Imagine your arrival at a large family reunion. Family members from all generations are meeting and greeting each other. You walk through the mingling crowd, listening to different voices and sometimes hearing similarities. You gaze at different faces and find familiar features on some. As the smaller family groups gather for a large reunion photograph, you notice how different each person and small group is, yet all are members of one big family. You soon realize that families are as varied as the individuals who are part of them.

What Is Parenting?

How would you describe the role of a parent? Parents are all different, and none of them are perfect. Yet most parents have certain qualities in common. They love their children, protect them, and guide them. They teach their children in many ways, helping them become capable, caring adults. It can be difficult to put all that goes into parenting into words, but here's one way to sum it up: **parenting** is providing care, support, and guidance that can lead to a child's healthy development. See Fig. 1-1.

Children are born to **biological parents**, but that is not the only kind of parent. Some children gain a **stepparent** when one of their parents remarries. **Adoptive parents** accept legal responsibility for children who were not born to them, raising them as their own. **Foster parents** accept temporary responsibility for children who would not otherwise have a safe, secure home.

Besides parents, other people may serve as **caregivers**—people in parenting roles who care for and guide children. A child's caregivers might include grandparents and other relatives, older siblings, and child care workers. Neighbors, teachers, coaches, and others may also help provide care and guidance. As you can see, many different people can play parenting roles in a child's life. For this reason, all kinds of people can benefit from learning about parenting—whether or not they actually become parents.

The Impact of Parenting

Parenting is perhaps the most important job anyone can have. Its impact is far-reaching—affecting individuals, families, and society not only in the present, but for years to come.

Shaping the Future. Imagine dozens of newborn babies in a large hospital nursery. Each baby is filled with possibility and potential. Now, fast-forward fifty years. What will each baby be like?

Fig. 1-1. Parents and others who care for children play a big part in a child's healthy development. **Why is spending time with a child an important part of parenting?**

Parenting Pointers

Making a Difference

Children look up to their parents, to other adults, and to teens like you. Here are some examples of ways to make a difference in children's lives.

- **Take time to listen.** Ask questions and let children talk about their day.
- **Share recreational activities.** Shoot baskets, read a story, or play games with a child.
- **Invest time.** Invite children to go on errands and help with tasks such as washing the car or walking the dog.
- **Show affection.** Share a smile or a hug.
- **Encourage children.** Tell them when you are proud of something they said or did.
- **Watch children play a game or demonstrate a skill.** Praise them for their efforts.
- **Share interests.** For example, read newspaper articles about interesting topics to children and ask their opinions.

Many of these babies will become happy, well-adjusted adults, even in the face of personal challenges. Others may lead troubled lives. What makes the difference? There is no simple answer. In many cases, however, the outcomes may be linked to the children's early lives and the quality of the parenting they received.

Even before a baby is born, the future parents imagine what their child's life will be like. They may ask themselves questions like these:

- What do we want our child to learn?
- How can we help our child reach his or her full potential?
- What kind of adult do we want our child to become?

Raising children is not easy, and the result is seldom exactly the way parents imagined in the beginning. Yet one fact is certain: through parenting, adults can have a huge impact on their children's lives. Children who are cared for by skilled, loving parents are more likely to become happy and self-assured adults.

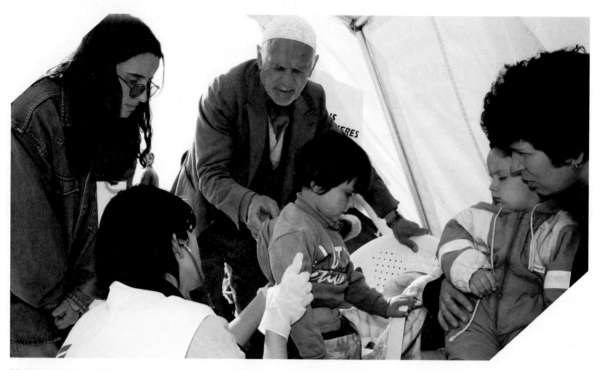

Fig. 1-2. You might choose a career that addresses a concern for children affected by global problems such as poverty, war, and famine. **How would parenting skills be useful in such a career?**

Building Strong Families. Like architects, parents design the blueprints on which their families are built. When laying the foundations for their families, parents need to commit to putting their families first. Just as strong foundations help buildings stand firm, families whose foundations are based on love, trust, and commitment are also likely to endure. In Chapter 2, you'll learn more about some of the ways in which parents can build strong families.

Building a Strong Society. One of the primary goals of parenting is to raise children who will become responsible, productive members of society. Although there are no guarantees, children who benefit from good parenting are less likely to engage in antisocial behavior such as vandalism and violence. They are more likely to make positive contributions to their community and the larger world. Strong families—led by responsible, caring parents—are the basic building blocks of a strong society.

Why Study Parenting?

There are many good reasons to study parenting. For example, you may want to:

- Gain information to help you decide whether you want to become a parent.
- Become a better parent if you do have children someday.
- Learn parenting skills that may be helpful in the career you choose. See Fig. 1-2.
- Update your skills and knowledge about parenting as new information emerges.
- Increase your understanding and appreciation of your own parents and caregivers.

Child & Family Services
CAREERS

▸ Youth Counselor

Youth counselors work with children in many different settings, such as:

- Adolescent treatment centers.
- State agencies.
- Juvenile justice or youth centers.
- Wilderness or outdoor programs for at-risk youth.

Depending on the setting, youth counselors may conduct individual or group counseling sessions or serve as part of a treatment team. They may develop case plans to address each child's problems and goals; maintain physical custody of youth; plan and supervise recreational, social, spiritual, and daily living activities for youth; and intervene in crisis situations.

"I'm a youth counselor for children ages 8 to 11. In my previous job I worked with teens in trouble, but this program is all about prevention. If we help these young kids and their families to create healthy attitudes and behaviors, we can prevent at-risk behaviors, such as teen pregnancy, later on. It feels good to be on the prevention end of the spectrum. Good listening skills are definitely a plus. Many of the kids I counsel have never had anyone who really listened to them before."

CAREER TIPS

- Take child development and parenting courses in high school.
- Volunteer as a camp counselor or mentor.
- Earn a college degree in social work, psychology, or a related field (required for some positions).
- Complete a first-aid and rescue-breathing course.
- Learn crisis intervention techniques.

Child- and Parent-Related Careers		
Career Areas	**Possible Occupations**	**Possible Settings**
Social Service	Adult day care worker Child welfare worker Children, youth, and family counselor Family intervention specialist Foster parent HIV health educator Juvenile officer Music or art therapist Substance abuse counselor Youth development specialist	Agencies (federal, state, county, city, private) Child abuse centers Drug abuse programs Family planning services Family and children's services Juvenile facilities Prisons Private practice Shelters
Education	Child care worker Children's librarian Coach School teacher or teacher aide Parent educator Recreation leader School counselor	Early childhood programs Public and school libraries Public and private schools Recreation centers VISTA/Peace Corps Youth organizations
Medical	Audiologist Dental hygienist Doctor Home health aide Nurse Physical therapist	Birthing centers Dental offices Hospitals and clinics Medical offices Private practice
Other	Author, children's books Camp counselor Consumer product safety specialist Parenting magazine writer Scout leader Youth minister	Camps Churches Federal agencies Private businesses Publishers Sports facilities

Fig. 1-3. Many careers, occupations, and entrepreneurial opportunities require knowledge of parenting. **What other child- and parent-related occupations can you name?**

Career Opportunities

You may be interested in having a career or occupation that requires knowledge of parenting. Some jobs require parenting skills or knowledge of child development for working directly with children or parents. Many career areas, such as teaching, require both.

Opportunities for jobs related to children and parents can be found in many career areas. Fig. 1-3 identifies some of these career areas and occupations, as well as the settings in which people work.

Parenting Yesterday and Today

People see their own lives—the good, the bad, and the neutral—at close range. That is why they sometimes think that days gone by were simpler or worry free. In fact, every generation of parents and children faces problems and challenges. In the past four hundred years, for example, children and families have endured:

- **Child apprenticeship.** In the early 1600s, children were often sent away from home to live with other families to learn a trade.
- **Child labor.** In the last half of the 1800s, many children worked in factories or other businesses for up to 16 hours a day, earning a few pennies an hour.
- **Child mortality.** Between 1890 and 1900, more than one in ten American babies died before their first birthdays. Until the invention of penicillin in 1950, many children died of infections that are well controlled today.

Fig. 1-4. In the past, children tended to have more opportunities to develop close relationships with older family members. **How can today's children develop such relationships?**

Current Issues Affecting Parenting

Parents in the United States today face challenges that parents living 100 years ago could hardly have dreamed of. Some of the issues described below may affect you and your family.

Working Parents. Many families today are under financial pressure, and most parents are employed outside the home. This often means day care or after-school care is necessary for the children. In the past, families often had relatives nearby to help in raising children. Today, many families live far apart, making it difficult for some parents to have that kind of family support. See Fig. 1-4.

Safety Concerns. Parents have always worried about their children's health and safety. Today, awareness of child abductions and other dangers can cause parents to have greater concerns about their children's safety. As a result, many children today have less freedom to roam—even around their own neighborhoods—than their parents had.

Technology. Television, video games, computers, cell phones, and pagers are familiar to many families today. There are some serious concerns associated with technology, however. For example, experts caution parents about letting children under age two watch television. Yet, in some families, television may become a cheap babysitter. For many children, sitting in front of a television has replaced physical exercise and creative play. See Fig. 1-5.

Technology offers many benefits, as well. For example, medical testing enables doctors to gather valuable information about the health of a pregnant woman. Educational technology, too, has created motivating and entertaining learning tools for children. Various adaptive tools, such as computer-aided voice devices, help children with disabilities communicate and learn. Many parents silently thank pagers and cell phones for helping them keep track of their busy teens.

Media. The good news is that television and the Internet provide instant access to world news and information that was not available just one or two generations ago. The bad news is that some of this information is too easily accessible to children, who may be negatively affected by it. Parents face enormous challenges in shielding their children from content they think is inappropriate. There is ongoing debate over whether this responsibility lies with the government, media decision makers, or parents.

Overscheduling. Most parents want their children to have opportunities they did not have themselves as children. As a result, some children are involved in dozens of activities: music, art, dance, and personal defense classes; swimming programs and scout camps; community youth groups, charity walk-a-thons, and after-school soccer leagues . . . all on top of homework! Is it any wonder that overscheduling has become a source of stress for some children? Like adults, children need regular "down time" to relax, rest, and recharge their batteries.

Fig. 1-5. Children who spend too much time watching television may be missing out on other activities that are needed for healthy development. **What are some possible consequences?**

Fig. 1-6. A special homecoming celebration brings family members together. **Which function of a family is being fulfilled in this situation?**

Functions of the Family

Despite all the challenges faced by families today, the idea of people forming family units remains strong, as it has throughout history. Why do people create family units? They do so for many reasons, such as:

- For physical safety and shelter.
- For love, affection, and emotional support.
- For raising children in a stable setting.
- For economic stability.
- For comfort and support when family members become aged or ill.

It is easy to take such family functions for granted, but fulfilling those functions is sometimes a difficult task. For various reasons, not all families are able to stay together and provide safety, security, stability, and support for each other.

At their best, however, families function like ports in a storm. Throughout life, many people turn to their families for safety, reassurance, help, and fun. People often celebrate births, graduations, and marriages; weather hard times; and grieve losses together as a family. Family stories, artifacts, and memories are often passed down through generations. See Fig. 1-6.

Another vital function of the family is to ensure that **values**—strongly held beliefs and ideas about what is important—are passed on from one generation to the next. Parents provide moral guidance by teaching their children values such as honesty, fairness, caring, responsibility, and respect for others.

Family Structures

You don't have to attend a family reunion to realize that there are many types of families. Just look around. Families are as different as the people who are a part of them. Here are four common types of family structures.

- A mother, a father, and one or more children form a **nuclear family**. The parents in nuclear families decide how to share responsibilities such as bringing in income, caring for the children, and doing household chores. See Fig. 1-7.
- Relatives other than parents and children comprise an **extended family**, which includes grandparents, aunts, uncles, and cousins. Sometimes extended families share a household and work together to fulfill family responsibilities.

- One parent and that person's children form a **single-parent family**. Single parents may or may not have help from other family members who share responsibilities.
- When a single parent marries, a **blended family** is formed. A blended family can include each spouse's children from previous marriages, as well as new children of the couple.

There are many variations of the four basic family structures. Some children are adopted into families. Some families care for foster children. Sometimes grandparents assume the role of parents to their grandchildren. In some cases, other family members and even older siblings may act as caregivers for younger children. There are many ways that responsible, caring adults can raise the children in their families. In all its many forms, the family is a vital part of society.

Fig. 1-7. Children in a nuclear family can look to both parents as role models. **What other type of family structure might include these children and their parents?**

Fig. 1-8. Friends and neighbors may have different ethnic and cultural backgrounds, but also share a common culture—that of the community in which they all live.

Families and Culture

In addition to having different structures, families vary because of cultural diversity. **Culture** refers to the customs and traditions of a specific group of people. Your cultural background can be a product of several factors, including your ethnic heritage, where your parents and grandparents lived, where you grew up, and where you live now. Ours is a multicultural society made up of people from many different cultures. In addition, many people have ties to more than one cultural group. See Fig. 1-8.

Families preserve and transmit culture by handing down customs and traditions from one generation to the next. This is reflected in many ways, from traditional foods to special holiday celebrations. Parenting practices, too, reflect cultural and ethnic diversity. People with different cultural backgrounds may have different expectations for how children should behave, for example, or place more importance on certain values. One culture's way is not better than another's, as long as family members' needs are met. In Chapter 2, you will learn how parents from all cultures fulfill certain roles and responsibilities.

The Family Life Cycle

There is no set pattern for family life. However, many families with children go through a series of stages that family researchers call the **family life cycle**. The family life cycle described on the following pages includes seven stages.

Stage 1—Individual

The individual stage takes place during young adulthood. During the individual stage, a person begins to separate from the family and gets ready to live independently. A person in the individual stage develops career skills, takes responsibility for his or her own care, and learns to make financial decisions.

Stage 2—Marriage

When one person joins another in marriage, they form the foundation of a new family. See Fig. 1-9. The couple blends their expectations, values, and vision of the future. They learn to deal with new issues, such as organizing finances as a couple. They learn about commitment and setting mutual goals. Learning to communicate, listen, and solve problems together enables them to cooperate to complete tasks as simple as preparing meals or as complex as remodeling a home.

Stage 3—Childbearing

When children are added to a family, a couple must adjust to their new roles as parents. This includes learning to meet their infant's physical and emotional needs while continuing to take care of themselves and nurture their relationship as a couple. They learn to deal with the physical and emotional stress—and the joy—of integrating a new member into their family. They may need to adjust their relationships with each other and sometimes with their extended families.

Stage 4—Parenting

Raising children can be challenging. Parents' commitment to each other and their communication, problem-solving, and decision-making skills become very important during this stage of the family life cycle. A growing child's health and development often depend on the parents' ability to provide a safe, stable, and loving environment.

Parenting adolescents can be especially challenging. To meet the challenge, parents need to help teens gradually gain independence while also establishing boundaries to support teens and keep them safe.

Fig. 1-9. A wedding is the start of a new stage of the family life cycle. **What adjustments will the newlyweds need to make during this stage?**

Fig. 1-10. The senior years can be very rewarding. **Why do you suppose so many seniors continue to stay busy and active?**

Stage 5—Launching

The launching stage begins when the first child leaves the parents' home and ends when the last child leaves. Children often leave home gradually, as parents continue to support and encourage them. In time, parents can step back and allow their older children to venture out into the world, yet return to the family for support. As their children reach adulthood and gain independence, parents often spend less and less time providing for their children's needs and more time thinking of their own.

Stage 6—Middle Years

After their adult children leave home and establish their own lives, parents often need to adjust to their *empty nest*, their home without children. They must also learn to relate to their grown children as adults. People in the middle years may take the opportunity to renew their own relationships, build their careers, and develop new interests. This can be quite a change for parents who might have neglected parts of their own development and marriage while raising their children. People in their middle years also might take on the responsibility of caring for their own aging parents.

Stage 7—Senior Years

The senior years are a time when many people look back over their lives and review all they have learned and experienced. During the senior years, some people retire from their jobs and enjoy a life of leisure. Others don't retire, but continue to pursue their careers for many years. Still others choose to begin a new career or take a part-time job. Some spend time as volunteers, contributing a lifetime's worth of skill and experience to helping others. See Fig. 1-10.

Many seniors like to share family history and stories with younger members of the family. Some strengthen a relationship with grandchildren by teaching them skills such as woodworking or cooking. Many simply appreciate having the opportunity and time to enjoy the company of their grandchildren and great-grandchildren.

Building Strong Families

A strong family is able to both carry out daily tasks and meet larger challenges. Building a strong family is usually no accident. It's often the intended result of much hard work. Here are some ways people can build a strong family at any stage of the family life cycle.

Express Love and Acceptance

In healthy families, children do not need to work to gain their parents' love and acceptance. The children are loved even when their actions are not always lovable! Knowing they are loved unconditionally gives children the self-confidence they need to cope with life and form relationships as adults. Even when children misbehave, parents can use kind, respectful, and loving ways to correct the undesirable behavior.

Spend Time Together

Spending time together is one way that family members can show how highly they value each other. Like a friendship, a strong parent-child relationship takes time to develop. Parents whose top priorities include spending valuable time with their children are likely to build strong family relationships. See Fig. 1-11.

Even in the midst of busy schedules, parents who are intent on building strong bonds with their children make sure they spend time together. Think about these situations: One parent outfits a child's playroom with expensive new toys, but rarely spends time with the child. Another parent takes time to interact with a child every day, yet spends no money doing this. Which parent-child relationship do you think might grow stronger?

Show Respect

Showing respect for others is a key to building healthy relationships, including strong family relationships. Parents strengthen the family when they show respect for their spouses, children, and others. They model courtesy and respect by treating family members and their possessions with care.

Fig. 1-11. A fun-loving person is often a fun-loving parent. **What do children learn when parents play games and have fun with them?**

Fig. 1-12. Traditions help strengthen family ties. **What family traditions would you begin or carry on as a parent?**

Parents teach self-respect by caring for their own health and by being true to their own values. Children learn to respect others by listening to the way their parents and other family members talk to each other and other people. For example, children can learn from adults how to listen politely, not interrupt, and accept others' views even when they don't agree with them. Showing respect for family members and others is a valuable trait both at home and in the community.

Build Trust

Building trust among family members is vital to building a strong family. Children learn to trust when they realize they can count on their parents to take good care of them, tell them the truth, and keep their promises. Consistency also builds trust. In families, adults can model and build trust by showing that they trust and respect each other's opinions and decisions. Learning to trust their parents and others helps children form strong relationships and make choices confidently as they get older.

Establish Traditions

Traditions are experiences that family members share and look forward to repeating. Following traditions is one way to strengthen family ties. Books, foods, songs, and special activities are a few elements that can become parts of family traditions. Many family traditions are linked to holidays and other special events, such as birthdays, marriages, and anniversaries. Family traditions can arise from smaller occasions, too, such as nightly dinners and weekly get-togethers. Having family traditions can draw family members together and help them to build lasting bonds. See Fig. 1-12.

Communicate

Building communication skills is another way to build strong family relationships. People of all ages want to be heard. They like to know that others understand and respect their views. Through healthy communication, information is exchanged among family members, and children receive guidance that fosters their development. When family members use good communication skills to discuss problems, they are better able to find sensible solutions.

Parents and caregivers strengthen the family by modeling communication skills for children. When communication skills are taught and practiced in childhood, the benefits often grow stronger as children grow into adulthood. Parents can foster family communication by:

- Talking, reading, and singing to children.
- Allowing children to try new things and express themselves in new ways.
- Listening and paying attention to all family members. See Fig. 1-13.

Resolve Conflicts

Most families have conflicts or disagreements at times. Families are strengthened when its members know how to settle conflicts in a loving and respectful way.

Parents can often lead the family through conflict resolution by listening to and respecting each person's opinions as they discuss a dispute. They can help family members reach an agreement by staying calm and keeping the discussion focused.

Fig. 1-13. Listening to family members helps them feel valued. **What might parents learn by listening to their children?**

Fig. 1-14. Schools and public libraries provide many programs, such as storytellers, to enrich the lives of children and families. **What recreational services are available to families in your community?**

Parents sometimes have to take a leadership role by settling disputes in ways that are best for the whole family. The result of effective conflict resolution is a stronger family that thrives despite disagreements.

Ask for Assistance

Part of building a strong family is solving problems when they arise. Even strong families need help at times to solve problems. Such times might be during a crisis, such as a family member's illness, or in the midst of a changing situation, such as moving to a new home.

Nearly every community has organizations that support parents' efforts to create a strong family. Extended family, friends, clergy, counselors, classes, and support groups are all possible sources of help. Sometimes parents need to seek the advice of a lawyer or obtain legal services. For example, parents who wish to adopt a child often speak with an attorney who specializes in family law.

Many families rely on community services. State and local health departments often run clinics and programs to meet family health needs. Other facilities offer assistance through family counseling, emergency aid, and housing programs.

In most communities, private agencies and religious institutions staffed by volunteers also offer assistance to families in need of food, clothing, and temporary child care. Many fraternal organizations, such as firefighters and police officers, hold fund drives to benefit families in need.

Many communities offer recreational services that enrich family life. For example, community park services may offer craft programs and nature walks. Often programs are available to help children explore dance, music, science, and the environment. Some groups help families grow strong together by organizing family bicycling, walking, and sports programs at local parks. See Fig. 1-14.

Although parents have the primary responsibility for meeting children's needs, society also shares that responsibility. A strong web of services and support run through communities that value families. A variety of programs, agencies, and individuals are ready and willing to provide help. Making use of these resources is one more way in which parents can build strong families and give their children a brighter future.

CHAPTER SUMMARY

- By using strong parenting skills, people who care for children can have a positive impact on individuals, families, and society.
- Studying about parenting can be helpful in a number of ways.
- Many challenges that parents face today are different from those of former generations.
- Although there are many different types of families, all family units have the same basic functions.
- Families with children typically go through a set of stages called the family life cycle.
- A strong family is able to carry out daily living tasks and effectively meet life's challenges.

Check Your Facts

1. What is parenting?
2. Describe three types of parents other than biological.
3. Besides parents, who may be caregivers for children?
4. How does strong parenting impact individuals, families, and society?
5. What can you gain from studying parenting?
6. Name six parenting-related occupations.
7. Compare these parenting challenges of today with their impact in the past: working outside the home; child safety; technology; and the media.
8. What is the potential problem with over-scheduling children?
9. Identify five basic functions of the family.
10. What are values? Give examples.
11. Describe four typical family structures.
12. How do families help preserve culture?
13. Summarize the seven stages of the family life cycle.
14. Describe at least four ways to build family strength through parenting.

Think Critically

1. **Contrasting.** Contrast the benefits and drawbacks of television and the Internet on families today.
2. **Making Predictions.** Through parenting, adults can have a huge impact on children's physical, intellectual, emotional, social, and moral development. Predict some possible outcomes for children who are not loved and cared for through thoughtful parenting.

Apply Your Learning

1. **Dual-Worker Families.** Today many parents work outside the home for various reasons. On one side of a sheet of paper, list advantages of working outside the home, and on the other side write disadvantages. Compare lists in class and discuss how this information might influence decisions that your generation will eventually make about working outside the home as parents.

2. **Conflict Resolution.** With several classmates, act out a scene that shows disagreement in a family and positive ways to settle the disagreement. In class, analyze the effectiveness of the methods used.

3. **Strong Families Brochure.** Join a team of students to design and create a brochure that promotes ways to build strong families. Present your suggestions in clear and simple language. Illustrate your brochure with drawings or photographs.

Cross-Curricular Connections

1. **Language Arts.** Write a thank-you letter to a relative, teacher, or other adult caregiver who has had a positive impact on your life.

2. **Social Studies.** Use Internet or print resources to identify at least four public or private policies—at the national, state, or local level—related to children and families. Choose one such policy to investigate further. How does it influence parenting? Share your findings with the class.

Family & Community Connections

1. **Traditions Old and New.** Talk to adults in your family about traditions they remember from their growing-up years. What events did they traditionally celebrate? How were those traditions carried out? Have they continued any of these traditions in your family today? Describe any new traditions you would like to start in your family now. What traditions would you like to follow in your own family someday?

2. **Community Resources.** What are some of the recreational services that enrich family life in your community? In what ways do they help? As a class, compile a list of ideas for other recreational services that would be beneficial for families in your community.

Responsible Parenting

CHAPTER OBJECTIVES

- Analyze the myths and realities of parenting.
- Identify basic rewards and responsibilities of parenting.
- Explain the legal rights and responsibilities of parents and other caregivers.
- Define child abuse and child neglect.
- Identify ways to report and prevent child abuse and neglect.

PARENTING TERMS

- potential
- nurture
- emancipated
- child care power of attorney
- guardian
- termination of parental rights
- child abuse
- child neglect

Does parenting begin on the joyful day when a baby is born? Does it end when the child graduates from high school? If you think it might start sooner and go on longer than that, you are right. Responsible parents begin planning for their family long before a baby is born. They know that parenting is a huge responsibility and takes long-term commitment. Even after a child leaves home, the parents' responsibilities continue in different ways. As you read, think about ways that parenting is a life-changing and lifelong responsibility.

Parenting Myths and Realities

Where do young people learn about being parents? Many have front row seats to see real parents in action; they learn about parenting by observing their own parents. Other views of parenting may be based on both myth and reality. For example, Brandi sees her neighbors and their children having fun at a local carnival, but that doesn't tell her everything about being a parent. Sam's aunt and uncle have several adopted children, and Sam visited the family one day last summer, but that wasn't enough time to learn much about the realities of parenting. Jake figures that parenting is the same as it appears in television comedies, which is not realistic at all!

Many people have ideas about raising children that turn out to be false. Learning about the myths and realities of parenting *before* becoming a parent can make it easier to understand what it means to be a responsible parent. See Fig. 2-1.

Common Myths

Shawna often daydreams about becoming a mother. She pictures herself holding her newborn baby boy—sweet, adorable, perfect. In Shawna's imagination, the baby is almost always sleeping, except when he's gazing into her eyes and cooing softly. He hardly ever cries, he never spits up, and his diapers never leak. As for herself, Shawna imagines a happy, peaceful life as a parent, with no real worries and a baby to give her all the love she wants.

Babies can be sweet and adorable, but not much else about Shawna's daydream is realistic. Like Shawna, many people have unrealistic expectations about parenthood. Here's how some of the most common parenting myths compare to reality.

- **Myth #1: Good parenting comes naturally.** It's true that no special degree or experience is required to be a parent. Instinct plays a part in parenting, but education, training, and experience are valuable to even the most intuitive parents. To be a responsible parent, a person must be mature, willing to learn, and able to make sacrifices when needed.

Fig. 2-1. Everyone has ideas about parenting. Some are realistic and some may not be. **What ideas about parenting do you have? Do you think they reflect reality?**

Fig. 2-2. This parent has adapted his schedules to meet his baby's needs. **Do you agree that, in the beginning, babies rule? Why or why not?**

- **Myth #2: Having a baby doesn't have to change a person's life.** Babies must be fed, burped, changed, held, cuddled, and loved day in and day out. Imagine being awakened every few hours, all through the night, by a crying baby who needs to be fed. No wonder parents of newborns look so tired! Because they don't get much sleep, they may find it hard to muster enough energy to get through the day.
- **Myth #3: Having children doesn't cost much.** The truth is, having a baby is expensive. In addition to delivery costs, babies need diapers, formula, bottles, clothing, and much more. All of these added items can cause parents' expenses to skyrocket. The money needed to feed, clothe, and care for a child is largely a fixed expense. This means you cannot choose to do without such items if you don't have the money. As children grow, they continue to need things that parents must provide for them.
- **Myth #4: Children can make up for whatever is missing from a person's life.** Some people believe that having a baby will fill a void, or empty place, in their lives and will provide unconditional love. This is not true. Babies bring with them a whole bundle of their own needs. Most of all, they need their parents to be there for them, not the other way around.
- **Myth #5: Children affect parents' lives for a short time.** Being a parent requires a lifelong commitment. Most American children remain with their parents for 18 years or longer. That means parents must consider their children's needs, and perhaps put their own personal dreams on hold, for a very long time. The greater reality is that parenting never really ends.

Real Parenting

In real life, new babies rule! For example, many new parents find that their baby sleeps best at home, so going out, even to a family member's home, can be difficult. Katy, a 17-year-old single mom, says that one of the hardest parts of parenting is seeing her friends go out dancing without her. Miguel and Kamala, who have two children, say they miss going snowboarding most weekends in winter. People who are ready to be parents are willing and able to handle these and many other changes in their lives. They are willing to make sacrifices for their children. See Fig. 2-2.

Parenting Rewards

When parents raise children responsibly, they increase their chances of reaping the rewards of parenthood. Here are a few possible examples of such rewards.

Youthful Perspective

Children give parents a wonderful gift: the opportunity to see the world through their eyes, lending a whole new perspective on life. For infants and toddlers, the world is totally new and life is a journey of discovery. By watching their children splash in puddles or blow bubbles, parents can regain a sense of wonder about everyday life. As children age, their changing perspectives help keep parents aware and growing. See Fig. 2-3.

Emotional Fulfillment

Most parents would say that, although raising children can be difficult at times, few experiences are as emotionally fulfilling as parenthood. The rewards of a child's smile or hug are deeply satisfying to most parents. The bond between parents and children is one of the strongest of all human connections. When parents strive to preserve and build on that bond, their life with a child becomes even more rewarding.

Fig. 2-3. Children give you a chance to see the world through their eyes. **What do you think a child might teach you about the world?**

Fig. 2-4. Honoring the traditions they learned from their parents, and passing them on to their own children, helps people to realize that they are a part of something larger than themselves.

Personal Growth

Parenting gives people exceptional opportunities for personal growth. People who learn good parenting skills and put them to work develop strengths and understandings they might not achieve in other ways. They gain the ability to empathize and to appreciate others as individuals. Putting a child first teaches self-sacrifice. A parent feels responsible for someone else and learns to focus on what's really important in life.

Parents can learn more about themselves and their own thinking through their children. Each child is a unique individual with his or her own opinions. Parents who discuss social issues with a teen, for example, may find that it helps them not only examine and express their own ideas, but expand their understanding of other viewpoints.

Sense of Pride

Most people take pride in a job well done, and parents are no exception. When children take their first wobbly steps, learn to read, improve their school grades, or help their sports team to victory, parents as well as children celebrate the accomplishment. Years later, as their children leave home, many parents feel a sense of satisfaction at having prepared them to live independently and give something back to the world.

Family Continuation

Many people are pleased to know that their family's traditions and values will live on in their children's lives and the lives of future generations. Family history and stories, special ways of celebrating holidays, treasured foods—all are examples of traditions linked to family. Parents feel gratified to see their children, and perhaps grandchildren and even great-grandchildren, continue these elements of their family heritage. See Fig. 2-4.

Parenting Responsibilities

Parenting is a complex job. Parents are responsible for meeting a child's needs, beginning with the most basic requirements. They are also responsible for nurturing, protecting, teaching, and guiding their children.

Meeting Children's Needs

Parents and caregivers are responsible for meeting children's many needs. Children need things as basic as food, clothing, and shelter, which responsible parents provide. They have more complex needs, too—such as intellectual, emotional, social, and moral needs—that are fulfilled by activities such as attending school, being part of a loving family, building friendships, and becoming responsible members of society.

Maslow's Theory. Many theorists, including psychologist Abraham Maslow, believe children's development is affected by how well their needs are met. Maslow theorized that every person has needs that must be met in a certain order, moving from the most basic to the more complex. Maslow's hierarchy of human needs is shown in Fig. 2-5.

The physiological needs at the bottom of the pyramid are absolutely essential to survival. Human beings could not live without food, water, air, sleep, and health. Being free from danger is also a basic need. Only after these are met can the higher-level needs be addressed.

Meeting higher-level needs is a process that continues throughout life. Maslow believed that not everyone reaches the highest level, which he called *self-actualization*. People who attain this level feel that they are fulfilling their life's purpose.

According to Maslow's theory, what happens when a child's basic needs are not met? Here are some examples. A child who is always cold and hungry will have difficulty feeling secure. A child who lives in a place where it's not safe to play outdoors may miss opportunities to develop friendships that meet social needs. In other words, unmet needs at any level of the pyramid interfere with meeting higher-level needs. By ensuring that essential needs are met, parents help make it possible for children to reach their highest level of development.

Maslow's Hierarchy of Human Needs

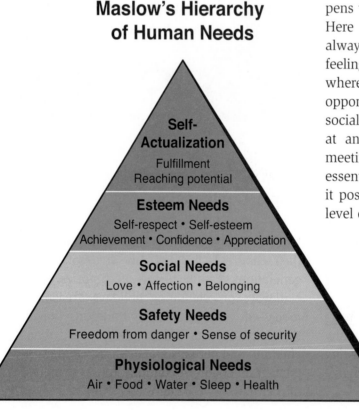

Self-Actualization
Fulfillment
Reaching potential

Esteem Needs
Self-respect • Self-esteem
Achievement • Confidence • Appreciation

Social Needs
Love • Affection • Belonging

Safety Needs
Freedom from danger • Sense of security

Physiological Needs
Air • Food • Water • Sleep • Health

Fig. 2-5. Each level in Maslow's hierarchy indicates people's needs. Needs near the bottom of the pyramid must be met before the higher-level needs can be dealt with. **What can parents do to meet a child's needs at each level?**

Fig. 2-6. Encouraging children to explore their own interests is one aspect of nurturing. **Describe other ways parents can nurture a child and foster healthy development.**

Nurturing Children

Every child is born with **potential**, which is the ability to reach a certain level of achievement. Whether or not a child lives up to this potential is due in part to the care he or she receives. Parents and caregivers **nurture** a child by providing the type of care that encourages healthy growth and development.

For a parent, nurturing involves meeting a child's basic needs, but there is much more to nurturing than that. Parents and caregivers are also responsible for nurturing children's emotional, intellectual, and social growth. They do this by listening to their children, playing with them, and encouraging them to explore their own unique interests and talents. See Fig. 2-6.

Protecting Children

Young children cannot protect themselves. They depend on the watchful eyes and quick reflexes of adults to keep them safe. Protecting a young, energetic child is not always easy. Parents and caregivers must constantly be on guard to keep young children safe while they play, eat, and sleep.

Children also need freedom to explore their environment and learn from it. One tricky aspect of parenting is protecting children while allowing them to explore. As children grow, parents teach them how to make their own safe and healthy decisions by gradually giving them more responsibility. This allows them to become independent and able to make wise choices as they grow into adulthood.

All parents want to keep their children safe. Here are some ways to protect children by teaching them to make wise choices about their safety.

- Insist that children always walk with a parent or buddy when they are away from home. Children who are out alone are more vulnerable to harm.

- Teach children that a "stranger" is any person the child does not know, even if the stranger claims to know the family.

- Warn children not to engage in conversation or get near a stranger who calls to them from a car.

- Tell children to run to a store, school, or public area if a stranger begins following them.

- Make sure young children know they should never go into public restrooms without a parent or other trusted person.

- Instruct children to seek out a store clerk or security guard if they become lost in a store or mall. Warn them never to go into the parking lot by themselves.

Teaching Children

A parent is a child's first teacher. Beginning at birth, children learn about the world from information taught by parents and caregivers. Many parents teach their children about their own cultural heritage and pass down family and cultural traditions to them. Parents also teach their children to solve problems of different kinds, so that when they become adults they may be confident problem solvers.

Guiding Children

Parents and caregivers are responsible for guiding children in their care. Guidance involves more than safety. Parents and other caregivers also guide their children by modeling strong values, such as compassion, honesty, and respect. An example of a simple value that parents can teach to children is kindness, such as kindness to other children, pets, and other living things.

Child & Family Services
CAREERS

▶ Teacher Aide

Teacher aides work in schools to provide instructional and clerical support to teachers, so teachers will have more time to teach and plan lessons. Teacher aides may also:

- Help children learn classroom material.
- Supervise students in the cafeteria and lunchroom and on the playground.
- Record grades, set up equipment, and stock teaching supplies.

Teacher aides work closely with the individual teachers to whom they are assigned. Their duties will vary somewhat according to the level of support the teacher requires and the age of the students. Educational requirements vary by state or school district; some require college training.

"I work as a teacher aide in an elementary school. I've always enjoyed young children. In high school, I worked after school in a child care center. I especially enjoy helping children learn small motor skills, such as safely using scissors and working with art materials. I've worked with the same teacher for the past three years and can usually anticipate what kind of help she needs even before she asks. I also closely watch the children so I can offer help right away. I feel my efforts to keep the classroom running smoothly are appreciated by the teacher and the students."

CAREER TIPS

- Gain experience working with children in after-school programs and summer camps.
- Take child development and parenting courses in high school.
- Develop good communication skills.

Legal Rights and Responsibilities

Do you know that parents and caregivers have legal rights pertaining to the children in their care? There are also consequences that may follow when caregivers do not meet their parenting responsibilities.

Parenting is like a contract. When you become a parent, you agree to provide for your children. When you do your job, society benefits as well. Healthy, happy children have a good chance of growing up to be well-adjusted adults who strengthen society.

Legal Rights

Parents have the right to control the care and upbringing of their children and to make decisions that affect them, such as where to live, what school to attend, and what medical treatment to obtain. Other caregivers have rights, too. School officials have rights regarding the conduct of students because they become temporary caregivers in the absence of parents during the school day. Laws in all 50 states address the rights of grandparents to have contact with their grandchildren. See Fig. 2-7.

Many parents speak out for rights that they feel are important in raising their children. They want safe schools and quality education, protection for their children when using the Internet, clean water and air, and family-friendly employment policies. Parents draw attention to their concerns by:

- Asking for flexibility and support from the workplace to help them meet the needs of their children and family.
- Speaking out for affordable child care and health care for children.

- Staying informed about laws and regulations that affect families, writing letters to newspapers and elected officials, and attending public meetings.
- Making sure their community has high-quality schools and programs that can meet the needs of a diverse population.
- Voting for candidates who share their views on how to strengthen and support families.

Emancipation. Parental rights continue until a child legally becomes an adult, usually at age 18. In some cases, a person younger than 18 may be legally **emancipated**, or freed from parental controls and support. In most states, teens age 16 to 18 may seek legal emancipation if they are married, financially independent, or members of the armed forces.

Legal Responsibilities

Parents are legally and financially responsible for the care of their children. Parents must provide their children with food, clothing, shelter, medical care, and education. Parents may also be financially responsible for damage to property or injury of another person caused by their child.

Under certain circumstances, the legal responsibilities of parents can be transferred to others. For example, parents who are serving in the military or traveling without their children may wish to designate someone to be legally responsible for their children's care during their absence. This can be accomplished using a legal document called a **child care power of attorney**. It temporarily gives an agent the power to act in place of the parent, such as by consenting to medical care in case of emergency.

When a child's parents have died or are unable to provide care, the court will appoint a **guardian** to take legal responsibility for the child. The child does not usually take the

Fig. 2-7. When their parents divorce, children often gain a sense of stability by staying in contact with their grandparents. **In what ways do grandparents' rights also reflect the rights of children?**

guardian's last name. The guardianship ends when the child legally becomes an adult, usually at age 18 or 21.

Termination of Parental Rights

If parents neglect or abuse their legal responsibility of caring for their children, they can forfeit their rights as parents. State and federal laws alike are made to protect children. When social service agencies, the police, and the court system get involved, it is because they suspect a child is in physical or emotional danger.

If parents neglect their duties, a judge may issue an order for **termination of parental rights**. This court order permanently severs all rights, powers, privileges, immunities, duties, and obligations between parent and child. Some parents choose to voluntarily give up their rights. In other cases, termination is involuntary, following court proceedings brought against the parent.

When termination of parental rights is established, children are taken from the parent or parents and placed in foster care or adoptive homes. Possible reasons for termination of parental rights include severe abuse or neglect, abandonment, and long-term alcohol or drug abuse.

Child Abuse and Child Neglect

The precise definitions of child abuse vary from state to state. In general, **child abuse** is intentional or neglectful physical, emotional, or sexual injury to a child.

- Physical abuse includes non-accidental injuries, such as bruises, burns, and broken bones.
- Emotional abuse includes severe rejection, loss of affection, and humiliation. It also includes actions intended to produce fear or extreme guilt in a child.
- Sexual abuse of a child includes any sexual act between a child and an adult.

Health & Safety

Shaken Baby Syndrome

Shaken baby syndrome is a pattern of severe head injuries an infant or child can suffer when shaken violently. The most common reason for shaking a baby is crying. Many infants cry for long periods in spite of all attempts to comfort them. If a caregiver gets frustrated or angry and shakes the baby, the baby's brain can bounce against the inside of the skull. The brain and blood vessels in the head may be damaged. The long-term consequences can include permanent disability or death.

- Forcefully shaking a baby for even a few seconds is long enough to cause damage.
- Signs of brain damage may include a change in behavior, lethargy, loss of consciousness, pale or bluish skin, vomiting, and seizures.

- Immediate emergency treatment is necessary. However, once the injury has occurred, the damage is already done.

If a baby won't stop crying, parents and caregivers can ask someone else for help or let the baby cry. Either option is better than risking the terrible consequences of shaken baby syndrome.

Child neglect is failure to meet a child's basic physical and emotional needs. For example, parents who leave young children alone or who don't provide adequate food are guilty of neglect. Some children suffer from both abuse and neglect. See Fig. 2-8.

According to the National Clearinghouse on Child Abuse and Neglect, abuse and neglect occur among people in all income and education levels, racial and ethnic groups, religions, and areas of the country. Some details are especially troubling:

- Children ages birth to three years have the highest rates of victimization.
- Many children die due to abuse or neglect. Most are younger than four years old.
- Those responsible for child abuse and neglect are often the parents.
- Siblings and other family members can also be abusers.

Fig. 2-8. Abuse and neglect can take various forms, but all have devastating effects. **What is the difference between child abuse and child neglect?**

Why Does Abuse Occur?

There is no acceptable reason for parents or others to commit child abuse or neglect. There are, however, avoidable or reversible factors that sometimes lead to child abuse or neglect. Here are some of those factors:

- Parents or other caregivers who become abusers may think that physical abuse is an acceptable form of discipline and guidance for children. This is often due to the type of discipline a parent experienced growing up. In other words, a parent who was abused or neglected as a child may, in turn, abuse or neglect children.
- Parents or caregivers may let anger and frustration get out of control. Adults are much bigger and stronger than children, and a screaming adult voice is frightening to a child. It is even more terrifying when coupled with the threat or occurrence of physical violence.
- Drug or alcohol use plays a role in many reported cases of child abuse.

Reporting Child Abuse and Neglect

If you suspect that a child is being abused or neglected, it is your responsibility to contact your local protective services agency, police, or emergency hotline. You do not have to give your name when you call. The child's safety is of prime importance.

Preventing Child Abuse and Neglect

Many local and national agencies and programs are working hard to prevent child abuse and neglect. To find the resources that are available to you, check the telephone directory, public library, or the Internet.

Crisis Intervention. Parents and others who feel they are losing control and might harm a child need to get help right away. In many communities, local agencies operate child abuse or domestic violence hotlines that can be called day or night. Some provide residential shelters where parents can take their children during a crisis. The National Domestic Violence Hotline, which has a Web site and a toll-free number, links individuals to local resources and help.

Support. Family members shouldn't wait until a crisis occurs to seek help. They can get support from resources such as:

- Anger management classes, which teach strategies for coping with frustration and anger.

- Substance abuse classes and support groups.
- Local support groups for new parents.
- Online parenting support groups found on the Internet. See Fig. 2-9.

Education. Parents and caregivers are less likely to become frustrated with children's behavior if they understand the developmental stages of childhood and have realistic expectations. They can educate themselves, and build their parenting skills, by:

- Reading practical books written by parenting experts.
- Taking parenting classes at a local school, hospital, or social service agency.
- Consulting Web sites that offer reliable information about child development and parenting.
- Asking for advice from experienced parents.

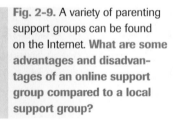

Fig. 2-9. A variety of parenting support groups can be found on the Internet. **What are some advantages and disadvantages of an online support group compared to a local support group?**

Modeling *CHARACTER*

Character Traits for Parenting

One of the best ways to learn about parenting is from people who are already good parents. Many families are filled with positive parental role models—people who demonstrate qualities of good parenting. Some people learn about parenting from a *mentor*, an experienced person who acts as a wise and trusted guide and advisor.

The best parental role models and mentors demonstrate not only parenting skills, but also positive character traits. *Character* is moral strength to do what is right. It is based on values such as:

- Respect.
- Fairness.
- Trustworthiness.
- Responsibility.
- Integrity.

These and other character traits provide a solid foundation for parenting. Throughout this text, you will read about ways to practice positive character traits and be a role model for others.

Think About It

Why is it a good idea to envision the character traits for the kind of parent you may want to be someday? What character traits do you think are most important for parents? Why?

CHAPTER **2** Review & Activities

CHAPTER SUMMARY

- Learning about the myths and realities of raising children helps build an understanding of what it means to be a responsible parent.
- By raising children responsibly, parents are more likely to reap the rewards of parenthood.
- Parents nurture children's physical, intellectual, emotional, social, and moral growth.
- Parental responsibilities include protecting, teaching, and guiding children.
- Parents and other caregivers have legal rights and responsibilities concerning the children in their care.
- Child abuse and neglect are serious problems that need to be prevented.

Check Your Facts

1. Explain three myths of parenting.
2. Describe five rewards of parenting.
3. Summarize the basic ideas in Maslow's hierarchy of human needs.
4. How do parents and other caregivers nurture a child?
5. Why are these parenting responsibilities important: protection, teaching, and guidance?
6. What are two legal rights and two legal responsibilities that parents have in raising children?
7. How does emancipation affect someone under age 18?
8. Why are parental rights sometimes terminated?
9. Explain the difference between child abuse and child neglect.
10. What can cause, but not excuse, child abuse?
11. What should be done if child abuse is suspected?
12. What actions occur through crisis intervention?
13. What support is available to people who worry about becoming abusive?
14. How can education help prevent child abuse and neglect?
15. Why are mentors helpful?
16. What is character?

Think Critically

1. **Analyzing a Myth.** Feeling lonely and unloved made one young woman yearn for a baby. What could happen in this situation? What advice can you offer?
2. **Drawing Conclusions.** Why do you think all 50 states protect grandparents' rights?
3. **Understanding Cause and Effect.** Why do you think child abuse often continues from one generation to the next?

Apply Your Learning

1. **Responsible Parenting Poster.** Work with a partner to create a poster about the responsibilities of parenting.

2. **Public-Service Message.** With a team of students, create a 30- to 40-second, public-service radio message that calls attention to shaken baby syndrome. Include the dangers to a baby and ways to prevent shaken baby syndrome from happening.

3. **Anger Questionnaire.** Research anger management and learn how to recognize when anger is out of control. Then, with a team of students, devise a questionnaire to help people determine whether they have an anger problem. For example, one question might be: "Do you tend to hold in angry feelings for a long time?" Use a scale for responses, such as 1 for never and 4 for frequently. Decide what total scores mean. What do you learn about yourself by answering the questions?

Cross-Curricular Connections

1. **Math.** Go to a Web site such as the National Clearinghouse for Child Abuse and Neglect. Find statistics on abuse and neglect to use in a graph, such as:
   - A bar graph showing deaths by age group.
   - A pie graph showing percentages of children affected by abuse and neglect.

2. **Language Arts.** Complete this sentence in writing: "I think the most important thing a parent can do for a child is …" Share sentences in class and discuss reasons for the responses.

Family & Community Connections

1. **Parenting Interview.** Interview a family member who has parenting skills you admire. Include the following questions and analyze responses in class:
   - What was the hardest part of parenting for you? How did you handle it?
   - What have been the most rewarding parts of parenting?
   - What advice do you have for new parents?

2. **Community Support.** Find information on an organization that helps families in crisis. Find out what services it provides and share what you learn with the class.

3

Personal Readiness

CHAPTER OBJECTIVES

- Assess your own maturity level and goals in relation to parenting readiness.
- Relate age and health to parenting readiness.
- Explain good and poor reasons for wanting to become a parent.
- Describe a healthy relationship needed for parenting readiness.
- Explain how finances relate to parenting readiness.
- Describe ways to learn more about parenting and to make a responsible choice.

PARENTING TERMS

- self-assessment
- emotional maturity
- self-esteem
- sexually transmitted diseases (STDs)
- abstinence

"*Ready, set, go!*" Well, not so fast. Those three little words need careful consideration when the subject is parenting. What does it mean to be *ready* for parenting? How do people make sure they are *set* for a future that includes children? When is it right to *go* ahead and become a parent?

It is vital to be ready and set—emotionally, physically, and financially—before becoming a parent. Those who are considering parenthood should assess their readiness for parenting and explore their reasons for wanting a child.

Self-Assessment

How well do you know yourself? One way to learn more about yourself is through self-assessment. **Self-assessment** is the process of examining your personal qualities, such as your level of maturity. It also involves thinking about your goals for the future and how you plan to reach them. See Fig. 3-1.

Assessing Your Emotional Maturity

Emotional maturity is the ability to understand and act on your emotions at an adult level of development. It's a key aspect of parenting

readiness. A person who is emotionally mature has the patience and self-control to remain calm when children are crying or misbehaving, for example. Emotionally mature parents accept their responsibilities and carry them out willingly. They will even put their children's needs before their own needs when necessary. In contrast, people who are self-centered, irresponsible, or unable to control their temper are not emotionally mature enough to be parents.

How can you tell whether you have the level of emotional maturity that raising a child requires? Here are some questions that can help you assess your emotional readiness for parenting:

- Do you accept responsibility without being pressured and without complaining?
- Can people depend on you to honor long-term commitments?
- Are you patient, sympathetic, and responsive to what others need?
- Can you set aside your own needs when someone else's needs are more important?
- Do you have high **self-esteem**—positive feelings about yourself?
- Are you willing to tackle problems instead of walking away from them?
- Can you take care of yourself and others, or do you expect others to take care of you?
- Can you control your emotions and manage stress when faced with difficulties?
- Do you have a positive outlook on life?

Fig. 3-1. Self-assessment helps you learn more about yourself and your readiness for parenthood. **What are some signs of parenting readiness?**

Fig. 3-2. People who are ready to become parents know they will often need to put their child's needs before their own. **Are you ready to make that kind of commitment?**

People who answer yes to most of these questions may be emotionally mature. They are not necessarily ready for the immense responsibilities of parenting, however. Parenting readiness requires constant use of emotional maturity in situations that involve children. Try to imagine yourself in the parenting situations listed below. How would you respond?

- You have a commitment to complete a project with co-workers, but the sitter you hired to care for your child while you're at work never shows up.
- You have to spend a week indoors and away from your friends and other activities to care for your sick child.
- You have to get up and go to work in the morning after the baby wakes up crying four or five times during the night.
- You learn that your new baby has a health problem that requires lifelong monitoring and treatment.

Just thinking about the parenting situations like these can overwhelm many people. Most parents do feel overwhelmed at times. However, the key to emotional maturity is not how a person feels, but how he or she copes with those feelings and responds in real-life situations. People who are not emotionally prepared to take full responsibility for their own lives are not ready to make a lifelong commitment to a child. See Fig. 3-2.

Assessing Your Goals

"What will you be when you grow up?" You may have heard this question when you were very young. What was your answer? Have your goals changed since then? Most people adjust or change their goals as they go through life.

What do you want out of life? Figuring out what you want to achieve and how you will reach your goals is a big step toward maturity. Striving to reach your goals is often a key to living life to the fullest, as well. See Fig. 3-3.

Here are some self-assessment questions about goal setting and parenting readiness:

- Do you set your own goals, and are you self-motivated to reach them?
- Are you in control of the direction your life is taking?
- Can you give up short-term comfort to achieve long-term goals?

- Do your career plans require education beyond high school? If so, how might that affect parenting decisions?
- Does your chosen occupation require long hours, or do you expect to work limited or part-time hours? What level of pay can you realistically expect? Will your job take you away from home a lot or be physically dangerous? How might these factors affect your family life?

Most teens who think about questions like these realize they have much to do before becoming parents. Many realize they need to become self-motivated and self-directed before they are ready to take on added responsibilities. Most want to finish their education, find a good job, and establish a sense of security before tackling parenthood. Parenting is a worthy goal, but it is rarely possible to consider it a sole occupation. It is usually best to make parenting a part of an adult life that includes other ambitions.

Fig. 3-3. The satisfaction of achieving a goal makes all the effort worthwhile. **How would your current goals be affected by a parenting choice?**

The Heartbreak of Fetal Alcohol Disorders

Alcohol consumption during pregnancy damages nerve cells in the developing baby's brain. A variety of problems, known collectively as *fetal alcohol disorders*, can result. Possible effects include:

- Mental retardation.
- Physical abnormalities, such as cleft palate (an opening in the roof of the mouth).
- Below-normal height and weight.
- Vision or hearing problems.

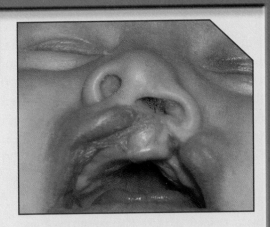

- Problems with learning, memory, attention span, and communication.

The damage from alcohol consumption can occur before a woman even realizes she is pregnant. Fetal alcohol disorders are irreversible, and their effects on the lives of children are permanent.

Age, Health, and Readiness

Age and health are big factors in physical readiness for pregnancy and parenting. Those who are too young or who don't practice good health habits increase the risk of problems for themselves and their children.

Teens and Health Risks

Teens are not the best candidates for pregnancy, giving birth, and becoming parents. Parenting can be physically demanding for anyone, at any age, whether male or female. However, pregnancy and childbirth pose serious added health risks for adolescents.

Teens who become pregnant have a much higher than average risk of death during pregnancy and birth. They are also more likely to develop health problems, such as obesity, high blood pressure, and painful bones and joints due to lack of calcium and other nutrients.

Because teens are still growing and maturing, their bodies need a lot of nourishment, even without pregnancy. Meeting a teen's extra nutrient needs during pregnancy can be tough to accomplish.

Children born to teen mothers are more likely to have health problems, too. Many are born too small, which puts them at risk for many serious, even life-threatening, disorders. Some don't survive their early weeks. Those that do face an increased risk of lifelong health problems, such as blindness, deafness, cerebral palsy (a group of disorders caused by brain damage), mental retardation, asthma, or learning disorders.

Other Health Issues

Teens are not the only ones who face health risks during pregnancy. For example, any woman who uses tobacco or alcohol during pregnancy risks harming the unborn child. Another risk is **sexually transmitted diseases (STDs)**—infections spread through sexual contact. Many STDs, such as herpes, gonorrhea, and AIDS, can affect children who are born to infected mothers. Also, women who become pregnant later in life face health risks, as do their unborn children. For these and other reasons, assessing health is an important consideration in evaluating readiness for parenting. You can read more about health considerations during pregnancy in Chapter 9.

Fig. 3-4. Adults who tackle the job of parenting will need maturity to succeed. **What do you think motivates parents to face the challenge?**

Choosing to Parent

All children deserve parents who are ready and happy to take on the huge job ahead of them. Parenting readiness means that adults have thoughtfully and purposefully chosen to become parents. It is sometimes possible for mature adults to have an unplanned pregnancy and still raise a happy, healthy, and much-loved child. Most of the time, however, it is best when parenting is a choice, not an accident. See Fig. 3-4.

Reasons for Having Children

Why do some people want to have children? There are so many possible answers to that question, it's impossible to list all of them!

Good Reasons. There are plenty of good reasons for choosing to become parents. Some people may say they want to be parents because they love children. Some may say they want to devote their lives to raising productive members of society. They may wish to pass on some part of themselves and their family traditions to a new generation. Couples in a thriving marriage may feel that having children is a way to make their relationship even more fulfilling.

Poor Reasons. There are also plenty of poor reasons for wanting to have children. Here are a few examples:

Fig. 3-5. In spite of what some people imagine, having children does not make life perfect. **If a couple decides to have a child to improve their life, what are some possible consequences?**

- **To prove adulthood.** Some young women and men choose to have children because they want to prove to their parents and friends that they are no longer children themselves. However, becoming a parent before being ready to take on all the responsibilities of parenthood is not a mature decision.

- **To please someone else.** For example, a young couple's parents say they desperately want a grandchild. Because young adults in this situation want to make their parents happy, they may choose to have a child even though their parenting readiness is not high enough.

- **For emotional benefits.** Having someone to love and to love you back sounds appealing, but it is not realistic. Babies need lots of love, but they do not give love the way they receive it.

- **For respect and status.** Families with children may sometimes seem to get more respect and have greater status in society, but this is a mistaken notion. Having a baby too early as an attempt to gain status and respect is not likely to work out that way. In fact, it could have the opposite effect.

- **To escape a situation.** Some people think that becoming a parent is a way out of a bad situation, such as poverty or an unfulfilling job. Having a child certainly changes a person's life, but it is not the solution to any problem. In fact, some problems, such as lack of money, are likely to become worse because of it. See Fig. 3-5.

- **Because society expects it.** Having a baby just because friends and people around you have children is not a wise decision. It is much smarter to achieve personal parenting readiness before deciding to have a child.

- **To improve a bad relationship.** Couples having relationship problems who think having a baby will bring them back together are mistaken. Adding a child to a troubled relationship is bound to make things worse, and the one who suffers is usually the child.

Healthy Relationships

Anyone who is thinking of parenthood owes it to the child to provide a secure home environment. One key to a secure environment is parents who form healthy and stable relationships. Here are some signs of a healthy relationship:

- **The relationship is satisfying.** Each member gains as much from the relationship as he or she gives to it.
- **Each person treats the other respectfully.** The couple are generally happy with each other's actions and respectful of each other's ideas. They communicate openly. See Fig 3-6.
- **The relationship is stable.** It has lasted long enough to ensure the couple have truly loving feelings for each other and are not just infatuated.
- **Both people work to resolve conflicts and reach compromises.** They sometimes agree to disagree and to respect each other's different opinions. Their discussions involve reasonable issues and don't revolve around petty arguments.
- **The couple share a common philosophy about having and raising children.** That is, they agree on issues such as how many children to have, how to divide responsibilities, and how to handle discipline, education, and religion.
- **The couple don't have serious differences or problems.** There are no issues with drug or alcohol abuse, for example. The couple resolve all major differences through reasonable discussions, avoiding shouting and the use of physical force.

Fig. 3-6. Talking openly and honestly enables a couple to build a good relationship. **What is the possible outcome of a relationship that is not built on honesty?**

Fig. 3-7. Having a child often means having little money to spend on entertainment and fun. **What activities do you think new parents typically have to give up?**

Financial Planning

If babies were born with price tags attached, you might be shocked at the cost of raising even an "economy model"! The financial burden of raising a child begins before birth and often lasts into the child's adulthood.

According to a recent government report, a two-parent family with average income spends about $10,000 per year to care for one child. That includes only basic costs such as housing, food, transportation, clothing, and health care. There are plenty of other costs to consider. For instance, some parents plan to help pay for their children's college education.

Just giving birth to a healthy baby can cost more than $6,000, and having a baby with health problems can cost much more. Because good health care during pregnancy often prevents serious health problems, it is essential to find and pay for that care. Health insurance,

if available, may not cover all the expenses. Sometimes public and private resources can help parents pay for health care during pregnancy and birth, but relatively few people qualify for aid.

Having a child not only increases parents' costs, but also may cause income to drop. For example, if one parent stops working temporarily to have a baby or to care for a child, the family's income can rapidly shrink.

When parents spend money on raising a child, as they must, it usually means they do not have as much money to spend on activities they enjoyed before having a child. See Fig. 3-7.

Meeting the Cost of Parenting

How can prospective parents make sure they are financially ready to have a child? They can ask themselves the following questions and carefully consider the impact their answers might have on their lives.

- Do we have a steady source of income? Is it enough to meet current expenses plus the additional expenses of having a child?
- How much has been set aside in savings?
- Are other resources available? For example, would relatives be able and willing to help out financially?
- What are the costs of pregnancy, birth, and health care for a child?
- Do we have health insurance? What costs will it cover? What will we have to pay for ourselves?
- If one parent plans to stay home with the baby, can we afford the loss of income? If both parents plan to work, how much will child care cost? How will we pay for it?
- Will a larger home be needed for a growing family? Can we afford it? See Fig. 3-8.

Educate Yourself

What is it like to be a parent? Although you can't truly know until you experience it, there are other ways to gather ideas about parenting and learn what it might be like. Think about ways you might educate yourself to help you decide whether or not parenting may be right for you.

Learn by Doing

There are many ways to get first-hand experience in caring for children. The experience you gain may help you assess your parenting readiness. To find out what it's really like, you might:

- Find a neighborhood child-care job (such as babysitting).
- Volunteer to work with children at a local community center, arts center, after-school program, or other supervised situation.

Learn by Observing

Another way to learn about parenting is to observe people who take care of children every day. Examples include teachers, child care workers, parents, and school counselors. You can ask to observe people as they care for babies and children. As you observe, ask questions about parenting and listen carefully to the answers. You may find this helpful in assessing your own level of parenting readiness.

Fig. 3-8. Couples who are considering parenthood should review their finances before making a decision. **What financial information might they want to gather and discuss?**

Parenting Pointers

Financial Planning for Future Parents

Prospective parents must figure out how to manage their financial resources in order to raise a child. They may need to:

- **Cut back other expenses.** A good way to start the financial planning process is to keep track of all expenses for at least several months. Then take a good, hard look at how the money is spent. Which expenses are truly necessary? What creative solutions could reduce some costs?

- **Reduce debt.** The less debt a couple has to deal with, the easier it will be to take on the added costs of raising a child. When paying off debt, start with high-interest credit cards.

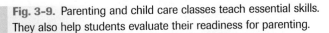

Fig. 3-9. Parenting and child care classes teach essential skills. They also help students evaluate their readiness for parenting.

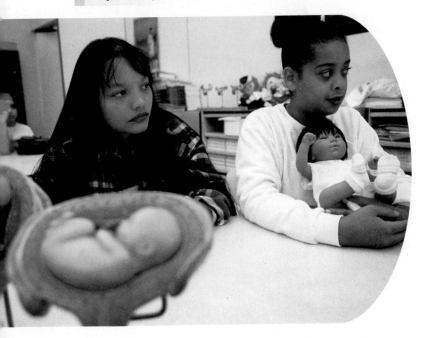

Learn Through Education and Training

You are already educating yourself about parenting by reading this book. You can take your education a step further through activities like these:

- Read other books about parenting and child care.
- Take additional classes about parenting, child development, child care, and related issues. See Fig. 3-9.
- When you're ready, attend workshops for parents-to-be and new parents at schools, hospitals, and other locations.

▶ Parent Educator

Parent educators work with parents to help them understand their children's developmental needs and to offer ideas on how to help their children develop physically, emotionally, socially, and intellectually. Parent educators are especially helpful to parents who face special challenges, such as raising a child with special needs or raising a child alone.

"I help parents gain the skills they need to help their children. For example, I worked with one family that thought their 10-month-old had developmental delays because he wasn't rolling, crawling, or bringing his hand to his mouth. After observing the family, I realized that his mother and sister held him all the time and did everything for him. He never had a chance to learn to do things for himself. I explained this to the family, and in just six weeks the child was able to roll, crawl, pull himself up to furniture, feed himself, and babble more sounds. His parents called me later to let me know their son was walking on his first birthday!"

CAREER TIPS

- While in high school, take courses on subjects like parenting and child development.
- Volunteer to work with children and their parents in community settings.
- Earn your bachelor's degree in an area like Early Childhood Education or Child Development.
- Consider interning with an organization like Head Start, which offers parent education services.
- Consider earning a Parent Education Certificate from a college or professional organization.

Fig. 3-10. Relationships grow stronger when couples take time to get to know each other. **In what ways does abstinence take pressure off couples?**

Make a Responsible Choice

Now that you have a better idea of what it takes to be ready for parenthood, consider your own situation. In what ways are you prepared for parenthood? In what ways are you not prepared? By now, you might feel that if you're not absolutely ready to make a huge commitment, you are probably not ready to be a parent.

Choosing Abstinence

There is only one way to be absolutely sure you won't become a parent too soon. **Abstinence**—refraining from any form of sexual activity—is a guaranteed way to avoid pregnancy. Abstinence can also offer other benefits. For example:

- By abstaining from any form of sexual activity, you avoid any risk of becoming infected with potentially harmful or deadly sexually transmitted diseases.
- Many people are pressured to have sex before they are ready. Some may engage in sex to avoid a confrontation. If you make a commitment to be abstinent, you are not likely to be coerced into having sex when you don't want to.
- For some couples, sex replaces talking and doing things together. As a result, the relationship never has a chance to grow. Abstinent couples may take more time to learn about one another's likes and dislikes, hobbies, dreams, goals, and concerns. See Fig. 3-10.
- When your relationship doesn't involve sexual activity, you learn to find other ways to express affection and show that you care about each other.

Child-Free Choices

Not everyone who is emotionally, physically, and financially ready to become a parent chooses to take on the responsibility. Many decide to wait before becoming parents. Some are not parents now but hope to have children someday when the circumstances are right. Others choose not to become parents at all.

Just as there are many possible reasons for becoming a parent, there are many possible reasons for choosing not to. Some people simply don't feel a strong desire to have children.

For some, activities such as a career, travel, or personal interests may provide a greater sense of fulfillment than parenthood would. Whatever the reasons, the decision to parent, or not to parent, is a very personal one. See Fig. 3-11.

Looking Toward the Future

Getting ready for parenthood takes time. You may want to see the world—or complete your education—before you settle down. You may want to start a career, build up your savings, or buy a home. You may want to try spending time with children—as a caregiver, educator, or volunteer—to get a better sense of your parenting skills. There is no reason to rush into parenthood.

Teens have a golden opportunity to think hard about the responsibilities of parenting. They are able to make informed decisions about whether or when they want children. Many decide to wait before having a child, and others may decide that they don't want to have a child at all.

The fact is, having children changes your life. It's impossible to predict what those changes will be for each family. Some things, however, are predictable. Being a parent will be the cause of significant personal growth for each person. Also, parents need to have the time, money, stamina, and patience that raising a child requires. The best time to choose parenthood is when a couple is physically, financially, and emotionally ready. That is when a child may become a wanted and most welcome addition to a family.

Fig. 3-11. Each couple must decide for themselves whether to become parents. **What factors might influence their choice?**

Modeling CHARACTER

Choosing Integrity

Teens who choose abstinence often face pressures that can make it difficult to carry out their decision. Just remember that acting according to what you value shows that you have *integrity*. By standing firm in your decision to do what you believe is right, you can be a role model for others.

How can teens stand up to pressure to be sexually active? Here are some suggestions.

- Avoid situations that could lead to sexual intimacy. Plan activities to include other people and meeting in public places.
- Discuss your feelings with the other person in your relationship before an intimate situation happens. Make sure each of you understands and respects the other's view.
- Say no firmly and convincingly. Don't wait to be asked.
- Practice ways to say no. Focus on the value of the relationship. Use reason. Try different messages to suit the situation. For example, you might say, "I don't feel emotionally ready to take on a physically intimate relationship."
- If you're tempted to give in, ask yourself: Will I be proud to recall this moment in a few hours, months, or a year? In five years? Will I be able to tell my parents what happened?
- Find others who have chosen abstinence. Knowing that others share your views can give you confidence.

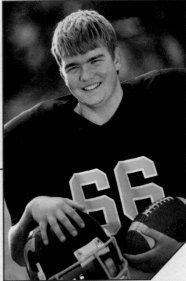

Think About It

What are the short-term and long-term benefits of choosing abstinence? How does this choice demonstrate the value of integrity?

CHAPTER SUMMARY

● Self-assessment is a way to examine emotional maturity and personal goals.
● Age and health issues affect physical readiness for parenting.
● Although people want to be parents for many good reasons, some want to be parents for poor reasons.
● A couple should establish a healthy relationship before deciding to have a child.
● Responsible parents are financially prepared to meet the expenses of raising a child.
● By learning about parenting and acting responsibly, people are better equipped to make decisions about whether or when to parent.

Check Your Facts

1. What is emotional maturity?
2. How can the following show emotional maturity: responsibility, commitment, and deferring personal needs?
3. When caring for an infant feels overwhelming, how does a parent show emotional maturity?
4. How might having a child too soon impact career and personal goals?
5. Why are age and health big factors in parenting readiness?
6. Describe three health concerns for pregnant teens.
7. What difficulties might a child born to a teen mother have?
8. What are two good reasons people might have for wanting children?
9. What are four poor reasons people might have for wanting children?
10. Describe four qualities of a healthy relationship.
11. Why is having a baby and raising the child a financial concern?
12. What are four financial questions to consider before having a baby?
13. What are three general ways to learn what parenting is like? Give examples.
14. What are two benefits of abstinence besides avoiding pregnancy?
15. Why do some couples choose not to have children?
16. How can a person stand up to pressures to be sexually active?

Think Critically

1. **Predicting Reactions.** Suppose you had to miss out on a special occasion planned with friends in order to take care of a younger brother or sister. How would you react? What would you say to friends and family? How would you treat the child? How does this situation relate to parenting readiness?
2. **Making Generalizations.** Why do teens tend to be less ready for parenthood than adults are?

Apply Your Learning

1. **Maturity Assessment.** With the class, create a questionnaire that can be used to assess emotional maturity. Include points in the chapter and other questions that you think help determine maturity. Answer the questions privately to analyze your own maturity level. How do the results relate to parenting readiness?

2. **You Be the Counselor.** Suppose you are a family counselor helping a couple. They are both age 19, have been married for six months, and are talking about having a baby. She says she wants a large family, and he frowns at this. He is taking technical courses and works full time at a discount store. She has a full-time job at a restaurant and can't wait to quit. What potential problems can you identify? What questions will you ask? How will you guide the couple?

Cross-Curricular Connections

1. **Language Arts.** Identify at least three of your personal and career goals. In writing, analyze what would happen to each of these goals if you became a parent before achieving each one. What do you learn about your parenting readiness?

2. **Math.** Research the estimated cost of raising a child from birth to age 18. How many different types of expenses will there be? Create a chart that breaks down the costs by category.

Family & Community Connections

1. **Goals and Parenting.** Talk to one or two adult family members who are parents about their goals and parenting. What were their personal and career goals when they were teens? In other words, what did they want to do and be after high school and beyond? When did they become parents? Did their goals change after becoming parents? If so, how? What impacts did this have on them and their life? Take notes and share your findings in a written or oral report.

2. **Parenting Educator at Work.** With a team of classmates, visit a parenting educator at work. Take notes as you observe the educator. What topics does the educator cover when working with parents? How does the educator help people prepare for parenting? Share your notes in class.

CHAPTER 4

Understanding Child Development

CHAPTER OBJECTIVES

- Describe the five areas of development.
- Explain basic principles of child development.
- Assess how heredity and environment impact development.
- Summarize theories presented by influential child development experts.
- Identify and describe the stages of child development.

PARENTING TERMS

- development
- physical development
- intellectual development
- emotional development
- social development
- moral development
- heredity
- environment
- theory
- infancy
- toddlers
- preschoolers
- puberty

Have you heard the expression "Knowledge is power"? Knowing the facts helps people make informed decisions. When it comes to parenting, people who learn about the stages of child development are more likely to have reasonable expectations for their children's progress. They are also better equipped to provide surroundings that are safe, supportive, loving, and healthy.

Principles of Child Development

Think of the difference between what you were like as an infant and what you are today. In between, an amazing amount of development has taken place. **Development** is a process that includes growth—becoming taller, for example—as well as progress in skills and abilities. See Fig. 4-1.

As children mature, they pass through various stages of development. During each stage, development occurs in several areas:

- **Physical.** Increases in size and weight, along with the increasing ability to control and coordinate body movements, are examples of **physical development**.
- **Intellectual.** The ways children develop language, solve problems, and remember what they learn are examples of **intellectual development**.
- **Emotional.** Learning to recognize feelings and express them appropriately is the process of **emotional development**.
- **Social.** Learning to relate to other people is the process of **social development**.
- **Moral.** The process of learning to distinguish between right and wrong is **moral development**.

Each child is unique. However, certain basic principles of development can be observed in all children.

Development Is Sequential

Would you try out for a hockey team if you didn't know how to ice skate? Of course you wouldn't. If you wanted to play ice hockey, you'd learn to skate first. Similarly, children master tasks in a logical order. The sequence of development follows recognizable patterns, including:

- **From simple to complex.** Before children can run, they must learn to stand, then walk. Before they speak in complete sentences, they learn to say simple words.
- **From head to foot.** A newborn's head is large compared with the rest of the body. Later, the development of the arms and legs catches up.
- **From the center of the body outward.** For example, babies first use their shoulder muscles to wave their arms at objects they want. Later, as they develop better control over their arms, hands, and fingers, they are able to grasp objects and pick them up.

Development Proceeds at an Individual Rate

If you have ever spent time with children, you know how different one child can be from another. It's normal for there to be a certain amount of difference in the rate of development among children in the same age group. Although descriptions of the "average" child can be useful, keep in mind that no child will fit that description exactly. General patterns of development hold true for most children, but the rate of individual development varies.

Development Is Interrelated

Progress in one area of development affects progress in others. For example, as a child develops intellectually by learning to read, he or she also gains a sense of accomplishment that contributes to emotional development. On the other hand, suppose a learning disability creates difficulty with reading. If the child feels discouraged and is teased by classmates, emotional and social development can be affected.

Fig. 4-1. As children develop, they gain new skills and take pride in their accomplishments. **What skills do you remember developing as a child? How did you feel when you mastered them?**

Development Continues Throughout Life

Many researchers believe that the first three years of life are a critical period in human development. From birth to age three, the brain develops rapidly. Emotional, social, and intellectual skills gained during this time are the foundation for later accomplishments.

However, development certainly does not end at age three, or even with childhood. Throughout your life, you can continue to develop new skills and abilities, make wiser choices, gain a deeper understanding of yourself, and forge stronger bonds with others. Life is a continuing process of development—which is one reason why human growth and behavior is such a fascinating area of study.

THE DEVELOPING BRAIN

Inside each newborn's brain are about 100 billion *neurons*, or nerve cells. These cells transmit information to one another by firing electrical signals across *synapses*—the junction points between neurons. Synapses allow each neuron to connect to thousands of others.

The connections between neurons are not fixed and unchangeable. Just as lifting weights can cause muscles to grow, enriching experiences cause neural connections to develop. The 50 trillion synapses an infant has at birth will grow to an astounding 1,000 trillion within the first several months of life. The final number of synapses can increase or decrease by as much as 25 percent, depending on the level of positive attention and interaction the baby receives. Talking to an infant, singing songs, playing patty-cake—all can help build the brain connections that are so important.

Factors That Influence Development

Every person has one-of-a-kind qualities—but where do those qualities come from? What causes each person to develop into a unique individual? Two major factors are at work: heredity and environment.

Heredity

Sondra's relatives often say that her wavy hair comes from her father and her brown eyes from her mother—and they're right. Scientists have long known that hair texture, eye color, and other physical traits are inherited. The biological process by which certain traits are transmitted from parents to their children is called **heredity**.

Each inherited trait is determined by a specific gene. A *gene* is a small section of a chromosome. *Chromosomes* are threadlike structures found within the nucleus, or center, of body cells. Each human body cell has 46 chromosomes, and each chromosome has hundreds, or perhaps thousands, of genes.

It's clear that some traits, like eye color, are determined solely by

Fig. 4-2. Cultural influences are part of a child's environment. **In what ways might they affect development?**

heredity. With many other traits, the answer is not so clear. Studies suggest that intellectual ability, for example, is influenced by both heredity and environment.

Environment

Environment refers to all the conditions and circumstances affecting a person's daily life. Many environmental factors can affect development.

The most influential part of a child's environment is the family. Many of your beliefs, attitudes, and habits probably come from your family—not through heredity, but through teaching and example. Even within the same family, the environment is slightly different for an oldest child compared to a middle or youngest child.

Other factors also play a role. The society and culture in which you live transmit values and customs that help shape the person you become. See Fig. 4-2.

Economic conditions, too, can influence development. However, a family doesn't have to be wealthy to provide an enriching environment. A loving atmosphere and plenty of positive interaction will do more to foster development than all the expensive toys in the world.

Having access to technology, such as the resources of health care facilities, may enhance certain aspects of development. In addition, each individual will be affected by the particular events that occur in his or her life. These are just some of the environmental factors that influence the person a child will become.

Child Development Theorists

Early in the 20th century, physicians and social scientists began studying children and working out theories about their development. A **theory** is a set of ideas based on observations and analysis. Many of the principles set forth by these child development theorists are still relied on today.

Maria Montessori

One of the first to develop a theory about how children learn was Maria Montessori (1870–1952). According to Dr. Montessori, learning takes place in three stages:

- Being introduced to a concept.
- Processing the information.
- Knowing the information well enough to easily express it or teach it to someone.

Montessori was one of several educators whose ideas about how children learn are built on a theory called *constructivism*. Constructivism is based on the idea that children build knowledge by actively participating in the learning process. Constructivist teachers use a wide variety of hands-on learning tools, such as cut-out shapes of alphabet letters. Their classrooms provide the freedom for children to explore various activities at different learning centers. See Fig. 4-3.

Arnold Gesell

Arnold Gesell (1880–1961) conducted studies which suggested that each child develops at his or her own rate, based on an "inner timetable" determined by heredity. Dr. Gesell felt it was useless to teach a skill to a child before he or she was developmentally ready. To determine which learning opportunities were best for individual children, Gesell developed tests for systematically evaluating a child's physical, social, and language development and ability to adapt to new situations. See Fig. 4-4.

Fig. 4-3. Maria Montessori believed classrooms should be child centered rather than teacher centered. Her method is still employed in countless Montessori schools around the world today.

Fig. 4-5. B. F. Skinner felt that learning should be structured and led by teachers. **In his view, how should the teacher structure learning?**

B. F. Skinner

B. F. Skinner (1904–1990) believed that behavior is predictable. He theorized that learning can be structured by setting clear objectives and providing positive reinforcement—responses that encourage children to repeat specific behaviors. Positive reinforcement might include praise, an excellent grade, or simply fostering the child's personal sense of pride.

Unlike constructivists, who believed learning should be child centered, Skinner and other *behaviorists* thought the teacher should clearly be in charge. Skinner also believed children learn best by committing facts to memory through practice and repetition. See Fig. 4-5.

Jean Piaget

Jean Piaget (ZHAWN pee-ah-ZHAY) (1896–1980) believed that learning occurs as children interact with their environment. He defined four stages of cognitive development that determine the way children are capable of learning at various ages. Later chapters of this book explain Piaget's stages.

Piaget theorized that learning should be fostered by putting children in situations that engage their minds. His principles have influenced preschool teachers and parents to provide young children with hands-on play objects. See Fig. 4-6.

Lev Vygotsky

Lev Vygotsky (1896–1934) worked out a social development theory of learning. This theory says that socializing with adults or more capable peers equips children with words, concepts, and techniques that help them learn.

Fig. 4-6. Many of Piaget's experiments related to the age at which children should be introduced to various logical and mathematical concepts.

Fig. 4-7. This child knows that pointing a finger can communicate "I want that." **According to Vygotsky's theory, how did the child gain this understanding?**

Like Piaget, Vygotsky believed that intellectual development is limited to certain skills at any given age. An infant does not realize the significance of pointing a finger, for example, whereas a two-year-old child understands the meaning of the gesture. See Fig. 4-7.

Albert Bandura

Albert Bandura (born 1925) is known for his social learning theory. This theory states that learning is based on a four-step process of watching and copying the behavior of others. The four steps are:

- Attention—watching or listening to the new behavior.
- Retention—remembering the behavior that was seen or heard.
- Reproducing—doing the behavior oneself.
- Motivation—wanting to continue the behavior.

Bandura believes that children are more motivated to reproduce a behavior if the outcome is something they value. In other words, they learn better if they expect a "payoff" such as parental praise, peer admiration, or a good grade in school. See Fig. 4-8.

Fig. 4-8. Albert Bandura's social learning concepts can be applied in many ways. **How might the producer of a television commercial use Bandura's ideas to make the ad more effective?**

Erik Erikson

Erik Erikson (1902–1994) studied emotional and social development. He theorized that all human beings progress through eight stages of psychosocial development. According to Erikson, each of these eight life stages is defined by a crisis or turning point. Only by resolving the crisis or reaching the turning point can an individual develop in a psychologically healthy way. You will learn more about Erikson's stages in Chapter 18. See Fig. 4-9.

Urie Bronfenbrenner

Urie Bronfenbrenner (born 1917) set forth a theory of development that he called "environmentalist." He believed that interacting with others in one's environment is crucial to development.

According to Bronfenbrenner, children experience four types of environments, each with different expectations for behavior:

- Microsystem—a child's daily environment, such as home and school.
- Mesosystem—connections between the home and school environments.
- Exosystem—an outside environment, such as a parent's workplace, that indirectly affects the child.
- Macrosystem—the larger environment, such as the country where the child lives.

Lawrence Kohlberg

Lawrence Kohlberg (1927–1987) studied moral development. He believed that individuals progress through three levels of moral development as they mature.

- The first level occurs throughout childhood, starting between the ages of six and ten. Children follow rules because they are told to do so by an authority figure such as a parent or teacher. See Fig. 4-10.

Fig. 4-9. Erikson's view of the stages of development sets him apart from others in his field.

Fig. 4-10. In Lawrence Kohlberg's view, the early stages of moral development depend on the influence of an authority figure. **Who were your authority figures when you were growing up?**

- The second level of moral development occurs in adulthood. Adults at this level abide by rules and laws because society expects it.
- At the third level of moral development, adults make moral choices because they truly care about how their actions will affect others. According to Kohlberg, some adults never reach this level. Kohlberg's theory and other ideas about moral development are discussed in Chapter 22.

Robert Coles

Robert Coles (born 1929) devoted his career to learning about the moral development of children. Unlike most other social scientists, who base their theories primarily on observations and experiments, Coles talked directly with inner city children and recorded their thoughts and feelings. His books aim to convey, in the children's own words, the reasoning they use to make moral decisions in their lives. See Fig. 4-11.

Fig. 4-11. Psychiatrist Robert Coles, a professor at Harvard University, blends scientific inquiry and personal interviews to learn about the inner lives of children in challenging circumstances.

Child & Family Services
CAREERS

▶ Mental Health Therapist

Mental health therapists treat mental and emotional disorders of individuals and families to help them develop the best possible outlook on life. They are trained to counsel people needing help with a variety of issues, including family issues, parenting concerns, poor self-esteem, depression, suicidal impulses, and alcohol and drug abuse. Some therapists specialize in helping families resolve emotional conflicts and enhance communication.

"After receiving my undergraduate degree in psychology, I decided to earn my master's degree in social work and seek employment as a family therapist. An advanced degree in psychology would also have qualified me for this work, but since I already had a psychology degree, I felt a graduate degree in social work would give me a broader perspective."

CAREER TIPS

- Volunteer to work with at-risk children through community programs.
- Get a college degree in social work, psychology, or counseling.
- Pass a state licensure exam.
- Apply for a position at several community, state, and government agencies.

Fig. 4-12. Infants reach predictable milestones when they are developmentally ready. **Why is it important for parents to understand this?**

Child Development Stages

Psychologists and other experts have observed and reported on the developmental stages that children experience. Knowing what to expect during each stage helps parents better understand and respond appropriately to their children's behavior and needs.

Infancy

Infancy is the stage that begins at birth and lasts through twelve months of age. As infants develop, they progress through a series of predictable milestones, such as rolling over or saying their first word. However, infants are individuals and reach milestones when they are developmentally ready to do so. Children who are born prematurely—that is, before their due dates—usually reach each milestone a bit later than full-term babies. See Fig. 4-12.

Physical Development. Infants undergo tremendous physical changes during their first year of life. Here are some of the milestones of an infant's physical development:

- At two months, most infants have grown about 3 inches and gained about 3 pounds. They can hold up their heads, but only for short periods when lying on their stomachs.
- By four months, infants have typically grown another 2.25 inches and gained 2 more pounds. Many can hold up their heads and bear some weight on their legs when held upright.
- By six months, most infants have gained another 2 pounds, doubling their birth weight, and grown another 1.5 inches. Their heads are bigger, too, to accommodate their rapidly growing brains. Most can roll over and sit with some support.
- Between six and twelve months, physical growth slows down and motor development speeds up. By seven months, most infants crawl and sit without support. By twelve months, many can walk with support, and some can walk a few steps alone.

Progression of Early Intellectual Development	
Age of Infant	**Milestone**
1 to 2 months	❑ Looks at people and objects ❑ Makes "ooh" and "aah" sounds
2 to 4 months	❑ Coos in response to others' speech ❑ Anticipates events (e.g., smiles when put in a stroller)
4 to 6 months	❑ Makes more sounds ❑ Recognizes own name
6 to 9 months	❑ Says "mama" and "dada" ❑ Understands more words ❑ Looks for a dropped object
9 to 12 months	❑ Adds 1 to 3 more words to vocabulary ❑ Imitates sounds such as "bow wow"

Fig. 4-13. Milestones in language and thinking skills are evident in the first year. **How do these milestones illustrate the basic principles of development?**

Intellectual Development. Infants' intellectual growth during the first year is just as astonishing as their rapid physical growth. Fig. 4-13 lists some intellectual milestones throughout infancy.

Emotional and Social Development. Infants' personalities begin to blossom during their first year.

- At one month, infants widen their eyes in recognition and smile at parents or caregivers.
- By four months, infants make and keep eye contact, wave their arms, smile, and often stop crying when a loved one picks them up.
- From four to six months, infants become more social. They laugh and love to cuddle. They make eye contact with friendly strangers.
- From six to nine months, the bonds infants form with loved ones grow stronger. They miss absent parents and develop a fear of strangers.
- From nine to twelve months, love bonds strengthen even more, and fear of strangers

grows. Infants this age may hide their faces when a stranger speaks to them and cry when an unfamiliar relative attempts to pick them up.

The Toddler Stage

One- and two-year-old children are often called **toddlers**. During this period, children move from the complete dependency of infancy to learning to walk, talk, and relate to others.

Physical Development. The rapid physical growth of infancy slows during the toddler stage. Since they need less energy for growth, toddlers tend to eat less. They may "graze" on small portions frequently throughout the day.

During these years, children lose their "baby fat." Their legs grow thinner and longer, making the head appear to be more in proportion to the body. At age two, the brain has grown to 55 percent of its adult size.

Toddlers are quite physically active. By fourteen months, most can walk without support. By age two, toddlers can walk, run, and climb.

Fig. 4-14. "Mine" is a word often used by toddlers. They typically think something belongs to them only as long as they hang onto it. **Why would this make it difficult for them to share?**

Intellectual Development. Toddlers are extremely curious and enjoy exploring their surroundings. They develop a sense of humor and can imitate animal sounds. They typically begin to speak at age one. By the time they are two, most toddlers can speak in two- or three-word sentences and sing simple songs.

Toddlers have a short attention span and are easily distracted. Wise parents capitalize on this characteristic by quickly diverting a toddler's attention when the child becomes frustrated.

Emotional and Social Development. Toddlers do become frustrated easily. One reason is that toddlers want to do things for themselves that they are not yet capable of doing. They try and try—and often cry and cry—until they master a task. Temper tantrums—fits of anger in which the child cries, screams, hits, or kicks—are common. However, they usually pass quickly if the toddler is presented with another activity or toy.

Toddlers are self-centered and have a hard time sharing their possessions. See Fig. 4-14. However, they enjoy playing near, if not always with, other children. They like to imitate adults, but still do not understand how their actions, such as refusing to do what they are told, affect others.

The Preschool Stage

The term **preschoolers** usually refers to children who are three, four, or five years of age. Preschoolers are eager for independence and want to show what they can do.

Physical Development. Preschoolers continue to progress in their physical skills. They enjoy engaging in active play that uses large muscles. Three-year-olds can stand on their tiptoes and stand on one foot. Four-year-olds can hop on one foot and skip. By age five, children are learning to jump, run, and throw. Preschoolers are also becoming more skilled at controlling the small muscles of their hands and fingers as they learn to write, draw, tie knots, and button clothes.

Intellectual Development. Preschoolers are interested in the world around them, are eager to learn, and have very active imaginations. Language skills increase rapidly. Whereas a two-year-old knows about one or two hundred words, five-year-olds typically have at least two thousand words in their vocabulary.

As their brains develop, preschoolers' mental skills become more sophisticated. Four- and five-year-olds begin to connect ideas logically. As their short- and long-term memory improves, they can recall short word lists read to them and describe past events in greater detail. They like to play "pretend," and they can play games that require following simple rules.

Emotional, Social, and Moral Development. Preschoolers are intent on developing self-confidence and separating from their parents. At the same time, they need the security of a parent nearby to encourage them and applaud their accomplishments.

By age three or four, children are able to play cooperatively with one another. However, they still prefer to have their own way. See Fig. 4-15.

Preschoolers are sensitive to their family's standards of "good" and "bad" behavior. They can anticipate adult reactions to inappropriate behavior.

Fig. 4-15. Preschoolers begin to interact with one another as they play. **How does playing together with toy animals demonstrate both social and intellectual development?**

Modeling CHARACTER

Encouraging Responsibility

Effective parents encourage the development of responsibility in their children. *Responsibility* includes being accountable for one's words and actions, accepting positive and negative consequences for those words and actions, and being willing to admit and correct mistakes. Here are some ways to encourage responsibility in children:

- **Have age-appropriate expectations.** It's not fair to expect a toddler to be as responsible as a six-year-old. Consider a child's age and stage of development.
- **Set fair, reasonable limits.** Responsibility develops when children make the choice to stay within their limits. For example, "You may ride your tricycle if you stay on the driveway."
- **Set reasonable consequences that children understand.** Children should know what to expect if they break a limit. "If you ride your tricycle off the driveway, I will take it away for the rest of the day."
- **Provide opportunities for children to correct their mistakes when possible.** This reinforces responsibility.
- **Reward responsibility.** Rewards do not have to cost anything. Sometimes just saying "I'm proud of you" is all the reward needed.
- **Model responsibility in your own behavior.** Keep your promises. When you make a mistake, admit it and accept the consequences. Even if you don't think children will notice, they do. By observing and following your example, children learn what it means to be responsible.

Think About It

How can having age-appropriate expectations encourage responsibility through all stages of child development? Give an example for each age level.

Middle Childhood

Children ages six through ten are developing greater competence in all areas of development. For most, entering school is a milestone that affects many aspects of their lives.

Physical Development. Changes in height and weight are very apparent in middle childhood. Another noticeable physical change is the loss of primary, or "baby," teeth and the growth of permanent teeth. This process begins at about age six and continues at a rate of about four teeth per year. See Fig. 4-16.

At this age, boys and girls are fairly evenly matched physically, as both grow stronger and more coordinated. Becoming proficient at a sport is a traditional way for children in this stage to develop physical skills as well as skills in other areas of development.

Intellectual Development. In middle childhood, children gradually begin thinking in more complex ways. They move from understanding simple sentences at age six to grasping fairly complicated ideas at age ten. Mathematical ability also becomes more developed. Though reasoning is still immature, children begin to think things through for themselves. However, they still think concretely in the "here and now" rather than dealing in abstractions.

Emotional and Social Development. Children from ages six through ten gradually begin to refine their emotional and social skills as they come into contact with new people at school and in the community. Establishing an identity separate from the family is a major task in middle childhood. Children this age try out behaviors on their peers as they develop a sense of who they are and what they stand for.

The self-centered viewpoint of early childhood begins to subside by age ten. Many children begin to develop the ability to put themselves in another's place. They are able to set their own immediate desires aside to help the team or the group.

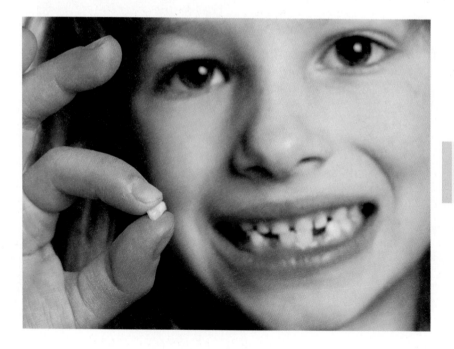

Fig. 4-16. Losing primary teeth and growing permanent teeth is a sign that young children are growing up.

Fig. 4-17. In early adolescence, the average height for girls is about an inch taller than that for boys. However, physical development varies widely among individuals.

Toward the end of this stage, children become choosier about their friends, developing relationships based on common interests. However, aggression can be a problem if a child's social skills have not kept pace with his or her growing physical strength.

Moral Development. Morally, children's sense of right and wrong continues to develop, but it sometimes conflicts with the desire to "fit in" with their peer group. Developing a conscience and learning responsibility and fair play are developmentally important for this age group.

Early Adolescence

The stage known as early adolescence lasts from about age eleven through about age fourteen. All areas of development—physical, intellectual, emotional, social, and moral—are more markedly different among individuals now than at any other stage. Not only are adolescents changing in every way, but they are often needlessly concerned that their changes are too fast, too slow, or abnormal in some other way.

Physical Development. Both boys and girls grow taller during this stage, but girls usually begin their growth spurt sooner. It's not unusual at this age for girls to be taller than boys. See Fig. 4-17.

It's also common for various body parts to grow at different rates. Early adolescents may worry that they have gangly arms and legs, huge feet, or a big nose. Most will eventually "grow into" their features as growth catches up in all areas.

Most eleven- to fourteen-year-olds enter **puberty**, the stage of physical development when sexual reproduction first becomes possible. Most boys show the first sign of puberty between the ages of ten and twelve when their testicles enlarge. Most girls begin to develop breasts between the ages of nine and eleven. Some are having regular periods by age eleven; others do not begin to menstruate until they are fifteen.

Body fat increases in females as they develop physically, but decreases in males as they grow taller. In both genders, the heart doubles in weight, and the lungs grow larger. Males grow facial hair, and both genders grow hair around the genitals and under their arms. Males' voices gradually deepen, often "cracking" and embarrassing them.

Intellectual Development. Young adolescents have a greater ability to perform more complicated mental tasks. At the beginning of this stage, they are still largely unable to think in the abstract and often fail to consider the consequences of their actions. By age fourteen, however, most can begin to think ahead by forming abstract concepts. Nevertheless, a teen's reasoning and judgment skills are still immature compared with an adult's, even though the teen may look physically mature.

Emotional, Social, and Moral Development. "Moody" is a word commonly used to describe early adolescents. Some are overwhelmed by hormonal and physical changes, and nearly all teens struggle to develop a sense of identity. "Am I normal?" and "Who am I?" are two questions that early adolescents ask themselves. Conflict with parents is common, as adolescents work at defining their own separate identity. Interest in dating increases. This, along with the desire for peer approval and a drive for independence, often conflicts with the parental need to continue to nurture teens.

THE DEVELOPING BRAIN

Brain growth in early adolescence is primarily in the frontal lobe, which controls reasoning, judgment, and self-control.

As early adolescents develop morally, they often test the rules set by parents and other authority figures. However, young teens are also developing ideals and seeking role models. They begin to show consistent evidence of being guided by a conscience. Relying on their conscience provides them with the courage to reject peer behavior that conflicts with their values.

Late Adolescence

From ages fifteen through eighteen, teens continue to develop at their own pace. Some look physically mature, while others are still growing. They vary in other areas of development, too. It takes some teens longer than others, but eventually they all complete this final stage of child development and enter the world of adulthood.

Physical Development. Research shows that females usually grow only another 1.5 to 2.5 inches taller following their first menstrual period. Males, however, generally don't begin their growth spurt until two years after puberty begins. Although their growth spurt begins later, it tends to occur faster and last longer than that of females. In late adolescence, most males surpass most females in height, weight, and strength, and both sexes achieve sexual maturity.

Fig. 4-18. Teens in late adolescence can use their growing intellectual skills to complete complicated school projects. **How would sequential logical thinking help a teen complete a research paper?**

THE DEVELOPING BRAIN

According to studies at the National Institute of Mental Health, the connections being made in teens' brains during late adolescence will affect the way their thought processes work for the rest of their lives.

Intellectual Development. Most teens from ages fifteen through eighteen are capable of sequential logical thinking. That is, they can project the logical consequences of their actions and juggle several concepts simultaneously. As mental abilities progress, writing, speaking, and mathematical skills improve. See Fig. 4-18.

Emotional and Social Development. Personal awareness of sexual feelings during late adolescence can have a strong effect on emotional and social development. Interest in romance and intimacy grows. However, acting on these feelings is a choice. Family, cultural, and religious values can have a strong impact on teens' behavior.

Moral Development. For many fifteen- to eighteen-year-olds, conflicts with parents decrease as teens gain more self-confidence and emotional control. Moral development spurs concern for others, as teens develop the ability to compromise and to delay gratification. Peer relationships are still important, but many teens place increased importance on determining the next life step, be it further education or employment.

Review & Activities

CHAPTER SUMMARY

- Human development is a process that includes growth as well as progress in skills and abilities. Development can be categorized into five specific areas.
- Both heredity and environment influence children's development.
- Physicians and social scientists have devised theories about how children develop.
- Children progress through certain stages of development. At each stage parents and other caregivers can use their knowledge of development to respond appropriately.

Check Your Facts

1. Describe the five areas of development.
2. What are three patterns that show sequential development?
3. Compare rate of development with patterns of development.
4. Give an example that shows how areas of development are interrelated.
5. What causes neurons to make connections in the developing brain?
6. What are heredity and environment as related to human development?
7. How do social scientists produce a theory of development?
8. Describe a Montessori classroom.
9. What is positive reinforcement? Give an example.
10. What is Piaget known for?
11. What are Kolhberg's three levels of moral development?
12. Identify the five stages of development and the ages they include.
13. What are typical ages for these infant accomplishments: a) holding up the head; b) rolling over; c) crawling; d) walking with support?
14. Why might a parent be easily frustrated by a toddler's behavior?
15. When do children first start learning the difference between right and wrong?
16. What can cause an early adolescent to be moody?

Think Critically

1. **Categorizing Information.** Learn more about the theories of the child development experts named in the chapter. Then categorize each expert according to who might believe heredity has more influence on development and who might say environment.
2. **Predicting Consequences.** Suppose a child isn't developing the physical skills and speech patterns that are typical for the child's age, but the parent doesn't know what is typical. Predict what might happen. How could knowledge of development make a difference?

Apply Your Learning

1. **Child-Centered or Teacher-Centered.** With a team of students, research one of the following: the child-centered classroom (promoted by Montessori) or the teacher-centered classroom (promoted by Skinner). Discuss the two approaches. Which method of learning do you think is more effective? Why?

2. **Development Chart.** Create a chart that shows how a person develops from infancy through adolescence. Include physical, intellectual, emotional, social, and moral development. Display the chart in your classroom for reference throughout the course.

3. **Preschool Advertisement.** Imagine you are planning the curriculum for a new preschool. Write an advertisement that highlights how activities will meet developmental needs of preschool children.

4. **The First Three Years.** Investigate why the first three years of life are thought to be critical to a child's development. Share your findings with the class.

Cross-Curricular Connections

1. **Language Arts.** On paper, list 15 to 20 human characteristics: for example, hair color, shyness, sense of humor, and intelligence. Then indicate how you think each one is acquired: beside each trait write *H* for heredity, *E* for environment, or both. Compare results in class. Then write a summary about how you think heredity and environment influence human development.

2. **Science.** Investigate genetics and heredity. What is the role of dominant and recessive genes? How do such genes influence development? Create visuals to use in an oral report for the class.

Family & Community Connections

1. **Family Games.** Ask family members what developmental games have been played with children in your family. Explore games from infancy and beyond, in recent as well as past generations. What were some family favorites? How did each game influence development? Which games would you use in your own family someday?

2. **Preschool Observation.** Visit a child-care center and observe one preschooler for at least 15 minutes. Take notes on the developmental skills you observe. What do you conclude about the child's age and development?

Effective Parenting Skills

CHAPTER OBJECTIVES

- Describe how parents can make use of various management skills.
- Explain the value of interpersonal skills in parenting.
- Relate personal qualities to parenting success.
- Compare the three basic parenting styles: authoritarian, authoritative, and permissive.
- Evaluate sources of parenting information.

PARENTING TERMS

- prioritize
- resource
- proactive
- mentoring
- consensus
- compromise
- negotiation
- mediator
- parenting style

Imagine that people had to apply for the job of parent. On their job applications, they would have to list their relevant skills and experience. If you were applying for that job, what would you list?

The skills and qualities needed to be an effective parent can be learned over time—not just by trial and error, but by making an effort to learn and improve. Take a closer look at what might qualify someone for the job of parent.

The Need for Parenting Skills

Think of the skills a parent might need. What comes to mind? You might think of a baby crying, and the ability of a parent to feed, clothe, or comfort the infant. You might think of a child running out in the street, and the ability of a parent to watch over and protect the child.

Parenting requires those skills and more. In fact, being a successful parent requires many of the same skills as being a successful student. To do well in school, a person needs to be able to solve problems, manage time, make good decisions, set and achieve goals, and communicate well. These skills are essential to good parenting, too. See Fig. 5-1.

In this chapter, you'll learn about some of the management and interpersonal skills that parents use to achieve success. You'll also learn why parents need to develop personal qualities such as patience, confidence, and a sense of humor. Finally, this chapter looks at different parenting styles and how parents choose among them.

The skills and qualities described in this chapter are not the only ones that parents and caregivers need, but they provide a good basis for developing other effective parenting skills. Make these your strengths, and you will have a head start when it comes to parenting.

Management Skills

Whether they realize it or not, effective parents use management skills all the time. Personal management skills include the ability to set priorities and goals, identify and use resources well, make decisions, and solve problems.

Setting Priorities

Good management starts with being able to **prioritize**—to set priorities by deciding what you consider to be most important. Priorities are often based on values. For example, parents may tell their children that doing homework has priority over watching TV. This decision is based on one of the parents' values: the importance of getting an education and being a responsible student.

Fig. 5-1. Parents and other caregivers put parenting skills to good use at home and in other settings. **Why do all caregivers need good parenting skills?**

Fig. 5-2. Parents need to set priorities in many aspects of family life. **What are some examples of how parents can set priorities for themselves and their family?**

Parents often need to juggle multiple, conflicting demands: the demands of work, of home and family, and of outside activities and interests. Learning how to prioritize can make it easier for parents to manage their multiple roles in a balanced way. Prioritizing also helps parents reach their goals and plan for their family's future. See Fig. 5-2.

Setting Goals

Once they know what their priorities are, parents are better able to set goals. A goal is like a target—it defines a specific outcome that you want to achieve. Setting goals can be a powerful management tool for parents, helping them accomplish more of what they want for themselves, their children, and the family as a whole.

Parents often set long-term goals, defining what they want to achieve years in the future. Long-term goals usually need to be broken down into short-term goals. For example, parents want to teach their children to be financially responsible. They can start with the short-term goal of teaching their children to manage their weekly spending. Through a series of small steps like this, the long-term goal will eventually be reached.

Managing Resources

A **resource** is anything that can be used to meet a need or to help achieve a goal. Resources for parenting include personal or human resources such as skills, knowledge, creativity, time, energy, and other people. They also include material resources, such as money, belongings, and technology. Schools, libraries, parks, and public transportation are examples of community resources. The ability to make good use of resources is a skill valued not only among family members, but in the workplace and in the community at large.

Managing resources means making the most of what you have, skillfully distributing your resources to meet many needs. Resourceful people focus on what they have, not on what they lack. They come up with creative ways of getting things done. Rather than always buying goods or services, for example, they might trade other resources for them. Parents might swap books or clothes as their children outgrow those things. One father might give a neighbor child guitar lessons in exchange for his child receiving tennis instruction. See Fig. 5-3.

Fig. 5-3. Parents with limited resources often find creative ways to manage what they have. **What are three creative ways that parents can trade or manage resources without spending much money?**

The Management Process

Sometimes parents want to accomplish a specific project, such as preparing a space in their home for a new baby. Successful project managers use a system called the *management process*. It includes four major steps: planning, organizing, implementing, and evaluating.

Planning. This step begins with stating your goals. The goals of a project often relate to time, money, and the quality of results achieved. Next, write down ideas about tasks that need to be completed and resources that can help you get them done. As you do, you may realize that not all of your goals can be met. In that case, prioritize or adjust them as needed.

Organizing. Getting organized prepares you to carry out the tasks. Create a schedule by figuring out how much time you need for each task and in what order the tasks must be completed. Then make sure your resources are on hand and ready to use. If other people will be involved in your plan, assign tasks and make sure everyone knows what to do.

Implementing. Next, it's time to carry out, or *implement*, your plan. With your resources at hand, follow the steps you've outlined in your plan. Of course, unforeseen events change a lot of plans. If that happens, be creative and use other resources.

Evaluating. Finally, evaluate how well your plan worked. Did you accomplish all of your goals? If not, try to identify what happened to keep you from reaching a goal. Did some tasks take longer than expected? Did you forget to include a step in your schedule? Was there a breakdown in communication? Think about how to do better in your next project.

Fig. 5-4. Decision making calls for assessing all the available options. **How might parents use the decision-making process to reach goals?**

The management process can help families achieve success in almost any type of project, from hosting a birthday party to moving across the country. Long-term or especially complex projects may need to be broken down into a series of shorter-term goals or smaller subprojects. Then apply the management process to each part.

Making Decisions

Parents are responsible for making many day-to-day decisions. These include decisions about meals, clothing, after-school lessons, playtime activities, and bedtime routines. Parents also make major decisions with far-reaching effects, such as where to live or what school their children will attend. Skilled decision making makes it possible to achieve goals and manage resources in an efficient manner. See Fig. 5-4.

The Decision-Making Process. Sometimes it's difficult for parents to be sure they are making a sound decision. That's where the decision-making process comes in. People can use the following six-step process to make all sorts of important decisions in life, in addition to decisions about parenting.

1. Identify the decision to be made. How you tackle a decision depends on how you define it. For example, "Should the kids sign up for the soccer league?" is a decision with limited options. "What after-school activities would best promote our children's development?" defines a goal and opens up more possibilities.

2. List possible options. You may need to do some research to identify your options. Think about what resources are available and how they might increase your options.

3. Weigh the pros and cons of each option. As you do, keep your values, priorities, and goals in mind. Consider the possible consequences for everyone involved.

4. Choose the best option. There may not be a perfect solution. Choose the alternative that has the most benefits and the fewest drawbacks.

5. Take action. Simply making a decision is not enough. Make a plan for carrying out your decision, then follow your plan.

6. Evaluate the decision. Look back at the results. Are you satisfied with the choice you made? Would you make a different decision next time? Either way, accept responsibility for your decision and learn from it.

Child & Family Services CAREERS

▶ Adult Day Care Worker

Adult day care workers provide services to adults who are not capable of full-time independent living. The people in their care may have physical or mental health issues that make it difficult to manage ordinary activities. Most adult day care workers are employed by state-licensed nonresidential facilities. They can have a wide range of responsibilities. They may develop programs, work with therapists, or help people to get services they need. They also may work directly with older adults, helping them to take part in daily activities.

"I was always interested in health care because I like making a difference in people's lives. I wasn't especially interested in pursuing math or science, so a degree in medicine or nursing wasn't for me. When my grandmother started to have health problems, my parents were able to get her involved at a senior center, and I met some of the adult day care workers there. Soon, I began volunteering. What I loved most about the work was the feeling of being needed. These folks really enjoyed having me around and missed my help when I couldn't be there.

"After high school, I went to college and took courses in social work, psychology, and gerontology. I also got a part-time job at a local senior center. When I graduated with my degree in social work, I found a job as a full-time adult day care worker."

CAREER TIPS

- While in high school, take classes in psychology and human development.
- Volunteer or get a job at a senior center or adult day care facility.
- Earn a college degree in social work, gerontology, or a related field.
- Apply for jobs in senior centers, adult day care centers, nursing homes, and rehabilitation centers.

Fig. 5-5. Parents face many challenges, big and small. They must solve some problems themselves. In other cases, like this one, they provide advice and guidance to help their children learn to handle their own problems.

Solving Problems

In addition to making decisions, parents have to deal with a variety of problems. Some, like a broken window, are short-term and relatively easy to handle. Others, like major financial difficulties or a family member's serious illness, can seem overwhelming. See Fig. 5-5.

One way to tackle a problem is to use a process similar to the steps in decision making. Another strategy, called *practical reasoning,* can help you examine complex problems. Practical reasoning involves looking at the situation from four different angles:

- **Context.** Think about the circumstances surrounding the problem. How do they affect the situation?
- **Desired ends.** Think about the results you want. What would have to take place in order for everyone involved to agree that the problem has been successfully solved?
- **Means.** Think about possible ways to achieve the desired results. What actions would need to be taken and by whom? What resources could be used?
- **Consequences.** Think about the consequences of the actions being considered. Who would be affected by them, either positively or negatively? Do the benefits outweigh the risks for all concerned?

Problems are by nature challenging, but they can't be avoided. When parents learn to successfully handle everyday problems, they gain a sense of accomplishment. They also build problem-solving skills that can help them handle life's larger challenges.

Preventing Problems. When parents take steps to solve a problem that has already occurred, they are reacting to a situation. Parents also need to be **proactive** by taking actions to prevent problems *before* they arise. For example, before children reach an age where drug use is a concern, proactive parents talk about the issue with their children. They discuss the harmful effects of drugs and the reality of drugs in schools. They teach their children specific techniques for dealing with the pressures to experiment with drugs. They can tell their children to call home for a ride whenever a situation becomes uncomfortable. These are all proactive steps that can help prevent a problem from occurring.

Another way for parents to be proactive is to monitor their children's activities. Monitoring is not spying; it is being aware. Parents should know the answers to questions such as:

- *Where* is my child?
- *What* is my child doing?
- *Who* is with my child and what do I know about that person?

- *Who* is supervising my child when he or she is a guest at a friend's house?
- *When* is my child leaving and when will she or he be home?
- *How* is my child getting to and returning from a destination?
- *Which* Web sites and online chat rooms is my child visiting?

Children need some freedom, but that freedom must be balanced with an appropriate level of parental supervision. The more parents know about their children and their children's friends, interests, and concerns, the better they will be at preventing problems. See Fig. 5-6.

Interpersonal Skills

Interpersonal skills include the ability to communicate well, promote teamwork, and act as a leader. When parents have strong interpersonal skills, all family members benefit.

Communication

Good communication skills are essential to strong relationships. Parents must be able to listen closely, give clear explanations and directions, and express what they want and need from others. They need to teach their children, through example and guidance, to communicate effectively as well. See Fig. 5-7.

Fig. 5-6. Getting to know their children's friends is a proactive step parents can take to prevent problems. **What else can a parent do to help a teen avoid risky or dangerous behavior?**

Fig. 5-7. Family members may stay in touch throughout the day by talking on the phone, leaving notes for each other, or by sending e-mail. **What forms of communication does your family use to keep in touch?**

One of the keys to good communication is listening. When someone is speaking to you, pay attention. Don't wander out of the room, pick up the phone, or otherwise show that you don't care about what the other person is saying. If you don't understand something, ask questions. Communicating with young children is an art in itself, and you'll learn more about it in Chapter 21.

Teamwork

Teamwork, or working well with others to reach a common goal, is a valuable skill no matter what a person does in life. Parenting is a team effort that requires cooperation and collaboration among many different people, including family members, teachers, close friends, neighbors, and other caregivers.

Just putting together the members of a team is not enough. Parents need to develop strong teamwork skills. Good team players support and encourage one another as they work together. They all do their part instead of expecting one person to carry the load. They treat their teammates with the same respect and appreciation they would want to receive. See Fig. 5-8.

Fig. 5-8. A team is strengthened when all its members find ways to work well together. **What might happen to a team if its members don't work well together?**

Leadership

Think of a great sports team you know. What makes it successful? You probably think of some star players, but don't forget the coach. Great teams have great leaders.

In families, the parents are the leaders. They assume overall responsibility for the team and make decisions that affect everyone. They set goals and guide the team members as they work toward realizing those goals.

The ability to motivate or inspire people is an essential leadership skill. One of the most powerful motivators for children is recognition and praise. Hearing words of encouragement from a parent or caregiver motivates children to do their best, especially when they face new tasks.

Role Modeling

Parents who are skilled at setting consistent and positive examples for their children are acting as role models. They behave as they want their children to behave. For example, if a parent talks about respect, but acts disrespectfully toward others, the child will get a mixed message. Eventually, the child may mimic the adult by saying one thing and doing another.

Children can be influenced by many things in life, but parents are the strongest influence overall. As family leaders, parents can model good character, values, and morality to their children. Children tend to mimic the examples set by their parents and others around them. They develop a sense of right and wrong when they see these principles at work in their parents' lives.

Mentoring

Mentoring means serving as a trusted guide, usually for someone younger or less experienced than you. Children can have many mentors—parents, teachers, coaches, even older siblings.

What do mentors do? They serve as positive role models, and much more. Mentors provide guidance based on the wisdom of their experience. When a child is struggling with difficult issues, a mentor is someone to turn to for advice and support. A mentor enables a child to see what success looks like and guides the child toward achieving similar success.

When parents are supportive and family bonds are strong, children naturally look to their parents as mentors. Effective parents also seek opportunities for children to benefit from other mentoring relationships. For example, Big Brothers Big Sisters is a program that pairs children with teens and adults who are willing to mentor them. See Fig. 5-9.

Fig. 5-9. A mentor may share familiar experiences or help a child blaze new trails in life. **What values would you pass on to a child if you were a mentor?**

Parenting Pointers

Skillful Role Modeling

A parent is the most important role model in a child's life. That's why it is so important for parents and other role models to pay attention to their own behavior around children. Here are some tips for being a good role model:

➤ **Follow your own advice.** If you tell a child to eat vegetables, but the only vegetables you eat are fries with ketchup, the child is more likely to learn by watching you than by listening to you.

➤ **Be consistent.** Children need to see that you always act according to your values. When you are respectful toward one person but scornful toward another, children may learn that only some people deserve respect.

➤ **Explain your actions.** For example, a child might wonder why you volunteer to help others. Explaining your reasons for doing so will help the child to understand and imitate your positive behaviors.

Resolving Conflicts

Conflict resolution involves settling disagreements in ways that are peaceful and fair. Parents need conflict resolution skills for many reasons:

- To resolve disagreements they may have with one another or with other adults.
- To maintain positive parent-child relationships when inevitable clashes occur.
- To help children settle arguments with siblings or playmates.
- To teach children how to resolve conflicts on their own—a skill they will need throughout life.

Goals of Conflict Resolution. Conflict resolution has two main goals. One is to reach a **consensus**—an agreement that is acceptable to everyone involved. The other is to preserve positive relationships. Parents who demonstrate conflict resolution skills show family members that they can continue to love and respect each other despite their disagreements.

One way to reach a consensus is by coming up with a **compromise**—an agreement in which each person gets some, but not all, of what he or she wants. Suppose two children are having a conflict on the playground: there is only one swing, and each child wants to use it. One possible solution might be for them to take turns. Both children give up something—the idea of having the swing all to themselves—but they both gain something by reaching an agreement.

Another possible solution might be for the children to choose another activity. Perhaps both of them would have just as much fun climbing the jungle gym. This is a *win-win solution*—both children "win" by getting to do something they enjoy. A win-win solution benefits everyone and has no real drawbacks for anyone.

Negotiation and Mediation. What processes can help people reach a consensus? The most basic tool for resolving conflicts is **negotiation**—discussing a problem in order to reach an acceptable solution. Generally, by age five children are able to discuss problems and take part in negotiation.

Younger children may not have the skills to negotiate a solution on their own. A parent may need to act as a **mediator**—an impartial third party who provides guidance to help settle a dispute. Older children, teens, and adults sometimes need this type of help, too. The role of a mediator is not to decide who is right or what to do. Rather, he or she guides the discussion, making sure that everyone stays calm and has a chance to be heard. The mediator helps those involved reach their own solution. See Fig. 5-10.

Whether a conflict is being settled by direct negotiation or with the help of a mediator, following these guidelines can make the process more effective:

- **Stay calm.** If a child starts to lose control, the parent could suggest, "Wait a minute. Slow down and take a deep breath. We're listening."
- **Stay focused.** Avoid getting sidetracked by unrelated issues.
- **Avoid personal attacks.** Blame and accusations don't help settle a conflict—they only make it worse.
- **Recognize all valid points.** All those involved need to feel that their wishes were fairly considered.
- **Acknowledge needs.** It's not enough to know *what* each person wants. Try to understand *why* he or she wants it.

Fig. 5-10. Parents often mediate when family conflicts arise. **When should adults step in and help children settle their differences?**

- **Be open to a compromise.** A parent might say, "I'm willing to change your bedtime to 9:30 if you agree that you'll go to bed on time without complaining."
- **Respect the final agreement.** Once consensus has been reached, both parties are responsible for following through as agreed.

Qualities for Successful Parenting

You've read about some of the management and interpersonal skills that parents need. But what *qualities*, or aspects of personality and character, make for successful parenting?

Patience

When it comes to parenting, patience is invaluable. Being a patient parent can mean reading the same story to a child for what seems like the hundredth time. It can mean waiting while a child struggles to put on a jacket "all by myself," knowing that you could do it in half the time. Being patient can mean not being in such a hurry for children to grow up, but enjoying them as they are right now.

For most people, patience is a skill that must be consciously developed over time. Fortunately, children offer parents the perfect opportunity to develop patience. When confronted with a frustrating situation, parents can learn to stop, take a few deep breaths, and relax.

Confidence

Confidence is a strong belief in oneself and one's abilities. Confident parents aren't afraid to make decisions. They gather information, listen to advice, and consider their options carefully. Once a decision is made, however, they don't waste time second-guessing their choice or worrying about whether they're doing the right thing. On the other hand, it is also a sign of confidence when parents are willing to ask others for help when it's needed.

Sensing that no one is in charge can make children feel insecure. Some children try to take charge themselves, which can lead to struggles and confusion over leadership that can disrupt a family. When children know that a confident adult is in charge, the family functions better and children feel more secure. See Fig. 5-11.

Much confidence comes through experience. To build your own confidence, try these suggestions:

- Identify your strengths and successes. Let them inspire you to seek new challenges.
- Talk over your self-doubts and setbacks with a positive, encouraging friend or family member.
- Increase your knowledge so you can make decisions more easily and confidently.
- Treat mistakes as opportunities to learn. Realize that you may have to try many times before you succeed.

Realistic Expectations

Is parenting an unending joy or an unending hardship? If you think realistically, you know that neither extreme is true. The reality lies somewhere in between.

Reasonable parents base their expectations on careful judgments about reality, not on what they might like reality to be. For example, parents cannot realistically expect a toddler to read a book or add numbers. They expect children to do those things eventually, but only after reaching more realistic goals, such as recognizing letters and numbers. Parents with realistic expectations guide their children through new experiences without frustrating or pressuring them. See Fig. 5-12.

Reasonable parents have realistic expectations for themselves, as well. They set challenging goals and approach them with a positive attitude, but they don't try to be perfect or expect success overnight.

A Positive Attitude

People with a positive attitude and optimistic outlook tend to see the bright side of things. As the saying goes, they tend to see the glass as half full, not half empty. They prefer to concentrate on what is there as opposed to what is lacking. Parents with a positive attitude tend to focus on what is good about their children and their lives. They view problems as challenges and opportunities to learn.

Fig. 5-12. Children feel good about themselves when they experience success. **How do realistic expectations on the part of parents contribute to that success?**

Children tend to pick up on this positive attitude and imitate it, just as they imitate other behaviors their parents model. A positive attitude on the part of parents teaches children to have confidence in themselves. It can be a powerful motivating force, inspiring children to reach for new levels of excellence and satisfaction. It can also help reduce tension and stress during difficult times.

A Sense of Humor

Seeing the lighter side of life benefits parents and children alike. Humor can ease a tense situation. When a heated discussion reaches the boiling point, for example, humor can help everyone let off steam.

Children generally love to laugh, and parents who model humor help children gain a healthy, balanced, and positive perspective on life. Research shows that laughter is good for health. When children enjoy laughter and learn to see the bright side of a situation, their emotional health blooms.

There is one important rule for using humor: You may laugh at yourself or a funny situation, but never another person, especially a child. A child's self-image often depends on a parent's approval, and children can be deeply hurt when someone laughs at them. Wise parents make sure that their sense of humor doesn't hurt their children.

Sensitivity

To be sensitive means to be aware of and responsive to what is around you, including the feelings of other people. All people, and children in particular, like to know that others understand and are sensitive to their feelings.

Sensitive parents try to see situations through their children's eyes. They think about why a child is saying or doing something and how the child feels. They may give

Fig. 5-13. Having a positive attitude does not mean ignoring or minimizing problems. It does mean focusing on what can be done to solve a problem or prevent it from happening again. **Why is this more helpful than dwelling on negativity and blame?**

the child a comforting pat on the shoulder or hand to show that they understand. They speak gently and imagine how the child might interpret their words.

Suppose a child's favorite toy is accidentally broken and the child reacts by crying. An insensitive person might respond harshly— "Stop crying!"—and throw the toy in the trash. A sensitive parent, on the other hand, first makes clear that he or she understands the child's feelings. The parent might wipe away the child's tears and, in a comforting tone, offer reassurance that these hurt feelings will mend. The parent might then examine the problem calmly and suggest possible solutions. For example, the parent might help the child think of a possible substitute for the damaged toy. See Fig. 5-14.

Parenting Styles

Every day, parents face choices about how to guide and influence their children. Over time, the choices that a particular parent makes form the pattern of his or her **parenting style**, or general approach to raising children. Researchers who have studied parenting styles have grouped them into a few broad categories. Although individual variations exist, most parenting styles tend to fit into one of these categories: authoritarian, authoritative, or permissive.

- **Authoritarian.** Parents who have an authoritarian parenting style emphasize obedience. They set clearly defined standards of behavior and expect their children to follow the rules without question. This parenting style provides a structured environment in which children know exactly what they can and cannot do. Their opportunities to make decisions on their own are limited.

- **Authoritative.** Parents who follow this style —which is sometimes called democratic— also set rules for their children. However, they are more likely than authoritarian parents to explain the reasons behind the rules. Rather than telling children exactly what they must do, these parents are more likely to offer a choice of several alternatives. If rules are broken, they may be more willing to take circumstances into account. They also tend to be more open to their children's input when making decisions. Still, the parents have the final say.

- **Permissive.** Parents who use this style emphasize giving children the freedom to make many of their own choices. Children are encouraged to think for themselves rather than always following rules established by others. The parents make limited demands and are generally accepting of their children's behavior. They feel that if children make poor choices, they will learn from their mistakes without parental intervention.

Fig. 5-14. A sensitive parent shows understanding for a child's feelings. Compare how a child might feel after a parent demonstrates sensitivity and after a parent demonstrates insensitivity.

Fig. 5-15. Parents choose the parenting style that they feel is best for themselves and their children. **When a child asks for a toy that isn't on the shopping list, how might parents respond based on their parenting style?**

Adopting a Parenting Style

No single parenting style is best for all parents or all situations. Parents adopt a style that is in harmony with their personality, values, priorities, and parenting goals. In addition, the personality and needs of their children may affect their choice of parenting style. Some children seem to thrive on structure, while others respond well to a more flexible environment. See Fig. 5-15.

Sometimes a specific situation calls for a specific parenting style. For example, in an emergency, a parent who is usually permissive may quickly switch to an authoritarian style and take charge of the situation. Parents may also find that they adapt their parenting style over time in response to a child's changing needs and maturity level.

Generally, however, parents stick with their chosen parenting style unless circumstances clearly require a change. Consistency in parenting style helps children know what to expect from their parents and what is expected of them. Couples who are considering parenthood should discuss their ideas about parenting styles ahead of time and reach agreement on the general approach they will take.

Building Parenting Skills

How can parents learn more about parenting styles and philosophies? How can they build the skills and qualities they need to be good parents? There are lots of ways to learn. Many organizations offer classes, publications, and support groups to help people learn and practice good parenting skills. Parents can get advice and support from friends, family, teachers, books and magazines, and from personal experience and observation. The Internet is a rich source of information for parents, as well.

Books and Magazines

Libraries and bookstores are filled with books and magazines about all aspects of parenting, from pregnancy through relationships with adult children. These materials present a variety of viewpoints. Evaluate the trustworthiness of the source by investigating the authors' education, experience, and reputation.

Experience and Observation

Parents often say that raising their second or third child was easier than raising the first. Why? After raising their first child, the parents had actual experience to draw on. They learned from their successes and their mistakes.

First-time parents can learn from the experience of others. They can talk to seasoned parents, asking for advice. They can become careful observers of parents whom they admire, noting what strategies and techniques they use. They can learn from other caregivers, too, such as teachers and child care workers. See Fig. 5-16.

Fig. 5-16. You can learn much about parenting by spending time with children and their parents, whether friends, neighbors, or family members. **If you don't have children nearby, what could you do to learn more about parenting?**

Parenting Classes

Many hospitals and schools offer classes on different aspects of parenting. Classes on childbirth, breastfeeding, infant care, and emergency aid are usually available at hospitals. Some hospitals also have parenting centers or offer other resources. There may be classes on topics such as positive discipline, sibling rivalry, and other issues that arise as children get older.

The Internet

The Internet is a rich resource for parents. Web sites and online forums can be excellent sources of information. It is very important, though, to choose online sources carefully. Don't assume that everything you read is true. There are no rules about who can post information or what they can say, sell, or recommend.

Using the Internet Wisely. It's not always easy to determine whether the information you get from the Internet is correct. Here are some suggestions for evaluating the reliability of Internet sources:

- Look for a statement of who runs the site or provided the information. The Web site of a well-respected parenting magazine, for example, is probably a more trustworthy source than a site run by an anonymous individual.
- Look for sites that present balanced information. Be cautious when using sites that seem to be selling a product or promoting a specific viewpoint.
- Keep in mind that parents you meet online are like parents that you meet anywhere else. They're not necessarily experts.
- Check with a doctor before following any medical advice you get online. Print out any interesting articles and show them to your health care provider before taking action.

A Lifelong Journey

Parenting is a lifelong learning process. No parents can ever say that they have finished learning everything they need to know in order to raise children successfully. Still, parents who prepare themselves by developing useful skills and qualities are giving themselves and their children an advantage in life. See Fig. 5-17.

As their children grow and learn, parents also grow in their knowledge and experience. You might say that parents and children support each other on a lifelong journey of development.

Fig. 5-17. Before this child arrived on the scene, his parents began learning the skills that they will need in the years ahead. **Why is this advantageous for both the child and the parents?**

CHAPTER 5 Review & Activities

CHAPTER SUMMARY

- Parents and other caregivers use management and interpersonal skills to deal with issues and problems, to interact with people, and to set examples for children.
- Such qualities as patience, confidence, and sensitivity help parents use parenting skills effectively.
- Parents adopt a parenting style—authoritarian, authoritative, permissive, or a combination of these—based on their values, priorities, and goals.
- Parents can learn more about developing parenting skills through publications, observation, classes and support groups, and other sources.

Check Your Facts

1. How does prioritizing help parents?
2. Why are short-term goals useful?
3. If money is limited, what can resourceful parents do?
4. Describe the steps in the management process.
5. List the steps in the decision-making process.
6. How does being proactive affect problems?
7. How can each of these interpersonal skills be valuable in parenting: communication, teamwork, and leadership?
8. In what ways can children benefit from mentoring relationships?
9. Distinguish between consensus and compromise in resolving conflicts.
10. How do negotiation and mediation help solve problems?
11. How can each of these qualities contribute to successful parenting: patience, confidence, sense of humor, and sensitivity?
12. Compare the three different parenting styles.
13. How can you evaluate the reliability of information in written materials and on the Internet?

Think Critically

1. **Making Predictions.** A child typically has multiple caregivers. Predict what might happen if these caregivers don't work as a team. How might the child and the caregivers be affected? How can teamwork be promoted?
2. **Drawing Conclusions.** You've read about personal qualities that promote successful parenting. What qualities might interfere with effective parenting? How could these be changed?
3. **Recognizing Points of View.** Based on your own observations, do you think males and females parent differently? How do you account for differences and similarities?

Apply Your Learning

1. **Values.** Make two columns on a sheet of paper. Under *Values*, list personal traits that are important to you. Under *Skills*, describe how you would instill each trait in a child, using the interpersonal skills in the chapter.
2. **Parenting Styles.** With other students, prepare and present a skit that shows parents using a specific parenting style as they interact with their children. Ask other class members to identify the parenting style.
3. **Web Sites.** Explore parenting Web sites, including these: government (*.gov*), organization (*.org*), and commercial (*.com*). Which sites are most helpful and why? Explain why some sites seem less helpful or less reliable.

Cross-Curricular Connections

1. **Language Arts.** A *philosophy* defines basic beliefs about something. Put your philosophy of parenting in writing by completing one of these statements: "I believe that a parent should…" or "To me, parenting means…"
2. **Science.** Observation is part of the scientific method. Find out what it means to write observations in objective language. Why is objectivity needed? Observe a child and write an objective account of what occurs.

Family & Community Connections

1. **Problem Solving.** Talk with a family member who is a parent. Explain that you are studying problem solving, as related to parenting. Ask the person to describe a past parenting problem and how it was solved. In looking back, would the parent do anything different?
2. **Parents in the News.** Scan newspapers for articles about positive parenting situations. For example, you might read about parents who coach children's athletic teams or who have large foster families. Share an article in class, pointing out parenting skills and qualities.

Teens and Parenting

CHAPTER OBJECTIVES

- Describe factors that contribute to teen pregnancy.
- Analyze risks of teen pregnancy and challenges for teen parents.
- Explain the effects of teen parenthood.
- Assess options available to teens facing parenthood.
- Explain teen parents' rights and responsibilities.
- Summarize sources of support for teen parents.

PARENTING TERMS

- prenatal care
- miscarriage
- stillbirth
- premature birth
- low birth weight
- paternity
- adoption
- closed adoption
- open adoption
- semi-open adoption
- in-family adoption
- WIC program

Parenting is one of the most difficult jobs in the world—just ask any parent. It can be hard enough trying to take care of your own physical, emotional, and intellectual needs. Add to that the responsibility of caring for a child who demands much more time and attention than an adult, and you have a real challenge on your hands. Teen parents live with that challenge 24 hours a day, every day. Many wish they had known the realities of teen parenthood before going down that road.

Parents Too Soon

Recent statistics show that more than 430,000 teens had babies in one year. This situation is often referred to as "children having children." See Fig. 6-1.

Responsible citizens are concerned about these statistics—with good reason. Although many teens manage their lives responsibly, few are ready for the emotional, physical, and financial demands of parenthood.

The teen years are a time to explore life's possibilities and prepare to meet its challenges. It is the time to finish high school, learn workplace skills, and plan for a career, higher education, or the military. Most teens still need time to develop the skills and qualities they will need to be capable, caring adults and parents.

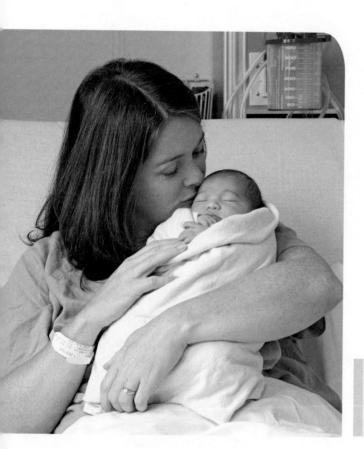

After reading Chapter 3, you know what parenting readiness means. A stable relationship, physical and psychological maturity, and financial security are all part of parenting readiness. Few teens have all three.

Factors Leading to Teen Pregnancy

Most teens don't want to become parents too soon. As one teen put it: "I have trouble giving up a weekend night for a babysitting job. How could I give up entire years of my life right now to care for a child?" However, some teens act against their better judgment and give in to the pressures that can lead to pregnancy.

Internal Pressures

The pressure to become sexually active can be very strong. Some of the pressure comes from within. Understanding what goes on inside the mind and body can help teens be prepared to cope with those pressures.

Sexual Feelings. The teen years are marked by deep and sometimes unpredictable feelings, including sexual desire. Often teens are not prepared for these strong new emotions. They may have urges to become sexually active, but they haven't yet learned how to recognize and manage those feelings. They may have trouble controlling their behavior, as can happen when psychological maturity lags behind physical maturity.

Fig. 6-1. About ten percent of all births in the U.S. are to teens. **What do you think a teen misses by becoming a parent too soon? Do you think most teens are ready to become parents? Why or why not?**

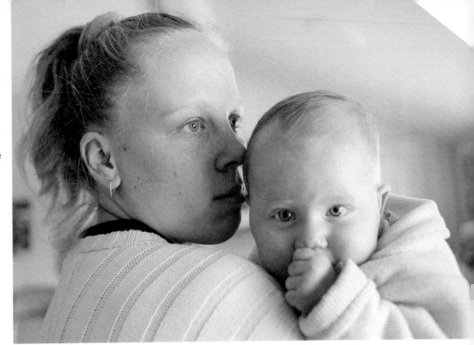

Fig. 6-2. Some teens think that a baby will provide them with the love they lack. **Why is this an unrealistic expectation?**

Reluctance to Communicate. Because they are still growing emotionally, many teens have trouble talking about serious subjects. Some are uncomfortable talking with adults about sexuality. Even teens who want to explain their thoughts and feelings to a partner may be embarrassed to do so. This is a warning sign that indicates that neither the teen nor the relationship is mature enough for successful parenting.

Mistaken Ideas. Misinformation about sex and pregnancy is common. Rather than admit their own lack of knowledge, teens may listen to myths and half-truths. Unfortunately, lacking information about sex and acting on misinformation can result in pregnancy.

Desire for Love and Attention. Most births to unmarried teens result from unintended pregnancies. Some teens, however, intentionally become pregnant to satisfy needs for love and attention. Teen mothers learn too late that in a mother-baby relationship, it is the baby that needs and gets the vast majority of the love and attention. See Fig. 6-2.

External Pressures

Outside forces also play a part in teen pregnancy. These influences come from several sources.

Societal Pressure. Popular culture is filled with sexual imagery. Songs, movies, television, and advertising repeatedly remind people of their sexuality. Sex is associated with pleasure, prestige, and romance, but rarely with responsibility, pregnancy, or sexually transmitted diseases. Teens who are good at thinking and analyzing are able to question what they see and hear. Those who understand the consequences of sexual behavior have a better chance of not falling for the wrong message.

Pressure from Peers. Many teens, both male and female, feel pressured by their peers to have sex. For males, having sex can be seen as the way to be a man. Nothing could be further from the truth. Being a man means having the maturity to act responsibly. A mature male teen does not want to have children he cannot support.

Females may feel that if they don't have sex, they are missing out or are less mature than their peers. If they have friends who are teen mothers, they may begin to think that motherhood is a typical way of life. Fortunately, many teens recognize that delaying parenthood can mean a more fulfilling life for themselves and their future children.

Pressure from Partners. Pressure to be sexually active also comes from partners. One argument, that "everyone is doing it," is flawed. Statistics show that sexually active teens are in the minority. Regardless of what others are doing, each person must make his or her own decisions.

The pressures to have sexual relations take many forms. One tactic is to imply that abstaining from sex is "childish" behavior. Another argument a partner might use is: "You would if you loved me." Anyone who demands sex as proof of love is showing a lack of love and respect for the other person. All teens should think ahead about how to say no effectively. See Fig. 6-3.

Health Risks of Teen Pregnancy

Teens need to give thought not only to the factors that can lead to pregnancy, but also to the reality of pregnancy itself. From the beginning of a pregnancy, a mother needs to care for her health and that of the baby. Because teens' bodies are still developing, pregnancy poses different health risks for them than for adults.

Risks to the Pregnant Teen

Pregnancy carries certain medical risks at any age, but pregnant teens face greater risks. For example:

- If a teen has poor eating habits, her body competes with the fetus for what limited nutrients are available. Neither mother nor child gets adequate nutrition.
- If a female's skeletal structure is not fully developed, she can experience problems with her spine and pelvic bones during pregnancy and birth.
- Teens are at risk for such health problems as pregnancy-induced high blood pressure, a potentially life-threatening condition.
- Teens whose bodies are still developing may have difficulty delivering a baby.

Fig. 6-3. Teens may feel pressure to have sex. **Would someone who loved and respected you force you to do something that you didn't want to do?**

Teen Pregnancy: Seeking Medical Care

Pregnant teens should see a medical professional as soon as they know they are pregnant. Teens who have limited funds can go to family health clinics. These can be found in the Yellow Pages under "Clinics" or "Medical Centers."

Medical professionals will run diagnostic tests to identify—and prevent—problems the mother or child could have, and they will monitor the health of both as the pregnancy progresses. The mother will receive counseling on how best to care for herself during pregnancy and how to deal with any specific problems.

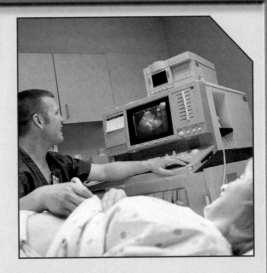

Ideally, a pregnant teen should see her doctor once a month for the first 28 to 30 weeks of the pregnancy, every two to three weeks until 36 weeks, then once a week until delivery. If a mother has any medical condition, the visits will probably be more frequent.

- The death rate from complications of pregnancy is much higher for teens under age fifteen than for adult women.

Regular **prenatal care**—medical attention given throughout pregnancy—improves the chances that both mother and child will come through pregnancy safe and healthy. Because they are such a high-risk group, teens need more prenatal care than adult women. Unfortunately, they are less likely to seek it. One-third of all pregnant teens receive no prenatal care. Many that do receive care do not seek it until the last three months of pregnancy, when it may be too late to correct many problems.

Risks to the Baby

The health risks of teen pregnancy can endanger the life of the unborn baby. Sometimes the result is a **miscarriage**—spontaneous loss of the pregnancy before the twentieth week. If an unborn baby dies during pregnancy after the twentieth week, the loss is called a **stillbirth**. Rates of both miscarriage and stillbirth are higher for teens than for adults.

Even after birth, infants born to teen mothers may still be in danger. Teen mothers are more likely to experience **premature birth**, in which the baby is born before the thirty-seventh week of pregnancy. (The normal length of pregnancy is 40 weeks.) Premature babies are born before their development is complete. Because their internal organs are underdeveloped, they often have difficulty breathing and regulating body temperature. They may not be able to fight infections as easily as full-term babies.

Another medical risk faced by newborns is **low birth weight**, defined as a weight of less than 5 pounds, 8 ounces at birth. Such babies are 20 times more likely to die in their first year of life than infants of normal weight. Their organs may not be fully developed at birth, leading to lung problems, bleeding in the brain, vision loss, and serious intestinal problems.

Fig. 6-4. Teen parents often feel isolated from their peers. **Why is it challenging for them to maintain close ties with friends?**

Challenges for Teen Parents

Apart from health risks to mother and child, teen parents face many other challenges. While still developing physically and emotionally themselves, they have to assume responsibility for the care and development of a child. Parenthood affects everything from their day-to-day emotions to their financial future.

Emotional Impact

Parenting takes an emotional toll on teen parents. Adolescence can be an anxious, confusing time, and it is made more difficult when pregnancy occurs. Pregnancy increases concerns about the future, forcing teens into decisions they aren't ready to make.

Teen fathers often react to a partner's pregnancy with feelings of shock, anger, or guilt. They may feel anxious about what to do and have the urge to run from the responsibility. Many make the mistake of doing that.

Teen mothers who are left to care for their children without the father's support feel abandoned, hurt, and upset. Whether or not they get support from the baby's father, teen mothers tend to feel isolated. Caring for their children adds stress and loneliness to their lives. They worry about what's ahead for themselves and their children.

Social Life

Teen parents usually don't have much of a social life. Most aspects of their lives revolve around their children and the responsibilities of parenthood. There simply isn't much time—or money—for activities such as sports, movies, or going to the mall with friends. Responsibilities such as caring for their children, earning a living, and finishing school become top priorities for most teen parents. See Fig. 6-4.

Child & Family Services CAREERS

▶ HIV Health Educator

An HIV health educator receives training in the skills needed to teach people about HIV (human immunodeficiency virus), the virus that causes AIDS (acquired immune deficiency syndrome). The HIV health educator learns:

- The medical facts about HIV and AIDS, including the various ways HIV is transmitted and risk factors for contracting HIV.
- Information about HIV testing and reporting.
- Techniques for speaking in public, leading discussions, and answering questions.

Training for an HIV educator varies depending on the specific program. It can be as basic as a short, intensive course, or it can involve college degrees (bachelor's and master's) and state certification.

"As an HIV educator, I may be called on to teach in a wide variety of settings, including schools, houses of worship, community centers, prisons, and clinics. My presentations cover everything from how HIV is contracted to resources available to people affected by this disease. AIDS is the leading cause of death for Americans between the ages of 25 and 44, according to the Centers for Disease Control and Prevention. By educating people about HIV, I can give them the tools they need to protect themselves and others."

CAREER TIPS

- Take parenting, health, psychology, and social studies courses in high school.
- Volunteer for charity outreach programs.
- Take college courses in psychology and sociology.
- Apply for positions in community health organizations, clinics, and hospitals.

Financial Responsibility

Financially, teens come up short. Most do not have enough earning power to provide for themselves, let alone a child.

Both the mother and father are legally responsible for providing financial support until the child is 18. Although some teen parents get financial help from their families, not all families are willing or able to provide it.

Teen mothers usually have limited financial resources, and many quickly fall into poverty. Government assistance, if available, doesn't allow the kind of lifestyle that many teens desire.

Teen fathers are seldom prepared to support a child financially either. A teen father is legally responsible for his child whether he marries the mother or never sees her again. A male who refuses to acknowledge **paternity**—biological fatherhood—can be forced to take a blood test or genetic test to determine whether the child is his.

The courts take a strong stand regarding financial responsibility. Child support payments may be automatically deducted from paychecks, unemployment benefits, and tax refunds. The child has a right to the parents' Social Security benefits, insurance benefits, inheritance, and military benefits.

Education and Employment

Having a child dramatically changes education and career goals for teen parents. The responsibilities of parenthood make getting a high school diploma—let alone higher education—a challenge. In turn, lack of education can limit career opportunities and future income.

School can be difficult enough for teens without children. Teen parents attending school have to cope with doing homework and caring for a child—often simultaneously. They are often exhausted, having been up caring for the child during the night. They have to arrange for child care while they are at school, which can be expensive. When a child or child care worker gets sick, parents have to make other arrangements, usually with very little notice.

Many teen parents need to work to earn a living. Having a job boosts income, but it also makes life even more complicated. The time spent at the job, in addition to traveling to and from work, leaves even less time for classes, schoolwork, and caring for a child. See Fig. 6-5.

Faced with these challenges, many teen parents drop out of school. That's unfortunate, because not having a high school diploma creates further obstacles to establishing a healthy and prosperous household.

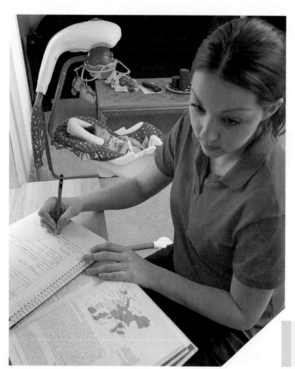

Fig. 6-5. Juggling a schedule of paid work, schoolwork, and caring for a child is a tremendous challenge for teen parents. **Why is it difficult to set priorities in this situation?**

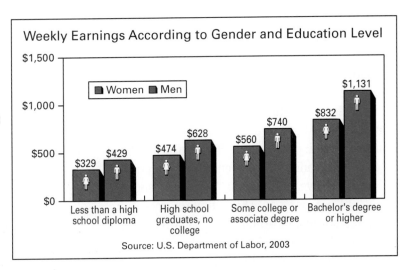

Fig. 6-6. This chart shows the differences in salaries between education levels. The figures shown are for full-time wage and salary workers ages 25 years and over. **According to this chart, by how much does a high school diploma increase yearly earnings?**

Weekly Earnings According to Gender and Education Level

Source: U.S. Department of Labor, 2003

According to U.S. Department of Labor statistics, earnings increase significantly as a worker's degree of education increases. Findings also show that unemployment is lower among those with more education and more skills. These are good reasons for teens to stay in school and achieve at least a high school diploma. See Fig. 6-6.

Wider Effects of Teen Parenthood

Teen parenthood affects many people, not just the teens themselves. It has far-ranging consequences for children, families, and society.

Effects on Children

Many children of teens face a discouraging future. Statistically, children raised by teen parents are at risk for a variety of problems. For example:

- They are more likely to be neglected, abandoned, or abused. One possible explanation is that many teen parents lack the emotional maturity to deal with the stress of parenting.

- Sons of teen parents are more likely to spend time in prison.
- Daughters of teen mothers tend to have sex and give birth at a younger age than other girls.

Teens can, of course, learn how to be good parents, and not all children of teens will experience these problems. Still, the statistics are enough to make most teens think twice about parenthood.

Effects on Families

Extended families of teen parents usually pay a price, too. Because teens are seldom ready to parent, the baby's grandparents or other relatives may have to step in to make sure the child receives proper care. Often this means providing a place to live, financial assistance, and hands-on help with child care tasks.

How might grandparents feel in this situation? In most cases, they are concerned about the future of their child and grandchild and want to do whatever they can to help. At the same time, they may feel resentment at having to postpone or sacrifice their own goals and desires. After spending years raising their own children, they may have dreamed of having more time for hobbies, travel, and relaxation. Instead, they find themselves back in the world of diapers and baby bottles, with all its stress and fatigue. See Fig. 6-7.

In many instances, a teen mother and her child live with her family. The baby is the legal responsibility of the teen, but the teen, if still under 18 years of age, is the legal responsibility of her parents. This situation sets the stage for confusion about each person's role. Conflict is likely to result, especially if the teen and her parents have different points of view about how to raise children.

Each teen parent may experience hostility, blame, and disapproval from his or her own family or from the other parent's family. When relationships become strained, those involved may need to talk to a professional counselor. A teen who lives up to his or her responsibilities is more likely to gain parental support and maintain strong, loving ties within the family.

Effects on Society

Teen pregnancy takes an enormous toll on society. Government and private organizations spend billions of dollars annually on expenses related to teen pregnancy. These expenses include temporary support for teen families, foster care for abused children, and tutoring and physical therapy for children with disabilities.

Lost potential of teen parents is also a great cost to society. Although some teen parents build an independent life for themselves and their children, many do not. Those who become parents as teens may spend years struggling just to raise their children and support themselves. Many never regain the opportunity to fully develop their minds and skills in ways that benefit them and society.

Fig. 6-7. Grandparents often have to fill in for teen parents. **How does taking care of a grandchild put pressure on grandparents?**

Options, Rights, and Responsibilities

When a teen pregnancy occurs, feeling frightened and confused is a normal reaction. Many teens at first try to ignore a pregnancy, but that doesn't change the reality of the situation. The best thing to do is to face up to the decisions that must be made.

Teens in this situation need time to think about all their options and plan what to do. They also need to understand their rights and responsibilities under the law. There are no easy answers, but seeking help and advice from trusted, responsible adults is a wise first step. Options to consider include single parenthood, marriage, and adoption.

Fig. 6-8. A successful marriage takes a lot of work. **How does having a child add to the effort needed to make a marriage succeed?**

Single Parenthood

Some teen parents choose to remain single and raise their children on their own. Before committing to this option, teens should be aware of the difficulties that go with it. The challenges of parenthood are even tougher when the other parent is not there to share the burden.

Consider the dilemma of a single teen mother—not just in the first few years, but in the long run. How will she support herself and her child? If she lacks higher education or specialized training, job opportunities are likely to be scarce and low-paying. If she finds a job, who will care for the child while she's at work? How much of her earnings will have to go toward child care expenses? Some teens assume they can get by on government aid, but programs and the funding for them change over time and are not a reliable source of adequate income. Nor is it realistic to expect family members to provide continuing financial support. It's possible to be a successful single parent, but it's not an easy road for anyone.

Marriage

Most people would agree that a strong and successful marriage benefits parents and their children. However, creating a strong, successful marriage is not easy—especially for teens.

They tend to have less education and lower incomes than couples who marry in their twenties or later. They often feel isolated from friends, but don't fit into the adult world either. Pressures like these contribute to a much higher divorce rate for teens than for more mature couples. See Fig. 6-8.

Adoption

Teens facing pregnancy and parenthood may consider the option of having another family adopt their child. **Adoption** is a legal process by which people acquire the rights and responsibilities of parenthood for children who are not biologically their own. An adopted child becomes a member of the adoptive parents' family, exactly as if he or she were born into that family. The adoptive parents take responsibility for raising the child to adulthood.

Putting a child up for adoption is a very difficult choice for many parents. It requires them to weigh their desires and what they could offer a child against the benefits of adoption, then decide what is best for the child. Such a decision calls for maturity and the desire to put the child's needs first.

Adoption has several benefits. It gives the child a good chance to be raised in a stable home. The adoptive parents are grateful to have a child to love and rear. In addition, the teen parents gain a fresh start. See Fig. 6-9.

Most adoptions are arranged through agencies. The agencies screen prospective adoptive parents to ensure they can provide a loving, stable home.

Through adoption agencies, parents can choose from several types of adoption.

- Some parents choose a **closed adoption**. This means the birth parents remain anonymous and do not have contact with the child after the adoption takes place.
- In an **open adoption**, the birth parents can maintain a close relationship with the child and the adoptive family.
- In a **semi-open adoption**, the birth parents can monitor the child's progress by receiving pictures and letters through the adoption agency or a mediator. The birth and adoptive parents know each other by first names only. All contact and correspondence is through the third party.

Another alternative is an **in-family adoption**. In this situation, a grandparent or other family member adopts the child. One benefit is that the child remains within the extended family. A potential drawback is that the lines of responsibility within a family can become blurred, causing tensions.

Legal Rights and Responsibilities of Teen Parents

As they consider their options, teens facing decisions about parenthood should understand their legal rights and responsibilities. These can vary from state to state.

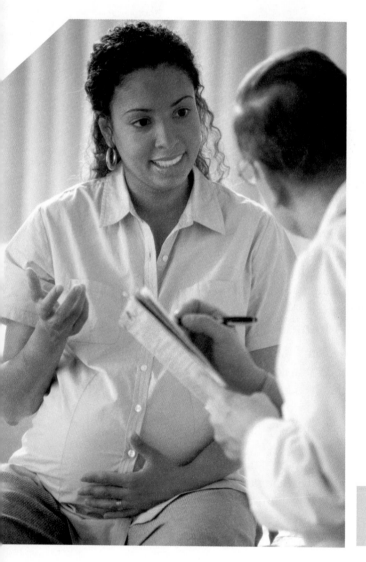

Fig. 6-9. Adoption is one alternative for teens facing parenthood. **How might adoption be a good alternative for the baby and for the parents?**

If teen parents choose to raise their child themselves, they assume all legal and financial responsibility for the child's care. If the mother is raising the baby on her own, the father is responsible for child support payments. In any case, if parents do not fulfill their responsibilities for the child's care, their parental rights may be legally terminated.

A father normally has the right to have contact with his child, even if he is not married to the mother. If he wishes, he may seek *shared custody*, an arrangement in which the child lives with each parent part of the time. He may also seek *sole custody*, in which he would be the primary caregiver. If the father does not have custody, he usually has the right to *visitation* or *parenting time*, meaning that he can visit with the child at prearranged times. However, before he can claim any legal rights, the father will need to establish paternity.

If adoption is chosen, both biological parents must give their consent. Most states don't allow parents to legally consent to an adoption until after the child is born. Some states require that parents wait three or four days before signing a consent form, and some also require that they go through counseling first. Many states also specify a period of time during which the birth parents can withdraw their consent.

Sources of Support

Those teens who have successfully raised their children are the first to say they could not have done it alone. They wisely sought help as soon as they learned they were going to become parents. See Fig. 6-10.

Fortunately, many people and organizations are willing to help teens in need. Pregnant teens and teen parents can seek advice and support from sources such as these:

Fig. 6-10. Many community organizations can help teen parents. **Can you think of any organizations in your community that offer support for teen parents?**

- **Parents and family.** Many teens are reluctant to tell their parents about a pregnancy. However, the truth cannot be kept hidden forever. The sooner parents know about the pregnancy, the sooner they can offer support and assistance.
- **School counselors.** High school guidance counselors can refer teens to community resources such as health clinics, counseling services, and classes about pregnancy and childbirth.
- **Religious leaders.** Members of the clergy can also offer guidance and advice to a teen facing pregnancy.

- **Health care professionals.** Doctors, nurses, and other health care professionals can provide the medical care a pregnant teen will need, offer guidance, and refer teens to other sources of help.
- **Social service organizations.** Help is available from publicly and privately funded groups. Some organizations offer advice about prenatal care, family planning, and adoption. Others help teens discuss the pregnancy with their parents. Social service professionals can recommend support groups when appropriate.
- **Legal aid societies.** These organizations provide free legal information, advice, and services to low-income families and individuals. They can give advice on a variety of matters, including paternity, adoption, and custody of a child.

- **Government programs and services.** Teen parents may qualify for government programs designed to help families in need. One such program is the Special Supplemental Nutrition Program for Women, Infants, and Children, better known as the **WIC program**. Women who are pregnant or have recently given birth, as well as infants and children through age five, qualify for this federal program if they are at risk for poor nutrition due to low income or other factors. The program provides supplemental foods, nutrition counseling, and referrals to health care services. See Fig. 6-11.

Support for Finishing High School

Finishing high school is one of the most important things teen parents can do for themselves and their children. Although pursuing this goal can be challenging for teen parents, options are available that can help make it a little easier.

By law, high schools must offer the opportunity to earn a diploma to pregnant and parenting teens. Some school districts offer alternative programs for teen parents. In addition to academic subjects, the curriculum usually includes courses in parenting, nutrition, and other family and consumer sciences topics. Some schools provide day care services for children of teen parents. Being in a school environment gives teens access to health care, counseling, and school-to-work programs.

Fig. 6-11. In most states, WIC participants receive checks or coupons that can be used to buy specific foods, such as infant formula, eggs, and milk.

Modeling CHARACTER

Teaching Perseverance

Setting a goal and sticking to it can sometimes seem overwhelming. For a teen parent, even finishing high school may seem like an impossible task. Few things are impossible, though, for those who have *perseverance*—the ability to keep going in spite of difficulties.

How can you develop perseverance? As you work toward a long-term goal, focus on one small step at a time. Expect some setbacks and don't let them steer you off course. Just adjust your plan if needed, then keep going!

When parents model perseverance, their children learn a valuable real-life lesson. Young children often feel frustrated as they try to master difficult tasks. It helps them to see that parents, too, face obstacles—but that they don't let those obstacles stand in their way. From parents who persevere, children learn that success comes not just to the smartest or the strongest, but to those who simply don't give up.

Think About It

Describe a time when you were successful in meeting a goal because of your perseverance. How would you teach your child to keep working toward a goal when things get tough?

For students who cannot attend school classes, a GED (Graduate Equivalency Diploma) may be an option. A GED offers the same advantages as a high school diploma. It is obtained by passing a lengthy test that covers English, math, science, and social studies.

Each state has its own rules about who can take the GED test. Ways to prepare for the test include taking a GED course at a school or learning institute, checking out study books from the public library, and watching GED courses on local public television stations.

CHAPTER 6 Review & Activities

CHAPTER SUMMARY

- Both internal and external forces contribute to teen pregnancy.
- Teen pregnancy poses risks to mother and child, and teen parenthood presents challenges to the parents.
- Teen parenthood affects not only the parents and child but also others in the family and society as a whole.
- Options for teen parents include single parenting, marriage, and adoption.
- Both fathers and mothers are legally and financially responsible for their children.
- Teens faced with pregnancy can turn to government and community sources for help.

Check Your Facts

1. Describe at least two internal pressures that contribute to teen pregnancy.
2. What external pressures can lead to teen pregnancy?
3. What health risks do pregnant teens face?
4. When and where should a pregnant teen go for prenatal care?
5. Compare these terms: miscarriage, stillbirth, premature birth, and low birth weight.
6. How do each of the following present challenges for teen parents: emotions, social life, finances, and education and employment?
7. How is paternity determined?
8. What do statistics show about the effects of teen parenting on children?
9. How does teen parenting affect society?
10. What difficulties might a teen who is a single parent have?
11. Compare these adoptions: closed, open, semi-open, and in-family.
12. If parents don't fulfill their responsibilities, what can happen?
13. Name at least four places a pregnant teen can seek advice or support.
14. What programs help teen parents get a high school education?

Think Critically

1. **Supporting Your Opinion.** What might be done to reduce the number of teen pregnancies? Explain your ideas and support them with examples, facts, and clear reasoning.
2. **Analyzing Options.** When pregnancy occurs, some teens choose adoption for the child. Analyze this choice. What personal values might encourage a teen to choose adoption?

Apply Your Learning

1. **Class Discussion.** Some people feel that the media has heavy influence on teen pregnancy. Do you agree? Explain why or why not.

2. **Grandparents.** Using library and Internet resources, and possibly interviews, do research on grandparents who raise grandchildren. What are the implications for the children, the grandparents, and society? Report your findings to the class.

3. **Brochures.** With a team of classmates, design a brochure about teen pregnancy. Choose a specific theme, such as "The Risks and Challenges of Teen Pregnancy," "Rights and Responsibilities of Teen Parents," or "Teen Pregnancy: Finding Support." Ask a guidance counselor how brochures might be made available to students.

Cross-Curricular Connections

1. **Language Arts.** Imagine a day in the life of a teen parent who goes to school, works, and cares for a child. Write a journal entry that describes a typical day. Include activities as well as emotions and feelings.

2. **Social Studies.** Research how another developed nation, such as England, Sweden, or Japan, handles teen parenting issues: for example, child care and medical care. Share what you learn with the class.

Family & Community Connections

1. **Families Working Together.** Does your family know a teen parent who could use some help? If so, talk about ways to lend support and then take action. You could provide child care for a few hours or prepare a meal to share. If you don't know a teen parent, think of another way to help, such as volunteering at a pregnancy care center.

2. **WIC Program.** Contact a community agency to learn more about the WIC program in your state. Find out about eligibility requirements, nutritional benefits and education, and the program's impact.

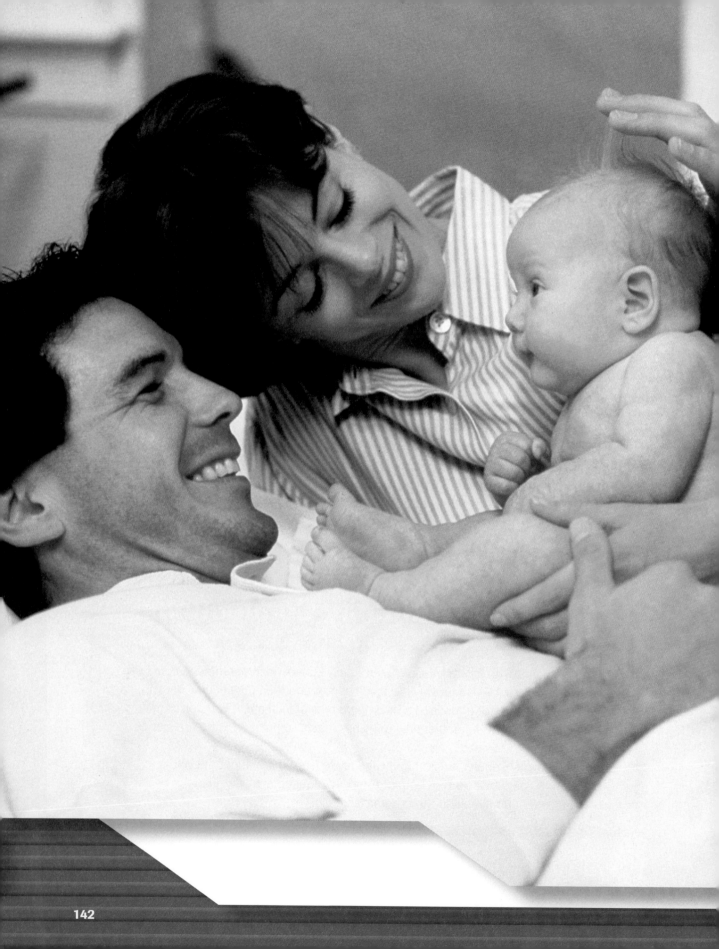

Becoming a Parent

CHAPTER 7

Planning a Family

CHAPTER OBJECTIVES

- Identify reasons for planning a family.
- Explain how to prepare for healthy parenthood.
- Explain the biological processes related to conception.
- Compare methods of contraception.
- Summarize basic principles of genetics.
- Describe alternatives to biological parenthood.

PARENTING TERMS

- ovaries
- uterus
- ovulation
- fallopian tubes
- sperm
- testes
- conception
- infertile
- contraception
- heredity
- genetics
- dominant
- recessive
- genetic disorders
- adoption
- foster parents

If children could choose their families, the most important quality would be parents who want them. Children whose arrival is planned are likely to be welcomed into a loving, supportive home by parents who are prepared to meet their physical, intellectual, emotional, and social needs.

Why Plan a Family?

Every day you see people plan for positive results, whether completing a homework assignment, searching for a job, or planning an event. When it comes to starting a family, however, many people give little thought to planning. Yet the family they create will likely be a central part of their lives for years to come. Shouldn't that family be formed with careful thought?

An essential first step in planning a family is choosing an emotionally mature and financially stable marriage partner. Together, the couple can develop a family plan that best meets their needs. See Fig. 7-1.

Planning a family, rather than leaving parenthood to chance, has several benefits. First and foremost, planning helps ensure that children are truly wanted. Children who are born by choice, rather than by chance, get a better start in life.

In addition, couples who plan can take time to build a solid relationship before becoming parents. They can make sure they are physically, emotionally, and financially prepared for the responsibilities of parenting, as discussed in Chapter 3. Together, they can discuss and reach agreement on important issues such as these:

- Do we share common values and beliefs about raising children? What are they?
- How soon do we want to begin a family? Do we want to focus on other goals first?
- Do we want to have more than one child? If so, how far apart in age would we prefer the children be spaced? Spacing children at least two years apart allows parents to adjust to parenthood before increasing the size of their family.
- How will we balance commitments to family and work? Will one person stay home to care for children? Will both work part time and share child-rearing duties?

Fig. 7-1. When people choose a marriage partner, they are also selecting a prospective parent for any children they may have. **What qualities would you look for?**

Health & Safety

Medications, Supplements, and Pregnancy

Women who are planning a pregnancy should:

- **Tell their health care provider about any medications or supplements they take.** Some could harm a developing baby.
- **Be sure to get enough folic acid.** If a woman does not get enough of this vitamin before conception and early in pregnancy, her baby has an increased risk of neural tube defects.

(The *neural tube* is the part of a developing baby that becomes the brain and spinal cord.) Many women do not get enough folic acid in their diet. For this reason, physicians often recommend folic acid supplements for all women of childbearing age.

Preparing for Healthy Parenthood

As you can see, parenthood involves many complex issues. It also involves matters as basic as good health. Couples that decide to start a family in the near future should prepare physically for a healthy pregnancy and parenthood. Here are some steps they can take:

- **Develop and maintain healthy habits.** Pregnancy and childbirth are physically demanding. Good health habits will help a woman get and stay in the best possible physical condition to meet those demands. She should eat a nutritious and balanced diet, get enough sleep, and exercise regularly. These habits are a good idea for prospective fathers, too.

- **Get a medical checkup.** Both prospective parents should have a checkup to be sure the reproductive system is healthy and there are no hidden medical problems.
- **Get vaccinated.** Couples planning a pregnancy should make sure they have received all needed *vaccinations*—shots given to prevent diseases. One particular concern is *rubella*, a common disease also known as German measles. If a pregnant woman comes down with rubella, it will make her only mildly ill, but it could cause serious problems for the unborn baby. A rubella vaccine is available, but it cannot be given to pregnant women. Before the pregnancy, both prospective parents should be tested for immunity to rubella and vaccinated if necessary.

- **Get a dental checkup.** The health of the teeth and gums can affect the health of the entire body. Having teeth cleaned and any cavities filled helps put prospective mothers in the best possible shape.
- **Kick unhealthy habits.** Anytime is a good time to stop using tobacco, alcohol, or other drugs, but giving up any harmful habits is especially important for prospective parents.

The Reproductive Process

Human reproduction is a function of the male and female reproductive systems. Knowing how the human reproductive process works will give you the terminology necessary to ask intelligent questions when talking with health care professionals about planning a family.

The Female Reproductive System

Females are born with thousands of reproductive cells, called *ova*, or eggs. (A single egg is called an *ovum*.) Ova are stored in a woman's **ovaries** (OH-vuh-reez), two oval-shaped reproductive organs. The ovaries lie near the **uterus** (YOO-tuh-russ), or womb, the organ in which an unborn baby develops. The uterus is lined with thick muscles that can expand to hold a developing baby before it is born and contract to help push the baby out during labor. See Fig. 7-2.

When a female reaches puberty, an ovum matures in one of her ovaries about once each month. The mature ovum is released by the ovary in a process called **ovulation**. It then travels through one of the two **fallopian tubes** (fuh-LOH-pee-uhn) that lie to the upper right and left of the uterus. Tiny hairs lining the

Fig. 7-2. The female reproductive system is designed to produce ova and to nourish and protect a developing baby. **Which organs perform each of these functions?**

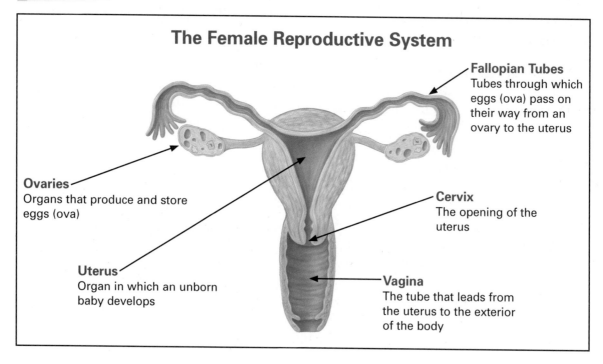

The Female Reproductive System

Fallopian Tubes
Tubes through which eggs (ova) pass on their way from an ovary to the uterus

Ovaries
Organs that produce and store eggs (ova)

Cervix
The opening of the uterus

Uterus
Organ in which an unborn baby develops

Vagina
The tube that leads from the uterus to the exterior of the body

passageways inside the fallopian tubes help push the ovum along to the uterus.

If the ovum is not fertilized by a male reproductive cell, it passes out of the uterus during menstruation, along with the lining of blood vessels and other tissue that forms each month. This cycle repeats itself every 28 days for about 40 years during a woman's reproductive lifetime.

The Male Reproductive System

Sperm are the male reproductive cells. Males begin producing these microscopic cells at puberty, and healthy males may produce sperm for the rest of their life. Sperm are produced and stored in the two **testes** (TES-teez).

The testes are oval shaped and grow to be about one inch long. The testes also produce *hormones* (natural body chemicals) that stimulate the production of sperm and cause males to become sexually mature.

During sexual intercourse, the male reproductive system releases sperm cells into the reproductive system of the female. The sperm cells travel from the testes through the *urethra* (yu-REE-thruh), a narrow tube inside the penis. Four to five hundred million sperm cells, surrounded by a protective milky fluid, are released at one time. The combined substance of the sperm and the fluid is called semen (SEE-men). See Fig. 7-3.

Fig. 7-3. The male reproductive system produces sperm. **Where are the sperm cells produced and stored?**

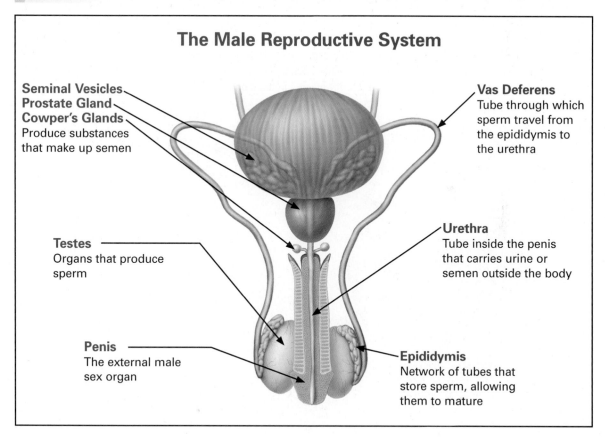

The Male Reproductive System

Seminal Vesicles
Prostate Gland
Cowper's Glands
Produce substances
that make up semen

Vas Deferens
Tube through which
sperm travel from
the epididymis to
the urethra

Testes
Organs that produce
sperm

Urethra
Tube inside the penis
that carries urine or
semen outside the body

Penis
The external male
sex organ

Epididymis
Network of tubes that
store sperm, allowing
them to mature

Conception

Conception occurs when male and female reproductive cells unite after sexual intercourse. During intercourse, sperm are deposited near the lower end of the female uterus. The sperm that enter the uterus quickly swim into the fallopian tubes. If an ovum is present, the sperm swarm the ovum and try to break through the surface. Only one sperm is successful. At this moment of fertilization, the surface of the ovum seals out the remaining sperm, which eventually die.

Deposited sperm can live for four or five days inside the female's body. An ovum might typically survive for about 24 to 48 hours in the female's fallopian tubes. Therefore, pregnancy can occur if intercourse takes place during the four or five days before the ovum is released and for about two days afterward.

Once the ovum has been fertilized, it attaches to the wall of the uterus. There the lining of blood vessels and other tissue remains to nourish the developing baby until birth. For almost all women, menstruation stops until the pregnancy is over. See Fig. 7-4.

Myths About Becoming Pregnant. Many people are uncertain about when conception can occur. Some common questions are:

- **Can pregnancy occur before a female has had her first menstrual period?** Yes. It's rare, but occasionally an ovum is released before the very first menstrual period begins.
- **Can pregnancy occur the first time a female has intercourse?** Yes. As long as an ovum and sperm are present and unite, it makes no difference whether it's the first time.

Fig. 7-4. The ovary produces an egg (1), which travels down the fallopian tube (2). Fertilization occurs when a single sperm cell unites with an egg (3). The fertilized egg begins to divide into two cells, then four, then eight, and so on (4 and 5). The clump of cells travels down the fallopian tube toward the uterus (6). About two weeks after conception, the cells that will eventually form the baby are firmly planted in the uterine wall (7).

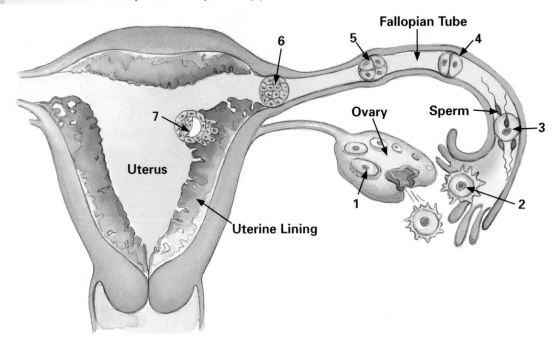

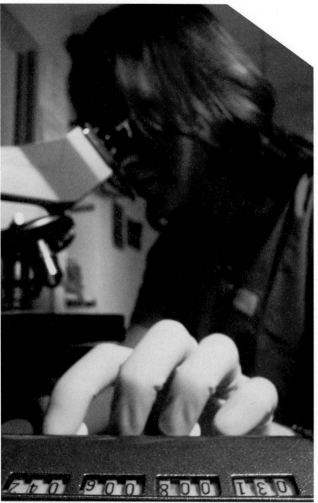

Fig. 7-5. With in vitro fertilization, an egg is fertilized in a laboratory dish. Only the healthiest sperm are used. Here a technician categorizes sperm according to their activity level before choosing those that will be selected for the process.

- **Can pregnancy occur during the menstrual period?** Yes. The ovum may be alive and present at this time.
- **Can pregnancy occur even if intercourse is incomplete?** Yes. A few sperm may be released, and only one is needed.

Fertility Problems

Once couples decide to have a child, they are understandably eager for pregnancy. Many are able to conceive within a few months. Others take considerably longer, and some are unable to conceive. Couples who are **infertile** are unable to conceive a child after trying for 12 months. About 8 to 12 percent of couples worldwide are infertile.

About 40 percent of fertility problems among couples are the result of male infertility. The three most common causes of infertility in men are low production of sperm, impaired delivery of sperm, and low production of a male sex hormone.

Infertility in women can have a variety of causes. For example, a hormone imbalance can prevent or delay ovulation. A woman's ova deteriorate in quality as she grows older, making it more difficult for her to conceive. The fallopian tubes may be blocked by scar tissue, preventing an ovum from reaching the uterus. Endometriosis, a condition in which tissue that normally lines the uterus is found in other locations, can lead to infertility in some cases.

Treatment for Infertility. Science has developed a variety of techniques to treat infertility. Physicians who specialize in fertility problems can conduct tests to find out the cause of infertility, then offer treatment options. See Fig. 7-5.

Depending on the cause of the infertility, one option might be *artificial insemination*. The physician helps the couple determine exactly when the woman ovulates. At that point, the physician uses a needle to implant sperm into the woman's uterus. The sperm may come from the husband or from a donor.

Another possible option is *in vitro fertilization*. In this procedure, an ovum from the woman is surgically removed, then combined in a laboratory dish with her husband's sperm. If the egg becomes fertilized, it is placed back in the woman's uterus.

Multiple Births

Many people wonder how twins occur, and why some twins look more alike than others. Twins can be either fraternal or identical, depending on how conception occurs.

- **Fraternal twins** occur when the ovary releases two separate eggs and each is fertilized by a different sperm cell. Fraternal twins may include a boy and a girl. Even if they are both the same sex, they will look no more alike than any other pair of siblings. The only thing that makes fraternal twins unusual is that they are born at the same time.

- **Identical twins** result when a single egg is fertilized, then splits into two separate parts, each of which goes on to develop into a baby. Because they develop from the same fertilized egg, identical twins are always both boys or both girls, and they look very much alike. Identical twins are more rare than fraternal twins.

Triplets, quadruplets, and other multiple births come about the same way as twins. The babies can be identical, fraternal, or a combination. See Fig. 7-6.

You have probably read or seen reports about women giving birth to as many as seven babies at once. Such occurrences are extremely rare. Most result from fertility treatments.

Multiple births carry increased risks of complications for the mother and babies. Mothers are more likely to deliver prematurely and to experience excessive bleeding after giving birth. Babies who are multiples are at a higher risk for having low birth weight and other problems. The greater the number of babies born at one time, the higher the risks. Fortunately, thanks to modern science, the survival rate for babies born together is very high.

Fig. 7-6. If children in a multiple birth are all the same sex, that doesn't necessarily mean they are all identical. **Do you think these triplets might be identical? Why or why not?**

Contraception

Many couples choose to delay pregnancy until they are financially secure. Others want to time a pregnancy around their careers or family responsibilities. They decide not to leave family planning to chance. Instead, they rely on some form of contraception. **Contraception** is the use of drugs, devices, or techniques to prevent pregnancy. Another term for contraception is "birth control."

Decisions about contraception are extremely personal. Religious beliefs, personal values, age, health, and a couple's economic situation all enter into their decision. Other factors to consider include:

- **Reliability.** How effective is the method in preventing conception from occurring?
- **Safety.** How effective is the method in preventing AIDS and other sexually transmitted diseases or infections?
- **Potential health risks.** Can the method cause side effects or injury?

When a couple decides to use contraception, both of them must be comfortable with the choice. They must also be committed to properly using the method every time they have sexual intercourse.

Types of Contraception. The only completely effective method of contraception is abstinence—choosing not to engage in sexual activity. Abstinence also prevents the spread of sexually transmitted diseases or infections. Other methods have varying degrees of effectiveness, as shown in Fig. 7-7.

Fig. 7-7. The effectiveness of any contraception method depends on whether it is used correctly. Abstinence is the only 100% effective method of preventing pregnancy.

Methods of Contraception			
Method	**Effectiveness**	**How It Works**	**Disadvantages**
Abstinence No sexual intercourse.	100%	Avoids any possibility of conception.	None. Abstinence is the only 100% effective way to prevent pregnancy and sexually transmitted diseases or infections.
Hormone Implant Capsules inserted beneath skin in woman's upper arm.	99%	Prevents monthly release of ovum for up to 5 years.	Doctor must insert. May cause irregular bleeding, missed menstrual periods, weight gain, headaches, mood changes.
3-Month Hormone Injection Injection given to woman once every 3 months.	99%	Prevents monthly release of ovum for 3 months.	Doctor or nurse must inject. May cause weight gain, headaches, abdominal pain, irregular periods.
Sterilization Surgical procedures.	99%	For female: tubal ligation clamps or seals fallopian tubes. For male: vasectomy cuts or ties tubes carrying sperm to penis.	Minor surgery with some risk of infection. Requires surgery to reverse, which is costly and doesn't always work.

(Continued on next page)

Methods of Contraception (Continued)

Method	Effectiveness	How It Works	Disadvantages
Oral Contraceptive Pill taken by woman daily.	94–97%	Prevents monthly release of ovum.	Prescription needed. Can cause weight gain, headaches, mood changes. Health risks for women who are over 35, smoke, or have family history of certain diseases.
Contraceptive Patch Adhesive patch worn on woman's body.	94–97%	Prevents monthly release of ovum.	Prescription needed. Can cause weight gain, headaches, mood changes. Health risks for women who are over 35, smoke, or have family history of certain diseases.
Monthly Hormone Injection Injection given to woman once every month.	94–97%	Prevents monthly release of ovum.	Doctor or nurse must inject. Can cause weight gain, headaches, mood changes. Health risks for women who are over 35, smoke, or have family history of certain diseases.
IUD (Intrauterine Device) Small plastic or metal device inserted into uterus.	94%	Prevents pregnancy by interfering with implantation of fertilized ovum.	Doctor must insert. Increases risk of pelvic infection. May increase menstrual flow and cramping.
Male Condom Latex sheath that fits over penis.	86–90%	Traps semen. Also reduces risk of sexually transmitted diseases or infections. Each condom is used only once.	Can break or slip off. Damaged by hot or cold and petroleum products.
Female Condom Polyurethane pouch inserted into vagina.	75–95%	Prevents sperm from reaching womb. Each condom is used only once.	Can break. Incorrect use decreases rate of effectiveness.
Natural Family Planning System for tracking the woman's monthly cycle to determine when ovulation occurs.	80–90%	If pregnancy is not desired, intercourse is avoided during the time when pregnancy can occur.	Requires accurate record keeping. Illness or irregular menstrual cycle can throw off calculations. Errors easily made.
Diaphragm Dome-shaped latex cup stretched over a flexible ring; inserted into vagina.	84%	Blocks entrance to uterus. Used with spermicide.	Must be fitted by health professional. Must remain in place for at least 6 hours after intercourse. Increases risk of bladder/urinary tract infections.
Cervical Cap Small latex or plastic thimble that fits snugly over cervix (narrow opening of the uterus).	82%	Blocks entrance to uterus. Used with spermicide.	Must be fitted by health professional. Difficult to insert. Must remain in place for at least 8 hours after intercourse.
Spermicide Foams, creams, gels, and vaginal inserts.	74%	Sperm-killing chemical. Used with condom, diaphragm, cervical cap.	Not very effective when used alone. May cause allergic reaction.

Fig. 7-8. Heredity determines, to a large extent, what a person looks like. **What are some physical traits children inherit from their parents?**

Understanding Genetics

"He has his mother's nose." "She must have gotten her musical talent from her grand-father." Comments like these are observations on **heredity**, the biological process by which certain traits are transmitted from parents to their children. See Fig. 7-8.

Genetics is the study of how traits are passed from parents to child through heredity. How does this process occur? It all starts with *chromosomes*, long, threadlike structures in the nucleus, or central portion, of each human cell. On each chromosome are hundreds or thousands of genes. A *gene* is a hereditary unit that determines a particular trait, such as eye color.

Almost all cells in the human body contain 23 pairs of chromosomes, or 46 in all. Ova and sperm cells are the exception. Each ovum or sperm contains only 23 chromosomes. When an ovum and sperm unite at conception, they create a single cell with 46 chromosomes—23 from the sperm and 23 from the ovum. Thus, for each inherited trait, the fertilized egg has two genes, one from each parent.

The number of possible combinations of genes is staggering. According to one scientific estimate, as many as 64 trillion different genetic combinations are possible.

Through the process of cell reproduction, the fertilized egg will multiply into the trillions of cells that make up the human body. Every resulting cell contains copies of those 46 chromosomes—the genetic blueprint for a unique individual.

Dominant and Recessive Traits

As you have read, a child receives two genes for each inherited trait. In some cases, both genes are the same. For example, if both the sperm and ovum carry a gene for brown eyes, the child will have brown eyes.

In many cases, however, the genes are different. One might be for brown eyes, and the other for blue eyes. What happens then? The stronger, or **dominant**, trait is expressed. In this example, the gene for brown eyes is dominant, so the child will have brown eyes.

A trait that is weaker, such as the one for blue eyes, is said to be **recessive**. To be expressed, a recessive gene must be inherited from both the mother and the father.

Could two parents with brown eyes produce a blue-eyed baby? Yes, if each parent carries a recessive gene for blue eyes. In that case, some of the mother's ova will have the gene for blue eyes and some will have the gene for brown eyes. The same is true of the father's sperm. If an ovum with the gene for blue eyes unites with a sperm that has the same gene, the child will have blue eyes.

Gender Determination

Will the baby be a boy or a girl? The answer is settled at the moment a sperm fertilizes an ovum.

Of the 46 chromosomes in each cell, two are specialized chromosomes that determine gender. In a female these are alike (XX). In a male, they are different (XY).

Each reproductive cell receives only one gender chromosome, either an X or Y. Since females have two X chromosomes, all ova will have an X. Since males have an X and a Y, sperm can contain either one of these.

If the sperm that fertilizes the ovum carries an X chromosome, the chromosome pair will be XX and the baby will be female. If the sperm carries a Y chromosome, the resulting pair will be XY and the baby will be male. As you can see, the father determines the child's gender. See Fig. 7-9.

Knowing whether a child is male or female before birth is an option that most parents have today. Some like to be prepared ahead of time. Others prefer a surprise at the time of birth.

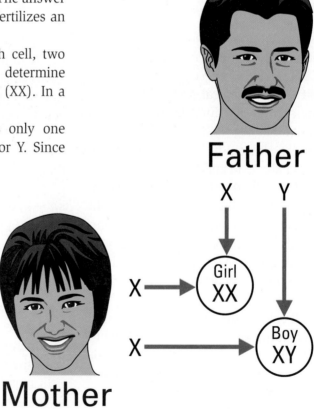

Fig. 7-9. The father determines the gender of a child. **Can you explain why?**

Fig. 7-10. Down syndrome affects more than 350,000 people in the United States.

Genetic Disorders

Genes contain instructions that give nearly all the information necessary for a living organism to grow and function. Most of the time, this mysterious process works amazingly well. Sometimes, however, a problem occurs. If genes carry the wrong instructions, body processes may not work as they should.

Genetic disorders are medical conditions caused by errors in genes or chromosomes. The error might be a mutation, or change, in the instructions encoded on a gene. In other cases, genetic disorders result from missing, damaged, or extra chromosomes.

Testing can identify most genetic disorders. Early diagnosis allows parents and medical professionals to do as much as possible to improve or manage the child's condition. Although many disorders cannot be cured at present, medical researchers continue to look for answers.

Nearly 4,000 genetic disorders afflict humans. Here are some examples.

- **Down syndrome.** A child born with Down syndrome has an extra chromosome 21. The effects vary, but include moderate to severe mental impairment. Many children with Down syndrome also have physical disorders such as hearing loss, impaired vision, and heart defects. Women over 35 are at greater risk for having a child with Down syndrome. The disorder can be detected before birth with genetic testing. Many people with Down syndrome benefit from special education services and physical therapy. See Fig. 7-10.

- **Cystic fibrosis.** This disorder is caused by inheriting a certain defective gene from both parents. Cystic fibrosis causes the body to produce an extremely thick, sticky mucus that clogs the lungs and causes lung infections. The mucus also interferes with digestive enzymes that are needed to break down and digest food. The expected lifespan for someone with cystic fibrosis is about 30 years. Diagnosis before birth is possible, and screening of at-risk newborns is recommended to prevent malnutrition and improve lung function.

- **Muscular dystrophy.** This is a group of genetic disorders that cause progressive weakness and degeneration of the skeletal muscles that cause movement. There are many forms of muscular dystrophy, which can be inherited from one or both parents. Signs of some forms appear as early as birth; other forms appear later in childhood, in adolescence, or in adulthood. Some types affect lifespan, while others do not. Respiratory therapy, physical therapy, and orthopedic appliances can help improve the quality of life.

- **Sickle-cell disease.** This blood disorder most often affects people of African or Middle Eastern descent. Hard, sticky red blood cells shaped like sickles clog the flow of blood. They then break apart, slowing the delivery

Modeling CHARACTER

Responsible Family Planning

One sign of *responsibility* is accepting the consequences of your actions. Another is considering the potential consequences before deciding what action to take. Bringing a child into the world has significant, long-lasting consequences for the child, the parents, other family members, and society. As they discuss and consider issues related to family planning, responsible couples:

- Recognize and accept that raising children, while rewarding, is also hard work.
- Agree that if they have a child, they will make whatever sacrifices are necessary to provide for the child's needs.
- Decide that they can be happy with either a son or a daughter.
- Talk with family members to learn if any genetic disorders run in the family, and seek genetic counseling if necessary.

Think About It

If prospective parents did not take the steps listed above, what consequences might result?

of oxygen to cells and causing pain, fatigue, and swollen joints. Medication can relieve the pain, but there is no cure, and early death may result. A blood test can screen for carriers and detect sickle-cell disease in newborns.

- **Tay-Sachs disease.** This rare disease occurs most often in people of eastern European Jewish descent. Affected infants appear to develop normally for the first few months, but they lack an enzyme that breaks down a certain fatty substance in the brain and nervous system. The fatty material soon builds up in the brain's nerve cells, causing the cells to rupture. As this occurs, the child gradually loses skills and eventually becomes blind, deaf, and unable to move or swallow. There is no treatment for Tay-Sachs disease. With the best care, some children live to age five. Both parents must be carriers to have an affected child. A simple blood test identifies parents who carry the defective chromosome.

- **PKU.** Phenylketonuria (fe-nul-KEE-tun-UR-ree-uh), or PKU, affects the body's ability to properly use protein. One of the enzymes that breaks down protein does not function properly, causing other enzymes to build up in the blood and tissue. The buildup of these enzymes prevents the brain from growing and developing normally. PKU occurs when a child inherits a gene for this disorder from each parent. PKU can cause mental retardation and other problems if treatment is not started within the first few weeks of life. Fortunately, a routine blood test of newborns identifies the disease. A carefully controlled diet can prevent or control the effects of PKU.

When a child has a genetic disorder, parents must work closely with health care professionals to ensure that the child receives proper

Fig. 7-11. An older relative often can provide useful information that can help doctors identify inherited disorders. **What questions would you ask a relative about family medical history?**

medical care. Parents also need to rely on their problem-solving skills to handle the added issues that the disorder may cause. With effort and a positive attitude, families can successfully manage the challenges. You can read more about parenting children with special needs in Chapter 25.

Genetic Counseling

Many people who have a genetic disorder in their family want more information about how the disorder may affect their lives and the lives of any children they might have. Genetic counseling can help. Genetic counselors are health specialists trained to provide information and support to families who are facing the possibility of genetic disorders. Those who already have a child or children with a genetic disorder usually seek counseling before having more children. See Fig. 7-11.

Genetic counselors help provide families with the information they need to understand genetic disorders. They begin by taking a detailed medical history of the families of both partners. In some cases, they arrange for testing to detect defective genes. They analyze the collected data and talk to prospective parents about their risk of having a child with a particular disease or disability. They then help the couple understand how this potential disability is likely to affect the child and the family. Based on this information, the couple can make an informed decision about their family planning options.

Fig. 7-12. Adoption provides a happy solution for children who need homes and people who want to love and provide for them.

Choosing Adoption

Biological parenthood is not the only option for those who want children and are ready to become parents. Many people begin or add to their family by adopting children. **Adoption** is a legal process by which people acquire the rights and responsibilities of parenthood for children who are not biologically their own.

Some children are available for adoption because their birth parents have died. In other cases, parental rights of the biological parents have been terminated by the court due to neglect or abuse. Most of the time, however, the birth parents chose adoption because they realized that they were physically, emotionally, or financially unprepared to provide what a child needs. They made the decision that was best for the child.

People adopt children for many reasons. Some couples who receive genetic counseling decide to adopt after analyzing the risk factors. Infertile couples may prefer to adopt rather than continuing to try to conceive. People who are single and those for whom pregnancy poses health risks may also choose to become adoptive parents. Some people adopt for no other reason than to provide a loving, stable home for a child who is without one. See Fig. 7-12.

The Adoption Process

Most people who adopt do so through a public or private adoption agency. These can be found in the telephone directory or through referrals from other social service agencies. After filling out application forms, the applicants must undergo a series of meetings with a social worker. The social worker will ask prospective parents about their income and the time demands of their jobs. He or she will also visit their home to make sure it is clean

Fig. 7-13. Many children from around the world have found a good home through international adoption. **What are some benefits and challenges of adopting a child from another country?**

and safe. A police report will be run to make sure applicants have not committed any crimes. Friends and business associates may be asked to write letters stating why applicants would be good parents.

There is a waiting period for all adoptions. The wait for adopting a healthy infant is longest—in some cases, between two and seven years. If parents are willing to adopt a child who is older or has special needs, the process is much faster.

After the child is placed with the adoptive parents, the social worker visits the home several times to ensure that the child is receiving proper care. The child lives with the adoptive parents for six months or more, as required by state law, before the adoption becomes final.

Private, or independent, adoptions—those in which an agency is not involved—are handled differently. The procedures for legal private adoptions vary from state to state. Sometimes the birth mother's lawyer simply draws up a legal agreement with the adoptive parents. In other states, the process is more complicated.

International Adoptions

In some countries, there are many more children needing parents than there are parents seeking to adopt them. Infants can be adopted from more than fifty countries in Latin America, Asia, Eastern Europe, and some

African countries. Most were born to poor mothers who cannot support another child. Half of all children adopted internationally are under the age of one. Nearly all are younger than four. See Fig. 7-13.

Procedures for foreign adoptions vary widely and are determined by the agencies within each country. Many parents adopting foreign children will be required to make one or more trips overseas before they can bring the child home. Others may be able to handle the paperwork long-distance, and their child may be brought to them.

Adjustments After Adoption

Adoption, like all major family events, requires some emotional adjustments. The nature of those adjustments depends on the situation. If parents adopt an infant, they must adapt to the new arrival just as they would to the birth of a biological child. An infant usually adjusts easily to a new environment.

When an older child is adopted, the transition for the child may be more difficult. Whatever the child's previous situation was, he or she is leaving behind familiar people and places. The adoptive parents should expect some ups and downs as the child adjusts. The best approach is to be patient, understanding, and supportive. It takes time, but the bonds that eventually form will be as strong as those between any other parent and child.

Children who were adopted before the age of two usually do not remember their previous home or family. Eventually, they must be told that they are adopted. There is no one best age at which to do this. Adoption experts offer suggestions ranging from age two to age eight, depending on the situation. Whatever the child's age, parents should discuss the adoption in a matter-of-fact, positive way. For example, an adoptive mother might say, "You were born like all babies, but I didn't give birth to you. A different woman did. She cared for you very much, but she wasn't ready to be a mommy. She chose to let Daddy and me be your parents. We were very excited and happy when you came to us. We love you so much, and we will be your parents forever."

Becoming a Foster Parent

Foster parents are adults who provide temporary care for children who have been removed from their homes. The removal may have been due to child abuse or neglect, or the parents may be facing problems that make it difficult for them to fulfill their responsibilities. Foster parents provide a temporary home until a permanent one can be found. This might take days, weeks, months, or even years. Some children in foster care will return to their own homes when their parents become able to take up their responsibilities again. Others will eventually be placed with relatives or an adoptive family. See Fig. 7-14.

Foster parents must be approved and licensed by the state. They receive a small monthly payment to help cover the cost of the child's food, clothing, and other basic needs. As with adoption, the arrival of a foster child requires emotional adjustments for everyone involved. Children in foster care have been through stressful experiences and often struggle with feelings of rejection, insecurity, and guilt. Some have emotional, behavioral, developmental, or physical problems. Despite the challenges, foster parenthood is rewarding and fills a great need. People who are interested in becoming foster parents should contact their local child welfare agency or state foster parent association.

Fig. 7-14. Some couples host several foster children at the same time. **How can foster parents help children?**

Child & Family Services
CAREERS

▸ Family Advocate

Family advocates act on behalf of children and families in need of social services. Some work through the courts or social service agencies to help young families adjust to parenthood. Others focus on getting neglected or abused children into safe homes. Still others work within the schools to help give students with discipline problems or those lacking life skills the tools necessary to succeed in the workplace.

"My degree in social work prepared me to apply for and pass the test necessary to receive a social work license. Because I work with children, I also had to pass a criminal history check. I was hired by a social service agency to work with young single mothers in need of various mental health, legal, and other social services. I find my work rewarding because I'm able to have a positive impact on people's lives."

CAREER TIPS

- Take parenting and psychology courses in high school.
- Volunteer at an after-school program for young children or teens.
- Earn a college degree in the field of human development, social work, or sociology.
- Pass a licensure exam.
- Apply for jobs with social service agencies.

CHAPTER SUMMARY

- Prospective parents are wise to plan the family they want to have.
- Couples who decide to start a family need to prepare for a healthy pregnancy and for parenthood.
- Conception occurs when reproductive cells from a male and female unite.
- Contraceptives allow couples to delay or prevent pregnancy.
- Genetic testing can alert couples to the possibility of genetic disorders in their offspring.
- Adoption and foster parenting are alternatives to biological parenthood.

Check Your Facts

1. Why should people plan their family?
2. What are five ways to prepare for healthy parenthood?
3. Use these terms to explain ovulation: ovaries, uterus, and fallopian tubes.
4. Define sperm and testes.
5. Explain the process of conception.
6. Identify at least three reasons why a couple may be infertile.
7. Compare fraternal and identical twins.
8. What are at least four factors to consider when choosing a method of contraception?
9. Summarize how traits are passed genetically from parents to child.
10. Genetically speaking, why are people unique?
11. Distinquish between dominant and recessive traits.
12. How does the father determine the gender of a child?

13. Why would a couple consult a genetic counselor?
14. What are three reasons why a couple might choose adoption?
15. What type of child custody do foster parents have?

Think Critically

1. **Supporting Your Viewpoint.** Do you think couples who plan their family will be more effective parents than those who don't? Explain your reasoning.
2. **Analyzing Information.** At what age do you think a child should be told that he or she is adopted? What circumstances might affect this decision? How would the explanation differ according to the child's age?

Apply Your Learning

1. **Family Planning Questionnaire.** Devise a questionnaire to help couples explore their plans for a family. Expand the questions on page 146, focusing each question on a specific point. Then combine ideas to create a class questionnaire.

2. **Contraceptives.** Compare the effectiveness rates of the contraception methods named in the chapter. Considering the disadvantages as well, what methods might be reasonable options for a young married couple who want to postpone parenthood? Choose two that you think would be best for them and explain why in writing.

3. **Identity of Birth Parents.** In the past, adopted children did not typically learn the identities of their birth parents. Today, they often do. List the advantages and disadvantages of each approach and compare ideas in class.

Cross-Curricular Connections

1. **Language Arts.** Suppose some teens decide to sign an abstinence pledge. Write a suitable pledge for them. Then share results in class. How could such a pledge be helpful to teens?

2. **Science.** Use print or online references to learn more about one of the following: fertility treatments; a genetic disorder described in this chapter; a genetic disorder not covered in the text. Report your findings to the class.

Family & Community Connections

1. **Family Planning Questionnaire.** Is anyone in your extended family (or a family friend) planning to be married or newly married? If so, ask the couple to complete the questionnaire developed in "Apply Your Learning" above. Find out whether the questionnaire was helpful to them and what improvements they would suggest.

2. **Community Service Project.** Contact a community center that helps women with unplanned pregnancies. Ask whether the center needs maternity clothes and baby items. Collect and donate these items to the center.

CHAPTER 8

Prenatal Development

CHAPTER OBJECTIVES

- Summarize growth and changes during prenatal development.
- Explain problems that can occur during prenatal development.
- Suggest ways of coping with the loss of a pregnancy.
- Describe prenatal tests.

PARENTING TERMS

- prenatal development
- trimesters
- zygote
- embryo
- fetus
- amniotic fluid
- placenta
- umbilical cord
- miscarriage
- stillbirth
- ectopic pregnancy
- birth defect
- premature birth
- ultrasound imaging
- amniocentesis
- chorionic villi sampling

Not long ago, pregnancy was a mysterious experience, hidden from view until the birth. People could only guess whether a baby would be a boy or a girl, how fast the baby was growing, and whether the baby would be healthy.

Today, advances in technology and medicine have made the inner workings of pregnancy more visible. Through medical testing, parents can learn about characteristics such as gender, growth rate, and health before their baby's birth.

Development Before Birth

Prenatal development is the process by which a baby-to-be grows inside the mother. This process normally takes about nine months for a *full-term* pregnancy, one that goes to completion. A full-term pregnancy typically lasts about 280 days (40 weeks), counting from the first day of the last menstrual period. However, it can be a little shorter or longer than this.

The timeline of pregnancy can be divided into three **trimesters**, or three-month time periods. Each is a time of remarkable growth and development.

First Trimester

During the first trimester—the first three months of pregnancy—an amazingly rapid sequence of prenatal development occurs. It begins at the moment of conception. As explained in Chapter 7, conception takes place when an ovum, or egg, is fertilized by a sperm.

The Zygote. At this very early stage, the developing life is called a **zygote** (ZIE-goat). The fertilized egg is a single cell, but it soon begins to divide—first into two cells, then four, then eight, and so on. After a few days, the zygote has grown to about 500 living cells that form a tiny, fluid-filled ball. This ball of cells travels through the woman's fallopian tube into her uterus, then implants itself in the lining of that organ. The ball of cells is still a tiny speck, barely big enough to be seen without a microscope, yet ready to grow into a fully developed human being. See Fig. 8-1.

The Embryo. From the time of implantation into the uterine wall through about the eighth week of pregnancy, the developing baby is called an **embryo** (EM-bree-oh). During this time, cells continue to multiply rapidly. In a few weeks the embryo is the size of the head of a pin.

Not only do new cells continue to form, but in addition, the cells begin to take on different functions. Three layers of cells form that eventually will develop into all the structures of the human body.

- The *ectoderm*, or outer layer of cells, becomes the skin, hair, and nails. It also forms the nervous system, including the brain, spinal cord, and nerves.
- The *mesoderm*, or middle layer, eventually grows into the bones, muscles, blood vessels, and some internal organs, such as the heart, kidneys, and reproductive organs.
- The *endoderm*, or internal cell layer, eventually becomes the other internal organs, such as the stomach, liver, and lungs.

Midway through the first trimester, the embryo has grown to the size of a small raisin. In two more weeks, it is about the size of a grape. The eyes and inner ears begin to form on the sides of the embryo's head, and the mouth and nostrils begin as small openings. Next, the eyelids begin to form and the nose, upper lip, and outer ears begin to take shape. The heart begins to pump blood cells,

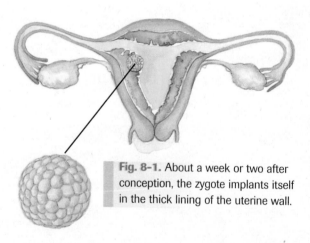

Fig. 8-1. About a week or two after conception, the zygote implants itself in the thick lining of the uterine wall.

although a heartbeat can't yet be heard. The digestive and respiratory systems start to form, and buds that will become arms and legs emerge. See Fig. 8-2.

THE DEVELOPING BRAIN

After about five weeks of pregnancy, a tiny cellular strand runs from the top to the bottom of the embryo. That strand later becomes the spinal cord, brain, and nervous system.

During early prenatal development, up to 100,000 new nerve cells are produced *every minute*. By the end of the first trimester, brain growth accelerates to a rate of nearly a quarter of a million new brain cells per minute. When the baby is born, it has about 100 billion nerve cells.

The Fetus. From the beginning of the ninth week until birth, the developing baby is called a **fetus** (FEE-tuhs). At the beginning of the fetal stage, the major organs are present but are still forming. The heartbeat of the fetus flutters rapidly and can be heard using a special instrument. The bones begin to form, taking on a skeletal shape, and the skull and jaws begin to harden. The muscles start to develop, as do the tissues that connect the muscles to the bones. The arms and legs lengthen. By now, a very thin skin covers the fetus.

At the end of the first trimester, the fetus is about 3 inches long and typically weighs about 1 ounce. All of the fetus's major organs are growing and developing. The intestines, which began forming in the umbilical cord, move into the fetus's abdomen. The ears and tightly-shut eyes move closer to their final positions. The liver begins to produce bile,

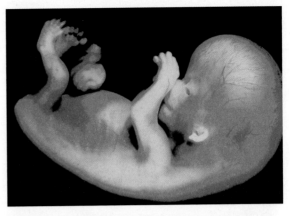

Fig. 8-2. About eight weeks after conception, many organs and systems have already begun to develop. **What features can you recognize in this picture?**

which later aids digestion, and the kidneys produce urine. The fetus can open and close its mouth and tiny fists, but the pregnant woman cannot feel those movements.

The Support System. During the first trimester, as the zygote becomes an embryo and then a fetus, the structures that will protect and nourish the developing baby also form. One of these structures is a protective sac that surrounds and encloses the developing baby. The sac is filled with **amniotic fluid** (am-nee-AH-tik), which cushions the developing baby from outside pressures.

Another support structure is the **placenta** (pluh-SENT-uh). This tissue, shaped somewhat like a pancake, is attached to the uterine wall and contains a rich network of blood vessels. The developing baby is connected to the placenta by the **umbilical cord** (uhm-BILL-ih-kuhl). For the rest of the pregnancy, blood will flow from the mother's body through the placenta and umbilical cord, carrying nutrients and oxygen to the developing baby. Wastes from the developing baby pass through the umbilical cord and placenta into the mother's

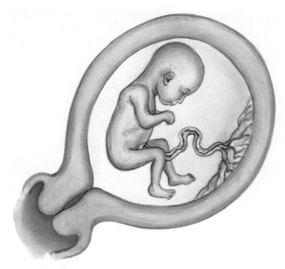

Fig. 8-3. The umbilical cord extends from the developing embryo to the placenta. **What is the function of the umbilical cord?**

bloodstream for processing and disposal. The placenta acts as a filter between the mother's and baby's bodies. See Fig. 8-3.

Second Trimester

During the second trimester—the fourth, fifth, and sixth months of pregnancy—the fetus grows dramatically. By the end of this period, the fetus will typically weigh nearly 2 pounds. Also during this time, the eyebrows and lashes appear, and fine hair, called *lanugo* (luh-NEW-go), begins to cover the fetus's skin. Fat tissue, which later will keep the newborn warm, begins to form under the skin.

At this stage, the fetus can move around and kick. The pregnant woman usually feels these movements, a milestone that is often called "quickening." Other muscle movements, such as prenatal thumb sucking, also begin during the second trimester. The lungs strengthen as the fetus "breathes" amniotic fluid in and out. The fetus also swallows amniotic fluid, and nutrients in the fluid pass through the

digestive system. However, most of the fetus's nourishment is still received from the mother's body through the placenta and umbilical cord. See Fig. 8-4.

In the second trimester, the senses—taste, touch, smell, sight, and hearing—steadily develop as nerve cells form more connections with the brain. The eyes, which had been sealed shut, now open and close. The fetus begins to hear sounds, including the mother's heartbeat and even some loud noises from outside the mother's body.

Third Trimester

During the third trimester—the seventh, eighth, and ninth months of pregnancy—the brain and other parts of the nervous system continue to develop. Brain scans by researchers

Fig. 8-4. During the second trimester, the fetus becomes very active. **What purpose do you think the fetus's activities serve?**

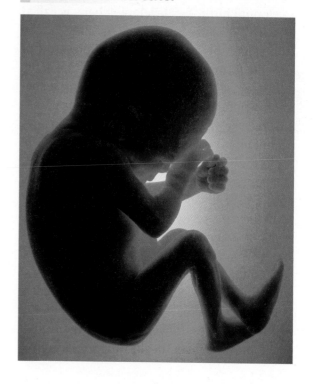

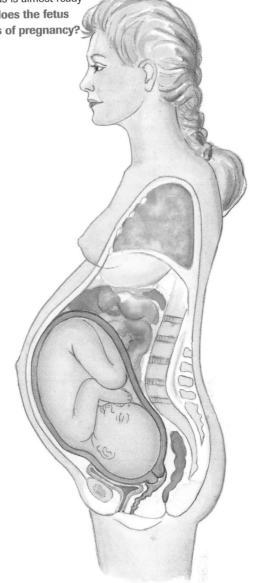

have shown that the fetus sleeps and may dream. The heart and other parts of the circulatory system also continue to mature in preparation for the newborn's independence from the woman's body. The lungs are almost fully developed by the ninth month, so they are ready to fill with air for the first time at birth.

The fetus steadily grows and gains weight until birth. The amount of vital fat tissue increases all over the fetus's body. During the third trimester, the fetus typically triples its weight. In the last few weeks before birth, the fetus gains around half a pound each week. A birth weight of 7.5 pounds is average. The head is the largest body part, accounting for one-fourth of a newborn's weight. The bones of the skull are still somewhat soft and pliable, allowing the fetus to pass through the birth canal.

During the eighth month, the fetus has less freedom of movement as it grows and fills the uterus. The fetus usually turns head downward during this month in preparation for a typical headfirst birth. In the ninth month, the still-growing fetus settles further down into the woman's pelvis. See Fig. 8-5.

In just nine months, an impressive amount of development has taken place. Fig. 8-6 on page 172 summarizes this amazing process.

Problems in Prenatal Development

Most of the time, prenatal development proceeds smoothly and results in the birth of a healthy baby. However, serious problems sometimes develop for various reasons.

Miscarriage and Stillbirth

Sometimes a pregnancy ends unexpectedly. A **miscarriage** is the spontaneous loss of the pregnancy after less than 20 weeks of fetal development. The zygote, embryo, or fetus dies and is expelled from the mother's body.

Miscarriage is not uncommon. According to researchers, between 15 and 20 percent of

Prenatal Development	
First Trimester	
Weeks 1 and 2	❑ Called a *zygote*. ❑ Single cell divides into about 500 cells in a few days. ❑ Ball of cells travels to uterus and implants there after 2 weeks.
Weeks 3 through 8	❑ Called an *embryo*. ❑ Cells multiply rapidly. One strand will become the spinal cord, brain, and nervous system. ❑ Buds of arms and legs emerge. ❑ Digestive and respiratory systems start to form, and heart begins to beat. ❑ Eyes, ears, mouth, and nostrils begin to form. ❑ Grows to about the size of a grape.
Third month	❑ Called a *fetus*. ❑ Bones begin to form. ❑ Muscles and tissues start to develop. ❑ Arms and legs lengthen. ❑ Covered by very thin skin. ❑ Grows to about 3 inches long and weighs about 1 ounce. ❑ Nearly a quarter of a million new brain cells form per minute.
Second Trimester	
Fourth month	❑ Skin is less transparent. ❑ Fine hair covers the entire body. ❑ Can suck its thumb, swallow, hiccup, and move around. ❑ Facial features become clearer.
Fifth month	❑ Hair, eyelashes, and eyebrows appear. ❑ Teeth are developing. ❑ Organs are maturing. ❑ Hands are able to grip. ❑ Becomes more active, which the mother can now feel.
Sixth month	❑ Eyes open and close. ❑ Muscles in arms and legs strengthen. ❑ Fat deposits appear beneath skin. ❑ Hears sounds (mother's heartbeat and loud sounds outside her body). ❑ Lungs strengthen as fetus "breathes" amniotic fluid in and out. ❑ Senses steadily develop as nerve cells form more connections with the brain. ❑ Grows to about 2 pounds.
Third Trimester	
Seventh month	❑ Covered by thick, white protective coating called vernix. ❑ Nervous, circulatory, and other systems mature. ❑ Periods of rest and quiet follow periods of activity.
Eighth month	❑ Has less freedom of movement as it grows. ❑ Usually moves into a head-down position.
Ninth month	❑ Increased fat under the skin reduces wrinkles. ❑ Lungs are becoming fully developed. ❑ Heart and other parts of circulatory system mature. ❑ Usually triples in weight during this trimester. ❑ Descends into the pelvis, ready for birth.

Fig. 8–6. Prenatal Development.

known pregnancies end in miscarriage. Many other pregnancies end before the woman even knows she is pregnant.

Myths about miscarriage persist. Physical activity, stress, and minor falls are *not* believed to cause the loss of a pregnancy. Miscarriages that occur very early in the pregnancy are usually due to a genetic abnormality. Most often the problem was not inherited, but simply occurred by chance. Couples in this situation should not blame themselves, since they could not have done anything to prevent the miscarriage. Many are able to have a successful pregnancy later.

Although many miscarriages have no known cause, some risk factors have been identified. Some researchers have found that the risk of miscarriage is increased by factors such as:

- Age (women over age 35 are at greater risk).
- Previous miscarriage.
- Family history of miscarriage.
- Certain diseases or infections.
- Exposure to hazards during pregnancy, such as alcohol, drugs, smoking, heavy caffeine use, or certain chemicals.

Health & Safety

Warning Signs During Pregnancy

When a woman sees her doctor for prenatal care, they usually talk about the warning signs of possible problems. These can include:

- Heavy bleeding.
- Sudden loss of fluid (prior to expected due date).
- Absence of movement after the fetus had been active.
- Intense or painful cramping or other abdominal pain.
- More than three contractions in an hour (prior to expected due date).

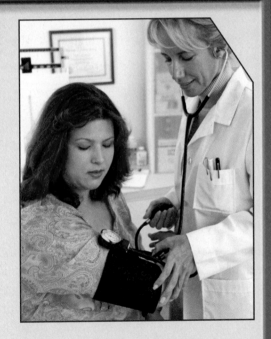

If any of these signs are noted, mothers- and fathers-to-be should *immediately* report them to their health care provider. In addition, they should talk to their health care provider if they have any other concerns about the pregnancy.

Parenting Pointers

Coping with the Loss of a Pregnancy

After a miscarriage or stillbirth, a woman's body needs time to heal. How long physical healing takes depends on how far the pregnancy had progressed. The woman should contact her doctor to get a physical exam and discuss her recovery.

The expectant parents must also cope with the grief of their loss. The process of mourning is different for everyone. Healing takes time, but there is no set length of time for grieving and no "right" way to grieve. Many people find the following suggestions helpful in dealing with loss, pain, and grief:

➤ Ask family and friends for help.

➤ Talk to a counselor, clergy member, or therapist who specializes in loss and grief.

➤ Join a support group for people who have been through a similar experience.

➤ Gather and read information to increase understanding.

➤ Write letters or poems as an outlet for emotions.

➤ Avoid making big decisions or life changes during the grieving process.

If the fetus dies after the twentieth week of pregnancy, the loss of pregnancy is called a **stillbirth**. This occurs in approximately one out of 200 pregnancies. The death can occur during labor or delivery, but more often it occurs before labor. Causes vary, and sometimes no cause can be found.

Ectopic Pregnancy

Sometimes a fertilized egg never reaches the uterus. In an **ectopic pregnancy**, a fertilized egg implants outside the uterus. In most cases, implantation occurs in the fallopian tube. For this reason, another term for ectopic pregnancy is *tubal pregnancy*.

Without the nourishment and protection of the uterus, the embryo cannot survive. In addition, ectopic pregnancy causes a serious risk to the mother's health. As the embryo grows, it may eventually burst the fallopian tube, which can cause life-threatening bleeding. For these reasons, when an ectopic pregnancy is discovered, a physician must end the pregnancy. In some cases, miscarriage occurs before the ectopic pregnancy is discovered.

Birth Defects

The complex structures and systems of the human body don't always develop as expected. Sometimes a birth defect is present. A **birth defect** is an abnormality that is present at or before birth and results in mental or physical disability. Birth defects may be caused by genetic factors, environmental factors, or a combination. Often the cause is unknown.

Genetic Causes. As explained in Chapter 7, errors in genes or chromosomes can result in genetic defects. Some are inherited. For example, when both parents carry the recessive gene

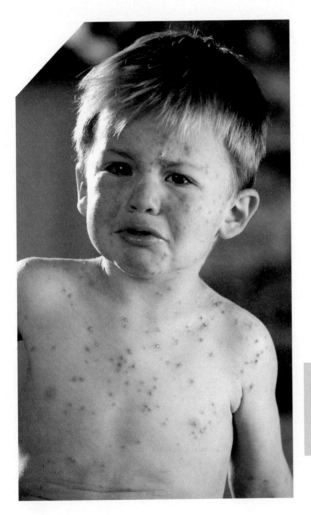

for cystic fibrosis, each of their children has a 25 percent chance of being born with the disease and a 50 percent chance of being a carrier. Genetic defects can also occur when specific genes or chromosomes are missing, damaged, or duplicated. An example is Down syndrome, caused by an extra chromosome 21.

Environmental Causes. Factors in the environment can also cause birth defects. What a pregnant woman eats, drinks, breathes in, or is otherwise exposed to has the potential to either help or harm her developing baby. Among the environmental factors that increase the risk of birth defects are:

- Poor nutrition during pregnancy.
- Use of tobacco, alcohol, or other drugs.
- Certain prescription and over-the-counter medications.
- Exposure to X rays.
- Certain illnesses, such as chicken pox and rubella (German measles). See Fig. 8-7.
- Sexually transmitted diseases and infections such as syphilis.

Prevention and Treatment. Good health habits during pregnancy can help prevent birth defects. Pregnant women should get proper medical care and take steps to avoid prenatal health hazards, as described in Chapter 9.

Fig. 8-7. In children, chicken pox is an uncomfortable but mild illness. If a pregnant woman is infected with chicken pox, her baby may be at risk for eye problems, poor growth, delayed development, and mental retardation. **What does this suggest about the importance of getting a medical checkup before pregnancy?**

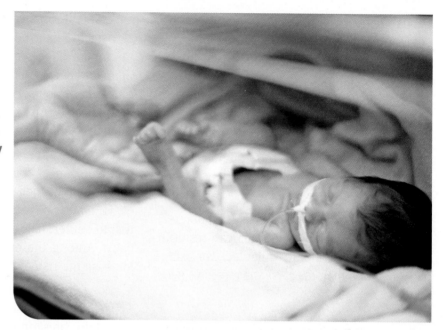

Fig. 8-8. Babies born prematurely have less time to develop in the uterus. **Why does the risk of health problems decrease as time spent growing in the uterus increases?**

Medical advances have made it possible to identify many types of birth defects before the baby is born. Some can be corrected before or soon after birth, through surgery or other means. Even if a cure is not possible, early diagnosis and intervention can help the child reach his or her full potential. Chapter 25 provides information about raising children with special needs.

Premature Labor and Birth

For various reasons, a pregnant woman will sometimes begin to go into labor sooner than expected. If this occurs before the thirty-seventh week of pregnancy, it is called *premature labor*. Sometimes doctors can delay premature labor by giving the woman medication.

If labor can't be stopped and the baby is born before the thirty-seventh week of pregnancy, it is considered a **premature birth**. About one out of every 10 babies is premature.

Premature babies have less time to develop in the uterus, which increases their risk of health problems. The risk decreases as the time spent growing in the uterus increases. Babies born before the twenty-sixth week of pregnancy and weighing less than 2 pounds usually have the most serious health problems. These can include underdeveloped lungs, fluid accumulation in the brain, seizures, and growth and learning delays. Those born between the thirty-fourth and thirty-seventh weeks of pregnancy may have short-term health problems, but in the long run they generally do as well as full-term babies. See Fig. 8-8.

Many premature infants survive and thrive with good medical care. You can read about the technology used to care for premature infants in Chapter 11.

A Healthy Pregnancy

CHAPTER OBJECTIVES

- Describe how pregnancy is detected.
- Explain prenatal care and why it is important.
- Suggest ways to cope with physical and emotional changes during pregnancy.
- Recommend daily practices that pregnant women should follow.
- Create and analyze meal plans for pregnant women.
- Explain the risks posed by prenatal health hazards.

PARENTING TERMS

- prenatal care
- obstetrician
- certified nurse-midwife
- Rh factor
- preeclampsia
- anemia
- nutrient dense
- fetal alcohol disorders

Have you ever heard that a pregnant woman shouldn't raise her arms over her head for fear of harming the developing baby? What about the idea that spicy foods bring on labor, or that after each pregnancy a woman loses a tooth? Each of these beliefs is a myth.

In this chapter, you'll learn the facts about promoting a healthy pregnancy. When a woman is pregnant, her choices affect not only her own health, but her baby's.

Detecting Pregnancy

When a couple are ready and eager to become parents, getting confirmation of a pregnancy is an exciting time. A woman doesn't know right after conception that she is pregnant. Within a few weeks, however, her body gives several signs that might make her wonder. These signs might include:

- A missed menstrual period.
- Nausea.
- Fatigue.
- Breast tenderness.
- Frequent urination.

Keep in mind that almost all of the possible signs of pregnancy can have other potential causes, so they do not always indicate pregnancy. The reverse is also true—a woman who is pregnant sometimes notices few of the usual signs.

The only reliable proof of pregnancy is a urine or blood test performed by a health care provider. Such laboratory tests are painless and quick. They are used to detect a hormone (body chemical) that is present only in the urine and blood of pregnant women. A blood test can reveal pregnancy as early as one week after conception.

Before getting a laboratory test, some women choose to use a home pregnancy test. These tests, which detect the same hormones as laboratory tests, are easy to use and yield immediate results. See Fig. 9-1.

Although home pregnancy tests are fairly accurate, they are less reliable than lab tests. Even when a woman is pregnant, it's possible for a home test to give a false negative result, causing the woman to postpone getting medical care. Whether the result of a home pregnancy test is positive or negative, it's best to follow up with a visit to a health care provider for confirmation.

Fig. 9-1. For accurate results when using a home pregnancy test, it's essential to follow directions exactly. **What are the advantages and drawbacks of using a home pregnancy test?**

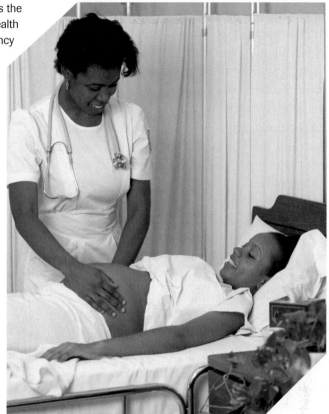

Fig. 9-2. Prenatal care greatly increases the chances of a healthy pregnancy. The health care provider who monitors the pregnancy usually delivers the baby as well.

Prenatal Medical Care

Prenatal care, or health care during pregnancy, is essential for the health of both the expectant mother and her developing baby. A woman who does not receive proper prenatal care places herself and her baby at risk. In contrast, a pregnant woman who seeks and actively participates in prenatal care benefits in many ways. With the help of her health care provider, she learns what steps she can take to give her developing baby the best possible start in life. She also receives advice about how to feel better during her pregnancy. Her health care provider monitors the pregnancy and can reassure her that all is well. If any problems do occur, they can be found and treated early. See Fig. 9-2.

For most families, health insurance covers many or all of the costs of prenatal care. Expectant mothers who are not covered by health insurance should contact a local social service agency and ask for a referral to sources of free or low-cost prenatal care.

Health Care Providers

A physician or other health care provider is a key partner in a healthy pregnancy. Some women obtain prenatal care from their primary care physician. Most women choose an **obstetrician** (OB-stuh-TRISH-uhn), a medical doctor who specializes in pregnancy and delivery. Another option is a **certified nurse-midwife**, a professional trained to care for women with low-risk pregnancies and to deliver their babies. In most states, a certified nurse-midwife works under the supervision of a medical doctor. Unlike most medical doctors, who deliver babies only in hospitals or clinics, many nurse-midwives offer the option of a home birth.

The choice of someone to provide prenatal care should be made carefully. The woman's primary care physician can provide a referral to an obstetrician or certified nurse-midwife. Family members and friends may also be able to recommend someone. Many county and regional medical societies offer lists of appropriate health care providers and the services they offer. However, options may be limited by the woman's health care coverage, where she lives, and other factors.

Prenatal Examinations

The first visit to a woman's health care provider takes longer than other visits because there are many things to do. The health care provider confirms the pregnancy, if this was not already done in a medical office. The pregnant woman's height, weight, and blood pressure are measured. The health care provider asks questions about the expectant parents' health habits and medical history. The expectant parents may also have questions they want to ask. See Fig. 9-3.

Next, the health care provider performs a complete physical exam. This includes an internal, or pelvic, exam to determine the size and position of the uterus. In addition, a Pap test is done by gently scraping cells from the *cervix*, the narrow lower end of the uterus.

Fig. 9-3. The first prenatal visit provides an opportunity to learn about prenatal development and what to expect during pregnancy. **What questions might a first-time expectant mother have?**

This routine test is done to check for cancer or pre-cancer of the cervix. An internal exam and Pap test may be a little uncomfortable, but are not painful.

Samples of the woman's urine and blood are taken for testing. Tests can reveal the presence of infections and other health conditions that might affect the pregnancy.

What Is the Rh Factor? Among other tests, doctors check the pregnant woman's blood type and Rh factor. The **Rh factor** is a protein found in the blood of some people. If the blood has this factor, the person has a *positive* blood type; if not, the person has a *negative* blood type. Problems can arise if the mother's Rh factor is negative and the baby's is positive. As the baby is born, the mother's immune system may produce antibodies against the baby's blood cells. The antibodies usually do not harm a woman's first baby, but they create risks for the fetus in any future pregnancies. If the woman's blood is not compatible with the fetus's blood, two injections are given to the woman to prevent problems in future pregnancies.

Calculating the Due Date. During the first visit, the health care provider will estimate when the baby will be born. For women with regular cycles, the due date is calculated from the first day of the last menstrual period. Other methods are used for women with irregular menstrual cycles. The due date is only an estimate, since a normal pregnancy can last anywhere from 38 to 42 weeks. Only about 4 percent of pregnant women deliver on their due dates.

Health & Safety

Working with a Health Care Provider

Expectant parents should be active participants in prenatal care. Here are some ways they can work as a team with the health care provider:

- Keep all medical appointments. Make this a priority.
- Bring pen and paper to prenatal checkups. Write down the health care provider's advice and instructions.
- Between visits, make a list of any questions as they arise. Take the list to the next appointment.
- Call the health care provider if any unusual symptoms or concerns arise between visits.

Regular Checkups. All health care providers establish their own schedules for prenatal checkups. After the initial consultation, visits are typically scheduled monthly for the first 28 weeks and every two weeks from 28 to 36 weeks. During the last month, visits are usually scheduled weekly to monitor the upcoming birth even more closely.

At each visit, the health care provider performs a physical exam. Some of the tests done at the first visit may be repeated, and additional tests may be performed as needed. Expectant parents are encouraged to bring up any questions or concerns when they see the health care provider. They can also phone the office if they have questions between visits.

Possible Complications

Most pregnancies are healthy, but various medical problems are possible. During prenatal checkups, pregnant women are monitored for signs of complications such as these.

Preeclampsia. About 5 to 10 percent of pregnant women develop **preeclampsia** (pree-uh-CLAMP-see-uh), a disorder that involves high blood pressure, protein in the urine, and fluid retention. Other names for this disorder are *pregnancy-induced hypertension* and *toxemia*. Preeclampsia is dangerous because it can keep the placenta from receiving enough of the blood that supplies the fetus with oxygen and nutrients. Left untreated, the condition may worsen into *eclampsia*, which can cause seizures and permanently damage the mother's health. A pregnant woman should immediately contact her health care provider if she notices any signs of preeclampsia. These include sudden weight gain, swollen hands and face, blurred vision, or severe headache.

Gestational Diabetes. *Diabetes* (dy-uh-BEET-us) is a disease that causes poor processing of sugars in a person's body. *Gestational* (jess-TAY-shun-uhl) means during pregnancy. Gestational diabetes affects about 3 percent of pregnant women. It usually begins during the second or third trimester and is detected by a routine glucose (blood sugar) screening test. Most women with gestational diabetes improve by following a doctor-recommended diet and exercise plan. Women who don't receive treatment are more likely to have a very large baby. Gestational diabetes usually disappears after the baby is born, but in some cases the mother develops lifelong diabetes.

Physical and Emotional Changes

Pregnancy is a time of great change—not only for the developing baby, but for both expectant parents. Everyone recognizes the enlarging abdomen of pregnancy, yet that's just one of the physical changes the mother-to-be experiences. Fewer people are familiar with the emotional changes that take place during pregnancy. Understanding the various physical and emotional changes makes it easier for expectant mothers and fathers to cope with them.

Weight Gain

During the first trimester of pregnancy, weight gain is usually minimal, although most women experience swelling of the breasts and abdomen. During the second trimester, women gain more weight and the pregnancy usually becomes apparent. See Fig. 9-4.

Most health care providers advise a healthy woman of normal weight to gain between 25 and 35 pounds during pregnancy. This allows 6 to 8 pounds for the baby and 14 to 24 pounds for the placenta, fluids, and other maternal weight gain. Adequate weight gain is important for the health of the baby. If a pregnant woman gains too little, her baby may have low birth weight, which increases the risk of serious health problems.

Maternity Clothes. By the fourth month of pregnancy, most women notice that their regular clothes

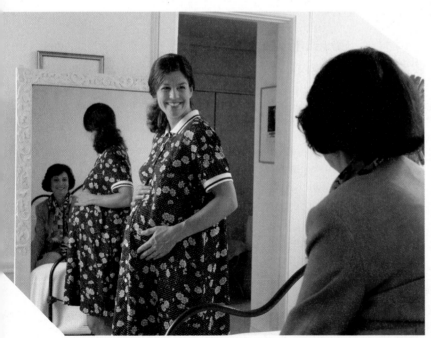

Fig. 9-4. Weight gain is a normal, healthy part of pregnancy.

Common Discomforts of Pregnancy	
Discomfort	**Suggestions**
Nausea Often called "morning sickness," but can occur at any time of day or night. Most common in the first trimester.	❑ Get out of bed slowly in the morning. ❑ Eat crackers and sip ginger ale. ❑ Eat frequent small meals throughout the day. ❑ Avoid strong odors, such as tobacco smoke and fumes from cleaning products.
Backache Increasing weight pulls the spine forward.	❑ Practice good posture. ❑ Exercise regularly. ❑ Wear supportive, low-heeled shoes. ❑ Try heat or massage.
Constipation Hormonal changes slow down the digestive tract.	❑ Drink plenty of fluids. ❑ Eat high-fiber foods. ❑ Exercise daily.
Leg cramps Muscle cramps may be caused by poor circulation.	❑ Exercise daily to increase circulation in the legs. ❑ Eat plenty of foods high in calcium. ❑ Stretch the calf muscles before going to bed.
Heartburn Hormonal changes slow digestion, and pressure on the stomach can cause acid to back up.	❑ Eat frequent small meals. ❑ Avoid foods that seem to trigger heartburn. ❑ Avoid lying down immediately after eating. ❑ Keep the head slightly raised when lying down.
Swollen ankles and feet Body fluids increase during pregnancy.	❑ Exercise daily. ❑ Avoid standing for long periods. ❑ Rest with the feet above heart level several times a day. ❑ Avoid tight clothing.

Fig. 9-5. Not all pregnant women will experience these discomforts, but many do. **Why is it helpful to be aware of discomforts that might occur?**

become uncomfortably tight around the chest and waist. When this happens, it is time to get maternity clothes, which are specially designed to fit pregnant women. Many maternity pants, for instance, have panels in the front that stretch to accommodate a growing midsection. As a result, the pants can be worn for the entire pregnancy and for some time after giving birth. Maternity clothes made of comfortable, easy-care fabrics are a good choice. Borrowing maternity clothes from friends and relatives is a way to save money and increase the variety of outfits.

Pregnant women should wear low-heeled shoes with good support. They often need shoes that are longer or wider than their usual size.

Discomforts of Pregnancy

Many women feel fine throughout pregnancy. It is not uncommon, however, for pregnant women to experience various types of discomfort. Some of these discomforts are caused by hormonal changes. Others result from the increasing size of the uterus. For example, pregnant women often feel the need to urinate more frequently as the expanding uterus creates pressure on the bladder. Around the eighth month, a pregnant woman may feel shortness of breath because the top of the uterus is pushing against her diaphragm. Fig. 9-5 lists some other common discomforts of pregnancy and suggestions for preventing or relieving them.

Mild discomforts are usually nothing to be concerned about, and simple self-care measures can help bring relief. However, a pregnant woman should immediately report any unusual or extreme symptoms to her health care provider.

Emotional Changes

Pregnancy is an emotional time for many women. A pregnant woman may worry about the unborn baby's health or be apprehensive about labor and delivery. During the final weeks of pregnancy, anxieties and fears may increase. See Fig. 9-6.

Mood swings are common during pregnancy. A pregnant woman might be cheerful one moment and irritable or tearful the next, for no apparent reason. Some of these feelings are caused by her hormones. However, researchers are not yet sure of the exact relationship between hormonal changes and emotional changes.

Managing Stress. The emotional upheavals of pregnancy can be worsened by stress. *Stress* is physical and mental tension that people experience as a result of changes and events in their lives. Since pregnancy is certainly a life-changing event, stress is to be expected. The key is taking steps to reduce stress so that it doesn't create problems. Stress-reducing strategies include:

- Getting plenty of sleep each night.
- Taking breaks to rest and relax throughout the day.
- Exercising regularly.
- Enjoying the company of family and friends.
- Making time for fun activities.

Emotional Difficulties. Some women experience serious emotional difficulties, such as depression, during and after pregnancy. Isolation, rejection, and lack of support can compound these problems. A woman's health care provider can refer her to sources of help. The sooner aid is sought, the better it is for

Fig. 9-6. Patience, support, and understanding can help expectant couples get through the emotional changes of pregnancy. **How might they show support for one another?**

Fig. 9-7. Short breaks help a pregnant woman stay rested and refreshed. **What are some of your favorite ways to rest and relax?**

the woman, her child, and those who are concerned about their wellbeing.

The Expectant Father's Emotions. Women and men share not just the joys of parenthood, but also the worries. A father-to-be may feel left out because so much attention is directed at the pregnant woman. He may also be worried about the woman's and the baby's health. Some men experience *sympathy symptoms*, such as nausea, appetite changes, weight gain, fatigue, and mood swings. Health care providers can help expectant parents with these and other concerns.

Daily Activities During Pregnancy

Many expectant couples wonder how pregnancy will affect the woman's daily routines. Should she restrict any of her activities? How long can she continue to work or go to school?

In general, a normal pregnancy requires few restrictions on activities. Most pregnant women can continue working throughout their pregnancy, unless their job poses physical risks. The Pregnancy Discrimination Act forbids discrimination on the basis of pregnancy. This means that pregnant women must be treated the same way as other job applicants and employees with similar abilities or limitations.

Although most pregnant women need not restrict their activities, their daily routines do deserve thought and planning. Pregnancy is a time to pay special attention to healthful habits, including getting enough rest and exercise.

Rest

Pregnant women need plenty of rest. In addition to sleeping at least eight hours a night, pregnant women should plan rest periods during the day. Rest can include whatever the pregnant woman finds effective, such as taking a nap, reading a book, listening to music, writing in a journal, or sitting outdoors and enjoying nature. See Fig. 9-7.

At times, pregnant women may have difficulty sleeping, perhaps due to hormonal changes. Engaging in relaxing activities in the evening and having a warm beverage or light snack before bed can make it easier to fall asleep. In late pregnancy, it may be difficult to find a comfortable sleeping position. Many pregnant women find that lying on the side with a pillow between the knees works well.

Exercise

Exercise is beneficial before, during, and after pregnancy. Pregnant women who are physically fit feel better and will have the strength they need for labor and delivery. Regular exercise

can boost energy, combating the fatigue that some pregnant women experience. As you have read, exercise also reduces stress and helps relieve many of the physical discomforts of pregnancy. Health experts recommend that pregnant women get 30 minutes or more of physical activity each day. See Fig. 9-8.

Types of Activities. Since different types of exercise have different benefits, it's best to choose a variety of physical activities. Low-impact, moderately intense activities, such as walking and swimming, are good choices to benefit the heart, lungs, and circulation. Stretching exercises help increase flexibility.

A special activity called the *Kegel exercise* helps strengthen and prepare the pelvic floor for delivery. This exercise also helps women recover from childbirth. The easiest way to learn how to do the Kegel exercise is to practice stopping and starting the flow of urine. Once a woman has identified the muscles needed to do this, she can squeeze and release them while seated.

Precautions. Pregnant women should be wary of activities that pose a risk of falling, including those that require sudden changes in direction or a significant need for balance. They should also avoid contact sports, as well as high-risk activities such as diving, surfing, or skydiving.

Fig. 9-8. Walking is good exercise for pregnant women. **What other forms of exercise do you think would be appropriate?**

Fig. 9-9. Food choices are always important for good health, but especially during pregnancy. **Why do people sometimes say that a pregnant woman is "eating for two"?**

Like everyone else, pregnant women should take sensible precautions during physical activity. A pregnant women should:

- Consult with a health care provider before beginning or changing an exercise routine.
- Drink plenty of fluids before, during, and after exercise.
- Take frequent breaks while exercising.
- Avoid exercising in very hot or humid conditions.
- Slow down or stop if she feels short of breath or uncomfortable.
- Never exercise to the point of exhaustion.
- Stop exercising immediately if she feels dizzy, has pain, or starts bleeding vaginally.

Personal Care and Hygiene

Most pregnant women's personal care and hygiene routines don't change. A generation ago, many people believed that taking baths wasn't good for pregnant women because the tub water could enter the uterus and cause an infection. Today, doctors generally agree that tub bathing is safe for most pregnant women. To reduce the risk of slipping and falling, a pregnant woman should be sure the tub has a nonslip mat and should get into and out of the tub carefully.

Nutrition During Pregnancy

Good nutrition is an important part of prenatal care and a key to a healthy pregnancy. If a pregnant woman does not get enough nourishment, her baby has an increased risk of long-term health problems. By eating right, a pregnant woman nourishes the fetus and keeps her own body strong and healthy, too. See Fig. 9-9.

Calorie Needs

Calories measure the energy provided by food or used in activities. A pregnant woman needs energy for her own body's needs and the needs of the growing fetus, too. Getting enough calories helps them both gain the right amount of weight. A pregnant woman usually needs an extra 300 calories per day during the last six months of pregnancy. However, energy needs vary, so she should follow the advice of her health care provider.

Nutrient Needs

Along with extra calories, a pregnant woman needs added nutrients for herself and her developing baby. The main nutrient groups include carbohydrates, proteins, fats, vitamins, minerals, and water. Each nutrient plays a special role in promoting health before, during, and after pregnancy. See Fig. 9-10.

Carbohydrates. The body uses carbohydrates as fuel to produce heat and energy. If a pregnant woman doesn't get enough carbohydrates, her body has to get its fuel from other nutrients or from reserve energy supplies, and she might not gain enough weight for a healthy pregnancy. Most of her energy should come from complex carbohydrates (starches) rather than simple carbohydrates (sugars). Foods high in complex carbohydrates include:

- Grain products such as breads, cereals, rice, and pasta. Those made from whole grains are preferable because they contain more of the grain's natural nutrients.
- Dry beans and peas.
- Other starchy vegetables, such as potatoes and corn.

All of these foods also provide fiber, which is plant material that the body does not digest.

Fig. 9-10. Healthful foods, such as fresh fruits and vegetables, are more than just good tasting. They provide vital nutrients needed for good health.

Vital Vitamins		
Vitamins	**Why Needed**	**Good Food Souces**
Vitamin A	❏ Aids vision ❏ Needed for healthy skin and hair ❏ Helps the body resist infection	❏ Eggs ❏ Liver ❏ Dairy products ❏ Dark green leafy vegetables, such as broccoli and spinach ❏ Deep yellow-orange fruits and vegetables, such as cantaloupe, apricots, carrots, and sweet potatoes
B Vitamins	❏ Help nerve and brain tissues work well ❏ Help the body produce energy ❏ Help build red blood cells ❏ Help the body resist infections	❏ Whole grain, enriched, and fortified grain products ❏ Meat, poultry, fish ❏ Dry beans and peas ❏ Dairy products ❏ Some fruits and vegetables
Vitamin C	❏ Helps keep body tissues and blood vessels healthy ❏ Helps the body resist infections ❏ Aids in healing cuts and bruises ❏ Helps the body absorb iron	❏ Citrus fruits, strawberries, cantaloupe ❏ Tomatoes, potatoes, broccoli, cabbage, green peppers
Vitamin D	❏ Aids the development of bones and teeth	❏ Fortified milk ❏ Egg yolks ❏ Fatty fish, such as salmon and mackerel
Vitamin E	❏ Helps the body form red blood cells and muscles	❏ Vegetable oils ❏ Whole grains ❏ Dark green leafy vegetables ❏ Dry beans and peas ❏ Nuts and seeds

Fig. 9-11. These and other vitamins perform important functions in the body. **How often do you enjoy the foods listed?**

Eating foods high in fiber, along with drinking plenty of water, can help prevent constipation and hemorrhoids. In addition to keeping the digestive system working properly, fiber also has other health benefits, such as reducing the risk of heart disease and cancer.

Proteins. Proteins are nutrients used to build and repair body tissues. They are vital for the growth of a developing fetus and to keep the mother's body healthy, too. Meat, poultry, fish, eggs, beans, nuts, and dairy products are high in protein. Some other foods, such as grains and vegetables, provide protein as well.

Fats. A limited amount of fat is part of a healthful diet. Fats provide a concentrated source of energy for the body and are needed to transport and store other nutrients. They also help regulate body temperature and growth. The healthiest fats are plant-based ones, such as olive oil and other vegetable oils.

Vitamins. Vitamins help the body function properly and are vital to good health. Fig. 9-11 summarizes the functions and food sources of several vitamins.

Folic acid, one of the B vitamins, is especially important before pregnancy and during the first trimester. Lack of enough folic acid can cause birth defects that affect the brain and central nervous system. Pregnant women should consume 600 micrograms of folic acid per day from fortified foods, supplements, or both.

Minerals. Minerals are important nutrients that regulate body processes, such as digestion, and form parts of many tissues, such as bones, teeth, and blood. Calcium and iron are two of the most important minerals for a pregnant woman and her growing fetus.

- **Calcium.** Along with phosphorous and magnesium, calcium builds strong bones and teeth. It also keeps the heartbeat regular and helps blood to clot normally after injury. A pregnant woman must consume enough calcium for both her own needs and those of the fetus. If she doesn't, the fetus will draw calcium from the mother's bones and teeth. Good sources of calcium include dairy products; dark green leafy vegetables; canned fish with soft bones, such as salmon and mackerel; and calcium-fortified foods. See Fig. 9-12.

- **Iron.** A pregnant woman needs extra iron. Her body uses iron to produce and maintain red blood cells, which supply oxygen to all the cells of both the mother and fetus. Lack of iron can result in a condition called **anemia**, in which there are too few red blood cells. Anemia during pregnancy increases the risk for premature birth and low birth weight. Pregnant women should eat plenty of iron-rich foods, such as meat, fish, poultry, dried fruits, and iron-fortified cereals.

Water. Pregnant women, like everyone else, should drink plenty of water. The body needs water to carry nutrients, eliminate waste, and regulate temperature. A pregnant woman needs 8 to 10 cups of fluid each day, but that doesn't mean she must drink that amount of water. Foods such as fruits and vegetables, which contain water, meet some of her fluid needs. She can also get fluids from milk, juices, soups, and other healthful liquids.

Fig. 9-12. In addition to dairy products, foods such as calcium-fortified orange juice can help build strong bones. **What can happen if a pregnant woman doesn't consume enough calcium-rich foods?**

Sample Food Needs for a Pregnant Woman*		
Food Group	**Foods Included**	**Daily Amount of Food**
Grain Group	Bread, pasta, oatmeal, breakfast cereals, tortillas, grits, and any other foods made from grains	7 to 8 ounce-equivalents
Vegetable Group	Any vegetable or 100% vegetable juice	3 cups
Fruit Group	Any fruit or 100% fruit juice	2 cups
Milk Group	Milk, yogurt, cheese, pudding	3 cups
Meat & Beans Group	All foods made from meat, poultry, fish, dry beans or peas, eggs, nuts, and seeds	6 to 6.5 ounce-equivalents

*The amounts shown assume that the woman's normal calorie needs, when not pregnant, are 2,000 calories per day and that she needs an extra 200 to 400 calories daily during pregnancy.

Source: MyPyramid.gov

Fig. 9-13. Food needs vary, so some pregnant women may need a little more or less food than shown. **What are some of the nutrients provided by the foods in each group?**

Healthful Eating Habits

A woman who is healthy and well-nourished before she becomes pregnant has a head start on a healthy pregnancy. Even when that's not the case, she can develop new eating habits by making simple changes, one step at a time. She might start by learning about nutritious foods and stocking the kitchen with them. Then she can look for simple ways to include a greater variety of nutritious foods in daily meals and snacks. For example, she might find that it's easier to get enough fruits and vegetables when she takes a nutritious lunch to work instead of grabbing a meal from a fast-food restaurant.

Pregnancy is definitely not the time to skip meals. Nor is it a time to lose weight through dieting, unless a woman's health care provider instructs her to do so for medical reasons. It *is* a time to make wise food choices.

One of the keys to good nutrition is choosing foods that are **nutrient dense**. That means their calories are packed with plenty of important nutrients. Examples of nutrient-dense foods include fruits, vegetables, whole grains, legumes, lean meats, and low-fat dairy products. In contrast, foods such as candy, cakes, cookies, and sugary soft drinks are filling but provide few nutrients. They can be enjoyed in small amounts, but should not take the place of nutrient-dense foods.

How can a pregnant woman make sure she gets the nutrients she needs for good health? The answer is simple—by eating a variety of nutrient-dense foods every day. Fig. 9-13 shows sample amounts from the five food groups, each of which provides essential nutrients.

Nutrition and Teen Pregnancy. A pregnant teen needs extra nutrients not only because of her developing fetus, but also because she is still growing and developing herself. Therefore, her nutritional needs are greater than those of an adult pregnant woman. To be sure she gets enough calcium, a pregnant teen may need extra amounts of dairy foods each day. She should also pay special attention to getting enough iron and protein.

Are Supplements Needed?

Although nutritious foods are the best source of nutrients, a woman's health care provider may recommend a vitamin or mineral supplement before, during, or after pregnancy. For example, many obstetricians prescribe an iron supplement and recommend a multivitamin that includes folic acid.

Pregnant women should not take supplements unless recommended by their health care provider. That's because getting too much of a nutrient can be as harmful as getting too little. Too much vitamin A, for example, can cause nerve and liver damage and contribute to birth defects.

Herbal supplements are also a cause for concern. Very little scientific research has been done on their safety during pregnancy. For this reason, pregnant women are advised to avoid herbal supplements and to limit their consumption of herbal teas.

Common Nutrition Concerns

Many women have questions about nutrition during pregnancy. Are food cravings normal? Is caffeine harmful? What about salt? Here are the facts.

Food Cravings and Dislikes. Many pregnant women develop food cravings and dislikes. Changing hormone levels are partly responsible. A pregnant woman may find that she can no longer stand the smell or taste of certain foods that she previously enjoyed. At the same time, she may crave other foods. As long as she's eating a balanced, nutritious diet, these changes are nothing to worry about. See Fig. 9-14.

Sometimes, however, a pregnant woman will crave nonfood substances, such as clay, ashes, or laundry starch. This condition, called *pica*, should be reported to a health care provider. It may signal a serious nutrient deficiency.

Caffeine. Scientists are still researching the possible effects of caffeine during pregnancy. Most health experts believe that moderate caffeine intake is not a cause for concern. To be on the safe side, however, many doctors advise pregnant women to limit their caffeine intake.

Salt and Sodium. It's not necessary to restrict salt or sodium during pregnancy. In fact, because sodium needs increase during pregnancy, cutting back could cause problems.

Fig. 9-14. You may have heard humorous stories about food cravings during pregnancy. As long as they use moderation and common sense, pregnant women can safely indulge most cravings.

Fig. 9-15. Pregnant women are more likely than other healthy adults to get listeriosis. Ready-to-eat foods such as hot dogs can be a source. **What precaution reduces the risk?**

Food Safety During Pregnancy

Pregnant women are at high risk for food-borne illness, which can cause symptoms such as diarrhea. One type of foodborne illness, called *listeriosis*, can cause premature birth, stillbirth, or infection in the newborn. To reduce the risk of foodborne illness, pregnant women should avoid the following foods:

- Raw (unpasteurized) milk and foods made from raw milk.
- Soft cheeses (such as Brie, feta, blue, and queso blanco) unless they have labels that clearly state they have been made from pasteurized milk.
- Raw or partially cooked eggs and foods that contain them.
- Raw or undercooked meat, poultry, fish, or shellfish.
- Unpasteurized juices.
- Raw vegetable sprouts.
- Cold cuts, deli meats, and hot dogs, unless they have been reheated to steaming hot. See Fig. 9-15.

Another concern is mercury, a heavy metal toxin that can harm a fetus's developing nervous system. Pregnant women should avoid eating fish or shellfish that are high in mercury. These include shark, swordfish, king mackerel, and tilefish.

Federal guidelines advise that women of childbearing age and women who are pregnant or nursing eat an average of no more than 12 ounces of low-mercury fish and shellfish per week. This includes shrimp, canned light tuna, salmon, pollock, and catfish. Of the 12 ounces, no more than 6 ounces should be albacore (white) tuna, which typically has more mercury.

Avoiding Prenatal Health Risks

Health risks during pregnancy can come from many sources. They include exposure to tobacco, alcohol, illegal drugs, certain medications, X-rays, chemical hazards, and infections. All of these are potentially harmful to the fetus.

Tobacco, Alcohol, and Illegal Drugs

Smoking cigarettes or using other forms of tobacco is dangerous because it limits the amount of oxygen the fetus receives. Research shows that secondhand smoke is dangerous, too, so pregnant women should avoid smokers. Premature birth, low birth weight, and other complications are linked to maternal smoking and secondhand smoke.

No amount of alcohol use by a pregnant woman is considered safe for the fetus. Alcohol use during pregnancy increases the risk of miscarriage, stillbirth, and low birth weight. It can permanently damage the fetus's brain, leading to serious problems called **fetal alcohol disorders**. The effects vary but may include mental retardation; defects of the head, face, limbs, heart, and central nervous system; vision and hearing disorders; and learning and behavioral problems.

Tremendous harm can come to a baby whose mother uses cocaine, heroin, LSD, or other illegal drugs during pregnancy. The newborn may be addicted to these substances at birth and is at risk for a stroke, brain damage, and death. Premature birth and low birth weight are likely, often leading to a lifetime of learning and behavioral problems.

Prescription and Over-the-Counter Medications

A drug does not have to be illegal to harm a fetus. A pregnant woman must inform her health care provider of any prescription medicines she is taking. If a drug is not safe to take during pregnancy, the health care provider may recommend a safe substitute. In addition, a pregnant woman should always consult her health care provider before taking any over-the-counter medication. Products as common as aspirin and antacids can sometimes be harmful. See Fig. 9-16.

Fig. 9-16. A pregnant woman should discuss any medical conditions with her health care provider. She may need to change her medications during pregnancy.

Child & Family Services
CAREERS

▶ Substance Abuse Counselor

People with a desire to help those who are troubled may be drawn to a counseling career in human and social services. Substance abuse counselors, for example, work with people who abuse alcohol and other drugs. They help abusers break free of their addiction. Many abusers have related problems, such as family conflicts, job loss, and physical illnesses. Counselors may refer them to other professionals for treatment.

Most substance abuse counselors have a college degree and may need other counseling experience to qualify for a position. Many states provide certification. Although some counselors work at home, they may also be employed by hospitals and clinics.

"As a substance abuse counselor, I see patients alone and in groups. Families may also be involved. I consult with the police, doctors, and other counselors to create a therapy plan for a patient's recovery. The plan is assessed at regular intervals. I also prepare documents for court and accompany clients to legal proceedings. Another part of my job is talking to groups that are concerned about drug and alcohol abuse.

"My job is challenging and takes patience, compassion, and persistence. I can't be judgmental, and I have to show restraint in what I say and do. Not every case is a success story, but when someone's life is reclaimed, it's a wonderful feeling for me."

CAREER TIPS

- In high school, take classes in biology, chemistry, public speaking, and psychology.
- Volunteer in a drug rehabilitation center.
- Earn a college degree in counseling.

X-Rays, Chemicals, and Lead

X-rays use radiation to make images of structures inside the body. High levels of radiation could damage the fetus. However, most X-ray procedures use a relatively low level of radiation that is unlikely to cause harm. Before having any X-rays, a woman should always inform the health care provider if she is pregnant or thinks she might be pregnant. If it is not possible to postpone the procedure, precautions can be taken to minimize the risk to the fetus.

Exposure to certain chemicals can be dangerous during pregnancy. Women who have contact with chemicals in their work environment should discuss the situation with their health care provider and employer. Most workplaces have safeguards to prevent excess exposure.

Lead is a naturally occurring metal that poses health risks, especially to unborn babies, infants, and young children. Some older homes contain lead-based paint or lead water pipes. If a pregnant woman has concerns about lead exposure, she should discuss them with her health care provider.

Common Infections

Some diseases that don't usually harm adults, and may not even be noticed, can seriously affect a fetus. Here are some examples.

Chicken Pox. Most people have chicken pox in childhood and cannot get it again. Having chicken pox during pregnancy, however, can lead to premature delivery, low birth weight, birth defects, or miscarriage. The risk is greatest during the first half of pregnancy. A pregnant woman who thinks she might have chicken pox should call her health care provider immediately.

Rubella. This illness, also known as German measles, is mild in adults. During pregnancy, it can cause severe damage to the fetus's brain, heart, eyes, and ears. The risk is greatest during the first trimester. People who have already had rubella are immune, and a vaccine can provide immunity to others. However, the vaccine cannot be given during pregnancy. A pregnant woman should have a blood test to determine whether she is immune. If she is not, she will be educated about symptoms and advised to avoid contact with anyone suspected of having the disease.

Toxoplasmosis. This infection is caused by a parasite found in raw or undercooked meat; within cats who eat raw meat, rodents, birds; and in cat feces. In pregnant women, toxoplasmosis can lead to miscarriage or birth defects. The infection usually does not have symptoms, but a blood test can determine its presence.

A few simple precautions can prevent toxoplasmosis. Meat and poultry should be cooked thoroughly, and any utensil that touches raw meat should be washed well before touching other foods. Pregnant women should ask someone else to clean cat litter boxes and shouldn't garden where cats have left waste. If they may have been exposed, pregnant women should see a health care provider.

Sexually Transmitted Diseases or Infections

Every year, almost two million pregnant women in the United States are infected by sexually transmitted diseases (STDs), also known as sexually transmitted infections (STIs). These diseases can cause devastating consequences for pregnant women and their developing babies. For the woman, long-term effects may include cancer, liver disease, pelvic inflammatory disease, and infertility. STDs can be transmitted

Self-Discipline During Pregnancy

Making and keeping a commitment to good health takes *self-discipline*. That's especially true when resolving to give up habits that are harmful, risky, or just not as healthy as they could be. Replacing poor health habits with good ones takes determination and inner strength, but the results are well worth it. To increase her chances of success, a pregnant woman can:

- Visualize how her choices will affect her baby.
- Enlist the support of the father-to-be.
- Surround herself with others who are equally committed to health and wellness.
- Think of herself as a role model of self-discipline and healthy living.

Think About It

What are some of the lifelong results of a woman's self-discipline during pregnancy?

---

from mother to baby before, during, or after birth. Here are some examples of STDs and their effects on the developing baby:

- HIV, the virus that causes AIDS (acquired immunodeficiency syndrome), can lead to serious illness and death.
- Genital herpes (HER-peez) can cause potentially fatal infections.
- Syphilis (SIFF-uh-luhs) can cause severe damage or stillbirth.
- Gonorrhea (gahn-uh-REE-uh) can cause blindness, joint infection, or a potentially fatal blood infection.
- Chlamydia (kluh-MID-ee-uh) can cause eye infections and respiratory infections.
- Hepatitis B can cause serious liver disease.

STDs can be prevented by avoiding risky sexual behaviors. People who think they might have an STD should tell their health care provider at once. Symptoms may include unusual discharge, pain in the abdomen, burning during urination, and swelling, blisters, open sores, or a rash in the genital area. Prompt treatment can cure some STDs and minimize the effects of others.

CHAPTER **9** Review & Activities

CHAPTER SUMMARY

- Most pregnant women experience signs of pregnancy, but the signs may vary.
- Prenatal care is health care during pregnancy. Visits to a health care provider are usually monthly for the first 28 weeks and then more frequent.
- Although most pregnancies are healthy, certain medical problems can arise.
- Understanding the physical and emotional changes in a woman during pregnancy makes it easier for expectant mothers and fathers to cope with them.
- Pregnancy is a time to pay special attention to healthful habits and avoid health risks.
- Good nutrition is an important part of prenatal care and vital for a healthy pregnancy.

Check Your Facts

1. What are five indications of possible pregnancy?
2. Why is prenatal care important?
3. Compare an obstetrician with a certified nurse-midwife.
4. What typically happens at a woman's first prenatal examination?
5. Why are pregnant women checked for the Rh factor?
6. What is preeclampsia?
7. What is the recommended amount of weight gain while pregnant?
8. How can three discomforts of pregnancy be prevented or relieved?
9. What are at least three ways that pregnant women can reduce stress?
10. Suggest rest and exercise recommendations for a pregnant woman.
11. How do nutrition needs for a pregnant woman differ from those of a woman who isn't pregnant?
12. How can anemia be avoided?
13. Suggest at least four guidelines for healthful eating during pregnancy.
14. What are at least five foods to avoid for food safety during pregnancy?
15. Name at least five prenatal health hazards.
16. What are fetal alcohol disorders?

Think Critically

1. **Predicting Consequences.** What might occur if a woman receives no prenatal care during pregnancy?
2. **Understanding Cause and Effect.** What situations might cause a woman to skip prenatal care during pregnancy? How could she overcome each of these in order to get the necessary care?
3. **Summarizing Information.** This chapter explains important actions to take to have a healthy baby. Summarize them with several general guidelines.

Apply Your Learning

1. **Problem Solving.** Discuss the following situation with a classmate and come up with suggestions for the couple. *A pregnant woman works part time and has a 14-month-old son. The child has problems with ear infections and often awakens in the night. The mother cries frequently over little things, such as an overcooked casserole. Her husband works full time and can't understand why so many things bother his wife. He is impatient and tries to avoid the situation by working extra hours.*

2. **Meal Plan Analysis.** Plan one week of meals for a pregnant woman, including recipes for dishes. Exchange meal plans with a partner, and analyze how well the plan fulfills a pregnant woman's nutrient needs.

3. **Due Date.** On the Internet, find a due date calculator. If a woman's last menstrual period began on February 20, what is her due date? How is the calculation computed?

Cross-Curricular Connections

1. **Math.** Create a profile of a pregnant woman, including her main activities. Then use catalogs to choose a basic maternity wardrobe for her. Compute the cost of the wardrobe and suggest specific ways to cut some costs.

2. **Language Arts.** A young woman who smokes and drinks alcohol is pregnant. Write three messages to her from these different perspectives: a) her physician; b) her husband; and c) the developing baby. What would each say to her and why?

Family & Community Connections

1. **Family Interview.** Interview a family member who gave birth ten or more years ago. Ask what advice she was given during pregnancy about physical activity, weight gain, nutrition, and other aspects of prenatal care. Discuss how this advice compares with the guidelines you have learned.

2. **Community Food Drive.** Conduct a food drive. Collect healthful foods, such as canned fruits and vegetables, whole grain cereals, and beans. Then donate them to a community food pantry or pregnancy care center.

CHAPTER 10

Preparing for Baby's Arrival

CHAPTER OBJECTIVES

- Propose ways to help children adjust to the arrival of a new sibling.
- Compare hospital birth facilities, birthing centers, and home birth.
- Evaluate the use of prepared childbirth and birth plans.
- Examine financial issues that expectant parents must consider.
- Analyze basic decisions to be made about baby care.
- Summarize what to consider when choosing furnishings, clothing, and other baby items.

PARENTING TERMS

- birthing room
- birthing center
- prepared childbirth
- birth coach
- birth plan
- parental leave
- pediatrician
- infant formula

Whether a new baby is joining the family through birth or through adoption, there are many decisions and preparations to be made. Expectant parents are suddenly very busy choosing names, shopping for necessities, and fixing up a space for the baby. They also face decisions about how they will meet the baby's needs—not to mention how they will fit the added expenses into their budget. Of course, pregnancy is a time to prepare for the birth itself, too. Wise parents plan ahead for the many changes that are in store for them.

Sharing the News

Becoming parents changes a couple's status with friends and family. It shows a new level of adulthood and responsibility. It can be particularly exciting for family members to know that their line will continue. News of a pregnancy can bring out all kinds of feelings, from happiness and excitement to anxiety or even envy.

Family members and friends often want to share in the preparations for birth. Having some extra help with housework, shopping, meal preparation, errands, and care of older children is a much-needed relief for expectant parents. Most family members and friends enjoy the feeling of participation and the opportunity to demonstrate their caring in practical ways.

Parents-to-be may want to designate one close relative or friend as the person they will contact at the time of the birth. This person might help the parents get to the birth facility or provide care for other children in the family. The parents should keep this person's phone number handy.

Helping Siblings Adjust

When the family already includes a child or children, parents must take special care to help them adjust to the new addition to the family before the baby arrives. Children may be excited about the prospect of a new baby brother or sister, but it's also natural for them to feel anxiety or resentment. After all, the security of their family routine will soon be disrupted, and they will have to share what they value most—their parents—with a newcomer. It's better to prepare children ahead of time than to wait until the baby is already there and demanding attention. See Fig. 10-1.

The unfolding events of pregnancy are a mystery to children. They have a natural interest in their mother's growing belly, and children's books about pregnancy and childbirth can help answer their questions. Many birth facilities offer tours and classes for siblings so they can visualize "where mommy will go to have the baby." Other ways to involve siblings include having them think of names for the baby, help pack the suitcase for the hospital, and choose coming-home clothes for the baby. Giving the older children extra attention and care during the pregnancy can reassure them that they are still valued members of the family.

Fig. 10-1. Preparing children in advance for the arrival of a new sibling helps them adjust more easily once the baby comes home. **Why might a child have mixed emotions about a new baby in the family?**

Parenting Pointers

Comparing Birth Facilities

Before making a decision about where the baby will be born, prospective parents need to gather information. They may want to visit several facilities and ask questions such as:

- What rooms are used for births? Can the mother go through labor, give birth, and recover in the same room?

- What types of comfort measures are offered? For example, is there a tub or shower in the birthing room?

- What types of medication are available?

- Who can be present for the birth? The father-to-be is welcome in any facility. Some also allow other relatives, friends, or children.

- Are cameras and video equipment allowed during the birth?

- What are the policies about caring for the baby? Can baby and mother stay in the same room?

- Can family members stay overnight? Is there an extra charge for this?

- What is the average length of stay?

Preparing for Childbirth

Wise parents-to-be take the time, well before their baby is due, to learn as much as they can about the process of giving birth. Books and Web sites about pregnancy and childbirth can provide useful information. Expectant parents can also learn from other parents, health care professionals, and childbirth classes. One of the first decisions to be made is where the baby will be born.

Choosing a Birth Facility

A pregnant woman may give birth in a hospital, a birthing center, or her own home. In some cases, options may be limited to what a particular health insurance plan will cover. Expectant parents should learn as much as they can about the options available to them.

Hospitals. Most babies are born in a hospital. An advantage of a hospital birth is that support personnel and technology are already in place to deal with any emergency situations that may arise. This is especially important in high-risk pregnancies.

A woman who gives birth in a hospital may go through labor in one room, give birth in another, recover from the birth in a third room, and then move to a fourth room for the rest of her stay. Some hospitals, however, offer the option of a **birthing room** in which the mother can remain before, during, and after giving birth. Birthing rooms are specially designed to provide everything needed for labor and delivery in a homelike atmosphere.

In order to deliver a baby in a hospital, a health care provider must have "admitting privileges"—that is, the right to practice in that facility. Thus, when a woman chooses a health care provider, she may also be choosing the place where her child will most likely be born.

Birthing Centers. A **birthing center** is a facility designed specifically to provide a homelike environment for giving birth. A birthing center may be a special part of a hospital, a separate building affiliated with a hospital, or an independent facility run by a health care provider. Birthing centers are designed for low-risk pregnancies, in which emergencies or unusual needs are unlikely. However, they can provide most emergency medical procedures if necessary, as well as care during delivery. Birthing centers tend to cost less than hospitals. Often, families are welcome to stay with the pregnant woman for the entire birth process.

Home Birth. Some women decide to give birth in their homes. Home birth is recommended only for women who are having low-risk pregnancies, do not have preexisting medical conditions, and are carrying only one fetus. Certified nurse-midwives, rather than doctors, most often care for women during home births. See Fig. 10-2.

Prepared Childbirth

Many parents take classes in **prepared childbirth**, an approach to giving birth in which the expectant parents understand and take an active

Fig. 10-2. Most certified nurse-midwives offer a variety of options for the birth setting, including giving birth at home. **Why might a couple prefer a home birth?**

Fig. 10-3. Techniques learned in childbirth classes may reduce stress during labor and delivery. **How else might childbirth classes help expectant parents?**

role in the birth process. Most prepared childbirth classes focus on one of two methods: the Lamaze method or the Bradley method. Both are based on the idea that women should work with the birthing process and not against it. Techniques such as rhythmic breathing are used to minimize discomfort and aid the birth process naturally. These techniques can reduce the need for pain medication.

Prepared childbirth also emphasizes the role of the **birth coach,** a person who helps the woman through the birth process. The birth coach is usually the baby's father, but it could be a relative or friend. During labor and delivery, the coach provides encouragement and support—for example, by helping the laboring woman focus on her breathing and the relaxation techniques she has learned. Studies show that childbirth is less stressful when the mother receives constant support through labor and delivery.

Hospitals, health clinics, and other health care groups offer childbirth education classes. Typically, parents register for a course sometime before the sixth month of pregnancy. Weekly classes begin around the sixth or seventh month. During these classes, parents-to-be learn what to expect and what to do during each stage of childbirth. They view films of birth and may tour the birth facility. Small class size—usually about eight to twelve couples—allows for questions and individual instruction. See Fig. 10-3.

Making a Birth Plan

Compared to couples several decades ago, couples today have more to say about how they want their childbirth experience to be. Once the parents-to-be have learned about childbirth, they can discuss their options and make informed decisions. They may want to prepare a **birth plan**, a list of preferences concerning birth options. The plan may cover such issues as:

- Who will be present during the birth.
- The role of the birth coach in labor and delivery.
- Whether the woman will receive medication to relieve pain.
- Under what circumstances certain medical procedures will be used.
- What position the woman wishes to be in for delivery.

This is only a partial list of issues related to childbirth. To make sure they do not overlook anything, first-time parents may wish to consult experienced parents, appropriate books, and other sources of information. They should also discuss their options with their health care provider well ahead of time.

A birth plan is only a guide. Because labor and birth are unpredictable, expectant parents must be flexible. In some cases, they may have to sign a release stating that in the event of an emergency, hospital or birthing center policy takes precedence over the birth plan.

Financial Planning

Decisions about where and how to give birth raise another issue for expectant parents: the medical bills that will arrive along with the baby. Medical costs are not the only financial matter they need to think about, of course. They must also decide what impact the birth of a child will have on their employment situation, and they must prepare for their long-term financial future as parents. See Fig. 10-4.

Medical Expenses

Having a baby involves several separate medical costs. These typically include:

• Fees charged by the woman's obstetrician (or other health care provider) for prenatal visits, laboratory tests, and delivering the baby.

• A separate bill from the hospital or birthing center for use of the labor and delivery room, any medications, room and board after the birth, and other items.

• In many cases, an additional charge for a doctor selected by the hospital to attend the birth and examine the baby.

The total cost of childbirth varies considerably by region of the country, but amounts to several thousand dollars even for a routine, uncomplicated birth. The cost increases if medical problems arise.

Fig. 10-4. A growing family means growing expenses. **What might happen if expectant parents did not review their financial situation before the baby's arrival?**

Health Insurance. Ideally, most of the costs of giving birth will be covered by health insurance. This insurance may be provided through the woman's employer, her husband's employer, or her parents' employer if she is living with her parents and covered under their health plan. Expectant parents should review their health insurance plan and note exactly what expenses it covers. If a pregnant woman does not have health insurance, she can purchase her own coverage. When that is not possible, she may qualify for government assistance. Otherwise, the new parents will be responsible for paying all medical bills.

Employment Decisions

Before the baby is born, parents-to-be must decide how they will balance the demands of work and family life. No one solution is right for every family. Some couples decide that one parent will care for the child while the other works outside the home. Some parents decide to work fewer hours so they can spend more time with their families. A mother may take some time off and then return to work part-time until the child is old enough for school. Parents can even work separate shifts so that one of them is always home with the child. See Fig. 10-5.

Parental Leave. A pregnant woman who is employed must take some time off from work to have the baby, whether or not she plans to return to work later. Many fathers also take time off when a baby is born. Time away from the job allows new parents to recover from the stress of childbirth and to settle the new baby into the home. They need time to establish a daily routine, adapt to the responsibilities of parenting, and build emotional bonds with the child.

Parental leave is a parent's paid or unpaid time off the job after the birth or adoption of

Fig. 10-5. Parents who work must consider how to meet their responsibilities to both their family and their employer. **Identify the pros and cons of one option they might choose.**

a child. It is sometimes referred to as *maternity leave* for the mother and *paternity leave* for the father. Some men start parental leave after the mother's leave ends, extending the time that at least one parent can be home full-time with the child.

For parents who have worked for at least 12 months (including at least 1,250 on-the-job hours) at a company that employs 50 people or more, parental leave is covered under the Family and Medical Leave Act. This law ensures that workers can take time off from work without putting their jobs at risk. Employees are allowed a total of 12 work weeks of unpaid leave during any 12-month period for any of several reasons, including the birth or adoption of a child.

Other Financial Concerns

In addition to medical costs, expectant parents face expenses for baby equipment and supplies. If both parents plan to work outside the home after the baby arrives, they will also need to pay for child care. If one of them is leaving a job, their expenses will be lower—but so will their income. Expectant parents must adjust their household budget to deal with the costs of raising a child. Chapter 26 provides tips for planning a budget.

Parents-to-be can also take other steps to help protect their financial future. One is to review their life insurance needs, since parents generally need more life insurance than people without children. They may also want to consider participating in a *flexible spending account*, if their employer offers one. In this arrangement, a certain amount of pre-tax income is set aside from each paycheck to be used for expenses such as child care and health care.

Baby Care Decisions

Expectant parents also have to make many decisions about their baby's care. They need to make arrangements for regular or occasional child care, select a doctor for their child, decide whether to breast-feed or bottle-feed the baby, and choose what type of diapers to use. Parents-to-be who start thinking about these issues early on will be prepared when the baby comes.

Making Child Care Arrangements

No matter what they decide about employment, most expectant parents need to give some thought to child care arrangements. If both parents will be working, the need for quality child care is crucial. Even if one parent plans to stay home to care for the baby, substitute care will be needed from time to time. See Fig. 10-6.

Finding suitable child care can be challenging. Sometimes family members, such as grandparents, can help provide care. Other options might include sharing child care responsibilities with other parents, having a paid caregiver come to the home, or taking the baby to an infant care center. Chapter 28 discusses these and other options, as well as factors to consider when choosing child care.

Fig. 10-6. Decisions relating to substitute child care are a major concern for many families. **Why should parents think about child care options before a baby is born?**

Choosing the Baby's Doctor

The health care provider that parents choose for their baby will play a major role in the early years of the child's life. Parents and child will visit this doctor regularly for both routine checkups and care during illness. The doctor will monitor and chart the child's growth and give the child vaccines to protect against diseases. He or she will address concerns and answer questions about the child's health, and will serve as a valuable source of information on all kinds of issues. Because parents rely so much on their child's doctor for care and advice, they need to find a doctor they trust and who shares their attitudes and beliefs.

Many parents choose a doctor for their child before the baby is born. That way, the health care provider who will be supervising the birth can share medical information with the baby's doctor before and after the birth. Some parents choose a **pediatrician** (PEE-dee-uh-TRISH-un), a doctor who specializes in the treatment of infants, children, and adolescents. Other parents decide to take their baby to a family practice physician or to a clinic.

For the parents-to-be, the first step in choosing a doctor is to find out whether their health plan restricts them to a list of certain medical providers. Next, they can ask for recommendations from their primary care physician, obstetrician, or certified nurse-midwife, as well as from relatives and friends who have children.

They may also wish to contact the Federation of State Medical Boards (FSMB) to make sure that there have not been any serious disciplinary actions against a particular doctor.

After identifying a possible doctor, it's a good idea to call the doctor's office and ask for some basic information. Questions to ask include:

- Does your office accept our health insurance?
- What are the typical costs of an office visit and a follow-up visit? Is payment expected at the time of service, or can it be made later?
- What are your office hours?
- What is the best way to contact the doctor with questions?
- Is someone on call for emergencies? Who covers for the doctor when he or she is away?

Parents may also want to visit the doctor's office in person. This gives them a chance to meet the staff and view the facility. See Fig. 10-7.

Choosing a Feeding Method

Whether to breast-feed or bottle-feed is a personal decision. Each method has its advantages and disadvantages. As long as the baby is thriving and the parents are comfortable with the method, they have made the right choice.

Breast-Feeding. Parents often choose breast-feeding because it is a safe and natural way to feed infants. Here are some benefits of breast-feeding:

- Breast milk is easy for babies to digest. Breast-fed babies rarely suffer from constipation, and because babies only nurse until full, they are less likely to be overfed.
- Breast milk carries disease-fighting agents called *antibodies* that help babies fight off infections and illness in the first couple of months. Breast-fed babies generally have fewer illnesses than bottle-fed babies and develop fewer food allergies as they grow.
- A mother's milk is ready at all times and is the right temperature. Mothers who are away from the baby during part of the day can express, or pump out, their milk and store it in bottles for later feedings.
- Breast milk is free.
- Breast-feeding benefits the mother by aiding the release of a hormone that stimulates the uterus to return to its pre-birth condition.
- Mothers who breast-feed often enjoy a special bond with their infant, which first-time mothers find especially encouraging.

Bottle-Feeding. For those who cannot or do not wish to breast-feed, bottle-feeding is a healthful alternative with advantages of its own.

- Bottle-feeding allows fathers and other relatives to share the work and rewards of feeding the baby.
- The mother has a chance to rest.
- The infant can be left for many hours at a time, if necessary. See Fig. 10-8.

Bottle-fed babies consume **infant formula**, a commercially prepared mixture of milk or milk substitute, water, and added nutrients. Formula is available ready to use or as a concentrate or powder that is mixed with boiled water. The baby's doctor can recommend a formula. If the infant is allergic to cow's milk formula, a soy substitute will be suggested. Babies should not be given pure cow's milk until they are one year old.

Fig. 10-8. Infant formula keeps babies well fed and satisfied. **What advantages does bottle-feeding have for parents?**

Diaper Pros and Cons

Type of Diapers	Advantages	Disadvantages
Cloth (Home Laundered)	❏ Economical. ❏ Softer than disposables. ❏ Free of chemicals that may irritate baby's skin.	❏ Initial purchase is expensive. ❏ Requires frequent laundering (which uses energy and water). ❏ Can cause diaper rash, especially if not changed frequently. ❏ Diaper pail is needed, which can smell unpleasant.
Cloth (Professionally Laundered)	❏ Convenient pick-up and delivery. ❏ Diapers are sanitized, which may reduce rashes.	❏ Service is expensive. ❏ Energy used for cleaning and delivering diapers raises environmental concerns. ❏ Some child care facilities refuse to use cloth diapers.
Disposable	❏ Convenient. ❏ Leakproof. ❏ Variety of sizes for growing baby.	❏ Expensive over time. ❏ Must be replaced regularly. ❏ Create a large volume of solid waste that does not break down naturally.

Fig. 10-9. Parents consider a variety of factors when choosing between cloth and disposable diapers. **Why might parents who use cloth diapers want to have some disposables on hand, and vice versa?**

Choosing Diapers

Happiness for a baby is a clean, dry diaper! Parents have the choice of washing cloth diapers at home, using a diaper service, or buying disposable diapers. Each option has its advantages and disadvantages, as summarized in Fig. 10-9.

Making Room for Baby

One of the most visible signs of getting ready for a baby's arrival is preparing a space for the baby to sleep. Some parents prepare a separate room for the baby. Others prefer having the baby sleep in their bedroom, perhaps in a curtained-off area to give both parents and child some quiet and privacy.

Choosing a Crib

No matter where the baby sleeps, the parents will have to provide a sturdy, safe crib. A 54-inch, safety-approved crib can serve a child until age three. Some models convert to a toddler bed that can be used until the child is about five or six.

A secondhand crib can cut costs, and an heirloom crib may have sentimental value, but both may also be unsafe. The Consumer Product Safety Commission first issued safety standards for cribs and other baby items in 1973. Cribs older than this may have safety hazards such as lead paint, which could poison an infant, or wide spaces between bars where a baby could slip through.

To make sure that the crib they choose for their baby is safe, parents should use the crib safety checklist shown on the next page. They can also look for the seal of the Juvenile Products Manufacturers Association, which indicates the cribs have gone through strict safety testing. Parents who have questions or concerns about cribs or other baby equipment can consult the Web site of the Consumer Product Safety Commission.

Bedding

A crib requires appropriate bedding. One item to look for is a bumper pad to prevent tiny arms and legs from poking through the bars of the crib. The pad wraps around the sides of the crib just above the mattress and should be securely tied in at least six places. Parents will also need several fitted sheets and a waterproof pad to protect the mattress.

One item a crib should *not* include is a pillow. It could accidentally cover the baby's face, creating a risk of suffocation. For the same reason, a crib should not contain stuffed animals, blankets, or other loose coverings.

Other Furnishings

In addition to the crib, parents will need a place to store baby clothes and supplies. Possible solutions include a chest of drawers, a set of open shelves, or inexpensive plastic crates. They will also need a changing table. In some cases, a waist-high chest of drawers can double as a changing table with the addition of a suitable pad and a safety strap to

Health & Safety

Crib Safety Checklist

A crib does not have to be expensive to be safe. Look for a reasonably priced model that meets these guidelines:

- Bars are no more than 2⅜ inches apart. Larger gaps can trap an infant's head. Decorative cutouts on end panels pose the same risk.
- Sides go up and down easily and can be operated with one hand.
- The mattress fits snugly in the crib. A baby can get stuck in a gap as small as the width of two fingers.
- If the crib has drop sides, they have a childproof locking mechanism.

- The sides of the crib reach at least 9 inches above the mattress support when lowered and 26 inches above it when raised. This prevents infants from rolling or climbing out.
- Corner posts have no decorative knobs that can snag an infant's clothing.
- There are no rough edges or exposed bolts. All bolts should stay securely tightened to prevent a choking hazard.

Baby Items Checklist	
Clothing	
❑ One-piece sleepers (gown or footed type) ❑ Undershirts or "onesies" (one-piece undergarments with snaps at the crotch) ❑ Daytime outfits ❑ Mittens (to cover the hands of babies who tend to scratch their faces) ❑ Socks	❑ Hats ❑ Sweater or jacket for cool weather ❑ Bunting (hooded sleeping bag) or snowsuit for cold weather ❑ Receiving blankets (small, lightweight blankets in which a baby can be wrapped)
Diapers and Changing Supplies ❑ *Cloth diapers:* 2–3 dozen diapers and 2–4 pairs waterproof pants ❑ *Disposable diapers:* At least a week's supply on hand (about 70 diapers) ❑ Baby wipes (unscented, alcohol-free) ❑ Petroleum jelly ❑ Cotton balls or gauze pads ❑ Ointment for diaper rash	**Feeding Equipment** *If breast-feeding:* ❑ Nursing bras and disposable nursing pads ❑ Breast pump ❑ 2–3 bottles for storing breast milk *If bottle-feeding:* ❑ 6–8 bottles (8-ounce size) ❑ Extra nipples and bottle caps ❑ Sterilizer (if not using a dishwasher) ❑ Bottle brush
Bathing Equipment ❑ Plastic baby bathtub ❑ Soft washcloths and bath towels ❑ Baby wash or mild soap ❑ Baby shampoo ❑ Baby lotion and/or baby oil ❑ Baby comb ❑ Baby nail scissors	**Travel Items** ❑ Car seat ❑ Baby carrier, stroller, or carriage (optional) ❑ Tote bag for supplies

Fig. 10-10. Although stores carry many special items for babies, parents can get by with just the basics. **What would you add to this list? Why?**

keep the baby from rolling off the surface. A rocking chair is a nice addition to a nursery, but is not a necessity.

Acquiring Other Baby Items

In addition to nursery furnishings, items needed for a new baby include diapers, clothing, and a variety of equipment and supplies. Expectant parents may receive some needed items as gifts, but will probably have to purchase others. Although most baby items are small, their cost adds up quickly. Expectant parents can save money by accepting hand-me-down items and shopping at secondhand stores and yard sales. However, they should check used items carefully to make sure they meet current safety standards.

Babies don't need fancy items or ones with designer labels. As long as the baby is safe and comfortable, parents should not feel guilty about choosing items that fit their space and their budget. Fig. 10-10 lists some of the items that expectant parents may need or want for the baby.

Choosing Clothing

Baby clothes should be comfortable, washable, and easy to slip on and off. Many parents find one-piece outfits that snap on to be the most functional and easiest to use. See Fig. 10-11.

For safety, baby clothes should be free of decorations such as buttons or ribbons that could choke or strangle a baby. Infants will put nearly anything in their mouths, and they cannot remove things that get wrapped around their necks.

Infant clothing is sized by age in months. Because infants grow rapidly, they outgrow clothes quickly. It is wise to buy only a few small-sized items and then add larger items as the baby grows. Also, think about when certain items of clothing will be needed. For example, a snowsuit purchased in the spring should be sized according to how big the baby will be the next winter.

All garments, as well as washcloths, towels, and blankets, should be washed before use in a detergent made especially for babies. Families that own or have easy access to a washing machine can get by with fewer clothes by laundering more often. Families that use a coin-operated laundry may save money and time by having more clothing.

Choosing a Car Seat

By law, babies traveling in a car must be in a car seat that meets current safety standards. A newborn riding home from the hospital must go in a car seat specifically designed for infants. Installing the car seat correctly is important for safety. Seats for newborns must be installed in the vehicle's back seat and must face toward the rear. Follow manufacturer's guidelines for correct installation. See Fig. 10-12.

Fig. 10-11. When choosing infant clothing, comfort and ease are more important than style or brand name. **Why do you suppose second-hand infant clothes are so plentiful?**

Fig. 10-12. By law, newborns must ride in the back seat and be buckled into rear-facing car seats. This provides the best protection in case of an accident.

Car seats should have the newest safety features, so be wary of used or hand-me-down car seats. Any car seat that has been in an accident, even a minor one, should be rejected. Although it may look undamaged, safety may be compromised. Parents can check the Web site of the Consumer Product Safety Commission for further safety information about car seats.

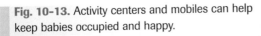

Fig. 10-13. Activity centers and mobiles can help keep babies occupied and happy.

Choosing Toys

Toys are not actually necessary for an infant. While babies do need stimulation to learn and grow, they can get it simply from interacting with their parents and other caregivers. However, since infants receive so many toys as gifts, parents need to be aware of safety issues related to infant toys. All toys should be carefully checked for hazards, such as lead paint, strings and cords, or small, loose parts that could cause choking. Babies should not sleep with stuffed animals or other soft toys that may pose a suffocation risk. Chapter 16 includes more information on toy safety.

Mobiles, mirrors, and activity centers that attach to the crib are popular. They should attach securely with devices that are well out of the infant's reach. For safety, parents should remove mobiles as soon as a baby can sit up and all other attached toys once the baby can stand. See Fig. 10-13.

Ready for Delivery

At least two weeks before the due date, expectant parents should pack a bag for the trip to the hospital or birth center. Items that may be needed during labor and delivery include insurance cards, a copy of the birth plan, and phone numbers of family and friends. Items that will be needed after the baby is born include a robe and toiletries for the mother and a going-home outfit for the baby. Parenting books and Web sites list other suggested items to pack.

Well-prepared expectant parents plan their transportation to the hospital or birth center in advance and have a car seat ready for the baby's ride home. They may also want to:

- Arrange for in-home help, if possible, for the first week or two after the mother and baby come home from the hospital.
- Stock up on household supplies and non-perishable groceries.
- Prepare and freeze meals in advance or collect menus from restaurants that deliver.
- Purchase or design birth announcements and stamp and address the envelopes.

All the preparation that parents have done prior to the baby's birth will help them reach their most important goal: a safe and healthy delivery. The only thing left for them to do is relax while waiting for the baby to choose an arrival date. See Fig. 10-14.

Fig. 10–14. When they have prepared as much as possible ahead of time, parents-to-be have fewer details to be concerned about when the big day arrives. **Why is it a good idea to pack a suitcase at least two weeks before the due date?**

‣ Home Health Care Aide

Home health care aides take care of disabled or elderly people in their homes. They may also care for children when a parent is sick or disabled. Aides work under the supervision of a registered nurse, physical therapist, or social worker.

Home health care aides spend many hours with their patients. They monitor and report on patients' conditions by keeping track of pulse, blood pressure, and temperature. They dispense medication and make sure patients take it on time. Nutrition is another important part of their job. Aides often prepare and serve food and make sure their patients eat. They also help keep the house orderly and clean. If a patient is bedridden, aides help with bathing and toileting. Health care aides provide emotional support and keep patients stimulated and mentally alert.

Training and certification to become a home health care aide varies from state to state. Some states require a high school diploma and some do not. However, all require aides to go through hours of specialized nurse aide training and pass an exam for certification. Aides may also receive federal certification.

"One of the things I love about my job is the feeling that the work I do has great value. By caring for my patients and helping them with daily living tasks, I make it possible for them to enjoy the dignity and comfort of living in their own homes. You really need dedication and a caring attitude to do this job well."

CAREER TIPS

- Take psychology and health science technology courses in high school. Courses in parenting and child development may also be helpful for aides who work with children.
- Volunteer at a hospital or senior center.
- Sign up for nurse aide training.
- Pass the certification exam.

10 Review & Activities

CHAPTER SUMMARY

- Parents need to help children adjust to the arrival of a new sibling.
- Mothers usually give birth in a hospital facility, in a birthing center, or at home.
- Prepared childbirth classes and a birth plan offer advantages to expectant parents.
- Parents-to-be must examine such financial issues as medical expenses and employment decisions.
- Planning for a newborn includes making decisions about child care, medical care, feeding methods, and diapering choices.
- Choosing furnishings, clothing, and other items is part of preparing for a baby's birth.

Check Your Facts

1. Identify at least four ways that parents can help children adjust to the arrival of a new sibling.
2. What is a birthing room?
3. Compare hospital birthing facilities, birthing centers, and home births.
4. What are three advantages of the breathing techniques learned in prepared childbirth?
5. What is the role of the birth coach?
6. Why do expectant couples often prepare a birth plan?
7. Identify three medical expenses related to pregnancy and childbirth and three ways to pay for these expenses.
8. What is parental leave?
9. Identify two ways that parents can protect their family's financial future.
10. What are four potential child care arrangements that parents might explore before a baby is born?
11. Why is a family's choice of health care provider for their baby so important?
12. Identify at least three advantages of breast feeding and three advantages of using infant formula.
13. What safety issues should be considered when choosing the following? a) crib; b) car seat; c) infant toys.
14. What are six actions that help a couple get ready for delivery?

Think Critically

1. **Drawing Conclusions.** Why do you think prepared childbirth classes are helpful for parents-to-be, especially for a first baby?
2. **Judging Relevance.** What situations might influence employment decisions when a baby is expected?
3. **Analyzing Options.** Analyze the information provided in Fig. 10-9 and decide which diapering option you think is best. Explain your reasoning.

Apply Your Learning

1. **Appropriate Responses.** How would you respond to these comments? **a)** "Since I have an obstetrician, I don't need a birth plan or birth coach." **b)** "My parents are giving me an antique crib for my baby." **c)** "Having a baby sister is going to take Jonah by surprise, but I'm sure he'll just love her."

2. **Room Design.** Design a baby's room. Use graph paper or software to draw the floor plan. Create a visual display of your design, including fabric and paint samples plus pictures of the furnishings.

3. **Product Safety.** Check the Web site of the Consumer Product Safety Commission to find consumer safety recalls. Explore the list of recalled items to find reasons why products for infants are recalled. What common reasons do you find?

4. **Infant Car Seats.** Investigate how to install an infant car seat correctly. Demonstrate for the class, using photos, drawings, or an actual seat.

Cross-Curricular Connections

1. **Math.** Investigate the costs of one of the following for infants: a) diapers; b) cribs and bedding; c) changing tables; d) clothing; e) car seats; f) toys. Include prices at low, moderate, and high levels. With the class, put the information together and compute what overall costs for baby equipment might be at each price level.

2. **Language Arts.** Prepare a one-minute, public-service radio announcement about a safety topic in the chapter. Possible topics are cribs, car seats, clothing, and toys. Play the recording in class.

Family & Community Connections

1. **Families Helping Others.** Does your family know anyone who is expecting a baby? Discuss ways you can help, such as giving attention to an older sibling or delivering a meal to store in their freezer until needed. Carry out at least one of your ideas.

2. **Community Support Project.** Collect any baby items no longer needed from relatives, neighbors, and friends. Check all the clothing and toys for safety and discard any that are questionable. Donate the remaining items to a community organization that helps those in need.

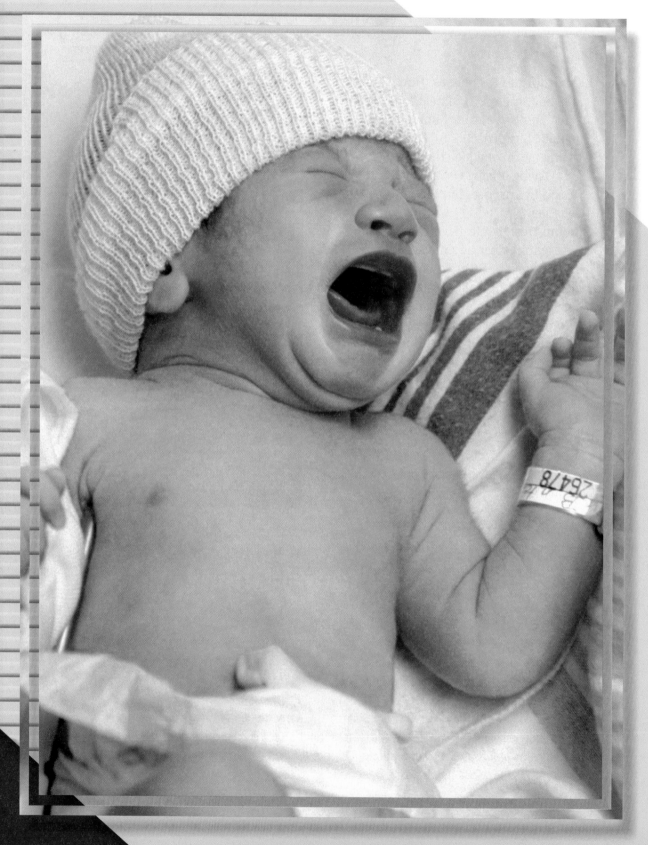

CHAPTER 11

The Birth Process

CHAPTER OBJECTIVES

- Distinguish between signs of real and false labor.
- Describe the stages of the birth process.
- Demonstrate ways that parents can bond with their new baby.
- Describe physical characteristics of newborns.
- Summarize postnatal care of the mother and infant.
- Compare different arrangements for the hospital stay.

PARENTING TERMS

- labor
- contraction
- fetal monitor
- transition
- anesthetic
- episiotomy
- breech presentation
- cesarean delivery
- vernix
- jaundice
- bonding
- Apgar scale
- rooming-in
- colostrum
- circumcision

If parents-to-be got all their ideas about child-birth from TV shows, they might be in for a surprise! Some shows play childbirth for laughs, with nervous parents becoming involved in endless mix-ups. Others paint an idealized view of the birth process: the expectant mother calmly says "It's time," and in the next scene is holding a perfectly beautiful infant. No matter how birth is portrayed in the media, in reality it's a messy, exciting, life-changing experience for everyone involved.

Signs of Labor

How does a woman know when her baby is about to be born? Various signs may occur before **labor,** or the process of giving birth, begins. Not every woman will experience all of these signs, but when they occur, they are a clue that labor is not far off.

- The woman may experience a feeling called *lightening*, when the baby drops lower into the pelvis. This can occur a few weeks before labor, or it may not happen until just before labor begins.
- In the last few weeks before birth, the cervix, or lower part of the uterus, becomes thinner in a process called *effacement*. The opening of the cervix also begins to widen, or *dilate*. A doctor will notice these signs during internal examinations.
- The woman may notice a pinkish discharge from her vagina. This sign is sometimes called "show." It results from a loosening of the mucus plug that sealed the cervix during pregnancy.
- Sometimes the amniotic sac—the protective, fluid-filled membrane surrounding the fetus—ruptures when labor begins. The amniotic fluid may gush out or leak in small amounts. This is often called "breaking of the waters." Most often, however, labor starts without the water breaking.
- When labor actually begins, the woman will feel contractions. A **contraction** is a tightening of the uterus muscles, followed by relaxation of the muscles. See Fig. 11-1.

Fig. 11-1. Contractions usually create a feeling of cramping, tightness, or pressure. They are mild at first. If labor is truly underway, they will become stronger and more frequent.

False Labor

Mild and painless contractions, sometimes called *Braxton Hicks contractions*, can normally occur any time throughout pregnancy. Often they are not even noticed by a pregnant woman. Sometimes, though, Braxton Hicks contractions are vigorous enough to notice and may even be painful. These "false labor" contractions can make the woman think she is going into labor when she is not.

Fig. 11-2. During early labor, the expectant mother should try to relax as much as possible. **What can the birth coach do to help?**

It can be difficult to tell the difference between real and false labor. Here are some clues:

- During false labor, contractions are irregular. Real labor contractions may be irregular at first, but then occur at regular intervals.
- During false labor, the contractions do not become stronger or more frequent. As real labor progresses, contractions intensify and come closer together.
- During false labor, the contractions generally stop if the woman walks around or shifts position. Real labor contractions, in contrast, are usually not affected by a change in position.
- During false labor, the woman feels pain in the lower abdomen. Real labor contractions most often start in the lower back and spread to the lower abdomen.

The Stages of Labor

Few pregnancies follow an exact pattern, but knowing what a typical birth is like can greatly relieve anxiety. Childbirth consists of three stages.

- First stage: Contractions cause the cervix to dilate.
- Second stage: The baby is born.
- Third stage: The placenta is expelled from the mother's body.

First Stage of Labor

The first stage of labor begins with a phase called *early labor*. During this phase, the pregnant woman's contractions are usually mild. They may last 30 to 40 seconds and occur every 20 to 30 minutes. The contractions may be irregular or they may seem to stop for longer periods of time. Gradually, however, the contractions grow stronger, last longer, and occur more often.

Early labor usually lasts about 8 to 12 hours, so there is no need to rush to the hospital or birthing center. The woman can rest or engage in light activity, such as walking around or taking a shower. See Fig. 11-2.

Active Labor. Once the cervix has dilated to about 3 centimeters, a phase called *active labor* begins. During active labor, which generally lasts three to five hours, the contractions become stronger and more frequent. The woman is usually advised to go to the hospital or birthing center when the contractions are five minutes apart or less. She may be advised to leave sooner if she lives far from the place where the baby is to be born or if this is her first baby.

After the expectant mother is admitted to the hospital or birthing center, she changes into a hospital gown. An identification band is attached to her wrist. The mother gives a brief medical history, signs routine forms, and gives a urine sample. A nurse or doctor does a pelvic examination—the first of several during labor—to check the degree of dilation and the position of the fetus.

As labor continues, the mother's pulse and blood pressure are checked regularly. She may be hooked up to a **fetal monitor,** a device that allows medical staff to keep track of the fetus's heart rate and watch for signs of stress. See Fig. 11-3.

Transition. Toward the end of the first stage of labor, a phase known as **transition** occurs. It lasts 30 minutes to two hours. Transition is often the most demanding part of labor, as the woman's contractions intensify. They last 60 to 90 seconds and occur every 30 seconds to two minutes. At the beginning of the transition phase, the cervix has dilated to about 7 centimeters (3 inches). During transition, the cervix continues to dilate until it is 10 centimeters (4 inches) wide.

Most women have the expectant father or another birth coach to help them with labor. Birthing professionals encourage the coach to participate during transition by offering emotional support. For example, the coach can offer the mother ice chips, wipe her face and arms with a cool washcloth, and tell her that she's doing a great job.

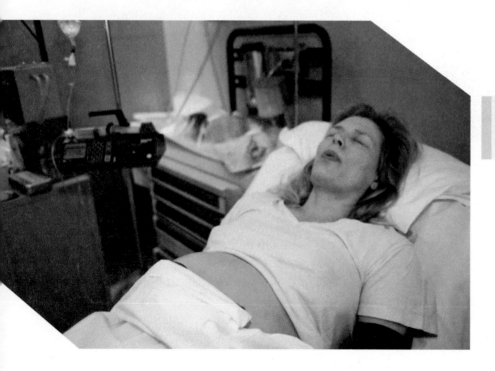

Fig. 11-3. One type of fetal monitor is a wide belt that wraps around the mother's abdomen.

Reducing Discomforts of Labor

Contractions can be uncomfortable or painful, especially as they become more intense. However, the experience is different for every woman. Discomfort may be lessened as a result of several factors:

- Having the support of loved ones often helps make the experience less stressful.
- Being well-rested gives a woman added tolerance and endurance during labor.
- Having eaten gives a woman strength. She should have light snacks early in labor, if permitted, and can suck on ice chips during labor.
- Knowing what to expect during the three stages of labor reduces anxiety and fear, which in turn can reduce pain.
- Using techniques taught in prepared childbirth classes can provide a sense of control and help a woman stay calm and relaxed. See Fig. 11-4.

If she chooses, the mother may be given medication to reduce or eliminate pain. The following types of medications are available:

- **Systemic drug.** Medication that helps relieve pain, tension, or nausea is injected into a muscle or vein.
- **Local anesthetic.** An **anesthetic** (an-ess-THET-ik) is a medication that causes loss of sensation. Local anesthetic is given by injection and numbs a small area.
- **Regional anesthetic.** This injection numbs a large area. An *epidural* anesthetic, the most common type given during labor, is injected in the space that surrounds the spinal cord in the lower back. It numbs the uterus and birth canal without stopping labor. The anesthetic can be regulated so the mother can still feel the urge to push.
- **General anesthetic.** This anesthetic produces unconsciousness. A regional anesthetic is usually preferred over a general anesthetic.

Second Stage of Labor

During the second stage of labor, the cervix is fully dilated and delivery of the baby begins. At this stage, the woman is allowed to bear down with her abdominal muscles and push the fetus out of the uterus and through the vagina. This part of labor lasts anywhere

Tips for the Birth Coach

The birth coach and other members of a woman's support team can make labor easier for her by following these suggestions:

➤ **Be supportive.** Help the pregnant woman get ready, and reassure her that she is in good hands.

➤ **Be prepared.** Know how to distinguish between true and false labor and what to expect during each stage of labor.

➤ **Be positive.** It is natural and understandable to be apprehensive about childbirth. A positive and encouraging attitude helps relax the laboring woman, which makes labor easier for her.

➤ **Stay calm.** Even if the labor takes an unexpected turn, members of the support team should try not to let their worries show. For example, people helping the woman should speak in low and reassuring voices.

from 20 minutes to two hours. Contractions last about 45 to 90 seconds and come every 3 to 5 minutes.

In some hospitals, the woman is usually moved to a separate delivery room at this stage. Otherwise, the room used for the first stage of labor is readied for delivery.

The woman's pelvic and vaginal areas are scrubbed with an antiseptic soap. The lower part of her body is covered with a sterile cloth. On a delivery table, she may lie on her back or lean forward. Some birth facilities allow alternative positions, such as kneeling, squatting, or lying on one side with the upper leg supported.

The birth coach, scrubbed and dressed in a sterile gown, can help by holding the woman's hand, supporting her back as she pushes the baby out, and offering words of encouragement. The coach helps the woman respond to her body's cues to breathe, bear down during the contractions, and relax when they are over.

During a typical birth, the baby travels down the birth canal head first and facing toward the mother's back. The baby's skull is made of flexibly joined plates of bone, allowing it to be temporarily molded into an egg shape as it descends through the narrow birth canal. As the head begins to emerge, the baby turns face upward. Fig. 11-5 shows how the baby travels down the birth canal.

To ease the passage of the baby's head through the vaginal opening, the doctor may

The Birth of a Baby

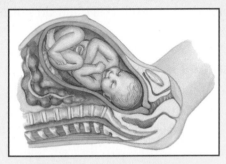

A. As labor begins, the fetus is head down in the uterus and the cervix is still narrow.

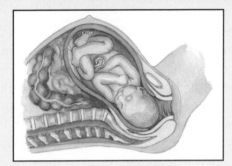

B. The cervix starts to dilate.

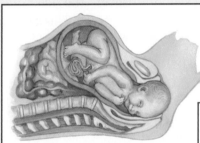

C. After the cervix is fully dilated, the muscles of the uterus begin to force the head through the birth canal.

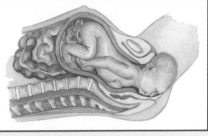

D. The head emerges and turns upward.

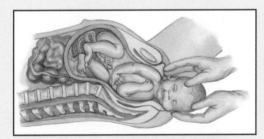

E. The shoulders emerge, helped by turning the baby's head. The baby exits quickly after the shoulders are out.

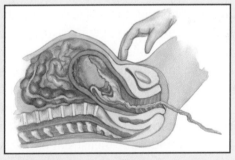

F. Delivery of the placenta occurs soon after the baby is born.

Fig. 11-5. The baby has just a short distance to travel, but the journey can take many hours. **Identify which of the three stages of labor is taking place in each picture.**

widen the opening by making a surgical cut called an **episiotomy** (eh-pee-zee-OTT-uh-mee). This cut is made after a local anesthetic is given.

When the head has fully emerged, an attendant suctions mucus from the baby's mouth and nose. The head expands the birth canal so the rest of the body can pass through. As the baby emerges from the birth canal, the baby's body rotates to one side, gently guided by the doctor. This enables the baby's shoulders to emerge one at a time. Usually, the mother gives a few more pushes and the baby slides out. If necessary, the doctor may use a suction device or *forceps,* a tong-like instrument, to ease the baby out of the birth canal.

The baby is still attached to the placenta by the umbilical cord. A medical attendant clamps or ties the umbilical cord in two places. Often the father or other birth coach cuts the cord between the two clamps, or a nurse does so. Neither the mother nor the baby feels the cut.

Once the baby is delivered, the parents are elated to welcome the newcomer. They often laugh and cry with joy and relief as the medical staff congratulates them.

Third Stage of Labor

During the third and final stage of labor, the placenta is delivered. The new mother experiences mild contractions, which separate the placenta from the uterine wall and move it into the vagina. Then the mother can push it out. A nurse massages the mother's abdomen to assist in this process, which usually takes about 10 to 30 minutes. A menstrual-like flow begins. It continues for at least several days and may last as long as six weeks.

If an episiotomy was done during the second stage of labor, it is stitched up after the placenta is delivered. The stitches are eventually absorbed into the body and do not need to be removed.

Variations in the Birth Process

Not all births follow the typical pattern just described. For various reasons, it may be necessary for medical staff to intervene in the natural birth process. Fortunately, they are trained and equipped to handle such situations.

Breech Presentation. Sometimes the baby does not rotate into the normal head-down position. Instead, the feet or buttocks are closest to the cervix. This position is called a **breech presentation**. See Fig. 11-6.

Fig. 11-6. In a breech presentation, the baby has not assumed the head-down position in the uterus. If the baby is delivered through the birth canal, either the buttocks or feet will emerge first.

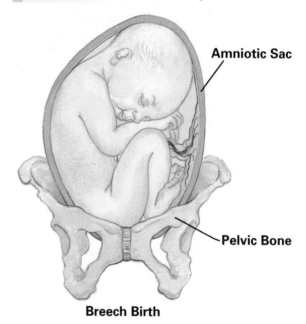

Amniotic Sac

Pelvic Bone

Breech Birth

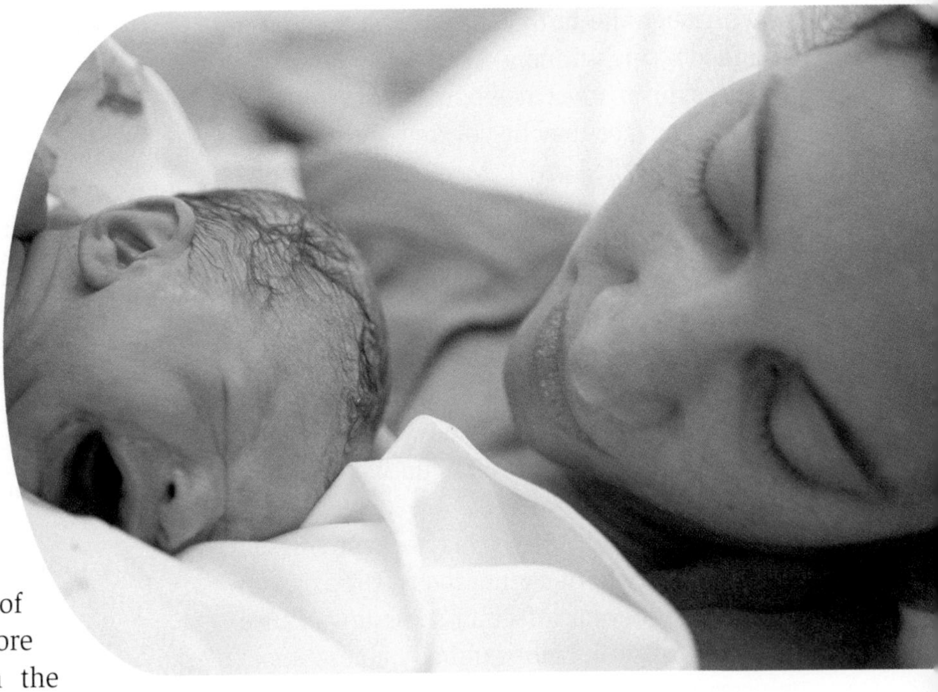

Fig. 11-7. Babies often look a little strange at birth. **How do they change over the next few days?**

Usually the doctor is aware of the breech presentation before labor begins. Depending on the baby's position, the doctor determines the safest way to proceed. Sometimes the baby can be delivered through the birth canal. In other cases, the doctor may decide to deliver the baby surgically.

Cesarean Delivery. A **cesarean delivery** (si-SAIR-ee-in), sometimes called a C-section, is a procedure in which the doctor delivers the baby through a surgical opening in the mother's abdomen. A cesarean delivery may be necessary when:

- The mother's pelvis is too small to deliver the baby.
- The fetus is in the breech position.
- The mother is carrying multiple fetuses.
- The mother has a preexisting medical condition that makes a vaginal birth unsafe.
- The placenta covers the opening of the uterus.
- A long labor threatens to harm the health of the baby or mother.
- The fetal monitor shows the fetus's heart rate dropping dangerously low.

Most of these conditions are known in advance. As a result, many cesarean deliveries are scheduled to take place before a woman goes into labor.

In most cases, the mother is given an epidural anesthetic during cesarean delivery. She is awake and alert, but does not feel any discomfort from the procedure. Often, the birth coach can be present.

Meet the Newborn

First-time parents who expect newborns to look picture-perfect are in for a surprise. The newborn's skin is covered with **vernix** (VUR-niks), a greasy white material. Vernix keeps the skin from getting waterlogged by amniotic fluid. See Fig. 11-7.

The newborn's head may look pointed or lopsided because of being squeezed on its way through the birth canal. It will take on a rounded shape within a few days.

The skin of most newborns looks blotchy at first. The face may be covered with pimple-like bumps called *milia*. Most skin conditions clear up on their own within the first few weeks of life.

One fairly common medical problem is **jaundice**. It occurs when a baby's liver is not yet able to break down a substance called *bilirubin*. This causes the skin to have a yellowish tint. Jaundice is treated with ultraviolet light, either in the hospital or with special equipment at home.

At first, the baby's eyes may appear crossed because a newborn cannot focus. Drops given at birth to prevent infection sometimes cause the eyes to swell. Light-skinned babies almost always have blue eyes at birth. Darker-skinned infants more often have brown eyes. Individual eye color develops over several weeks or months.

Bonding

Many health care providers allow parents to hold their baby immediately after delivery. Lying on the mother's stomach or in her arms, the newborn feels her skin and heartbeat and hears the father's voice. As the parents talk to the baby and caress it, they begin the process of forming an attachment, or feeling of close connection, between parent and child. This process is called **bonding**. See Fig. 11-8.

The term bonding originated in the 1970s. At that time, some studies showed that separating a mother and her newborn posed a threat to their lifelong relationship and the infant's future relationships to others. However, the concept came to be misunderstood. This caused unnecessary worry for parents who were unable to hold a child immediately after birth because the mother or baby required medical procedures.

Fig. 11-8. Whether it happens immediately or takes time to develop, bonding results in a close emotional tie between parent and child.

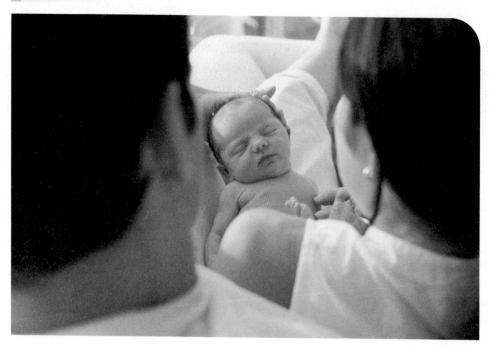

Apgar Scale			
Sign	**Points**		
	0	1	2
Heart Rate	Not detectable	Below 100	Over 100
Breathing	None	Slow, irregular	Good (crying)
Muscle Tone	Limp	Some movement in arms and legs	Active motion
Reflex Response	No response to nasal irritation	Grimace	Cough or sneeze
Color	Pale, grayish, or blue all over	Normal color in body; limbs grayish or blue	Normal color all over

Fig. 11-9. Using the Apgar scale, newborns are given a rating based on five key signs of health. **Why is crying considered a good sign?**

Later studies have shown that parents bond with their children under many different circumstances. Bonding can occur in the first hours, days, weeks, or months of life together. Some experts believe that bonding doesn't take place until the baby is at least six months old. Adoptive or foster parents, who may not meet their children until they are well out of infancy, still form bonds with them.

Postnatal Care

After the baby is born, both mother and newborn require postnatal care. (*Postnatal* means after the birth.) Some postnatal care procedures must be done right away. Others can be delayed for a while to allow the new parents time to bond with their baby. If expectant parents have preferences about the timing of postnatal care, they should discuss them with their health care provider ahead of time.

The Apgar Scale

Minutes after delivery, the newborn is given a medical checkup to detect any problems that require immediate emergency treatment. The checkup consists of rating the infant's physical condition using the **Apgar scale**, named for its inventor, Dr. Virginia Apgar. As shown in Fig. 11-9, the newborn receives a score of 0, 1, or 2 for various signs that are assessed. The scores are recorded at one minute and five minutes of life.

Newborns who score a total of seven or more points are in good to excellent condition. Those who score between four and six points may need some assistance, such as administration of oxygen or suction to help them breathe. Newborns scoring less than four points may require emergency life-saving measures.

Routine Newborn Care

After the Apgar test, medicated drops are put into the newborn's eyes to prevent possible infection. The baby is also given a vitamin K injection and a hepatitis B vaccine. The baby is weighed, measured, and washed.

Before the baby leaves the delivery room, an identification band that matches the mother's band is placed on the baby's wrist or ankle. The infant's footprints are recorded for the hospital records. These procedures are done to ensure that mother and child are correctly matched when they leave. See Fig. 11-10.

Neonatal Intensive Care

Most births go smoothly, and most babies are born healthy. However, infants who were born too soon, are too small, or have serious medical problems require special care immediately after birth.

About ten percent of all pregnancies in the United States result in premature birth, which is birth at less than 37 weeks of development. Because they are born before prenatal development is complete, premature infants often face numerous health problems. For example,

they often have breathing problems because their lungs are immature.

Many premature infants have *low birth weight*, which means they weigh less than 5.5 pounds. Some babies who are not premature also fall into this category. They, too, face an increased risk of health problems.

Premature infants and those with low birth weight often require specialized care in a *neonatal intensive care unit*, or NICU (*nik-you*). There they receive constant monitoring and attention. Premature infants are often placed in an *incubator*, an enclosed crib in which temperature, humidity, and oxygen levels are carefully controlled. See Fig. 11-11.

Infants who are premature or have low birth weight have an increased risk of long-term health problems and disabilities. However, advances in medical care are helping more of these children survive and thrive.

Postnatal Care of the Mother

Right after the birth, while one team of health care professionals is caring for the baby, another team is taking care of the new mother. They monitor

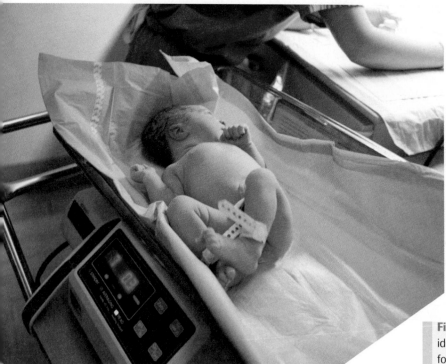

Fig. 11-10. Being weighed and wearing identification bands are routine experiences for newborns in hospitals.

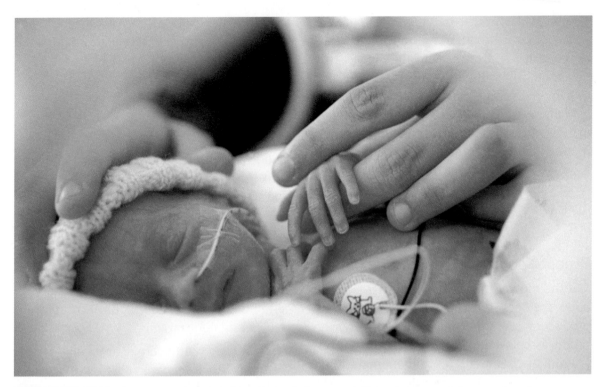

Fig. 11-11. Babies born prematurely may have to stay in the neonatal intensive care unit for several weeks. Medical technology has increased the chances of survival for premature infants.

the mother's vital signs, including blood pressure, pulse, and breathing rate. That's because significant changes in any of the mother's vital signs after she gives birth could indicate complications.

Now that the long process of labor is over, the new mother may feel chills and thirst. She may also be hungry. In a hospital or birthing center, she is usually taken to a recovery room before being taken to her regular hospital room. At that time, she is often given a light snack, such as toast or crackers and juice.

The Hospital Stay

How long do the new mother and her baby stay in the hospital? A generation ago, the average hospital stay following a vaginal birth was five days. Today, mother and baby are usually discharged a day or two after a normal vaginal delivery. Some go home sooner. A woman who undergoes a cesarean birth may stay several days.

Rooming-In Options

Rooming-in is the practice of allowing the baby to be cared for in the mother's room rather than in the hospital nursery. Rooming-in offers several benefits. It allows mother and baby to spend more time together, which helps them get to know each other and bond. Rooming-in also helps the mother become accustomed to caring for her newborn. For instance, she learns to recognize and respond to the signals that mean the baby is hungry. Nurses are available to help the mother learn to care for her baby.

Many hospitals offer the option of *full rooming-in*, in which the baby stays in the mother's room full time, day and night. With *partial rooming-in*, the baby stays in the mother's room most of the time, but is taken to the nursery periodically so that the mother can rest. See Fig. 11-12.

Breast-Feeding

If the mother has chosen to breast-feed the baby, she does so frequently to stimulate milk production. For a few days after delivery, she produces **colostrum** (kuh-LAHS-trum), a yellow fluid rich in nutrients and antibodies that protect newborns from infection.

Circumcision

Some newborn males undergo a **circumcision** (sur-kuhm-SIH-zhun). In this surgical procedure, part of the foreskin is cut away from the tip of the penis. Circumcision is usually done on the second day after birth.

Circumcision may be done for several reasons. It is part of a religious rite in some faiths. Some people believe that it confers health advantages, making the penis easier to keep clean. Some fathers who are circumcised choose to have the procedure done so their sons look the same as they do. The decision whether or not to circumcise an infant is left to the parents.

Birth Certificate

After the birth of their child, parents should be sure to receive a birth certificate. The hospital does the paperwork of registering the birth with the appropriate office of vital statistics. The office then issues the birth certificate.

A birth certificate should be kept in a safe place with other important documents because it is the child's proof of identity. A child cannot get a Social Security number without a birth certificate, and thus may not qualify for certain financial benefits. A birth certificate is also essential for proving:

- **Legal age.** A birth certificate enables people to prove their age when getting married or obtaining a driver's license, for instance.
- **Citizenship.** A birth certificate is necessary to obtain a passport.
- **Relationships.** A birth certificate may be used to establish family relationships.

Fig. 11-12. Babies in a hospital nursery are cared for by nursing staff. Nursery care may be necessary if the mother had a difficult birth and needs time to rest and recover.

Child & Family Services CAREERS

▶ Obstetrician

An obstetrician is a medical doctor who treats women throughout pregnancy, labor, and postnatal care. Most obstetricians are also trained as gynecologists—doctors who assess and treat patients with disorders of the reproductive system.

Many obstetricians work in their own medical practices or with a group of other doctors. Others work in clinics, hospitals, or public health settings. Some choose subspecialties, such as high-risk pregnancies.

"After graduating from medical school, I completed a four-year obstetrical residency program. Then I had to pass the medical board tests, including a combination of written and oral exams. I'm continually learning and must be recertified every ten years.

"If you're considering a career in this field, spend some time in a doctor's office or hospital to see a little of what it's like day to day. My job is stressful and requires a lot of stamina and commitment. Obstetricians need good people skills as well as good analytical skills."

CAREER TIPS

- Take classes in biology, chemistry, math, and child development or parenting.
- Volunteer in a hospital or a doctor's office.
- Earn a college degree in a pre-med program.
- Graduate from an approved medical school.

CHAPTER SUMMARY

● The birth process takes place in stages. A woman can use several signs to help her determine when labor has begun.

● Some circumstances during the birth process cause the need for a cesarean delivery, which is a surgical method.

● Babies look very different at birth than they do after a few days.

● Bonding can take place at various times, depending on the circumstances.

● Postnatal care includes care given to both the newborn and the mother.

● During a hospital stay, the mother may have the newborn in her room if she wishes.

Check Your Facts

1. What are five signs of labor?
2. Compare false labor with true labor.
3. What are the stages of labor?
4. Why is transition the most demanding part of labor?
5. How can the birth coach help during transition?
6. What are four types of medications available to a mother?
7. Describe what happens to the baby during a typical birth process.
8. What is the purpose of an episiotomy?
9. What happens to the placenta at birth?
10. What is a breech presentation?
11. In what situations might a cesarean delivery be medically necessary?
12. What is vernix and what is its purpose?
13. Describe how a newborn looks.
14. What is bonding?
15. What is the Apgar scale?
16. Why is premature birth dangerous?
17. Describe the care given to a premature baby.
18. How is the mother cared for after delivery?
19. Compare different rooming-in options.
20. Why is colostrum advantageous?
21. Who makes decisions about circumcision?

Think Critically

1. **Identifying Alternatives.** Crystal has been to the hospital twice with false labor in the last week. Now she feels that she's in labor again. What should she do?
2. **Analyzing Viewpoints.** Marc has a weak stomach and isn't sure he wants to be in the delivery room. His wife wants his support. How should they handle this situation?
3. **Identifying Alternatives.** Sometimes a mother cannot make it to the hospital in time for delivery. What should those who are with her do in such a situation?

Apply Your Learning

1. **Stages of Labor.** With a team of students write single facts that describe the three stages of labor, putting each fact on a separate index card. Mix the cards up and exchange sets with another team. Without looking at the chapter, sort the cards into the three stages and put them in the order that they occur. Check the chapter to confirm the accuracy of your handling.

2. **Different Opinions.** Learn how opinions differ concerning these birth practices: a) inducing labor; b) the use of anesthetics; c) episiotomies; d) filming the birth. Explain the points of view and the reasons for them to the class. What do you think?

3. **Bonding.** Using an infant doll, demonstrate how a mother and father can promote bonding with their baby. What do you think might happen if family members make no effort to bond with an infant?

Cross-Curricular Connections

1. **Social Studies.** In the United States, birth tends to be a relatively private event, although this is not always the case. Learn about common birth customs in various cultures. Report what you discover.

2. **Language Arts.** Complete one of these writing ideas: a) Seeing a baby born can be awe-inspiring; write a poem from a parent to his or her newborn baby. b) Suppose you just became a parent; write a letter to a relative that describes the birth events and your emotions before, during, and after the birth.

Family & Community Connections

1. **Birth Defects.** Learn about organizations that give support to people who are dealing with birth defects. As a family, carry out an activity to earn money, such as recycling cans, selling baked goods, or mowing lawns. Donate your earnings to one of the organizations you researched.

2. **Birth Locations.** Where in your community can a mother give birth? Suppose a couple live in a rural area. What route would they take to the nearest birthing location? What potential delays might be met along this route? Would time of day matter? Plot routes from other locations as well. How much time do you think should be allowed for the trip to the birthing location using these routes?

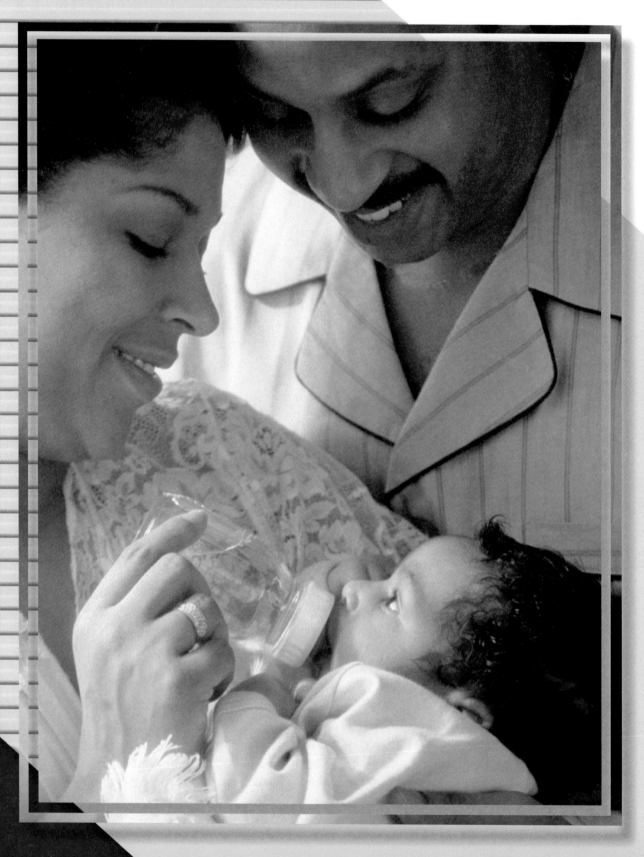

Adapting to Parenthood

CHAPTER OBJECTIVES

- Describe the physical and emotional changes a new mother experiences.
- Propose ways to manage the challenges encountered by new parents.
- Demonstrate how communication skills can help new parents.
- Suggest ways to help siblings adjust to a new baby.
- Explain the special parenting challenges faced by single and adoptive parents.

PARENTING TERMS

- lochia
- baby blues
- postpartum depression

Excitement, love, joy, concern, fatigue—all are normal reactions to the arrival of a new member of the family. First-time parents, in particular, face major adjustments. They are often surprised at the many changes they must make in their lives to meet the needs of their new son or daughter. Even parents who already have children must adapt to each new arrival.

Recovery After Childbirth

Giving birth is a normal, but extremely strenuous, experience. As one new mother said, "Now that I've gone through it, I understand why it's called labor!" Recovery from childbirth involves both physical and emotional adjustments. See Fig. 12-1.

Physical Changes

After the birth of a child, the mother's body must recover and shift back to its normal nonpregnant state. One of the first physical changes a new mother notices is a vaginal discharge called **lochia** (LO-kee-a). Lochia is the normal discharge of blood, tissue, and mucus from the vagina. The discharge continues for several weeks after a woman gives birth. It is nature's way of cleaning out the uterus after pregnancy.

A new mother's uterus slowly shrinks back to its previous size and location inside her body. A woman may sometimes feel the uterus contracting, especially if she is breast-feeding. As the uterus shrinks, her abdomen tightens as well.

During pregnancy, the woman's body takes on additional fluid. After birth, new mothers perspire more and urinate more frequently to rid the body of that excess fluid.

Women who had an episiotomy during childbirth may experience some physical discomfort for a few weeks. The incisions of those who had a cesarean delivery will also feel sore. Health care providers can recommend measures to ease these discomforts.

Postnatal Care

During the *postnatal* (after childbirth) period, a new mother needs to take good care of herself. Her own needs must be met so that she has the physical and emotional energy to meet the needs of her baby.

Rest and Sleep. Proper rest helps a new mother recover from childbirth and gives her the energy to care for her newborn. Since her nights will probably be interrupted by feedings, she must take advantage of opportunities to rest and sleep during the day. Sleeping whenever the baby sleeps is a good strategy.

Fig. 12-1. After giving birth, a new mother needs to recuperate and regain her strength. **What support might the father offer during this time?**

Fig. 12-2. Exercise, combined with a healthful diet, can help new mothers lose the weight gained during pregnancy. **What are some other benefits of being physically active?**

Nutrition. Eating nutritionally balanced meals and snacks provides energy and helps the mother's body recover. A new mother should choose a variety of healthful foods: whole-grain breads and cereals, vegetables, fruits, low-fat or fat-free dairy foods, and lean sources of protein. She also needs plenty of liquids. They help the body function better and can lessen fatigue. Water, milk, fruit juices, and vegetable juices are good choices.

A mother who is breast-feeding needs an extra 300 to 500 calories daily to maintain an adequate supply of milk. For her own and her baby's health, she should avoid alcohol, tobacco, and illegal drugs. The harmful substances they contain can be passed through breast milk to the baby. So can some medications. A breast-feeding mother should ask her health care provider for further advice.

Postnatal Checkup. About four to six weeks after childbirth, the mother has a postnatal medical examination. This checkup is usually done by the health care provider who oversaw prenatal care. The doctor or nurse-midwife makes sure that the new mother's uterus is returning to normal, that any incisions are healing properly, and that there are no complications affecting the mother's health. Women can discuss weight loss, birth control, and other issues at the postnatal checkup. New mothers should wait until after this checkup to start an exercise routine.

Exercise. Physical activity tones muscles, increases strength and energy, and aids the return to pre-pregnancy weight. It also helps improve mental and emotional well-being. The new mother's health care provider can give guidance on an appropriate level of physical activity. At first it may be limited to stretching and other gentle exercise. Later, the woman can begin to increase her level of activity. See Fig. 12-2.

Weight Loss. New mothers can expect the return to their pre-pregnancy weight to take several months. That's true whether or not they breast-feed. Moderate exercise combined with a healthful diet will yield weight loss of about a pound a week. Strict dieting should be avoided.

Hormones and Emotional Changes

Hormones—the body's powerful chemical messengers—cause and regulate changes in the mother's body during pregnancy, childbirth, and the postnatal period. These hormonal shifts affect a mother's emotions as well as her physical recovery.

It's not uncommon for new mothers to experience periods of moodiness, with feelings of anxiety, sadness, fear, guilt, and even anger. These periods of negative feelings are often called the **baby blues**. They stem from a combination of hormonal changes, fatigue, lack of adequate sleep, and the stress of new roles. The baby blues may occur in the days and weeks shortly after birth and then go away. See Fig. 12-3.

For some mothers, the problem is more severe. Feelings such as sadness, anger, or frustration can become strong enough to interfere with daily life for an extended period of time. When this occurs within a year after giving birth, doctors may diagnose a mood disorder called **postpartum depression**. Symptoms may include an inability to sleep or complete everyday tasks, feelings of worthlessness, withdrawal from family and friends, loss of interest or pleasure in activities, or fear of hurting the baby. Postpartum depression may begin days, weeks, or months after childbirth. It's important to seek medical help as soon as this problem becomes apparent.

In rare cases, some new mothers have experienced a dangerous form of mental illness.

They become very agitated, behave strangely, and may lose touch with reality. Some with this condition hear voices that aren't there. They may be at risk of hurting themselves or others. Immediate treatment is essential.

Most of the time, however, recovery from childbirth goes fairly smoothly. For many new mothers, the biggest challenges are not a result of childbirth, but rather the need to take on new responsibilities as a parent.

Fig. 12-3. It's normal for a new mother to feel sad or upset from time to time. If her mood changes are severe, she should talk to her health care provider.

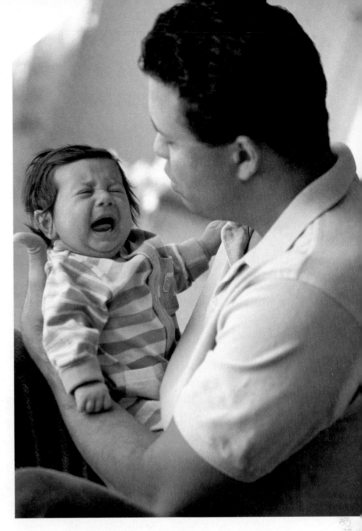

Fig. 12-4. New parents spend a lot of time comforting the baby, who cries to communicate needs. **Why might a father want to take parental leave after the baby's birth?**

Challenges for New Parents

Both new mothers and new fathers face many challenges, especially if they are welcoming their first child. Assuming the role of parent changes life dramatically.

Adapting to New Routines

Once a new baby comes home, the parents may feel as if their life has turned upside down. Newborns sleep just a few hours at a time, whether it's day or night. They need to be fed ten to twelve times a day, around the clock, plus have about the same number of diaper changes. For awhile, uninterrupted sleep becomes a thing of the past. All this occurs at a time when the mother is still recovering from delivery, and both parents are likely to be very tired. See Fig. 12-4.

Help from family and friends can be a real boost during this time. New parents should not hesitate to accept offers of assistance. Having someone prepare a meal or do a load of laundry frees parents for time with the baby or much-needed rest.

Eventually the baby will sleep through the night, and the whole family will settle into a routine. Still, life will never be the same as it was before the baby's arrival. Time spent caring for an infant necessarily takes time away from other things, such as hobbies or going out with friends. Work schedules may have changed, especially if one or both parents leave a job temporarily or permanently. Adjusting to these lifestyle changes takes time.

Handling Mixed Emotions

New parents may be surprised by mixed emotions. Joy at the baby's arrival is often mixed with anxiety over the enormous responsibilities of parenthood. Aside from immediate care tasks, there is the future to think about. Being completely responsible for a tiny new life—not just for the moment, but for years to come—may feel frightening and overwhelming. Financial worries often add to the concern. Many parents feel resentment of their new role at times, as well as guilt for having these negative feelings.

All these emotions are natural. If anything, they show that parents have a realistic understanding of both the joys and challenges of caring for a child. In time, they will adapt to their new roles, and parenthood won't seem quite so overwhelming. Meanwhile, they can focus on taking practical steps to address their concerns. For example, to reduce anxiety about finances, they can set realistic goals for spending and saving.

Gaining Confidence

Parents—especially first-time parents—often worry about whether they are providing the right care. Confidence as a parent is not inborn. It comes only with time and practice. Getting

tips and advice from experienced parents helps, as does reading books or taking parenting classes. Mainly, though, confidence grows through hands-on experience. As parents spend time caring for and getting to know their child, they will become more self-assured in their new role.

Strengthening the Parent-Child Bond

When a new baby arrives on the family scene, is it love at first sight? Surprisingly, it might not be. Many parents expect to be overwhelmed by feelings of love as soon as they see their newborn. Actually, the lifelong bond between parent and child develops gradually.

As you read in Chapter 11, bonding is the process of forming an attachment between parent and child. One of the main ways in which parents bond with their newborn is by meeting the baby's needs promptly and with love. Daily loving care, such as feeding, bathing, and cuddling, helps babies and parents get to know each other and develop a close connection. See Fig. 12-5.

Managing Multiple Roles

With the birth of a child, life becomes much more complicated. Even parents who successfully juggled work and personal life before the baby often find themselves feeling overloaded. Additional responsibilities call for improving personal management skills, such as:

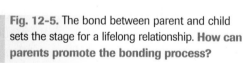

Fig. 12-5. The bond between parent and child sets the stage for a lifelong relationship. **How can parents promote the bonding process?**

Fig. 12-6. Caring for a child and maintaining the household require good time management skills. **What strategies do you use to manage your time effectively?**

- **Setting priorities.** With the arrival of a new baby, parents experience a major shift in their priorities. They must accept the fact that caring for the baby—and themselves—comes first. Certain other things just aren't as important as they used to be. Tidying the house can wait—feeding the baby can't!

- **Using time effectively.** Even when priorities are set, most tasks can't be put off forever. The list of things to be done may seem endless, but each day still has only 24 hours. Parents soon become adept at combining activities, such as folding clothes and talking to the baby while heating soup for dinner. See Fig. 12-6.

- **Getting organized.** Babies add a lot of belongings to a home, from bottles to diapers to tiny socks. Having a designated place for items helps keep parents from wasting time looking for them. Another useful organizing strategy is to develop routines for tasks that are done frequently. Many people schedule certain tasks for certain days of the week. If parents know a chore will be taken care of on Tuesday, they don't have to worry about it on other days.

- **Managing stress.** Life with a child is filled both with wonderful moments and with difficulties that cause stress. Too much stress is not good for anyone, but parents, in particular, must be careful how they handle stress. Taking it out physically or emotionally on a child is *never* appropriate. On especially hectic days or when the baby won't stop crying, it helps to take a deep breath and realize that "this, too, will pass." A sense of perspective—and a sense of humor—can go a long way in relieving the stress of parenting.

Developing a Support System

A strong support system can be a lifesaver for new parents. Parents need people in their lives that they can trust and rely on to help them with the challenges of caring for children. Seeking support when needed is not a sign of poor parenting. Just the opposite—it shows a person's commitment to good parenting.

Family and friends are the backbone of most support systems. Grandparents and other relatives, if they live nearby, may be willing to lend a hand. Neighbors and close friends might give advice or take care of the baby when parents must be gone. However, parents should be careful not to take such assistance for granted. Asking for help only when needed is better than simply expecting it to be given. Expressing appreciation and offering help in return also keep a support system strong. See Fig. 12-7.

In some cases, new parents have mixed emotions about relatives. They appreciate the support, but they also want to protect their own role as parents. If relatives try to take over or offer too much advice, the baby's parents can gently but firmly say they need to make their own decisions. Being kind and diplomatic helps prevent hurt feelings.

Couples as Parents

At the same time as they are adjusting to new roles as parents, couples must continue to nurture their relationship as husband and wife. Defining and becoming comfortable in new roles within an established marriage can be challenging. Cooperation and mutual support are key.

Sharing Responsibilities

Many years ago, most people assumed that caring for children was the responsibility of mothers rather than fathers. Today, couples work out the arrangement that suits them best. Child care might be handled mainly by the mother or the father, or it might be shared.

Most couples find that even if one parent is the primary caregiver, it's beneficial for the other parent to also be involved in the child's care in some way. As you have learned,

Fig. 12-7. Grandparents and other relatives often enjoy helping to care for a baby, but parents should not take their support for granted. **How might they express their appreciation?**

Fig. 12-8. A father's attention is the greatest gift he can give his child. **What benefits does the father gain from being involved in his child's care?**

providing care helps new parents gain confidence and promotes bonding between parent and child. When both parents participate in caregiving, both of them gain these benefits. Research has shown that children, too, fare better when both parents are involved in their lives. See Fig. 12-8.

Couples should discuss and agree on the division of child care and household tasks rather than simply making assumptions. Some couples start out with the idea that they will divide responsibilities equally, but soon discover that "equal" is not easy to define. A better approach is to decide what's fair based on each person's skills, energy, and schedule. Does one parent have more responsibilities outside the home than the other? What tasks is each person best suited for? This approach frees each person to contribute and to appreciate the other's contributions, without trying to keep an exact count of chores done or time spent.

Whatever the couple decides about sharing responsibilities, reviewing those decisions from time to time can help identify problem areas. It can also help protect the relationship by preventing resentments from building up.

Discussing Parenting Philosophies

Most couples discuss parenting before the child arrives. Even so, it's not unusual for new parents to disagree about childrearing philosophies, such as the parenting styles described in Chapter 5. Many find their ideas changing after the baby is born. That's why it's important to talk about these issues on a regular basis.

Making Time for Each Other

While caring for children is a high priority, so is a couple's relationship. One of the best things parents can give children is a loving, peaceful home. When parents have a solid relationship, children feel more secure.

Suppose you were so busy that you had no time for your best friend. Eventually, you might find yourselves drifting apart. The same thing can happen to new parents if they don't make time for each other. Some couples set aside a certain time to spend together, such as the first hour after the baby is put to bed each evening.

New parents should not feel guilty about occasionally leaving their child in someone else's care so that they can go out and enjoy themselves. If they're concerned about the cost of hiring a caregiver, they might consider alternatives such as:

- Accepting offers from friends and family members to watch the baby.
- Trading off child care duties with a neighbor who also has a baby or small child.
- Attending community events and activities at which free or low-cost child care is provided.

Communicating as a Couple

It's easy for parents with very busy lives to overlook the need to really talk with each other. Ongoing communication is vital to the health of any relationship. Without it, the feeling of deep attachment between two people

Modeling CHARACTER

Playing Fair on the Parenting Team

If you've ever played sports—or even just watched sports—you know that the game is more enjoyable when everyone plays fair. It's the same with parenting. When parents practice *fairness* with one another, the whole family benefits. Here are some ways parents can play fair:

- View parenting as a team effort, not a competition. Don't keep score of who changed how many diapers. Just pitch in and help each other when needed.
- Even though you're not keeping score, make sure you do your share. Don't take unfair advantage of the other person.
- Talk about concerns with one another instead of complaining to friends or relatives. Be open-minded and willing to listen.
- Don't play the blame game. When a problem arises, focus on how you can solve it together, not on who's at fault.

Think About It

How can parents be fair to each other without "keeping score"?

Fig. 12-9. Participating in the new baby's care helps siblings adjust. Parents should supervise them and be careful not to give children more responsibility than they can handle.

can be lost. Many problems and misunderstandings come from a failure to communicate clearly and often. Couples who communicate well make better decisions by sharing and discussing ideas. They are able to listen to one another's concerns and work together to find solutions.

Helping Siblings Adjust

Imagine that you're three years old. As the only child in the family, you're used to a comfortable daily routine and lots of attention. All that changes when your parents bring home a squalling baby. Everyone is fussing over the newcomer, and no one seems to have much time for you anymore. How would you feel?

When a new baby joins a family that already has children, the reactions of siblings vary, depending in part on their age. Very young children may not understand what has happened. They just know that suddenly someone else is receiving more attention. Jealousy is a common reaction for children under five, who are still very dependent on their parents.

Wise parents help siblings adapt to the arrival of a new baby brother or sister. To make the adjustment easier, parents can:

- **Involve siblings in the baby's care.** Pushing a carriage, talking to the baby during diaper changes, or fetching a towel at bath time helps siblings feel they have an important new role to play. See Fig. 12-9.
- **Spend some time alone with each older child.** This enhances the original parent-child bond and helps prevent resentment of the new baby.
- **Tolerate some babyish behavior.** Siblings, especially those who are young, may regress to earlier developmental stages. Parents should realize that this is a natural expression of the child's need for attention.
- **Praise more mature actions.** A parent might say, "Thank you for singing to the baby. You are such a good big brother!"
- **Encourage siblings to talk about their feelings.** Allow them to be honest and express negative emotions. Be clear, however, that they are never allowed to hurt the baby.
- **Tell them that they are loved.** Siblings need frequent reassurance that their place in the family is secure.

Special Parenting Situations

For the most part, adjustments to parenthood are similar for all parents. However, single parents and adoptive parents may face some special concerns.

Single Parents

As they face the challenges of parenthood, single parents have no spouse to share the load. Time and energy are usually stretched thin for singles, who are often full-time workers or students as well as full-time parents. Management skills such as setting priorities, planning, and organizing are vital.

No matter how good their management skills are, successful single parents don't try to do everything alone. Instead, they become skillful in finding the help they need. Perhaps even more than couples, single parents need a strong support network. For example, one single parent was called to work unexpectedly to deal with an emergency situation. She asked a trusted neighbor to stay with her child until she returned. Because she and the neighbor had already established that relationship of trust, the single mother was able to handle the situation effectively.

Many communities have support groups for single parents. Meeting and talking with others who face the same challenges can help keep single parents from feeling alone. See Fig. 12-10.

Adoptive Parents

Parents who adopt a child sometimes face special challenges. They may worry that the child's birth parents will try to regain custody. Parents who have been through a long, difficult process to adopt a child may feel an extra measure of guilt at the negative feelings that all new parents occasionally experience. Some adoptive parents must deal with relatives who treat the adoptive child differently from birth children in the family. Parents who adopt children from overseas may have to help them adjust to a new culture and language. Some parents must deal with the emotional problems of adopted children who come from troubled backgrounds.

Such issues can be resolved. Support groups and information networks are available to offer guidance on issues of concern to adoptive families. Time helps parents, children, and family members adjust to the adoption and feel more secure.

Fig. 12-10. Single parents who are teens face even greater challenges in financially supporting and caring for a baby. **What support systems are available for teen parents in your community?**

Child & Family Services CAREERS

▸ Parenting Magazine Writer

Parenting magazines are popular sources of advice for new parents. Some of their articles are written by staff writers—full-time or part-time employees of the magazine. Others are submitted by self-employed freelance writers.

Writers sometimes propose their own topics on parenting or family-related issues. Often, however, they are assigned topics by the magazine's editors. Before beginning an article, writers must gather information about the topic. They might interview experts or talk to parents who have experienced a relevant situation. Writers must conduct careful research and keep a record of all sources they consulted while gathering information.

"I became interested in writing when my English teacher recognized my skills and suggested I write for the school newspaper. This experience gave me an under-standing of the preparation required for writing a solid article. It quickly became apparent that I couldn't just sit down and write my own thoughts on the subject the editor assigned. Luckily, I found I enjoyed interviewing people and doing research. In college, I majored in journalism and minored in psychology. After graduation, I jumped at the opportunity to work as a staff writer for a parenting magazine, because the job suits both my interests and my skills."

CAREER TIPS

- Take parenting and creative writing courses in high school.
- Maintain proficient computer skills.
- Write for a school or community news-paper or magazine.
- Earn a college degree in journalism, English, or communications.

CHAPTER 12 Review & Activities

CHAPTER SUMMARY

- All women undergo physical and emotional changes following childbirth.
- Parenthood is as life-changing for new fathers as it is for new mothers.
- A number of challenges accompany the role of new parent, such as handling new routines and managing multiple roles.
- Married couples should work as a team to support each other and provide the best possible care for their new baby.
- Parents can take specific steps to help siblings adjust to a new baby in the family.
- For single and adoptive parents, parenting comes with some unique challenges.

Check Your Facts

1. What physical changes occur in a mother's body after birth?
2. Why does a new mother need to rest when the baby sleeps during the day?
3. Suggest three nutrition guidelines for a new mother.
4. Explain how hormones can affect a woman's emotions after giving birth.
5. How does a newborn affect routines?
6. Why do some new parents have mixed emotions following the birth of a baby?
7. How can parents become more confident about parenting?
8. What are four management skills parents need in order to manage multiple roles?
9. How can parents keep their support system strong?
10. Should child care and household tasks be shared equally by a couple? Explain.
11. Why should parenting philosophies be discussed regularly?
12. What can happen to new parents who don't take time for each other?
13. Why is communication vital to a couple?
14. Identify six strategies that help siblings adjust to a new baby.
15. Besides relying on family and friends, where can single parents turn for help?
16. What are three typical worries of adoptive parents?

Think Critically

1. **Predicting Consequences.** Suppose a new mother is afraid to tell anyone about her feelings of depression. Predict what could happen if she continues to feel depressed and refuses to seek treatment.
2. **Making Generalizations.** In general, is it possible for mothers and fathers to play identical roles in their newborn's life? Why or why not?

Apply Your Learning

1. **Communication Skills.** Work with a partner to practice effective communication. Create dialogues that demonstrate what you would say to a spouse in the following situations. Consider "I" messages, tone, and tact. **a)** Holly has gone back to work but still does most of the baby care and housework. She is frustrated. **b)** Brent feels that his wife is more interested in the baby than in him. He misses the time they used to have alone together.

2. **Menu Ideas.** Create a week of menus and snacks for a new full-time mother. She is breast-feeding and has little time and energy for fixing food. Menus should be nutritious and easy to prepare.

3. **Relationship Strength.** How can a couple keep their relationship strong after children are born? Work with a partner to think of ways. Include simple ideas that are inexpensive. For example, a midday how-are-you-doing phone call could be part of their routine.

Cross-Curricular Connections

1. **Math.** Create a pie chart that shows how a parent who is taking care of a newborn might spend a typical day. First, divide all of a day's activities into categories (examples: sleeping, eating, changing diapers). Then assign the number of hours each category takes. Convert these to a pie chart and compare charts in class.

2. **Language Arts.** Make a list of adjectives (descriptive words like *happy*) that describe the parent of a one-month-old baby. Share lists in class. How did positive and negative words compare? Why?

Family & Community Connections

1. **Caring for Baby.** Discuss with family members how they would feel about helping with a new baby in the family. To what extent would they like to be involved? Do job, distance, and time have impact? Would they like to be heavily involved in care or prefer to limit their contact to social events that are more fun than work?

2. **Mental Health Support.** Where could a new mother who is experiencing emotional problems after the birth of a baby find help in your community? Check the telephone directory for possibilities. Look in the Yellow Pages under "Mental Health," "Social Services," and "Counselor" to get ideas.

Caring for Children

CHAPTER 13

Understanding Infants

CHAPTER OBJECTIVES

- Describe typical patterns of growth and physical development during the first year.
- Relate sensory stimulation to brain development and learning.
- Summarize a typical infant's emotional and social development.
- Identify temperaments that infants may demonstrate.
- Explain what moral development means during infancy.
- Identify developmental characteristics in an infant.

PARENTING TERMS

- fontanels
- reflexes
- motor skills
- large motor skills
- small motor skills
- pincer grasp
- sensorimotor period
- object permanence
- stranger anxiety
- attachment behavior
- self-esteem
- temperament

Newborns come into the world with some built-in abilities. They can turn their head from side to side and move their hands to their mouth. Full-term babies are able to cry and to use their sucking reflex to receive nourishment. But that's just the start. Other milestones—laughing, sitting up, crawling, babbling—will soon follow. Knowing what behaviors to expect from their baby can make parents feel more relaxed and confident. Understanding the "why" behind some of the baby's actions can make family life easier, too.

Infant Growth and Development

Infancy, the period between birth and one year, is a fascinating time because so much happens so quickly. It is a time of tremendous growth and development. *Growth* refers to an increase in a baby's size and weight. *Development* refers to increases in physical, intellectual, emotional, and social skills. See Fig. 13-1.

Fig. 13-1. The rapid growth and development that occurs in the first year is exciting for both parents and infants. **What is the difference between growth and development?**

By studying babies around the world, researchers have identified average age ranges for milestones in growth and development. Knowing the average ages for these milestones helps parents track their baby's progress. While monitoring a baby's progress is part of parenting, it is important to remember that each infant is unique and may develop faster or slower than the average. If an infant appears to be significantly lagging behind, however, the parents should consult the baby's doctor.

Physical Development

Physical development includes growth in size and weight, as well as the increasing ability to control and coordinate body movements. Never in a person's lifetime will there be more rapid growth and physical changes than during infancy.

Growth and Proportion

Most newborns lose a few ounces of weight in the first few days. Within a short time, they are back at their birth weight and begin to grow. Gaining one or two pounds per month is typical during the first six months. During the first year, the average infant triples in weight and grows 50 percent taller.

As an infant grows, body proportions change, too. A newborn's arms and legs seem small in comparison with the rest of the body, and the head seems large. In fact, the head represents about 25 percent of a newborn's total length. In contrast, an adult's head accounts for only 12 percent of total height. More than half of the total growth of the head occurs during the first year. Long after the head has reached its full size, the torso, arms, and legs continue to grow. See Fig. 13-2.

Health & Safety

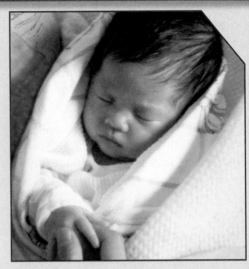

Failure to Thrive

When an infant's rate of growth is significantly below average, doctors may use the term *failure to thrive*. Not only is growth affected, but skill development is often delayed as well.

Possible causes range from medical problems to poor nutrition to hazards in the environment. Failure to thrive can also be caused by unmet emotional and social needs. If an infant is not held, cuddled, talked to, and provided with stimulation, he or she may not grow and develop normally. Babies not only enjoy receiving attention—they thrive on it!

The Fontanels. Newborns have a "soft spot" at the top of their head. Most also have a smaller soft spot in the middle of the head toward the back. These are the **fontanels** (fahn-tuh-NELZ), the areas between the bone plates of the skull. During birth, they allowed the head to change shape as it squeezed through the birth canal. Afterwards, they allow the head to grow.

The fontanels are covered with tough, fibrous tissues. They are safe to touch, although a direct blow would be dangerous. When a baby is quiet, these areas may

Fig. 13-2. An infant's head grows rapidly in the first year to accommodate the developing brain.

seem sunken, but they may pulsate when the baby cries. Between the ages of six and eighteen months, the bones of the skull gradually grow together and the fontanels disappear.

Reflex Behavior

At birth, an infant's movements are controlled by **reflexes,** which are automatic responses to stimulation. Some reflexes, such as blinking and sneezing, remain for life. Others are temporary. Several infant reflexes are described in Fig. 13-3.

Development of the Senses

Most mammals have poorly developed senses at birth. A puppy, for example, is born with its eyes and ears tightly shut. The eyes open after about one week, and eyesight begins to develop. The puppy's ears open about a week later, and it begins to hear sounds.

As you know, human babies are very different. They are prepared from birth to experience the world around them because their senses are fully or partially developed before birth. Infants use these developing senses to see, hear, smell, taste, and feel whatever comes near. Every waking minute, they experience the world around them through their senses. From birth through early childhood, most of their learning comes through the five senses—vision, hearing, touch, taste, and smell.

Vision. At birth, babies can focus only at close range, a distance of 8 to 10 inches. Conveniently, this is the approximate distance between babies and those holding them.

Newborns can detect light and dark, but cannot see all colors. Faces and simple black-and-white patterns are of greatest interest. Within a few weeks, a baby can *track*, or follow by sight, the movement of an object.

Fig. 13-3. The presence of reflexes at birth indicates normal brain and nerve development. **How might knowing about reflexes be helpful to new parents and caregivers?**

A Newborn's Reflexes			
Reflex Name	**Stimulation**	**Infant's Behavior**	**Approximate Age when Reflex Ends**
Babinski	Stroking the sole of the foot	Toes fan out; foot twists in	6 to 12 months
Moro (startle)	Loud noise or sudden change in baby's position	Extends legs, arms, and fingers; arches back; throws head back	4 to 6 months
Palmar grasp	Stroking the palm of the hand	Makes a fist over the person's finger	3 to 5 months
Placing	Back of feet drawn against flat surface	Withdraws feet	1 month
Rooting (sucking)	Stroking the cheek	Head turns, mouth opens, sucking begins	3 to 4 months
Stepping	Held under arms with bare feet touching flat surface	Makes stepping motions that look like walking	2 months
Swimming	Placement on stomach on a blanket	Well coordinated movements that resemble swimming	6 months
Tonic neck	Placement on back	Head turns to one side; arms and legs on preferred side are straightened and those on other side are bent	4 to 5 months

By three or four months, babies have a wider field of vision. *Depth perception*, the ability to see objects as three-dimensional, starts to develop around the second month and is fully developed by the seventh month. By one year, most babies have very good vision.

Hearing. Babies are able to hear even before they are born. Newborns pay attention to their parents' voices and may even stop moving when a conversation starts. When an individual talks to a baby often, the baby learns to recognize that person's voice. Newborns are startled by loud noises, but are often able to sleep soundly even when a doorbell rings or a dog barks in the same room.

Touch. The sense of touch is fully developed at birth. When newborns cry, cuddling often helps them calm down. Some babies feel comforted when held close to the parent's chest or wrapped snugly in a blanket.

Taste. Newborns have a well-developed sense of taste. Researchers have found that within hours of birth they can distinguish among sweet, sour, and bitter tastes. Not surprisingly, they prefer sweet ones.

Smell. The sense of smell develops very soon after birth. Within the first few days, babies show a preference for their mother's smell. As early as six days of age, breast-fed babies can recognize the smell of their own mother's milk. Since babies are so sensitive to smells, parents should avoid exposing them to strong odors.

Motor Skills

Motor skills are abilities that depend on the controlled use of muscles. **Large motor skills** (sometimes called *gross motor skills*) involve the muscles of the back, legs, shoulders, or arms. Crawling is an example. **Small motor skills** (or *fine motor skills*) involve

THE DEVELOPING BRAIN

Infants are not born with depth perception. Their vision is two-dimensional, or flat, rather than three-dimensional. During the first month of life, certain neurons in the brain are assigned to one eye or the other. This enables them to maintain two slightly different images of an object. The brain processes and integrates these two images into one three-dimensional image. This makes it possible to perceive distance and depth.

the muscles of the fingers, wrists, or ankles. Drinking from a cup, for example, is a small motor skill.

Motor control follows a specific sequence, based on the increasing strength of a baby's muscles. It starts with head and trunk control, which enables babies to lift their heads. A newborn's head is wobbly, but a six-month-old controls the head very well.

Most infants are able to roll over completely by the age of six months. The feat may startle them the first time! After that, they are able to pull themselves into an upright sitting position. Crawling, standing, climbing, and walking soon follow.

As with large motor skills, small motor skills develop in sequence. Infants progress from batting at objects with their hands to being able to grasp a rattle or block. Later they master the **pincer grasp**—the ability to take hold of small objects between thumb and forefinger.

Fig. 13-4 on the next page summarizes some of the milestones of physical development. Keep in mind that because no baby is completely typical, the ages at which milestones are reached vary in real life.

Motor Skills Development in Infants

Approximate Age	Large Motor Skills	Small Motor Skills
3–4 months	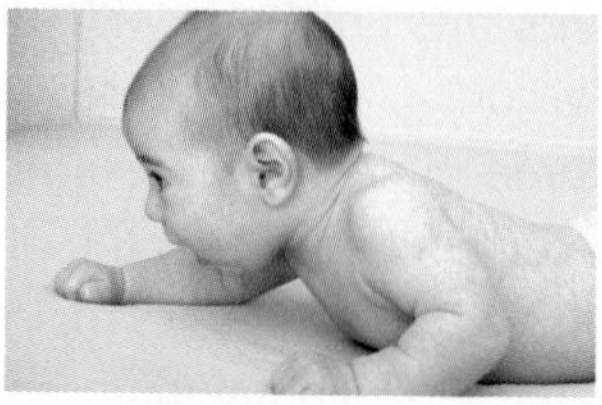 ❏ Lifts head and chest when lying on stomach ❏ Rolls over from stomach to back	❏ Swipes at objects ❏ Shakes rattle
5–6 months	 ❏ Rocks on stomach while kicking legs and waving arms ❏ Sits with support	❏ Reaches out and grabs objects ❏ Puts objects to mouth with hand
7–8 months	 ❏ Stands with assistance ❏ May begin creeping on belly	❏ Transfers objects from one hand to the other ❏ Bangs blocks together
9–10 months	 ❏ Sits unaided ❏ Crawls well ❏ Pulls up to a standing position	❏ Puts objects in containers ❏ Points with index finger
11–12 months	 ❏ Side-steps holding on to furniture ❏ Stands unaided ❏ May take a few steps	❏ Grasps with thumb and forefinger (pincer grasp) ❏ Holds a cup and drinks from it

Fig. 13 4. These milestones show how a typical baby's physical development progresses during infancy. Remember, however, that each baby develops at an individual rate.

Tooth Development

While a baby is developing in the mother's uterus, the first set of teeth is forming under the gums. Typically, they break through the gums when the baby is about six to ten months old. However, some babies get their first tooth at three months; others at one year old. Teeth usually emerge in pairs. In general, the lower front teeth appear first, followed by the upper front teeth.

The first set of teeth, called the baby teeth, are not permanent. They will fall out later to accommodate the larger, permanent teeth.

Most babies experience *teething pain* as their teeth erupt. They may be cranky and even run a fever. The baby's doctor can give advice on how to help alleviate the discomfort. See Fig. 13-5.

Intellectual Development

Intellectual development has to do with the ability to think, understand, learn, remember, develop language, and solve problems. Experts have learned that infancy is a critical time for this development.

Brain Development in Infancy

A newborn is truly a work in progress. At birth, the brain performs only physical maintenance tasks, such as regulating heartbeat and controlling reflexes. The areas of the brain that perform high-level thought processes aren't yet developed.

As you learned in Chapter 4, newborns have about 100 billion *neurons* (NER-onz), or brain cells, but few of them are organized and connected at birth. Researchers have learned that in order to build brain connections, sensory stimulation is required. When brain cells are stimulated by experiences, they "talk" to one another through *synapses* (suh-NAP-seez)— communication connections between neurons. As an infant's brain processes the flood of information from the senses, new connections form and existing ones are strengthened. Connections that are not reinforced eventually disappear. This is why infants deprived of stimulation don't progress the way they otherwise might.

How Infants Learn

In response to sensory stimulation, infants begin to organize the information they receive. Their minds and bodies work together. For example, they look in the direction of a sound they find interesting. They watch objects and form ideas about their shape and size over time. Within a few months of birth, research has shown that infants can group objects into simple categories, such as round or flat. They become curious about new objects that feel different or make sounds they haven't heard before. See Fig. 13-6.

A baby's sensory and motor experiences enable the baby to "fine tune" brain responses to outside stimulation. For instance, babies rely on their keen sense of smell to recognize their mothers. If they detect similar smells, they will associate those odors with their mothers. Stimulation from parents and care-givers helps babies make such associations and develop their thinking skills.

Everyday activities help infants learn by trial and error. For example, almost all babies enjoy playing the "drop food on the floor" game. By dropping their bottle or other objects and watching others repeatedly pick them up, infants learn about the appearance, disappearance, and reappearance of objects. They also have an early lesson about gravity!

Development of Memory

A baby's ability to remember things is a sign of intellectual development. Researchers now believe that even three-day-old babies remember recurring events. They rely on their senses of vision, hearing, smell, taste, and touch to recognize their parents.

As early as eight weeks, some babies show they expect their feedings at certain times. Some six-month-old babies can recognize an object by seeing only a part of it. By about eight months, infants can imitate behavior they saw the previous day.

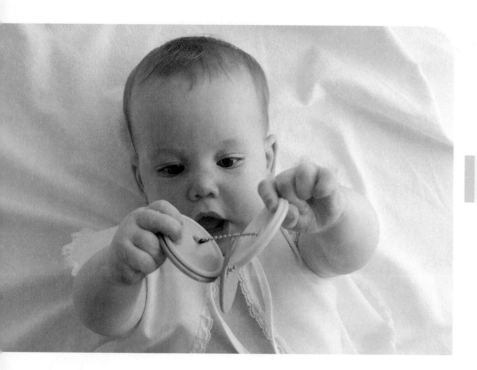

Fig. 13–6. Infants learn by using their bodies and senses. **What might this baby be learning?**

Piaget's Sensorimotor Period

Swiss psychologist Jean Piaget developed an influential theory of intellectual development. He observed that infants, children, and adults use different thought processes to learn. Piaget categorized children's intellectual development into four periods, each more advanced than the one before. Because development is gradual, the end of one period may overlap with the beginning of the next.

Piaget called the first major period of intellectual development the **sensorimotor period**, lasting from birth to about age two. During this time, infants and toddlers use their senses and movement to explore and learn about their surroundings. See Fig. 13-7.

Piaget further divided the sensorimotor period into six stages. The first four stages typically occur during infancy. As you read about each stage, think about how it corresponds to the infant's physical development at that age.

- **Stage 1: Birth to one month.** Reflexes are the primary means through which the newborn learns about the world. Through the palmar grasp reflex, for example, babies learn about the textures of objects, but only those objects that happen to touch their hands.
- **Stage 2: One to four months.** Through greater use of their senses, babies begin to sort out their environments. They start to make simple, yet deliberate actions.
- **Stage 3: Four to eight months.** Babies start to use and manipulate objects. These actions, combined with use of the senses, allow babies to begin learning about cause and effect. For instance, they might discover that pushing a button on a toy means that they will hear a certain noise.
- **Stage 4: Eight to twelve months.** The ability to combine actions allows babies to act more purposefully. Advanced motor skills

Fig. 13-7. In the sensorimotor period, babies learn by exploring their surroundings. **Why is "sensorimotor" an appropriate name for this period of development?**

allow them to explore, and they become more aware of the outside world.

In Chapter 17, you'll read about the last two stages of the sensorimotor period. You will also learn about the three other periods of intellectual development that Piaget identified.

Object Permanence

During the sensorimotor period, infants develop an understanding of **object permanence**, the concept that objects continue to exist even when they are out of sight. This understanding typically develops between six and nine months of age.

Six-month-old Chandra was happily playing with a stuffed bear. When her father covered the bear with a blanket, Chandra stared at the blanket for a moment, then turned and picked up another toy. To her, the bear no longer existed because she could not see it. A few months later, when Chandra and her father were playing with the same bear, he again covered it with a blanket. This time Chandra quickly looked under the blanket and found the bear. Her actions showed that she knew the bear still existed, whether she could see it or not.

Object permanence applies to people, too. At around nine months, infants are able to keep people in mind when they are out of sight. Babies begin to understand that, when their parents are not immediately visible, they can cry to get their needs met because their parents may be nearby.

Language Development

The ability to understand language and produce speech is one of the most impressive skills that human beings possess. Many language researchers believe that the human brain is preconfigured to learn language. In other words, the structure of language is built in. Researchers believe this because babies from around the world acquire language similarly.

During the first two months of life, a baby's vocal tract is still developing. Infants this age cry, grunt, and sigh. Between two and five months, they add coos and laughs. Babbling begins between seven and eight months. Babies the world over make the same babbling sounds, such as *ba-ba-ba* and *dee-dee-dee*. Babbling is a baby's way of mastering the sounds of language.

Babies copy the sounds, speech patterns, accents, and words they hear. Responding to their sounds and reading to babies promotes their language development. See Fig. 13-8.

Fig. 13-8. Looking at pictures while hearing the sounds of words helps infants learn what the words mean. **What are some other ways in which infants might benefit from being read to?**

Emotional Development

Children and teens may feel love, joy, anger, jealousy, and fear—all in the course of an afternoon. Newborns don't possess such a wide range of emotions. They alternate between two basic emotional states: contentment and distress. Over the first year, the infant's emotions become more varied and distinct, eventually including such feelings as delight, elation, affection, anger, disgust, and fear.

The ability to feel emotions is inborn, but not the ability to recognize those emotions and identify their source. Infants acquire these abilities as they interact with important people in their world and as their brains develop. They learn to link emotions to specific sensations, such as hunger, or circumstances, such as attention from their parents.

At about nine months, most babies can recognize situations that they interpret as threatening. They usually begin to fear unfamiliar people, a stage called **stranger anxiety**, between six and ten months of age.

Key Tasks of Emotional Development

Physical and intellectual development are marked by the development of certain key skills, such as crawling or babbling. Later development builds on these skills. Similarly, healthy emotional development is marked by progress in certain key areas. These developmental tasks are the foundation of emotional development throughout life. They include:

- **Forming attachments.** Between three and six months of age, infants begin to recognize and trust their caregivers. Babies become excited when their caregiver appears and show distress when the person leaves. This is called **attachment behavior**. Attachment

Fig. 13-9. A child's relationship with a trustworthy and caring adult is a foundation of emotional and social development.

is key to emotional and social development. Babies who form strong attachments are better able to handle their emotions, create and maintain relationships, and cope with stress. Research has shown that confident children had a firm attachment to a caring person during infancy. Therefore, infants need at least one caring person who meets their needs during the first year. See Fig. 13-9.

- **Learning to give and receive affection.** Parents who give their babies ample affection are educating their children about giving and receiving love. This enables children to form strong attachments as they grow and mature.
- **Developing self-esteem.** Children need to develop **self-esteem**—positive feelings about themselves. A healthy sense of self-worth gives them confidence to try new things. Parents can foster self-esteem by hugging and cuddling their infants and meeting their needs. When parents respond promptly to their baby's cry, babies learn that their needs will be met. This responsiveness confirms that they are important. Consistent reinforcement will help ensure that the child's sense of self-worth continues through life.

Temperament

Although infants follow a general pattern of emotional development, they can seem quite different in their emotional makeup. That is because all babies have their own individual **temperament**, or general way of reacting to the world around them. See Fig. 13-10.

- Some babies seem especially sensitive to changes in their environment. They tend to be easily upset and may be difficult to soothe.
- Other babies might be called placid or easygoing. They seem to take change in stride with a minimum of fuss. Relatives might comment on how "good-natured" they are.

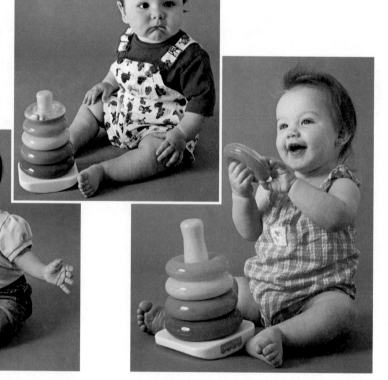

Fig. 13-10. Even when exposed to the same toy, these infants all react differently. **How would you describe the temperament of each baby?**

Fig. 13-11. Social development is strengthened as parents interact and play with their infants.

- Some babies tend to be cautious or passive. They may withdraw from new situations and often prefer to watch rather than participate.
- Still other babies respond eagerly to new people or events. They love activity and may seem strong-willed at times. They might be termed active or aggressive.

These are not the only possible variations in temperament, so not all babies will fit neatly into these categories. Remember, too, that no baby is always happy or always crying. Even a normally placid baby can become upset or withdrawn under certain circumstances. Over time, however, temperament can be observed as a general pattern of the baby's reactions.

When interacting with an infant, parents and other caregivers may have to make adjustments based on the baby's temperament. For example, at his sister's birthday party, Chase's parents allow him to watch from the sidelines rather than seating him alongside the unfamiliar five-year-old guests. They recognize that he is more sensitive and cautious than his siblings were as babies.

Parents may also have to think about whether their own temperament is markedly different from their child's. For instance, active parents might have to relax and slow the pace for a baby with a passive temperament. The most important thing is to nurture and give loving attention to the baby, no matter what his or her temperament is like.

Social Development

Close physical contact with a child—through holding, bathing, cuddling, and playing—aids the development of many skills. One of the most important is social development—learning to relate to other people.

As they begin to smile around the age of six weeks and then begin to laugh, babies quickly become social beings. Well before they are six months old, babies recognize their parents and show pleasure at their appearance. By nine months, many babies enjoy waving goodbye. Parents reinforce their baby's developing social skills by smiling, making eye contact, talking to the baby, picking the baby up, and playing games such as peek-a-boo. See Fig. 13-11.

Maintaining a pleasant environment at home aids a baby's social and emotional development. Babies are sensitive to other people's moods and can easily pick up on tension.

Siblings as well as parents can help a baby's social development. Babies enjoy contact with siblings and other children because they are fascinated by the speech and actions of people closer to their own age and size than adults. Encouraging siblings to play together can help them to develop lifelong ties and social skills.

Moral Development

Some researchers believe that moral development—the process by which children learn to distinguish right from wrong—actually begins in infancy. It starts as an outgrowth of social development. Babies eventually learn that social interaction includes rules that are gently reinforced by parents and caregivers. While babies should not be expected to share their toys or to know right from wrong, they can understand the concept of "no." For example, eleven-month-old Adrian is learning that she should not hit the family cat. Her parents put the pet in another room and explained in a sad tone of voice that it hurts the kitty when she pats her too hard. You will read more about moral development in Chapter 22.

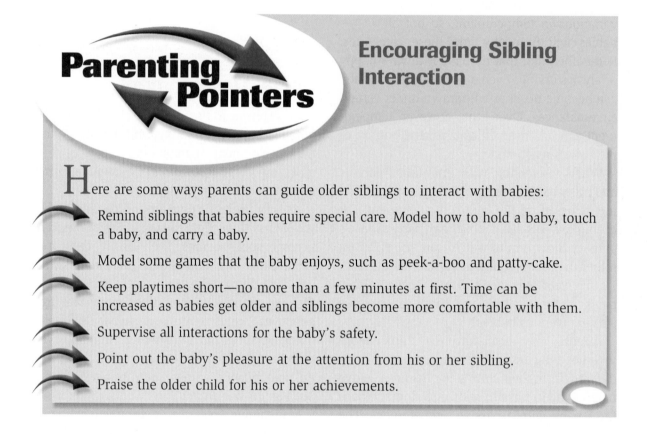

Parenting Pointers

Encouraging Sibling Interaction

Here are some ways parents can guide older siblings to interact with babies:

- Remind siblings that babies require special care. Model how to hold a baby, touch a baby, and carry a baby.
- Model some games that the baby enjoys, such as peek-a-boo and patty-cake.
- Keep playtimes short—no more than a few minutes at first. Time can be increased as babies get older and siblings become more comfortable with them.
- Supervise all interactions for the baby's safety.
- Point out the baby's pleasure at the attention from his or her sibling.
- Praise the older child for his or her achievements.

Child & Family Services
CAREERS

▸ Neonatal Nurse

Neonatal nurses care for critically ill infants in the neonatal intensive care unit (NICU) of a hospital. The tiny patients may be premature, have a birth defect, or have a critical medical condition, such as withdrawal from their mother's drug addiction. Neonatal nurses assess the infant's condition, provide hands-on care, and evaluate different treatment options. They work under the direct supervision of *neonatologists*, doctors who specialize in the care of critically ill infants during their first ten days of life.

Neonatal nurses must earn a bachelor's degree in nursing or science. Most NICUs also require neonatal nurses to obtain state or national certification. Knowledge of medications and the latest treatments for critically ill infants is essential, as is the ability to maintain accurate medical records.

"As a neonatal nurse, I must be able to clearly communicate medical information, not only to my professional colleagues but to the infants' parents. I also have to react calmly and effectively in emergencies.

"Working with seriously ill infants can be emotionally and physically draining. However, the work also provides enormous emotional rewards when the babies go home with their families."

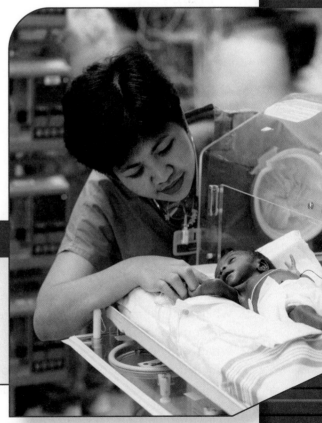

CAREER TIPS

- Take high school classes in biology, parenting, and child development.
- Volunteer at a hospital.
- Obtain a college degree in nursing and the required certification.
- Be prepared to relocate if necessary.

CHAPTER SUMMARY

- Although infants develop at varying paces, their progress can be evaluated by considering typical physical and behavioral characteristics.
- Many aspects of an infant's physical growth and development, including reflexes, motor control, and tooth development, follow a specific sequence.
- Infants learn through vision, hearing, touch, taste, and smell.
- Attachment is important for an infant's healthy emotional and social development.
- Adjusting to the temperament of an infant benefits both parents and baby.
- Infants do not understand the difference between right and wrong.

Check Your Facts

1. What is the difference between growth and development?
2. How does an infant change in growth and proportions during the first year?
3. What is the purpose of the fontanels?
4. Choose four reflexes a newborn has at birth. Tell how each reflex is stimulated and how the baby reacts.
5. Summarize how each of the five senses develops in an infant.
6. Distinguish between large and small motor skills.
7. What is the pincer grasp?
8. Why is sensory stimulation important for infants?
9. What occurs during each stage of Piaget's sensorimotor period?
10. What is object permanence?
11. Why is it important for babies to babble?
12. What is stranger anxiety and when does it usually develop?
13. How do you instill a sense of self-worth in an infant?
14. Describe four basic temperaments of babies.
15. What are two signs that an infant is developing socially?

Think Critically

1. **Drawing Conclusions.** Baby Samantha babbles and laughs. She screams when she is angry. She can sit up by herself but hasn't started to crawl. How old do you think she is? Why?
2. **Analyzing Behavior.** A ten-month-old baby pulled up to a low table and knocked over a vase, which broke. The parent reacted angrily. Whose fault was it that the vase broke? Under the circumstances, what should the adult reaction have been? What might have prevented this situation? What role does safety play here?

Apply Your Learning

1. **Clip and Comment.** Cut a picture of a baby from a magazine and mount it on paper. Add labels that point out signs of the baby's physical development. Show your picture to the class and give an age estimate. Do classmates agree? What other developmental characteristics would the baby likely have?

2. **Brain Building.** Interaction with an infant is critical for brain development. Make a list of specific ways to interact with an infant through talking and playing: for example, singing a lullaby and making silly faces. Combine lists in class to create a master list of ideas.

3. **Infant Observation.** Find an opportunity to observe an infant. Document signs of the baby's development in these areas: physical, intellectual, emotional, and social. Summarize your observations in a chart, including the baby's age.

Cross-Curricular Connections

1. **Math.** At birth, Julia weighed 6 pounds and was 18 inches long. Research typical weight and height gains during a baby's first year. Based on your research, predict the baby's weight and length at 3 months, 6 months, 9 months, and 12 months.

2. **Language Arts.** When a five-month-old cried, one parent picked the baby up right away. The other parent said, "You're going to spoil that child." Write a response from the first parent that explains why such action is not spoiling. Compare responses in class.

Family & Community Connections

1. **Remembering Infancy.** Interview a family member who knew you as an infant. Ask about milestones in your physical, intellectual, emotional, social, and moral development. Record specific anecdotes in a journal.

2. **Music and Brain Development.** Studies show that music and rhythm have a positive impact on brain development. Find and read several articles that discuss this topic. Then volunteer with a team of students to provide musical stimulation to infants in a child care center. You might find appropriate songs to sing, play instruments, or hold infants while you move to recorded music.

CHAPTER 14

Caring for Infants

CHAPTER OBJECTIVES

- Explain how to respond to a baby's cues.
- Describe food and feeding methods during infancy.
- Demonstrate care skills related to feeding, diapering, clothing, and bathing an infant.
- Explain how to keep infants safe and to protect them from illness and disease.
- Summarize signs that indicate an infant needs medical attention.
- Demonstrate ways to interact with an infant in order to promote development.

PARENTING TERMS

- colic
- demand feeding
- colostrum
- infant formula
- weaning
- puréed
- diaper rash
- cradle cap
- sudden infant death syndrome (SIDS)
- immunizations
- vaccines

What do infants need most? Enough to keep parents busy around the clock! Nourishment, warmth, comfort, clean diapers, dry clothing, a safe place to sleep, and regular check-ups are high on the list of musts. Most first-time parents realize they have a lot to learn. Just physically caring for a newborn takes a variety of skills. In the words of one first-time father, "Baby gifts are nice, but what we really need is an owner's manual!"

Handling an Infant

Newborns are fragile. They must be handled gently and carefully. One primary concern is that the baby's head and neck be supported. A newborn's neck muscles are weak, and the head is relatively large in proportion to the body. When picking up and holding a new baby, support the child's head and neck with the palm of your hand or with your inner forearm. See Fig. 14-1.

Most babies love to be held and handled. In fact, their hunger for touch is nearly as strong as their hunger for food. Newborns will react to touch by moving their arms and legs, turning their head, and making sounds.

While it may seem that newborns can do little more than wiggle, at times they can move surprising distances just by wiggling. That is why caregivers must never leave them alone even briefly on an elevated surface, such as a changing table or a crib with the side rail down. Similarly, putting a baby on a regular bed to sleep is not safe. If a young baby does fall, seek medical help.

Responding to an Infant's Cues

Infants often give cues that signal their needs and wants. Learning to recognize their baby's cues enables parents to respond to meet the baby's needs.

Crying and Comforting

Babies and crying seem to go together. Crying is one of the few ways newborns can communicate their needs. They may also thrash, fuss, and eventually get red in the face. For new parents, it can be difficult at first to figure out what different cries mean.

Hunger is the most frequent reason for crying. Parents usually get the message loud and clear! Babies also cry or fuss when their diapers need changing, when they feel pain from indigestion, and when they are feeling tired or lonely. The Parenting Pointers feature on the next page suggests ways to comfort a crying baby.

Fig. 14-1. A newborn is not yet strong enough to hold up its own head. **How does handling a baby safely change as the baby grows?**

How To Comfort a Crying Baby

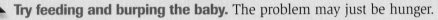

When a baby is tired but continues to cry instead of falling asleep, parents can try several strategies to soothe and quiet the baby.

Try feeding and burping the baby. The problem may just be hunger.

Check the diaper. A new diaper may be needed sooner than expected.

Check clothing. An article of clothing may need adjustment.

Swaddle the baby. *Swaddling*, or snuggly wrapping the baby in a blanket, will keep the baby warm and secure.

Sing or play music. Listening to gentle music or hearing a parent's voice sing a lullaby can relax an infant.

Move with the baby. Walk and sway while holding the baby, or try putting the baby in a stroller for a walk. Some parents strap the baby in a car safety seat and take a short drive.

Crying for several hours at a stretch with no apparent cause, often at the same time every day, is known as **colic**. It usually gets worse in the evening. Colic is frustrating for parents but is not a serious medical condition. Some colicky babies respond to touch and motion. Parents might gently rub the baby's stomach or hold the baby while walking or rocking.

Sometimes parents who have ruled out all the obvious reasons for a baby's cries are completely stumped when their newborn continues to wail. Parents often feel helpless and frustrated, but it's a common experience. If there are no signs of pain or illness, simply holding and trying to soothe the baby is usually the best course of action. Dealing with frequent or prolonged crying requires patience and the ability to stay calm.

Interaction Cues

In addition to signaling their discomfort, babies also signal when they are interested in a person or object and want to interact. A baby's eyes widen and brighten as they focus on some attraction. Babies often stop what they have been doing to focus on the stimulus. They may even stop sucking as they try to locate the source of the sound or track a face or object as it moves. Babies may turn toward the person or thing they are interested in. Parents should respond to these cues and interact with the baby by talking and cuddling.

Parents can also learn to recognize cues that the baby has had enough play and interaction for awhile. Babies who are overstimulated may turn away, avoid eye contact, or close their eyes. They may tense up or become irritable. They may try to comfort themselves by putting their fingers or fists in their mouth.

A baby who seems tense or irritable can often be soothed by rubbing his or her back and speaking softly. A baby who is calming down often stops fussing, nestles in a parent's arm, and may even sigh with content.

Feeding an Infant

Frequent feeding is needed for newborns to grow and thrive. A newborn's tiny stomach holds only about two to three ounces of liquid. That is why newborns "ask" to be fed every one to four hours. An infant who falls asleep full and contented usually wakes in a few hours, crying with hunger.

Most authorities recommend **demand feeding**, which means feeding infants whenever they are hungry rather than keeping a fixed schedule. This helps keep babies from being hungry and uncomfortable.

A newborn's "hunger clock" may be irregular and unpredictable at first, but feedings soon become more regular and less frequent. By age seven months, most babies need three to five feedings of solid food a day.

Breast-Feeding

Many new mothers decide to breast-feed their babies. Breast-feeding is usually begun shortly after birth and, at first, may be needed ten to twelve times each day. The first breast milk, called **colostrum**, is high in the calories and the types of protein and fat a newborn needs. It also provides some protection from illnesses. See Fig. 14-2.

Parents can learn more about breast-feeding by attending birth and parenting classes. Lactation consultants are often available to assist new moms with breast-feeding soon after the baby is born. Experienced friends and the La Leche League, an organization that promotes breast-feeding, can offer advice as well.

A nursing mother should eat nutritious foods and drink plenty of fluids. Some babies are sensitive to foods that the mother eats because some flavors and substances are passed to the baby through breast milk. Nursing mothers may find

Fig. 14-2. Breast-feeding provides a newborn with perfect nutrition. **What other infant needs are satisfied while mothers feed their babies?**

Fig. 14-3. Any family member or caregiver can bottle-feed a baby. **How else can fathers and other family members be included in feeding and infant care?**

they need to avoid eating chocolate, spicy foods, and strong-flavored vegetables. A baby may be sensitive or allergic to some foods, such as milk products, vitamins, or food additives.

At first a new mother who breast-feeds may experience some physical discomfort, such as soreness around the nipple. The feeling usually disappears within a few weeks. Warm showers may help in the meantime.

Bottle-Feeding

Many parents decide to bottle-feed their babies or to use bottle-feeding when breast-feeding is not convenient. A bottle-fed newborn is likely to eat every three or four hours. As with breast-feeding, the baby needs the physical contact of being held close during feeding. See Fig. 14-3.

For bottle-feeding, a pediatrician usually recommends a specific **infant formula**, a commercially prepared mixture of milk or milk substitute, water, and added nutrients. Formula is available as a ready-to-use liquid or as a liquid concentrate or powder, which must be mixed with water before being fed to the baby. Some formulas have added nutrients to make them more like breast milk. Parents can discuss the use of such formulas with their doctor or other health care provider.

Formula must be prepared exactly according to directions. Bottles, nipples, and other equipment must be washed thoroughly in hot, soapy water and rinsed several times in hot water. Items are sterilized by applying high temperature, usually by boiling in water, to kill germs that cause illness. A dishwasher with very hot water may also be used. A health care professional can advise parents on how to sterilize feeding equipment.

Prepared formula should be kept refrigerated and used within two days. To warm for feeding, the bottle should be placed in a pan of hot tap water until the formula is warm. A drop or two of formula on the inside of the caregiver's wrist should feel pleasantly warm. Don't heat a bottle in a microwave oven, because it can heat unevenly. Even though the formula may feel just right when it is tested, hot spots could burn the baby's mouth and throat.

A newborn may consume up to three ounces of formula at one feeding. To meet the infant's demands and increasing nutritional needs, the amount is gradually increased to six to eight ounces during the first year of life. Physicians advise against giving juice to babies under six months old. Older babies should be given 100 percent juice, rather than juice drinks.

Experts caution parents not to put babies to bed with a bottle. Using the bottle as a pacifier can cause a variety of problems:

- Formula or juice can pool in the mouth while the baby sleeps, causing serious tooth decay.
- Ear infection could result from liquid dripping into the back of the throat and entering the tube between the throat and ears.
- If the baby is allowed to suck on an empty bottle, air bubbles can form in the abdomen and cause discomfort.
- An association between food and anxiety relief can lead to eating problems later in life.

Burping Techniques

Babies often swallow air while drinking. If it isn't released, the trapped air causes discomfort. Breast-fed babies should be burped about every five minutes during feeding. Burp a bottle-fed baby after two ounces of formula have been consumed.

To burp a baby, hold the baby against your shoulder, face down across your lap, or in a sitting position on your lap. Place a clean towel where it can catch any expelled milk. Gently pat or rub the baby's lower back until the air is expelled. See Fig. 14-4.

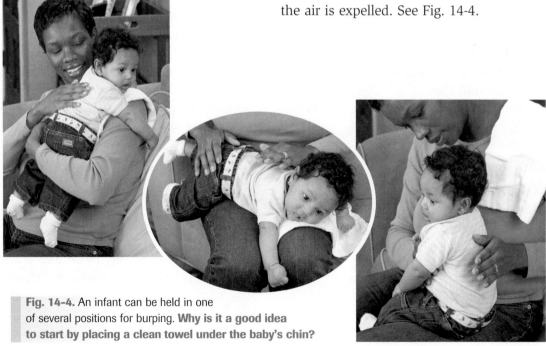

Fig. 14-4. An infant can be held in one of several positions for burping. **Why is it a good idea to start by placing a clean towel under the baby's chin?**

Fig. 14-5. Swallowing solid food is a skill that takes practice. **How can a parent or caregiver help babies make the transition to eating solid foods?**

Spitting Up

Most babies spit up at times, usually right after eating or when they are burped. It doesn't mean that they are sick. It may be that they swallow too much at one time or eat too fast. Sometimes a baby spits up because of an allergy or sensitivity to a food, medication, or vitamin supplement. Spitting up is most common in formula-fed babies, but breast-fed babies can spit up too. It is usually harmless and painless for babies, and they usually outgrow it after four to six months. When should the doctor be consulted? Discuss the issue if the baby spits up after every feeding or if there is a more serious problem, such as weight loss.

Weaning

Replacing bottle-feeding or breast-feeding with drinking from a cup is called **weaning**. Infants may begin to show less interest in bottle-feeding or breast-feeding around nine to twelve months. Experts recommend that babies give up bottle-feeding entirely by about twelve months.

To begin weaning, the child can be given formula or juice from a cup, slowly decreasing bottle-feeding or breast-feeding over time while increasing the amount of cup feeding. First try holding the cup so the baby can practice sipping. Eventually, let the baby hold the cup. Special covered cups with handles and spouts reduce spills. A pediatrician or other health care provider can give parents specific advice about weaning.

Introducing Solid Foods

A baby's first experience with solid food often follows this pattern: An eager parent puts a small spoonful of food in the hungry baby's mouth and the baby pushes the food right back out. The action of swallowing solid food is a new skill that takes practice for babies to master. Once they learn to enjoy solid food, babies will open their mouths wide at feeding time, until they feel full. They eat more some days than others. Most babies instinctively know when they have had enough to eat. Closing the mouth and turning away is a sign that the baby is full. See Fig. 14-5.

When introducing solid foods, experts have several recommendations:

- **Don't rush solid foods.** Most doctors advise feeding a baby only breast milk or formula for the first four to six months.

Both are easy to digest and nutritionally complete. They give babies all the nutrients and calories they need for those first months.

- **Introduce foods gradually.** New foods should be introduced one at a time, three to five days apart. That way, parents can identify any food that causes a reaction such as a rash, stomach pain, vomiting, or diarrhea.
- **Start with cereal.** Most parents start with iron-fortified, single-grain cereals, beginning with rice cereal. Strained yellow vegetables such as sweet potatoes and carrots can then be introduced. Simple strained fruits (apples, bananas, peaches, and pears) come next; then green vegetables, other fruits and vegetables, strained meats, and vegetable-meat combinations.
- **Choose nutritious foods.** A healthful diet is important. The most nutritious foods are those with the fewest added ingredients. Plain pears, for example, are a better choice than pears in heavy syrup.
- **Be patient.** Starting a baby on solid food takes patience. The baby may need time to adjust to the new experience. There is a wide variety of baby foods from which to choose. Some babies develop definite likes and dislikes. Others refuse a new food several times before deciding to accept it.

Commercial Baby Foods. Many parents like the ease of using commercially prepared baby foods. They are labeled according to the stage of the child for whom they are designed, such as "infant" or "toddler." Foods for young babies are blended into a smooth consistency for easier swallowing. Those made for older babies have more texture. If you have tasted baby food, you know that it tastes bland. That's because it lacks additives such as salt.

Homemade Baby Foods. Some parents prefer to make baby food at home. By doing so, they can control the ingredients in the food and usually save money.

An easy way to make baby food is to steam fresh fruits and vegetables by cooking them over boiling water in a steamer basket until they are soft. Parents can also simmer chicken or beef in a little water or broth until it is tender. Then it can be mashed with a fork, food processor, or blender.

As with purchased baby food, begin feeding single foods in case the baby has a food allergy. Later, foods that the baby likes can be combined. For example, some babies find puréed chicken with sweet potatoes delicious. To make baby food from a meal prepared for the family, separate the baby's portion before adding spices or seasonings.

Food can be prepared ahead of time and frozen in small portions. An ice cube tray makes ideal portion sizes for babies and toddlers. Be sure to label and date each package before placing it in the freezer.

Table Foods. Babies like to join family meals. They may be offered tastes of certain soft foods from the table such as applesauce, pasta, and

THE DEVELOPING BRAIN

Brain growth is strongly affected by an infant's diet. For instance, iron is needed to maintain the production of oxygen-rich red blood cells, which in turn promote brain growth. Experts say that bottle-fed babies should receive formula that contains iron. Breast-fed infants should begin to receive iron-enriched foods, such as fortified infant cereals, when they are about six months old.

mashed potatoes. By about age one, they can eat many of the same foods as the rest of the family. Check with a doctor for advice on giving milk products, however.

Preventing Choking. Babies should be sitting up when they eat. Table food should always be thinned and **puréed**—blended into a smooth consistency—before being served to an infant who is starting solids. Once the baby is old enough to chew solid foods, large pieces such as grapes and hot dogs must be cut into small pieces to prevent choking. Bread needs to be broken into small pieces, too. Even soft bread can be a choking hazard because it absorbs saliva and could stick in the baby's throat. For safety's sake, parents should never leave the room while a baby is eating.

Learning to Self-Feed

Self-feeding usually begins around nine months of age. Babies are still developing their motor skills and coordination, so parents should not be surprised by messy eating habits. Also, at this age, food is for exploration as much as for eating.

Finger foods are best for first attempts at self-feeding. Small pieces of soft fruit, cooked vegetables, cheese, soft toast, and hard-cooked egg yolks are good starter foods. Cooked, crumbled meat can also be given. Raw vegetables or hard raw fruits should not be given because they might cause choking. See Fig. 14-6.

Diapering and Clothing Needs

Regular diaper changes keep a baby dry and comfortable. They help prevent **diaper rash**, a skin irritation caused by contact with stool or urine in the diaper, diaper material, or laundry products. Plan on changing a diaper after every bowel movement and whenever the diaper is obviously wet. A healthy newborn wets at least six to eight diapers a day.

Ten changes a day or more may be needed for the first month or two. All told, that can be about 4,700 diaper changes while a child is in diapers!

Changing a Diaper

You should not leave a baby unattended once you start the changing process, so gather all the supplies so they are within easy reach. These include:

- A changing pad or towel to lay the baby on while changing.
- Clean diapers.
- A bowl of lukewarm water and a baby washcloth, or pre-moistened disposable baby wipes.
- Medicated ointment, if necessary.

Place the baby on the changing pad or other clean surface. Some parents attach the baby to the table with the safety strap to reduce squirming. With or without a strap, parents should never step away from the baby.

Remove the dirty diaper and set it out of the baby's reach. To prevent skin irritation or a diaper rash, clean the diaper area before putting on a fresh diaper. This can be done with warm water and a soft cloth or packaged moist "wipes." Baby soap may be needed after a bowel movement. Pat the area dry with a cloth diaper or another washcloth, or let air dry briefly. If the baby has a diaper rash, apply a medicated ointment to the affected area.

If a newborn boy was circumcised, gently apply petroleum jelly to the area after each diaper change. It is normal for the site of the surgery to appear red and swollen for up to a week. The petroleum jelly prevents the scab that forms over the circumcision from sticking to the diaper.

Put a clean diaper on the baby, following the instructions learned in childbirth class or those printed on the diaper package. Fasten the diaper so it is snug, but not tight enough to pinch the baby's legs or abdomen. See Fig. 14-7.

After changing a diaper, clean the changing surface by wiping with a mild disinfectant solution or a baby wipe. A soiled cloth diaper should be rinsed in the toilet and then soaked with other diapers in a soapy solution in a covered

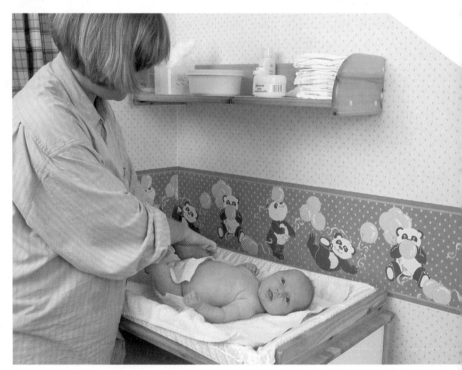

Fig. 14-7. Diaper changing keeps a baby comfortable and dry. As babies get older, squirming and wiggling may make diaper changes challenging. Be patient and keep your sense of humor.

diaper pail until they are laundered. Disposable diapers should be folded over, tightly re-taped, and tied in a plastic bag for disposal in a trash can. If you are visiting someone else's home, ask where you should put the wrapped diaper. Always wash your hands after changing a diaper.

Dressing an Infant

Have you seen a baby bundled up on a warm day? As a general rule, young babies need about one more layer of clothing than an adult at the same temperature. At first, newborns' circulatory systems aren't very efficient, and their hands and feet can quickly grow cold. Booties and a blanket can help them stay warm. No matter what clothes they are wearing, most newborns seem to find it comforting to be wrapped in a light blanket.

Babies need soft clothes because their skin is delicate. One-piece sleeper garments made of cotton knit are a good choice. They are comfortable, stretchy, and have a closed bottom or feet to keep the baby warm. They usually have a long front opening with a zipper or snaps, making it easier to change clothes.

It's easiest to dress babies while they are lying down—for example, after a diaper change. Gather everything you need so you don't have to stop to search for a missing undershirt or sock. If the air is chilly, it's a good idea to keep a blanket handy to drape over the baby.

Sleepers with feet are put on feet first. The garment is then slipped up over the baby's back. Next, guide the baby's arms through the sleeves of the sleeper. Then snap or button the sleeper's leg and front openings. See Fig. 14-8.

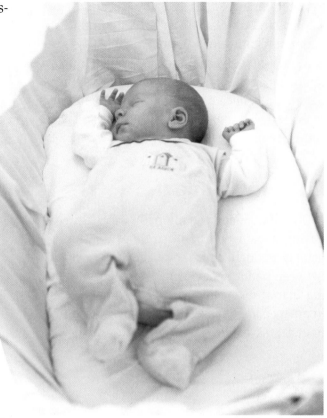

Fig. 14-8. Babies do not need shoes until they are old enough to stand up. **Why do many infant clothes and sleepers completely cover the feet?**

To put on a shirt or gown, gather the shirt from top to bottom and hold the neck open with two hands. Some have shoulder snaps to make the neck opening larger. First, put the shirt over the back of the baby's head. Then stretch the shirt over the head, being careful not to scratch the baby's face. Next, gather each sleeve and guide the baby's arms through, one at a time, taking care not to bend the baby's fingers. Finally, pull the shirt or gown downward to its full length and fasten any snaps or other closures.

Watch for signs that the baby has outgrown a garment. Babies will not be comfortable or happy in clothes that are too small.

Adjust the baby's temperature by adding or removing clothing. Depending on the weather, parents may decide to dress their baby in two or more layers of clothing. That way, a layer can be removed as the air becomes warmer.

Bathing an Infant

Do babies need a daily bath? Not really—having a bath two or three times a week is usually enough until they begin to crawl. In between baths, spot cleanups are needed during diaper changes and after feeding. As an infant becomes more active, daily bathing is fine as long as the skin doesn't become dry.

Giving a Sponge Bath

Newborns should not be given tub baths until the stump of the umbilical cord has fallen off and the navel heals, usually within three weeks of birth. Until that happens, it's sufficient to simply wipe the baby's head, face, hands, and diaper area with a clean, damp washcloth. This is sometimes called a *sponge bath*. See Fig. 14-9.

Giving a Tub Bath

To give a baby a tub bath, you'll need a small, plastic baby tub. There are many inexpensive tubs that are shaped to fit a baby's body and facilitate bathing. Place the tub on a table or counter top at a comfortable height, in a warm, draft-free place. The regular bathtub should not be used until the infant can sit up unaided.

Fig. 14-9. Sponge baths are the best way to clean a newborn. **When can a baby begin having tub baths?**

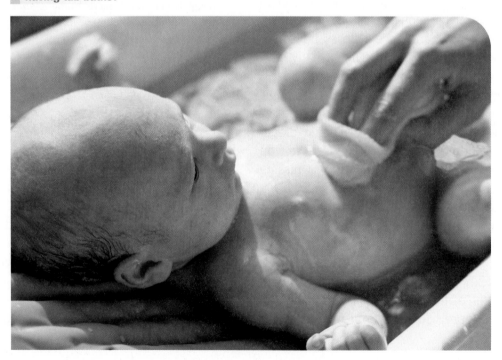

Bath Time Safety

Most babies love bath time, but slippery soap and hot water are hazards. Take these precautions so bath time is safe:

- Make sure electrical outlets and appliances are out of reach and out of splashing and spilling range.
- Put all needed items where you can reach them but the baby can't.
- Put only about two or three inches of water in the tub.
- Water should be warm, but never hot. If using a regular bathtub, make sure the faucet does not feel hot.

- With a baby too young to sit up, keep one arm around the baby at all times.
- Never leave the room or even turn away. Ignore the phone and doorbell or take the baby with you. It takes only a second for a baby to slip under the water.

Never leave a baby unattended in a tub, where drowning is always a danger. To avoid this, assemble the bath supplies—mild soap, baby shampoo, bath toys, washcloth, and towel—before you begin. Place them close enough that you can reach them with one hand while holding the baby with the other.

Put a few inches of lukewarm water in the tub. Check the water temperature with the inside of your elbow—it must not be too hot.

Until the baby is old enough sit up independently, you will need to hold the baby with one arm and hand during the bath. With your arm wrapped around the baby's shoulders, support the neck and head with your forearm and hold the baby's arm with your hand. Your other hand is free to bathe the baby.

Use a soft washcloth to wash the baby's face with warm water (no soap). Then soap and rinse the rest of the body. Rinse by continually pouring cupfuls of warm water so the baby doesn't get cold.

Once or twice a week, shampoo the scalp, rinsing well without letting water splash onto the baby's face. If soap or shampoo gets in the baby's eyes, use a washcloth and lukewarm water to rinse it away.

Finally, wrap the baby in a soft towel and gently pat the skin dry. A hooded towel can help keep the baby from getting chilled.

If the baby's skin is drying out too much, apply a small amount of unscented baby lotion after the bath. Some infants develop **cradle cap**, an oily, yellowish, patchy scalp condition. If it occurs, massage a little mineral oil onto the scalp before shampooing. If cradle cap worsens or becomes infected, parents should consult a pediatrician.

Sleeping Needs

Babies require plenty of sleep to fuel their rapid growth. Most newborns sleep 16 to 20 hours a day for the first month. They are likely to wake every two to four hours for feedings and diaper changes.

Newborns are able to fall asleep and stay asleep regardless of what's going on around them. They alternate periods of deep sleep with periods of restlessness that can occur as often as once an hour. During the restless periods, the newborn will twitch, wiggle, and make sounds. Left alone, the infant will most likely fall back into a deeper sleep.

Newborns meet their need for sleep during both daylight and nighttime hours. The result is that new parents typically get little undisturbed sleep. "She seems to have her days and nights mixed up," is a common lament of parents of newborns.

Fortunately, this is not a permanent sleep pattern. After the first month, babies tend to sleep more at night and less during daylight hours. Most babies begin to sleep through the night by about three months of age. By the fifth month, the average baby sleeps a total of about 14½ hours out of every 24, including three or four hour-long naps during the day. During the following six months, the pattern usually changes to one nap in the morning and one in the afternoon. After the first year, a single daytime nap is typical.

Putting Baby to Bed

Babies often fall asleep in an adult's arms. They may doze off after being fed or calmed by a parent. Once asleep, babies can be placed in a crib or bassinet. The trick is to not wake or startle the baby. Carefully lower the sleeping baby into the crib, face up. Then, gently slide your hands out from under the baby and stand up. Stay nearby for a moment. If the baby starts to wake, give comfort with a soft touch or pat. See Fig. 14-10.

Fig. 14-10. The safest way for a baby to sleep is on its back. **What other baby safety tips have you learned?**

Fig. 14-11. Between routine checkups, parents can keep a list of questions they have for the health care provider. **What are some questions parents might have?**

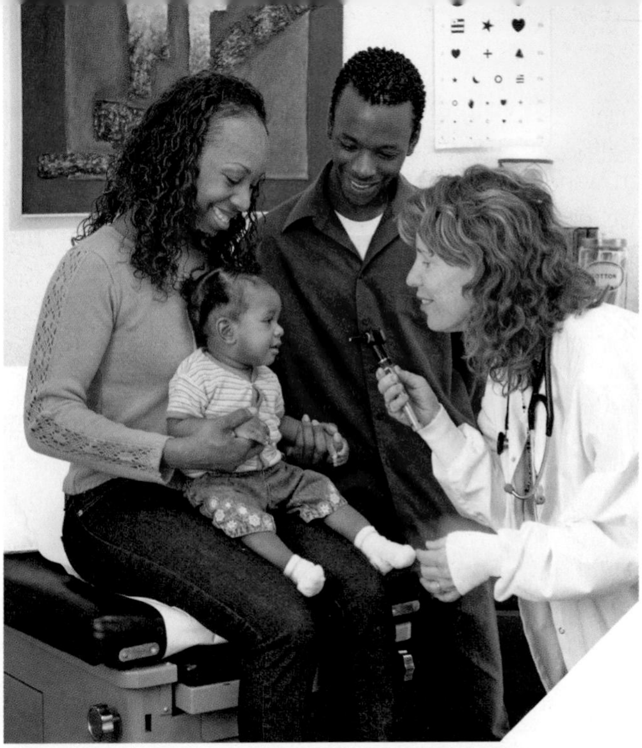

Bedtime Safety

It can be easy for tired parents to fall asleep next to a sleeping baby on a sofa or bed, but the practice should be avoided. Tragedy can result when a sleeping adult rolls too close to the baby.

Babies—especially newborns—should *always* be placed on their backs rather than on their stomachs. This measure may help prevent **sudden infant death syndrome (SIDS),** or "crib death," the death of a baby under one year old with no known cause. Babies who die of SIDS seem healthy but die in their sleep. Parents can take these safety steps to lower the risk of SIDS:

- Always place a baby on his or her back to sleep. This is the safest position.
- Place the baby on a firm mattress, not a soft surface such as a waterbed.
- Remove soft toys and loose bedding from the baby's crib.
- Make sure the baby's face stays uncovered. Keep blankets away from the nose and mouth.
- Don't allow anyone to smoke around the baby.
- Don't let the baby become overheated during sleep. Keep the baby warm, but not too warm.

Medical Care for Infants

Babies need relatively frequent checkups by a health practitioner during the first year. This may be a pediatrician, family physician, nurse, or well-baby clinic. Many states, counties, and private not-for-profit organizations offer help if paying for the checkups is a problem. The following information gives some idea what to expect, but parents should follow their doctor's recommendations for the schedule of visits and what happens at each visit.

Well-Baby Examinations

A newborn's first medical checkup is usually within 24 hours of birth. The baby is checked again before being released from the hospital and at the doctor's office or clinic about one week after birth. Regular checkups, called well-baby visits, are recommended at one, two, four, six, nine, and 12 months of age. See Fig. 14-11.

At each visit, the baby's weight, length, and head size are measured and recorded on a growth chart. Motor skills, vision, and hearing are checked. The baby is thoroughly examined. Both parents should go to the checkups, if possible. They will be asked questions about how the baby is eating and sleeping and whether they have noticed any changes in behavior.

Immunizations

Infants and children can be protected from a number of diseases through **immunizations**, doses of vaccine given by injection (shots) or by mouth. **Vaccines** are preparations containing a small amount of a dead or weakened disease germ. They allow the body to form defenses against the germ without getting sick.

Immunizations are available from the baby's doctor or clinic or a county health service.

Fig. 14-12. While this chart shows a suggested timetable for immunizations, parents should follow the recommendations of the doctor or county health service. **Why might the timetable change?**

Recommended Immunization Schedule Through Age Six		
Name of Vaccine and Diseases Prevented	**Number of Doses Needed**	**Recommended Timing of Doses**
HepB vaccine Hepatitis B	3	Birth to 2 months 1 to 4 months 6 to 18 months
DTaP or DTP vaccine Diphtheria, tetanus, and pertussis (whooping cough)	5	2 months 4 months 6 months 15 to 18 months 4 to 6 years
HiB vaccine Bacterial meningitis, pneumonia, and certain other infections caused by H. influenza type B	4	2 months 4 months 6 months 12 to 15 months
Polio vaccine Polio	4	2 months 4 months 6 to 18 months 4 to 6 years
MMR vaccine Measles, mumps, and rubella	2	12 to 15 months 4 to 6 years
Pneumococcal vaccine Pneumococcal disease	4	2 months 4 months 6 months 12 to 18 months
Varicella vaccine Chicken pox	1	12 to 15 months
HepA vaccine Hepatitis A	1	2 to 6 years

Fig. 14-13. If a baby gets sick, it is best to call a doctor. **What information should parents take with them when taking a sick child to the doctor's office or hospital?**

Some babies have a mild reaction to immunizations, such as redness or swelling at the injection site or a slight fever. Health care providers can tell parents what to do if a reaction occurs.

Parents should keep a careful record of all the immunizations a child receives. Many require several doses over time. A recommended schedule for immunizations is shown in Fig. 14-12 on page 296.

When to Call the Doctor

Even the healthiest baby is bound to get sick at times. Parents should ask questions when they have concerns. If a baby has a problem, it is best to get early treatment. See Fig. 14-13.

Parents often call the doctor or medical clinic seeking advice for problems like these:

- **Abdominal pain.** Common causes of abdominal pain in babies and toddlers include stomach flu, gas from overfeeding or milk intolerance, and constipation.
- **Excessive sleeping.** Call the doctor if a newborn sleeps for longer than 10 hours at a time or cannot be awakened easily.
- **Feeding difficulty.** Parents should call a doctor if their baby skips more than three feedings or has difficulty eating.
- **Fever or temperature change.** The doctor should be alerted if a baby has a temperature above 100.4°F.
- **Stomach virus.** A stomach virus can cause vomiting, diarrhea, and fever. Vomiting usually stops within 12 hours. Diarrhea may last for a few days or longer.

Emergencies

If an infant or child exhibits any of the following signs, emergency treatment is needed. Parents should call 911 or other emergency service immediately and follow the responder's directions if they see any of these signs of serious trouble:

- Blue color when the baby isn't cold. Babies turn blue when the blood carries less oxygen through the body. This may be a symptom of breathing problems, heart problems, or seizures.
- Signs of severe dehydration. These can include extreme sleepiness or difficulty waking, dry mouth and tongue, sunken soft spot (fontanel) on top of the head, sunken eyes with no tears, fast breathing and rapid heartbeat, or no urination for more than 12 hours.

- Signs of *shock*, a condition in which the vital organs cannot get enough blood. Possible signs include cool and clammy skin that looks pale or mottled, shallow and rapid breathing, listlessness and lack of interest in activities, difficulty waking, a lack of response, unusual jerky movements (possible seizure), or a weak and rapid heartbeat.
- Signs of difficulty breathing, such as very fast breathing or grunting with each breath; use of the neck, chest, and abdominal muscles to breathe; or a need to sit up and lean forward or to tilt the nose up to breathe.
- Head injury with symptoms afterward, such as vomiting more than three times after a blow to the head.
- Poisoning, or indications (such as vomiting) that the baby has eaten a toxic substance. Common poisons include household cleaning products and pesticides.
- Severe reaction to an immunization, such as trouble breathing or swallowing, hives or rash, changes in alertness within seven days, a seizure, collapsing, a fever of 104.5°F or higher, or redness and swelling for more than 48 hours after an injection. See Fig. 14-14.

Promoting Infant Development

Just as parents take care of their infant's basic needs, it is important that they also help promote the baby's development. As explained in Chapter 13, lack of attention, interaction, and stimulation can actually prevent infants from growing and developing as they should.

Promoting Physical and Intellectual Development

Appropriate and interesting experiences involving all five senses—sight, sound, smell, taste, and touch—can help stimulate development of the baby's brain and body. Here are some suggestions to help infants grow and learn:

- **Play infant exercise games.** Patty-cake and similar games help babies learn new ways to move their legs, arms, and hands. The personal interaction also supports social development.

Fig. 14-14. Parents should call 911 immediately if they see any sign of serious illness or injury. **Why is it important for parents to keep accurate records of a child's health history?**

Fig. 14-15. At first babies do not recognize their reflection in the mirror. **What do they see in the glass when they move their arms or legs?**

- **Provide new experiences.** Infants need to see, touch, taste, smell, and listen. Parents can aid development by providing an environment that stimulates all the senses. For instance, visiting neighbors and relatives, the supermarket, or the self-service laundry brings new sights, aromas, and sounds.

- **Encourage visual development.** Make eye contact while cuddling and feeding so the baby can see your expressions. Hold babies in comfortable positions that allow them the best view of faces, objects, and activities. To help babies learn to track movements with their eyes, parents can use toys with distinct black and white patterns; the contrast makes these easier for newborns to follow. Show babies what they look like in the mirror. See Fig. 14-15.

- **Provide toys.** Toys do not have to be elaborate or expensive. Simple toys help babies coordinate kicking, reaching, grasping, and pulling skills. In the crib, hang a mobile that the baby can see and reach for, at a distance the baby can barely touch. Colorful wall decorations and music boxes stimulate vision and hearing. At around four months, infants can shake rattles and squeeze soft toys. An older infant enjoys tossing balls and pounding with a rubber hammer. Musical toys stimulate listening skills, and brightly colored balls invite crawling.

- **Support crawling and walking.** When babies begin to crawl and pull themselves up on furniture, parents can make sure the area is safe by moving objects that might fall and covering sharp corners of furniture. They can hold a baby's hands to help the baby practice walking. In this way, parents encourage the child's natural desire to use new skills.

- **Encourage language skills.** It may feel silly to talk to a baby who can't talk back. However, research shows that a steady stream of loving verbal communication from another person (*not* voices on television!) helps infants develop language skills more easily. Talk to and mimic the baby, repeating the baby's name and the names of objects. Singing songs, using rhymes, and demonstrating rhythm add to the appeal of language.

Promoting Emotional and Social Development

Being gently touched, held, and physically comforted the first months of life doesn't spoil a baby. It builds the trust needed for later relationships. Appropriate care and communication go hand-in-hand. By combining care with positive verbal and nonverbal communication, parents and other caregivers help babies develop emotionally and socially.

The responsibility to promote a child's emotional and social development begins at birth. Here are some guidelines:

- **Hold the baby.** Physical contact is important to an infant's emotional development. Infants who are frequently held, hugged, and cuddled develop feelings of safety and love. Walk around, dance, or rock while holding the baby in your arms. A parent's face is probably the most important visual stimulus for an infant. A baby learns from the close, one-on-one interaction with a parent or caregiver. Infants also need someone to play with them and talk to them about what they see. This helps them learn about the world around them.

- **Smile often and use loving words.** Infants need attention from caregivers to learn and develop emotionally and socially. When parents show approval by smiling, an infant feels loved and encouraged. Using loving words and expressions makes babies feel secure. Nonverbal communication, including hugging, kissing, touching, rocking, and smiling, actually helps babies grow. Encourage the baby to make gestures to communicate even before the baby starts making speech-like sounds. See Fig. 14-16.

- **Encourage social development.** Infants learn to relate to others through daily activities that include positive interactions. Babies especially need contact with the people who are most important in their lives—their parents, siblings, other family members, and caregivers. Parents promote social development by providing positive examples. Early lessons about manners begin in infancy when parents teach children to say "hello," "thank you," and "bye-bye." This early positive interaction provides a foundation for getting along in the world as children grow and begin school.

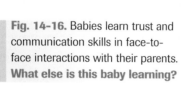
Fig. 14-16. Babies learn trust and communication skills in face-to-face interactions with their parents. **What else is this baby learning?**

Child & Family Services
CAREERS

▶ Interagency Caseworker

Caseworkers help people deal with personal and family problems. They work for government agencies, school systems, and private facilities that help people in need.

An interagency caseworker may be assigned to a family that has overlapping problems, such as unemployment and financial concerns that arise when a parent needs to care for a sick child. The caseworker may help clients identify their needs and find solutions and resources, such as financial aid and medical care. Caseworkers may visit clients at home to keep track of their progress and to arrange for services that help clients address their problems. They may give advice about nutrition, cleanliness, and household management.

"As an interagency caseworker, I often work independently, but I need to develop good relationships with coworkers in various agencies as well as with my clients. That's why I have to be a good listener and communicator. I respect the private information my clients provide, and I need to be fair and objective in handling my cases. I have to be well organized and keep careful records about my clients because I regularly write reports about my cases. I also expect to face certain job pressures, such as time limits and emotional stress. It's important to be emotionally mature to deal with all the responsibilities of my job."

CAREER TIPS

- In high school, take psychology and college-prep courses.
- Earn a bachelor's degree in a field such as social work.
- Meet licensing and certification or registration requirements.

14 Review & Activities

Check Your Facts

1. Suggest four actions that might soothe a crying baby.
2. Why is demand feeding encouraged?
3. Why is putting a baby to bed with a bottle not advisable?
4. If an infant spits up, when should the doctor be consulted?
5. How is an infant weaned?
6. In what order are different types of foods introduced to an infant?
7. Compare commercial and homemade baby foods.
8. How can you prevent choking when serving foods to a baby?
9. What should you do after changing a diaper?
10. Compare a sponge bath with a tub bath.
11. What should a parent do if cradle cap occurs?
12. How does an infant's need for sleep change from birth to one year?
13. Why shouldn't you sleep beside a sleeping infant?
14. What are at least three ways to lower the risk of SIDS?
15. What are immunizations and why are they needed?
16. List three signs in an infant that tell a parent to call the doctor and three signs that require a call to 911.
17. What can you do to help a baby develop positive emotions?

Think Critically

1. **Understanding Cause and Effect.** Would you serve any of these foods to an older baby: peanut butter, bread, grapes, or lollipops? Explain your reasoning.
2. **Predicting Effects.** Suppose an infant is seldom held and lives with people who smile very little and are angry a lot. What effects do you think this might have on the personality of the child in later years?

Apply Your Learning

1. **Care Skills Demo.** Using a baby doll that is close to life size, demonstrate the following: **a)** holding a newborn; **b)** burping a baby; **c)** changing a diaper; **d)** dressing a baby; and **e)** bathing a baby.

2. **Toys for Development.** Make a chart with five columns, headed *Toys*, *Physical*, *Intellectual*, *Emotional*, and *Social*. Using toy catalogs, choose 6 to 10 toys that you think are outstanding for infants. Write the name of each toy in the first column. Then in the other columns, explain how each toy promotes development.

3. **Infant Interaction Demo.** Arrange to play with an infant for at least 20 minutes. Plan age-appropriate activities that promote development. Report on your plan, the development you aimed to promote, and the infant's reactions.

Cross-Curricular Connections

1. **Math.** Research the cost of disposable diapers for the year of infancy. Using inexpensive diapers, calculate for each of these averages: 6, 8, and 10 changes per day. Do the same for more expensive diapers. Chart and compare results. How might diaper quality impact actual use?

2. **Language Arts.** Write a description of an infant who shows signs of illness, without saying who should be called. Exchange descriptions with a partner. Write whether you would call the doctor or 911 and why. Discuss in class.

Family & Community Connections

1. **Infant Emergencies.** Talk to a family member who is a parent about experiences with infant care. Did the person ever face an emergency situation? How did he or she respond? What was the outcome? What advice would the person give to new parents? Take notes and discuss the experiences in class.

2. **Infant Accommodation.** Survey public places in your community, such as stores, malls, supermarkets, restaurants, community centers, and medical clinics. What accommodations are made for infant care? For example, consider diaper changing, places to sit and feed, available strollers, wide aisles for strollers, and safety seats. What improvements would you suggest?

CHAPTER 15

Meeting Children's Physical Needs

CHAPTER OBJECTIVES

- Identify physical growth patterns in children and adolescents.
- Explain how to promote good nutrition, fitness, and motor development in children.
- Plan nutritious, age-appropriate meals and snacks for children.
- Identify major milestones in a child's motor development.
- Suggest ways to promote good hygiene and sleep habits in children.
- Summarize criteria for selecting children's clothing.

PARENTING TERMS

- manual dexterity
- growth spurts
- puberty
- large motor skills
- small motor skills
- eye-hand coordination
- ambidextrous
- sphincter muscles
- enuresis
- flame resistant

Watching a child grow is one of the most amazing and satisfying experiences of parenthood. This constant transformation can be a source of wonder and concern. Parents who know what to expect at different stages of development, and how to nurture and guide their child's development during each stage, will be better equipped to deal with all these changes. In this chapter, you'll learn how to care for the physical needs of growing children.

Physical Growth and Development

A baby's first birthday is a milestone for both baby and parents. It seems that suddenly the infant has become a child! Just the advance from crawling to walking changes a child's world remarkably—and the parents' world as well. Development proceeds quickly in the next few years, propelling the child toward greater independence and the parents toward new joys and challenges. See Fig. 15-1.

Parents can anticipate certain physical changes as children grow. However, every child grows at his or her own rate, which can vary substantially from child to child. For instance, at 16 months, one toddler may be the size of an average two-year-old, while another the same age is much smaller. There is a wide range of what is considered "normal" for a child at any age. See Fig. 15-2.

Toddlers

During the toddler years—from the first to the third birthday—children grow at an impressive rate. By age two-and-a-half, the average child has reached half of his or her adult height. Fig. 15-3 lists average heights and weights for children ages two through six years.

As children get taller, their physical proportions change. Arms and legs lengthen relative to the head and torso. Baby fat begins to disappear. Arms and legs become thinner, faces more defined, chests flatter; even the feet lose their pads of fat. These changes redistribute a toddler's weight, improving balance and posture.

Other physical changes are also evident in the toddler years. **Manual dexterity**, the ability to manipulate objects with the hands, improves dramatically. Between the ages of seven months and 33 months, children's primary teeth come in.

Fig. 15-1. A baby's first birthday is an occasion of great joy. **What are some milestones the baby may have accomplished by the end of that first year?**

Fig. 15-2. In any group of children of the same age, some will be larger or smaller than others. **How can parents help children feel good about their growth?**

Preschoolers

Preschoolers—children ages three through five—often grow faster in height than they do in weight, resulting in a lanky appearance. The abdomen flattens, shoulders widen, and the neck and legs grow longer. The lower jaw becomes more defined, while the upper jaw widens to make room for the permanent teeth that will come in later.

As their muscles and skeletal systems develop, children are able to move more freely. Now they can run, jump, ride a tricycle, and kick a ball. Their manual dexterity also improves; they gain in ability to manipulate smaller objects such as shoelaces and buttons.

School-Age Children

Growth slows as children enter the school years. The percentage of body fat increases, especially in girls, in preparation for the faster growth of adolescence.

	Average Height and Weight for Young Children			
	Females		Males	
Age	Height	Weight	Height	Weight
2 years	35 in.	28 lb.	36 in.	30 lb.
3 years	38 in.	32 lb.	38 in.	35 lb.
4 years	40 in.	37 lb.	41 in.	39 lb.
5 years	43 in.	43 lb.	44 in.	44 lb.
6 years	45 in.	47 lb.	46 in.	49 lb.

Fig. 15-3. Growth is rapid throughout the toddler and preschool years. **Would you expect all children to grow at the average rate? Why or why not?**

Now as throughout childhood, growth is not a steady progression. Weeks or months of slower growth alternate with **growth spurts**, during which a child grows more quickly. Growth tends to be a bit faster in the spring than during the rest of the year. Otherwise the spurts seem random. They are usually accompanied by an increase in appetite. See Fig. 15-4.

During a growth spurt, parts of the body tend to grow at different rates. The legs, arms, hands, and feet often grow most quickly, followed by the child's torso. Consequently, the child may look and feel awkward and clumsy.

Growth rates and physical abilities vary substantially from one healthy child to another. Children may notice how their growth differs from that of their friends. Some children compare themselves negatively to their friends, wondering why they are different. Parents can encourage children to take pride in their achievements without making comparisons or drawing attention to unusual height or weight.

As part of a child's regular physical exams, health care providers chart growth rates and compare these with norms, or what is considered "normal" for the child's age. They may recommend specialized tests for children whose growth is very different from the norm, to assess growth speed and pattern.

Children begin to lose their primary teeth and gain their permanent teeth around age six. By age 13 they usually have all their permanent teeth except for the third molars (also called wisdom teeth), which typically appear around 17 years of age.

Adolescents

Adolescents undergo another major growth spurt during **puberty**, or the onset of sexual development. Puberty typically begins for girls between the ages of nine and 11; for boys, about age ten to 12. Over the next two to five years, children undergo the enormous changes of sexual development: the growth and development of sex organs, the appearance of pubic and underarm hair, and, in girls, the onset of menstruation.

During adolescence, muscles and bones may grow faster than the tendons and ligaments that connect them. As a result, these connective tissues tighten, causing some adolescents

Fig. 15-4. Often the first sign of a growth spurt is a child growing out of clothes that fit just a few months before. **What are some characteristics of a growth spurt?**

pain in their knees and lower legs. Stretching, especially before playing sports, can help relieve or prevent the pain. See Fig. 15-5.

These years are often a time of confusion and doubt. Adolescents' bodies are no longer familiar to them, and they are flooded with new feelings and drives. They tend to compare themselves constantly with their peers. Parents can help by directing adolescents' focus away from physical appearance to other strengths and achievements.

Promoting Nutrition and Fitness

Proper nutrition is essential to a child's physical and mental development. A healthful diet provides energy for growth, for daily activities, and for resistance to disease. In combination with physical activity, good nutrition helps children maintain fitness and appropriate weight.

The U.S. government has a program to help low-income families buy nutritious foods for children through age five. See page 138 for a description of the WIC program.

Nutrition Needs

It's important for a parent to be aware of ways nutritional needs change as children grow. Children need to consume adequate liquids and the same essential nutrients as adults, in forms and servings appropriate to their age.

- **Protein.** Meat, fish, poultry, beans, and dairy products such as milk and yogurt are good sources of protein, necessary for growth and tissue repair.
- **Carbohydrates.** Starchy foods such as bread, rice, wheat, corn, and potatoes provide carbohydrates, the main source of the body's energy.

Fig. 15-5. Proper stretching is always a good idea before engaging in strenuous activity. **Why is this especially true during adolescence?**

- **Vitamins and minerals.** Fruits and vegetables contain important vitamins and minerals that help build bodies and develop resistance to disease. Calcium-rich foods such as milk, yogurt, cottage cheese, and leafy green vegetables help build strong bones and teeth. Lean red meats, poultry, fish, and whole-grain bread are sources of iron, which is needed to

The Food Groups

Food Group	Foods Included	Selection Tips
Grain Group	Bread, pasta, oatmeal, breakfast cereals, tortillas, grits, and any other foods made from grains	At least half the grains eaten should be whole grains. Look to see that grains such as wheat, rice, oats, or corn are referred to as "whole" in the list of ingredients.
Vegetable Group	Any vegetable or 100% vegetable juice	Include dark green vegetables, orange vegetables, dry beans and peas, starchy vegetables, and others.
Fruit Group	Any fruit or 100% fruit juice	Choose whole or cut-up fruit more often than juice.
Milk Group	Milk, yogurt, cheese, pudding	Choose fat-free or low-fat milk, yogurt, and cheese.
Meat & Beans Group	All foods made from meat, poultry, fish, dry beans or peas, eggs, nuts, and seeds	Select fish, beans, peas, nuts, and seeds more often. Choose lean or low-fat meat and poultry, and bake, broil, or grill it.

Fig. 15-6. Each of these food groups has a role to play in good nutrition. **How might you teach a child about the food groups?**

absorb nutrients and carry oxygen throughout the body. Vitamin C—found in most fruits and green leafy vegetables—helps the body absorb iron, among its other jobs.

- **Fats.** These concentrated sources of energy also enable the body to use certain vitamins, cushion vital organs, and help maintain body temperature.
- **Water.** Every cell in the body must be bathed in water in order to live. Water is essential to many chemical reactions and helps carry other nutrients throughout the body.

In general, nutrition needs increase as a child grows. For example, children ages four to eight require 800 milligrams of calcium daily, while children ages nine to 18 require 1,300 milligrams daily. Two exceptions are fats and iron. Children from one to three years old need more fat than adults, and the need for iron is greatest in children between ages four and eight.

Food Choices for Children

Any food can be part of a healthful diet, in moderation. For balanced nutrition, children —like adults—need a variety of nutrient-packed foods from the food groups shown in Fig. 15-6.

How Much Food for Children? The amount of food needed from each food group depends on an individual's overall calorie needs. Calories are a measure of food energy. Daily calorie needs vary depending on age, gender, and activity level. In general, younger children need fewer calories than older children, and less active children need fewer calories than more active children of the same age. In some cases, boys need more calories than girls. See Fig. 15-7.

Fig. 15-7. MyPyramid is an interactive food guidance system developed by the U.S. government. It provides personalized recommendations for how much to eat daily from each food group.

MyPyramid.gov
STEPS TO A HEALTHIER YOU

Fig. 15-8. Snacks can help fill in the amounts needed from each food group. **What snacks might appeal to children?**

When children are offered nutritious foods, they can usually be allowed to decide for themselves how much to eat. It's best to serve small portions and let children have seconds if they are still hungry.

The amount that toddlers eat may vary widely from meal to meal and from day to day. For example, children who are busy with an activity at midday may eat only a little lunch and later be very hungry for supper. It is normal for a toddler to be very hungry one day or week and not at all the next. During growth spurts, children's appetites increase and they eat more. How much a child eats at any one meal matters less than the total over several days and the nutritional value of the foods eaten.

Snacks. With their high energy level and small stomachs, most young children need snacks. Snacks should be spaced between meals. Snacking just before mealtime dulls the appetite for the meal, and giving snacks too soon after a meal encourages children to skip meals in favor of snacks.

Snacks should be foods that are packed with nutrients and easy for children to handle. Fruits, vegetables, whole-grain bread and crackers, and low-fat cheeses make good snacks. Children often enjoy dipping raw or steamed vegetables into a low-fat yogurt dip. See Fig. 15-8.

Foods to Avoid. To avoid choking, children younger than four years old must not be allowed to eat:

- Small, hard foods such as nuts, seeds, popcorn, chips, pretzels, raw carrots, and raisins.
- Slippery foods such as whole grapes, large pieces of hot dog, hard candy, and cough drops.

Parenting Pointers

Helping Children Learn to Self-Feed

Toddlers want to become independent, especially when it comes to feeding themselves. Some start trying to use a spoon between the ages of 12 and 18 months. By age two, most toddlers say "more" or "all done." Two-year-olds begin to want more of a voice in choosing what to eat. Here are some ways to make the process of learning to self-feed easier for toddlers and parents alike.

Provide the child with special utensils. A small, plastic-coated toddler spoon reduces the potential for injury. Plastic toddler cups are designed to reduce spills: they are weighted at the bottom, have two handles, and are covered with a "sippy" lid. A third useful item is a sturdy bowl with a nonskid base. Toddler utensils are inexpensive and readily available in grocery and baby stores.

Provide foods that are soft and easy to eat with a spoon. Mashed vegetables, cottage cheese, applesauce, and cooked cereals are toddler-friendly selections.

Cut larger chunks of foods into bite-sized portions. Smaller portions are easier for toddlers and young children to manage.

Give toddlers dry cereal. This is a fun food for toddlers because it's easy for them to pick up. Dry cereal is also easier than wet foods to clean up!

Be ready for some mess. Place a bib around the child's neck. Lay newspaper or plastic on the floor under the high chair to catch spilled or thrown food.

Promoting Good Eating Habits

There are many ways to help children learn positive lifelong eating habits. Start by serving foods with an appealing variety of colors and textures. Think about how good a platter of crisp apple slices, soft golden mangos, and a smooth yogurt dip would look and taste! See Fig. 15-9.

Introducing New Foods. Encourage variety by introducing new foods one at a time. Children's natural curiosity makes it easier to introduce new foods. Model the behavior by eating the food first, commenting on its good taste, and then offering some to the child. Introduce only small tastes of new foods, and don't insist that children eat something they find repulsive.

Fig. 15-9. Children who learn to enjoy the colors, textures, aromas, and flavors of nutritious foods are well on their way to developing healthful eating habits.

In general, children are more likely to try new foods that are:

- Served separately rather than combined, as in a casserole.
- Mildly flavored.
- Served at room temperature.
- Attractive or fun, such as finger-sized portions or food cut into shapes. See Fig. 15-10.

Teaching and Modeling Good Nutrition. Teach good eating habits by example. Model serving yourself only the amount of food you will eat and taking seconds only when you're hungry. Choose nutritious foods from all five food groups, and be open to trying new foods.

Teach children directly about good nutrition by explaining why people need specific foods for good health. You can also point out the nutritional value of foods from the information given in recipes and on food boxes. Discuss which foods are the most healthful and why.

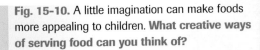

Fig. 15-10. A little imagination can make foods more appealing to children. **What creative ways of serving food can you think of?**

Fig. 15-11. Preparing a salad can be a fun learning experience. **Why are children more likely to eat foods that they have helped prepare?**

Children are more likely to develop good eating habits if they are involved in making their own food choices. When possible, let children choose the food for some meals. Even young children can help grow their own vegetables and fruits in a garden outside or an indoor pot. Older children can help prepare meals and snacks. See Fig. 15-11.

Making Mealtime Pleasant. One of the best ways to promote good eating habits is to eat meals together as a family and to make mealtimes a positive occasion. A relaxing, reassuring atmosphere not only aids digestion but also encourages children to associate food with pleasant experiences. To keep mealtimes from becoming pressured, avoid using food as a reward or a punishment, and don't insist that children finish everything on their plate. See Fig. 15-12.

Handling Finicky Eaters. Some children are finicky eaters. Parents can feed their children without sacrificing nutrition or making mealtimes unpleasant by remembering these tips:

- Offer a variety of foods to increase the chances that a child will find something to enjoy.

Fig. 15-12. Meals should be positive, nurturing times. **What can parents do to make mealtimes pleasant?**

- Try serving a rejected food in a different form. Lightly steamed broccoli florets might be more appealing to a child than chopped broccoli in sauce—or vice versa.
- If child still won't eat a particular food, offer substitutes that provide similar nutrients. For instance, if a child won't eat red meat, offer eggs, tofu, or poultry.

- Serve finger foods as a fun alternative to traditional mealtime foods.
- Don't force children to eat foods they dislike. Forcing a food won't make a child like it and makes mealtimes unpleasant for everyone.
- Don't be overly concerned with children's food phases; they are temporary.

Health & Safety

Obesity in Children

Seriously overweight (obese) children are more likely to become obese adults, often leading to health problems such as diabetes and heart disease. Over 15% of children in the U.S. are considered obese, more than twice as many as in the 1970s. Here are some ways that parents can prevent and treat obesity in children:

- Create an environment that fosters physical activity.
- Encourage and model good eating habits for everyone in the family.
- Provide nutritious foods and healthy snacks, such as fruits and vegetables.
- Avoid fasting or extreme dieting for yourself or your child.
- Eat at home more often than in restaurants, which commonly serve large portions.
- Emphasize the positive value of fitness and nutrition rather than the problem of weight.

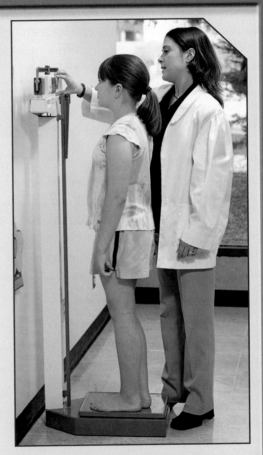

- If you think a child has a weight problem, consult a health care professional. You may be advised to limit soft drinks and foods that are high in fat and sugar.

Promoting Physical Activity

Regular exercise helps children maintain wellness. Exercise strengthens bones, improves heart health, and controls weight. Study after study indicates that when children become physically fit through exercise, they have the energy they need to learn and achieve.

Do children of physically active parents tend to be more physically active than other children? Many educators and researchers think so. In this as in so many other areas, a parent's example is a powerful motivator.

THE DEVELOPING BRAIN

Physical exercise strengthens the brain as well as the body. It increases blood flow to the brain, carrying oxygen needed for mental activity. Researchers have also found that exercise raises levels of a brain cell growth hormone. Thus physical fitness helps children think and learn.

Parents who clearly enjoy regular physical exercise are good role models of healthy behavior. For example, parents who take a walk after dinner, play catch as a family, or enjoy long bicycle rides demonstrate to their children the pleasure and benefits of being fit. These activities are also a good source of family fun. See Fig. 15-13.

Being active is an easier task when the weather is warm and there are plenty of opportunities for outdoor activities. But don't let cold weather keep you inside and inactive. Fig. 15-14 suggests some enjoyable ways that the entire family can become physically active year-round.

Fig. 15-13. Physically active parents set a positive example for their children. **What message about physical fitness do you think these parents are sending to their children?**

Promoting Motor Development

Motor skills are abilities that involve moving muscles. As they grow, children continuously develop two different kinds of motor skills: large and small. Some motor skills come naturally, such as a baby's ability to crawl. Others have to be taught for children to do them well and happily. To develop such skills as throwing and catching a ball, children need guidance and practice.

Large Motor Skills

Large motor skills (also called *gross motor skills*) use the large muscle groups, such as those in the arms, legs, abdomen, and back. These skills include walking, climbing, and running. Healthy infants practice their large motor skills when they kick and crawl. Toddlers further refine their large motor skills by walking, running, and climbing steps—leading with the same foot on every step and bringing the other foot up to join it. Most preschoolers can run with even strides and hop on one foot. They climb stairs by alternating feet, one foot to a stair.

Parents can encourage large motor skill development in young children by creating safe places for them to play. Caregivers should remove potential obstacles from the home and yard and move breakable objects out of a toddler's reach. Toys such as swings and riding toys help preschoolers develop strength and coordination. Preschoolers are developing large motor skills when they play simple running games such as "Tag" and "Red Light, Green Light."

School-age children are ready for activities requiring finer coordination, such as swimming and skating. Many teens continue to hone their skills in specific sports.

Ball Skills. Throwing and catching are not as easy as they may look. Parents who teach their children how to do so properly are giving the children skills they can enjoy their whole lives.

The ability to throw and catch develops gradually. Many children have trouble learning to follow a ball with their eyes as it moves through space, so as to be in position to catch it. Parents can begin by rolling large balls to the young child. The next step might be to have the child practice catching "slow balls" such as balloons or big bubbles.

Physical Activities the Family Can Enjoy Together
❑ Walk the kids to school and the library.
❑ Go roller skating or ice skating.
❑ Take the stairs instead of the elevator.
❑ Go sledding.
❑ Take a family swim in a local pool.
❑ Dressed in rain gear, enjoy a long walk in the rain.
❑ Play hopscotch on the sidewalk.
❑ Shoot hoops with a basketball.
❑ Build a snowperson.
❑ Rake leaves.
❑ Play softball, volleyball, or soccer.
❑ Do errands by bicycle instead of car or bus.
❑ If the weather is very bad, walk in a big store or mall.
❑ Jump rope together.
❑ Hike in the woods.

Fig. 15-14. Options for family activities may vary depending on the season, climate, and community. **What other factors might affect a family's choice of physical activity?**

Toddlers catch a large ball by scooping it up in their arms and trapping it in a bear hug. Preschoolers can throw a small ball, but probably cannot catch it. At first, the child tosses the ball and steps off with the foot that is on the same side as the throwing arm.

By about age six, children can be taught to step off with the foot opposite the throwing arm, to increase strength, momentum, and aim. By age seven to eight, a child can learn to do an over-arm throw and to catch a softball in a glove. Older children may continue to improve their skills for use in a particular kind of ball game.

Fig. 15-15. Children should wear helmets when riding tricycles and bicycles. **What other precautions should parents take to ensure children's safety during outdoor play?**

Tricycles and Bicycles. Riding tricycles and bicycles can help children develop both large motor skills and a sense of independence. Many children learn to ride a tricycle during their third year. At first, they may straddle the seat and walk. With parental assistance, they learn how to pedal the tricycle. See Fig. 15-15.

By age five, most children are ready to learn how to ride a bicycle. Parents may attach training wheels to the bike to help a child develop balance and gain confidence.

Small Motor Skills

Small motor skills (also called *fine motor skills*) involve coordination of the small muscle groups, such as those in the fingers, wrists, and ankles. Small motor skills improve as children develop manual dexterity and refine their **eye-hand coordination**, the ability to move the hands accurately in response to what the eyes see.

Young children improve eye-hand coordination and manual dexterity as they play with blocks, building sets, large pop beads, clay, finger paints, sand, and simple puzzles. Parents may also let them play with selected unbreakable household items, such as metal or plastic containers with lids. Young children love to put objects inside each other and then take them apart. Teaching children to feed and dress themselves, according to their abilities at a given age, also teaches small motor skills. See Fig. 15-16.

Fig. 15-16. Many activities for young children develop small motor skills. **Can you think of other games preschoolers play that help improve these skills?**

Typical Motor Skills Development, Ages One to Five		
Age	**Large Motor Skills**	**Small Motor Skills**
One-Year-Old	❑ Walks haltingly ❑ Walks up stairs with help	❑ Self-feeds using fingers ❑ Picks up objects ❑ Holds objects in fist
Two-Year-Old	❑ Walks and runs ❑ Walks up and down stairs	❑ Self-feeds using spoon ❑ Scribbles with fat markers in specific directions ❑ Can undress self if wearing slip-on clothing
Three-Year-Old	❑ Balances on one foot ❑ Rides a tricycle	❑ Builds towers with blocks ❑ Draws circles ❑ Unzips clothes
Four-Year-Old	❑ Hops and spins in place ❑ Walks backward ❑ Throws and catches a ball	❑ Uses safety scissors ❑ Attempts to draw shapes ❑ Dresses and undresses with supervision ❑ Handles buttons
Five-Year-Old	❑ Runs heel-to-toe ❑ Imitates dance steps	❑ Eats with greater skill and assurance ❑ Prints own name ❑ Writes numbers 1–5 ❑ Dresses and undresses without help, including shoes

Fig. 15-17. Large and small motor skills do not always develop at the same rate. **How does mastery of motor skills affect a child's self-concept?**

Remember that children develop at different rates. If a child seems to be lagging seriously behind many benchmarks, parents should consult a health care provider. Some motor delays resolve themselves as the child matures, while others require therapy or other treatment. Fig. 15-17 identifies some of the typical milestones of motor skills development.

Hand Preference. By about age six, 85 percent of all children prefer to use their right hand for most activities, a trend that continues into adulthood. Others prefer the left hand. A few children become **ambidextrous** (am-beh-DEK-struhs), or able to use both hands equally well. Parents should never try to convince children to use one hand instead of the other.

Promoting Hygiene Skills

For children, learning hygiene skills is both a practical and emotional milestone. Caring for one's personal needs is basic to independence. Brushing teeth, bathing, and toileting are significant accomplishments that make a child feel competent and confident—as well as clean!

Dental Care

Dental care should begin at birth. Before a child has teeth, gently wash his or her gums with a piece of gauze or a clean, damp washcloth twice a day. As soon as a child has teeth, brush them with a soft, child-sized brush. Begin flossing as soon as two teeth are touching.

Brushing and flossing help a child retain primary teeth, which helps ensure proper spacing for permanent teeth.

Children can practice brushing with a small amount of toothpaste, about the size of a pea. The brushing motion of the toothbrush is more important than the toothpaste. Some parents buy toothpaste made especially for kids because its flavor may encourage more frequent brushing. Children should be able to brush and floss their own teeth reliably by the time they are seven or eight years old.

Bathing

Creating a happy bath experience builds positive associations with hygiene. Some parents like to make bath time a relaxing evening ritual, complete with floating toys. See Fig. 15-18.

Young children must be supervised whenever they bathe. Even if they wash, rinse, and dry themselves, preschoolers must have an adult in the bathroom. Children can drown very quickly in a very small amount of water. School-age children do not need to be supervised (nor should they be) and may prefer a shower to a bath.

Around age seven, some children show less interest in hygiene. Nonetheless, parents must make sure that children clean themselves regularly. By adolescence, children are more aware of their bodies, more sensitive to peer approval, and typically more concerned about hygiene. At every age it's best to make showering or bathing a pleasure, not a chore.

Toileting

Children are ready to be taught to use the toilet when they can control their **sphincter muscles** (SFINK-tuhr), the muscles in the bowel and bladder regions that regulate elimination. Most children develop the necessary muscle control between 18 months and three years of age. More important than chronological age, however, is a readiness to learn. Parents should watch for common readiness signals. Generally, a child is ready to learn toileting when he or she:

- Is aware of the process of elimination.
- Complains about wearing a soiled diaper.
- Has predictable bowel movements.
- Has at least two hours between elimination events.
- Takes pride in accomplishments.
- Imitates other people's behavior.

Fig. 15-18. Toys help children enjoy bathing. **How else can parents make bath time fun?**

Fig. 15-19. Some children are more comfortable on a child seat attached to the toilet, while others prefer a separate potty chair. **How can parents encourage toileting?**

- Has a name for urine and bowel movements.
- Can follow simple directions.

A child-size potty seat or chair makes the learning process easier. See Fig. 15-19.

After the child has become comfortable flushing the toilet and talking about the process, place the child on the toilet or potty seat whenever he or she signals a need to go. Signals may include a sudden change in facial expression or stopping play. It also helps to place the child on the potty at regular intervals, perhaps every two hours. While the child is on the seat, stay in the room. Reading aloud or chatting together makes potty time enjoyable. Praise the child whether or not elimination occurs, and do not express disappointment if it doesn't.

Learning to use the toilet can take just a few days or several months. Don't punish the child for having an accident. At first, most children gain control over their bladder and bowels only when they are awake. Control during sleep comes later, so diapers may still be needed at nap time and overnight.

Bedwetting. Most children achieve the bladder control to stay dry all night by the time they are four, five, or six years old. However, it is not uncommon for bedwetting to continue into the school years. More rarely, it may still occur in the teens. Two out of three bed wetters are boys.

Bedwetting is a form of **enuresis** (en-you-REE-sis), which is the medical term for lack of urinary control. It's important to know that enuresis is a physical problem and not an emotional one. The condition tends to run in families that, doctors believe, may simply have smaller than normal bladders. It may also be related to the size of the tubes that carry urine.

Bedwetting is a humiliating problem and one that should be treated with sympathy and practical support. Parents should:

- Have the child's doctor perform a thorough physical exam to make sure the child does not have a bladder infection.
- Work with the child and doctor to develop behavior modification techniques that train the child to wake up and use the toilet when the bladder is full. Very sound sleepers may need to be awakened during the night to use the bathroom.

- Limit the amount of fluid the child drinks in the evening.
- Encourage the child to use the toilet immediately before going to bed.
- Provide adequate lighting for a child to find the bathroom at night.
- Put older children in charge of changing their sheets, not as punishment but as an opportunity to assume responsibility for their own needs.

If the problem persists despite the child's best efforts, talk with the doctor about medication that helps control the problem.

Fig. 15-20. To a child, bedtime fears are very real. What might be the problem with reading an exciting or frightening story at bedtime?

Promoting Good Sleep Habits

Regular, sufficient sleep is critical to a child's healthy development. Most toddlers sleep about 11 to 13 hours daily. Two- and three-year-olds may stop wanting to take a nap; this is all right so long as they don't get cranky. Preschoolers tend to sleep about ten to 12 hours a night. Sleep needs decrease gradually. The average 12-year-old still needs about ten hours of sleep, and teens need more than nine hours. Teens in particular tend to get less sleep than they need.

Shortage of sleep can cause mood swings, lack of attention, and misbehavior. Unfortunately, many children strongly resist bedtime. Younger children in particular may not want to leave the excitement and pleasure of their waking world or the company of the ones they love.

Bedtime Routines

From birth onward, parents need to establish bedtime schedules and routines that become positive habits. Limit TV time and rule out scary, violent content. Providing a bedtime snack, reading together, and talking about the child's day help children of all ages relax and feel safe when it's time for bed.

Dealing with Sleeping Problems

Two common sleeping problems are fear of the dark and nightmares. Children's imaginations develop more quickly than their ability to reason. It is important that parents respect their children's feelings and not try to dismiss their fears. Rather, they should help the child develop skills to deal with those fears. See Fig. 15-20.

Fig. 15-21. Children's clothing should be "kid-friendly" as well as practical for parents. **Why might a parent want to buy a larger size than the child currently wears?**

Fear of the Dark. Many children are afraid of the dark. Some are helped by having a nightlight in the bedroom or a light in the hall. Others are soothed by having the door left open so they are able to hear people. Many are comforted by sleeping with a beloved stuffed animal or blanket.

Sometimes parents need to use more imaginative ways to help a child deal with fears. Before saying goodnight, they can do a "monster sweep" of the bedroom, looking under the bed and in closets. They can position a stuffed animal outside the door as a guardian. Lying in bed with a child in the dark and recalling pleasant things that have happened during the day, or just looking out the window, can make the dark seem less frightening and ease the transition to sleep.

Nightmares. Children can have nightmares at any age. They are most likely to mention nightmares between the ages of three and five. Many children are not able to distinguish dreams from reality, particularly when they are very young.

Again, parents need to respect their children's feelings. They should comfort children and assure them that they are safe from harm. A parent can leave a light on for the child and make sure there is nothing in the room that might look frightening, such as clothes hanging over a chair.

Soothing bedtime routines can help reduce nightmares. Parents should make sure that children eat only bland foods in the evening and are not excited before going to bed. Any conflicts or upsets should be talked out, and parents should reassure children that they are loved and safe before saying goodnight.

Choosing Clothing

Buying children's clothing can be expensive, especially because children grow so fast. As a result, it's important to shop carefully for safe, durable, and comfortable clothes that are easy to care for. See Fig. 15-21.

Safety

Safety is more important than style when it comes to choosing children's clothing. Fire is one safety concern. Federal standards require that all children's sleepwear sizes nine months to size 14 be **flame resistant**. Flame-resistant garments are treated with chemicals that will self-extinguish if they catch fire. Other safety guidelines for children's clothing include:

- Make sure that pants fit well to allow children to move freely without tripping.
- For small children, avoid clothing with trim and buttons that can be pulled off and swallowed.
- Avoid long strings, scarves, and skirts that can catch on playground equipment and bicycle wheels.
- Be sure that hoods and hats don't obscure vision.

Ease of Dressing

Children are eager to dress themselves. Their ability grows as motor skills improve. Most four-year-old children can dress and undress themselves with little assistance. Choosing age-appropriate clothes for ease of dressing will help children develop confidence and independence.

Big shirts are easier to slip on and off than tight ones. Buttons and zippers are much easier to manipulate on the front of the clothing than in back. A child who is learning to use the toilet will benefit from pants with elastic waistbands instead of buttons, hooks, or zippers. Children can put on shoes with hook-and-loop tape closings long before they know how to tie shoelaces.

Other Clothing Considerations

Many other factors may affect clothing choice, including the family budget, the local climate, school requirements for school-age children, and—especially as children get older—the children's preferences. Be sure to consider:

- **Durability.** Active children need clothing made of sturdy woven or knit fabrics, such as denim. Reinforced seams and knees help clothes last longer. Adjustable straps provide room for growth.
- **Comfort.** Garments should be cut to allow freedom of movement. Also look for clothing made with natural fibers such as cotton or wool. These fibers absorb moisture and allow air to pass through.
- **Easy care.** Children's clothing should be economical and easy to wash and dry. Fabrics that don't require ironing save time. Cotton blends—cotton mixed with small amounts of synthetic fabrics such as polyester—shrink and wrinkle less than 100% cotton. Information about fabric content and care can usually be found on one of the inner labels of a garment. See Fig. 15-22.

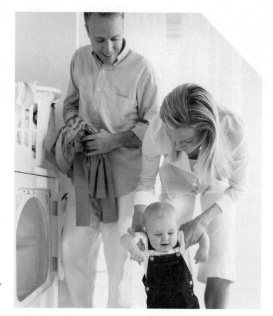

Fig. 15-22. Ease of care is an important consideration when choosing children's clothing. **What other guidelines does this child's outfit illustrate?**

▶ Physical Therapist

Physical therapists (sometimes called PTs) provide services that help restore function, improve mobility, relieve pain, and prevent or limit permanent physical disabilities resulting from injury or disease. They work in hospitals, offices, schools, and homes. Their patients may include accident victims, people recovering from surgery, and those with disabling conditions such as low back pain, arthritis, heart disease, or cerebral palsy. Increasingly, professional athletes work with physical therapists to prevent injuries.

Therapists review patients' medical histories and assess their physical abilities. They set goals for recovery, develop treatment plans, and document progress. To strengthen and retrain muscles, physical therapists often lead their patients through exercises. They also use various means to relieve pain, such as electrical stimulation and massage, and teach patients to use devices such as crutches and wheelchairs as needed.

Physical therapists must first earn a college degree, then get a postgraduate degree from an accredited physical therapist educational program. Some earn advanced certification in subspecialties such as pediatric care. Before they can practice, physical therapists must pass a state licensing exam.

"It's such a joy to see people regain use of physical abilities they need for everyday life. I can't do it for them; it takes teamwork between the patient and me. That means I have to know about bodies, but I need people skills as well."

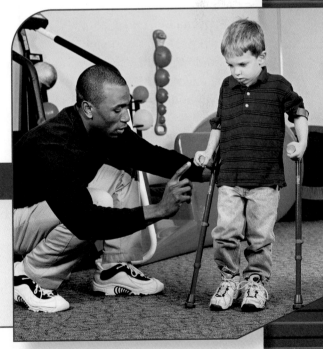

CAREER TIPS

- In high school, take classes in biology, chemistry, and physics.
- Volunteer in the physical therapy department of a hospital or clinic.
- Earn a college degree in physical therapy.
- Get a physical therapy license.

15 Review & Activities

CHAPTER SUMMARY

- From infancy through adolescence, children follow predictable physical growth patterns, although individual variations occur.
- Proper growth and development depend on nutritious foods and physical exercise.
- Motor skills develop through play that makes use of large and small muscles.
- Children need to learn hygiene skills that include bathing, dental care, and toileting.
- With skillful handling, parents can help children develop good sleep habits.
- Parents must consider safety when making clothing choices for children.

Check Your Facts

1. Describe in general the physical growth of toddlers and preschoolers.
2. Why does clumsiness often accompany growth spurts?
3. What is puberty?
4. What functions do each of the five nutrients provide in the body?
5. Should a child eat the same amount of food each day? Explain.
6. What should a mealtime atmosphere be like?
7. Identify benefits of physical exercise.
8. Name two large and two small motor skills that children typically gain each year from one to five.
9. How can large and small motor skills be promoted? List four activities for each.
10. What is eye-hand coordination?
11. What does ambidextrous mean?
12. What safety rule is essential when bathing young children?
13. Why does a parent need to understand what enuresis is?
14. What do sleep shortages cause?
15. What are at least six guidelines for selecting children's clothing?

Think Critically

1. **Analyzing Behavior.** Despite her parents' pleas, Maggie, age four, routinely refuses to eat at mealtime. When she asks for food later, they give it to her. Analyze why Maggie behaves as she does.
2. **Evaluating Actions.** A 14-month-old is placed on the potty chair for a few minutes at regular times during the day. The child doesn't seem to understand but doesn't object. Is this technique effective? Examine advantages, disadvantages, and possible consequences.
3. **Categorizing Information.** What actions and attitudes in the chapter can be instilled in children through a parent's example? What actions are typically promoted in other ways?

Apply Your Learning

1. **Menu Ideas.** Plan a week of meals and snacks for a preschooler. Keep safety in mind. Exchange menus with another student and evaluate them on nutrition and appeal.

2. **Parenting Dilemmas.** How would you respond as a parent to the following situations? **a)** Pedro, age two, wants to help his father prepare dinner. **b)** Teresa, age five, refuses to eat vegetables. **c)** Alicia, age six, is overweight for her age. **d)** Nick, age four, has trouble using his fingers for simple tasks. **e)** Ellie, age two, is afraid of the bathtub. **f)** Ben, age five, has wet the bed for the fifth night in a row. **g)** Anna, age four, screams every night after she is put to bed.

3. **Photo Essay.** Use magazine photos of children to create a photo essay on a chapter topic. Possibilities include the growing child, building motor skills, or practical clothes for children. Display your photos and explanations creatively.

Cross-Curricular Connections

1. **Language Arts.** With a partner, plan an engaging way to serve nutritious food to a child: for example, a clown face made with a pear half and bits of vegetables. Then write step-by-step directions on how to prepare your creation. Compile all ideas into a booklet to share.

2. **Social Studies.** Explore how changes in technology might affect parenting. What technological advances have made raising children easier than a generation ago? Which have made it more difficult? Why?

Family & Community Connections

1. **Development Memories.** Ask adults in your family about your childhood progress in the areas described in the chapter. What stories can they tell? Were there awkward times? Did any of the skills or situations described in the chapter take extra attention? What techniques that they used were effective?

2. **Exercise for Children.** Work with a team of students to plan a series of half-hour exercise periods for a group of preschoolers or school-age children. Investigate old and new game ideas. Create ideas of your own. What physical skills will you emphasize? Arrange to lead children in a trial run of your program.

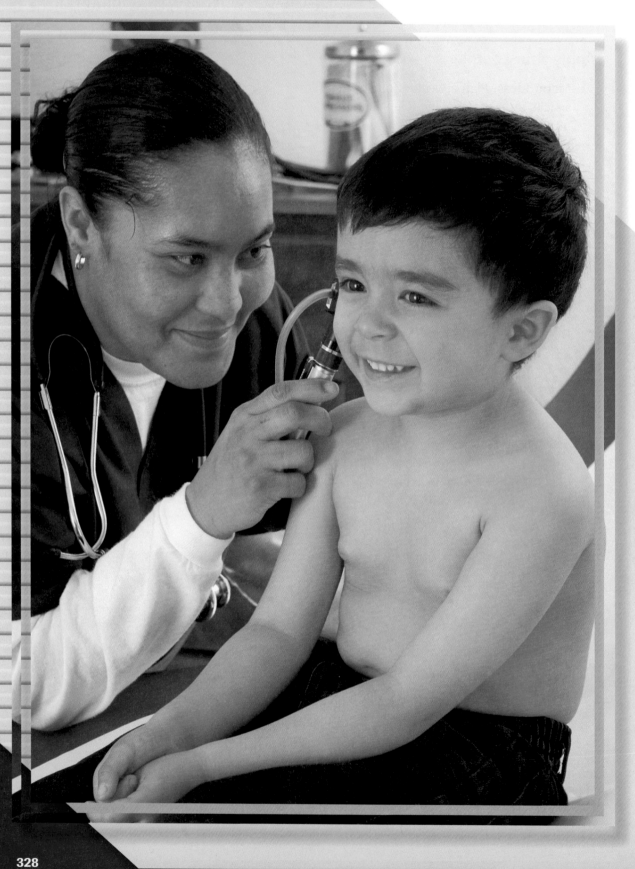

CHAPTER 16

Health and Safety

CHAPTER OBJECTIVES

- Explain preventive health care for children.
- Describe symptoms of common childhood illnesses and treatments for these illnesses.
- Identify safety guidelines that help protect children from harm both in and away from the home.
- Describe how to treat common injuries in children.
- Demonstrate how to handle medical emergencies involving children.

PARENTING TERMS

- wellness
- developmental screening
- orthodontist
- chronic
- convulsions
- shock
- first aid
- CPR

Parents often wish they could protect their children from everything that could possibly harm them. Unfortunately, this just isn't possible. No parent can keep a child from ever catching a cold or scraping a knee. However, parents can make sure their children receive medical care. They can pay attention to safety at home and away. They can learn how to care for children who are ill or injured and what to do in an emergency. In these and other ways, parents can promote their children's health and safety.

Preventive Health Care

A lifetime of good health is something all parents want for their children. They can increase the chances of good health by teaching their children to practice wellness. **Wellness** is an approach to life that emphasizes taking positive steps toward overall good health. Wellness strategies include maintaining good nutrition and hygiene, being physically active, getting adequate rest and sleep, managing stress, and having good personal and family relationships.

Another key wellness strategy is preventive medical care. Parents can prevent many serious problems by scheduling regular medical and dental checkups for their children and immunizing them against diseases.

Medical Checkups

Children should visit a health care provider at regular intervals, not just when they are sick. The American Academy of Pediatrics advises that infants should have their first well-baby checkup at two to four days old. After that, infants and toddlers should have checkups at one month, two months, four months, six months, nine months, 12 months, 15 months, 18 months, and 24 months. From that point until age 21, routine checkups should be scheduled once a year. Children with health problems, of course, will have to see their doctor more often.

For children under five, a checkup may include **developmental screening**. This is a process that medical professionals use to determine whether a child is developing at a normal pace. Regular screening can help identify whether children have any physical, mental, or emotional problems that require attention. Diagnosing such problems early can be the key to treating them successfully.

Some children are afraid of going to see a health care provider. Parents can help reduce fears by choosing a health care provider the child likes and trusts. They can also explain procedures and treatments to their children in simple, honest terms, emphasizing how they will prevent health problems or help children get better. See Fig. 16-1.

Fig. 16-1. Many doctors' offices provide toys and books to help small patients feel at home. **How can parents help children develop positive feelings about visiting the doctor?**

Fig. 16-2. Just like brushing teeth, visiting the dentist should be a routine part of a child's health care and hygiene. **When should a child see the dentist for the first time?**

Immunizations

As explained in Chapter 14, all children need to be immunized against specific diseases. For most of these diseases, children will receive their first shot before they reach one year of age. Around the time of their first birthday, they will receive their first shots for varicella (chicken pox) and the combined vaccine for measles, mumps, and rubella (German measles). They will also need "booster" shots of various other vaccines at this time.

Children continue to receive additional immunizations at various points up through age 18. The child's health care provider will establish a schedule for each vaccine. Parents should also check with their child's school or state health department for a list of immunizations required before each school year.

Some vaccines may cause mild side effects. However, the benefits of immunization greatly outweigh the health problems that may arise.

Dental Care

Good dental care begins at birth. In addition to brushing and flossing their teeth at home, children should see a dentist on a regular basis. See Fig. 16-2.

Parents should schedule a dental checkup around the child's first birthday and then regularly thereafter, as suggested by the dentist. Children should see a dentist immediately if they receive a blow to the mouth, even if there is no bleeding.

If a child's teeth do not come in correctly, parents can take the child to an **orthodontist** (OR-thuh-DON-tist), a dentist who specializes in straightening and realigning teeth. This process usually involves putting braces on the child's teeth. Braces can be uncomfortable, and some children may feel self-conscious about the way they look. In the long term, however, braces can make a significant improvement in health, appearance, and self-image.

When Illness Strikes

When small children are sick, they cannot always explain what's wrong with them. While an older child can say "My throat hurts" or "I feel sick to my stomach," younger children may lack the verbal skills to describe their symptoms. Parents often must rely on subtle clues to figure out when their child is ill. For example, a child who tugs on his or her ear and cries may have an ear infection. However, another child with the same illness might stop eating, have trouble sleeping, or just become a bit cranky. Learning how to recognize the signs of illness, as well as how to respond to them, can help parents find and take care of a problem before it becomes severe. See Fig. 16-3.

Common Childhood Illnesses

Certain problems—such as colds, fever, rash, vomiting, and diarrhea—are quite common in children and are not necessarily cause for alarm. In most cases, parents can deal with these problems at home. If symptoms are severe or persistent, however, parents should call their child's health care provider.

Fig. 16-4 on page 333 lists guidelines for recognizing and treating some common conditions that affect children. These guidelines are not hard and fast rules. When in doubt, parents should call a health care provider.

Caring for a Sick Child. Children who are ill need the care and companionship of an adult caregiver. Here are some general guidelines for caring for children who are ill:

- **Give fluids.** Good choices include water, clear broth, and (except in cases of diarrhea) fruit juices.
- **Modify the child's diet.** Children with a sore throat or upset stomach should have soft, bland food until they feel better. Children who don't have any restrictions on their diet may find it comforting to have some of their favorite foods while they are ill.
- **Check medications.** Do not give a child any medication without checking with a health care provider. Many over-the-counter medications that are safe for adults can be dangerous for children.
- **Avoid aspirin.** Unless otherwise instructed by a health care provider, do not give children aspirin or products that contain aspirin. They have many potentially dangerous side effects for children.

Fig. 16-3. Because young children cannot always explain how they feel, parents must pay close attention to subtle signs. **What are some signs that could alert parents that a child is sick?**

Treating Common Illnesses		
Illness	**Symptoms**	**Treatment**
Cold	Runny nose, sneezing, coughing, possibly fever	Give fluids. Use a cool-mist vaporizer, making sure to clean it thoroughly after use. Do not give medication unless instructed by health care provider.
Diarrhea	Loose stools, upset stomach	Give plenty of clear fluids to prevent dehydration. Avoid giving fruit juices, soda, and other sugary drinks, as too much sugar can make dehydration worse. Put the child on a BRAT diet (bananas, rice, applesauce, and toast without butter) until symptoms subside.
Ear infection	Pulling on ear, crying, sore throat, irritability	Call health care provider for an examination.
Influenza (flu)	Fever, head and body aches, fatigue, chills, sore throat, nausea	Call health care provider, who may prescribe medication. Make sure the child gets rest, a bland diet, and plenty of fluids.
Sore throat	Difficulty swallowing, red throat, irritability	Give soft food. Call health care provider for a throat culture to check for strep throat. Antibiotics may be prescribed.

Fig. 16-4. Many illnesses common during childhood can be treated at home. **When is the attention of a health care provider needed?**

- **Follow instructions.** Give any prescribed medication exactly as the physician directs. Be sure that the dosage is correct. With some medications, it's important that the child finish the entire prescription, even if he or she feels better in a few days.
- **Keep sick children home.** Children who have a fever, bad cough, or runny nose should stay at home. Do not send them to school, take them shopping, or let them play with other children. A child recovering from a fever should have a normal temperature for 24 hours before going out.

Chronic Illnesses

Some children have a **chronic** illness, one that lasts a long time or frequently recurs. Living with a chronic illness involves learning to manage symptoms so that they interfere as little as possible with normal daily activities. Examples of chronic illnesses that may affect children include allergies, asthma, and diabetes.

Allergies. An allergy is the body's overreaction to a triggering substance, called an *allergen*. Common allergens include dust, mold, pet hair, and pollen. Some children are allergic to certain foods or plants. Reactions may include itching, sneezing, nasal congestion, watering eyes, vomiting or other digestive problems, and breathing difficulties. Most allergic reactions are only uncomfortable, but some are serious and can even be fatal if not treated immediately. A parent who suspects a child has an allergy should consult a physician. Some allergies can be managed by medication. In other cases, avoiding the allergen is the only sure way to prevent a reaction.

Asthma. This condition is characterized by attacks in which the muscles around the windpipe tighten and its lining becomes inflamed and congested. Wheezing, coughing, and shortness of breath can result. Attacks may be severe or mild and occur daily, monthly, or less often. Medication can lessen and sometimes prevent asthma attacks. When symptoms do occur, parents must remain calm and reassuring.

Diabetes. In this disorder, the body either does not make enough of a hormone called *insulin* or cannot use it effectively. As a result, the body cannot adequately control blood sugar levels.

Parenting Pointers

When to Call a Health Care Provider

Anxious parents looking after a sick child may worry about whether they need to call a doctor. It may not be obvious whether the child's condition is serious or not. Here are a few signs that can alert parents that it's time to call a health care provider:

- **Unusual behavior.** Possible signs of trouble include sleeping much more than usual, speaking less clearly than usual, unusual crying or screaming, or difficulty moving.

- **Severe pain.** While older children may be able to describe the pain, young children may show their discomfort by crying or by changing their behavior. Be on the lookout for pain that interferes with a child's normal activities.

- **Unusual symptoms.** For instance, if the child has what appears to be a simple cold, but then develops a rash as well, the condition may be something more serious.

- **Persistent symptoms.** Call a health care provider if a child's illness lasts longer than expected or if the child does not respond to treatment within a reasonable time.

- **Negative reactions to medication.** Depending on the reaction, the health care provider may decide to prescribe a different drug.

Levels that are too high can cause a variety of problems, such as damage to the eyes, kidneys, and nervous system. With the help of medical professionals, parents can manage their children's diabetes. Careful monitoring of diet, exercise, and blood sugar levels is usually required. It may also be necessary to give regular injections of synthetic insulin. School-age and older children can be taught to manage their own diabetes.

Hospital Care

Many children will have to stay in the hospital at some time. Hospitals can be strange and frightening places for children. They need their parents to be with them, to explain what is going on, and to reassure them. See Fig. 16-5.

Preplanned hospital stays are, of course, the easiest for a parent to handle. Parents can help children become familiar with the hospital environment by taking them on a preadmission tour. During the tour, children have a chance to meet the hospital personnel, ask questions, and see what goes on at the hospital. Becoming familiar with the hospital and some of the staff members helps build trust and gives children a sense of control.

On the day of admission, parents can bring along the child's favorite toy, blanket, or article of clothing. Most children feel much better if their parents stay with them and answer their questions honestly, in simple and reassuring terms.

Safety in the Home

The old saying, "Better safe than sorry," certainly applies to raising children. Young children love to wander around and explore, but they can easily hurt themselves in the process. Wise parents take reasonable precautions to prevent accidents and injury.

Childproofing the Home

Accidents are the leading cause of death for children over one year old. Protecting a child from accidents needs to start at home, as soon as a child is able to crawl. Begin making the home safe by seeing the world from a child's point of view. Get down on your hands and knees and look around. You'll discover that seemingly harmless household objects can be dangerous traps for curious children. Here are some general tips for childproofing a home:

- Cover all electrical outlets with caps or shields made especially for this purpose.
- Keep electric fans and heaters out of reach.
- Lock up dangerous items such as guns, ammunition, and power tools.
- To prevent poisoning, store household chemicals in high and securely locked cabinets.

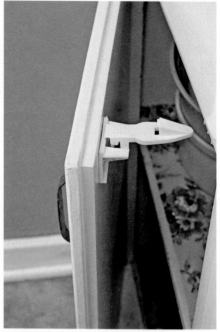

Fig. 16-6. This type of childproof latch lets the cabinet door open slightly. Adults and older children can then undo the latch, but infants and toddlers cannot.

- Use childproof latches to keep children out of low cabinets. See Fig. 16-6.
- Close the covers on the washer and dryer when not in use.
- Use window guards, available at hardware stores, to make sure that windows cannot be opened more than six inches.
- Ensure that furniture cannot be tipped over.
- Cushion edges on tables with foam pads.
- Use baby gates for places that need to be blocked off, such as staircases.
- Get rid of poisonous houseplants or move them out of children's reach.

In the Kitchen. If the handle of a pan is sticking out over the edge of the range, a young child can reach up and grab it, possibly pulling it down and spilling its hot contents. To reduce this risk, use rear burners when possible, and always turn pan handles toward the back of the range.

Sharp objects can also be hazardous. Keep all knives and other sharp utensils off of countertops or any other surface where a child could reach them. To prevent a hazard from broken glass or pottery shards, try to use unbreakable cups and plates when children are at the table, and keep breakable items out of reach. Avoid tablecloths that hang over the edge of the table—a child could grab the edge of the cloth and pull it right off, plates and all. For the same reason, unplug and hide the cords of appliances that could be pulled off a table or counter.

In the Bathroom. Even the bathroom holds hazards for young children. For example, if they climb into the toilet, they can drown. To prevent this, install a latch on the toilet lid. Make sure that all medicines—both prescription and over-the-counter—have childproof caps and are stored in high cabinets with safety latches or locks.

Around Heat Sources. Young children should be kept away from radiators, space heaters, and fireplaces. Installing guards over fireplaces can keep small children out. As soon as children are old enough to understand, they should be warned about the risk of burns from heat sources.

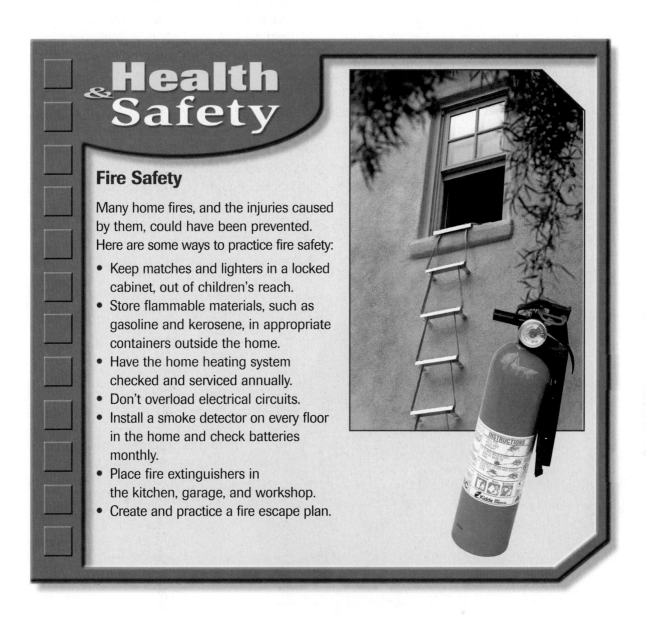

Health & Safety

Fire Safety

Many home fires, and the injuries caused by them, could have been prevented. Here are some ways to practice fire safety:

- Keep matches and lighters in a locked cabinet, out of children's reach.
- Store flammable materials, such as gasoline and kerosene, in appropriate containers outside the home.
- Have the home heating system checked and serviced annually.
- Don't overload electrical circuits.
- Install a smoke detector on every floor in the home and check batteries monthly.
- Place fire extinguishers in the kitchen, garage, and workshop.
- Create and practice a fire escape plan.

Bathing Children Safely

For most children, bath time is a lot of fun. To make baths safe as well as enjoyable, parents should supervise baths for children until they are at least five years old. Do not leave the bathroom while a child is in the tub, even if the phone rings or someone comes to the door. Even when two children are bathing together, they should not be left on their own. An older child does not have the skill to supervise a younger one. See Fig. 16-7.

To prevent electric shock, unplug and put away electrical appliances, such as hair dryers, before filling the tub. Another concern is that hot water can scald a child. Test the water temperature before putting the child in the bath, and swish the water with your hand to distribute the hot water evenly. Don't turn on the hot water when the child is in the tub. To further reduce the risk of scalding, consider installing faucets that have anti-scald valves.

Preventing Falls

Toddlers have softer, more flexible bones than adults. As a result, they often escape injury from minor falls. However, left unsupervised, toddlers may suffer major falls that can cause serious injury. They often lose control of speed and direction when running, so rooms and play areas must be kept free of such hazards as loose rugs, sharp protruding surfaces, and slick or sticky spills.

Toddlers like to climb, which can set them up for a dangerous fall. Parents need to be firm in setting and enforcing rules against climbing on furniture and cabinets. They should get in the habit of closing drawers, since children can use drawers that are left open as "stair-steps" to climb a piece of furniture. Parents should not leave anything near a window that a child might climb to reach the window. Since a determined child may still manage to climb onto a window ledge, parents should install latches and safety gates over windows to prevent the child from falling through.

Fig. 16-7. Bath time can be fun, but parents must always remember that safety comes first. **What should a parent do if the phone rings while children are in the bathtub?**

Fig. 16-8. Toddlers want to explore their world, sometimes by trying to climb out of their cribs. **What safety measures should parents take to prevent this?**

To prevent toddlers from tumbling down stairs, parents can either block staircases with gates or keep the doors leading to the stairs closed and latched. Parents need to teach toddlers how to walk up and down stairs, supervising them until they have mastered the skill. Even preschoolers and school-aged children may need to be reminded to walk slowly and carefully on stairs, taking one step at a time and holding on to the handrail.

Making Cribs and Beds Safe. A toddler who is three feet tall can climb out of a crib—and often wants to! To stop toddlers from climbing over the railing, parents can set the mattress to its lowest possible level within the crib and remove any objects that might help the toddler reach the railing. See Fig. 16-8.

As the child grows and moves from a crib to a bed, safety rails around the bed will prevent the child from falling out. The bed should be at least two feet from windows, heating vents, lamps, and drapery cords.

Parents can also take other steps to keep children from injuring themselves at night. A night-light will prevent the child from bumping into things in the dark, and a gate across the doorway of the child's bedroom will keep him or her from wandering out. Some parents use a child-monitoring device to alert them when a child wakes up.

Keeping Mealtimes Safe. In a high chair, a toddler feels on top of the world—and is in danger of falling. To prevent falls, parents should fasten the child in the seat with the chair's safety strap and keep a watchful eye on the child. The high chair should be placed in a safe part of the kitchen, away from the range, tables, counters, and door handles. Children can grab onto such objects and tip over the high chair. Any hot food or liquids should also be out of the child's reach.

Large pets should not be allowed to roam freely when toddlers are being fed because they can tip over high chairs. Toddlers may even encourage this behavior by feeding the pet or accidentally dropping food.

Preventing Suffocation

Many toddlers find plastic bags entertaining. They like the noise the bags make, and they enjoy pulling them over their heads—unaware that plastic can quickly suffocate them. This is why all large plastic bags have a warning printed on them, reminding people of the danger of using them as toys. Any plastic bag can pose a threat to children, so safety-conscious parents keep all plastic bags away from children. They poke holes in bags they don't need and dispose of them immediately. Many parents tie knots in the bottom of dry cleaning bags hanging in closets so that children cannot get inside them.

Choosing Safe Toys

Toys are an important part of a child's development, but inappropriate or poorly made toys can be dangerous. More than 200,000 children a year are treated in hospital emergency rooms for toy-related injuries. The following guidelines can help parents choose safe and age-appropriate toys for their children.

- **Read the label.** A toy that is safe for a five-year-old may be dangerous for a two-year-old. To make sure toys are age-appropriate, always read a toy's warning label before buying it. The label will specify what ages the toy is appropriate for and whether adult supervision is required. See Fig. 16-9.
- **Use common sense.** Age recommendations are based on general development levels for each age group. However, every child is different. Thus, a toy that is right for one child might not suit the skills and needs of another. Parents must be careful to match the toy to their child's abilities.
- **Think big.** To prevent choking, make sure that all toys and their parts are larger than the child's mouth. Avoid toys that have small batteries because young children can remove the batteries and choke on them.
- **Look for quality.** Choose toys that are well made. When buying stuffed toys, make sure the eyes, nose, and other small parts are sewed on securely. Remove loose ribbons and strings. Avoid toys that have sharp points and edges.
- **Avoid toxic materials.** Check that paint sets, crayons, and markers are labeled "nontoxic."

Fig. 16-9. Whether a toy is safe for a child depends partly on the child's age and abilities. **How can parents determine whether a toy is age-appropriate for their child?**

Fig. 16-10. Outdoor play equipment should be sturdy, and elevated platforms should have guardrails. **What else should parents look for to ensure that a playground is safe?**

Preventing Lead Poisoning

Toxic lead poses a major hazard to children. If they ingest even a small amount of lead, they can suffer long-term brain and nerve damage. Symptoms of lead poisoning include stomach problems, irritability, and sluggish behavior.

The principal source of lead poisoning in the home is lead-based paint, especially if it is in poor condition. Children may breathe or swallow tiny particles of peeling and chipped paint. The federal government banned lead paint in 1977, but homes and apartments built before 1978 may contain lead paint. Local or state health or environmental agencies can provide information about testing for lead hazards. If present, lead paint must be removed by a certified professional.

Lead may also be present in dirt and dust, so cleanliness can help guard against lead poisoning. Wash children's hands, bottles, pacifiers, and toys often, and regularly clean floors, windowsills, and other surfaces.

Safety Away from Home

The home is, of course, not the only place where children can be injured. The outside world has dangers all its own—and they are much harder for parents to control. The best way for parents to protect their children away from home is to keep an eye on them at all times. They can also check out the environment for possible hazards and teach their children some basic safety rules.

Playground Safety

Not surprisingly, many children get injured on playgrounds. To prevent such injuries, parents should not only supervise their children while they play but also make sure that the playground is safe before their children play on it. Playground equipment should be in good repair, and the area should be free of trash and any sharp objects, especially glass. Playground equipment should not be installed over concrete or asphalt, but rather over a softer, more cushioning surface such as sand or wood chips. Today, federal regulations require these and other safety measures. See Fig. 16-10.

Fig. 16-11. Teaching children to swim enhances their safety while giving them a chance to enjoy the water. **Why are precautions still needed even if a child can swim?**

Water Safety

Each year, accidents in swimming pools cause hundreds of deaths and thousands of injuries to children under five. Pool accidents involving children happen fast: a child can drown in the time it takes to answer a phone. Often children drown before they even have a chance to call for help.

Never allow a child to swim alone or to play near water without adult supervision, even if the child can swim. Don't let a child dive unless someone has checked to make sure that the water is deep enough and that there are no underwater hazards. At a public pool or beach, make sure a lifeguard is on duty before children enter the water. Always have a child wear a life preserver in a boat. Ensure that the life preserver fits the child properly, as one that is too large may not help in an emergency.

Younger children can drown in small amounts of water, so beware of ponds, ditches, fish bowls, and even buckets of water. Always drain and put away small "kiddy" pools after each use. Don't allow young children in spas and hot tubs; they could drown or become seriously overheated. Watch children carefully while they are playing at the beach, as unseen tides and currents can quickly pull a child into the water. See Fig. 16-11.

Safety on the Road

Motor vehicle crashes kill more children under age 15 than any other cause, claiming nearly 1,800 lives and resulting in more than 274,000 injuries each year. Most of those deaths and injuries occur because children are not buckled in safely. To prevent injuries in motor vehicles:

- Make sure children are securely fastened into approved, age- and size-appropriate safety seats properly installed in the vehicle's rear seat.
- Model safety precautions by insisting that everyone—adults and children alike—have a seat belt or other restraint on before the vehicle begins to move.
- Drive carefully and defensively, obeying all traffic laws.
- Never allow children to move around freely in a vehicle.
- Avoid driving while distracted. If something happens to distract your attention, pull over, stop the vehicle, and deal with the distraction before driving on.

Choosing a Car Seat. The guidelines for selecting the right car safety seat are based on the child's age and size. Infants up to 12 months and 20 pounds should always be placed in a rear-facing safety seat. When they outgrow an infant seat, children are best protected in a forward-facing child seat with its own harness. A child who has reached a weight of 40 pounds and a height of 40 inches should be moved to a booster seat to help the adult-sized safety belt fit properly. Only when children are adult-sized should they use a car's standard seat belts. They are considered large enough when the lap belt fits low over the child's upper thighs and the shoulder belt rests on the child's shoulder, not across the neck or face.

Fig. 16-12. A car seat will not protect a child unless it is used correctly. Parents must read the owner's manual carefully and follow the instructions exactly.

No one car seat is best or safest. Choose the seat that best fits the child and can be installed correctly in your vehicle. Some can be converted from rear-facing to front-facing seats. Price does not always indicate quality, since expensive car seats may have features that are unnecessary or difficult to use. Whatever car seat is chosen, be sure to install and use it correctly. See Fig. 16-12.

Bicycle and Pedestrian Safety. Kids who are too young to drive are likely to do a lot of traveling on foot or on a bicycle. They need to be aware that, like cars, bikes have to follow traffic laws. Cyclists should ride close to the curb, with the flow of traffic, and they should never ride into a street without looking first for cars and pedestrians. In addition to these safety rules, most states require that bike riders wear helmets. Make sure that helmets fit properly and are securely fastened.

Pedestrians need to follow safety rules, too. Instruct children to stop and look both ways for traffic before crossing a street. Teach them to recognize signals such as stop signs, walk signs, and traffic lights. Younger children should hold an adult's hand when crossing a street. A group of children can form a line, holding hands, behind the adult who is supervising them.

Safety with Strangers

One of the most terrifying thoughts for parents is the possibility that another person could deliberately harm their child. A parent's or trusted caregiver's close supervision can ward off such danger when children are very young. As they grow, however, children need to assume more responsibility for their own safety. Parents can follow these guidelines to help protect their children from strangers who might harm them:

Modeling CHARACTER

Teaching Responsible Behavior

Perhaps the best way for adults to teach children to behave responsibly is to be responsible themselves. Actions, in many cases, speak louder than words. For example, a parent who always tells children to wear their seat belts, but never puts on his or her own belt, is sending mixed signals. The message the children may get is that when they grow up, they won't need to wear safety belts either.

A parent who always wears a helmet when riding a bicycle, by contrast, is teaching by example. Children will learn that wearing a bike helmet is the right thing to do for everyone. Parents can reinforce this behavior by explaining how wearing a helmet protects them from injury in case they fall. Children will have more respect for safety rules if they understand the reasons behind them.

Think About It
What are some other situations in which a parent could model responsible behavior?

- Know where children are, and with whom, at all times.
- Teach young children their names, addresses, and telephone numbers, as well as the first and last names of their parents or caregivers.
- Never leave a child alone in a car, even for a short period of time.
- Teach children never to accept a ride from a stranger and never to enter anyone's home without parental approval.
- Tell children that if anyone attempts to grab them or give them a ride, they should scream, run away, and tell a parent or other trusted adult immediately.
- Tell children never to give any information over the phone, especially their names and addresses, or to indicate that they are alone at home.
- Caution children who are home alone to keep the doors locked and admit only authorized people.
- Don't drop older children off alone at public places such as malls, arcades, or parks.

Abuse. In many cases, the person who harms a child is not a stranger but someone the child knows and trusts. To protect children from sexual abuse, parents must teach them that certain parts of their body are private and that there is "good touching" and "bad touching." Children need to know that if anyone touches them in a way that makes them feel uncomfortable, they should walk away and tell a trusted adult immediately. Teachers or family counselors can tell parents how best to communicate these ideas to their children in an age-appropriate fashion. Parents who suspect abuse can contact the police, an emergency hotline, or a local protective services agency. Chapter 2 gives more information about child abuse.

Injuries and Emergencies

Would you know what to do if a child fell and broke an arm? What if a child with a high fever began to have **convulsions**—strong and involuntary contractions of the muscles? All parents and caregivers should be prepared to handle a variety of situations, from minor injuries to serious emergencies.

Treating Minor Injuries

No matter how many safety precautions parents take, no child gets through life without a few bumps, scrapes, and bruises. Fortunately, most childhood injuries heal with only a gentle cleansing, a bandage, and a comforting hug. See Fig. 16-13.

Fig. 16-13. By far, the most common injuries during childhood are minor ones. **How should a minor cut be treated?**

Children may also experience nosebleeds, splinters, and other mishaps. Most are minor, although parents should watch for signs that they are more serious. Fig. 16-14 describes how these and other common injuries should be treated.

Preparing for Emergencies

A quick and appropriate response in an emergency can mean the difference between life and death. To be ready for a crisis, parents should keep a list of emergency numbers by the phone. If the phone has a speed dial feature, parents can program the emergency numbers into it. Children should be taught how to call for help and what to say in an emergency. See Fig. 16-15.

Handling Emergencies

If a situation appears to be more serious than just a minor injury, what should you do? Here are some basic guidelines:

- Stay calm and assess the situation.
- Call for medical help if necessary.
- Reassure the child in a calm manner.
- Do not move the child unless it is necessary for safety reasons.
- Keep the child warm and still to prevent **shock**, a dangerous drop in blood flow caused by serious injury.

Many emergencies require **first aid,** immediate care provided until medical help arrives. Fig. 16-16 describes first aid for specific medical emergencies.

Treating Common Injuries

Injury	Treatment
Animal bites	Apply pressure to stop bleeding. Wash the wound with soap and water. Call a health care provider for advice. If the animal is someone's pet, find out whether it has been vaccinated for rabies. If it was a wild animal, call the local animal control department to have the animal trapped for testing.
Bumps and bruises	Apply a cool cloth or cold pack for ten minutes. For a bump on the head, call a health care provider if the child loses consciousness, becomes drowsy or irritable, complains of a headache, or vomits. Also call a health provider if a baby falls or is dropped from any height.
Burns (minor)	Run cold water over the burned area for about five minutes. Then keep the area dry and clean. Do not apply ointment.
Cuts and scrapes	Apply pressure to stop bleeding, if needed. (Small wounds usually stop bleeding on their own.) Wash the wound with soap and water. Dry the area, then apply antiseptic and a bandage.
Insect bites	Wash the area with soap and water, dry, and apply antiseptic.
Insect stings	Scrape or brush off the stinger with a straight-edged object, such as a credit card. Don't try to pull it out with tweezers or your fingers, as this may release more venom. Disinfect the site and apply ice or cold packs. If the child shows signs of a severe reaction (difficulty breathing, swelling throat or lips, faintness, confusion, rapid heartbeat, hives, nausea, cramps, or vomiting), call emergency services.
Nosebleed	Have the child sit with the head tilted slightly forward. Pinch the lower half of the nose between thumb and finger. Hold firmly for ten minutes, then release. If bleeding has not stopped, apply pressure for ten more minutes. Get medical help if bleeding continues.
Splinters	Wash the area. Remove the splinter with a sterilized needle or tweezers. Clean with an antiseptic. Call a health care provider if the splinter remains embedded after a few days, or if skin reddens.

Fig. 16-14. Some injuries can be treated at home, while others require professional attention. **What are some signs that medical assistance is needed?**

Fig. 16-15. Children should be able to tell rescuers their name, telephone number, address, and their parents' names. **Which emergency numbers should be listed by the phone?**

CPR. Giving first aid may include performing **CPR**—cardiopulmonary resuscitation, a technique used to keep a person's heart and lungs functioning until medical care arrives. The rescuer breathes into the injured person's mouth and applies pressure to the chest to force the heart to pump. Because CPR can cause serious damage if done incorrectly, only trained, certified individuals should perform it.

Rescue Techniques for Choking. What do a small plastic toy, a bottle top, and an ice cube all have in common? Each could be the culprit in a choking accident. Parents can take steps to prevent choking by keeping small objects

First Aid for Medical Emergencies	
Bleeding (serious)	Apply direct pressure to the wound for at least ten minutes, using sterile gauze or a clean cloth. If possible, elevate the wounded area so that it is above the heart. Get help if bleeding does not stop in ten minutes, if the cut is large and deep, or if the child is pale, dizzy, or unconscious.
Bone fracture	Keep the child still. Place a pillow under the injured limb. Call your health care provider.
Burns (serious)	Get medical help immediately. If the skin is charred or destroyed, do not touch the wound or try to remove charred clothing. If clothing is on fire, smother the flames by wrapping the child in heavy material, such as a rug or coat, and rolling the child on the ground.
Choking	If the child can cough, speak, or make noise, the airway is only partially obstructed. Wait for it to clear on its own. If the child cannot cough, speak, or make any noise, the airway is completely obstructed. Use the appropriate rescue technique (see pages 348-349).
Convulsions	Guide the child to a clear space on the floor, and place a cushion or folded towel under the child's head. When the convulsions have passed, turn the child to one side, allowing saliva to drain from the mouth, and call a health care provider.
Electric shock	First, turn off the electric source that caused the shock. If this is not possible, separate the child from the current with a dry stick—never with any metal object. Get emergency help. CPR may be required.
Poisoning	Call emergency services or poison control center. Do not take any action until instructed by medical personnel. If the poison is known, save the container if possible.

Fig. 16-16. In an emergency, a quick and correct response may mean the difference between life and death. **When is the best time to learn how to handle emergencies?**

such as these away from young children and by reminding older children to take moderate-sized bites when eating. In case an emergency occurs, parents should also know how to perform the rescue technique for choking. The maneuver varies according to the victim's age, as shown in Fig. 16-17 below and Fig. 16-18 on the next page.

Rescue Technique for Choking Infants

Step 1: Place the infant stomach-down across your forearm, using your thigh or lap for support, and hold the infant's chest in your hand and jaw in your fingers.

Step 2: Point the infant's head downward and give up to five quick, firm blows to the infant's back with the heel of your hand.

If this procedure fails to expel the object that is causing the choking, follow these steps:

Step 3: Turn the infant face up. Lay the infant on your thigh or lap, and support the infant's head with your hand.

Step 4: Using your other hand, place two fingers on the middle of the infant's breastbone just below the nipples. Give up to five quick downward thrusts.

Step 5: Continue giving five back blows followed by five chest thrusts until the object is dislodged or the infant loses consciousness.

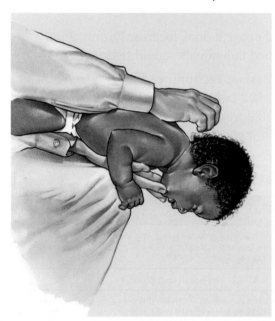

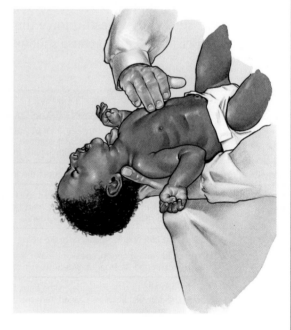

If the child does lose consciousness or starts to turn blue, immediate cardiopulmonary resuscitation (CPR) is needed. Have someone call 911, and begin CPR if you have been trained. Also, look into the infant's throat. If you can see the object that is causing the choking and think you might be able to grasp it, try to remove it with a finger.

Fig. 16-17. The rescue technique for choking in infants differs from that used for older children and adults. **What are the differences?**

Fig. 16-18. There's no substitute for taking a first aid class and regular refresher sessions. **Why should a person receive training before attempting to perform CPR or the rescue technique for choking?**

Rescue Technique for Choking Children and Adults

If the victim is standing or sitting:

Step 1: Stand behind the victim. Make a fist with one hand and place it, with the thumb toward the victim, just above the victim's navel.

Step 2: Grasp the fist with your other hand.

Step 3: Thrust your fist upward and inward quickly. Repeat the technique until you dislodge the object.

If the victim is unconscious:

Step 1: Position the victim on his or her back, and look inside the mouth. If you can see the object, use a sweeping motion with your index finger to remove it.

Step 2: If not, kneel over the victim, place the heel of one hand in the middle of the abdomen just above the navel, and place your other hand on top of the first hand.

Step 3: Give five quick thrusts, pressing your hands in and up.

Step 4: Open the victim's mouth again, and sweep the area again to try to remove the blockage.

Step 5: Repeat these steps until the object is expelled or help arrives.

Step 6: If the victim stops breathing, begin CPR if you have been trained in this technique.

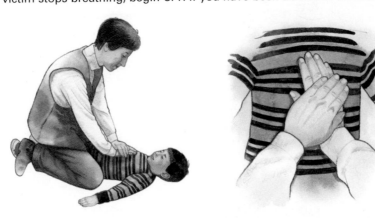

Preparing Caregivers for Emergencies

When choosing a temporary caregiver for their child, parents will want to know that the caregiver is able to handle a medical emergency. Parents can check to make sure that the caregiver knows basic emergency procedures, such as how to administer first aid for choking.

When leaving a child with a caregiver for the first time, parents should make sure to discuss whatever health issues the child has, including any medications the child is taking. They should give the caregiver detailed written instructions for administering the medicine. They should also leave a written list of emergency information, including:

- The address and phone number (including area code) of the place where the parents will be.
- Their cell phone number, if they have one. The cell phone should be left on.
- The names and phone numbers of two trusted people the caregiver can call if a parent cannot be reached.
- Phone numbers for the child's physician and for emergency services, including a poison control center. See Fig. 16-19.

Fig. 16-19. When parents have confidence that their children's caregivers can handle emergencies, they have greater peace of mind. **If you were caring for someone else's children, what questions would you ask the parents?**

▶ Consumer Product Safety Specialist

Consumer product safety specialists are the people who make sure that the products you use every day are safe. They perform various tests to determine that equipment is sturdy, foods and drugs are safe to consume, and chemicals are not harmful to the environment. Because there are so many different ways to test products, people who work in this field have a variety of different job titles: investigator, inspector, engineer, and statistician, to name a few.

Consumer product safety specialists work in many different areas. Some work for government agencies such as the Consumer Product Safety Commission (CPSC). Others are employed by private companies such as toy makers, cosmetic companies, homebuilders, pharmaceutical firms, and clothing manufacturers.

"When you buy something in a store, you have a right to know that it won't harm you, your loved ones, animals, or the environment. Individual consumers can't be expected to test every product they buy; they don't have the knowledge. That's where we come in. We're trained to understand consumer safety laws, and we have the background to verify that the information manufacturers provide about their products is accurate, valid, and complete."

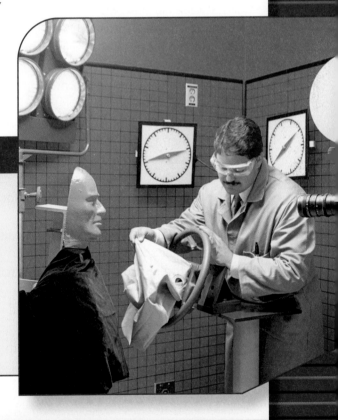

CAREER TIPS

- In high school, take classes in business and consumer law, if available.
- Pursue a college degree in a field that interests you, such as health care, chemistry, business, or manufacturing. All these fields are involved in different aspects of consumer safety testing.
- Consider an internship at the Consumer Product Safety Commission or a related government agency.

CHAPTER SUMMARY

- When parents teach their children to take positive steps toward overall good health, they teach the concept of wellness. Preventive medical care is part of wellness.
- Parents need to know the symptoms of common childhood illnesses and how to treat them.
- By following safety guidelines, parents protect children in and away from the home.
- Treating children for injuries is a common occurrence for parents. Many injuries are minor, requiring only basic first-aid procedures.
- Serious emergencies are handled by providing emergency first aid and seeking help.

Check Your Facts

1. What kinds of preventive medical care promote wellness in children?
2. What is the purpose of developmental screening?
3. What should a parent do to provide good dental care for a child?
4. Why do parents often struggle to figure out whether a child is ill?
5. How would you treat a child who has a cold and one who has diarrhea?
6. List six general guidelines for caring for children who are ill.
7. What are five signs that indicate a health care provider should be called?
8. Describe three chronic illnesses that may affect children.
9. How would you prepare a young child for a hospital stay?
10. How can a parent prevent poisoning in the home?
11. Suggest five tips for preventing falls.
12. How can you tell that a playground is safe for children?
13. What is the most important rule for child safety around water?
14. What causes the most deaths and injuries for children in vehicle crashes?
15. Are the people who sexually abuse children always strangers? Explain.
16. Describe how to treat at least five common injuries.
17. What are five basic guidelines for handling serious injury situations?
18. What emergency information does a babysitter need from parents?

Think Critically

1. **Identifying Examples.** Describe a toy that would be unsafe for a three-year-old, and explain why it is unsafe.
2. **Predicting Consequences.** If a parent doesn't remain calm in an emergency, what are several things that could happen?

Apply Your Learning

1. **Kitchen Safety Model.** Make and display a model of a childproof kitchen. Use labels to point out specific safety precautions.

2. **Parenting Advice.** What would you recommend to parents in the following situations, and why? **a)** The phone rings while Erin, age three, is in the bathtub. **b)** Will, age ten months, can crawl and often heads down the hall near the top of the stairs. **c)** Andy, age two, tries to climb out of the high chair. **d)** Lily, age two, plays with toys stored in several plastic bags. **e)** From her playpen Amelia, age one, picks at chipping paint on the wall.

3. **Emergency Responses.** Demonstrate how to handle the medical emergencies in Fig. 16-16.

4. **Caregiver Interview.** With a partner, conduct a mock conversation between a parent and babysitter. Highlight basic health and safety issues the babysitter needs to know.

Cross-Curricular Connections

1. **Language Arts.** Suppose you are a pediatrician. Some parents tell you they've heard that immunizations can cause autism in children. Research immunizations and write a handout for parents, explaining how facts support the need for immunizations.

2. **Science.** Learn about fire extinguishers and report how they work. What is a fire? How are they put out? What are the different types of fire extinguishers?

3. **Language Arts.** Write a dialogue in which a parent teaches a child about stranger safety. Check the Internet for ideas.

Family & Community Connections

1. **Fire Safety Awareness.** Discuss the fire-safety tips you learned in this chapter with family members. Does your home meet the guidelines? Work with your family to make any changes that will improve your home's safety.

2. **First-Aid Classes.** Contact at least three local public health clinics, hospitals, or other medical facilities to find out what classes they offer in first-aid techniques. List the name, contact information, and available classes for each place you contacted. Present your findings to the class.

UNIT 4

Nurturing Children

CHAPTER 17

Helping Children Learn

CHAPTER OBJECTIVES

- Summarize brain development through adolescence.
- Describe patterns of intellectual development.
- Identify signs of intellectual development in young children.
- Explain a parent's role as teacher.
- Propose ways to help children learn skills related to concepts, thinking, language, and math.
- Explain the value of music and art experiences.

PARENTING TERMS

- neurons
- synapses
- concepts
- classification
- seriation
- centration
- conservation
- reversibility
- incidental learning
- learning style
- articulation
- bilingual

Two-year-old Jackson and his parents are in a sporting-goods store. Every time Jackson sees a ball, he points and yells, "There ball!" He eagerly points out a bin of soccer balls, boxes of golf balls, and a display of round fishing floats. Jackson is excited about his ability to find balls everywhere.

Jackson might as well be wearing a hat printed with the message, "Brain development in progress!" Children's minds grow and develop in remarkable ways, and parents can take steps to nurture that development.

Brain Development in Progress

Research on brain development shows that a child's brain grows at an amazing rate. The brain triples in weight during the first two years of life, then continues to grow. Throughout this process, brain cells, called **neurons,** branch and grow into dense connective networks. As the neurons become coated with an insulating layer, they are able to send messages to each other more quickly and efficiently. See Fig. 17-1.

In the past, scientists believed that the brain stopped growing in early childhood. However, new brain research has uncovered another wave of gray-matter production that occurs around age 11 or 12. This growth spurt occurs in the *frontal lobes,* the part of the brain that governs impulse control, planning, and reasoning. The shift to frontal-lobe brain activity leads to more reasoned decisions and increased perception and performance.

After this wave of growth, the brain continues to develop in other ways. Some regions of the brain, such as the emotional (limbic) system, are not completely wired until puberty.

During adolescence, the number of **synapses,** or connections between neurons, decreases. This "pruning" process is a healthy one for the brain. Unneeded connections are weeded out, strengthening those that remain. While the brain of a three-year-old has about 1,000 trillion synapses, an adult brain has only about half this number.

The pruning process illustrates that brain cells and the connections between them must be used in order to survive. Thus, a person's interactions in the world help shape his or her brain.

While some areas of the adolescent brain are mature, full development of the frontal lobes does not occur until the late teens or early twenties. Researchers see this fact as strong evidence that teens need to protect their brains from harmful substances, because the adolescent brain is still a work in progress.

Fig. 17-1. An infant's brain is full of potential. Positive, stimulating experiences during the early years build and reinforce neural connections. **How can parents aid this process?**

Piaget's Four Periods of Intellectual Development		
Period	**Age Range**	**Key Characteristics**
Sensorimotor period	Birth to 2 years	❏ Using the senses to explore and learn ❏ Object permanence—the understanding that objects continue to exist when they are out of sight ❏ Beginning of symbolic thought
Preoperational period	2 to 7 years	❏ Conceptual thinking ❏ Classification ❏ Seriation ❏ Centration ❏ Symbolic thought
Concrete operational period	7 to 11 years	❏ Beginning of more complex thinking ❏ Conservation ❏ Reversibility ❏ Some awareness of other people's perspectives
Formal operational period	11 years and older	❏ Logical and abstract thought ❏ Forming hypotheses ❏ Predicting consequences ❏ Use of reason and creativity to solve problems

Fig. 17-2. Piaget divided a child's intellectual development into four periods. **During which period do children begin to understand the meaning of symbols?**

Patterns of Intellectual Development

There are many theories about how thought processes develop during childhood and adolescence. In Chapter 4, you read about the theories of social scientists and physicians such as Maria Montessori, Arnold Gesell, and B. F. Skinner. Perhaps the best-known theory of intellectual development is the one developed by Jean Piaget, a Swiss psychologist.

Piaget's Theory

According to Piaget, children advance through a series of intellectual stages that use increasingly complex thought processes. These stages occur in a fixed order and at approximately the same ages in all children. Development is gradual, so the end of one stage may overlap with the beginning of the next. Piaget identified four main periods of intellectual development, as summarized in Fig. 17-2.

Sensorimotor Period. This developmental period, which is divided into six stages, takes place from a child's birth to age two. The first four stages, which all occur during infancy, were described in Chapter 13. Stage 5 begins around a child's first birthday. Piaget called Stage 5 the "little scientist" stage because of the way young toddlers explore. They like to experiment, repeatedly turning a light switch off and on or poking their fingers into every morsel of food on their plates.

Before they reach the age of two, children progress to Stage 6. This stage marks the beginning of *symbolic thought*—the ability to use symbols to represent objects and experiences. This ability eventually helps children recognize that words and numbers are symbols that can stand for objects and ideas.

Children in Stage 6 can begin to solve simple problems using an ability that Piaget called "mental combination." For example, whenever 22-month-old Rosa washed her hands, she used a small stool to reach the bathroom sink. One day, she wanted a cookie from the kitchen counter but couldn't reach it. She solved her problem by pushing a kitchen chair over to the counter so that it could be used as a stool. She was able to mentally combine her understanding of how a stool works with her current situation and the chair that was on hand.

Preoperational Period. This period lasts from about age two to age seven. During this time, children learn to organize information into **concepts**, or general mental categories of objects or ideas. In conceptual thinking, children learn to group objects according to some quality they share and to see relationships between objects.

Fig. 17-3. Some toys are designed to let children practice skills such as seriation. **What characteristics is this child focusing on as she sorts objects?**

During the preoperational period, children begin to use two methods of organizing information. The first, **classification**, involves grouping objects by common traits. For example, two-year-old Jackson has formed a concept of a ball. If his parents open up his toy box and tell him to find all the balls, Jackson will pull out every object that has a spherical shape. Soon he will begin to display **seriation**, arranging objects in order by size or number. When his parents ask him which ball is biggest, he will be able to pick out the largest one. See Fig. 17-3.

By about age six, Jackson will be able to pick all the blue balls from a box of red and blue balls and line them up by size. But he won't be able to pick out the blue balls from a box of red and blue balls *and blocks*. His classification skills will be limited by **centration**, the ability to focus on only one quality at a time.

During this period, children also become skilled in symbolic thinking. When a parent puts on a coat, for example, it symbolizes "going out." Pajamas, a story, and a hug and kiss may symbolize "bedtime."

Period of Concrete Operations. Around age seven, children enter the period of concrete operations. They take short "hops" into complex thinking. Their thought processes are restricted to working with concrete (solid) objects. For example, eight-year-old Chelsea understands the idea of adding numbers, but she solves a problem by counting on her fingers.

Children take big leaps in logical thinking in this period. For example, they understand the principle of **conservation**, that an object's physical properties stay the same even when its appearance changes. A liter of water remains a liter, whether it is in a tall, skinny bottle or a short, wide bottle. Once children master conservation, they also understand **reversibility**—changing something back to its original state.

Multiple Intelligences

Intelligence	Description	Examples
Linguistic	Ability to learn and use languages	Poet, writer, lawyer
Logical-mathematical	Ability to understand scientific or mathematical principles or operations	Scientist, mathematician, computer programmer
Spatial	Ability to represent the spatial world in the mind	Sculptor, painter, architect, scientist working in a field such as anatomy
Bodily-kinesthetic	Ability to use the whole body to solve a problem or create something	Athlete, performing artist
Musical	Ability to think musically, to hear patterns, to keep music in the mind	Musician, composer
Interpersonal	Ability to understand other people	Teacher, salesperson, counselor, politician
Intrapersonal	Ability to understand oneself well	Leaders in many fields
Naturalist	Ability to identify living things or natural features	Botanist, chef

Fig. 17–4. According to Gardner, each person has specific strengths and weaknesses in different areas of intelligence. **Which types of intelligence might be most important for a carpenter?**

They understand that water from the short, wide bottle can be poured back into the tall, skinny bottle again.

At this age, children also start to realize that other people experience things differently than they do. For example, a four-year-old might pick up an apple in the kitchen and call out to his mother in the living room, "Can I have this?" A few years later, however, the child will understand that his mother cannot necessarily see what he sees.

Period of Formal Operations. This last period begins around age eleven. As formal operational thinkers, adolescents can think logically, abstractly, and systematically. They can discuss theoretical issues, form hypotheses, and predict consequences. These skills help them become better decision makers. In addition, adolescents learn to use reason and creative thinking to solve problems. However, not everyone develops such skills at the same time or masters them to the same degree.

Gardner's Multiple Intelligences

What is intelligence? Is it the ability to do mental math or speak a foreign language? Are you intelligent if you know how to rope a calf or dance a tango? If you said, "All of the above," you are probably right. Intelligence is the ability to acquire and use knowledge.

Piaget's theory of intellectual development focused on those aspects of intelligence related to symbolic thought. Many other scientists have thought about intelligence along similar lines. Traditional intelligence tests have typically measured strength in language and logical-mathematical abilities. Harvard professor Howard Gardner, by contrast, holds a broader view of intelligence. Gardner theorized that the brain has eight areas of intelligence. Fig. 17-4 lists these eight "intelligences" and gives examples of professions that might make use of each area.

The theory of multiple intelligences suggests that, although all people share these eight areas of intelligence, each person has strengths and weaknesses in specific areas. For instance, a child might have high musical intelligence but be weak in the spatial realm. It is important that parents value their children's unique strengths and help them to recognize and develop their abilities. See Fig. 17-5.

Methods of Learning

Parents can better promote intellectual development if they understand how children learn. Unlike you, very young children don't learn by studying a textbook! Children from ages one to three learn by four main methods:

- **Imitation.** Toddlers are excellent observers of their environment. They learn to use a spoon or open a door by watching and imitating their parents. They learn language by listening to and imitating the people around them. This is why good role models are important. Parents can teach their children quite a lot just by modeling the skills they want the children to learn.

- **Repetition.** Young children love repetition. They enjoy stories and games that have repeating lines. Repetition strengthens children's ability to predict outcomes, which makes them feel safe and competent. Parents may need to learn to be patient with requests to play the same game or read the same story time after time.

- **Trial and error.** Toddlers are the masters of learning by trial and error, which they combine with repetition. For example, a toddler may try several ways of holding a cup in a stream of water before hitting on the method of directing the stream into the mouth of the cup. As they grow older, children learn how to predict outcomes based on prior experience and knowledge, rather than having to repeat an event.

- **Incidental learning.** Every new experience provides opportunities for **incidental learning**—unplanned learning that stems from other activities. For example, while drawing with a crayon, a child may learn that pressing too hard causes the crayon to break.

Fig. 17-5. When children are given opportunities to utilize their strengths, they gain a sense of achievement and confidence. **What areas of intelligence does rock climbing call upon?**

Learning Styles

As children grow, they gain additional ways to learn, such as by reading and writing. At some point along the way, methods of learning become more individual. According to some theorists, each person has a particular **learning style**, or preferred method of taking in and processing information. For example, some people are visual learners who need to write information down in order to learn and remember it. Others are auditory learners—they learn best by hearing information or saying it aloud to themselves. Observant parents recognize and respect each child's unique learning style.

Parents as Teachers

Parents can have a great influence on their children's early learning. They can promote intellectual growth by giving their children appropriate stimulation—different experiences and materials to encourage their blossoming imagination and curiosity.

Parents need to keep in mind that every child is different. They should allow each child to learn at his or her own pace and not worry if a child seems "slow" in some area. Most children catch up in their own time. What is important is to keep learning fun. That way, children enjoy and look forward to it. See Fig. 17-6.

Nurturing the Desire to Learn

Children love to learn. For them, learning new concepts is fun, challenging, and exciting. Many parents find that sharing in their children's excitement and curiosity is one of the most satisfying aspects of parenting.

Parents can stimulate learning in a number of ways. For one, they can model an enthusiasm for learning in their own lives. Children will

Fig. 17-6. Playing with children is a way to guide their learning. **What concepts or skills might a child learn by "playing store"?**

pick up on their parents' interest in learning about people, places, things, and ideas.

Parents can also encourage children's natural curiosity. Giving them the time and space they need to investigate new things, as well as encouraging them to ask questions and seek information, shows an appreciation of their urge to learn. By praising children for their curiosity, parents can show them that the ability to learn is within their grasp.

Opportunities for learning can come up at just about any time. For example, a parent who is at the grocery store with a young child might point out the different colors and shapes of the packages on the shelves. With an older child, the parent might read the labels or ingredients lists aloud. By taking advantage of such "teachable moments," parents can make just about any experience a learning opportunity for their children. See Fig. 17-7.

What About Television?

Parents often wonder whether television viewing benefits or hinders intellectual development. Research is continuing, but so far, the answer seems to be that it depends on the age of the child.

Because the early years are such a critical period for brain development, many child development experts recommend that children under the age of two not watch any television. Some studies suggest that daily TV viewing before the age of three leads to poorer reading and math skills at ages six and seven. One possible explanation is that when TV becomes a habit, it reduces the amount of time spent on more beneficial forms of stimulation, such as interacting with caregivers and exploring the environment.

On the other hand, there is evidence that quality educational programs can benefit children between the ages of three and five. Still, parents should be careful to choose age-appropriate programming and balance it with other forms of play and learning.

Fig. 17-7. A family camping trip can be a rich opportunity for learning. **How might a parent turn this into a "teachable moment"?**

Fig. 17-8. Basic concepts are the building blocks of learning. **What everyday objects could safely be used to help teach a child basic concepts?**

Promoting Concept Development

Children begin a lifetime of learning by mastering certain basic concepts and skills. Some of your favorite childhood books, songs, and games probably introduced you to such concepts and skills as counting, identifying shapes and colors, classifying, comparing and contrasting, perceiving position, and grasping elementary concepts of time. See Fig. 17-8.

Here are some ways that parents can promote the development of basic concepts:

- **Classification.** Children under seven can classify items by one characteristic only. Older children can perform more complex tasks. Parents can help their children learn to classify objects by sorting socks on laundry day or stacking magazines and newspapers in separate piles. For school-age children, making a family tree is a more elaborate exercise in classification.

- **Shape.** Comparing or experimenting with shapes helps children notice similarity and difference, an important skill for reading. To build this skill, parents might encourage children to cut shapes out of modeling clay using cookie cutters, or to make pictures by combining shapes cut out of paper or felt.

- **Size and space.** Grasping concepts of size and space paves the way for understanding the principles of seriation and conservation. Children can track their growth on a height chart or respond to requests involving space relationships, such as "Put the spoon next to the plate." Older children can work on more advanced size and space relationships by drawing a map of their neighborhood to send to an out-of-town relative.

- **Number and quantity.** The ability to understand numbers develops gradually. Through everyday activities, parents can help children learn basic counting concepts, such as the idea that each item in a group is counted only once. Parents and children might count individual pieces of fruit in the supermarket or count plates while setting the table.

- **Time.** Until about age five, children link the passage of time only to their own needs and to immediate, familiar events. By the time they start school, most children can tell time using a digital clock and recite the days of the week in order. Activities such as putting pictures of past events in a family photo album or growing plants from seeds can help children grasp the concept of time.

Promoting Thinking Skills

As children grow and learn, they develop a variety of basic thinking skills. They learn to perceive the world around them and focus their attention. They gain the ability to remember and process information, to reason, and to solve problems. At the same time, they also develop abundant curiosity, imagination, and creativity. Parents can nurture all these different types of thinking skills in their children.

Memory

The ability to remember develops very early. Infants as young as two months of age may come to expect a feeding at a certain time of day. Parents can strengthen a toddler's memory by playing games such as "Which hand?" The parent picks up a small object, such as a pebble, in one hand. Then the parent closes both hands and asks, "Which hand is the rock in?" By pointing to the correct hand, the child demonstrates the ability to keep an object in memory for a short period of time. See Fig. 17-9.

Toddlers can also remember the location of certain items that are always kept in the same place. Eighteen-month-old Tyler looks for a toy at his grandparents' house in the place it was the last time he was there. Parents can help children practice this skill by creating specific places for children's possessions to be stored. For example, a coat might be hung on a hook at the child's eye level. When it's time to go out, the parent can ask, "Can you find your coat?"

By age three, preschoolers begin to remember events that are significant to them. However, they may remember events out of sequence or forget the main idea, because they tend to remember the part of an experience that most

Fig. 17-9. Games such as "Which hand?" test a toddler's memory skills. **What are some ways to strengthen memory in older children?**

Fig. 17-10. Allowing children to evaluate options for themselves empowers them and gives them a sense of responsibility for their decisions.

captures their attention. At the circus, they may remember eating peanuts but forget having seen the elephants. However, they can usually remember a general sequence of events, such as going to the store or taking a bath. To strengthen a preschooler's memory, parents can read books aloud and ask questions for the child to answer. Children can also show that they remember where things belong by helping their parents put away laundry or toys.

During their school years, children begin to understand the *process* of memorization. They can figure out strategies for memorizing math facts or lists of spelling words. Parents can help foster memory skills in school-age children by asking them to tell about the day's events in order, or by helping them create routines for doing homework and chores.

Reasoning and Problem Solving

Young children have a limited ability to solve problems through reason. As they grow, their reasoning abilities develop in response to their experiences. Of course, practice helps children develop these skills more fully. Parents can encourage children to use such reasoning skills as naming, classifying, comparing and contrasting, identifying cause and effect, and generalizing.

To promote reasoning skills, parents can ask open-ended questions, such as "How do you think we could…?" and "What do you think might happen if we…?" In responding to these questions, children may draw on a variety of skills, such as making inferences or predicting outcomes. Parents can discuss the children's responses with them and guide them to see which answers are best supported by facts.

Parents can encourage young children to think about cause and effect by asking "why" questions. For example, while reading a picture book to a three-year-old, a parent might ask, "Why is that girl carrying an umbrella?" or "Why do you think that baby is crying?" The content of the child's answers is not as important as the process of learning to think about cause and effect.

With older children, parents can promote decision-making skills by helping children evaluate the pros and cons of a situation. If children ask for advice, parents can help them list the options and guide them in predicting the possible outcome of each one. See Fig. 17-10.

Curiosity, Imagination, and Creativity

Children are naturally curious. They are eager to explore and learn about the world around them. Parents can support their children's thirst for knowledge by responding patiently to their endless "why" questions.

Fig. 17-11. Through imagination and creativity, this father and son have found a way to enjoy a "fishing trip" in spite of obstacles. **How do you use your creativity and imagination to solve problems?**

They can do their best to explain why the sky is blue or why a cat has claws in simple terms that children can understand. If they aren't sure of the answer to a question, they can say, "I don't know, but I'll try to find out." This response leaves the door open for further exploration. Situations like this can also be an opportunity to show children how to find and use resources. Children who see their parents look up unfamiliar words in the dictionary or type queries into an Internet search page will learn how to use these resources to answer their own questions.

Curiosity is linked to imagination. Curiosity leads children to wonder about the world, and imagination leads them to dream up reasons why it is the way it is—or to envision other ways that it could be. Imagination and creativity help children find solutions to problems, bring insight to situations, and perceive things in unusual ways. See Fig. 17-11.

One way for parents to nurture these abilities in their children is to display imagination and creativity themselves. Even little things, like substituting tuna for chicken in a recipe, can show children that it is possible to solve problems by looking at things in a new way. Parents can help children learn to see possibilities by letting them play with ordinary household objects, such as a large cardboard box. In a child's mind, that box could turn into anything from a schoolhouse to a spaceship.

Parents should be careful not to stifle children's creativity. When young children make up stories for fun, parents should listen and accept them as flights of imagination rather than "lies." Older children and teens often want to show their individuality through their food and clothing choices. As long as these choices are not harmful or offensive to the parents' moral values, parents can accept them as another sign of creativity.

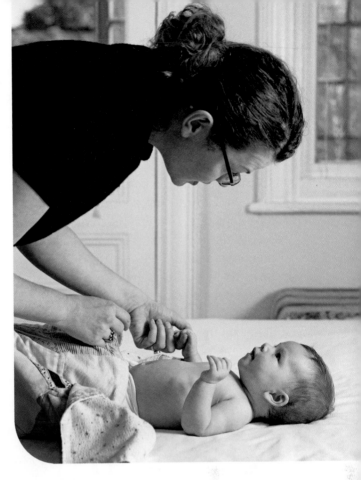

Fig. 17-12. Infants are fascinated by the sound of the human voice. **Why is it important to talk to babies, even before they can understand what is said?**

Promoting Language Skills

Years before they enter first grade, children are already developing the language skills they will need to succeed in school and in life. They begin as infants, learning to recognize and make sounds and eventually to understand and use words. Later, they will build on these basic language skills as they learn to read and write.

Understanding Language

Children begin to absorb and understand language long before they can produce it. During the first few days of life, a newborn begins to recognize important sounds in his or her environment, such as the sound of a parent's voice. Research has shown that by six months of age, most infants recognize the basic vowel sounds of their native language. Babies begin to comprehend their first words around nine months of age. See Fig. 17-12.

Talking and singing to children—right from birth—is very important in developing the parts of the brain that deal with sound and language. It's natural for parents to want to coo at infants in a high-pitched voice. Beyond infancy, however, "baby talk" is not necessary or effective. Once children reach the toddler years, it is much more useful to speak to them clearly and distinctly. Not only does this promote understanding, it also helps children develop good **articulation**—the ability to pronounce words clearly—as they learn to speak.

Speaking

At around one year, most children begin using words with meaning. At first, they use words singly: "bottle" or "more," for example. In their second year, most children can string together two-word phrases or sentences, such as "Doggy run" and "All wet." By age three, they may be speaking in complete sentences.

Once children begin to speak, they acquire new words at an amazing rate. At age two, most children have about 50 words in their speaking vocabulary. By age three, they use about 300 words; by age four, about 1,500 words; and by age five, about 2,200 words. At each age, children understand more words than they use in speaking.

The more words children hear, the more words they learn to use. Here are some ways parents and caregivers can help children build their vocabularies:

- Point out objects and name them. Young children have an amazing capacity for learning names.
- To prepare children for a new experience such as a trip to the zoo, read books and look at pictures, naming the things they will see. While at the zoo, encourage children to identify what they see.
- Read rhymes and poems aloud to children so they hear the sound and rhythm of words. Young children also love songs.
- Take children to the public library for story times and puppet shows.

As children learn to speak, they make a lot of mistakes in grammar and in pronunciation. These mistakes are a normal part of the learning process. Rather than correcting the child, parents should just rephrase the idea correctly. For example, if a child says, "Kitty runned away," a parent would respond by saying "You're right. The kitty ran away from the big dog." Listening to children and responding respectfully encourages them to express themselves.

Bilingual Skills. People who are **bilingual** can speak two languages. At one time, researchers believed that teaching young children a second language would limit their skills in their primary language. Parents who were bilingual were encouraged to speak only one language to their children.

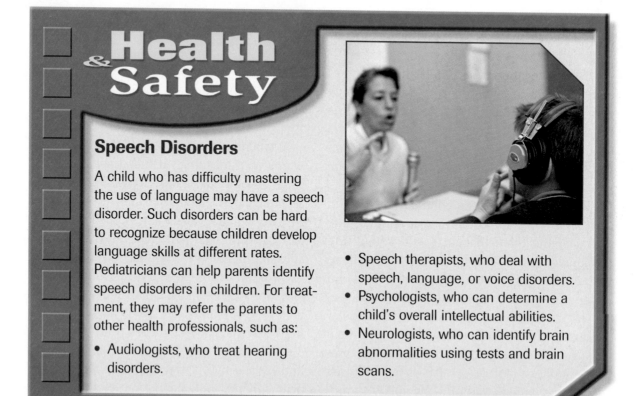

Health & Safety

Speech Disorders

A child who has difficulty mastering the use of language may have a speech disorder. Such disorders can be hard to recognize because children develop language skills at different rates. Pediatricians can help parents identify speech disorders in children. For treatment, they may refer the parents to other health professionals, such as:

- Audiologists, who treat hearing disorders.
- Speech therapists, who deal with speech, language, or voice disorders.
- Psychologists, who can determine a child's overall intellectual abilities.
- Neurologists, who can identify brain abnormalities using tests and brain scans.

More recent research, however, suggests that speaking two languages actually helps children learn. It not only aids language skills, but also improves abstract thinking abilities—the type involved in higher thought. Parents who speak two languages should encourage their children to learn them both. Knowing a second language is a definite advantage in today's global society.

THE DEVELOPING BRAIN

Brain research suggests that a three-year-old child can learn a second language more quickly than an adult. In an adult brain, the neurons responsible for language have already connected in a set pattern. The best time for learning new languages is in early childhood.

Reading

Reading strengthens a number of intellectual skills: language skills, memory, imagination, attention to detail, capacity for symbolic thought, and reasoning abilities. It also contributes to a child's ability to solve problems and predict outcomes. Mastering reading will not only help children do well in school, but also enable them to function well as adults in society.

A U.S. government report, based on the findings of more than 10,000 studies, concluded that reading to children is the single most important factor in their success as readers. Parents and teachers share the responsibility for helping children become readers. Children learn reading skills in school much more quickly if they have been exposed to reading at home. If a home has books, and if children are read to and see others reading, chances are they will grow up to be readers themselves. See Fig. 17-13.

Fig. 17-13. Parents who share books with their children are setting the stage for a lifelong love of reading. **What are some other benefits of reading to children?**

Children of all ages love being read to. Even infants can enjoy nestling close to their parents, hearing the sounds and rhythms of their voices, exploring the feel of the books, and looking at the pictures. Preschool children love certain books and want them read over and over. They may even correct adults who skip a page or miss a sentence! Though this repetition may become tedious for adults, it is essential in order for children to master the language.

Story time should be a natural part of the daily routine. It should not be offered as a reward for good behavior or withheld as punishment. When the experience of being read to is enjoyable, children will welcome it. Active children may prefer to listen while coloring or playing on the floor rather than sitting still. Choose books that are age-appropriate, keeping in mind that most children are not ready for long books until about age four or five. Don't continue to read a book a child doesn't like, no matter how highly recommended it may be.

As children grow older, reading on their own gradually replaces being read to. Parents can encourage older children to discuss what they are reading, and the parents can do the same. Reading can be a wonderful, shared journey into new worlds for both children and parents.

Here are some other ways to encourage reading in children of all ages:

- Model reading for pleasure and for information. Read all kinds of things to children—books, newspapers, magazines, greeting cards, shopping lists, signs.
- Introduce children to the library at an early age. Make regular visits to the library with children, and let them choose the books they want to take out.
- Visit bookstores and allow children to browse.
- Give children books and magazines as gifts.

Parenting Pointers

Choosing Books for Young Children

How can parents select the best books for their children? Start by visiting the local library. Most have a children's librarian who can recommend books children will like. Look for books that:

- Tell an enjoyable story with an appropriate theme.

- Have a simple, understandable plot.

- Include familiar situations and likable characters.

- Are respectful of diverse cultures and beliefs.

- Use basic, but descriptive language. Pleasing rhythms and rhymes help children remember words.

- Are illustrated with pictures that capture attention and help explain the words.

- Are well constructed. For toddlers, sturdy cloth or cardboard books with large pages are best.

Writing

Children like to imitate adult behavior, and writing is no exception. Children's first scribbles on paper show they are learning the function of writing and developing small motor skills. Adults can help by providing plenty of writing materials and perhaps colorful stickers to decorate the pages. They may let children write "letters" and, later, stories to send to relatives and friends.

It's never too early to start a habit of writing. For example, after children begin talking, they can dictate thank-you notes for birthday presents. An adult can write down what the child says and read it back to the child. Once children learn to write, adults can reverse roles and dictate things to children, such as grocery lists or the names on party invitations or gift tags.

For school-age children, a little adult help with writing assignments is often welcome. While parents should never write children's papers for them, they can help out in other ways. For example, they can provide a sounding board for children to "bounce ideas off" before beginning to write. A parent can also read a child's work and offer suggestions for improvement.

Promoting Math Skills

Many of the basic methods involved in teaching concepts to young children will also help them prepare for the study of mathematics. For example, lining up and counting objects, from blocks to socks, is a way to introduce the concept of numbers. Simple rhymes and songs that involve counting up or down can lead to an understanding of addition and subtraction. Games that teach concepts such as sorting, counting, matching, and measuring can also help children develop math skills.

After children start school, parents can help them succeed in math by giving them chances to use math skills on a day-to-day basis. For instance, on a trip to the grocery store, a parent might show a school-age child how to compare prices or use coupons. Parents can also assist their children with homework assignments and guide them through math concepts that are giving them trouble.

Providing Music and Art Experiences

Although academic skills such as reading, writing, and math are essential for success, they should not be the sole focus of learning. Parents can also promote their children's intellectual development by stimulating interest in music and art.

Enjoying Music

Children of all ages enjoy music. Infants often stop crying to listen to a song, and toddlers may enjoy dancing or clapping to the beat. Preschoolers will often make up songs or tunes to accompany their play—a habit that some carry with them all the way into adulthood.

THE DEVELOPING BRAIN

Research has revealed some interesting connections between music and mathematics. Preschoolers who were given piano and singing lessons were asked to work mazes, draw geometric figures, and copy patterns. These children demonstrated better spatial reasoning skills—the ability to perceive relationships between objects—compared with children who had no music lessons. Researchers suspect that this phenomenon, called the "Mozart effect," occurs because neurons exercised by listening to music also strengthen the circuits used for mathematics.

Parents don't have to be musicians to provide musical experiences for their children. They can start by exposing children to music and dance from different cultures and helping them imitate and describe what they see and hear. Moving to music helps children develop physical agility and learn about rhythm. Parents can encourage their children by playing and singing recorded music, including recordings made specifically for children to sing along. Young children can accompany the music by beating on pots, pans, or other nonbreakable household items. For older children, taking up a musical instrument provides an opportunity to explore music in more depth. See Fig. 17-14.

Enjoying Art

Art teachers note that the most important aspect of art activities for young children is "process, not product." In other words, the creative process itself has more value for children than the actual artworks they produce. Thus, parents shouldn't worry about whether their child's art is "any good." The creative urge is worth encouraging for its own sake.

To promote art activities, parents can provide safe, nontoxic art supplies for children. Examples include crayons, felt markers, paper and white glue, modeling clay, finger paints, tempera paint and brushes, and scraps of fabric or paper that can be used in collages. Setting aside a specific area for art activities is wise, especially for young children. Protect the area with newspaper or plastic coverings, and give the children smocks or old clothes to wear.

Parents can encourage their children's efforts by giving them positive feedback. Even if they aren't sure what a drawing is supposed to be, they should avoid disappointing a child by asking, "What is it?" Instead, they can praise the use of color or line and ask the child to tell them more about the picture. Describing their work will aid children's language skills, as well. Parents should resist the urge to "correct" their children's work. At this age, mastering technical skills is not the point of art activities. Art is simply one more opportunity to stimulate intellectual development.

Fig. 17-14. Children can be introduced to playing an instrument at a young age. **What do you know about the benefits of early music instruction for children?**

▶ Preschool Teacher

Preschool teachers are entrusted with the care and safety of parents' greatest treasure—their children. As caregivers, preschool teachers play a critical role in children's early development. They help children develop confidence in their abilities, learn to solve problems, and get used to being away from home.

Preschool teachers must possess positive work habits and attitudes, good management and leadership skills, sound ethics, and emotional maturity. They must be good observers to see early signs of developmental or emotional problems that require a specialist's attention. In such cases, they must know how to work together with parents to serve the child's best interests. Preschool teachers also need the ability to communicate with children and see them as unique individuals. They know that whatever children learn in these early years can shape their views of themselves for years to come. They must want each child's preschool experiences to be positive ones.

"Let me tell you, I wear a lot of hats! I have to organize indoor and outdoor activities, create a rich learning environment for children at different levels, provide quiet time, organize field trips, assist with toilet learning, teach readiness skills for reading and math, foster creativity, act as a nurse, and model appropriate social behavior. Some days the energy level of these kids is overwhelming! But I love this job. I consider it my life's work."

CAREER TIPS

- Take high school courses in parenting and early childhood development.
- Volunteer at a preschool.
- Job shadow preschool teachers in action.
- Get a college degree in early childhood education.
- Investigate different types of preschool programs and specialties.

CHAPTER 17 Review & Activities

CHAPTER SUMMARY

- Experiences help a child's brain develop rapidly.
- Theories of intellectual development help explain how mental abilities expand.
- Parents promote intellectual development by providing stimulating activities.
- As young children learn basic concepts, they build a foundation for future knowledge.
- Parents can use many simple techniques to help children learn thinking, language, and math skills. By promoting music and art, they also stimulate intellectual development.
- Skills learned in early childhood are keys to future success in school.

Check Your Facts

1. Summarize how the brain develops through adolescence.
2. What is symbolic thought and when is it first learned?
3. Explain these terms: *concepts, classification, seriation,* and *centration.*
4. Explain the link between the concepts of conservation and reversibility.
5. Summarize Gardner's theory of multiple intelligences.
6. What are the four learning methods used by children ages one to three? Give an example of each.
7. Compare visual and auditory learners.
8. Describe at least three ways to nurture a child's desire to learn.
9. Write television-watching guidelines for children under age six.
10. Identify five developmental concepts that children learn and an activity that could strengthen each one.
11. How does memory develop throughout childhood?
12. How would you help a child learn about cause and effect?
13. Name at least four ways to help a child learn language and speaking.
14. What are at least three ways to promote a desire to read in children?
15. Suggest at least three ways to help a child learn math skills.
16. What does the expression "process, not product" mean?

Think Critically

1. **Making Comparisons.** Which of the following statements would better strengthen a young child's concept of time, and why? **a)** "Dinner will be ready in twenty minutes." **b)** "After you take your bath, we'll eat dinner."
2. **Forming Ideas.** Many ordinary places offer learning opportunities for young children. How would you turn these into learning experiences: **a)** supermarket; **b)** ride in the car; **c)** yard or park; **d)** cooking?

Apply Your Learning

1. **Learning Stimulation.** Suppose a four-year-old girl is fascinated by plants and animals. How could you stimulate her interests and intelligence without spending much money? Develop an enrichment activity and present it to the class.

2. **Book Search.** Find two books for young children that are good for each of the following: **a)** teaching concepts; **b)** appealing to humor; **c)** bedtime reading; **d)** teaching moral lessons; **e)** educational information. Why is each book effective?

3. **Reading Demo.** Using a book for children, demonstrate how you would read it to a child. Afterwards, analyze your use of inflection and rhythm.

4. **Parental Responses.** How should a parent respond to these situations? **a)** Darius, age four, makes grammatical mistakes. **b)** Kayla, age four, dumps the toys out of the storage tub and plays in the tub. **c)** Patrick, age two, beats on a coffee table with a metal spoon. **d)** Rachel, age five, draws an unrecognizable picture.

Cross-Curricular Connections

1. **Science.** Cochlear implants and digital hearing aids help hearing-impaired children communicate. Research how these devices work and list any advantages and disadvantages. Use an image of the inside of the ear to show the class how one of these systems works.

2. **Math.** Is there evidence of the "Mozart effect" in your school? Develop survey questions to learn about students' musical and mathematical abilities. Get permission to have students take the survey anonymously. Analyze results and graph them. Why is the study of music worthwhile?

Family & Community Connections

1. **Multiple Intelligences.** Discuss Gardner's theory of multiple intelligences with your family. Have family members analyze where their strengths fit into the eight areas of intelligence. How might a mixture of strengths be useful in a family?

2. **Intellectual Development.** Observe young children in a community setting. Take notes on their activities and skills. Report on skills you saw that were consistent with Piaget's descriptions of intellectual development.

CHAPTER **18**

Meeting Children's Emotional Needs

CHAPTER OBJECTIVES

- Compare the stages of emotional development.
- Explain Freud's and Erikson's theories of development.
- Describe ways to promote independence, self-esteem, and healthy emotional development in children.
- Analyze strategies for handling difficult emotions in children.
- Explain how to help children manage stress.
- Identify signs of serious emotional problems in children and sources of help.

PARENTING TERMS

- egocentric
- self-image
- self-esteem
- empathy
- separation anxiety
- temper tantrum
- negativism
- anxiety disorder
- anorexia nervosa
- bulimia nervosa

Have you ever seen how grapevines grow? A young plant throws out vines that coil stubbornly around the nearest support. Gardeners provide a sturdy frame to train the plant to grow in the right direction. Otherwise, the vine will cling to whatever is available. When parents and caregivers care for their children, they have a similar responsibility. If they provide positive models and guidance, they can direct a child's emotional growth in a way that benefits the child and society.

Emotional Development

A variety of forces shape emotional development. Some traits appear to be inborn. For example, infants seem to have a tendency toward a certain *temperament*, or general way of reacting emotionally, as described in Chapter 13. Environment and life events also play a role.

While every child is unique, healthy emotional development follows a pattern from infancy through adolescence, as children grow in their ability to express and handle emotions. Knowing what to expect can help parents and caregivers respond appropriately to children's emotions.

- **Infants.** Over the course of the first year, a baby's emotional range expands from distress and contentment to include delight, anger, sadness, fear, disgust, and affection.
- **Toddlers.** By the time children are two years old, they are capable of a full range of emotions, including complex feelings such as pride and jealousy. Children under the age of five are **egocentric,** or self-centered—not yet capable of thinking beyond themselves.
- **Preschoolers.** Although preschoolers begin to learn about sharing and taking turns, they still see things only from their own point of view. Their emotions are usually extreme and short-lived. They may rage instantly at minor frustrations, then calm to contentment very quickly. Fears become more intense in most preschoolers.
- **School-age children.** By the time children reach school age, they are less self-centered and better able to recognize other people's feelings. Moods tend to be more even and predictable. Outbursts decrease as a child gains emotional control. See Fig. 18-1.
- **Adolescents.** In adolescence, physical and personal changes cause emotional swings. A twelve-year-old might leave for school feeling cheerful and optimistic but arrive quiet and withdrawn. Preteens are alternately excited and apprehensive about new freedoms and expectations.

Theories of Personality

Many theorists have explored similarities and differences in people's inner natures—the feelings and motivations that "make them tick." To explain these similarities and differences, they have developed a variety of ideas, often called *theories of personality*.

Fig. 18-1. The school-age years are often a relatively calm period in emotional development.

Erikson's Eight Stages of Development

Stage	Favorable Outcome	Unfavorable Outcome
Trust versus Mistrust Birth to about eighteen months	Infants learn to trust when their needs are consistently met. They view the world as safe and themselves as worthy.	Infants who are neglected feel insecure about their world and their place in it.
Autonomy versus Doubt Eighteen months to age three	Children strive for *autonomy*, or independence. They delight in learning self-sufficiency.	Toddlers who do not feel autonomous start to doubt their abilities and themselves.
Initiative versus Guilt Preschool age	Children begin to develop *initiative*, the readiness to start a task on their own. They feel pressure to act acceptably.	If children feel their actions are improper, guilt can stifle their initiative.
Industry versus Inferiority School age	Children feel the pull of *industry*, wanting to be productive, master skills, and contribute.	Failing to master productive skills causes feelings of inferiority.
Identity versus Diffusion Adolescence	Adolescents answer the question "Who am I?" and find an identity they are comfortable with.	Adolescents who lack a sense of self feel *diffused*, or mixed up.
Intimacy versus Isolation Young adulthood	Young adults begin to experience true intimacy through enduring friendships and marriage.	Young adults who are unable to relate closely to others become alone and isolated.
Generativity versus Self-absorption Adulthood	Adults produce, or *generate*, through their marriages (bringing children into the world) and in their jobs (benefiting society).	Adults who are unable to find meaning outside themselves become self-absorbed.
Integrity versus Despair Older adulthood	Having resolved all the preceding crises brings mature adults to *integrity*, or satisfaction with their lives and accomplishments.	If some of these crises remain unresolved, the older adult may be filled with despair for what is seen as a wasted life.

Fig. 18-2. According to Erikson, emotional development takes places in stages. **What might happen if a teen does not successfully master the challenge of the adolescent stage?**

Freud's Theory. Sigmund Freud defined three distinct aspects of thought and feeling: the id, the ego, and the superego. These are not parts of the brain, but levels of awareness affecting emotions and how they are handled. They are added in succession as the child develops.

- **Id.** According to Freud, infants are born with only this level of awareness. The id is focused on the demand to satisfy strong physical needs such as hunger and thirst.
- **Ego.** Between the ages of one and four, the ego becomes involved. It represents conscious reason and realistic thought. If the id has caused a hungry three-year-old to cry, the ego enables the child to stop crying once he or she knows food is on the way.

- **Superego.** By about age five, the third level of awareness, the superego, develops. This is the internal conscience that knows the difference between right and wrong. The superego matures as a result of lessons and modeling by parents and caregivers.

Erikson's Theory. Psychologist Erik Erikson proposed that social and emotional development is shaped by how a person handles a series of eight emotional challenges over a lifetime. Mastering one stage leads to a favorable outcome and progress to the next stage. If a challenge isn't mastered, emotional and behavioral problems make it difficult to tackle the next challenge. Fig. 18-2 outlines the stages described by Erikson.

Toward Independence

Erikson noted the importance of toddlers striving for independence. Emotionally healthy children are eager to become independent. However, growing up can be overwhelming at times. Understanding parents encourage a child's efforts without pushing too fast.

Stages of Independence

Each child progresses toward independence at a different rate. Some children may seem utterly helpless one day and remarkably competent the next.

Fig. 18-3. By patiently helping children learn new skills, parents can promote independence. **How can parents encourage children who have a difficult time mastering new skills?**

- **Young children.** "I want to do it myself!" is a cry familiar to most parents. New motor and intellectual skills spur toddlers and pre-schoolers to do more for themselves. For example, as small motor skills—such as finger movement—improve, young children can master dressing and undressing. This increases their independence and boosts their self-confidence. Still, toddlers and pre-schoolers waver between dependence and independence. Daily experiences often remind young children how much they still need parents. See Fig. 18-3.
- **Older children.** School-age children have mastered most personal care skills. Their feelings of independence come from accomplishing physical feats, such as riding a bicycle and running races, and from success in school activities. Lack of success can lead to feelings of inferiority, especially when children compare their abilities to those of classmates.
- **Adolescents.** Just as young children waver between dependence and independence, so do adolescents. One day they want nothing to do with their parents and other adults in authority; the next day they look to them for security and advice. In general, though, teens seek independence while developing their own identity.

Encouraging Independence

The drive for independence is inborn, but independence does not come naturally. Parents can promote independence by creating an environment that encourages a child to practice skills and try new things. For example, parents can:

- Teach children skills they need when they are developmentally ready for them.
- Choose clothes and utensils that encourage self-dressing and self-feeding.

- Let children select what they want to wear.
- Provide age-appropriate toys and low shelves for storage.
- Allow children adequate time to do chores and learn new skills without rushing them.
- Encourage them to practice and reinforce skills on their own.
- Resist the urge to do things for children that they could do for themselves.
- Ask children questions that encourage them to solve problems. A parent might say, "Which goes on first, your shoes or your pants?"
- Praise a child's efforts rather than criticize failure, slowness, or clumsiness. Whether successful or not, children can be instilled with a spirit to "try and try again."

Leading children toward independence is a growth experience for the parents as well. In teaching children to move beyond dependence, parents must draw back from always taking charge. Children can learn responsibility only as parents gradually let them assume it.

Self-Image and Self-Esteem

How do you see yourself? After considering everything about yourself—abilities and skills, strengths and weaknesses—the way you view yourself is your **self-image**, also called *self-concept*. A self-image can be positive or negative. People with a negative self-image see themselves in terms of their mistakes and weaknesses. People with a positive self-image recognize their strengths and treat their mistakes as learning experiences. See Fig. 18-4.

Gender Identity

As part of their development of a self-image, children develop a concept of their identity as boy or girl. Around the age of two, children become aware of gender. By preschool age, they know their own gender and begin learning male and female roles by watching family.

When parents provide toys and books that show men and women in both traditional and nontraditional activities and professions, they show children that gender roles can be broadly defined. Parents also can help children develop interests and abilities regardless of common gender images. For example, they can encourage both boys and girls to develop physical skills, engage in healthy competition, express emotions, and give and receive love.

The Need for Self-Esteem

A positive self-image can lead to high self-esteem. People with high **self-esteem** have positive feelings about themselves. They feel satisfaction, pride, and respect for who they are. Believing they are capable makes children —and adults—more willing to try things and learn from their mistakes. As a result, they often achieve more than people with low self-esteem.

How children feel about themselves influences the way they behave and the choices they make every day. When they succeed at something challenging, their self-esteem grows. Greater self-esteem usually brings about still more success.

Some typical behaviors of children with high and low self-esteem are contrasted in Fig. 18-5.

The behaviors of children with high self-esteem make it likely they will do well in life. The outlook is not as bright for children who think poorly of themselves.

Finding a Balance

Self-confident does not mean self-centered. A healthy, positive self-image involves respect for oneself *and others*. It combines realistic self-knowledge with understanding that one doesn't have to be "the best" to be a worthwhile person.

Parents who understand the importance of high self-esteem want to do all they can to make sure their children feel good about themselves. However, research shows that people who think too highly of themselves may develop problem behaviors. For one thing, they may become aggressive when someone criticizes them. After all, if children are raised to believe everything they do should be admired, they won't be pleased when admiration doesn't come.

Fig. 18-5. Children with high self-esteem behave in noticeably different ways than children with low self-esteem. **What are some characteristics of children with high self-esteem?**

Self-Esteem Affects Behavior	
Children with High Self-Esteem	**Children with Low Self-Esteem**
Make friends easily.	Feel uncomfortable making new friends.
Feel excited about new activities and challenges.	Avoid trying new things for fear of failure.
Enjoy sharing their ideas with others.	Feel no one will care about their ideas.
Show good self-control.	Lack self-control.
Think positively.	Think negatively.
Handle frustrations well.	Become easily frustrated.
Can be a positive influence on others.	Are easily influenced by others.
Accept responsibility for their mistakes.	Blame others for their mistakes.
Plan for their futures.	Don't like to plan because the future doesn't look bright.

Self-esteem must function within the framework of other important qualities. Without love, understanding, caring, compassion, humility, respect, self-control, responsibility, and other positive traits, high self-esteem can backfire. It's up to parents to find the balance.

Building a Positive Self-Image and Self-Esteem

How can parents encourage a realistic, positive self-image and high self-esteem in their children? There are many ways.

- **Be accepting.** Parents who accept a child's personality, abilities, appearance, and gender provide a solid core for developing self-esteem. Feeling loved "as is" gives children a sense of security.
- **Correct misbehavior.** While parents should accept their child, they should never accept intentional misbehavior. Avoiding appropriate guidance techniques is a serious mistake. Children who think they are above the rules won't learn how to behave responsibly.
- **Criticize the behavior, not the child.** After a child has lied, an appropriate response is, "I was disappointed to find out you lied to me. Lying is wrong." Do not attack the child's sense of worth by saying, "You are a liar" or "You are a bad boy."
- **Offer praise appropriately.** When handled carefully, praise and admiration are useful. Tell a young soccer player, "You did a great job blocking that shot," not "You're the best player on the team." Be specific and mean what you say.
- **Offer help tactfully.** If a well-meaning parent says "You're doing that all wrong—let me show you the right way," a child is likely to hear the words as criticism. "Would you like me to show you a little trick I've learned?" is a more positive approach. See Fig. 18-6.

Fig. 18-6. The way suggestions are given can boost or lower self-esteem. **How can parents help children learn to accept constructive criticism?**

- **Commend effort, not necessarily achievement.** After a child has worked hard but failed to achieve a goal, parental approval is reassuring. Children need to feel loved for themselves, not for their accomplishments.
- **Allow healthy risks and mistakes.** Within the limits of safety, resist the temptation to jump in and rescue a child. Trying to tackle new challenges builds confidence. Parents can help children find the right level of challenge and learn that making a mistake or failing is not the end of the world.

- **Avoid comparisons.** Telling children they are worse—or better—at something than other children sets up unreasonable expectations. A child's achievement learning to play the piano is just as much an achievement whether or not another child plays the piano better.
- **Encourage participation.** Children who have a chance to participate in clubs, organizations, and lessons develop abilities and skills that boost their confidence.

Fig. 18-7. A parent can help build a child's self-esteem by sharing enjoyable activities together. **Why is a parent's time an invaluable gift to a child?**

- **Model appropriate self-esteem.** Parents who show respect for themselves and others while comfortably admitting their mistakes set a healthy example for their children.
- **Give children time, attention, and respect.** The quality of the parent-child relationship influences a child's sense of self-worth. Parents foster self-esteem by being involved and taking interest in the child's life and activities. See Fig. 18-7.

Encouraging Affection and Empathy

Parental affection is essential for infants' emotional development. It helps them learn trust in relationships.

THE DEVELOPING BRAIN

Infants thrive on affection from parents or other caregivers. Without it, areas of the brain where feelings of emotional closeness originate may not develop.

With encouragement, toddlers begin to give affection also. When T.J.'s father says, "Give me a hug," T.J. gives him one and gets a smile of approval and a hug in return. T.J. learns that giving and receiving love and affection feels good.

This example illustrates something else. Parents teach a child not only *to* show affection but also *how* to show it. T.J. and his father hug. In some cultures, they might kiss. Parents need to show positive expressions of love: hugs, kisses, praise, and kind deeds and words.

Developing trust and affection in infancy provides a basis for **empathy**, the awareness

Modeling CHARACTER

Teaching Compassion

Teaching children compassion can enable them to make strong and healthy emotional connections throughout their lives. *Compassion* is demonstration of care and concern for another. It grows out of empathy, the ability to imagine oneself in someone else's situation and to understand how that person feels. People show compassion when they make efforts to relieve the suffering of others. Parents and caregivers can teach compassion through modeling and encouragement. For example:

- Pay attention to those in need.
- Point out your own feelings of compassion and ask how a child feels.
- Guide a child to see a situation from another person's viewpoint.
- Discuss ways to help people, then carry out the suggestions whenever possible.
- Praise the child for demonstrating compassion.

Think About It
Why is compassion so important to emotional health?

of other people's needs and feelings. In general, children who routinely feel empathy for others are more tolerant, compassionate, and understanding than those who do not.

To encourage empathy, parents need to remind young children that others have feelings. "Abdul is happy that you gave him a turn on your tricycle." "Kim is crying because he fell and hurt himself. Remember how it hurt when you fell?"

Handling Difficult Emotions

As children grow, their parents influence how they learn to handle uncomfortable emotions. Parents can encourage children to recognize and talk about their feelings by listening to them, sharing their own feelings, and responding with warmth and love.

It's easy to think that positive emotions are "good" and negative emotions are "bad."

Children learn to handle emotions better, however, when parents don't pass judgment on feelings. Instead, wise parents acknowledge that even unpleasant emotions are legitimate. At the same time, they offer reassurance and guide children to express emotions in acceptable ways.

Jealousy

Jealousy is a typical emotion for children. Toddlers may be jealous when they see a parent spending time with the other parent or a brother or sister, especially a new baby in the family. Including children in a new baby's care and in special activities of their own helps them feel more connected and secure. Preschoolers, too, may resent attention given to their siblings. See Fig. 18-8.

Jealousy over parental attention is less noticeable after age five, as children begin to form close relationships outside the home. New rivalries may develop. Children may be jealous of peers who appear more capable, more popular, or more privileged. They may grow possessive of friendships, protesting if a friend plays with another child.

It is helpful to praise children's accomplishments and let them know they are loved just as they are. Avoid comparisons, and talk more about what is good in life than what is missing or what other people have. Children need to understand that, while only one person can be the best student or the fastest runner, human worth is not measured by a single quality.

Fear

It's only natural that children will occasionally encounter people and situations that frighten them. Fear is a helpful emotion when it drives children away from real dangers and toward a parent's protection. Young children also have irrational or exaggerated fears. In time it is important to overcome irrational fears, but this is not possible until children are capable of reasoned, logical thinking.

Patience helps in dealing with fears, and so does a little indulgence. As irrational as some fears seem to adults, they are quite real to children. Parents can reassure young children who have these common fears:

- **Fear of the dark.** Many young children develop a fear of the dark, causing bedtime to become especially frightening. Some children's fears trigger nightmares. By talking patiently and soothingly, parents may restore the child's sense of security. A nightlight may also help.
- **Fear of bathing.** Among children ages two to five, fear of bathing is a common problem. It's not so much that they fear water, though some do. It's that they are afraid of being sucked down the drain when the water is let out of the tub. A simple solution is to remove the child from the tub before letting the water out.

Fig. 18-8. A child who feels left out may become jealous. **How might this parent help her older child feel included?**

Respecting Childhood Fears

Until children are developmentally ready to address their fears, sensitive parents find other creative ways to help children cope with fears. To build the child's trust:

➤ **Comfort instead of lecturing.** It's all right to mention that the object of fear is not really dangerous, if that is true. However, young children cannot be reasoned out of their fears. What they need is reassurance that their parents will keep them safe.

➤ **Never force children into situations that frighten them.** This destroys children's trust in parents who are supposed to protect them.

➤ **Never ridicule children's fears.** Saying "Big kids aren't afraid of the dark!" won't eliminate the fear. It only humiliates the child and teaches the child not to seek a parent's help.

➤ **Never lie to children about their fears.** Don't say, "When the doctor gives you a shot, you won't even feel it!" Instead, help children prepare for a potentially painful situation by talking about it honestly beforehand.

➤ **Don't ignore children's fears.** Children don't always talk about their fears. Respectful parents notice their children's nonverbal responses to stressful situations and ask how they can help.

- **Fear of thunderstorms.** Positive modeling helps prevent some fears. When a storm approaches, Keiko and her three-year-old daughter Ami watch together out the window. "Look at the beautiful lightning," Keiko says as the sky lights up. "Now wait for the thunder. Listen… There it is!" Just as Keiko predicted, Ami laughs as thunder rumbles. With a mother so confident, Ami has nothing to fear.
- **Fear of dogs.** Respect this fear. Staying away from strange animals and unknown people is a healthy instinct. If excessive fear persists, parents can gradually desensitize the child, first showing pictures of dogs and later letting the child pet a gentle, familiar dog under close supervision.
- **Fear of loud noises.** Information helps eliminate some fears. One preschooler cringed at the screaming sound of a fire engine. His mother explained, "The fire engine is rushing to put out the fire. The siren warns cars to move over and let the engine go by."
- **Imaginative fears.** To a preschooler, a wild animal living in the zoo could just as easily live in the basement. A child who is afraid

of wild animals might sleep better after Mom or Dad sets a cardboard box "trap" in the basement. By the time children are seven or eight years old, they will become concrete thinkers and outgrow most irrational fears.

Separation Anxiety

When children are very young, they feel closely linked to parents. Their first realization that parents have to be away from them can produce **separation anxiety**. This is a stress that infants or toddlers feel when separated from familiar people, usually parents.

Separation anxiety generally begins around the first birthday. Children at that age have little concept of time and don't know when the parent will return. They may react with crying, anger, and withdrawal. Separation anxiety is a stage that usually passes in a few months. Meanwhile, these steps can make parting less painful:

- **Avoid leaving when the child is asleep or distracted.** If this is not practical, tell the child in advance what will happen.

Fig. 18-9. When parents handle difficult situations with patience, they model good anger management skills for their children to imitate. **What do children learn when their parents do not manage anger well?**

- **Discuss the separation matter-of-factly.** Even before the child can talk, a parent can say, "I know you don't want me to go. I love you and I'll be back before you go to bed."
- **Spend time together before leaving.** This reassures the child and makes parting feel less like abandonment.
- **Involve the child in an interesting activity.** Returning to the activity after the parent leaves occupies the child's mind.
- **Be consistent.** Create a routine including a loving and firm good-bye. Children feel more secure with a predictable ritual and the knowledge that the parent will not sneak away.
- **Leave quickly, with a smile and a wave good-bye.** Lingering indicates a parent's own separation anxiety.

Anger

Everyone feels anger at times. Teaching a child how to manage this basic emotion is part of good parenting.

Toddlers are most likely to feel angry when they don't get their way. Anger becomes less frequent and less physical by the preschool years. Toddlers and preschoolers can be taught how to express anger acceptably. For instance, when Belle tries to kick her father, he tells her calmly and firmly, "I understand why you're angry, but I won't let you hurt me. If you want to kick something, you can kick your ball in the backyard."

By school age, children tend to show anger by trying to hurt feelings more than bodies. They may threaten and call names. Adolescents may hide their anger by pretending indifference. It isn't unusual for them to gradually retreat inward until they suddenly lose their temper.

Both school-age children and adolescents need more mature strategies to deal with anger. For example, they should be encouraged to talk about why they are angry. See Fig. 18-9.

Fig. 18-10. Temper tantrums are not fun for a parent, but toddlers eventually outgrow them. **What is the best way to respond to a toddler's temper tantrum?**

Temper Tantrums. Have you ever seen a toddler drop to the floor, arms and legs flailing, and wail miserably? If so, you have witnessed a **temper tantrum**, a fit of anger accompanied by crying, screaming, hitting, or kicking. See Fig. 18-10.

Toddlers are tantrum-prone for several reasons. They want to be independent, but that wish collides with adult authority. They want to describe how they feel, but they lack the verbal skills. Parents may find these suggestions helpful in responding to a tantrum:

- Speak softly, remaining calm and objective. Say, "I understand you're angry, but this is not the way to show your anger. Stop."
- Be sure children do not harm themselves, others, or possessions.
- At home, ignore the tantrum if there is no danger of injury. Generally, the less attention given tantrums, the less often they occur.
- In public, take the child to a quieter place, such as a restroom. Children quickly learn that having an audience helps their cause.
- Save explanations for a calmer time. In the midst of a tantrum, a child isn't listening.
- Don't reward a child for ending a tantrum.

Negativism

Toddlers usually go through a period of **negativism**, or opposition. "No" becomes their favorite word. Negativism is just another way for toddlers to express their growing independence. Although this is a perfectly normal stage of emotional development, it is a trying time for parents. Fortunately, negativism usually decreases by about the third birthday. In the meantime, parents can try these suggestions:

- **Redirect the child.** If the toddler won't leave the dog alone, draw attention to a nearby toy.
- **Don't scold or punish for saying no.** Focus on whether the child's actions are appropriate.
- **Don't take it personally.** The toddler is testing limits, not being disrespectful.
- **Don't offer a choice where none exists.** How do you think a toddler would answer the question, "Would you like to go to bed now?" Instead, offer genuine choices: "Pick out a book for your bedtime story."
- **Model a positive response.** Limit the number of times you say "no" yourself. It is possible to remain firm with different words, such as "Cookies are for later, after dinner."

Children and Stress

Growing up may seem like a carefree time, but it's a time of changes and challenges for a child. These changes and challenges bring on *stress*, or physical and mental tension. Since stress is an unavoidable part of life, parents must help children learn to manage stress.

Sources of Stress

Stress comes from many sources. Some major causes of stress include death of a loved one; divorce, separation, or remarriage of a parent; moving to a new community; and family violence. Chapter 27 gives suggestions for coping with major changes and crises.

Most of the time, stress creeps into the lives of children in smaller, everyday ways. For example, young children can sense tension in their parents, affecting their feelings of security. Another common cause of stress in young children is any change in routines.

Older children and adolescents face pressures in many areas of their lives. They may worry about their grades and schoolwork, their appearance, their athletic abilities, and their classmates' opinions of them.

Health & Safety

Negative Effects of Stress

Too much stress in a child's life causes problems. Since young children don't know what stress is or how to manage it, parents should watch for these signs:

- Behavior such as bed-wetting, over-eating, undereating, and stuttering.
- Physical complaints such as headaches and stomachaches.
- Nervousness, fear of sudden noises, or anxiety with no apparent cause.
- Nervous habits, including nail-biting, thumb-sucking, teeth-grinding, and hair-twisting.
- Lying or stealing.
- Unusual shyness.
- Poor sleeping habits or nightmares.
- Explosive crying or screaming.

If these symptoms persist, parents should consult the child's doctor.

Fig. 18-11. Everyone needs time to unwind. **What may happen in a home where every minute is scheduled?**

Reducing Children's Stress

Stress can surface when children feel too much pressure from their parents. Periodically, parents need to evaluate their expectations. Are they being reasonable, or do they expect their child to be perfect? By setting their standards too high, parents can cause stress. By adjusting their expectations, parents can reduce stress.

Parents can reassure young children by talking, listening, hugging, and spending time with them. Above all, by being calm themselves, parents can have a calming effect on their children.

At times, just cutting down on outside activities and simplifying hectic schedules can relieve stress for every family member. Young children need unstructured playtime. Older children and teens benefit from having a chance to unwind and relax. See Fig. 18-11.

Helping Children Manage Stress

Since stress can't be entirely avoided, children must learn to manage it properly. Parents may need to work on their own stress management skills to be supportive models and guides.

Children who get plenty of sleep each night handle stress better than their peers. Many studies have found that teens need more sleep than they routinely get. In our fast-paced world, the value of a good night's sleep gets overlooked.

Children who are anxious and tense need to talk about it, but they may not know where to begin or even exactly what is bothering them. It usually doesn't help to ask, "What's wrong?" Even a more specific question such as "Is something at school troubling you?" may not get an answer. Parents sometimes get better results by sharing stories from their own youth. This show of empathy may help their children cope.

Adolescents should be encouraged to find healthy ways to deal with stress, These might include physical exercise, relaxation techniques, journaling, music, or hobbies.

Emotional Problems

How children feel affects the way they think and act. It's perfectly normal to feel sad or worried for a few days. However, if a child's behavior is affected for weeks, there may be underlying emotional problems. It's estimated that between five and 15 percent of children face emotional problems such as anxiety and depression.

Anxiety

From time to time, most children experience anxiety—strong feelings of worry and fear. Many times just talking with a parent can help them feel better. See Fig. 18-12.

If anxiety becomes so extreme it begins to interfere with everyday life, it may be an **anxiety disorder**. School-age children and teens with anxiety disorders may have excessive worries about almost every area of their lives, including school, families, and health. Some have an extreme fear of social settings. When they try to start a conversation, answer a question in class, or take part in a performance, they have actual physical symptoms such as sweating, a racing heart, and dizziness. After experiencing a trauma such as a natural disaster or death of a loved one, some children have nightmares and flashbacks, which interfere with sleep and concentration. All of these symptoms indicate a need to seek professional help.

Eating Disorders

How many people do you know who look like a model or a movie star? Some children and teens who idealize those ultra-thin figures consider themselves fat, whether or not they are. Why this leads to eating disorders

Fig. 18-12. Children want someone to listen to them. **How might children feel if no one responds to their needs and moods?**

Fig. 18-13. Everyone has sad moods from time to time, but depression is marked by more intense and longer lasting feelings of sadness.

in some cases is not known. Risk factors include low self-esteem, perfectionism, and dissatisfaction with one's body. Those who have a close relative with an eating disorder, or participate in certain competitive activities such as ballet, skating, or fashion modeling, are also at increased risk. Adolescent females are affected most often, but eating disorders also occur in males.

Parents can reduce the risk by accepting their bodies and those of their children. If weight is a real problem, encourage more exercise rather than drawing attention to weight or appearance.

Different types of eating disorders exist. **Anorexia nervosa** involves an extreme urge to lose weight by self-starvation. In **bulimia nervosa**, bouts of extreme eating are followed by vomiting or taking laxatives to lose what was eaten. Both conditions are medically dangerous. Symptoms may include sudden weight loss, below-normal weight, preoccupation with food and calories, compulsive exercise, and an unrealistic self-image. Those affected will insist they do not have an eating disorder. Parents who suspect they do should get them to a doctor right away.

Depression

Childhood depression is more than just "feeling down." It is a treatable illness that affects about five percent of all children. A child who is depressed has an overwhelming feeling of sadness that interferes with abilities to handle emotions and enjoy life. See Fig. 18-13.

Parents should watch for signs of depression, although a child may be depressed and only exhibit a few of these signs. Possible signs of depression include:

- Frequent crying.
- Lack of energy.
- Lack of concentration.
- Difficulty getting along with others.
- Irritability.
- Problems at school.
- Headaches and stomachaches.
- Running away from home or threatening to run away.
- Increasing anger.
- Withdrawing from friends, family, and interests.
- Marked personality change.
- Talking about death and suicide.

Suicide

Untreated emotional problems or substance abuse can distort judgment, leading some young people to think life is too painful to continue living. Thoughts of suicide are a health emergency. Important guidelines for parents are:

- Be aware of the signs of depression listed on the previous page. Depression can lead to suicidal thoughts.
- Keep communication open. Don't appear angry, upset, or shocked by what the child says.
- Don't dismiss feelings that seem minor to you. To a child, they may be overwhelming.
- Discuss suicide in a straightforward way. It won't put ideas into a child's head that aren't already there.
- Recognize that a comment like "Everybody would be better off if I were dead" may be a cry for help.
- Seek help if you have the slightest suspicion a child might be suicidal.

Where to Go for Help

Parents need to get help for children who are suffering from emotional problems, just as they would for a broken bone or an ear infection. With professional help, children who suffer from anxiety disorders, eating disorders, depression, suicidal tendencies, and other emotional problems can be treated successfully. The treatment plan may include counseling, medication, or a combination of the two.

The family doctor or pediatrician can offer suggestions and make referrals. That's a good place to start. Schools have counselors and psychologists who are trained to deal with childhood emotional problems. See Fig. 18-14.

Other sources of help include:

- Community hospital or children's hospital.
- County mental health department.
- Medical college's psychiatry department.
- Local and state mental health associations.
- State psychological association.
- National organizations such as the National Mental Health Association or Federation of Families for Children's Mental Health.
- Professional organizations such as the American Psychiatric Association or the American Academy of Child and Adolescent Psychiatry.

Life can seem confusing and difficult to children. Parents need to guide and encourage children as they learn to deal with their emotions. When children feel respected and loved by their parents, they will more easily be able to relate to other people.

Fig. 18-14. Professionally trained counselors can help a struggling child or teen see that there are always options. **How can choices help a situation look more hopeful?**

Child & Family Services
CAREERS

▶ Art Therapist

Art therapists use different forms of art to help those suffering from emotional, physical, mental, or developmental disorders. Because it doesn't rely on words, art therapy is especially helpful for people who cannot or will not communicate. Through the artistic process, they are able to express their thoughts and emotions.

Art therapists provide art materials and instruction, focusing each session on the needs of the individual or group. Successful art therapists are sensitive to the needs of others. They are observant, patient, good listeners, and aware of the complex workings of the human mind.

"I love working with people of all ages who face all kinds of challenges. I've helped elderly stroke victims and young children recovering from trauma. Whether they are working with a piece of clay or using finger paints, they become absorbed with the creative process. I especially remember one young girl who had been rescued from a fire. For her, art became a means to work through her grief. I was able to give her the tools and the opportunity to heal inside. That was one of my most memorable moments in this field—seeing her smile again through her art."

CAREER TIPS

- Take art and child development courses in high school.
- Volunteer as a teacher's aide in a community art class.
- Obtain a bachelor's degree in psychology, art therapy, or art education.
- Obtain a master's degree in art therapy.
- Complete the required number of direct contact hours to become a certified or registered art therapist in your state.

CHAPTER 18 Review & Activities

CHAPTER SUMMARY

- Different stages of emotional development occur from infancy through adolescence.
- Psychologists have proposed theories about emotional and social development.
- Parents can use positive strategies to foster independence, self-esteem, and healthy emotional development in their children.
- Understanding children's jealousy, fear, and anger helps parents respond effectively.
- Parents need to help children learn how to manage stress.
- Help is available for parents who see signs of emotional problems in their children.

Check Your Facts

1. Compare the stages of emotional development.
2. According to Freud, how do the id, ego, and superego interact in a person?
3. Briefly explain Erikson's theory of social and emotional development.
4. How do young children, older children, and adolescents display independence?
5. Suggest at least six ways to encourage independence in children.
6. How do children learn gender roles?
7. What are at least six ways that parents can build a child's self-esteem?
8. Why do children need to learn empathy?
9. How can parents limit jealousy in children?
10. How can fear be useful to a child?
11. What is separation anxiety?
12. Describe at least three things parents can do to handle a child's temper tantrum.
13. What are five ways parents can deal with a toddler's negativism?
14. What are at least four things parents can do to help children manage stress?

15. What is an anxiety disorder?
16. What is anorexia nervosa?
17. Name at least five signs of depression in children.
18. How should a parent respond when a child expresses suicidal thoughts?
19. What are at least three sources of help for children's emotional problems?

Think Critically

1. **Making Predictions.** If a child grows up never seeing any affection shown between his or her parents, what effect do you think this could have?
2. **Making Comparisons.** Do you think children have more stress today than in past generations? Why or why not?
3. **Understanding Cause and Effect.** At what age do you think girls start to pick up social messages about body image? How are the messages conveyed, and what can result? What solutions do you suggest?

Apply Your Learning

1. **Self-Esteem Description.** Describe a fictitious child's behavior by completing the following in writing: "Aaron (or any name) has low self-esteem. I first noticed this when…" Exchange papers and suggest ways to help the child described.

2. **Parent-Child Scenes.** With a partner, act out one of these parent-child scenes: **a)** dealing with a two-year-old's temper tantrum in a busy store; **b)** handling a child's fear of the dark; **c)** talking to a daughter of average weight who complains that she is fat; **d)** taking a young child to a child care center and handling separation anxiety; **e)** talking with a child who has just fought with a close friend. Analyze strategies in class.

3. **Cartoon Strips.** Working with a partner, create a cartoon strip that shows parents mishandling an emotional situation with a child. Then show an effective way. Combine class cartoons in a parenting skills booklet.

Cross-Curricular Connections

1. **Social Studies.** How do people with high self-esteem and low ethical principles affect society? How do such personalities develop? Discuss your thoughts with a few other students and summarize them for the class.

2. **Language Arts.** At a children's soccer game, parents engage in a long angry yelling match, with raised fists and name-calling. Write a letter from the children to the parents, explaining how this affects them. In class, discuss how such situations can be avoided.

Family & Community Connections

1. **Flashback on You.** Ask an adult who knew you as a young child to describe what emotions you displayed then. Were you fearful, jealous, bold, timid, negative, easygoing, or hot-tempered? How did adults respond? Someday, if your child has similar qualities, how would you respond?

2. **Child in Need.** Children who struggle with schoolwork, are afraid of bullies, or are troubled in some other way need someone to support them. Reach out to a child near you. You could befriend a child who seems lonely, ask parents if you might tutor a neighbor child, or volunteer to play ball with a child at the park. Report to the class on how your actions affected you as well as the child.

CHAPTER 19

Helping Children Relate to Others

CHAPTER OBJECTIVES

- Explain why socialization is important for children.
- Summarize ways to build positive relationships within the family.
- Describe how peers interact at various ages.
- Propose ways to help children handle peer relationships.
- Analyze techniques that help teach social skills to children.
- Explain how to help children appreciate diversity.

PARENTING TERMS

- socialization
- sibling rivalry
- peers
- parallel play
- cooperative play
- bullying
- peer pressure
- clique
- assertiveness
- stereotype
- cultural bias
- prejudice

Have you ever thought how many social interactions you have during an ordinary day? Morning may start with passing the milk at the breakfast table and negotiating turns in the bathroom. Whether you walk or ride to school, getting there in one piece requires cooperation among drivers, bicyclists, and pedestrians. Interactions with peers and adults fill the school day and after-school jobs or activities. Children are not born knowing how to relate well to others. They learn through experience and the guidance of caring adults.

Socialization

A large part of parenting consists of the **socialization** of children, or teaching children how to get along well in society. The process of socialization begins at birth and continues throughout life. As children grow and mature, they learn how to relate to even larger and more diverse groups of people. Parents help build social skills by establishing a solid and healthy relationship with their children and by nurturing their children's emotional wellbeing. They model social skills and establish clear guidelines. They help children learn problem-solving skills for addressing the many difficulties that can arise in all relationships. See Fig. 19-1.

People who do not acquire appropriate social behaviors during childhood often have problems later in life. Children who lack social skills may interact poorly with family members and other adults, feel uneasy in groups, and have trouble making friends. The quality of children's social skills often corresponds to how well they will do in school, academically and socially. Children with social difficulties are more likely to drop out of school. As adults, they may not be able to hold a job and are more likely to get in trouble with the law.

THE DEVELOPING BRAIN

Researchers have found that neural connections necessary for learning develop through healthy interactions with other people. As children grow, social skills such as taking turns and listening are essential for academic success.

Fig. 19-1. Learning social skills begins at home. **What do children learn by interacting with other family members?**

Fig.19-2. As children grow, they learn how to make friends and get along with others. **What behaviors do you think help children enjoy each other? What behaviors alienate others?**

Social Learning

Children begin the long process of learning social skills at birth. Contact with people—being held, nursed, given a bath, kept warm, talked to—teaches an infant about relating to others. If that contact is warm and loving, the infant will begin to learn to relate well. If not, he or she will retreat from relationships. Unless children feel cared for, they won't learn to care for others.

Emotional and social well-being develop together as children gain trust, affection, and confidence in themselves and others. Children tend to repeat social behaviors that meet their needs and gain approval. If, for example, reaching out results in being cuddled, children will continue to reach out.

Children also learn acceptable social behavior by imitating their parents and others they admire. Parents need to model the kinds of behavior they want to see in their children. They also need to directly teach specific social skills, such as how to be considerate of others.

As children grow, they need to learn how to get along not just with family members, but with people outside the home as well. They have to learn how various groups of people get along. They must learn how to balance their own needs with those of others, whether on a team, at school, or in the neighborhood park.

As children grow older, they develop an understanding of broader social expectations. They learn the importance of honesty and respect for people, property, and the environment. These skills will help them get along in a society of many different people with many different wants and needs. See Fig. 19-2.

Relating to Family Members

A family is a child's first social group. It is within the context of the family that children first learn how to relate to others, how to get their needs met in appropriate ways, and how to express care and concern for others.

Parent-Child Relationships

Children's relationships with their parents form the foundation for all other relationships in life. Parents who build a secure, nurturing relationship with their children teach them how to be responsive to others, respect themselves and others, and deal with problems successfully.

Fig. 19-3. Sibling relationships can be a testing ground for the development of social skills. **What can siblings learn from healthy competition with each other?**

To strengthen relationships with their children, parents can:

- Respond consistently to children's needs.
- Reassure children when they are frightened.
- Share children's excitement and joy.
- Be active listeners, giving children periods of undivided attention.
- Say "I love you" often, even (perhaps especially) after an argument.
- Observe a special bedtime ritual.
- Help their children only as much as needed, rather than doing everything for them.
- Let their children help them.
- Eat meals as a family.
- Turn off the TV and listen to each other.
- Spend one-on-one time with each child.
- Respect their children's choices, within reasonable limits.
- Trust their children and let them make mistakes, within reasonable limits.

Sibling Relationships

For many people, the longest-lasting relationship in life is that with a brother or sister. It may also be one of the closest. Parents should encourage siblings to play and work together, while allowing them to have friends, interests, and possessions of their own. If children are spending all their time together, parents may want to guide them into separate activities so each has opportunities for independent development.

Children learn a tremendous amount about relationships from their siblings. Sibling relationships may be where children first learn essential social skills such as sharing, playing by the rules, and standing up for oneself. Older siblings may also model social skills, such as making new friends, that younger ones imitate. See Fig. 19-3.

Parenting Pointers

Fostering Individuality Among "Multiples"

Twins, triplets, and other "multiples" need to define themselves as individuals, separate from their same-age siblings. Parents can foster individuality among multiples and other siblings by:

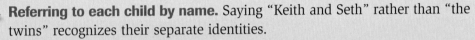

- **Referring to each child by name.** Saying "Keith and Seth" rather than "the twins" recognizes their separate identities.

- **Offering choices of clothing and hairstyles.** If siblings do choose to dress alike, suggest (but don't insist on) different colored accessories, such as backpacks or socks.

- **Providing separate possessions for each child when practical.** Multiples need their own personal items as much as other siblings do.

- **Encouraging individual interests.** More than other siblings, multiples may need "permission" to be different. Encourage each child to express personal feelings and pursue personal interests.

Handling Sibling Rivalry. *Rivalry* is competition, and **sibling rivalry** refers to the competition between brothers or sisters. All siblings exhibit sibling rivalry at various times. They compete for parents' attention and for status in the family. This competition is often fiercest among toddlers, preschoolers, and young school-age children, especially between siblings of the same gender who are close in age. Typically, rivalries fade as each child develops outside interests and a surer sense of his or her own identity.

It's important not to deny jealous feelings by saying things like "You don't really mean that. You know you're very proud of your sister." Although a degree of rivalry can be expected in any sibling relationship, parents can take steps to minimize its occurrence. Recognizing each child as an individual with unique talents and needs helps the child develop a distinct sense of self. Parents can remind children of the areas in which they excel, and reassure them that they are loved no matter what. Parents should never label or compare siblings: "Gina is so graceful, but Diego is the brains of the family." Comparisons tend to reinforce rivalry because children then feel they have to compete for attention and status.

Parents should treat children fairly, not equally. Children are individuals with different wants and needs. When one child gets extra attention during a period of illness or stress, it's helpful to remind siblings of other occasions when they have received extra attention.

Spending "alone time" with each child separately, even just a few minutes a day, can make a big difference. When children receive special time with a parent, they are less inclined to constantly compete for a parent's attention.

Responding to Sibling Conflict. All siblings have conflicts with each other. Teaching children how to communicate their feelings ("I feel mad when you don't share your toy") and how to reach an agreement ("I'll play with the toy for five minutes, and then you can play with it") can minimize parental involvement.

Parents can define and enforce clear limits about what behavior is permitted between siblings. Within those limits, it's usually best to let children work out their own quarrels. When children come to parents about a conflict, parents can take the opportunity to guide them through a conflict resolution process like the one explained later in this chapter. That

Health & Safety

Sibling Abuse

Physical, emotional, or sexual abuse by a brother or sister–called *sibling abuse*– is a serious matter. Unlike normal sibling rivalry, it often leads to physical danger and lasting psychological problems. Parents should be alert for signs of possible sibling abuse. Is one child always the attacker while another is always the victim? Does one child avoid his or her sibling or show a sudden change in behavior, such as nightmares? Abused children may also act out abuse or inappropriate sexual behavior during play.

To reduce the risk of sibling abuse, parents should:

- Try to minimize competition between siblings.

- Stay actively involved in children's lives.
- Make and enforce clear rules against violence, threats, and cruel forms of teasing.
- Limit children's exposure to violence or inappropriate sex on TV or online.
- Teach children anger management and conflict resolution.
- Spend private time with each child after children have been alone together.

helps children learn ways to resolve their own issues in the future.

If sibling conflicts become vicious, physical, or frequent, parents need to look at underlying causes. What stresses may be affecting the child? Parents can identify a child's hurtful behavior and ask the child to talk about his or her feelings and motives. By connecting feelings to actions, children can often discover another, more positive, way to have their needs met.

Relationships with Other Relatives

Relationships between children and members of the extended family can bridge the gap between the immediate family and the outside world. Cousins who live nearby can be valuable playmates, especially if a child has no siblings close in age. Aunts and uncles can offer guidance, just as teachers and other authority figures do.

A child's relationship with grandparents is often very special. Hearing a grandparent tell stories about when a child's mother or father was young can deepen a child's sense of family. Parents can encourage their children's relationships with their grandparents through regular visits, if possible. See Fig. 19-4.

When extended family members live far apart, maintaining relationships is still important and takes creativity. Parents can encourage children to keep in touch through letters, phone calls, e-mail, photos, or videos.

Relating to Peers

As children grow and develop, so does their ability to relate to an ever widening circle of people. An infant's most important relationships are with parents and other caregivers. As children grow and mature, they like and need the company of their **peers,** or those who are about their age.

Fig. 19-4. Relationships with relatives enrich a child's life. **How can grandparents, aunts, and uncles contribute to socialization?**

Friendship Patterns

The nature of children's friendships changes over time. As children develop physically and emotionally, they also develop socially. Parents who know what to expect at different developmental stages are better equipped to nurture their children's social growth.

Toddlers. Most one-year-olds and two-year-olds enjoy being around other toddlers, although they don't yet know how to share and interact. Large groups overwhelm them, so play groups of two or three are best. At this age children engage in **parallel play,** playing side-by-side (parallel) with each other. During parallel play, toddlers observe and imitate each other's movements. They may also take each other's toys because they see the other child having fun with them. Toddlers don't yet understand that the other child has feelings. Parents can encourage happy parallel play by offering enough similar toys to go around. See Fig. 19-5.

Preschoolers. By the age of three or four, most children have the language and social skills needed for **cooperative play**. In cooperative play, children interact and cooperate with one another. They agree on what they are doing—building a fort or playing "house." They begin to take turns and share.

The "pretend" play that preschoolers love is a tool for learning a number of social skills. Children explore different emotions and ways to handle them, an essential skill in forming friendships. They develop empathy by playing different roles.

Many children invent imaginary friends during this period. They react to these invisible playmates as they react to real ones, and expect parents to do the same. They may insist on setting a place for the "friend" at meals and act as a go-between to make the friend's wishes known. Like a favorite toy or blanket, imaginary friends can help children cope with times of loss, insecurity, or stress. This is not a cause for worry or argument. Even if they won't admit it, children know their imaginary friends aren't real. The need for imaginary friends fades as children grow older and more secure. In most cases, parents should indulge the "presence" calmly and matter-of-factly. They should consult a doctor, however, if a child spends much of each day in an imaginary world and has trouble playing with real children.

School-Age Children. Most five- and six-year-olds are outgoing and talkative. They have become much better at sharing. They play well in groups of four or five, and they play more complicated games. They may play team sports

Fig. 19-5. During parallel play, toddlers play side by side but with little interaction. This is a natural step in development, not a sign of poor social skills.

but are not necessarily "team players." Personal success matters most.

School-age children value peer approval. They begin to choose some peers as friends and exclude or reject others. A small group may organize as a club. The club acts as a micro-society in which children try out social roles: leader, follower, peacemaker, or individualist.

Most friendships in elementary school are between children of the same gender. Boys this age tend to form large friendship groups. Girls tend to form more intense friendships with one best friend and a few other close friends. See Fig. 19-6.

Adolescents. In general, adolescence is a time of "breaking away" from the family and establishing a separate identity with a peer group. To many adolescents, relationships with family members seem much less important than their relationships with their friends. They spend much more time with peers than younger children do.

Although adolescents sometimes act rebellious as they strive to develop a separate identity from their parents, they often conform to the norms of their peer group. Friendships often involve building loyalty and sharing inner thoughts and secrets. Adolescents spend more time with friends of the opposite sex, often in large groups, and dating may begin.

Peer Relationship Concerns

As children grow, their personalities become more defined. They become aware of similarities and differences among their friends. They choose to play with one child and not another. Social skills such as cooperation and consideration enable children to make friends.

Even children with strong skills and friendships run into difficulties in their relationships, however. Parents need to be aware of what happens in their children's peer relationships

Fig. 19-6. As children grow, friendships become closer and more long-lasting. **Why is it important for children to spend time with friends?**

and give children the support and tools they need for dealing with problems.

Teasing. Being teased is part of growing up, so all children need to learn how to cope with it. Parents can teach children these strategies to cope with teasing:

- **Ignore it.** When teasing provokes anger or tears, it is likely to continue. By not responding or by walking away, a child can defuse the teaser's power.

- **Visualization.** By picturing the words bouncing off them, children learn that they don't have to accept what is said.
- **Positive self-talk.** Children can say to themselves, "I don't like being teased, but I can handle it." They can also focus on their positive traits to counteract the negative message.
- **Humor.** Sometimes it is simplest to respond by saying "So?" or making a joke.

If teasing becomes severe or prolonged, parents may need to intervene. If necessary, they can enlist the help of school staff or other caregivers.

Bullying. Bullies deal with their feelings of inferiority and insecurity by trying to gain power over others. **Bullying** can include a variety of behaviors, ranging from verbal taunts, threats, and intimidation to deliberate physical injury. Whatever form it takes, bullying is a serious issue. Studies show that children who bully others are more likely to take part in criminal behavior as adults. Those who are bullied suffer emotionally and physically. They often live in fear and feel powerless to escape the abuse. They may even blame themselves, feeling that they deserve what they get. Bullying is believed to be a factor in a significant number of youth suicides.

Many schools have adopted anti-bullying programs. Successful programs address the problem using multiple approaches: counseling for the bullies, support for the victims, and education for the entire school community. See Fig. 19-7.

Children who are victims of bullies need to know that parents and other adults are willing to listen to their concerns and to support them. All children should know how to report incidents of cruelty, threats, or violence among their peers, as well as the presence of weapons. Anti-bullying programs provide specific procedures to report bullying behavior.

Parents of a bully must take a firm stand, without appearing to reject the child. An insecure child who bullies needs love and understanding, but must also be held accountable for mistreating others.

Fig. 19-7. With adult support, children who are bullied learn they do not have to suffer in silence. **What strategies can children use to deal with bullies?**

Fig. 19-8. Peer pressure can show itself in the fashions that children choose. **What are some other examples of peer pressure among children?**

Peer Pressure. As their relationships with friends grow in importance, children experience increasing **peer pressure**—social pressure to conform or behave in certain ways in order to be accepted by their peers. Sometimes this pressure may be a positive force. For example, children may learn a new skill in order to play with their friends. Other times it may be harmless, as when children all want to wear similar clothes. In such cases wise parents seek a balance, allowing children to fit in while encouraging them to express their individuality. See Fig.19-8.

Peer pressure can also be a negative force, leading children to become involved in harmful, destructive, or risky activities. The pressure to go along with friends may override knowledge that an action is wrong. To help children resist negative peer pressure, parents can:

- Help children develop healthy self-esteem, as discussed in Chapter 18.
- Encourage children's independence of thought and expression.
- Show genuine interest in their children's activities, keeping lines of communication open.
- Apply clear rules and high expectations.
- Get to know their children's friends and, if possible, meet the friends' parents.
- Know where children are and with whom.
- Express concerns in terms of behaviors, not children's choice of friends.
- Discuss particular situations and listen to their children's views, even if they disagree.
- Act out conversations that let children practice saying "no."

Rejection. Even if children have strong relationship skills, they will not be protected from one of the most difficult of all social problems: rejection. Whether it's a case of being turned away by potential playmates, receiving an angry response to a friendly greeting, or simply being ignored by peers, rejection hurts.

Children with healthy self-esteem are better able to handle rejection when it occurs. Parents can discuss what may be happening with the child who is doing the rejecting. They might say, "Sometimes kids just want to be alone" or "Maybe she was mad about something else." Parents should neither dismiss their children's feelings nor encourage them to dwell on these feelings.

If a child experiences frequent rejection from many different children who are not part of one group, parents may need to evaluate the cause. They should consider the possible need to teach the child more effective social behaviors. In any case, parents should reaffirm their love and encourage the child to focus on the friends he or she does have.

Groups and Cliques. Being part of a group is a normal, healthy part of growing up. It provides a sense of identity and belonging. It offers a context in which children may practice new social roles and skills. A group with flexible membership may form around shared interests such as sports, artistic pursuits, or computers. One child or teen may belong to several such groups.

Fig. 19-9. Adults outside the family can be a great inspiration to children because they are neither parents nor peers. **Why might children sometimes feel more comfortable talking about a problem to a trusted adult who is not a parent?**

When groups become rigid and deliberately exclude some people, they turn into cliques. A **clique** is a small, exclusive friendship group that restricts who can join. Cliques typically form during adolescence. They can present several problems:

- In a school or other large group setting, rival cliques may come into conflict. At best, there is little communication between them.
- Cliques intensify peer pressure. In most cliques, members tend to dress similarly, express the same opinions, or otherwise mimic one another to gain a sense of security and identity. Members who try to go against the pattern may find themselves threatened with being dropped from the group.
- Cliques also intensify rejection, since being excluded from a clique cuts a person off from an entire group at one time.

Whether their children are part of a clique or excluded from it, parents can encourage them to form friendships outside the clique, perhaps in another setting. The suggestions given previously for resisting peer pressure can also help.

Relating to Adults Outside the Family

Children benefit from positive relationships with adults other than their parents and relatives. Teachers, counselors, babysitters, mentors, coaches, and friends of the family can provide emotional support and help children learn a variety of skills. Parents can nurture adult-child bonds by involving children in after-school activities or community groups led by positive adult role models. See Fig. 19-9.

Children need to learn socially appropriate ways to interact with adults outside the family. These interactions are different from interactions with peers. Parents need to teach their

Fig. 19-10. Waiting for a turn is one of the most basic social skills children learn. **How can parents help children learn how to take turns?**

children to show respect for their elders and for authority figures. At the same time, parents should encourage children to tell them right away if an adult does anything that makes them uncomfortable.

Teaching Social Skills

Forming and maintaining healthy social relationships is a learned process. Children must be taught basic social skills, such as sharing, courtesy, cooperating, and conflict resolution.

Taking Turns and Sharing

Waiting in the cafeteria line, you probably don't congratulate yourself on practicing a social skill. Taking turns, basic to you, is at first incomprehensible to a toddler.

Janet helped her son learn this skill through everyday activities. While reading to him, she turned one page and then let Tim turn the next. They took turns with puzzle pieces and picking up toys. She set a timer to help Tim understand that each person's turn lasts the same amount of time. Like most children, Tim was not consistent about taking turns until he was about three. See Fig. 19-10.

Sharing is more socially taxing than taking turns. It takes generosity, empathy, and a sense of fair play to let others enjoy something that belongs to you.

Toddlers are often confused about the concept of ownership. Three-year-old Leroy sees that "his" plate is "his" only for as long as he eats from it. He may think his toys are his only for as long as he plays with them. His confusion is deepened at the child care center, where

toys are for everyone. To help Leroy learn that his possessions are his permanently, his parents label them with his name and provide special places to store them: a shelf for his toys, a closet for his clothes.

Using Good Manners

The essence of good manners is consideration for others. Teaching children good manners helps them get along with others and be liked. When teaching manners, parents should:

- **Explain the reason for a rule.** Parents need to explain how rules of good behavior demonstrate respect for others.
- **Set age-appropriate expectations.** Preschoolers can't manage several utensils at one meal, but they can chew with their mouths closed. A seven-year-old should know how to make introductions.

- **Practice in real life and during make-believe.** Making a pretend phone call during play time gets children used to proper phone manners. Children can answer real phone calls occasionally and practice certain phrases, such as "Just a minute, please."
- **Acknowledge efforts.** Thanking children for showing consideration reinforces thoughtful behavior.
- **Set a good example.** Parents should model good manners by treating children and others with courtesy.

Cooperation

Around age four, children are ready for cooperative games in which players work together for a common goal. Each player has a chance to succeed, and there is little competition. For example, everyone wins when the group keeps a large balloon afloat. In cooperative activities, the whole group succeeds by resolving conflicts, listening, sharing, and encouraging. Children need these skills for successful relationships.

Parents can help children learn to play cooperatively by teaching them to follow rules, take turns, share, and help others. By playing cooperative games with their children, parents give the children practice in cooperation and strengthen the bonds between parent and child.

Handling Competition

By about age eight, children become interested in competition. They like simple activities, such as board games and running races, which offer the possibility of winning. Competition helps children identify their talents and encourages them to try their best. Team competitions can be as effective as cooperative games at teaching teamwork and leadership skills. See Fig. 19-11.

However, competition can also divide children into "winners" and "losers." Children who are just learning how to do something may feel intimidated by competition. Parents should evaluate whether a child is ready to participate in a particular competitive situation.

Fig. 19-11. Team sports teach children about teamwork and sportsmanship. **What lessons for other social settings might this child learn from playing a team sport?**

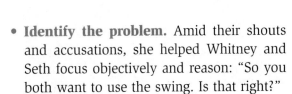

Fig. 19-12. Working out disagreements is part of growing up. **How might conflicts between children be solved without fighting?**

When children are ready to compete, parents can stress the importance of doing one's best and being graceful about winning and losing. Parents can admit their own defeats, without blaming others, and point out what they learned. From this example children see that everyone fails, even parents, yet they try again. People need not be perfect to be loved.

Similarly, parents need to model humility in success. They can share credit for achievements and avoid criticizing those who didn't fare as well.

The sensitive parent is careful when observing competitive games. Shouts from the sidelines should encourage and support all players, rather than belittling anyone for mistakes.

Resolving Conflicts

Only one swing was unoccupied. Whitney reached it first, but Seth hopped aboard and shoved her aside. Whitney shrieked and pushed Seth off. The fight was on.

Although conflicts like this occur every day, they do not have to lead to fights. See Fig. 19-12. Seth's mother helped the children use the conflict resolution process to settle their disagreement. She spoke calmly and respectfully, listening to each child. She let them take the lead when possible. Her goal was to give the children experience resolving conflicts by having them:

- **Identify the problem.** Amid their shouts and accusations, she helped Whitney and Seth focus objectively and reason: "So you both want to use the swing. Is that right?"
- **Suggest possible solutions.** She listened to every answer, from "It's not his swing!" to "I want to fight, I was winning."
- **Evaluate each suggestion.** She helped the children see the outcome of each choice. "You could keep fighting," she agreed, "but then neither of you will get to swing."
- **Choose the best solution.** She guided Whitney and Seth to agree to one of the choices. They decided to swing for five minutes each, using a timer.
- **Check to see if the solution worked.** Later, she asked, "Did you like the way you shared the swing?"

Overcoming Shyness

Periods of shyness are a predictable but difficult part of emotional and social growth. Parents should encourage, not force, children to overcome shy feelings.

Toddlers often react to people they don't know by clinging to a parent, hiding, or refusing to talk. This is a natural way for young children to handle a social situation in which they are unsure. Even though this shy behavior may embarrass parents, the best response is to accept it as a part of social development. Most often, toddlers outgrow their shyness around strangers as they learn social skills. See Fig. 19-13.

Parents can help a shy child by describing social situations in advance and practicing techniques for starting conversations. Parents may also be able to encourage friendships that bring out a child's social side. Some children

Fig. 19-13. It's not unusual for toddlers to feel shy around strangers. **How can parents help a shy child to feel more comfortable?**

blossom with the admiration of a younger friend. Others feel more comfortable with an older one who can take the lead.

Shyness that persists into preschool or grade school can hamper a child's happiness and success. If a child has few friends or withdraws at social events, parents may want to consult a teacher or school counselor.

Becoming Assertive

Children are born with a natural *temperament,* or general way of reacting to the world around them. Some children tend to be quiet and passive. Some tend to be loud and aggressive. Others seem to strike a balance between the two extremes. Most children alternate among different styles of behavior, depending on the circumstances.

When they want to avoid conflict, some children may behave passively, allowing other people's needs and wants to come before their own. In contrast, at times some children behave aggressively by assuming that their needs and wants matter more than those of others. A third type of behavior, called **assertiveness,** means showing equal respect for oneself and others. In American culture, assertive behaviors include making requests and expressing opinions firmly and confidently; making eye contact; listening to others respectfully; and responding directly and calmly.

Learning to be assertive boosts children's self-confidence. It can help them get along with others and resolve conflicts. Parents can help children develop assertiveness by nurturing both self-esteem and compassion. If children know that their thoughts and feelings matter in their family, they are more likely to feel that they matter in other groups.

Fig. 19-14. Children who have opportunities to play with peers from many different backgrounds learn to appreciate diversity. **What are some ways parents can teach children to avoid stereotyping others?**

Appreciating Diversity

As children spend more time outside the home, their relationships expand. Sooner or later they meet people whose appearance, language, or religion is different from their own. If parents help children appreciate diversity, children will get along better with all kinds of people. See Fig. 19-14.

Around age four or five, children use physical differences and differences in abilities to help define themselves in relation to their peers. They also see people from many different cultural groups and with varying physical abilities, in the media and perhaps in their own community. Young children tend to accept such differences as a matter of fact. They do not feel one quality is better than another—until someone tells them otherwise. To help children continue to accept and appreciate diversity, a parent can:

- Show books and videos from diverse cultures.
- Visit art exhibits and museums that celebrate diversity.
- Answer questions about differences with facts that are free from judgment: "People use wheelchairs because they can't walk."
- Discuss ways that people who have differences are alike. For example, everyone feels emotions; everyone eats food, whether it is beans and rice or bread and borscht.

Stereotypes

A **stereotype** is a fixed, oversimplified mental image of a group of people. Stereotypes presume that all individuals who share one characteristic are the same in other ways. Even positive stereotypes harm by oversimplifying. Parents can teach children to reject stereotypes by reminding children about people who defy a stereotype: "Some people say older people are grouchy. Grandma Clark is older, and you have a lot of fun with her."

Cultural Bias

People of all ages make assumptions about others. **Cultural bias** occurs when people make assumptions, based on their own culture, to judge and predict people's behavior. For example, behavior that is respectful in one culture may be considered rude or unfriendly in another.

Reading and discussing stories about people in different cultures can help children realize that many assumptions differ from culture to culture. Spending time with people from other cultures and discussing differences can also reduce the effect of cultural bias.

Combating Prejudice

Giving children many opportunities to play with children from different ethnic backgrounds helps to prevent **prejudice**, a negative opinion that is not based on fact or experience. It can also help children distinguish between truths and myths regarding other cultures.

Parents need to take a stand against prejudice, starting with their own attitudes and behaviors. Do they treat all people fairly and with respect? By teaching children to respect all people, all cultures, and all religions, parents instill dignity and respect in children.

Modeling CHARACTER

Teaching Tolerance

Tolerance, respect for the right of others to have different beliefs and customs, is a powerful tool in preventing anger and hatred. How can parents teach tolerance? Start by setting a good example. Children notice whether parents respect or ridicule the way others dress, the religious practices they observe, their disabilities, or the color of their skin. They are likely to follow that example.

Parents can also point out situations that require tolerance. They can talk with children about the importance of respecting differences and being considerate of other people's feelings. They can create opportunities for children to interact with or learn about people of different cultures—for example, by visiting cultural fairs or hosting an exchange student.

Think About It

Suppose you're the parent of a child who complains that a new student at school "talks funny." How would you use this as an opportunity to teach tolerance? What would you say?

Child & Family Services CAREERS

▶ Behavioral Specialist

Behavioral specialists provide counseling, skill training, and support services to individuals with, or at risk for, significant behavior problems at school, home, or work. Behavioral specialists begin treatment by assessing a child's problems and how those problems may be affecting school performance or other aspects of the child's life. They develop and implement behavior management plans that often involve multiple caregivers, such as teachers, family members, and specialists.

Behavioral specialists work in schools, hospitals, and private practices. Most work under the supervision of a clinical psychologist or other qualified professional. Behavioral specialists often work with children who have chronic, intense problems. Some children may have multiple problems, such as both mental and physical disabilities.

"In my job, I have to work with all kinds of people—not just my clients, but their families and teachers, medical professionals, and specialists. I really like the combination of interpersonal and management skills my job requires."

CAREER TIPS

- Take child development, parenting, psychology, and health science technology courses in high school.
- Obtain a bachelor's degree in psychology or social work.
- Consider obtaining a master's degree in counseling, marriage and family therapy, psychology, or social work. Some behavioral specialist jobs require a post-graduate degree; others do not.

CHAPTER SUMMARY

- Social development begins at birth and continues throughout life.
- By building a nurturing and responsive relationship with children, parents teach them how to develop positive social relationships.
- Children go through predictable stages of social development.
- Parents can teach children ways to cope with bullying, peer pressure, and rejection.
- Children must be taught to share, be courteous, cooperate, and resolve conflicts.
- By showing an appreciation for diversity, parents teach children respect for others.

Check Your Facts

1. Why is socialization important for children?
2. How do young children learn acceptable social behavior?
3. Identify at least eight ways to strengthen parent-child relationships.
4. Describe at least three ways that parents can reduce sibling rivalry.
5. Should parents solve children's conflicts for them? Explain.
6. Who are a child's peers?
7. Compare parallel play with cooperative play.
8. In team activities, what matters the most to school-age children?
9. How do relationships change in adolescence?
10. Why is bullying a serious issue?
11. List at least five ways parents can help children resist peer pressure.
12. What negative effects do cliques have?
13. List five ways to teach manners.
14. How can parents help children be positive about winning and losing?
15. What process can parents teach children to resolve conflicts?
16. Describe assertive behavior.
17. Define the terms *stereotype*, *cultural bias*, and *prejudice*.
18. Identify at least two ways parents can help children appreciate diversity.

Think Critically

1. **Comparing Roles.** How do parents, other adults, and peers influence a child's social development? Compare their roles.
2. **Evaluating Choices.** When would a parent let a child make social mistakes? When would a parent step in? Why?
3. **Recognizing Relationships.** Children need to feel good about themselves (an emotional need) in order to reach out for friendship (a social need). What other examples show how social and emotional needs interact?

Apply Your Learning

1. **Skill Identification.** A fourteen-year-old slips ahead of others in the theater line. What social skill or skills has the teen not learned? Discuss when and how such lessons should be taught.

2. **Cooperative Games.** Look for children's games that teach cooperation rather than competition. Teach one to a group of children. Describe the game to the class and report on the experience.

3. **Parenting Skills.** Write how you would handle these parenting situations and analyze ideas in class: **a)** Your ten-year-old wants a violent computer game and pleads, "All my friends have it." **b)** Your five-year-old pushes past an older woman in order to get through a doorway. **c)** Your eight-year-old is devastated after the team loses a gymnastics meet. **d)** Two young siblings are fighting about who broke a toy. **e)** Your three-year-old clings to you and hides her head when meeting someone.

Cross-Curricular Connections

1. **Social Studies.** Locate studies that deal with the effects of too much television watching on children. Summarize what you learn for the class. Discuss in class how too much television watching might affect a child's developing social skills.

2. **Language Arts.** Nineteenth-century poet Ralph Waldo Emerson said, "The only way to have a friend is to be one." Write how you, as a parent, would help a child learn this principle.

Family & Community Connections

1. **Diversity Exploration.** Teach a child in your extended family or neighborhood about diversity. Plan a cultural event to share with the child. You could visit a museum display, attend a cultural fair, read books about different cultures, or cook an ethnic dish. If you wish, pair up with another student and child for this activity.

2. **Teach and Reach.** Schools and communities are concerned about students who are teased or bullied and feel like outsiders. These students are often hurting, and some react violently. How can you and others be a positive force in solving this problem? Plan an elementary or high school campaign that *teaches* those who need to be more sensitive and *reaches* out to those who are troubled.

CHAPTER 20

The Value of Play

CHAPTER OBJECTIVES

- Describe the stages of play.
- Summarize how play benefits children.
- Explain the extent of parental involvement in children's play.
- Identify appropriate toys for children.
- Describe ways to guide children's play.
- Plan and demonstrate appropriate play activities for children.

PARENTING TERMS

- repetitive play
- constructive play
- symbolic play
- exploratory play
- facilitate
- dramatic play

Have you ever heard someone say "That's child's play," meaning that a task is simple or easy? Play comes easily to children, that's true. But in terms of its developmental benefits, play is far from simple. As they play, children are increasing their skills and abilities, learning about their world, and exploring roles and rules. By supporting children's play, parents encourage not only fun and enjoyment, but also healthy development in all areas.

Understanding Play

How would you describe what play is? The concept of play may be hard to define in words, but it's easy to recognize in action. When they're playing, children feel free to explore whatever absorbs their interest. They go wherever their imagination leads them. To a child, crumbling dry leaves is just as much fun as pushing a toy truck.

Children don't have to be taught what play is, how to play, or why play is beneficial. They simply enjoy playing. To a young child, even an activity that adults think of as a chore, such as washing a car, can become play. A child is enthralled with the bubbles, the rainbow from the hose spray, and the quantity of water. Helping wash the car, pouring water, spraying the hose, talking, and listening are learning opportunities that the child experiences as play and fun. See Fig. 20-1.

Stages of Play

As children grow up, their interests and styles of play develop and change. A five-year-old child plays very differently from a three-year-old child. According to child development experts, all children go through the same developmental stages of play in a specific order.

Repetitive Play. Infants enjoy **repetitive play**, the simple joy of doing an activity over and over. Through this repetition, babies discover that their actions have results. They learn, for example, that pushing a ball makes it move or that shaking a rattle makes a noise. Thus, they begin to grasp the basic concept of cause and effect.

Constructive Play. By 18 months of age, toddlers use materials to achieve a specific goal or purpose. This is called **constructive play**. Children at this age are drawn to such play activities as building and knocking down a

Fig. 20-1. Children and adults do not see work and play the same way. **Why might a child see this chore as fun? How can adults regain that sense of play?**

block tower, fitting pieces into a simple puzzle, and hooking plastic links together to make a chain.

Symbolic Play. Children between the ages of three and five engage in **symbolic play**. Common objects can become symbols for whatever they imagine. For example, a stick can symbolize a magic wand, and a sheet can represent a superhero's cape. See Fig. 20-2.

Game Play. Around age five, children become interested in formal games with rules. They begin to play team sports and board games, and they demonstrate an interest in competition. All the types of development—physical, intellectual, emotional, social, and moral—are incorporated in this stage. This final stage of children's play development is refined through adolescence and sets the stage for a lifetime of play.

Benefits of Play

Play is the means by which children develop physically, intellectually, emotionally, socially, and morally. Through playing, children actively explore the world and develop new skills.

Physical. Play has numerous physical benefits for children. Large muscle groups are exercised by walking, chasing balls, riding bicycles, and participating in sports. The heart and immune system are strengthened. Weight is controlled and stress is reduced through activity, and coordination and motor skills are improved. Young children develop small motor skills and eye-hand coordination by pouring water, stringing beads, or molding play dough.

Intellectual. As children interact with their environment, they grow intellectually. Through **exploratory play,** children use their senses to learn about the world around them. They explore how things look, smell, sound, taste, and feel. An infant explores a rattle by trying to chew it. A toddler explores the concept of volume by filling containers of varying sizes with sand. A preschooler uses exploratory play when using fingers to paint. See Fig. 20-3.

Other types of play also have intellectual benefits. For example, symbolic play stimulates creativity and abstract thinking. Some games for young children help them learn color names, animal sounds, or numbers. Games of strategy give older children an opportunity to solve problems, practice reasoning skills, and sharpen their ability to think logically.

Emotional. Play can build self-esteem by providing opportunities for real and imagined success. Pretending to be firefighters, for example, allows children to feel "big." They gain a sense of control needed for emotional health. Children can choose to do those activities in which they excel. Play also provides a way to explore and express feelings. A fear of starting school, for example, can be explored in the safety of a make-believe world. Stuffed animals are good "playmates," helping children practice how to treat others. Having a doll or stuffed toy helps children cope with fears and gain self-control.

Social. Children learn and practice social skills when playing with others. As explained in Chapter 19, these skills develop slowly over time. Two- and three-year-old children engage in *parallel play*, playing near each other but not together. They tend not to share toys or cooperate very well. At three to four years of age, children begin to interact during *cooperative play*. They are learning about give-and-take, sharing, taking turns, and negotiating with each other. By age five, children play together well. They acknowledge common goals and rules of play and become interested in competing with one another. Through group play, they learn communication, cooperation, conflict resolution, and how to follow rules.

Moral. Through play, children can practice the values their parents teach and model. Preschoolers learn the concept of fairness by sharing toys with other children, taking turns, and following the rules of a game. Children learn how to care for others by taking care of dolls or stuffed animals.

Fig. 20–3. Exploratory play can help a child develop intellectually. **How might building sand castles develop intelligence?**

Modeling *CHARACTER*

Demonstrating Fairness

It's a scene familiar to many parents: a group of children are happily playing a game until one of them cries out, "That's not fair!" The complaint might be "Who says you get an extra turn?" or "Why does she always win?" Children must learn that *fairness* does not necessarily mean "everyone gets the same thing." True fairness has to do with playing by the rules and respecting others. Here are some ways in which parents can model fairness:

- Follow the rules yourself, not only in games but in life: "The library books are due tomorrow, so let's make sure we return them today."
- When children break the rules of the family, apply consequences that are just.
- If children complain that they don't receive exactly what their siblings do, explain that each person in a family has different needs that must be met.
- Before settling a dispute, consider all sides. Make it clear that the decision is based on merit, not on emotion or prejudice.

Think About It

Two children are fighting over a toy. How might a parent demonstrate fairness in guiding them toward a resolution of the problem?

Parents' Role in Play

In every culture, a child's first playmates are his or her parents. At first, parents engage in repetitive play such as singing and clapping games with their infants. As children get older, play becomes more goal-oriented. The best play is freely chosen, open-ended, and directed by the child. Parents need to encourage play without being controlling.

Facilitating Play

Imagine a child exploring a large cardboard box. A parent says, "You could make a boat with that. I'll get an old blanket for a sail, and my old fishing pole. You can pretend you're fishing at sea." Now imagine another child and parent in the same situation. This parent says, "I'll bet you could have fun with that big box. What do you think you could do with it?"

The difference between the first and second parent is the difference between directing a child's play and facilitating it. Parents **facilitate** play when they aid children's play without giving them specific instructions.

When parents facilitate play, children learn by doing most of the work. If you were the second parent, for instance, you might suggest very general ideas for using the box: as a clubhouse, a train, or a cave. You might provide the materials needed to help create whatever the child has chosen. You might prime the child's imagination with comments or questions, such as "Where is this train going?"

Creating a Play Environment

Providing space at home is a basic way to facilitate play. Children don't need a specific playroom. However, whatever arrangements parents make should feature:

- **Well-defined boundaries.** Children should know exactly where and when certain play activities are permitted. A parent might say, "Keep your paint and pictures on the table" or "You may play your drums only until Hayley's nap. Then it's quiet time."
- **Safety and accessibility.** Play space should be located within easy view of adults so that children can be supervised. It should not, however, be too close to hazards such as a hot stove or a downward stairway. Nor should children at play, or their toys, block the normal stream of traffic in a home.
- **Inviting furnishings.** A comfortable chair and lamp encourage quieter activities. A small table and chairs truly make the space a child's own. Colorful furnishings appeal to children.
- **Suitable flooring.** Infants and young children spend a lot of time playing on the floor. Carpeting or an area rug can create a warm, comfortable surface for activities such as playing with blocks or dolls. See Fig. 20-4.

Fig. 20-4. Playing on the floor gives children room to use their toys in creative ways. **What desirable features does this play area include?**

Fig. 20-5. Parents can help create opportunities for children to play with others their age. **Why is having playmates beneficial for children?**

Helping Children Find Playmates

After the age of two, most children need playmates. Parents can arrange play dates, host play groups, or let their children know that they are welcome to invite friends over to play. On nice days, parents can supervise neighborhood children playing together outside. See Fig. 20-5.

In addition to bringing children together to play, parents can teach children how to approach new friends in a variety of situations. Parents may suggest ways to ask for a turn on a swing or to invite a new schoolmate to join a game of tag.

Keep in mind that not all play requires other children as playmates. At times, children may prefer to play by themselves. They may sometimes exhibit *onlooker play*, observing from the sidelines while others play. Children also enjoy playing with parents.

Participating in Play

Playing together is an opportunity for parents and children to deepen their bond. Parent-child play can have other benefits, too. Children reveal interests and abilities during play, which observant parents can then guide and encourage. If a child enjoys pretending to be a dinosaur, for example, a parent might make a mental note to check out dinosaur books from the library or visit a museum to see dinosaur bones. Play can reveal how development is progressing, too. Parents may learn just how well their child can hop while they pretend to be rabbits together.

While participating in play can be beneficial, parents must be selective about joining their children's play. Play can be a way for children to take a break from the world of adult authority. Parents should give children the opportunity to make their own decisions about play.

An adult doesn't need any special tools, toys, or materials to enter the imaginative world of a child's play. The right attitude and a willingness to play according to the child's rules are all that are needed. Adults should follow the child's lead. Playing with a preschooler, for example, may involve acting out the roles of different characters. A parent may be asked to be a bear one minute and a princess the next. Parents should approach play positively and enjoy the opportunity to act like a child again.

Choosing Toys

Providing appropriate toys is a way for parents to facilitate play. Whether purchased or homemade, carefully chosen toys promote development as well as fun.

Age-Appropriate Toys

When choosing toys, parents must make sure they are appropriate for the child's age and developmental level. Children benefit most when toys challenge their skills without frustrating them. Most five-year-olds, for example, would be bored by a toddler's set of stacking rings, but frustrated by a complex model kit designed for a twelve-year-old.

Safety is another factor when evaluating whether toys are age-appropriate. Toys with small parts are not suitable for children under age three because they create a choking hazard. Chapter 16 gives additional toy safety guidelines.

The age recommendation found on toy packages is usually a good guide, but parents should consider the child's level of development before making a decision. Fig. 20-6 suggests some toys that are generally appropriate for different age groups.

Less Is More

When it comes to toys, parents should remember the principle, "less is more." Children don't need mountains of toys, and toys need not be high-tech or expensive.

Children who have fewer toys tend to get more use from each one. They are motivated to be inventive. Having too many toys can actually cause children to lose interest in them or feel overwhelmed by their choices. If parents find their children are accumulating too many playthings, they might try rotating toys. Toys seem new and fresh after they've been kept on the shelf a while. Little-used toys that are in good shape might be given to charity.

Age-Appropriate Toys	
Age Group	**Toy Ideas**
Infants	Mobiles, blocks, shaker toys, squeeze toys, plush toys, plastic blocks, nesting toys, jack-in-the-box
Toddlers	Push toys, pull toys, riding toys, building blocks, child's tape player, spools to string, containers and items to fill them
Preschoolers	Water-play toys, dolls and accessories, beads to string, hand and finger puppets, alphabet blocks, magnetic letters and numbers, child's tape recorder
School-Age Children	Board games, chess and checkers sets, dominoes, backgammon, card games, child's chemistry sets, beginner needlecraft sets, age-appropriate computer and video games

Fig. 20-6. Many toys for older children are not suitable for toddlers. The reverse is also true. **What are some appropriate toys for school-age children?**

Parents should keep in mind that battery-operated toys are not always the best choices. An action figure that says five phrases when a button is pushed does not allow children to be as creative as when they have to imagine what the action figure would say.

Resourceful parents find ways to save money on toys. A group of parents might form a toy co-op, buying toys together and rotating them among their children. Used toys can often be purchased inexpensively at garage sales and secondhand stores. Be sure to carefully check used toys for safety.

Everyday Objects as Toys

Some of the best toys are everyday items found around the home. These may include plastic measuring cups and containers, old clothes used for dress-up, and paper towel tubes. Toddlers love to bang on pots and pans with spoons. A blanket makes a great tent. Plastic utensils such as colanders and cups are fun in the bath, as are large sponges. Old socks make fine puppets. Empty egg cartons are good for sorting or mixing paints. Toys and playthings are everywhere! Children should be encouraged to explore the everyday objects that are available to them. See Fig. 20-7.

Computer and Electronic Games

Many children love to play computer and electronic games. They love the vivid graphics and sounds, as well as the immediate feedback and sense of control. Computer games help children develop eye-hand coordination, reasoning skills, and memory strategies. Games that can be played by several children at once help develop certain social skills. Many electronic games, though, can be played by only one child at a time. Parents should balance the time their children spend playing solitary games with time spent playing with others. They should

Fig. 20-7. Many household objects make terrific toys. **How many different ways might a toddler play with these kitchen items?**

also remember that there is no substitute for physical play, which develops children's minds and bodies in ways not possible with electronic games.

Storing Toys

Having a system of organized toy storage helps when teaching children to put their playthings away. All storage should be child-height and child-accessible. For example, a low shelf can hold shoeboxes for small toys and books. Laundry baskets or milk crates can hold larger toys.

Toy chests with lids or doors should comply with Consumer Product Safety Commission standards to ensure children aren't trapped by accident. Hinges should ensure that a chest stays open when the lid is raised, and there should be no latches that might trap a child inside when closed.

Guiding Play Activities

Children need many different kinds of play activities, such as riding bicycles, playing instruments, and dressing up in old clothes. Variety in children's play is as important as variety in their diet.

Active Play

Children need plenty of opportunities for active play. That means play activities that are primarily physical—playing tag, throwing and catching a ball, or jumping rope, for example. Active play helps build muscles and improve motor skills.

Parenting Pointers

Choosing Appropriate Toys

When choosing toys for their children, parents should consider:

Sensory appeal. Bright colors, contrasting textures, and lively sounds hold a child's interest and stimulate learning.

Versatility. The more ways a child can use a toy, the better. Simple toys are often the best. A mound of clay may become a work of art one day and a plate of meatballs the next.

Care and maintenance. Toys should be washable to prevent the spread of germs. Consider how much maintenance, such as replacing parts and batteries, a toy requires.

Learning potential. A toy should spur children to use their minds and bodies. Building blocks, for example, let a child create structures while developing small motor skills.

Values. Toys can send messages about behavior and relationships. Does a toy promote violent play or cooperation? What ideas about age, gender, ethnicity, or beauty does it reinforce?

Economy. An expensive toy may be worth the extra cost if it is well made and will be used for many years. Toys can also be acquired inexpensively at second-hand stores or as hand-me-downs from friends and relatives.

Safety. Any toy given to a child must be safe. Never give toddlers toys with parts small enough to fit into their mouths. Toys should not have broken parts or sharp edges.

Health & Safety

Playground Hazards

Before allowing their children to play in any playground, parents should inspect it for hazards such as:

- Metal and moving parts that can pinch small fingers.
- Poorly spaced bars in which children's heads can get caught.
- Toddler swings that do not have safety straps.
- Metal slides that get hot in the sun.
- Lack of adequate cushioning material under playground equipment.
- Wood-framed structures that have been left untreated and that have splintered. Older wooden parts may have been treated with arsenic, a poison that can rub off on children's hands.
- Sandboxes that are left open at night. Stray cats often use these as litter boxes.

When children have access to a yard, playground, neighborhood green space, or a nearby public park, they can enjoy active, noisy play more often. If weather or other circumstances prevent children from playing outdoors, parents must find ways to bring active play indoors. For example, they might provide soft foam balls and designate a room where they can be thrown safely. Large cardboard boxes can be arranged into twisting, turning tunnels to crawl through.

Many parents who have outdoor space install play equipment for their children. It's important to choose sturdy equipment that's appropriate to children's ages and ability levels. A low slide is fine for a toddler with supervision, but a high one adds to the risk of injury. Equipment must be installed correctly. That means it is anchored to the ground correctly and securely. The area beneath the equipment should have a thick layer of shock-absorbing material to cushion falls. Sometimes shredded tires are used for this purpose.

Tricycles, bikes, inline skates, and similar equipment may also present hazards. Inspect them regularly to make certain they are in good condition. Children must wear safety helmets—and other protective gear, as appropriate—when using such equipment. Parents should set a good example by wearing their own safety gear. Enforcing these and other safety rules from an early age can help prevent severe injuries.

Quiet Play

Quiet play includes activities that engage a child's mind and small motor skills. Parents can inspire exploration with many quiet but stimulating activities. Parents can show children how to make shadows on the wall with their bodies and various objects. Magnets can provide hours of entertainment. For school-age children, models, puzzles, and card games are challenging yet relaxing forms of quiet play. See Fig. 20-8.

When quiet play is spontaneous and child-initiated, parents need to be patient and supportive. A toddler in the bathtub might pour water from one container to another, comparing the amount each one holds. The tolerant parent not only waits until the child's curiosity is satisfied but provides another container for an additional round of "tests."

Fig. 20-8. Quiet play is just as important as active play. **What are some benefits of quiet play?**

Dramatic Play

Most children are natural actors and playwrights. They love to pretend. In **dramatic play**, children assume different identities and take part in make-believe events. Dramatic play has several benefits. It allows children to work out what is going on in their real lives, perhaps expressing difficult emotions such as sibling rivalry. Dramatic play also allows them to explore adult roles such as husband and wife or manager and employee. It may even reveal undiscovered interests and talents as children pretend to be scientists, construction workers, or teachers, for example.

Children satisfy their appetite for make-believe as the need arises. A story, a movie, or a real-life event such as a wedding can inspire hours and days of dramatic play. Although children rarely need a parent's help in creating dramas, they do appreciate certain parental support, such as providing props or taking on the role of a character. See Fig. 20-9.

When a group of children are involved in dramatic play, parents should involve themselves only minimally. They should supervise the children's safety, of course. They can redirect play that seems to be growing violent or hurtful or that reinforces negative attitudes. Resolving conflicts and solving problems should be left to the children as much as possible. This is part of their learning.

Art Activities

Art teachers say process, not product, is what makes art activities so beneficial for children. By this they mean that the creative process, and what children learn from it, is more important than any product the child makes. For parents, this means encouraging and praising a child's efforts to create something, rather than focusing on the quality of what he or she makes.

The creative process is often a messy one—which may be part of its attraction for children. An art area should be protected with newspaper, plastic, or drop cloths. Children should be protected too, if necessary, with smocks, aprons, or old clothes.

Children progress from simpler activities, such as drawing basic shapes, to those that demand finer muscle control and concentration, such as making a collage. When planning an art project, a parent should make sure it is appropriate for the child's skills. Some common art activities for young children are described in Fig. 20-10.

Fig. 20-9. Children often imitate the roles they see in adults. **How can parents facilitate dramatic play?**

Parents need to exercise some care in responding to what children produce artistically. A child's drawing may be hard to identify, but asking, "What is it?" is apt to disappoint a child who has labored long over a creation. A very general, enthusiastic response usually works, such as, "What a beautiful picture! I love the way you used those bright colors. Tell me about this picture."

Choosing Art Activities		
Activity	**Suggested Supplies**	**Tips for Success**
Drawing	Crayons, washable felt markers, chalk, drawing paper, brown wrapping paper, computer paper	Encourage children to create their own drawings rather than using coloring books.
Painting	Tempera paint, large paint brushes, sponges, yarn pompons, unused flyswatters, newspaper, computer paper, paper bags	Supply a separate painting tool for each color.
Finger Painting	Commercial finger paints, colored wheat paste, freezer paper, egg cartons	Let children paint in the bathtub, which can be cleaned up easily after they are done.
Making Collages	Magazines, greeting cards, gift wrap, fabric scraps, twigs, leaves, pine cones, uncooked pasta, dry cereal	Use sturdy backing material, such as cardboard, and white glue thinned with water.
Modeling and Shaping	Play dough or modeling clay, rolling pin, cookie cutters, coins, buttons, shells	Make homemade play dough from recipes in parenting books or magazines.

Fig. 20-10. Many simple items can be used as art supplies. **What other household items might make good art supplies?**

Parents must also resist "improving" a child's artwork. Learning a technical skill is not the aim of art activities. If a child thinks a creation is beautiful, who is to say otherwise?

Music Activities

Children at every age enjoy music. Distressed infants will often calm down when they hear music. Toddlers take an active interest in music by marching, dancing, and clapping to the beat. Preschoolers enjoy singing, often making up songs to go along with their play.

A parent doesn't need musical talent to provide musical experiences. Infants love a parent's singing voice, regardless of its musical quality. They are delighted by toys that make sounds.

Young children develop coordination and a sense of rhythm by moving to music. Parents can encourage them by singing, playing instruments, and playing recorded music. Some recordings by children's artists are specifically made for singing along. Parents can provide rhythm instruments in the form of pots, pans, and other nonbreakable household items. For older children, joining a school band or a choir can be a pleasant way to explore a musical interest.

Making Play a Priority

Too often, parents think of play as strictly "kid's stuff." Yet sharing fun and good times is one of the best ways to build closeness and communication in families. Oftentimes it's the silly and enjoyable experiences that families recall and laugh about for years. Fun and laughter create a resilient bond. Even though adult life can be very hectic, parents need to make time to play with their children. To paraphrase a familiar saying, "The family that plays together stays together." See Fig. 20-11.

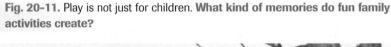

Fig. 20-11. Play is not just for children. **What kind of memories do fun family activities create?**

Child & Family Services CAREERS

▸ Play Therapist

Play therapy sounds like fun, but it is serious business. A play therapist is a trained mental health professional who uses play as a medium to help children who have been through difficult experiences or have emotional problems. A play therapist may work in a school, a clinic, a hospital, or private homes.

To become a play therapist, a person must earn a master's degree in a medical or mental health discipline and receive specialized training in play therapy. He or she then must practice many hours of clinical therapy before being licensed as a Registered Play Therapist (RPT).

A play therapist must be good at communicating with adults and children. He or she also must be tolerant, emotionally strong, and self-aware. Careful recordkeeping and good organizational skills are a must.

"As a play therapist, I have to be good at listening to children and interpreting their feelings. Children act out issues and emotions through play all the time. A child who is afraid to show anger toward a sibling, for example, will often act out that anger using toys. Through my therapy, I help children deal with difficult issues in a healthy way."

CAREER TIPS

- Take child development, language arts, psychology, and health science courses in high school.
- Gain experience working with children.
- Get a college degree and apply for an appropriate graduate program.

CHAPTER SUMMARY

- As children grow and mature, the way they play changes.
- Play helps children develop physically, intellectually, emotionally, socially, and morally.
- Parents can use a number of techniques to help children benefit from their playtime.
- Toys should be chosen carefully to be sure they are safe and appropriate for the child's age.
- Parents can find suitable toys for children without spending too much money.
- Children need and enjoy varied play that includes both active and quiet activities.

Check Your Facts

1. Why is play important for children?
2. Describe and give examples of repetitive, constructive, and symbolic play.
3. Identify at least three ways children develop physically through play.
4. How does exploratory play promote intellectual growth?
5. How do children develop emotionally and socially through play?
6. How does a parent facilitate play?
7. What are four features of a suitable play environment for children?
8. Who should make the decisions when an adult and child play together?
9. Suggest two age-appropriate toys for each of these: infants, toddlers, preschoolers, and school-age children.
10. What are two benefits of giving children fewer toys?
11. What guidelines about computer and electronic games should parents follow?
12. Describe a safe toy chest.
13. Distinguish between active play and quiet play, and suggest three ways to guide each of these types of play.
14. What are the benefits of dramatic play?
15. Suggest a tip for success when children draw and finger paint.
16. What are at least three activities that promote musical skills?

Think Critically

1. **Judging Relevance.** Suppose a five-year-old is confined to bed after surgery. What specific play ideas would you plan for the child?
2. **Analyzing Information.** A babysitter has a new job caring for a four-year-old girl and a five-year-old boy. The sitter wants to make a good impression on the parents and children in order to be hired again. What personality traits should the sitter display with the children? What play activities would you recommend?

Apply Your Learning

1. **Appropriate Toys.** Look through newspapers, magazines, and catalogs for toy ads. Select appropriate toys for infants, toddlers, and preschoolers. Show pictures in class of toys for each age group, and explain why they are good choices.

2. **Everyday Objects.** Demonstrate how to use simple household items as toys. Identify the ages of children who could play with these improvised toys.

3. **Parenting Advice.** Suppose you write a parenting advice column for a magazine. Write a response to this query: "My four-year-old is cranky all the time. I take her to music, art, and gymnastics classes. We often go to the museum and zoo, too. Why doesn't my child seem happy?"

4. **Creative Activities.** Demonstrate an art or music activity that a parent could share with a child. Bring any necessary supplies you need to class. Discuss how the activity stimulates creativity, imagination, and learning.

Cross-Curricular Connections

1. **Social Studies.** Research games played in another country or culture or games played by American pioneer children. Demonstrate one game for the class. What development was promoted with this game?

2. **Language Arts.** Create an interactive puppet show for children. Choose a specific safety, health, or moral lesson as the theme. Write the script, make the puppets, and design props and scenery. Include music in the production, and perform it for an age-appropriate group of children.

Family & Community Connections

1. **Playtime Memories.** Ask adults in your family what memories they have of favorite games and toys. Did they save any childhood toys or games that they could show you? Research antique toys on the Internet together, looking for toys older family members may recognize. How has play changed over the years?

2. **Community Safety.** Visit a playground in your community. Using the guidelines in this chapter and Chapter 16, evaluate the safety of the playground and equipment. Report your findings in class and discuss what can be done about any unsafe community playgrounds.

UNIT 5

Guiding Children

Communicating with Children

CHAPTER OBJECTIVES

- Explain the benefits of effective communication between parent and child.
- Describe how parents can send appropriate nonverbal and verbal messages.
- Demonstrate how to communicate well with children of different ages.
- Summarize how to use listening as a communication tool.
- Suggest ways to promote open communication with children.
- Identify how to model and teach respectful communication to children.

Parents may have great ideas and solid guidelines for their children, but if they don't know how to put the message across, their children just won't get it. Good communication between parent and child builds their relationship and the child's self-esteem. In addition, parents who communicate effectively give their children a gift for life: a model for how to communicate well with others.

Benefits of Effective Communication

Communication is the process of sharing information, thoughts, and feelings. That's more complicated than it sounds. The process uses words and actions, plus ideas and emotions. Communication between parent and child goes in two directions. Parents communicate support, guidance, love, and discipline to their children not only by what they say, but also by how they respond to what children tell them.

Effective parent-child communication has many benefits, including these:

- Strong, positive family relationships based on trust.
- Clarity and reduced risk of misunderstanding.
- Promotion of healthy self-esteem.
- Support for the child's intellectual, emotional, and social development.
- Training for the child to communicate well in school, work, and the community.

Sending the Right Message

Communication between parent and child can take many forms. They may talk on the phone, write notes, or exchange e-mail. Most often, though, parents and children communicate face-to-face. These conversations take place on two levels: verbal (in words) and nonverbal.

Nonverbal Messages

In **nonverbal communication**, messages are sent with the tone of voice, eye contact, gestures, facial expressions, and body language. In other words, it's not just *what* you say, but *how* you say it. Often, people are not even aware of the nonverbal messages they're sending. See Fig. 21-1.

When interacting with children, parents need to be especially aware of the nonverbal messages they send. Suppose a parent says to a crying child, "What's wrong?" If the words are spoken softly while the parent kneels down

Fig. 21-1. People express feelings nonverbally as well as verbally. **Which kinds of nonverbal communication, if any, can reach a listener over the telephone?**

Parenting Pointers

The Power of Touch

Touch sends a powerful message to a child—a message of acceptance, protection, and love. The physical comfort of a parent's hug or pat on the shoulder affects children's emotional growth. It builds a sense of security and trust. Here are some recommendations for parents:

➤ Touch a child gently on the shoulder to get his or her attention before starting to talk.

➤ Hold a child's hand. While this is often necessary for a young child's physical safety, it also communicates the parent's emotional protection and support.

➤ Hold a child in your lap as you read together. Peacefully sharing books and stories together in this way creates a memorable bond.

➤ Cradle a child's face in your hands. If you have something important to say, get down at eye level. Then place both hands on the child's cheeks and embrace them lovingly as you speak.

➤ Encourage a child in difficult moments with a gentle pat. When things aren't going well, a pat on the back can be comforting.

➤ Nudge gently to move a child toward something the child is avoiding. The power of touch can be positive and affirming, even in an uncomfortable situation.

➤ Continue hugging children through the adolescent years. They will never outgrow the need for this message of love, even when they are trying to detach themselves emotionally.

and touches the child on the shoulder, the child feels comforted. In contrast, if the parent whirls around sharply and barks out the words, the child is likely to react with fear or feel hurt.

When verbal and nonverbal messages do not match, children may become confused by the mixed messages or "hear" a message the parent didn't intend. Suppose a parent says, "Go on—I'm listening," but then turns away and starts doing something else. A lack of interest is the nonverbal message the child receives. Another child who hears a put-down accompanied by a wink and a smile may not recognize that it was meant as a joke.

Parents can make the most of nonverbal communication with their children by:

• Speaking in a respectful tone of voice—not yelling or mocking.

- Making sure the verbal and nonverbal messages match.
- Maintaining eye contact.
- Touching the child while talking.

Choosing Words with Care

Children can be very sensitive to the words in a message and the tone used to convey them. An unthinking outburst from a parent may lead children to feel worthless or unloved. Parents who communicate effectively with children phrase their messages with care.

- **Use positive language.** Trying to control behavior with too many "don'ts," "can'ts," and "shoulds" doesn't work well. Of course, an exception is when a child is in danger.
- **Comment on actions, not personalities.** Children can react quite strongly to remarks containing judgments that parents might not think twice about, like "You're crazy!" They can take these judgments quite seriously.

- **Be polite.** Adding such expressions as "please" and "thank you" models consideration and teaches children courtesy.
- **Avoid comparisons.** Comparing children to others or to how parents were as children is unfair and often belittling.
- **Avoid "never" and "always."** Safety rules and other family rules may be absolutes. In describing a child's behavior, however, it is best to focus only on the current event. See Fig. 21-2.

Using "I" Messages

Many parents learn to use **"I" messages** with children of all ages—and with adults as well. An "I" message from a parent expresses how the child's behavior affects the parent, rather than labeling the behavior as good or bad. The message gives a clear explanation without attacking. In this way, the child's self-esteem is preserved. Parental "I" messages

Put Your Best Words Forward	
Say This...	**Instead of This...**
"Thank you for just looking at these beautiful ornaments. They are very fragile."	"Don't touch anything in here. You'll break something."
"This game looks like a lot of fun. Please play it outside where you can run around and be noisy."	"Shut up! Stop running around!"
"Try putting less cereal in the bowl, and it won't spill."	"You are the clumsiest child I've ever seen. Can't you do anything right?"
"I can see you are disappointed because you wanted to see a different movie, but this time it was Anna's turn to choose. Thanks for being a good sport."	"Why are you always such a whiner if you don't get your way?"
"I know you want candy for a snack, but your choice is either an apple or cheese and crackers. Which would you like?"	"Candy is bad for you. How many times do I have to tell you that? You need to eat healthier foods and stop eating junk."
"I was so worried when you didn't come home at the time we agreed on, and you didn't call me."	"You're totally irresponsible and think only about yourself. It's impossible to ever count on you for anything."

Fig. 21-2. Carefully chosen words preserve a child's self-esteem while making a clear point. **What communication principles does each example illustrate?**

have three components: how the parent feels, the child's behavior that triggered the feelings, and the reason for those feelings. Here are some examples:

- "I was worried when you didn't call to let me know you went to Jacob's house because I had no idea where you were."
- "I was embarrassed by the way you complained about Uncle Bob's cooking because I thought his feelings might be hurt."
- "I feel frightened when I see you playing near the street. Even though you say you'd never run into the street, I worry that you might forget and be hurt."
- "I'm proud of you for petting the dog so gently. The dog seemed to really like it."

Simply putting "I" before a statement does not automatically make it an "I" message. Some very hurtful statements begin with "I." ("I just hate that you've become such a slob by making a mess everywhere you go.") Effective "I" messages are worded positively in a way that does not threaten or attack the child's character. See Fig. 21-3.

Children and teens learn by example how to use "I" messages in their communication with parents and others. An adolescent might say, "Mom, I care about your opinion. I want to tell you an idea I have. It's really important to me that you listen and not judge it right away. Just think about it, okay? Then later we can talk about it."

Age-Appropriate Communication

Children improve their ability to understand and convey messages as they develop. Parents should tailor their communication to a child's developmental stage.

Fig. 21-3. "I" messages allow the speaker to communicate without seeming to attack or judge. **In what situations might "I" messages be particularly effective?**

Infants

Research has demonstrated the benefits of talking to children from birth. One study linked the number of words babies and toddlers heard with aptitude test scores from ages three and nine. Babies in "talkative homes," where they heard as many as 2,100 words per hour, scored much higher than babies in homes where only 600 words were spoken per hour. Interestingly, radio and television voices did not have the same effect.

THE DEVELOPING BRAIN

Neuroscientists have found that early communication is critical to children's mental as well as emotional growth. Parents who talk with, read to, or otherwise verbally interact with children stimulate their children's linguistic skills. Because language is fundamental to nearly all cognitive development, talking and listening to children is one of the best ways of maximizing the important brain-building years.

Babies enjoy conversation about anything! Parents and caregivers can read aloud or sing to babies. They can discuss their plans for the day or what they are cooking. See Fig. 21-4.

While talking to an infant, remember to smile, touch, hold, rock, and make eye contact. Pause to allow the infant to respond with coos or babbles. Watch for cues that a baby does not want to "talk" anymore, such as turning away.

Parents the world over talk "baby talk" to infants—and the infants seem to appreciate the high-pitched tones and silly, babbling words. Babies also love it when people imitate the sounds they make. For instance, they delight when parents coo after they coo. Babies love to hear singing as well.

Toddlers and Preschoolers

Children outgrow "baby talk" by the time they are toddlers. They also grow in their ability to have two-way conversations. When speaking with toddlers and preschoolers, parents should:

- Talk in a normal tone of voice.
- Use simple words that children will understand, or define new words for them.
- Keep sentences short and clear. For example, this sentence is too long: "If it's really cold outside, it's good to wear your sweater, because otherwise you might catch a cold." Instead say, "If you go outside, please put on a sweater."
- Avoid or explain figurative language. Children at this age tend to interpret language literally. For example, if a preschooler's big brother says, "Mom's going to kill you for letting the cat out," the child may very well fear what mother may do. By age ten, most children know such statements are only expressions that shouldn't be taken literally.

Fig. 21-4. The act of talking to an infant is more important than what you talk about. **How does being talked to benefit infants?**

- Wait to give instructions until the time the child should follow them. Young children are easily distracted and tend to live in the moment. They forget easily.
- Get down to the child's eye level by squatting or sitting when possible. To strengthen the communication, also maintain eye contact and touch the child's hand, arm, or shoulder. See Fig. 21-5.

Older Children and Teens

As children develop, parents need to adapt their communication style. Listening to older children and teens and encouraging them to share feelings and thoughts help keep communication doors open. Respect and courtesy are essential. Children and teens need to know that parents value what they have to say and respect their thoughts and feelings, even when different from those of the parents.

Listening to Children

The ability to listen well is a powerful communication tool. Listening is not the same as hearing. Whereas hearing is a physical process, listening involves paying attention and understanding a message. Parents who listen to their children demonstrate consideration and build their children's self-esteem.

Here are some general guidelines for listening to children:

- **Pay attention.** Stop whatever you're doing and focus on the child. Turn off the radio or television. Make eye contact, and relax as you listen. Ignore distractions.
- **Be patient.** It may take some time for children to express themselves. Don't rush them, interrupt them, or finish sentences for them.

Fig. 21-5. Communication with young children is often most effective when adult and child talk eye-to-eye. **How might getting down to the eye level of a young child affect communication?**

- **Consider the context.** If a child says "My stomach doesn't feel so good" while riding in a car on a twisty road, parents can probably assume the child is suffering from motion sickness. If a child says this on the first day of school, however, a wise parent may suspect that the child is nervous about school.

Active Listening

When psychologists and counselors work with clients, they actively draw people out and acknowledge their feelings. They try to understand both verbal and nonverbal messages, without attempting to judge or correct. This technique is called **active listening**. It's a very effective tool for parents, as well. See Fig. 21-6.

With active listening, a parent tries to understand the child's point of view and reflect it back to the child. The technique does *not* mean agreeing or disagreeing, praising or blaming, distracting or minimizing, lecturing or explaining, or giving advice or directions. Active listening helps children accept uncomfortable feelings and solve their own problems.

Parents who are active listeners do the following:

- Try to understand both content and emotions. Active listening has been called "listening with the heart" because you pay attention to the feelings and intent behind the child's words, as well as the words themselves.
- Invite the child to say more, using such words and phrases as "Really?" and "You did, huh?" These phrases keep a child talking because you aren't being judgmental.
- Try to understand the child's point of view. For example, a child says, "I hate Tommy—he broke my truck." An active listener replies, "I know you loved that truck, and I know you're mad at your brother for breaking it."

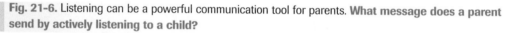

Fig. 21-6. Listening can be a powerful communication tool for parents. **What message does a parent send by actively listening to a child?**

Fig. 21-7. Acknowledging how a child feels is an important part of active listening. **Why is learning to accept negative feelings important to children's emotional development?**

- Acknowledge a child's right to opinions and feelings without labeling them as right, wrong, or unimportant. Children who are upset are soothed by having their feelings recognized, identified, and accepted. Never say "You shouldn't feel that way" or "You don't mean that." See Fig. 21-7.

Opening Doors to Communication

The process of building strong parent-child bonds through effective communication is ongoing. Parents encourage this communication in several ways. They provide opportunities for children to share thoughts and feelings, and they encourage expression. At the same time, they promote openness and honesty.

Making Time to Talk

Parents should make themselves available for one-on-one conversations with a child. They need a good time and place to listen to children. When a parent or child is preoccupied, rushed, hungry, or tired, conversations aren't meaningful. Many children like to talk as they are tucked into bed, when it is calm and quiet and they have their parent's complete attention. Riding in a car can provide private, uninterrupted opportunities to talk.

Some families enjoy conversation while eating dinner or playing a game together. See Fig. 21-8.

Sometimes parents "schedule" a time to talk. When you're too busy at the moment, you can set a time to talk later. Comments like these let children know you value what they have to say: "I need to get to the dentist right now, so we'll talk when I get back." "Let's talk about that after your nap." "Be sure to tell me more while I'm fixing dinner tonight."

Encouraging Children to Express Themselves

Once parents have provided an opportunity for children to communicate with them, how do they get children to open up? Conversation openers encourage children to share thoughts and feelings. An open-ended question or comment like these might work: "You seem upset; what's bothering you?" or "Tell me about your day today."

Asking questions shows that parents value what the child has to say. Even a quiet child may respond. Many parents ask questions while reading to a child and then relate the story to real life. A parent might ask, "Why do you think the girl in the story is worried?" After the story, the parent could say, "Does anything ever worry you the way it did Maggie in the story?"

How parents phrase questions affects the success of a conversation. Open-ended questions are better than yes or no questions. A parent who asks, "Did you have a good day at school?" might hear a response such as "Uh-huh" or "It was okay." This is a better starter: "What was the best thing that happened at school today?" As the child responds, continue the conversation by asking questions that repeat words the child has just used.

Keeping informed about what a child is doing in school or at child care is useful. Parents should get to know teachers, playmates, and other

Fig. 21-8. The best conversations are usually in relaxed settings free from distractions or interruptions. What are some good opportunities for family members to talk?

Fig. 21-9. As children reach adolescence, more and more of their activity takes place away from their parents. **How might a parent benefit from having established an atmosphere of open, honest communication?**

parents. With this information, parents are more apt to understand what a child says and be able to show interest in the child's life outside the home. Thinking of appropriate conversation openers is also easier.

Promoting Openness and Honesty

Children tend to express feelings openly and truthfully unless they find that such expression is not valued. Strong parent-child relationships are based on honesty and openness, which build understanding and trust. When children feel safe sharing their thoughts and feelings with their parents, fewer misunderstandings arise. See Fig. 21-9.

Honesty begins with truthfulness about events ("Yes, I accidentally broke the plate"), but it doesn't end there. With these techniques, parents can promote open, honest communication:

- Try to recognize your own feelings and examine what causes them. Awareness of your own feelings is the first step toward open communication.
- Accept children's thoughts and feelings, trying not to judge or criticize. Distinguish ideas and emotions from behavior; it is all right to feel angry, even though it is not all right to hit.
- Let children know that you recognize what they are feeling and thinking.
- Be open and honest with children in appropriate ways. Sometimes this may mean saying, "I understand that you feel that way, although I see it differently."
- Express appreciation when children are open and honest. "Thank you for letting me know you were disappointed when I had to miss the school play."

Teaching Respectful Communication

Effective communication not only strengthens the parent-child relationship but also helps children develop skills they need in life. Whether in the family or the wider community, a key to communicating effectively is respect. Parents can teach respectful communication by example and by teaching children basic conventions and principles.

Social Conventions

Social conventions are rules for behaving in society. Using them keeps relationships smooth, especially between people who don't know

Modeling CHARACTER

Modeling Respect Through Listening

People who listen to others demonstrate respect for the speaker's thoughts and feelings. You do not have to wait until you are a parent to upgrade your listening skills. Engage a young child, someone your age, or an adult in conversation and then answer the questions listed below. Your answers will help you see how you might improve the way you show respect as well as the quality of your listening skills.

- Can you summarize the other person's main points in your own words?
- Did your mind wander into judgment and criticism? Were there times when you were busy thinking of a response instead of listening respectfully?
- Did your own biases and beliefs prevent you from listening with an open mind? Could you identify any biases in the other person?
- Did the other person's body language give you any clues about his or her feelings or emotional state?
- Did the other person convince you to think differently in any way? If so, how?

Think About It

Who do you consider to be the best listener you know? What makes this person so skilled at listening and showing respect? How does this person model respect through effective communication?

Fig. 21-10. Children benefit from being taught such conventions of polite communication as making introductions. **What other basics of respectful communication might a parent teach a child?**

each other well. Some basic conventions that parents can practice and teach their children include these:

- Don't interrupt. Allow the other person to finish speaking.
- When it's your turn to talk, speak briefly.
- Give everyone in the conversation a chance to speak.
- Talk in a voice that others can hear, but not too loud.
- Call people by name: "Hi, Mr. Moto." "Thank you, Aunt Susan."
- Say "please" and "thank you."
- Know how to make an introduction. See Fig. 21-10.

Cultures have different conventions about respectful communication. For example, direct eye contact is considered impolite in many Asian cultures. In most Hispanic cultures, people stand very close together when speaking. Make children respectfully aware of differences as they arise.

Other People's Feelings

Children may confuse being open and honest with saying whatever they want, whenever they want, however they want. Parents need to help children understand the difference. Thinking about people's feelings is the best guide. Children can tell parents they don't like the new teacher, but it's not appropriate to say to the teacher, "I don't like you."

Upsetting Topics. Parents should teach children not to raise topics that might upset someone ("I heard your brother is in prison") or hurt a person's feelings ("Your house looks haunted"). Sometimes a child really needs to talk about an upsetting topic: for example, to straighten out a hurtful misunderstanding with a friend. Parents can suggest ways to be open and honest without making the friend feel attacked. These include choosing words with care, using "I" messages, listening actively to understand the friend's point of view, choosing a quiet time to talk privately, and assuring the friend that the child values the friendship.

Speech and Language Issues. Laughing at the way a person speaks or making fun of speech is never appropriate. Whether a person is learning the English language or has an accent, bad grammar, or a speech defect, respectful listeners focus on the speaker's content and emotions rather than the choice or sound of the words. Parents and caregivers can teach children to ask questions if they don't understand what was said. When someone doesn't understood them, they should answer questions freely before continuing.

Interruptions. While some children need encouragement to open up, others need to learn that there are times to be quiet. Just as children must be taught to wait for a turn to speak in a conversation, they must also learn to wait until people are available for talking. A parent might say, "Wait till Maria finishes her homework to tell her about the party" or "You know how you like to play with your friends? Well, Mrs. Sanchez is my friend, and I want to talk to her now." Children can learn to say "Excuse me" when an interruption is essential.

Fig. 21-11. Children need to know that they are loved. **How might parents communicate unconditional love for their children?**

The Most Important Message

Effective parent-child communication includes expressions of love, acceptance, and support. Providing encouragement is vital for children at all stages of development. Parents who express confidence and faith in their children's abilities instill a positive sense of self in them. Those children feel worthy and tend to be optimistic about life.

Encouragement is especially important when children try something new. Knowing that their parents have confidence in them helps inspire children to do their best. Encouragement leads to *motivation*, an inner desire to act or behave in a certain way to reach a personal goal. Children with high motivation learn and achieve more and feel better about themselves.

Parents can communicate acceptance without words, as well. Sometimes it's best to allow children to discover things on their own and make their own mistakes. When parents show confidence in children by allowing them to try things on their own, they indicate that children can learn and take care of themselves.

The most important message parents must communicate to children is that they love them. Children need to feel that they are accepted and loved unconditionally. They need to know that their parents are there for them even when they misbehave or make mistakes. Children who feel loved are much better equipped to face life's challenges. See Fig. 21-11.

Child & Family Services CAREERS

▶ Child Care Worker

Child care workers have the important job of nurturing children and keeping them safe. They have jobs in child care centers, businesses, nursery schools, preschools, private homes that provide child care, and in before-school and after-school programs.

Most child care workers provide basic care and also teach children. They help children learn to take turns and use words to tell people how they feel. They introduce basic mathematics skills by counting and measuring, and they read aloud and introduce alphabet games to teach pre-reading and language skills. They encourage motor development through physical activities and introduce the joy of art, music, dance, and nature. They feed children nutritious meals and snacks and provide opportunities for active group play as well as quiet time.

"I began working in child care after I got my GED. First I cared for three children in my home; in my state that required a license. Later, I went back to school and got an Associate of Science degree in early childhood development. Now I work in a child care facility for a large corporation. The best part of my job is seeing children develop confidence and positive self-esteem. They will take that with them into kindergarten as excited, happy learners."

CAREER TIPS

- Take child development, parenting, and health science courses in high school.
- Volunteer at a child care center or after-school program.
- Get an associate's degree and pass the licensure exam for your state, if needed.
- Consider a special focus, such as a program for children who have special needs.

CHAPTER **21** Review & Activities

CHAPTER SUMMARY

- Effective parent-child communication includes both nonverbal and verbal methods.
- Parents should use age-appropriate communication as children grow.
- Parents show they understand a child's messages when they use active listening.
- Openness and truthfulness are two vital components in parent-child communication.
- Teaching children respectful ways to send messages gives them skills to use in many social situations.
- Children learn and achieve more when parents and other caregivers motivate them by offering encouragement.

Check Your Facts

1. List at least three benefits of effective parent-child communication.
2. What is nonverbal communication?
3. What can result from giving children negative messages?
4. Give an example of an "I" message.
5. Besides saying words, what should also be done when talking to an infant?
6. Suggest four recommendations for communication with young children.
7. Why is listening to older children and teens worthwhile?
8. What is the difference between hearing and listening?
9. What are three general guidelines for parents as they listen to their children?
10. How can a parent be an active listener?
11. What can prevent meaningful conversations between a parent and child?
12. What is the value of an open-ended question when talking with a child?
13. List at least three techniques parents can use to promote honest communication.
14. What are at least four social conventions that keep relationships smooth?
15. What should you teach a child about other people's feelings?
16. What is the most important message a parent can send to a child?

Think Critically

1. **Analyzing Information.** Suppose a mother is talking on her cell phone at length while helping her four-year-old play on equipment at the park. Analyze the use of communication in this situation.
2. **Inferring Meaning.** Whenever seven-year-old Josh's parents accuse him of breaking something, making a mess, or starting a fight with siblings, he always becomes fearful and defensive, so he lies. Why does he react this way? How should the parents communicate with Josh to help avoid such reactions?

Apply Your Learning

1. **Communication Practice.** Work with a team of four students to evaluate parent-child communications. After two students act out a situation, the other two should suggest improvements. Then switch roles as actors and evaluators. Possible situations: **a)** A three-year-old constantly asks "why." **b)** A five-year-old interrupts while a parent talks with a friend. **c)** A five-year-old is sad and won't say why. **d)** A six-year-old says, "I hate that doctor!"

2. **Creative Communication.** Imagine you are a parent who works evenings. You see your children, ages eight and fourteen, before school and on weekends. Make a list of creative ways to maintain a loving bond of communication with each child.

3. **The Role of Humor.** How can parents use humor in messages? Write humorous responses to these situations: **a)** Two children are picking on each other in the car. **b)** A six-year-old doesn't get ready for school on time. **c)** A twelve-year-old leaves personal items on the floor. **d)** A ten-year-old forgets to feed the dog.

Cross-Curricular Connections

1. **Language Arts.** Write "I" messages a parent could use in these situations: **a)** An eight-year-old slams the door again. **b)** A five-year-old tears up a parent's magazine in anger. **c)** A seven-year-old brings home a happy-face report from school.

2. **Social Studies.** People in society once believed that "children should be seen but not heard." Compare that philosophy with today's view. To what extent are children "heard" today? Should they be heard more or less? Discuss your ideas in class.

Family & Community Connections

1. **Active Listening.** With your family, discuss what you've learned about active listening. For one day, listen actively to each other. Then evaluate the results. What changes in communication, if any, would family members like to make?

2. **Communication Help.** In many counties, programs help parents learn communication techniques. Some workshops, for example, teach about signing with very young children before they are able to put their thoughts into words. Find out what programs your county has and report to the class.

CHAPTER 22

Building Children's Character

CHAPTER OBJECTIVES

- Explain the impact of character on individuals and society.
- Summarize theories of moral development.
- Describe effective techniques for teaching values to children.
- Explain how to teach children and teens to make wise ethical choices.
- Analyze how outside influences can affect children's character development and how parents should respond.

PARENTING TERMS

- character
- moral development
- conventions
- empathy
- conscience
- values
- work ethic
- compassion
- citizenship
- ethical choice

Think about your most deeply held beliefs about how people ought to behave. Where did you learn them? For most people, parents are the first role models and teachers. Later, children begin to pick up ideas about behavior from schoolmates and what they see on television. The more effectively parents teach children their own beliefs about right and wrong, the more likely the children will be to maintain and follow those beliefs when other influences come into their lives.

What Is Character?

Character is moral strength to do what is right. People with character show, through actions as well as words, their commitment to qualities such as respect, fairness, trustworthiness, responsibility, and integrity.

A sign of true character is being motivated to do the right thing simply because it's right, without thought of reward or punishment. For example, when a teen defends a classmate from bullying because bullying is wrong, without regard to how other friends will react, that teen demonstrates character.

Why Shape Character?

When parents take an active role in shaping children's character, the children are the ultimate winners. They will be better equipped to make responsible decisions. Their social relationships will be more successful and relatively free of serious misunderstandings. As adults, they will be able to find and keep responsible jobs because of their sense of responsibility and willingness to work hard. They will obey laws and help improve their community. Finally, when children whose characters were shaped effectively during their formative years become parents, they will be able to model and shape character in their children. See Fig. 22-1.

Moral Development

Moral development is the process of learning to distinguish between right and wrong. Psychologists and other researchers have observed that this process follows certain patterns. The moral development theories of Kohlberg and Bronfenbrenner are widely known.

Kohlberg's Theory

Researcher Lawrence Kohlberg identified three levels of moral development. These levels of development relate to a person's understanding of **conventions,** or socially accepted standards of behavior.

Fig. 22-1. Parents who nurture character in their children can look forward to seeing these children become successful, responsible adults. **How can families pass on lessons of character from generation to generation?**

Fig. 22-2. When children begin to understand society's conventions, they develop a sense of fairness and cooperation. **At what age might a child be willing and able to play by the rules of a game?**

Kohlberg further divided each level into two stages. These stages refer to how people reason about right and wrong, regardless of whether they act according to that reasoning. Kohlberg believed that all people progress through the six stages in order, although not everyone achieves the final stage. He believed that resolving conflicts within each stage prepares a person to advance to the next stage or level of moral development.

- **Pre-conventional level.** Young children have little or no understanding of socially accepted standards of behavior. They lack a clear sense of right and wrong and tend to equate moral behavior with doing what they are told. In the first stage, the toddler associates moral behavior with obedience. The second stage involves more calculated self-interest, such as gaining rewards and avoiding punishment.

- **Conventional level.** Somewhere between about nine and 15 years of age, children begin to understand honesty, gratitude, and trust. They become sensitive to others' thoughts and feelings. In the first stage of this level, they seek approval by living up to others' expectations. When they reach the next stage, they have a sense of rules and fairness. See Fig. 22-2.

- **Post-conventional level.** The first stage of this final level involves a genuine interest in others and an understanding of the larger social need for people to help each other. It is the second stage of this level that Kohlberg felt many people fail to achieve. This final stage requires a respect for and willingness to live by universal principles, such as the equality of all people. In this final stage, people think in abstract terms and view others with respect.

Bronfenbrenner's Theory

Psychologist Urie Bronfenbrenner studied school children in different cultures. His research led him to define five different ways people might focus their thinking about right and wrong. Children all over the world begin with self-interest, he concluded. As they move beyond that, however, some cultures put more emphasis on obedience to authority, some on peer pressure, and some on serving the larger society. See Fig. 22-3.

Forming an Inner Moral Sense

According to both Kohlberg's and Bronfenbrenner's theories, children get their first knowledge of right and wrong from the people around them. Over time they develop a more internal moral sense. They can feel what they should do, even if it conflicts with the views of the people around them.

Empathy. The popular expression "Walk a mile in his shoes" is a reminder to understand and appreciate another's situation. **Empathy** is an awareness of other people's needs and feelings. Recent research suggests that empathy develops in the first years of life. A nine-month-old baby becomes tearful when another baby

Moral Orientations		
Moral Orientation	**Description**	**Example**
Self-oriented morality	❑ Wants to satisfy personal needs and desires. ❑ Considers others only if they help or hinder the satisfaction of personal needs.	A child grabs the last cookie on the plate without asking whether everyone has received a cookie.
Authority-oriented morality	❑ Accepts decisions of authority figures about what's good and bad.	A child puts a toy back on the shelf in the store because that is what her parents say to do, without understanding why.
Peer-oriented morality	❑ Accepts decisions of peers about what's right and wrong in order to conform.	A man signs a petition started by coworkers protesting a new company policy, even though he has no strong personal opinion about the policy.
Collective-oriented morality	❑ Places the group's goals and interests over personal interests. ❑ Feels strong duty and loyalty to group or society.	Student Council members work many after-school and weekend hours to raise funds for various school activities.
Objectively-oriented morality	❑ Accepts universal values without regard to criticism or differing opinions from some individuals.	A young woman gives her scarf and mittens to a homeless person, despite the objections of a friend.

Fig. 22-3. Bronfenbrenner believed that different cultures emphasize different moral orientations. **What are some examples of peer-oriented morality among American high school students?**

Fig. 22-4. Awareness of other people's feelings helps children develop kindness and understanding. **How can parents model empathy and encourage it in their children?**

cries. At 15 months, a child will bring a favorite toy or blanket to comfort a playmate. See Fig. 22-4.

As children mature, feelings of empathy grow in proportion to the ability to identify and accept one's own and others' feelings. Parents aid the development of empathy when they acknowledge children's feelings: "I can see how hurt you are by Brad's comment. His remark was thoughtless, and I can understand why you are upset."

Conscience. As children mature, they develop a **conscience** (KAHN-shens). This is an inner sense of right and wrong that prompts good behavior and causes feelings of guilt about bad behavior.

Experts believe that children develop a conscience when they're about five to seven years old. Prior to age five, appropriate behavior is usually triggered by a parent's reminder or correction. Between the ages of five and ten, children develop the ability to consider the impact their actions have on other people. Conscience leads children to:

- Feel guilty about negative behavior—"It was wrong of me to hurt my friend's feelings."
- Avoid negative behavior—"If I run away from home, my parents will worry."
- Recognize negative behavior in others— "He shouldn't do such a mean thing to a defenseless animal."

Teaching Values to Children

Moral development is strengthened when parents teach their children values. **Values** are strongly held beliefs and ideas about what is important. They guide people's thoughts, words, and actions, and they give life meaning and purpose. Families and cultures transmit values in the form of customs, traditions, beliefs, and attitudes about what is important in life. Values are the foundation of character.

While some values differ from family to family or from culture to culture, certain values are considered to be universal. Fig. 22-5 lists several of the values that nearly everyone would agree are important.

Universal Values	
Value	**How Children Live These Values**
Trustworthiness	❏ Tell the truth; don't mislead, cheat, or steal. ❏ Act reliable; keep their promises. ❏ Show loyalty to their friends, family, and country.
Responsibility	❏ Keep trying and do their best. ❏ Use self-control and self-discipline. ❏ Accept the consequences of their actions.
Fairness	❏ Play by the rules. ❏ Share and take turns. ❏ Don't take advantage of others' weakness or ignorance.
Respect	❏ Show good manners toward others. ❏ Accept differences with tolerance. ❏ Stay peaceful in the face of anger and disagreement.
Compassion	❏ Behave kindly toward people and animals. ❏ Express thanks and forgiveness. ❏ Help people in need.
Citizenship	❏ Obey rules, laws, and people in authority. ❏ Volunteer at school and in the community. ❏ Help protect the environment.

How Children Acquire Values

Children begin to acquire values almost from birth. Babies observe their parents' behavior. By the time they are toddlers, children are beginning to imitate their parents. They are also learning what makes parents say "yes" or "no." As toddlers learn to share, to play nicely with others, and to obey their parents, they are practicing the values of generosity, cooperation, and respect.

Teaching values is an important part of a parent's job description. What happens if parents don't teach children values? Other people will, and their values may not be the same. If parents want a child to share their values, they need to teach those values. These strategies can help:

- **Model values.** Even young children question why Daddy or Mommy can say bad words and they can't. It takes thought, time, and effort to "practice what you preach." However, it is very important, because children imitate the behavior they see in their parents.
- **Discuss values.** Conversation helps children understand the values being modeled. Some parents and schools pick a "Value of the Week" as a focus of discussion. Young children might talk about why it is important to be kind or honest. Older children will find it more interesting to explore moral dilemmas. For example, should a student stop to help a lost child if it means being late to school? Discussing such questions builds skills in moral reasoning.

Fig. 22-5. These values are shared in cultures around the world. **What other values can you think of that are probably universal?**

Fig. 22-6. Parents should stick to their commitments, such as attending a school play, and avoid making promises that they can't keep. **Aside from modeling, how might parents teach their children to be reliable?**

- **Use stories.** Psychologist Robert Coles liked to use stories to initiate discussions. Young children can identify good and bad behavior by characters in books. *Aesop's Fables* and other folktales convey specific moral lessons. Television programs or news broadcasts can trigger values discussions with older children. Parents can ask questions: "What do you think motivated his action?" "How would you settle this argument?"

- **Point out values in action.** It's easier for children to learn about values if they can relate them to events that they experience or understand. A creative parent teaches values by pointing them out in people and situations that the child encounters. For example, discussing loyalty when a child faces betrayal from a friend helps reinforce the child's understanding of why loyalty matters.

Teaching Trustworthiness

One of the universal values that parents try to instill in their children is trustworthiness. A trustworthy person is one in whom others feel able to place their confidence. What makes people trustworthy? They must be honest, loyal, and reliable. They must also demonstrate integrity—a quality that can be summed up as "what you see is what you get."

Honesty is the foundation of trust. When children lie, parents can encourage them to talk about why they lied. Then parents might invite children to imagine what would happen if people could not trust each other to be telling the truth. This can help the children understand the saying, "Honesty is the best policy."

Reliability is also part of trustworthiness. Someone who is reliable can be counted on to live up to promises and commitments. Parents can model the importance of reliability by following through with their commitments to children. See Fig. 22-6.

Teaching Responsibility

Responsible people are easy to recognize. When work needs to be done, they pitch in and do it willingly. They do the best job they can instead of the minimum needed to get by. They understand that sometimes it's necessary to put needs before wants, or to put someone else's needs before their own. When they make a mistake, responsible people accept the results instead of trying to put the blame on someone else.

To begin teaching responsibility, parents can help children become responsible for themselves. Children should be taught and encouraged to take care of personal hygiene and belongings. Older children may learn responsibility by taking care of a pet.

Chores and Homework. One of the best ways to build responsibility in children is by assigning age-appropriate chores. Parents should acknowledge children for doing those chores, even if the results are not perfect. Praise is often the best reward. See Fig. 22-7.

When children feel that they make successful contributions to a group (such as the family), they'll want to continue. In this way, children develop a strong **work ethic**, an appreciation for the value of work and its ability to build character. Children with a strong work ethic know the importance of working hard on schoolwork and volunteering in the community.

Parents should support children's efforts to be responsible, making sure that children have adequate time to complete homework and other commitments. Parents can monitor their child's progress and behavior in school. Both performance and behavior at school are signs of how well a student accepts responsibility.

Accountability. Another sign of responsibility is being accountable for one's own actions and their consequences. That means accepting criticism and suggestions, as well as credit. When they make a mistake or are unable to keep a promise, responsible people admit it: "I forgot to take the garbage out this week. I'm sorry." When they do not like the consequences of a decision or choice they have made, they accept that the result came from their own action or decision.

Parents can help children become accountable by allowing the children to experience the natural consequences of their actions. A child may learn to be more careful with toys, for example, if parents do not immediately replace toys that get lost or broken.

Parents can also help their children learn to accept responsibility for what they've said and done. People of all ages shift blame. "Officer, I had to speed to pass that lady. She was holding up traffic." "I failed the test because my little brother was bothering me last night so I couldn't study." Accepting responsibility in such cases is often uncomfortable, but it is important to maintaining trust and solid relationships. An apology is preferable to making excuses.

Fig. 22-7. Children who take responsibility for simple duties when they are young learn attitudes that will help them in a career someday. **Why is it important for parents to assign children chores that are age appropriate?**

Parenting Pointers

Teaching Kids to Manage Money

Teaching children to manage money responsibly will help them all their lives. Children learn by having some money to spend as they wish. If they waste it, they can learn from their mistakes. Here are some suggestions for parents of children in different age groups:

- **Elementary school age.** Give a small weekly allowance, which the child may spend or save. Discuss with the child possible reasons to save toward a larger purchase.

- **Middle school age.** Give the child money for school clothes and a voice in how it will be spent. Help the child open a savings account.

- **High school age.** Help the teen open a checking account and draw up a budget. Discuss the pros and cons of working at a part-time job after school or over the summer break.

Teaching Fairness

Sharing is an easy way for parents to model and teach fairness. Taking turns is another. Parents who make sure everyone has a first serving of a food before anyone gets a second, or give children turns choosing a book or television program, give their children examples of being fair.

When children become upset about situations or decisions they think are unfair, parents can help them determine whether their perception is accurate and what they might do about it. Perhaps the quiz was fair, but challenging because the child hadn't studied the assigned material. In another instance, children and parents might decide a decision wasn't fair. Parents can help the child examine the options: contesting the decision in an appropriate time and manner or accepting a decision he or she cannot change.

Teaching Respect

Everyone should be treated with dignity and good manners. Courtesy among family members models and teaches respect in the home. While enforcing their rules and values, parents can show respect by listening to children's feelings and opinions. When possible, parents can wait to reprimand a child until they can do so in privacy, instead of embarrassing the child in front of others.

Particular respect is due to figures of authority, such as police, school officials, coaches, clergy, and government officials. Sometimes children disagree with the behavior or decisions of authority figures. Parents can discuss these situations, helping the child distinguish between respect for the position and disagreement with the individual who fills the position.

Teaching Compassion

Compassion is demonstration of care and concern for another. A compassionate child may use allowance money to buy a gift for a sick friend. Children also experience compassion for people they don't know but may read or hear about. For example, some compassionate children raise funds to help the victims of an earthquake in another part of the world.

Jeanette and Paul model compassion by donating blood to the Red Cross and volunteering at a homeless shelter. They also invite their sons to help them rake their elderly neighbor's lawn and to visit nursing home residents. Teens transition into caring adults by observing and participating in compassionate efforts. Sometimes adults choose service careers (such as social work or the ministry) because of their early experiences with compassion.

Kindness to Animals. Learning to be kind and gentle toward animals is a lesson in compassion. Pets are often social "starter kits." Children who learn to feel love, kindness, and empathy for animals transfer those feelings to people. See Fig. 22-8.

In contrast, cruelty to people in adult life often begins as cruelty to animals as a child. Parents need to take such behavior very seriously. Children who abuse animals may need counseling to solve problems that might worsen.

Teaching Citizenship

Citizenship refers to a person's membership and participation in a particular group, such as a nation, school, or family. When people belong to a group, they need to follow the group's rules.

Parents begin teaching children to follow group rules by setting family rules. For example, they might set a family rule that conversation should not be interrupted unless an emergency arises. They model this rule with all family members and expect their children to do the same.

Fig. 22-8. Children learn compassion by caring for pets. **What other lessons in values can children learn from interacting with animals?**

Modeling CHARACTER

Being a Good Citizen

Parents who want their children to be constructive, law-abiding members of society need to watch their own behavior.

- Does Mom litter, or does she keep her trash until she can throw it away in an appropriate place?
- Does Dad observe traffic laws and drive within the speed limit, or does he drive carelessly so long as there is no police car in sight?
- Does the household participate in community recycling programs and other volunteer projects? Volunteering together is an excellent way to teach and model good citizenship.

Think About It

How else might parents set an example of good citizenship for their children to follow?

Citizenship goes beyond just following rules. Good citizens also stay informed, participate in community affairs, show civic pride, and work to improve their neighborhoods, schools, and communities. Parents can convey these principles through teaching and example. For example, they can talk about the importance of voting and of being informed about candidates and issues. They can encourage school-age children and teens to participate in student government or to hold offices in other organizations.

Ethical Choices

Character involves not just understanding and adopting values, but applying them in everyday life. One way to do that is by making ethical choices. An **ethical choice** is a decision for action based on one's moral values and principles. For example, Ann makes a conscious decision not to join Sally and Joe in ridiculing a boy's hairstyle. Ann is making an ethical choice based on her belief that making fun of others is wrong. Other examples of ethical choices are turning down a friend who asks to copy homework, refusing a ride from someone who does not have a driver's license, and staying away from a party where there may be drugs and alcohol. A person who makes choices that are true to his or her moral values, despite social consequences, has developed a code of ethics.

Some ethical choices are straightforward. In spite of temptations or social pressures, it is clear what would be the right thing to do. Other choices are more complicated. When should one report other people's rule violations, and when is it better not to be a "tattle tale"? When should one keep a friend's secrets confidential, and when is it important to tell an adult?

Parents who have made a practice of discussing values with their children have established a solid foundation for discussing such complex issues. They can help children evaluate the risks and possible results of each alternative. Once the children have decided the right course of action, parents can encourage and support them in acting on their ethical choice.

Outside Influences

Although parents play a very important role in shaping their child's character, they are not the only influence in the child's life. When children leave home—for a child care center, school, friends' homes, parties—they interact with people who may have different values. Parents may both appreciate and worry about the broadening of children's experience. The influence can be positive when contact with people of diverse cultures and backgrounds teaches values that parents share but have not chosen to emphasize. On the other hand, children are almost certain to encounter people whose values conflict with their family values. Parents must be prepared to deal with children's questions and struggles when they encounter conflicting value systems.

Peer Influences

As children mature, they spend more time with friends and less with their parents. One father complains, "She doesn't listen to me anymore; I'm just her parent! Her friends are the ones she goes to for guidance and direction." While this is a normal part of child development, many parents rightly become concerned when children choose friends with different values. See Fig. 22-9.

Fig. 22-9. As children become more independent, they spend more time away from their families. **How can parents encourage children to choose friends with positive values?**

What can parents do if their child's new friend has very different values? A parent may be able to select playmates for very young children. As children mature, this form of control is harder and may even backfire, making the "undesirable" friend seem more attractive. Some researchers believe that the most effective parents in this situation are those who have established a close, nurturing relationship with their children while being clear about their ethical standards. Their children may be willing to approach them with concerns about a friend's behavior. By listening and asking questions, parents can help the child decide how to respond to the friend. They can help the child to define clear limits for his or her own behavior and perhaps to find settings for meeting children with values more like theirs.

Media Influences

How many parents invite a stranger into their home and ask their children to accept whatever the stranger says or does as truthful and appropriate? Very few, if any. In a way, however, some parents "invite strangers" into their home every day when they fail to monitor what children are learning from television or the Internet.

Television. Parental guidance regarding television viewing is needed for several reasons. Most learning research suggests that children under the age of two should not watch television. Children from age two to about seven often confuse fantasy with reality, becoming frightened by cartoon violence. Older children may imitate behavior they see onscreen. Commercials can challenge all ages, promoting values the family may not share.

THE DEVELOPING BRAIN

Children's first two years are critical for brain development. For healthy mental, physical, social, and emotional growth, young children must explore their world and interact with parents or others—not sit in front of a screen. The American Academy of Pediatrics recommends *no television at all* for children below age two.

Networks rate the suitability of programs for various age levels based on violence, language, and sex. By law, most newer television sets include a *V-Chip*, technology that allows parents to block certain categories of programming. This is only a beginning, however. With children two and older, parents might:

- Limit television viewing to specific times or programs. Children should understand that other commitments, such as feeding the dog and doing homework, come first.
- Teach children to monitor their television viewing. Encourage them to avoid or turn off programs (however popular) that make them uncomfortable or upset.
- Be aware of what children are watching. Parents should sample any programs that children watch regularly, to be sure the content is appropriate for children in their family.
- Watch together with children if the program might be disturbing or depict questionable behavior. Then parents can discuss the content with the children.

Internet. The Internet is a fingertip resource and learning tool. However, there are dangers associated with unsupervised Internet use.

Not all sites are reliable or harmless. Because most children are trusting, they easily assume that information and people they encounter on Internet sites are trustworthy. Before children use the Internet, parents should teach these safety guidelines:

- Never disclose personal information such as name, address, phone number, or school.
- Never trade photographs with someone met over the Internet.
- Never respond to threatening or inappropriate messages.
- Always tell a parent about any message or interchange that feels uncomfortable.

If there is a computer in the home, parents can program it to block undesirable sites and "bookmark" often-used sites for children to find without searching. For easy monitoring, the computer should be kept in a common area instead of the child's bedroom. See Fig. 22-10.

Celebrity Role Models. It is not uncommon for the behavior of movie stars, entertainers, politicians, and professional athletes to conflict with some values taught in the family. It is unrealistic for parents to ignore or attempt to shield their children from such celebrities. Parents can, however, discuss value differences with their children as situations arise. Understanding their parents' beliefs will help children resist following poor role models.

Character and Society

Shaping character in children has far-reaching effects for the family, community, nation, and world. Imagine a world in which decisions were made by people who had no sense of fair play, honesty, loyalty, or compassion. The solutions to many of today's problems require not only logic but ethical choices. Decisions to help a starving nation, to respect different cultures and ideas, and to cooperate for everyone's benefit can be made only by people of character.

Fig. 22-10. The Internet is a remarkable information resource. **How can parents shield children from undesirable sites and dishonest users?**

Child & Family Services CAREERS

▶ Youth Development Specialist

Thousands of youth organizations serve young people in the United States today. While many of the adults who work with them are volunteers, professional leaders can be very helpful. Youth development specialists provide trained leadership for youth programs. They may work with community recreation programs, 4-H, Boys and Girls Clubs, faith-based youth programs, or not-for-profit organizations dedicated to developing the potential of a community's youth.

Youth development specialists need skills in communication, leadership, management, problem solving, conflict resolution, and interacting with individuals and groups. Many such jobs require volunteer experience and a bachelor's or master's degree in youth development, education, social and human services, or a related field. A college graduate may choose to study for a Youth Development Specialist Certificate, which requires less time to complete than a master's degree.

"Growing up, I was very active in my hometown youth center. When I went to college, I realized that I wanted to stay involved in youth programs. Getting a degree in youth and child development was the best decision I ever made. In my job, I coordinate after-school programming for elementary children, leadership training for middle school and high school students, and cultural enrichment programming for children of all ages."

CAREER TIPS

- Take parenting, child development, and health science courses in high school.
- Volunteer at a children's after-school or mentoring program.
- Spend a summer as a camp counselor or volunteer coach for a sports program.
- Pursue a bachelor's or master's degree or a certificate in Youth Development.

CHAPTER SUMMARY

- Character is the moral strength to do what is right.
- Moral development follows identifiable patterns as children mature.
- From the time they are born, children learn values as they observe parental behavior.
- Universal values include trustworthiness, responsibility, fairness, respect, compassion, and citizenship.
- Moral values help people make straightforward as well as complex ethical choices.
- Outside influences, including peers and the media, influence character development in children and teens.

Check Your Facts

1. How do people show true character?
2. Why should parents shape the character of their children?
3. What is moral development?
4. Define *conventions*.
5. Describe Kohlberg's levels of moral development.
6. Summarize Bronfenbrenner's theory.
7. What is a conscience?
8. What three things occur in children once they develop a conscience?
9. Compare values in general with values that are universal.
10. What will happen if parents don't teach values to children?
11. What are four ways to teach values?
12. What qualities relate to trustworthiness?
13. Should parents protect children from the consequences of mistakes? Explain.
14. How would you teach fairness to a young child?
15. Identify one ethical choice for a teen.
16. How can parents help a child who is struggling with an ethical choice?
17. Should parents choose their children's friends for them? Why or why not?
18. How should parents manage a child's television watching?

Think Critically

1. **Drawing Conclusions.** The immigrants who helped build America were said to have a strong work ethic. Do you think the same can be said of people today? How can parents instill this trait in children?
2. **Understanding Cause and Effect.** How does having respect for authority benefit children, teens, and adults?
3. **Recognizing Stereotypes.** A father won't let his eight-year-old daughter play with a child whom he calls a "foreigner." Analyze this parenting situation.
4. **Making Comparisons.** Compare empathy with compassion.

Apply Your Learning

1. **Children's Books.** Locate books that teach moral lessons to children. Review one for the class. Explain the principle taught and how the message is conveyed.

2. **Proactive Parenting.** How would you, as a parent, respond to the situations listed here? Analyze ideas in class and choose the best approach for each. **a)** A five-year-old has been caught several times hitting and kicking a cat. **b)** After a five-block walk from the store, a parent discovers a six-year-old has taken a candy bar. **c)** A seven-year-old blames a sibling for making the baby cry. **d)** An eleven-year-old is found viewing inappropriate material on the Internet.

3. **Program Analysis.** Analyze a television comedy or drama for its suitability for an eight-year-old. Consider subject matter, language, characterization, and dress. Present your analysis to the class.

Cross-Curricular Connections

1. **Language Arts.** Write a description of someone you know who displays one of the universal values described in the chapter: for example, fairness, compassion, or citizenship. Include specific examples that show how the person's actions demonstrate this value.

2. **Social Studies.** Team with other students to discuss how society is shaped by the character of its citizens. Come up with at least three ways society is affected. Then compare ideas in class.

Family & Community Connections

1. **Citizenship in Families.** How can a family practice good citizenship? Ask your family for ideas, and then put one into action. Some possibilities are recycling items at home, attending a city council or school board meeting, displaying the flag, or volunteering in your community.

2. **Character Education.** In many schools and businesses, people have started character education programs. Why do you think such interest exists? Use the Internet to learn about these programs, and then check on whether schools and businesses in your community have them. Plan and implement a program for your classroom or school.

Promoting Positive Behavior

- Compare discipline with punishment.
- Explain principles of positive guidance.
- Explain how to set and communicate limits that are age-appropriate.
- Describe ways to encourage positive behavior.
- Suggest techniques that prevent behavior problems.
- Relate confidence to effective parenting.

PARENTING TERMS

- discipline
- positive guidance
- self-discipline
- limits
- positive reinforcement
- redirection

Imagine taking several children to visit an older relative who has a collection of china figurines on the coffee table. Would you just hope nothing gets broken, or would you take steps to prevent a problem? With a toddler, you might move the figurines to a high shelf during your visit. You might tell preschoolers, "Please don't touch," and bring along some toys to hold their attention. Older children might need only a reminder to be careful. Finding the most effective ways to promote positive behavior is part of the art of parenting.

Discipline and Positive Guidance

Discipline is guidance that helps children learn to behave appropriately. It involves teaching and promoting positive behavior as well as discouraging negative behavior. It requires both firmness and understanding on the part of parents.

Many people confuse the word "discipline" with punishment. The two are not the same. Punishment refers to penalties for inappropriate behavior. As you will learn in Chapter 24, enforcing reasonable consequences for unacceptable behavior is indeed one aspect of discipline. However, that is not its sole focus. Effective discipline encompasses many other techniques, such as setting clear expectations, modeling positive behavior, and taking steps to prevent negative behavior. You will read about these and other guidance techniques in this chapter.

Another problem with the word "punishment" is that it tends to bring to mind actions that are harsh or hurtful. Thus, for people who link discipline with punishment, the word "discipline" takes on many negative associations. The truth is, discipline can and should emphasize the positive side. Guidance that focuses on teaching children positive behavior in a clear, firm, yet loving way is more effective than punishment.

Because of possible misunderstandings of the word "discipline," many people prefer to use the term **positive guidance** instead. After all, the purpose of discipline is to guide a child to behave appropriately. When parents provide positive guidance, they give direction that encourages appropriate choices and behavior.

Goals of Positive Guidance

Some people view discipline, or positive guidance, with their focus only on the present. They are mainly concerned with whether the child is behaving appropriately at any given moment. Of course, parents do want their children to behave in ways that are safe and acceptable. However, positive guidance has long-term goals that are equally important.

The ultimate goal of positive guidance is to help children develop **self-discipline**—the ability to manage their own behavior. When they are young, children rely on parents or other caregivers to teach and remind them how to behave. As adults, they will be responsible for their own choices and actions. This change does not occur overnight on their eighteenth or twenty-first birthday. Self-discipline develops gradually as children mature. See Fig. 23-1.

Fig. 23-1. As children mature, they grow in ability to make responsible decisions for themselves. **How can parents help children learn self-discipline?**

Positive guidance can help accomplish other long-term goals as well. If parents do their job well, positive guidance helps children:

- Develop self-confidence, self-esteem, and a healthy self-concept.
- Function independently in new situations as they get older.
- Get along well with others and show consideration for others' feelings and needs.
- Develop good character.
- Become socially responsible adults who make positive contributions to the world.

Parenting with Consistency

Children need *consistency*—predictable patterns from those they look to for guidance. Parents who enforce a rule some nights—a firm bedtime, for example—but fail to enforce it other nights when they are tired or distracted are not being consistent. Without consistency, children become confused about what they are supposed to do, and as a result feel anxious and insecure. Consistency from parents helps children feel secure. They know, from one day to the next, what behavior is expected of them. See Fig. 23-2.

Adopting a Parenting Style

Consistency in parenting style is important, too. As you learned in Chapter 5, parents choose the parenting style that works best for themselves and their children. The parents' choice of an authoritarian, authoritative, or permissive style of parenting will affect how they approach discipline. Although parents may adapt their parenting style as children mature, on the whole children need the security of knowing what to expect.

Parents should consult each other and agree on their general parenting style, as well as specific rules, expectations, and consequences.

Fig. 23-2. Consistency is an important part of positive guidance. **What are the benefits of consistency in promoting positive behavior?**

By conferring before a situation arises, they can avoid giving the child mixed messages or setting up a situation that tempts the child to play one parent against the other.

Starting Young

Positive guidance can and should begin in simple ways during infancy and continue through each stage of a child's development. Parents who begin to shape their children's behavior early are likely to have fewer problems and frustrations with their children later. Unfortunately, parents who fail to guide their children when they're young often have little or no control when the children are older. Establishing control where none existed previously can be difficult.

Defining Positive Behavior

Before they can promote positive behavior, parents need to decide exactly what behavior they want to encourage. They need to first give careful thought to how they want their children to behave, while making sure their expectations are reasonable. Then they can set specific limits and clearly communicate those limits to their children.

Deciding What Matters

When thinking about how they want their children to behave, parents should take a long-term view. What kind of adults do they hope their children will become? Most parents hold similar hopes for their children. They want them to develop positive values and character traits such as the ones discussed in Chapter 22: trustworthiness, responsibility, fairness, respect, compassion, and citizenship. Parents may also have other positive values they want to emphasize.

Modeling CHARACTER

Caring in Friendships

One of the best ways for children to make and keep friends is to show their friends that they care about them. People who are *caring* are kind and compassionate. They find ways to show their concern and appreciation for others. Parents can model caring in friendships by how they treat their own friends:

- Comfort a friend who is upset.
- Be available in an emergency.
- Speak kindly to a friend.
- Express gratitude when a friend does something nice, and return the favor as soon as you can.

Think About It

What are some other ways in which parents can show children how to express caring in friendships?

Having specific values and character traits in mind can help parents decide on the day-to-day behavior that they want to encourage. For example, in order to encourage a preschooler to be caring, parents can model and teach how to treat friends with kindness.

Age-Appropriate Expectations

Wise parents realize their children won't act like miniature adults from the day they can walk. Expectations must be reasonable and age-appropriate. Thus, effective guidance depends on an understanding of child development. In order to set reasonable expectations, parents need to have a basic understanding of what abilities and challenges are typical at each stage. As children develop from one stage to the next, parents' expectations for their behavior can and should change.

All types of development—physical, intellectual, emotional, social, and moral—affect the behavior that parents can reasonably expect. For example:

- Physically, most eighteen-month-olds feed themselves, but should you trust them to hold a fragile object? Probably not, because they're likely to drop it. Rather than trying to teach careful handling to children so young, it's more appropriate to distract their attention and move the object out of reach.
- A mother of a two-year-old should know that toddlers are at a stage of development in which they play alongside each other, but not with each other. If she doesn't realize this, she might frustrate herself and the toddlers by trying to make them interact. If a school-age child invites a friend to play, however, it is reasonable to expect the child to include the friend in his or her activities during the visit.
- A couple who leaves their tearful twelve-month-old with a babysitter for an evening

THE DEVELOPING BRAIN

The brains of young children have very limited memory capacity, so they cannot remember many rules or rules that have many parts. In addition, parts of the brain responsible for judgment and impulse control are not well developed in young children.

is reassured to know that separation anxiety is common at that age. They won't try to teach the baby that crying is unacceptable.
- Parents can expect a kindergartener to share toys with a friend, but it may not be reasonable to expect the same child to offer to donate toys to a charity. Compassion for invisible strangers does not come until a later stage of development.

Even when parents understand that certain behavior can or can't be expected at a certain age, they may still need to address that behavior with parental guidance. Knowledge of child development helps parents decide how to provide that guidance in the most effective way. Knowing that young children have limited impulse control, a parent can restrict ball-playing to an area away from the street. Knowing that teens are striving to define their identities, a parent may choose to have a conversation with the teen about the reasoning behind family rules. For young children, a very simple explanation is more appropriate.

Setting Limits

With a clear understanding of age-appropriate expectations, parents are ready to set specific limits for their children. **Limits** are rules that define the boundary between acceptable and unacceptable behavior. When parents provide reasonable limits for children, they teach children what is safe and acceptable for them to do. For example, five-year-old Lauren is allowed to play in the swimming pool when a responsible adult is present. If no responsible adult is with her, Lauren must stay out of the pool. This limit will help keep her safe.

Children for whom limits have been set from an early age feel more secure than others who've had no limits imposed on them. Parental limits give children a solid structure; they know what is allowed and what is not. They can trust that their parents will keep them safe. They're less likely to make serious mistakes that could result in unexpected, unpleasant consequences. Children who are not given limits are often frustrated, confused, or hurt when their actions turn out to anger, disappoint, or frustrate others.

When setting limits, parents can keep these practical guidelines in mind:

- **Keep limits reasonable.** If limits are too loose, a child could be in danger. If limits are too restrictive, a child's skills for independence may not develop normally. A young child who is given too many limits will not be able to remember them all.
- **Make sure limits have a teaching or guiding purpose.** They should not simply be for the convenience of adults. For example, it is not reasonable to make children stay in bed until 10:00 on Saturday morning so that both parents can sleep late. However, telling children to play quietly while one parent is sleeping can teach good lifelong habits for deciding when and where to make noise.

Health & Safety

Setting Safe Limits

Many limits that parents define for children are safety measures: wear a helmet when you ride your bicycle; always tell a parent where you are going. A challenge is how to balance keeping children safe with offering them greater independence as they mature.

Young children need clear and simple safety rules. Parents might teach how to behave around hot stoves, busy streets, and broken glass. As children mature, they can remember more rules, but they also need opportunities to develop judgment and self-direction. Over time this means making rules less restrictive. Learning to make safe decisions is an important part of growing up.

- **Expand limits as children gain maturity.** Some limits that are reasonable for very young children will not be so for older children and teens. An 8:00 bedtime is suitable for a second grader but not for a tenth grader. When parents set limits, they may mention that the limit will change as the child matures. "While you're in elementary school, Joseph, your bedtime will remain 8:00. When you're older, you'll be able to stay up later."

- **Consider the individual child.** Some children may be more prepared to handle responsibility and expanded limits than other children the same age. One child may be able to walk to the bus stop alone at age ten, while another lacks the personal safety skills to walk alone without great risk. Parents must know their children as individuals and set limits accordingly.

- **Consider the setting.** Limits may need to be adjusted to fit a particular environment. Is it appropriate for a nine-year-old to ride his or her bike to a park? That depends on whether the park is just down the street in a small town, or several blocks away through city traffic.

- **Make limits consistent.** Consistency makes limits enforceable. Children shouldn't be required to get dressed before breakfast for a few days in a row, and after that only from time to time. Infrequent exceptions can be made for special occasions, but keeping rules consistent helps children know what to expect.

- **Make limits specific.** It's easy for a parent to think, "I'll know a problem when I see it," but that gives a child no way to anticipate the parent's reactions. Parents need to define limits and expectations clearly in their own minds before they can communicate them to a child.

Fig. 23-3. Limits and rules should be specific. Why might some limits change over time?

Communicating Expectations

Children can't be expected to meet expectations that they haven't been told about or don't understand. If limits are too vague, expectations are unclear. If a caregiver does not think it safe for a child to play alone in the front yard, it is not enough to say, "Why don't you play out back?" The child might think using the back yard is optional or just for today. To be clear, the caregiver might say, "When you're playing by yourself, you must stay in the back yard. You can play in the front yard only when an adult is with you." See Fig. 23-3.

Young children in particular need limits explained clearly and simply. When possible, parents should tell children what they *should* do, instead of what they should *not* do. For example, "After you play with the toys, you must put them away" is more effective than "Don't leave your toys all over the floor." The words you want to form an image in the child's mind are "put them away," not "toys all over the floor."

As children mature, parents too often assume that children can figure out the meaning of a vague instruction. "Come home on time from the movie." "Help around the house." Both of these expectations are too general. What's "on time"? What specific help is needed? While older children can handle multiple expectations, those expectations must still be clear and specific. "The movie ends at 9:15. I expect you home by 10:00." "Please unload the dishwasher, set the table, and fold the basket of clean clothes before dinner."

Encouraging Positive Behavior

Once parents have defined and stated the positive behavior they expect, there are many ways to encourage it. These methods are generally effective when used consistently.

Modeling

Steve and his son Daniel were at the bank when an older man dropped a folder full of documents. Steve immediately said, "Here, let me get those for you," and knelt down to pick up the scattered papers. The next day, Steve was not surprised when Daniel immediately went to help a friend who had fallen off his bike. Steve knew that his son watched him closely and was likely to imitate his actions.

Parents who accept the responsibility of modeling positive behavior realize that they need to pay attention to, and possibly modify, their own behavior. If children are supposed to pick up after themselves, their parents must also model that behavior. "Practice what you preach" is key in successful modeling. See Fig. 23-4.

Fig. 23-4. Parents can encourage children to behave appropriately by setting a good example. **Why might a child be more likely to write a thank-you note if she sees a parent doing the same?**

Parenting Pointers

Encouraging Children to Pick Up Toys

It's a lot of fun to play with toys, but cleaning up is usually not a child's favorite task. Creative parents can find ways to motivate children:

- **Make a game of it.** Sing a clean-up song together. Race to see who can put the blocks away the quickest. Challenge a child to put away all the crayons before you count backwards from ten.

- **Follow the job with fun.** "When you're done picking up your cars, we'll read your favorite story together."

- **Establish a routine.** In some families, everyone works together to make sure that all the toys are picked up before bedtime. If this routine is established when children are young, in later years they will clean up out of habit.

- **Show appreciation.** When a toddler puts a toy in the toy box, give the child plenty of praise. When older children put their toys away, be sure to say thank you, and let them know you appreciate their help in keeping the home neat.

Teaching and Coaching

Children must be taught some of the behaviors parents want them to practice. Parents can do this by talking about why a behavior is important. For example, when a parent tells a three-year-old to stay out of the street so as not to get hit by a car, the parent is teaching the child a specific behavior.

Coaching is also something parents do often. A child receives a gift from a grandparent, and the parent asks, "What do you say?" The parent is coaching the child to say thank you. Coaching can work only after the behavior has been well taught, so that all the child needs is a quiet reminder. Otherwise the child may be confused and embarrassed, unsure of how to interpret the parent's "hint."

With older children, parents can offer a comment or prompt that does not tell the child what to do. For example, a parent might say, "Sam hasn't had a turn on your scooter yet." This helps the child realize his or her turn has gone on long enough, but lets the child take the initiative in offering Sam a turn. Coaching that is done in a gentle way without causing children to feel embarrassed or criticized is an effective parenting tool.

Positive Reinforcement

Children, like adults, enjoy having others acknowledge their achievements. Verbal or visual recognition makes children feel good about what they've done and eager to do it again. Such recognition is **positive reinforcement**—a response to a desired behavior that makes the behavior likely to be repeated. Several common forms of positive reinforcement can be effective.

Praise. Thanks and praise make people of all ages feel good about their accomplishments. A word of appreciation is especially helpful for very young children, who feel a strong need for approval from parents and other caregivers. Parents should praise a child for doing something well. "You did a good job of handling the little kitty gently." "Thank you for wheeling your bicycle into the shed." See Fig. 23-5.

Recording Achievements. Acknowledgement can be visual as well as verbal. Some parents create chore charts, which they post in prominent places for children to see. When a child successfully completes a chore, a sticker (such as a star) is placed on the chart to acknowledge the child's success. A child who has a chart full of stars has earned the right to be proud of the achievements the stars represent. Parents need to be consistent in maintaining the chart and enforcing the assigned chores.

Guidelines for Positive Reinforcement. If positive reinforcement is used inappropriately, it loses its power. These guidelines can help parents make sure the positive reinforcement they give is effective:

- **Be specific.** When praising a child, parents should be specific about the particular good behavior. Instead of saying, "You were well-behaved on our shopping trip," parents can say, "I like the way you listened and stayed right next to me in the store."
- **Be sincere.** Children know when adults are saying something they don't mean.

Fig. 23-5. Praise and approval make children feel good about what they have done. **Why is praise from parents particularly important for young children?**

Fig. 23-6. Parents should avoid leading children to expect large material rewards for everyday appropriate behavior. **How can parents make sure they are using positive reinforcement rather than bribery?**

- **Be timely.** Children should receive positive reinforcement for an action as soon as possible after they do it.
- **Be selective.** A child who receives praise equally for jobs done well or poorly learns to assign little value to praise. A parent who lavishly praises every little thing a child does can make the child immune to praise, as well as give the child an inflated sense of self. However, a simple "thank you" is almost always appropriate.
- **Be aware of the child's needs.** A child who is naturally timid needs praise for asserting herself, but not for being quiet. A four-year-old may be thrilled to get a big hug in public

for good behavior, while a ten-year-old might find it embarrassing.
- **Avoid bribery.** There is a big difference between positive reinforcement and bribery. When a parent says, "You can have ice cream if you stop running through the house," the parent is bribing the children to behave. It gives the children a motive to run through the house again tomorrow, in the hope of getting ice cream again when they stop. In contrast, positive reinforcement would be showing appreciation for quiet behavior when it occurs, whether the children were running earlier or not. See Fig. 23-6.

Preventing Problems Before They Begin

Experienced parents and caregivers know that there are ways to head off inappropriate behavior. This is especially important with younger children, because they have less ability to remember all the rules and control their impulses. Preventing trouble before it occurs can help eliminate conflict between child and parent, unpleasant consequences for the child, and damage to a child's self-esteem.

To prevent negative behavior, parents need to be aware of situations in which children tend to behave inappropriately and understand how children respond to guidance. There are several techniques for preventing negative behavior.

Provide a Child-Friendly Environment

The right kind of environment can prevent negative behavior. Putting breakable figurines out of a toddler's reach, as in the example at the beginning of the chapter, eliminates frustration on the part of both parent and child. If you don't want children to throw balls inside the home, provide a time and place to throw balls outside. Are children tossing their jackets and backpacks on the floor when they get home from school? Perhaps part of the problem is that there isn't a specific place to put these items. Providing child-height hooks just inside the front or back door makes it easier for children to be neat. See Fig. 23-7.

Redirect Attention

Sometimes a child can be distracted from an activity to avoid a problem. This technique is called **redirection.** As a toddler moves toward the family cat with an open hand and a determined look, you might redirect the child to a favorite toy. If the running footsteps of several preschool visitors might disturb the neighbors downstairs, you could seat the children at the table for a snack or an art project.

Fig. 23-7. Children are more likely to behave appropriately when the environment is child-friendly. **How can a child-friendly environment help shape children's behavior?**

Fig. 23-8. Introducing young children to interesting activities reduces the likelihood of misbehavior. **What might the long-term payoffs include?**

Offer Constructive Activities

Boredom can lead to unacceptable behavior for children of all ages. Children who are happily occupied are less likely to misbehave. That doesn't mean that parents should assume the role of full-time recreation director, making sure that children always have a video to watch or a toy to play with. Children need to learn how to occupy themselves. However, if children seem bored or restless, parents can be ready with suggestions for constructive, age-appropriate activities, such as art projects, playing dress-up, or a game of hide and seek.

Parents can also invite children to help with adult activities, such as washing dishes, dusting, washing the car, or gardening. Parents who model full, active, interesting lives encourage children to find activities that suit their own interests. See Fig. 23-8.

Offer Choices

Children sometimes resist being told what to do. To encourage positive behavior, parents should offer choices when possible. At times children respond better when they feel they have some control over a situation.

When offering choices, parents should keep two things in mind. First, limit the number of choices. Two options is enough for young children; more will overwhelm them. Second, parents must be sure they are willing to live with whatever choice the child makes. For example, Shana's mother said, "It's chilly outside. Would you rather wear your hooded sweatshirt or your red jacket?" Since she wanted Shana to be warm enough, she did not offer the choice of going out in shirtsleeves.

Avoid Problem Situations

Another way to prevent problems is to avoid putting children in situations where they are bound to behave in undesirable ways. A child who misses an afternoon nap may be tired and cranky later. This would not be the ideal evening to expect the child to sit nicely in a restaurant for dinner. Most children would find it difficult to sit through a long graduation ceremony. If children must attend such events, it's helpful to bring small, age-appropriate, quiet toys for them to play with.

Long car trips are sometimes a challenge because children get restless and aren't free to move about. Bringing along travel games and books can help keep children entertained and out of trouble. Many parents introduce word games, songs, or discussions of scenes out the car window to reduce boredom.

Supervise Children

Trouble often occurs when children are not adequately supervised. Two four-year-olds may be able to play in the sandbox alone, but a caregiver should be nearby to help resolve any disagreements and make sure no one gets hurt. A toddler is more likely to color on the walls when no one is watching than she is if Daddy is in the room to stop her. See Fig. 23-9.

Guiding with Confidence

In order to guide children effectively, parents must be confident in their efforts to do what is best for their children. Children need rules and limits, so parents must set them and stick to them. Doing so does not always make parents popular, but that's part of the job. Parents must not try so hard to be the child's "friend" that they fail to give the positive guidance the child needs from a caring adult. Ultimately, it is more important to be trusted and respected than liked.

Children feel more secure and show better behavior when they understand the expectations and limits placed on them. Loving, consistent discipline not only helps keep a child safe, but also provides the basis for the child to grow into an independent, responsible, self-disciplined adult. In the next chapter, you will read about another aspect of discipline: effective ways to respond to a child's negative behavior.

Fig. 23-9. Providing adequate supervision can keep a child out of trouble. **How can a parent supervise and still allow a child enough freedom?**

Child & Family Services CAREERS

▶ Recreation Supervisor

Recreation supervisors plan, organize, and supervise recreational programs in a variety of settings. They might work in hospitals, community and senior centers, military bases, or nursing homes. Their clients might include children, teens, adults, or those with special needs. The recreational programs they develop may include a wide range of activities: music, arts and crafts, dance, cultural arts, nature study, swimming, social recreation and games, or camping, for example. The work that recreation supervisors do benefits the physical, mental, and emotional wellbeing of their clients. It also adds to the overall quality of life in a community.

"As a recreation supervisor, I coordinate all youth and adult sports programs in my community, as well as special events. I work with everyone from children to seniors in helping create programs that serve their needs. They give me so many ideas that, coupled with all the ideas of my own, it's hard to turn my brain off at the end of the day!"

CAREER TIPS

- Take child development, art, and parenting courses in high school.
- Participate in sports.
- Volunteer to help a children's after-school or sports program, or a hospital or nursing home recreation program.
- Obtain a bachelor's degree in recreation administration, physical education, leisure services, therapeutic recreation, or a related field.

CHAPTER **23** Review & Activities

CHAPTER SUMMARY

- When parents guide children's behavior appropriately, children behave in ways that are safe and acceptable.
- Parents must decide on age-appropriate limits and clearly communicate those expectations to their children.
- Wise parents model, teach, and reinforce positive behavior.
- Preventive strategies can keep undesirable behavior from occurring.
- Although children may object to some rules, they need limits in order to feel secure and grow into responsible adults.

Check Your Facts

1. Compare discipline with punishment.
2. What is the goal of positive guidance?
3. How does positive guidance benefit children?
4. What can happen when parents are inconsistent?
5. Why are some parents unable to control older children?
6. What do parents need to know in order to have age-appropriate expectations?
7. Why are limits needed for children?
8. Explain at least five guidelines for setting limits.
9. What basic guideline helps parents communicate expectations well?
10. Compare modeling with coaching.
11. Why is positive reinforcement effective?
12. Describe two types of positive reinforcement.
13. List six guidelines for positive reinforcement.
14. Why does a child-friendly environment promote positive behavior?
15. Give an example of redirection.
16. Why is it effective to offer a young child a choice between two options?
17. Should a child who misses a nap be disciplined for misbehavior? Explain.

Think Critically

1. **Analyzing a Situation.** What would you say to a spouse who uses very little positive reinforcement? How could you make your point without offending?
2. **Analyzing Behavior.** How would you handle a two-year-old who is screaming for another child's toy?
3. **Predicting Possible Outcomes.** What might happen if a parent lacks the confidence to guide a child's behavior? In other words, the parent fails to send the message, "I am the parent here."

Apply Your Learning

1. **Response Analysis.** Analyze these parenting situations: **a)** After a child played very poorly during a soccer game, the parent decided to use positive reinforcement and said, "Great game, honey." **b)** A father said to an adolescent, "No, you can't go to a midnight movie." The mother said, "Oh, it'll be fine if she sleeps in on Saturday." **c)** A four-year-old's parents left a concert early because the child was disturbing others. **d)** A parent of a three-year-old built a model airplane, which he displayed on a low shelf. **e)** A parent asked a four-year-old, "What do you want for lunch?"

2. **Setting Limits.** Work with a team to create a list of limits for a child who is one of these ages: four; eight; ten; or fourteen. Consider safety, play, household responsibilities, manners, and health as you work on the list. Compare lists with other teams. Do the lists show greater expectations as children grow older?

Cross-Curricular Connections

1. **Language Arts.** Someone once said, "When parents don't mind that their children don't mind, the children won't." Write what you think this means. Share ideas in class.

2. **Social Studies.** Talk with someone from another country about the behavior expected of children in that culture. Compare responses with behavior expectations in the United States. Do you think Americans expect too much or too little of children? Why?

Family & Community Connections

1. **Family Discipline Then and Now.** Ask two older relatives (or older neighbors or friends) who have children how their parents handled discipline when they were growing up. Did they alter any of these techniques with their own children, and if so, why? Put class results together to reach a conclusion on whether discipline methods have changed.

2. **Positive Guidance Observation.** Spend time in a public place observing how parents interact with their children. Describe three examples of positive parenting to the class. Why do you think these were effective? Describe at least two situations that you think should have been handled differently. Based on what you've learned, how would you have handled them?

Handling Negative Behavior

CHAPTER OBJECTIVES

- Analyze reasons for negative behavior in children.
- Describe appropriate and inappropriate ways to respond to negative behavior.
- Explain effective ways to handle specific negative behaviors.
- Summarize what to do when children have serious behavior problems.
- Evaluate responses to behavior.

PARENTING TERMS

- natural consequences
- logical consequences
- restitution

Two-year-old Ethan finds a marker and uses it to scribble on the coffee table. Sergio, age four and a half, spies an expensive toy while on a shopping trip with his mother and won't stop whining about how much he wants it. Sixteen-year-old Jennie, who knows she is not supposed to stay out past 9:00 p.m. on weeknights, comes home half an hour late one night. All of these are examples of negative behavior. Yet they are three very different situations, and each requires a different parental response.

Understanding Negative Behavior

No matter how well parents promote positive behavior, no child is perfectly well behaved. Helping children develop self-discipline is a long learning process, and both children and parents make mistakes along the way. Undesirable behavior on the part of a child does not necessarily mean that parents have not done their job.

The key is whether parents respond appropriately to negative behavior. When they do, children can learn the judgment and self-control they will need as independent adults. In order to respond effectively to their child's undesirable behavior, parents need to understand the child, the situation, and some basic reasons why children don't always behave the way parents want them to.

Reasons for Negative Behavior

Negative behavior may occur for many reasons. One possibility, of course, is that the child has not received consistent, appropriate guidance from parents. However, even when parents do an excellent job of providing positive guidance, unwanted behavior is almost certain to occur at times. Why? It could be because the behavior is normal for the child's stage of development. For example, almost all toddlers have temper tantrums. It might also be because the child:

- Has never been told that a particular behavior is unacceptable.
- Has been given a rule or limit, but does not fully understand it.
- Has not yet mastered the self-control needed to behave appropriately at all times. See Fig. 24-1.
- Temporarily has less self-control than usual because of being tired, hungry, or ill.
- Is testing the limits to see whether they will be enforced.
- Is bored and unwilling or unable to find anything constructive to do.
- Is misbehaving to get attention.
- Has a serious physical or emotional problem affecting behavior.
- Is involved in drug or alcohol use.

As you can see, this list—which is by no means complete—covers a wide range, from normal development to serious disorders. Whether or not the explanation is a cause for concern, identifying it is the first step in deciding how to respond.

Fig. 24-1. The capability for self-control develops gradually as children grow. **What temporary factors can cause a child to have less self-control than usual?**

Fig. 24-2. A parent might talk to a preschooler about why certain behavior is not acceptable. **Why is this approach likely to be ineffective with a toddler?**

Finding a reason or explanation for negative behavior doesn't necessarily excuse it. Nor does it mean that parents should not provide guidance and discipline in response. However, analyzing reasons for negative behavior can help parents choose an appropriate response. As you read the rest of this chapter and learn about ways to respond to negative behavior, notice how the choice of response relates to the reason for the behavior.

Relating Development to Behavior

The choice of response also depends on the child's age and level of development. As explained in Chapter 23, parents need to take those factors into account when setting expectations for positive behavior. The same is true when responding to negative behavior.

Suppose fourteen-month-old Marcus bites another child who was trying to take a toy from him. At this age, Marcus does not yet have the self-control to stop biting—he simply acts on impulse. Nor does he understand that biting is wrong; the process of learning that lesson is just beginning. At such a young age, it would not be effective to have a talk with Marcus about why biting hurts the other person. Instead, his parent's response might be to say no and direct Marcus to another activity.

If a four-year-old did the same thing to a playmate, the parent would choose a different response, to make the child think twice before biting in the future. In general, preschoolers know that biting is not acceptable and should be mature enough to express their feelings in a more appropriate way. See Fig. 24-2.

Staying Focused on Behavior

When dealing with any behavior issues, parents must make sure to stay focused on just that: the child's actual behavior. A child who says "I don't like playing with Krissy" is simply telling her parents about her feelings. She has not behaved inappropriately. If she taunts Krissy by calling her cruel names, however, then her way of expressing dislike becomes a behavior issue.

Children should never be reprimanded or punished for having emotions such as dislike, fear, anger, or sadness. These are all normal emotions, and children have the right to experience and express them. They can, however, be expected to express their feelings in appropriate ways.

Fig. 24-3. Emotions are neither good nor bad, but there are good or bad ways to express them. **How would you explain to a child the difference between acceptable and unacceptable ways to express anger?**

Suppose a child gets angry at his brother and hits him on the arm. The parent's response should focus on the behavior of hitting, not the emotion of anger. The parent can make it clear that while everyone gets angry at times, it is never acceptable to hit others. The parent can suggest or model more appropriate ways to express anger: "Whenever Dylan makes you feel this way, you can tell him that you're angry, but you may not hit him." See Fig. 24-3.

Analyzing Behavior

What should a parent do when a child behaves inappropriately? Unless the child is risking his or her own safety or the safety of others, the first step is to analyze the situation in order to determine how to respond. The answers to these questions will play a role in how parents react.

- **What is the child's developmental level?** Some behavior, such as reaching across others for food at the dinner table, might be tolerated in younger children but not in older children. Other behavior, such as kicking someone hard under the table, is unacceptable at any age. Still, the parent's response should be based on the child's level of understanding and maturity.

- **Is the behavior within the child's control?** Children cannot be held accountable for behavior that they truly cannot control. For example, children of any age should never be scolded or punished for toileting accidents. Many children have not developed enough physically to prevent these accidents from happening. In some cases, a medical problem may be interfering with control. Punishment would not solve the problem; it would only make the child feel guilty and ashamed for something that can't be helped.

- **Does the child know that the behavior is wrong?** Suppose a parent shows a young child how to pick dandelions. Later, the child innocently picks flowers from the neighbor's flowerpot and presents them to the parent as a gift. The child does not understand that some blossoms are for picking and others are not. It would not be fair to punish her for breaking a rule that she didn't know about.

- **Was the child following the rules and limits that were set?** Suppose you are a parent who has set a limit that it's all right to be noisy while playing outdoors, but not indoors. One day you have a bad headache, and the shouts from your children as they play tag outside your window make it worse. It's fair to explain how you feel and ask the children to please find something quieter to do. It's not fair to scold them for being noisy, since they were following the rule that had been set.

- **Was the behavior intentional?** Having to wait for food at a restaurant may make a hungry two-year-old cry. That's understandable behavior that can probably be ended with a few crackers. The child is not intentionally doing anything wrong. A six-year-old who is throwing sugar packets is a different story. Similarly, if a vase gets broken because a child accidentally bumps it in passing and knocks it over, that's a different situation from an incident in which the child deliberately breaks the vase. See Fig. 24-4.

- **What factors may have contributed to the behavior?** Asking themselves this question may help parents see that something about the situation needs to be changed. A child who acts up just before lunch may need to have a lesson in appropriate behavior, but also needs to be fed. If a child feels frustrated by a too-difficult jigsaw puzzle

Fig. 24-4. Children often make a mess without meaning to. **Do you think behavior the child didn't intend should ever be penalized? Why or why not?**

and throws the pieces across the room, the parent might say, "We don't allow throwing in this house," but also may need to guide the child to a more age-appropriate activity.

Appropriate Responses

After analyzing negative behavior, parents must choose an appropriate response. There are many different possibilities; some are described below. In general, responses to negative behavior should include a goal of encouraging positive behavior. As children learn that their behavior is inappropriate, they should also be learning what to do instead.

Ignoring Some Behaviors

Most children crave attention from their parents. For some, the attention they get when they misbehave is better than no attention at all. When this appears to be the child's motive, parents can try ignoring the misbehavior. If children's behavior is not "rewarded" with attention, they may stop it on their own. If the behavior continues, parents need to use another approach. See Fig. 24-5.

Ignoring inappropriate behavior should be used sparingly. It does not work with some children, who may have different motives or simply strive harder to get the attention they crave. It is most effective with relatively minor undesirable behavior, such as baby talk or whining. However, parents must work to curb even these behaviors if they occur in settings where they are disturbing to others. Of course, behaviors that endanger anyone should never be ignored.

If parents notice a pattern of frequent intentional misbehavior, they should consider whether they are giving the child enough positive attention. They might need to make an effort to spend more time with the child and to remember to praise the child for positive behavior.

Redirecting Behavior

In Chapter 23, redirection was presented as a way to prevent inappropriate behavior. Redirection can also be used after the behavior begins. Because it addresses the immediate need without teaching a long-term lesson, redirection is especially suitable if the child is very young, no established rule is being broken, or the situation is unlikely to recur. When three-year-old Ella starts playing with the family budget worksheets her parents have spread on the table, her mother moves her to a children's table nearby with a coloring book and crayons.

Fig. 24-5. Some behavior, such as sulking, can simply be ignored. **What does the principle of positive reinforcement suggest may happen if parents respond?**

Parenting Pointers

Dealing with Dawdling

"Aren't you dressed yet—what's taking so long? Hurry up or we'll be late!" Dawdling is a behavior that often frustrates parents. When children move more slowly than an adult would like, they are not intentionally misbehaving. Children take longer to complete tasks and are more easily distracted than adults. Also, children live in the present. They are not concerned about being late for preschool or making their parents late to work.

Parents can make it easier for children to pick up the pace:

➤ **Plan to take longer.** Knowing that children need more time, parents can plan accordingly. Waking ten minutes earlier gives a child ten extra minutes to get ready in the morning.

➤ **Provide notice.** Children need time to make the mental and physical shift between activities. Give notice in terms that make sense to a child. Instead of saying, "We're leaving in five minutes," say "You can listen to that song once more, and then it's time to go."

➤ **Make the transition inviting.** The transition itself can be an enjoyable experience. Having a race from the front door to the car can encourage a child to move faster.

➤ **Make the goal appealing.** Find something the child will find interesting in the next event. "If we hurry to school, we'll have time for you to show me the hamster in your classroom."

➤ **Use good management.** Teach children basic management skills, such as how to organize toys and how to lay out clothes the night before.

Giving Reminders

In some cases, when a child breaks a rule, it may be appropriate for the parent to remind the child of the rule rather than immediately reacting with a penalty. This is especially true when a child is just learning a new rule or limit. It takes time for children to learn the difference between acceptable and unacceptable behavior and for positive behavior to become a habit.

For example, if a child leaves toys scattered on the living room floor and starts to go off to another activity, the parent might say, "Remember, you must put your toys back in the toy basket now." The younger the child, the more reminders are needed. Whether the rule is new or longstanding, parents must be consistent about enforcing it, first with reminders and later with consequences.

Using Natural Consequences

Ignoring behavior is not always appropriate, and redirecting or reminding is not always enough. Children may need to experience the consequences of their negative behavior. Consequences help children learn that both positive and negative behaviors produce results.

As their name implies, **natural consequences** are results that follow naturally from a behavior, without being imposed by a parent or caregiver. For example, a doll that is left out in the rain gets wet. A friend who is treated unkindly doesn't want to play. Natural consequences also include penalties imposed by adults outside the family as part of an established system. Examples include library fines, tardy slips, poor grades as a result of not studying, and penalties for unsportsmanlike behavior in athletics. See Fig. 24-6.

Although it may be difficult for parents to watch children and teens suffer natural consequences, it is often necessary. Natural consequences are, in many cases, the most effective consequences, provided they don't put the child's safety at risk. Consequences help children learn from their mistakes.

Imposing Logical Consequences

In some instances, behavior doesn't produce immediate natural consequences, or the natural consequences might be dangerous. Then it is necessary for parents to come up with **logical consequences**. These are consequences imposed by the parent that make sense in relation to the undesirable behavior. For example, if a seven-year-old does not put his dirty clothes in the hamper, a logical consequence would be for his clothes to not be washed. Ten-year-old Ella disregarded a rule about playing ball too close to the house, and the ball broke a window. A logical consequence would be that Ella must help pay for the window to be repaired.

Loss of privileges can be an effective type of logical consequence. The privilege should be closely related to the undesirable behavior; otherwise it is not a logical consequence. For example, if a teen violates a family rule by watching television before doing homework, the teen may lose the privilege of watching television for the next three days. If a toddler keeps throwing her toy train, the privilege of playing with the train may be taken away for a specified amount of time. See Fig. 24-7.

Fig. 24-6. Natural consequences are not imposed by the parent; they happen as a direct result of the behavior. **Why are natural consequences especially effective in shaping behavior?**

Fig. 24-7. Taking away a privilege, such as watching a favorite TV show, can be an effective consequence. **What are some other effective consequences?**

Guidelines for Logical Consequences. Although some people use the word "punishment" for consequences imposed by a parent, that word de-emphasizes the teaching and learning aspects of the penalty. Logical consequences are most appropriate and effective when they follow these guidelines:

- **Consequences should be related to the undesirable behavior.** When a child leaves a bicycle on the driveway, an appropriate consequence would be to take the bicycle away for the day. An inappropriate consequence would be to cancel a trip to the water park, because that has nothing to do with what the child did wrong.
- **Consequences should be important to the child.** Taking away a privilege a child really enjoys can be an effective consequence.
- **Consequences should be proportional to the undesirable behavior.** If a child behaves inappropriately in a minor way, the consequences should also be minor. On the other hand, if the child displays serious misbehavior, the consequences should be more serious as well.
- **Consequences should be timely.** They should be imposed as soon after the misbehavior as possible. For very young children, delaying consequences for more than even a couple of minutes can make the consequences ineffective.

Using Time-Out

Time-out is another type of consequence used by some parents, especially with three- and four-year-olds. If you've ever watched a hockey game, you know that a player who breaks the rules of the game too many times will be sent to the penalty box. Time-out is a similar concept.

The "penalty box," or time-out area, is—from a child's viewpoint—the most boring place in the house. It has no toys, books, or television to hold the child's attention. It might be a chair facing the wall in a hallway, or a room not equipped to entertain children.

Time-out should be used only for intentional misbehavior that the child knew was against the rules. Before imposing time-out, the parent should warn the child and give an opportunity to stop the forbidden behavior. If the behavior does not stop, time-out goes into effect immediately.

The parent calmly sends the child to the time-out area for a stated number of minutes.

One minute is long enough at first; a minute can seem like an eternity to a child. If the unacceptable behavior resumes after the time-out, the time can increase gradually up to five minutes. The parent places a timer or clock where the child can see it. Time-out starts over if the child screams, cries, or leaves the time-out area.

Time-out has several advantages as a teaching tool. It gives both parent and child a chance to calm down. It motivates the child not to repeat the behavior that earned the time-out. In addition, in completing the time-out the child learns self-control. As with other responses to negative behavior, parents need to keep themselves calm and controlled while enforcing the time-out.

Modeling CHARACTER

Teaching Self-Discipline

When parents yell, children learn to yell. When parents hit, children learn to hit. In order to avoid modeling negative behavior, parents need *self-discipline*. When self-discipline is lacking, feelings such as fear, anger, discouragement, frustration, or temptation can lead people to act in ways that conflict with their values. For that reason, self-discipline is a key to strength of character.

How can parents model self-discipline? They can learn and practice ways to manage stress so that they can handle the frustrations of everyday life without losing self-control. When children are angry or upset, parents can talk calmly with them, accepting the children's feelings while showing and insisting on appropriate behavior.

Think About It

What are some other ways in which parents can model self-discipline?

Avoiding Abuse

Few parents want to harm their children, but in the heat of the moment some parents cross the line from "consequences" or "penalties" to physical or emotional abuse. This occurs especially when parents were themselves abused as children. No circumstance or misbehavior can ever justify intentionally injuring, terrifying, or humiliating a child. For more information about child abuse, see Chapter 2.

Dealing with Conflict

Enforcing consequences for unacceptable behavior can lead to conflicts between parents and children. It is common for children to feel angry. When anger flares, parents should discuss the situation with the children and allow them to speak about their feelings. Parents should make sure children understand why the consequences were necessary.

Inappropriate Responses

Some responses to negative behavior should never be used by parents. They are either ineffective or likely to be harmful.

- **Making idle threats.** Threatening a consequence and not following through with it teaches children that parents don't mean

what they say. Don't tell children that you're going to give all of their toys away to charity if they don't clean them up—unless you plan to do it.

- **Shaming or belittling the child.** This includes calling a child names or saying things that make a child feel worthless. Loss of self-esteem can aggravate negative behavior.

- **Yelling or using harsh words.** Yelling can be frightening for young children. Scaring children is not the purpose of consequences. Speaking harshly toward teens can make them feel that parents don't respect or understand them.

- **Withholding love.** No matter what happens, children should always know that their parents love them. Withholding love only breaks down bonds between parents and children.

Managing Parental Anger

Sometimes parents become angry with children. Anger is normal, but parents must not let it influence how they respond to children's behavior. Parents can do several things to manage their anger:

- Walk away from the situation for a short period of time.
- Take a deep breath before speaking or acting on impulse.
- Count to 10, or even 100.
- Take a walk or a warm bath, if someone else is there to watch the child.
- Call a friend who is willing to listen.
- Pause to imagine how the child will feel hearing an angry outburst.
- Don't take a child's behavior personally. Imagine how a well-qualified child care worker would react. He or she would not get upset about the behavior, but simply deal with the situation calmly.

A parent who continues to find anger a problem may need professional help. Counselors can help parents learn strategies to gain control of their anger and express it in constructive ways.

When Parents Make Mistakes

Despite parents' best efforts to be fair, consistent, reasonable, and logical when guiding their children's behavior, they sometimes make mistakes. That's just part of being human.

Even the best parents occasionally handle a discipline issue inappropriately. It becomes a problem if parents continue to make the same mistakes with little or no effort to change. Parents should not try to hide mistakes, pretend they didn't happen, or blame someone else. It's okay to let children know that parents aren't perfect. When a parent does something inappropriate, he or she should admit the mistake and apologize. See Fig. 24-8.

Handling Specific Negative Behaviors

Parents who study child development realize that some undesirable behaviors tend to come with certain stages of development. Even though these behaviors are common, they can be difficult to handle. For example, Chapter 18 explains how to respond to temper tantrums. It's helpful for parents to know effective ways of dealing with other common undesirable behaviors in a competent, matter-of-fact manner.

Fig. 24–8. Sometimes parents make mistakes when they respond to children's misbehavior. **What does a child learn when a parent apologizes for a mistake?**

Inappropriate Language

Inappropriate language, such as swearing and using vulgar words, is common among school-age children for a variety of reasons. These may include a desire for acceptance in a peer group, a wish to copy an admired role model, or a need to express defiance against authority figures. Here are some appropriate ways for parents to handle this problem:

- **Model appropriate language.** Children imitate people they admire. Parents often top that list, especially for young children.
- **Don't respond with shock.** Some children use inappropriate language to get a reaction from parents. Parents must remain calm but firm in their response: "We don't use that language in our family."
- **Suggest alternative words.** Sometimes children want to express strong emotions and feel that inappropriate language best conveys their feelings. Parents can suggest more appropriate words for children to use to express the depth of their feelings.

Lying

Children lie for a number of reasons. They may want to avoid unpleasant consequences or to get others to like them. There are many ways parents can discourage lying and respond appropriately when children lie:

- **Model honesty.** Parents should let children see honesty in action by being honest themselves. Admitting their mistakes is one way for parents to model honesty.

Fig. 24-9. Fear of a parent's reaction can motivate a child to hide the truth. **What can parents do to promote honesty?**

- **Lead children to truthful responses.** Giving children the facts offers them an opportunity to tell the truth. A parent might say, "There was no stain on this carpet five minutes ago, and you were drinking juice in this room." Asking, "What happened to the carpet?" leaves an opening for a lie.
- **Respond appropriately to unacceptable behavior.** Children may lie to cover up mistakes if they think they will be punished harshly. Parents who are understanding and administer reasonable, logical consequences make it easier to be honest. See Fig. 24-9.
- **Praise truthfulness, especially when the news is bad.** Telling children, "I'm proud of you for admitting that you lost your glasses," encourages children to trust parents in difficult situations, even when they know their honesty may bring unpleasant results.

Children who continue to lie or who consistently refuse to admit misbehavior may need outside help. Parents can consult a child psychologist, school counselor, or another qualified professional.

Aggression

Nearly all children between the ages of one and four occasionally act aggressively. Very young children commonly bite, hit, or kick to show displeasure or to gain control over a playmate. At this age, children seek immediate satisfaction of needs and wants. Although they're thinking, "I want that toy," very young children can't express their thoughts, so they just grab!

When children display aggressive behavior, parents must respond. Here are some effective tips for handling aggression:

- **Recognize appropriate social behavior.** Use comments such as, "You shared so nicely with the boy at the park."

- **Never reward aggressive behavior.** Giving in to an aggressive child reinforces the idea that aggression is a successful way to get what you want.

- **Refuse to tolerate aggressive behavior.** *Always* enforce consequences for displays of aggression, and do so quickly and consistently.

- **Never use aggression in response.** Parents who wish to teach appropriate social behavior should not use harsh, aggressive behavior with their children.

- **Help children control aggressive impulses.** Give suggestions that will help children solve problems without being aggressive.

- **Seek professional help for children whose behavior consistently threatens the safety of others.** A child development specialist can help a child learn to control aggressive behavior.

Cheating

To a toddler, cheating doesn't exist. All ways of reaching a goal are equal. Preschoolers may understand that cheating means breaking a rule, but it may not bother them, since they obey rules only to please caregivers and avoid consequences. By age seven, children are more aware of right and wrong. As children get older, they may feel pressure to cheat, as winning games and getting good grades are important to them. See Fig. 24-10.

Parents must be careful about sending the right message regarding achievement. While encouraging a child to do well, parents must stress that it's more important to do what is right. Upon learning that his daughter failed a math test for cheating, one father said, "I'm sorry you copied your friend's answers, but not because you got a zero. I'm sorry because you cheated. Copying answers is unfair. Even if you got a good grade by cheating, you

Fig. 24-10. The temptation to cheat can be strong when students are under pressure to get a good grade or simply to pass a course. **What can parents do to discourage cheating?**

Fig. 24-11. Children need to learn that there are ways to acquire items honestly. **What other lessons do children learn by saving up their own money for a future purchase?**

wouldn't have earned the good grade. Next time you are having trouble with math, ask your teacher or me for help. I'm proud of you when you try your best, even if you get some answers wrong."

Stealing

It's not uncommon for very young children to help themselves to an item off the shelf in a store. Toddlers cannot comprehend the idea of ownership. Therefore, they see nothing wrong with taking something they want or need without asking. Telling toddlers that they may not have something is enough information for them.

Preschoolers begin to learn the concept of using money to buy things they want. Allowing preschoolers to buy small items with their own money teaches them the proper way to get items they want. By the time children are in early elementary school, most are developmentally capable of understanding that taking another person's property is wrong.

Knowingly taking another's possessions without permission is stealing, and parents need to address it. When responding to a child's theft, parents should:

- **Discover the reason.** Did the child plan to steal? Was it an impulsive act? Why did the child consider this item to be necessary?
- **Discuss alternative ways of fulfilling needs and wants.** Can the child think of other, more appropriate ways to get the item? Perhaps the child could put the item on a holiday wish list or earn money to purchase it. See Fig. 24-11.
- **Find ways to eliminate the behavior.** When shopping, parents should closely supervise children who are impulsive or who have stolen in the past.
- **Apply consequences.** A logical response to stealing is **restitution**, the act of paying back the loss in some way. The child might return or replace the stolen item, or repay it with cash.

Professional Help for Children with Behavior Problems

Children who display serious behavior problems may need professional help. Occasionally, parents' reasonable responses to negative behavior are ineffective. Serious underlying problems may need to be addressed as part of the process of promoting positive behavior.

Professional help for children who have severe behavior problems should not be embarrassing to either the child or parents. Also, it should not be seen as a sign that the parents have failed. It is, in fact, recognition that parents love their children and wish to provide for their children's needs, using whatever method or resource is necessary. See Fig. 24-12.

Even with the benefit of professional help, changing negative into positive behavior can be a long, difficult process. Parents should realistically acknowledge this fact to themselves and to their child. That way the child and the parents are less likely to be discouraged by setbacks or lack of progress.

If other family members are involved in the process, they should be encouraged to be positive, helpful, and supportive. Parents should not allow siblings to tease a child for receiving professional help or to share this information outside the family without the child's permission.

Most communities have many professional resources for helping children who have serious behavior problems. These resources include child and adolescent psychologists, psychiatrists, family therapists, residential treatment facilities, and others. Parents can consult their family physician, a pediatrician, or a school counselor for names of child specialists in their community.

Fig. 24-12. Sometimes families are included in counseling for children who have behavior issues. **How can family members help the progress of a child who has severe behavior problems?**

Child & Family Services CAREERS

▸ Child Psychologist

Child psychologists provide mental health care, including therapy and counseling, to children and their families. They work in private offices, counseling centers, schools, and hospitals. Child psychologists often administer personality, aptitude, and intelligence tests to gather information about the child and to help determine the best approach to treatment. In most cases, they also interview the child's parents and observe family interactions.

One of the positive aspects of the profession is being able to help children work through problems and grow into healthy adults. Child psychologists often get to know children and their families very well. Every child is different, so this career is filled with new challenges and rewards. No two days are the same.

"After ten years of university study, I received a license to practice in my state. Besides counseling individual children and their families, I teach a weekly parenting class at a local junior college. This career keeps me very busy, but I love the opportunity to make a positive difference in children's lives."

CAREER TIPS

- Take child development courses in high school.
- Volunteer to work with children in a group or individual setting.
- Investigate the licensing requirements in the state where you want to practice.
- Pursue a doctoral degree in psychology, counseling, or educational psychology.
- Get supervised experience and pass any exams required by your state.

CHAPTER **24** Review & Activities

CHAPTER SUMMARY

- Negative behavior in children occurs for many different reasons.
- Parents should analyze negative behavior before deciding how to respond.
- A variety of techniques can be used by parents to respond effectively to their children's negative behavior.
- Parents need to realize that certain kinds of responses to children's behavior are never appropriate.
- Specific forms of unacceptable behavior in children can be challenging to handle.
- If behavior problems become very serious, parents can turn to professionals for help.

Check Your Facts

1. What are at least five reasons for negative behavior?
2. Should emotions be punished? Why or why not?
3. What are at least four points to consider when analyzing behavior?
4. Why should some behavior be ignored?
5. When is it okay to give reminders?
6. Compare natural consequences with logical consequences.
7. Explain four guidelines for making logical consequences effective.
8. Why is time-out useful?
9. What are four inappropriate responses to a child's behavior?
10. List at least four suggestions for managing anger.
11. What should a parent do after realizing that he or she has not been fair to a child?
12. What is an effective response when a child uses unacceptable language?
13. List at least four tips for handling aggression in a child.
14. How can parents model honesty?
15. What is restitution as a logical consequence for theft?
16. Is seeking professional help for a child a sign of parental failure? Explain.

Think Critically

1. **Analyzing Viewpoints.** A child does something wrong and then tells the truth about it. Should you or should you not discipline the child? Why?
2. **Understanding Cause and Effect.** Incidents of cheating are common in society today. What examples show this? What are the effects in society? How can future parents improve the situation?
3. **Recognizing Relationships.** Why is modeling such an important technique in dealing with the specific negative behaviors described in the chapter?

Apply Your Learning

1. **Logical Consequences.** Write responses to these behaviors: **a)** A four-year-old hits a parent. **b)** An eight-year-old repeatedly neglects to feed the cat she promised to care for. **c)** A twelve-year-old who is home alone after school invites friends over, which violates family rules. **d)** A four-teen-year-old ignores her schoolwork and gets a poor report card.

2. **Parental Communication.** Evaluate these statements from parents: **a)** "If you don't get in here right now, you're going to be grounded for a month!" **b)** "I'm sorry I yelled at you when I was tired. Let's do something fun now that the dishes are done." **c)** "I don't love you when you do things like that!" **d)** "Since you took your sister's notebook, you will have to buy her a new one."

3. **Your Abilities.** How well could you handle problem behavior in a child? Examine your personality, knowledge, and skills, and write what you think.

Cross-Curricular Connections

1. **Science.** Locate research on problem behavior in children. Then narrow the scope of your search. You might focus on the effects of diet on behavior, how violence on television impacts children, or childhood mental illness. Write a report that summarizes what you learn, using authoritative sources of information.

2. **Language Arts.** Write a skit involving a parent and a teen who has broken a family rule. Show how the parent confronts the situation and resolves it.

Family & Community Connections

1. **Difficult Age.** Ask family members this question: At what age do they think behavior of children or adolescents is most difficult to handle? Why did they pick this age? Share responses in class. Were responses similar or varied? How can you use this information if you decide to become a parent someday?

2. **Out of Control.** Suppose you are the parent of a child whose behavior is getting out of control. You have tried everything you can think of, but the behavior is getting worse. Look in the telephone directory, and make a list of people and places that might be able to help you. Discuss in class what specific behavior problems might cause you to choose one resource over another.

Parenting Concerns

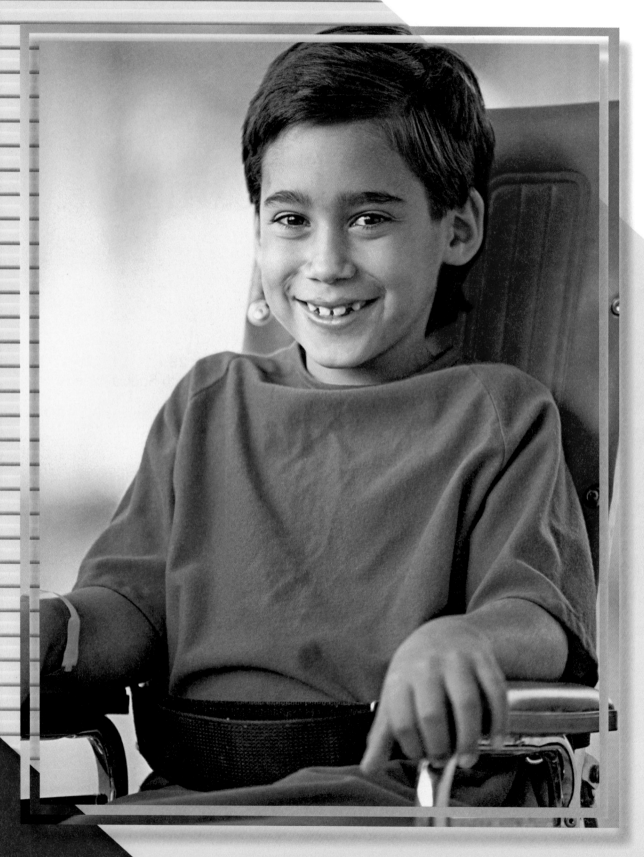

CHAPTER 25

Children with Special Needs

CHAPTER OBJECTIVES

- Summarize conditions that cause children to have special needs.
- Describe various disabilities.
- Suggest ways for parents to assist children who have special needs and to advocate for them.
- Explain how a child's disability affects parents and other family members.
- Identify resources available to families that have a child with special needs.
- Describe strategies that promote the development of gifted and talented children.

PARENTING TERMS

- congenital
- disability
- early intervention
- cognitive impairments
- orthopedic impairments
- learning disorders
- dyslexia
- attention deficit hyperactivity disorder (ADHD)
- pervasive developmental disorders
- autism
- advocates
- inclusion
- gifted

Children differ—physically, intellectually, emotionally, and socially. As a result, their needs also differ. This chapter focuses on parenting children who have needs outside the average or normal range. Some children have impairments or disorders. Some have exceptional gifts or talents. The same child may have impairments in one area and remarkable gifts in another. Whatever their special needs, children need good parenting most of all.

Understanding Special Needs

Every child is unique, but some might be called *exceptional*. One child might have an unusually high level of skill or ability in a certain area. Another child might have difficulty doing things most children can do. In both cases, the difference in ability results in some special needs.

Precisely because these needs are "special," they vary from child to child. One child may need special equipment such as a wheelchair or hearing aids. Another may need a specially arranged home. Some may need medication, physical therapy, or counseling. They all need diagnosis or identification, individualized attention, and targeted educational programs. At the same time, these children need the same things every child needs from parents and caregivers, such as love, security, and guidance. See Fig. 25-1.

Why Do Abilities Differ?

Both heredity and environment contribute to shaping every person. Conditions that give rise to special needs fall into three broad categories in terms of cause, although many involve a combination of causes. The cause of some conditions is unknown.

Hereditary Conditions. Some conditions or tendencies may "run in the family." Scientists are learning more about genes and chromosomes that make some people more likely to develop certain conditions than other people.

Congenital Conditions. Conditions that are present at birth, but not inherited from parents, are called **congenital** conditions. They may develop during pregnancy. Some hereditary or congenital disorders can be detected before birth using prenatal diagnostic tests, as discussed in Chapter 8. Others are discovered at birth. Still others emerge when children are young or when they begin school.

Acquired Conditions. Some conditions are not present at birth, but are acquired later, perhaps as the result of an accident or illness. For example, a fall or a blow to the head can cause brain damage, which, in turn, may cause mental and physical impairments.

Fig. 25-1. Whatever their abilities, all children need love and care. **What else do children with "different" abilities need from their parents?**

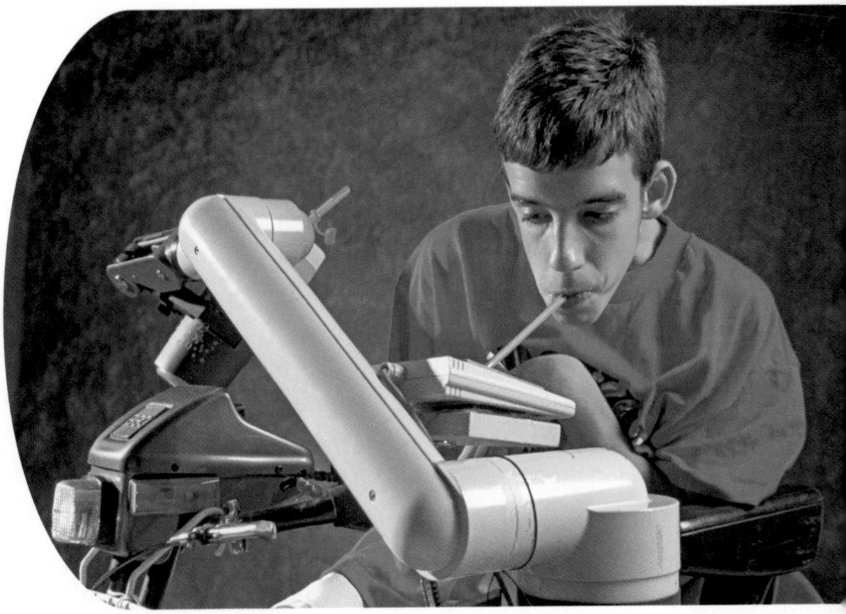

Fig. 25-2. Equipment for children with special needs is constantly improving. This boy uses a mouth stick to operate a keyboard. **What are some other ways modern science helps children with special needs and their families?**

A Balancing Act for Parents

Parents of a child with special needs can feel as though they're trying to perform a balancing act as they attempt to:

- Understand, accept, and meet their child's specific needs.
- Provide opportunities for ordinary childhood experiences.
- Find practical and emotional support for themselves.
- Meet the needs of other family members.
- Work closely with doctors, teachers, and other professionals.
- Stay confident that, as parents, they know their child best.

What Are Disabilities?

A **disability** is any physical, mental, or emotional condition that limits one or more major life activities to a large extent. Examples of disabilities include mental retardation, deafness, blindness, impaired mobility, speech or language impairment, and serious emotional disturbances. Two or more disabilities may occur in combination.

Once a condition has been diagnosed, treatment can begin. It's important for parents to realize that although many conditions cannot be cured, treatment can bring improvement. **Early intervention**—identifying and providing for a child's special needs as soon as possible—is a key element in successfully managing many conditions. There are specific therapies and tools for dealing with each disability, and many sources of support for children and their families. New means of helping children are being discovered all the time. In particular, rapid advances in technology promise better lives for those who have disabilities. See Fig. 25-2.

Many specific types of disabilities exist. They can be grouped into general categories such as the ones that follow.

Cognitive Impairments

Children with **cognitive impairments** (also called *mental retardation*) show significantly below-average intelligence and skills in self-care and communication. They function mentally well below other children their age. They are usually very slow to develop speech and motor skills. Basic academic skills, such as reading and math, come slowly, if at all.

Cognitive impairments may become evident at birth or anytime during childhood. Many children with cognitive impairments look quite normal. Unexplained slow development in a child below age three is generally called *delayed development* rather than impairment, as the child may possibly catch up with peers in a few years.

Down syndrome, which is described in Chapter 7, is one cause of cognitive impairment. Down syndrome is a combination of birth defects characterized by distinctive physical features, poor muscle tone, delayed speech and language development, and an increased risk of certain health problems, such as heart defects. Although there is no cure, children with Down syndrome can benefit from physical therapy, special education classes, and regular medical care.

Physical Disabilities

Children with physical disabilities have impairments in areas such as hearing, vision, or mobility. In order to accomplish daily tasks that most people take for granted, they may need specialized adaptations. For example, a child who is deaf may need to use hearing aids, sign language, or both. Early intervention is critical to help these children function well in spite of their limitations. See Fig. 25-3.

A *sensory impairment* is a loss of function in any of the five senses, especially hearing and seeing. Hearing impairments, which can range from mild hearing loss to total deafness, can make it hard for a child to learn and produce spoken language. Inability to hear words clearly may result in delayed speech. A child with impaired vision has eyesight that cannot be corrected to a normal level with glasses. The child may not be able to see objects clearly, may be able to see only a very narrow area at one time, or may be totally blind. Regular screenings help doctors diagnose hearing and vision impairments early.

Fig. 25-3. Children can adapt remarkably well to physical disabilities, such as blindness, when they receive support tailored to their special needs. **Why is early intervention so important?**

Modifying the Home

Families of children with orthopedic disabilities need to pay special attention to safety and mobility issues in their homes.

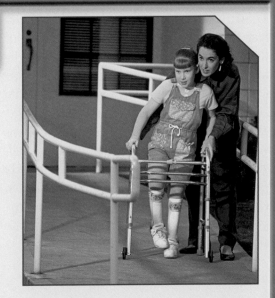

- **Doorways.** The home of someone who uses a wheelchair should have level entrances or ramps, not stairs. Doorways may need to be widened to accommodate wheelchairs and walkers, or replaced with doors that slide into the wall.
- **Bathrooms.** Install a roll-in or walk-in shower with a seat, a flexible shower hose, and a hand-held shower head. Install soft, nonskid surfaces on bathtub bottoms and shower floors to minimize the danger of slipping.

- **Supports.** Grab bars and handrails stabilize children as they sit, stand, and move around. They are especially helpful near chairs, toilets, and beds.
- **Multistory homes.** If possible, reduce the need to use stairs by placing a bathroom and the child's bedroom on the ground floor. Alternatively, install a chairlift or an elevator.

Orthopedic impairments may affect any or all parts of a person's skeletal system, including limbs, bones, muscles, and joints. For example, a child might be born with a missing limb or become partially paralyzed in an accident. Children with *spina bifida*, a birth defect involving an improperly formed spinal column, have full or partial paralysis and may have difficulty controlling their bladder and bowel functions. The effects of *cerebral palsy*, a group of conditions caused by brain damage, vary greatly.

Children with cerebral palsy may have stiff movements, coordination and balance problems, uncontrolled movements, a body that seems limp, or a combination of these and other symptoms. Depending on the condition, special needs of children with orthopedic impairments may include a combination of physical therapy, assistive devices such as wheelchairs, and in some cases surgery.

Learning Disorders

Learning disorders affect children's ability either to interpret what they see and hear or to link information from different parts of the brain. Children with learning disorders may have difficulty learning to read, write, or do math. They may have problems with language, reasoning, or memory. Some learning problems involve difficulty with motor coordination, self-control, or attention. Children with **dyslexia** (dis-LEK-see-uh), a type of learning disorder, have difficulties with skills such as recognizing words, spelling, and decoding letters into sounds. See Fig. 25-4.

Emotional and Behavioral Disorders

Every child gets upset and misbehaves from time to time. It becomes a disorder if the child displays one or more of the following over a long period of time, severely enough to affect the child's school performance:

- Inability to build or maintain satisfactory interpersonal relationships with peers and teachers.
- Inappropriate behaviors or feelings under normal circumstances.
- A general mood of deep unhappiness or depression.
- A tendency to develop physical symptoms or fears associated with personal or school problems.

Fig. 25-4. The earlier a child with a learning disorder gets help, the better. **How might parents recognize a learning disorder in their child?**

Children with **attention deficit hyperactivity disorder (ADHD)** have trouble controlling their behavior or paying attention. ADHD is believed to affect 3 to 5 percent of American children. A child with ADHD may be unable to sit still, control his or her impulses, or listen to the teacher. Since almost all children show these symptoms from time to time or under stress, ADHD can be hard to diagnose. Treatments may involve medication, counseling, or both.

THE DEVELOPING BRAIN

"White matter" in the brain is made up of fibers that connect one region of the brain to another. Using brain imaging technology, scientists have found that the brains of children with ADHD have significantly less white matter than the brains of other children the same age—provided the children with ADHD have not taken any medication for it. Children taking medication for ADHD, however, have the same amount of white matter as children without the disorder.

Pervasive Developmental Disorders

Pervasive developmental disorders are a group of disorders that involve delays in the development of social skills and communication skills. One example is **autism**. Children with autism do not communicate well and do not want to be held or cuddled. They do not respond to affection or engage in imaginative play. They often show repetitive patterns of behavior, interests, and activities. While many children with autism also have some degree of cognitive impairment, some do not.

People with *Asperger's syndrome,* another pervasive developmental disorder, have average to above-average language, thinking, and coping skills. Unable to relate socially, they tend to get deeply absorbed in a few special interests.

Parenting a Child with Disabilities

No one expects to have a child with a disability. When they are thinking about starting or adding to their family, couples envision having perfectly healthy children. Adjusting to the unexpected situation puts stresses on every member of the family. A wide range of emotions is natural. In a sense, the entire family experiences special needs.

The Diagnosis

Even before a disability is diagnosed, parents often sense that a child is not developing typically. Although all children develop at different rates, parents need to consult a doctor if their child seems to lag far behind others of the same age. The earlier a condition is diagnosed, the earlier treatment can begin, and the better the chances for future health and improvement.

If the doctor identifies a disability, he or she will give the parents a detailed diagnosis. The parents may be referred to appropriate health specialists and caregivers. A specialist will discuss treatment options and outline what the parents should do for the child at home.

Parents know their own children best. They are a child's primary **advocates,** or the ones who speak up to protect and defend the child's welfare and rights. If they feel confused or uncertain about a diagnosis, they should seek additional professional assistance.

The Road to Acceptance

Parents who find out that their child has a serious, and in many cases lifelong, condition go through a series of difficult emotional adjustments. Many parents react to the initial news with fear, anger, or denial. Most then pass through a time of mourning for the loss of the "normal" child—and the "normal" family life —they had hoped for. Parents often feel a sense of guilt, as though the disability is somehow their fault. Many parents continue to feel anxiety about their child's welfare and their ability to parent the child adequately.

Parents should expect such an adjustment process. They should also understand that other family members will be going through it too, and that they may not all be in the same stage of adjustment at the same time. One of the most important things parents can do is to realize they are not alone. They should seek out as much support as possible from family, friends, and the governmental and community resources discussed later in this chapter.

Impact on the Family

A child's disability affects not only the child but also every other member of the family. Because children with special needs often require extra attention, there is a risk that they will become the center of attention in a family. Other family members may then feel deprived. Parents need to learn how to balance the needs of their child with their own needs and those of the rest of the family.

Parents often feel strained beyond their limits, especially if one is providing most of the hands-on care. First and foremost, they need to take care of their own physical and emotional health. The divorce rate among parents of children with disabilities tends to be higher than usual. It is very important for parents to nurture their relationship and to seek whatever support they may need.

Siblings may feel neglected and angry. Living with a brother or sister who has special needs can be a confusing source of mixed emotions: anger, resentment, joy, isolation, guilt, and pride. Younger siblings may misunderstand the disability, feeling they caused it or afraid they might "catch" it. Older siblings may worry about the reactions of their peers or the possibility of passing the disability along to their future children. Many also feel pressure to be exceptionally successful or mature, to "make up for" their brother or sister. See Fig. 25-5.

Wise parents talk openly with all family members about a child's disability and how it affects everyone. They share information about the disability with their other children in age-appropriate ways, and they clearly communicate their expectations for all their children.

Fig. 25-5. The needs of siblings can sometimes be overlooked. **What are some of the emotions that might arise in siblings of children with special needs?**

Parenting Pointers

Balancing Siblings' Needs

Parents of children with special needs must be careful not to shortchange the needs of their other children. These suggestions can help them find the right balance:

- Let each child know that he or she is special. Encourage and reward individual character traits, skills, and accomplishments.

- Try to spend a few minutes each day alone with each child.

- Encourage children to express themselves, including whatever negative thoughts and emotions they may be feeling. Let them know it's normal to feel anger and resentment sometimes.

- Give each child specific tasks and responsibilities, including the child who has special needs.

- Be careful not to expect or encourage the other children to shoulder adult responsibilities. They need to be kids, not caregivers.

- Encourage cooperation rather than competition. Assign tasks to children as a group, set goals that children can reach as a group, and engage in family activities that everyone enjoys.

- Help children meet and spend time with other children who have differently-abled siblings.

Special in Some Ways, Not in Others

Although children with disabilities may be special in certain ways, in most ways they are just like all other children. Parents do not look at their child and see a disability—they see a person they love. Along with the extra work the disability may require, wise parents take time to relax and enjoy the child just the way he or she is.

To a considerable extent, parents can—and should—treat a child who has special needs like any other member of the family. Like their siblings, children with disabilities should be asked to assume certain personal and household responsibilities within their capabilities. They should follow schedules and do chores as would any other responsible family member. Coddling or overprotecting children does them no favors —in fact, it can hinder development.

Resources for Meeting Special Needs

It's not unusual for parents to be overwhelmed at first by the special needs of a child with a disability. They can seek information and support, as well as help for themselves and their child, from a variety of community resources.

Finding Information

As the child's primary advocates, parents have a responsibility to learn as much as possible about the nature of their child's particular needs. They also need to learn as much as they can about the different treatment, educational, and support options available.

There are many ways to discover what resources are available. One of the most reliable is to visit the local public library. Librarians can help parents locate and make sense of a wealth of information. Most libraries also offer Internet access as well as use of printers, so that people can look up information online, print it out, and take it home. See Fig. 25-6.

Parents can find it very helpful to have a good system for keeping track of all the information they gather. Many write everything down in a notebook, including notes from conversations with specialists, educators, and other caregivers. Parents should be sure to keep files containing their child's medical records and other professional evaluations, to document eligibility for special programs. Many parents also keep files of information about sources of support for their children, themselves, and their families.

Educational Resources

Both the federal and state governments guarantee certain support to children who have disabilities. The federal Individuals with Disabilities Education Act (IDEA) assures a free and appropriate public education for children with diagnosed disabilities. This education must be provided in the least restrictive environment consistent with meeting the child's needs.

Services for Infants and Toddlers. Under IDEA, children under three years of age with diagnosed disabilities, or developmental delays that put them at risk for disabilities, are eligible for a state-managed early intervention program. Qualified professionals work with parents to design an Individualized Family Service Plan (IFSP) for the child and his or her family. The IFSP identifies the family's priorities, concerns, and resources. It provides for professionals to work with the child in the child's home or at a school, library, or child care center. It describes not only the services the child will receive, but also the services available for parents and siblings. The plan is reviewed at least once every six months.

Fig. 25-6. A public library is an excellent place to begin research about ways to meet a child's needs. **What questions might a parent ask the librarian?**

Fig. 25-7. All children benefit when their parents become involved in their education. **Why is this especially important for children in special education programs?**

Special Education. With the transition from toddler to preschooler (ages three to five), the focus under IDEA shifts toward readiness for learning in a school environment. While parents remain actively involved, the child may spend more time in a preschool setting with other children who also have special needs.

Under IDEA, school-age children with disabilities are eligible for special education programs targeted to their special needs. Children who are unable to attend school may receive services at home. Usually, however, children attend public schools. The school district pays for all necessary services, such as those provided by a special education teacher, a speech therapist, an occupational therapist, a school psychologist, a social worker, a school nurse, and a classroom aide.

Children in special education programs may spend at least part of their school day in regular classrooms and activities alongside children who do not have special needs. The educational practice of mixing children with and without special needs in the same classroom is called **inclusion**. Its philosophy is that the opportunity to interact benefits all the children.

By law, the public schools must design an Individualized Education Program (IEP) for each child who received special education services. The IEP describes the goals for the child and sets up the service delivery system to meet those goals.

Parents play a critical role in creating their child's IEP. The plan should reflect agreement between parents and specialists on the child's needs and how to address them. Parents are asked to attend a meeting in which the plan is developed. Others attending this meeting may include a special education teacher, a general education teacher, and a representative of the public schools. Whenever practical, the student should be included in the team. See Fig. 25-7.

Child & Family Services
CAREERS

▸ Special Education Teacher

Special education—or "special ed"—teachers work with students of all ages who have special needs, from infants to adults. Special education teachers help develop, implement, and document a personalized instructional plan for each student. They work with students to develop behavioral and life skills as well as academic ones.

The majority of special education teachers are employed by public schools. They work as part of a team that includes general education teachers, school administrators, psychologists, and other professionals. About ten percent of special education teachers work in private schools, hospitals, residential facilities, or homes.

Education and training for special education teachers varies. Some states require a master's degree in special education. Many states offer alternative licensing programs. Special education teachers may study to become specialists in one area, such as speech-language pathology.

"My work draws on all my creative skills to help children with so many different learning issues. Because many of the children are included in regular classrooms, I often adapt existing materials to meet their specific needs. My work is both physically and emotionally demanding. I have learned to take satisfaction from any signs of a child's progress, large or small."

CAREER TIPS

- Take child development courses in high school.
- Talk to special education teachers in your local school system about their work.
- Complete a bachelor's degree and an approved teacher preparation program.
- Investigate state requirements for a teacher's certificate or license.

Fig. 25-8. Many children with disabilities play sports. How might playing an individual or team sport benefit a child who has special needs?

Other Educational Resources. In addition to the free public education guaranteed to all children with disabilities, there are organizations that offer financial aid for other types of education. Many communities offer free or low-cost tutoring services.

Extracurricular Activities. Depending on the particular disability, children can and should participate in activities outside of school. They can join sports teams, drama groups, bands—whatever other children do. All children need creative and physical outlets as well as the opportunity to be part of a group or team and excel on their own merits. Parents who encourage this kind of participation help a child achieve confidence and new skills. See Fig. 25-8.

Private and Community Resources

Many other resources are available to help children with disabilities—and their families—cope with a complex and often difficult situation.

Therapies. A family's primary care physician will refer parents to appropriate specialists—and, acting as the child's advocates, parents can research other therapies available. Some of this care will be funded by governmental sources or the family's medical insurance. Parents should consult with their insurance companies and doctors to make sure they understand the full extent of the coverage available to them under their particular insurance policy.

Community Support Services. Many communities offer support services to the families of children who have special needs, including child care services, transportation, and classes. Once again, parents can turn to their local librarians or school personnel for help in locating these resources.

Family and Individual Counseling. Many families of children who have special needs find essential support through counseling. Individual counseling, marriage counseling, and family therapy have all proven effective in helping people learn how to make the most of a difficult situation. Parents can ask friends, members of support groups, and various professionals—doctors, educators, community resource specialists—for referrals to a therapist who can provide the guidance they might need.

National Organizations. For every special need, there are multiple national organizations dedicated to supporting, educating, and speaking up for the people affected by it. Some of these groups are organized around a specific condition, such as the Cystic Fibrosis Foundation. Others, such as the Social Security Administration, help people find support for their individual needs. See Fig. 25-9.

Support Groups. Many families of children who have special needs find support groups very helpful. Support groups are groups of people sharing similar life situations who meet to discuss problems and solutions and to share information. There are support groups for all varieties of people touched by a child who has special needs: parents, siblings, relatives, and caregivers. Some of these groups are organized by a community resource such as a community center, school, or religious organization. Many of these meetings are moderated by someone experienced in dealing with specific special needs and in leading group discussions.

A number of support groups are available online. Parents can join an e-mail group and receive messages about different topics. There are also message boards and live chat rooms in which they can participate.

Fig. 25-9. A number of organizations provide service dogs for people with disabilities. The dogs are trained to do tasks such as opening doors, flipping light switches, and picking up dropped items. Just as important, they are also faithful companions.

Fig. 25-10. Gifted children perform much above their age level in some areas. **What are some examples of different gifts or talents?**

Gifted and Talented Children

A **gifted** person is someone who demonstrates, or has the potential for demonstrating, an unusually high level of performance in one or more areas. The term "gifted" is used to describe a wide variety of outstanding abilities. Some of these may be very general, such as intellectual or leadership skills. Others may be very specific, such as an exceptional ability or talent in music or mathematics. According to some estimates, about three million children in the United States are considered gifted or talented. See Fig. 25-10.

Gifts and talents may become evident very early in a child's life—child music prodigies are one such example. They may also show up later, when the child first gains exposure to an area such as science. Gifted children will perform well beyond their age level in their area of talent. To make the most of their gifts, they may need educational and other support beyond what is routinely offered in many school classrooms.

Parenting Gifted and Talented Children

Parents often react to discovering that their child is gifted with a mixture of pride, fear, and excitement. Like the parents of children with disabilities, they must make certain adjustments in their lives. They need to recognize and support their child's gifts while treating him or her like any other child. They must balance the needs of all family members, making sure siblings with average abilities feel equally valued. Parents of a gifted child must act as the child's advocates, making sure that their child's abilities are accurately identified and cultivated.

Nurturing a Gifted Child

Parents can nurture gifted children by recognizing their needs for:

- In-depth, intense pursuit of interests and information.
- Respect for their insights and opinions.
- Association with other gifted individuals.

- Guidance when they encounter situations and information that they understand but are emotionally unprepared to handle.

Like all children, gifted children benefit from frequent and positive interaction with parents and other caring individuals. See Fig. 25-11.

Parents can help their gifted child understand the difference between excellence and perfectionism. While pursuit of excellence is healthy, an attitude that everything must be perfect can cause tremendous stress. Often people who are perfectionists are so afraid of making mistakes that they are unwilling to take any risks. Parents and other adults can help by assuring gifted children that their worth does not depend on performance. Like all children, gifted children need to know that they are loved unconditionally.

Developing Social Skills

The rapid intellectual development of gifted children sometimes leads adults to expect them to act more grown-up in other ways as well. However, they are more likely to mature physically and emotionally at about the same rate as their peers, putting different aspects of their development "out of sync." While some are poised and well-adjusted, others show the strain of feeling "different" from their classmates. Socially, gifted children may act:

- **Seemingly immature.** Adults sometimes interpret the actions of gifted children as immature because they expect emotional maturity to match up with intellectual abilities. They need to accept age-appropriate emotional behavior from gifted children. Parents can help children to identify behavior that is likely to provoke negative reactions.

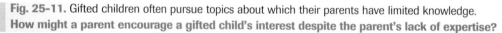

Fig. 25-11. Gifted children often pursue topics about which their parents have limited knowledge. **How might a parent encourage a gifted child's interest despite the parent's lack of expertise?**

Fig. 25-12. Some cities have schools designated for gifted children with special interests, such as performing arts. **How might such a school benefit a gifted child?**

- **Superior.** Parents can teach respect for others and acceptance of exceptional ability as a gift to be used wisely. They can also point out that friends do not need to be intellectual equals.
- **Demanding.** Gifted children have a need for energetic, challenging pursuit of information. Families and others should accept this need, but can help children learn to express it in appropriate terms and at appropriate times.

As children become older, family meetings can be a good way to communicate, to learn to share responsibility, and to develop negotiation skills. As with children who have disabilities, gifted children must function as responsible members of a family.

Meeting Educational Needs

Gifted children need parents who are responsive and who are their best advocates. Parents must be willing to go to bat for their children to make sure their talents are nurtured outside as well as inside the home.

Customized educational opportunities for gifted children are not required by federal law, as they are for children with disabilities. Some schools have excellent gifted programs, while others have none. It is up to parents to make sure that their gifted children receive a good formal education. Parents should find out what special programs are available through their schools and other organizations. Many schools offer *accelerated* classes, or classes that teach subjects at a faster rate and greater level of complexity than the standard classes. Other schools offer special in-school and after-school programs for gifted students.

Many cities have schools that offer specialized education for students who have specific abilities, such as a talent for science or visual arts. Many colleges offer weekend and summer programs for gifted children. There are also distance-learning programs available on the Internet. See Fig. 25-12.

Parents of children with special needs and gifts face special challenges. Everyone in a family is affected, and parents need to take action to meet and balance everyone's needs—including their own. All children can be a source of joy to parents who love and value them for who they are, regardless of the children's abilities.

CHAPTER SUMMARY

- Children who have disabilities and those who are gifted have abilities outside the normal range, giving rise to special needs.
- Types of disabilities include cognitive, physical, learning, emotional and behavioral, and pervasive developmental disorders.
- Parents need to act as advocates for a child who has a disability.
- Balancing the needs of all family members is a concern when a child has a disability.
- Many resources are available to help families who have a child with special needs.
- Parents can use positive strategies to promote the development of gifted children.

Check Your Facts

1. Compare special needs with the needs of all children.
2. Explain three broad conditions that may cause special needs.
3. What are six responsibilities of parents who have a child with special needs?
4. What is a disability?
5. Why is early intervention important?
6. Compare cognitive impairments with physical disabilities.
7. What treatment can benefit a child with Down syndrome?
8. What is cerebral palsy?
9. How might orthopedic impairments be treated?
10. What is dyslexia?
11. Why is ADHD hard to diagnose?
12. What is autism?
13. How do parents act as advocates?
14. How do parents typically react to a disability diagnosis in their child?
15. How should parents keep track of information about their child?
16. What is the purpose of each of these: IDEA, IFSP, and IEP?
17. What is inclusion?
18. List five types of private and community resources.
19. How can gifted children be helped socially and educationally?

Think Critically

1. **Understanding Cause and Effect.** What are specific ways for a parent to prevent other children in a family from resenting a sibling with a disability?
2. **Judging Relevance.** Some people believe ADHD is overdiagnosed, leading to unneeded medication. How would you respond to this diagnosis in your child?
3. **Predicting Possible Outcomes.** What could happen if parents are overly protective and permissive with a child who has a disability?

Apply Your Learning

1. **Parenting Responses.** Write how you would handle these parenting situations: **a)** Your child shows signs of a learning problem, but your spouse says, "Don't be silly; he's just fine." **b)** Your child comes home crying because children made fun of her disability. **c)** Your child seems bright but is often in trouble at school. **d)** Your nine-year-old confuses b's and d's.

2. **Adaptive Tools.** Investigate adaptive tools and equipment for physical disabilities. Describe one item to the class. How is it used and what does it cost?

3. **Community Resources.** Identify local resources for children with special needs and their families, including local offices of national organizations. Create a brochure that lists the resources, explains the services they provide, and supplies contact information.

4. **Game Creation.** Work with other students to invent a game for young gifted children. The game should promote social or intellectual development. Demonstrate your game in class.

Cross-Curricular Connections

1. **Language Arts.** Learn about American Sign Language (ASL), a communication tool for people with hearing impairments. Explain and demonstrate ASL for the class.

2. **Science.** Learn more about autism. What are possible causes, and why do some people believe this disorder is becoming more prevalent? What is being done to meet the needs of children and families affected by autism? Share your findings in class.

3. **Language Arts.** Write a description of a parent who successfully cares for a child with special needs.

Family & Community Connections

1. **Family Outreach.** Does your family know a child who has special needs? Think of ways to reach out with assistance, and put an idea into practice. For example, could you entertain the child to give parents some free time? Could you spend time with siblings? What other ideas does your family have?

2. **Accessibility.** Choose a location in your community to evaluate on accessibility. Look at streets, sidewalks, parks, and buildings (offices, stores, and schools). What changes should be made? Where can you take any concerns?

Managing Life as a Parent

CHAPTER OBJECTIVES

- Explain the causes and effects of role conflicts.
- Summarize ways to manage work, family, personal, and community responsibilities.
- Describe management tools and strategies that help people manage their lives effectively.
- Describe workplace policies that are helpful to families.
- Identify sources of support for parents.

PARENTING TERMS

- role conflicts
- prioritize
- work ethic
- materialism
- dovetail
- multitask
- budget
- flextime
- job sharing
- telecommute

Have you ever wondered how parents do it all? Juggling so many different things at once is tough. Parents have to make sure their children are developing in healthy ways. They have to work hard to provide for their family. They also need time to pursue their own personal interests and friendships. On top of all that, they're often involved with community activities. It can be a challenge for parents to give enough time and attention to all their roles, but they can learn strategies to help them succeed.

The Challenge of Multiple Roles

Everyone plays multiple roles in life, based on the different relationships they have with other people. Theresa is a parent, but she is also a spouse, household manager, employee, daughter, sister, friend, and neighbor. Part of what makes life interesting is this variety of roles. However, the variety can add stress and cause conflicts.

Role conflicts occur when one role negatively affects another role. Jordan, a high school senior, worked late one night at a part-time job. He came home too tired to study for a test. The next day, feeling angry about the test, he ignored

a friend after class. What happened? Jordan's work life affected his academic life, which in turn affected his personal life. Stress from one area of his life carried over to other areas, creating role conflicts.

Similar role conflicts often happen to parents. Sometimes pressures at work spill over, affecting family life. At times, problems in family life can influence work performance. See Fig. 26-1.

Factors that Increase Role Conflicts

In almost all families, role conflicts result from the need to provide care for children while one or both parents also earn income. Until children are able to care for themselves, parents either stay home with them or find quality, affordable child care. Both alternatives cause role conflicts. Parents at home give up the role of pursuing an outside career, and working parents sacrifice some of their parenting role.

In addition, some families face situations that tend to further increase role conflicts and create family stress. Examples of such situations include:

- **Single parenting.** The burdens of parenting are often greater when shouldered by single parents. Because they're typically alone in handling family responsibilities, single parents may have a harder time keeping problems in one role from carrying over into other roles.
- **Challenging work schedules.** Some people have jobs that make extreme demands on their time or energy. Some work two jobs to make ends meet. Still others work the late shift or have unpredictable work schedules that make planning difficult. Work situations such as these can have a negative impact on other roles.

Fig. 26-1. When parents undergo stress in one area of life, it often influences their performance in other areas. **How might having to work late affect family life?**

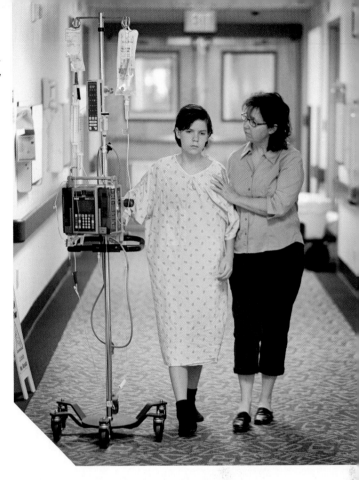

Fig. 26-2. Providing support for a family member who is ill can be physically and emotionally draining. **Why is it important for caregivers to care for themselves?**

- **Caring for ill or aging family members.** Additional role conflicts can occur if a caregiver has to spend work time dealing with the health and care of an ill or aging family member. When a caregiver has to devote extra time to one family member, other family members may feel neglected, adding stress to family life. See Fig. 26-2.
- **Family crises.** While one handles a family crisis, other areas of life suffer. It's hard to work productively or interact happily with friends and family when facing a crisis such as divorce. Chapter 27 provides suggestions to help families cope with challenges and crises.

Effects of Role Conflicts

What happens when people have role conflicts? When roles interfere with one another, the effects can include internal, external, and interpersonal problems.

Internal. Unresolved role conflicts can affect how a person feels inside. If problems are kept hidden, stress can build up, triggering symptoms such as headaches and digestive problems. Worrying can cause sleepless nights, which in turn lead to exhaustion.

Sometimes role conflicts produce feelings of guilt. For example, when working parents are dissatisfied with the quality of their child care provider, they may feel guilty for working (even if it's a financial necessity) or for not being able to afford better quality care.

External. Role conflicts can also have some noticeable external effects. What happens if a parent has to work overtime? Time spent in other roles—such as cooking meals or performing volunteer work—is cut short. When there's just not enough time, dishes can pile up, hobbies may be forgotten, and other interests may fade.

Interpersonal. Unfortunately, role conflicts often cause interpersonal problems, affecting relationships with others. If parents are too busy with work and child care to spend much time with each other, their marriage may suffer. If a parent is involved in too many community activities and outside interests, children may feel neglected and act up to get the parent's attention.

Finding the Right Balance

According to psychologists, to maintain good physical and mental health, it is important for individuals to have balanced lives. That means making room for different roles and areas of their lives in a way that works for them.

When thinking about a way to balance life, though, remember that *balanced* doesn't necessarily mean *equal*. Each role does not automatically get equal time. Imagine dividing your day equally between school or work, family, personal time, and community activities. Could you spend four hours a day on each? School alone requires more hours than that, so the other areas will get less time.

Balanced also doesn't mean that the most important role gets the most time. Parents would probably agree that their family life is most important. Yet, if they hold a full-time job to support their family, they will end up spending more time at work than interacting with family members. However, they can make sure that the time they do spend with family is meaningful.

A balanced life is one in which each role is given the time and attention needed. Sometimes the demands of one role may require sacrificing the others for a short time. But in general, all areas are included on a regular basis, and no role is neglected for long periods. See Fig. 26-3.

Setting Priorities

Work, family, personal, and community responsibilities are all important areas of life. While managing activities in these areas, it helps to **prioritize** them, or rank them in order of importance. When setting priorities, all areas of life should be considered so that no area is ignored for long.

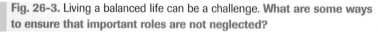
Fig. 26-3. Living a balanced life can be a challenge. **What are some ways to ensure that important roles are not neglected?**

Once priorities are set, that doesn't mean they are unchangeable. Flexibility is the key. Some days, work may take priority. At other times, family may take priority. When children are sick, their care becomes a clear priority.

Be Realistic. When setting priorities, consider whether your expectations for yourself and others are realistic. It's not possible to be a "perfect" parent who attends every school activity, coaches the child's team, and has a spotlessly clean house and a great career. When people set impossibly high standards, they will only be frustrated and disappointed not to reach their goals.

Avoid Overcommitment. Society offers so many choices that demands on your time can pile up. Knowing when to say no increases your control over life.

People often have a hard time refusing requests for their time, energy, and money because they want to be liked and don't want to let others down. However, taking on new commitments may disrupt the balance of people's lives and lead to frustration and stress. Parents should not feel guilty about saying, kindly but firmly, "Sorry, I can't."

Balancing Work and Family

Most parents would say that family is their top priority. Usually, however, the welfare of the family depends on one or both parents earning income. Employment, therefore, supports the goal of family life. Work can also have other benefits. Earning money and respect through hard work is satisfying. People can be proud of contributing to their community by doing their job well.

The belief that work is valuable and beneficial in its own right is called the **work ethic**. Work is necessary, beneficial, and rewarding. People with a strong work ethic enjoy a sense

Fig. 26-4. Work can bring the satisfaction of a job well done. **How does the work ethic benefit both individuals and society?**

of accomplishment from working hard and completing tasks well. See Fig. 26-4.

Working long hours now and then may not interfere with other areas of life. When it happens more often, however, overwork creates problems. Achieving the right balance may require a reduction in work hours. Parents must think about the benefits of work, including pay and feelings of satisfaction. Do the benefits outweigh the costs?

Costs of Overwork. Overwork can be a health hazard. People who work long hours may not take time to eat right, exercise, or relax. They may feel stressed and tired, yet won't take time off. These poor health habits leave them more vulnerable to ailments, from headache to heart disease.

Long hours are also a problem when relationships are neglected. Family members feel hurt and angry. Friends may find others to replace the friendship.

Work *is* important, but most careers can be reasonably paced. People who discover that overwork is causing problems in their lives need to make changes. They may need to find a different job or just learn how to enjoy other areas of life. See Fig. 26-5.

How Much Is Enough? Some parents try to justify long working hours by pointing out what the extra income allows them to buy for their children. If managed wisely, extra income can give parents a financial cushion and allow them to save for the future. Too often, however, the money is quickly spent on items that have little importance in the long run. Advertising and other societal pressures encourage an attitude of **materialism**, the belief that money and possessions bring happiness. As a result, people tend to want more and more—more clothes, more expensive vehicles, more and snazzier electronic devices.

Parents should look closely at what they give up in order to buy more. Which is more important: another hour working to earn money to buy a desired item, or an hour spent with a child? Few would argue that what children need most from parents is time and attention. When these are lacking, possessions can't make up the loss.

With that fact in mind, parents may want to review their options. Should they take lower-paying jobs that leave them more family and personal time? Could the family get by on one income so one parent could be home with the children? Could they reduce expenses by choosing to live more simply? After careful

Fig. 26-5. To enjoy family, friends, and good health, both now and in the future, it's essential to nurture them all along the way.

Fig. 26-6. Money and possessions can never replace time spent with family, especially when children are young. **How can families make more time for each other?**

thought and planning, some parents decide to sacrifice income for family time, instead of the other way around. See Fig. 26-6.

Setting Boundaries

To keep all areas of life balanced, it helps to set boundaries. By maintaining boundaries between work, family life, personal activities, and community involvement, people are more attentive and productive.

At Work. It's not possible to function well at work while receiving a constant flow of personal calls or e-mail messages. During work hours, focus on work and keep family and personal interruptions to a minimum. Job security and satisfaction depend on reliable effort.

With Family. In the same way, during family time, minimize work interruptions. Unless required to be on call, turn off cell phones or pagers to eliminate distractions. Make plans for specific family times and stick to them. Family members feel more loved and appreciated when they receive undivided attention.

Personal Time. Everyone needs time to pursue personal interests. Whether you enjoy kick boxing, stamp collecting, or tracing family history, set aside a specific time at least once a week to enjoy such activities. By spending time on your own interests, you'll be refreshed and renewed for other tasks.

Community Involvement. Community sports, charity events, classes, volunteer work, theater productions—communities today are active and alive! By getting involved, you can develop new interests and friendships while enriching your own community. Remember, however, to set boundaries. In this area of life, saying no can be especially difficult, but it is often necessary.

Management Tools and Strategies

Why do some people seem better able to cope with multiple roles and demands than others? A large part of the answer lies in management techniques. By using proven strategies, people can more successfully manage the different areas of their lives.

Using the Management Process

One tool that can help busy families is the four-step management process discussed in Chapter 5. Here's how Maronda used this process to host a surprise 13th birthday party for her daughter, Elise.

- **Plan.** Maronda thought about her goals for the party: to surprise Elise, provide a good time for her and her friends, and keep the preparations simple. She asked her sister, Joli, to help. Together they discussed what they would need to do to get ready, such as inviting Elise's friends and preparing refreshments.
- **Organize.** Maronda and Joli divided up the tasks that would need to be done. They created a reasonable schedule for accomplishing the tasks.
- **Implement.** By following their schedule closely, Joli and Maronda were able to complete their tasks by the time of the party. When they ran into a problem, such as not being able to find the kind of decorations they wanted, they adjusted their plan.
- **Evaluate.** On the afternoon of the party, the games and food were ready as planned, and Elise's friends were waiting for her. Elise was truly surprised, and everyone had fun. As they cleaned up, Maronda and Joli agreed all their hard work paid off. The management process made the difference.

Sharing Responsibilities

Have you ever heard that "many hands make light work"? When chores are divided or shared, it's easier to get things done. Daily jobs such as washing dinner dishes might be divided or rotated among individual family members. Accomplishing bigger tasks might require the help of everyone working together. See Fig. 26-7.

Fig. 26-7. In most families, doing work around the home is a shared responsibility. **What does a young child learn when the whole family pitches in to help?**

How Single Parents Can Succeed

Without a spouse to share the load, single parents can find caregiving and household responsibilities extra challenging. Successful single parents suggest ways to meet this challenge:

- **Find the best quality child care you can afford.** Parents can function better at work knowing their children are well cared for.

- **Get help from family and friends.** Assign children household tasks in keeping with their age and abilities. Establish a network of extended family members and friends who can offer practical support, such as occasional or regular child care.

- **Join an organization for single parents.** Sharing information, ideas, and concerns with other single parents can be encouraging.

- **Look for youth programs that can enhance family life.** YMCA activities, religious youth groups, scouting, and other community programs are designed to help children develop in healthy ways. Organizations like these can also offer appropriate male or female role models, essential for children from homes lacking either a father or mother.

- **Plan get-togethers and getaways with other single-parent families.** Children will enjoy getting together with friends, and the parents can share expenses and child care responsibilities.

- **Maintain a positive attitude.** Feelings are contagious. When a parent is optimistic and hopeful, children will be too.

Jobs can't always be divided equally, but they should be divided fairly. Consider each person's age, available time, abilities, and preferences. For example, an early riser might pour juice and set out cereal for the rest of the family. Someone who regularly passes a supermarket could be assigned grocery shopping.

Some parents can afford to hire others to help with some household tasks. If that's an option, they should weigh the costs and benefits carefully. Some parents may decide that it's well worth the expense of hiring help to take care of tasks that they don't have the time, energy, or skill to do well. Others prefer to do certain tasks themselves, even if they can afford help. Each family must decide based on their resources and priorities.

Getting Organized

In general, parents who are organized manage their roles more efficiently. They get things done more easily and with less stress. Getting organized includes strategies such as reducing clutter, working ahead, and establishing simple routines. Here are some examples:

- Discard, recycle, or give away things that haven't been used during the last year.
- Find specific places to keep the things that are left. Then get in the habit of putting them away after each use.
- Maximize and organize storage space using crates, boxes, bins, baskets, or underbed storage boxes. See Fig. 26-8.
- Go through incoming mail each day instead of letting it pile up. Toss out unwanted items immediately.

- Set aside a certain day or time each week to pay bills, file receipts, and take care of other household recordkeeping.
- Plan and shop for meals weekly. Once a month, cook and freeze meals ahead.
- Make a checklist of tasks for children to do each morning or evening: make bed, feed pet, and so on. This not only helps ensure nothing is forgotten, but also teaches children skills for organizing their own lives.
- To ease the morning rush, prepare as much as possible the night before. For example, before they go to bed, children can lay out the clothes they will wear the next day.

Managing Time

Time management—using time efficiently to achieve goals—offers mental as well as practical benefits. By using time well, you complete needed tasks, feel a sense of accomplishment, and feel more in control of your life.

Basic time management starts with making a list of tasks to accomplish. Having a written list helps you stay focused and set priorities. Some people prioritize tasks by marking each one either A (highest priority), B, or C (lowest priority).

A calendar or day planner is another basic time management tool. Write down appointments and other scheduled events as soon as you know about them. Each morning, or the night before, take a few minutes to plan the upcoming day. Look at what's on your calendar and how much unscheduled time you have available. Plan how to use that time effectively

Fig. 26-8. By providing well-organized storage, parents can teach children to keep things in order. **Why would it help children to learn organizational skills early?**

Fig. 26-9. Parents can use travel time to catch up on small tasks. **What can children learn by watching their parents use time wisely?**

to work on the tasks you need to complete. Start with highest-priority tasks first. Lower-priority tasks not completed today might get higher priority tomorrow. Throughout the day, check items off your list as you complete them.

Here are some additional time management tips:

- **Eliminate time-wasters.** For example, if calling a friend often leads to an hour-long conversation, wait until after high-priority tasks are completed. You could also try setting a timer or practicing ways to end the conversation.
- **Use scraps of time.** With a few spare minutes, you can complete small tasks or make progress on larger ones. See Fig. 26-9.
- **Group similar tasks.** For example, plan to do errands on the way to and from work or school instead of making a separate trip.
- **Dovetail or multitask when appropriate.** To **dovetail** means to go back and forth between the steps of two or more different tasks, such as washing dishes and making soup. To **multitask** means to do two or more things at the same time, such as folding laundry while listening to a radio talk show. Use both techniques with caution. Trying to do too much at once can be stressful and lead to mistakes. Some tasks, such as driving, require undivided attention or serious accidents can result. Children, too, often need and deserve parents' undivided time and attention. Parents may have to let some tasks wait so they can focus on their children's needs.

Managing Stress

No matter how well parents manage their time, they will still experience the physical and mental tension of stress. A certain amount of stress can be a positive part of life, stimulating people to solve problems and get things done. However, if stress gets out of hand, it can cause physical and emotional problems. For example, too much stress can cause headaches, muscle aches, digestive problems, and sleep disorders. It can cause people to be short-tempered and irritable.

No one can avoid stressful situations completely. The key is to manage stress so it doesn't become overwhelming. Here are some ways to manage stress:

- **Take care of your health.** Eat nutritious foods, exercise regularly, and get plenty of sleep.

- **Stay positive.** Focus on what's good in your life and what you can be thankful for.
- **Put things in perspective.** When days are tough, realize that "this, too, will pass." Don't get upset over things that aren't really important.
- **Relieve tension.** Breathe deeply to calm yourself. Have a good cry—or a good laugh. Look for the humor in frustrating situations.
- **Allow time to relax and have fun.** Leave room in your schedule for some unhurried moments. Make time for activities you enjoy, too—they're essential to your wellbeing.

- **Go easy on yourself.** Avoid comparing yourself to others. Remember that no one is perfect.
- **Get help when needed.** Talk things over with an understanding family member or friend. Trade babysitting time with other parents so everyone can enjoy other interests.

Managing Finances

Money management is another important part of managing life as a parent. Practicing sound money management helps families live within their income and avoid excess debt. It

Health & Safety

Parents and Stress

It's easy for parents to focus so much on caring for their children and other family members that they forget to take care of themselves. Yet if they don't take care of themselves, they won't be able to parent effectively. When parents make time to rest, relax, be with friends, and enjoy themselves, they aren't being selfish. They're caring for their own and their children's wellbeing.

Certain warning signs may indicate that stress is interfering with the ability to parent effectively. These signs may include overreacting to minor irritations, acting impulsively, feeling anger toward the children, frequent mood swings, and using alcohol or drugs to cope with stress. It's wise to seek professional help if these signs are noted.

Fig. 26-10. Reviewing past expenses can help parents analyze their spending habits. **How might they use this information?**

also helps them set aside money to meet future goals and be prepared for emergencies. Parents who manage money well have less stress and feel more in control of their financial future.

Getting Started. A good way for parents to begin managing their finances is by reviewing their current financial picture. How much do they have in their bank accounts and any investments? How much do they owe on home loans, car loans, credit cards, and other debt?

Next, they can review financial records such as pay stubs, checking account registers, utility bills, and credit card receipts. How much income do they receive each week or month? Where does their money go? If they don't have clear financial records, now is the time to start compiling them. Keeping track of income and expenses for a month or two can reveal patterns of spending and saving. See Fig. 26-10.

When reviewing spending, parents should think about the difference between *needs* and *wants*. Needs are things you must have—such as food, housing, and clothes. Wants, on the other hand, are things you would like to have—such as an expensive cut of steak, a bigger house, or clothes with designer labels. Good money managers prioritize their needs and wants to ensure that needs are met before money is spent on wants.

In addition, parents should think about their financial goals, both long-term and short-term. A short-term goal might be purchasing school clothes for the children in three months. Typical long-term goals include saving for education expenses that are years in the future and preparing for retirement.

Using a Budget. A **budget** is simply a plan for saving and spending money. Setting a budget and sticking to it can help parents meet their financial goals. Basic steps in planning a budget include:

- Estimate the amount of income that will be received each month.
- Estimate expenses, using past spending as a guide. Group expenses into categories such as food, housing, utilities, insurance, child care, and entertainment. Treat savings like another expense category—identify a certain amount of each paycheck to put into a savings account.

- Add up the estimates for income and expenses. If the expense total is higher than the income total, identify realistic ways to reduce expenses or increase income.

Once the budget has been planned, the key is to follow through with it. Recording income and expenses as they occur allows parents to compare the actual amounts with the budgeted amounts. If they find they are overspending in some categories, they can look for ways to adjust their spending habits. Small changes can make a big difference. For example, if they spend $20 less each week by taking lunches to work, they can save $1,200 over a year's time. Sticking to a budget takes self-control and determination, but the benefits make the effort worthwhile.

Controlling Debt. In today's society, it's easy to adopt a "buy now, pay later" philosophy. However, when the amount owed on credit cards and other debt mounts up too high, families can face serious financial problems. The best way to avoid these problems is to keep from racking up too much debt in the first place. Here are some tips for controlling debt:

- Use no more than one or two credit cards.
- Don't carry a credit card unless you plan to make a purchase.
- Save up for purchases instead of using a credit card to buy on impulse. Reconsider purchases that aren't necessary.
- If you do overcharge, pay off the debt as quickly as possible instead of letting interest charges mount up.

Using Technology

Technology can help parents manage their household and their multiple roles. For example, cell phones help parents and children stay connected. Some parents store information in an electronic planner that allows them to see their schedules at a glance. Personal computers can be useful for many tasks, such as planning a budget and keeping track of spending, as well as for accessing useful information and resources on the Internet. See Fig. 26-11.

Because technology can be costly and changes so rapidly, each family has to make practical decisions. Evaluate the benefits of an electronic device compared to its cost. As a rule, choose the simplest system to meet the family's needs.

Fig. 26-11. Computers can be useful tools for parents. **How might they be used to enhance parenting skills?**

Fig. 26-12. Employers are finding that a family-oriented approach benefits them as well as their employees. **Why would this be the case?**

Family-Friendly Workplace Policies

Traditionally, workers have tailored their lives around the nine-to-five, five-days-a-week schedule. To help employees balance work and family life, some employers offer alternatives such as:

- **Flextime.** When an employer offers **flextime**, employees can choose their own work hours, within certain limits. For example, a parent might choose to start work at 6:30 in the morning in order to be home at 3:30 in the afternoon when children get home from school.
- **Job sharing.** In a **job sharing** arrangement, two workers share the duties, hours, and pay of one job. They might work alternate days or split the workday into two shifts. Job sharing can make it possible for a parent to work part-time at a company that prefers having full-time employees.
- **Compressed workweek.** An employer might allow an employee to work four ten-hour days instead of five eight-hour days each week. This arrangement can give parents an extra day for family and personal activities.

- **Rotating shifts.** In workplaces that have several shifts, employees may alternate between them, so that all workers have some time with family.
- **Telecommuting.** Some workers are able to **telecommute**. They work from home while staying in touch with a central office using technology such as telephones, computers, and fax machines. This allows a more flexible schedule and saves travel time.

Companies have found such family-friendly policies in greater demand. In addition, many businesses offer employee benefits that support families, including:

- Health insurance plans that cover workers and their families. See Fig. 26-12.
- On-site child care facilities or assistance in paying for outside care.
- Wellness programs for employees' families.
- Personal time to be used as needed, including illness of children.
- Parental leave for special circumstances.

A federal law, the Family and Medical Leave Act, requires certain employers to give workers up to 12 weeks of unpaid leave for the birth or adoption of a child, or for illness in the family. This law has some eligibility restrictions and applies only to companies with 50 or more employees.

Sources of Support

At times, the demands of everyday life may seem overwhelming, but no one has to face challenges alone. Wise parents identify resources to help them cope.

- **Family.** As they try to juggle their many roles, parents can ask for help and support from family members. Talking openly about problems and concerns is a good start. Assess who is doing what, who is doing too much, and who can do more. This can benefit busy parents as well as help children feel more responsible and mature. Extended family members can support one another by providing practical help, such as child care, as well as emotional support.

- **Friends and coworkers.** Having friends available to listen and provide encouragement is especially comforting in tough times. Coworkers can do the same, as well as pitch in on the job as needed. Whether it's helping out during busy times or covering responsibilities while a parent cares for a sick child, coworkers can make life easier for each other. Just be sure to return the favor when the time comes. See Fig. 26-13.

- **Community resources.** Communities offer many resources to families. For example, clinics provide affordable medical care at convenient hours. County mental health departments offer counseling. Cooperative extension services inform on a variety of home management topics. Libraries are brimming with information, including lists of other resources. Another source of help is a support group—a group of individuals with common concerns who offer each other emotional support, practical information, and encouragement. Most support groups meet regularly, but some are available online. By helping families cope with problems, they provide an invaluable service.

Fig. 26-13. Coworkers can be a source of support. Remember, however, that employees should not spend time discussing personal issues during working hours. **What are some appropriate ways for coworkers to support one another?**

▶ House Parent

A house parent offers support and supervision to children living away from home. The setting may be a fairly large campus that includes many small individual homes or simply a large building with different wings. However, no matter what the setting or what the reason they are away from home, children need nurturing. This is a house parent's vocation.

"Being a house parent isn't easy, but I wouldn't trade places with anyone. I've always worked with children, but living with them day in and day out gives us the chance to connect on a different level.

"We have eight 13-year-old girls in our cottage that will be living here for at least two years. They've come to us from families facing crisis situations. Our daily schedule includes meals, chores, classes, homework, physical fitness, individual interests such as sports or music, skill building, and free time.

"Sometimes it's a real challenge to bring together individuals with such different backgrounds, personalities, and needs. There's nothing more satisfying to me than seeing these girls interact well, growing independently and as a group. No, I wouldn't trade places with anyone!"

CAREER TIPS

- Take parenting, child development, and psychology courses.
- Work with children in group settings such as camps and YMCA programs.
- Get training in conflict resolution and anger management.
- Volunteer in a setting that employs house parents.

CHAPTER 26 Review & Activities

CHAPTER SUMMARY

- Role conflicts occur when one role a person has negatively impacts another role.
- To manage different roles, people need to give each one time and attention, without neglecting any role for long periods.
- Setting priorities and maintaining boundaries between different areas of life help parents manage their responsibilities.
- A number of management tools and strategies can simplify tasks and make daily living easier.
- Parents can turn to support systems for help in meeting the demands of life.

Check Your Facts

1. What is an example of a role conflict?
2. What are four situations that can increase role conflicts?
3. Explain the three basic effects of role conflicts.
4. How can you prioritize tasks?
5. Why do people often end up with too much to get done?
6. What problems are linked to overwork?
7. What boundaries should people set?
8. Summarize the management process.
9. Suggest at least five guidelines for getting organized.
10. Describe four time management tips.
11. What are at least five ways to manage stress?
12. What are three basic steps in planning a budget?
13. What could a family save in a year if they reduced weekly expenses by $15 for eating out and $10 for entertainment?
14. Suggest two tips for buying electronic devices.
15. Describe at least three family-friendly work policies.
16. How can flextime benefit families?
17. What is telecommuting?
18. Identify three sources of support that parents have.

Think Critically

1. **Analyzing Behavior.** Why do people often find it difficult to say no when they really don't have time for something?
2. **Making Comparisons.** What is the difference between time for relaxing and wasting time? Cite examples of these in your routine. What changes would you make? Why is this distinction important in parenting?
3. **Drawing Conclusions.** Why do you think many families carry heavy debt loads? How is debt load related to wants and needs?

Apply Your Learning

1. **Prioritized Tasks.** Write your to-do list for the next few days. Then prioritize the tasks. Use the list to get things done, and report on its effectiveness.

2. **What Would You Say?** Write a parent's response to each of the following and discuss in class: **a)** *Boss:* "I want you to work Saturday. I know you worked late a couple nights, but I need you here." **b)** *Child's teacher:* "Can you take a day from work to help chaperone the field trip next week?" **c)** *Neighbor:* "Will you take Ty to ball practice with you on Tuesdays since you have to take your son anyway?" **d)** *Friend:* "You always do such a good job heading committees, could you lead the fundraising committee again?"

3. **Stress Relief.** Learn about relaxation techniques for relieving stress, such as soft music, deep breathing, and simple stretches. Teach some to the class. Then spend ten minutes every day for two weeks on these techniques. Evaluate the effects.

Cross-Curricular Connections

1. **Math.** Create a budget that a young couple with a baby could follow. Evaluate budgets in class.

2. **Social Studies.** What new technologies have had an impact on people's daily activities and schedules? Choose one technology to analyze for a class presentation. How does the technology help families manage? In what ways is it a drawback?

3. **Language Arts.** Turn a chapter idea into a catchy slogan: for example, "With tasks to do, they're more fun with two." Post slogans and discuss what they mean.

Family & Community Connections

1. **Shared Tasks.** Talk with your family about managing household tasks. Who handles various responsibilities in your home? What changes could prevent anyone from feeling overburdened? What could the family do to make some tasks easier or more enjoyable? Try out your ideas for two weeks and then get together to discuss the results and make adjustments.

2. **Workplace Policies.** Find out what an employer in your community offers to help people manage work and other responsibilities. Check on work schedules, benefits, and other policies. Compare information with what other students learn.

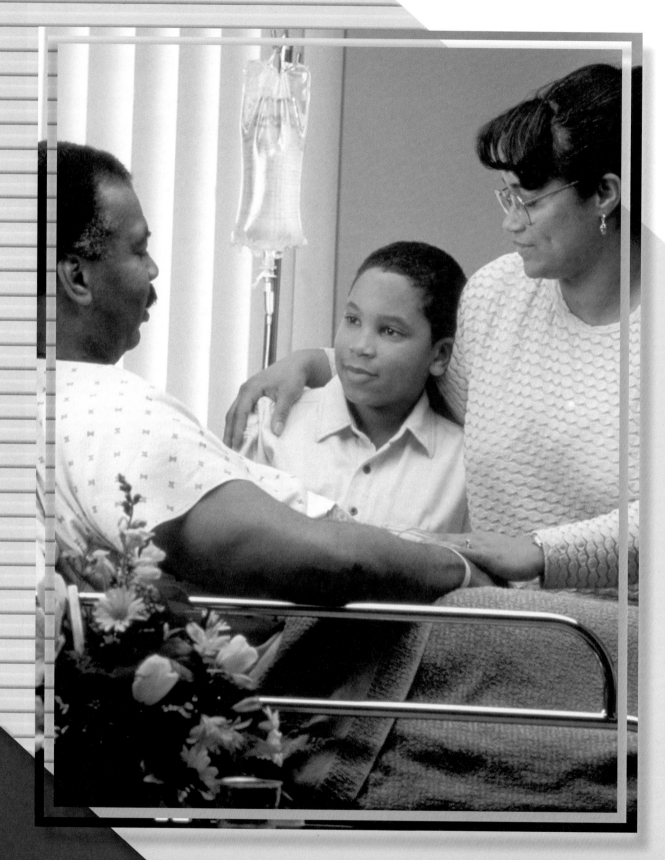

CHAPTER 27

Facing Family Challenges

CHAPTER OBJECTIVES

CHAPTER OBJECTIVES

- Explain the effects of change and crisis on parents and children.
- Describe challenges that families may face.
- Summarize how parents can help children cope with various changes and crises in life.
- Identify resources available to families at challenging times.

PARENTING TERMS

- crisis
- regressive behavior
- custody
- child support
- blended family
- family violence

" Wow! I always thought they were the *perfect* family! Who knew they had problems just like the rest of us?" Every family faces challenges. Money problems, health problems, and relationship problems between parents affect the children too. Emergencies create stress for every member of the family. Parents and children who learn effective coping skills can deal positively with life's challenges and become stronger and more resilient.

Coping with Change and Crisis

Changes happen all the time. Children grow older, parents change jobs, households relocate, and favorite pets die. Every change brings stress, even the changes people choose. In the process of maturing, most people develop coping skills to deal with the stress of predictable life events.

A change becomes a **crisis** when it is so overwhelming that one's usual coping mechanisms are not enough. A crisis causes severe stress. An incident that is a manageable change for one person or family may be a crisis for another, depending on the circumstances and individual coping skills.

Some challenging situations can have both positive and negative aspects. A mother's job promotion helps the family financially but may require her to work longer hours, keeping her away from the family. A new apartment may be bigger than the old one, but it's not in the familiar neighborhood.

Parents can expect that any major change will put stress on themselves, their children, and relationships within the family. They need to be aware that changes they consider positive may make children fearful or unhappy. Parents must recognize that children will pick up on their stress, whether or not they talk openly about the situation. While parents try to deal with a crisis themselves, they should remember that children need an extra dose of tender loving care in times of major change. See Fig. 27-1.

Parental Stress

If you have been on an airplane, you may have heard a flight attendant say that in case of emergency, you should put on your own oxygen mask before helping anyone with you who needs assistance. In the same way, parents must begin coping with a crisis themselves in order to help their children cope.

Fig. 27-1. Children need a parent's presence and attention during times of crisis. **What are some ways parents can "be there" for children during a crisis?**

Fig. 27-2. Changes in behavior can signal parents that a child is under stress. **How can parents reassure a child who shows signs of stress?**

Although many parents are able to rise to a crisis, the related stress can bring a complicated mix of emotions. These can make it harder to think clearly and make sound decisions. It is wise to recognize the emotions and take positive action to address them.

- **Denial.** Wanting to ignore a problem or deny that it exists is a natural reaction, but not a helpful one. It's better to acknowledge the situation and seek possible solutions.
- **Fear and anxiety.** Coping with these feelings is easier if they're out in the open. Discuss concerns and feelings with a trusted friend, family member, member of the clergy, or professional counselor.
- **Guilt, sadness, and depression.** Talk with others who have experienced a similar crisis to learn how they coped. If these feelings persist, get professional help.
- **Anger.** People sometimes take out their feelings of anger about a stressful situation on other people. Counseling can help them recognize the true cause of the anger and find ways to manage it.

Coping Skills. Because crises are very challenging, coping skills must be particularly effective. The management skills you read about in Chapter 5 can help parents deal with changes and crises. Stress management and problem-solving skills are especially important. While stress cannot always be avoided, it can be minimized by facing one issue at a time, trying to keep up some normal routines, talking with trusted friends, eating well, and getting enough sleep and exercise. Solving problems related to the crisis generally becomes less difficult after stress and extreme levels of emotion begin to subside.

Effects on Children

Children are especially vulnerable during a family crisis. They may experience the same mix of emotions as adults. They feel anxious and wonder if life will ever be the same. Some may feel they caused the problem or that it's their responsibility to fix it.

Children can't always tell parents how they feel, but their emotions can have a variety of outward effects. Timid children may become clingy and dependent. Older children and teens may become aggressive. Anxiety can bring on physical complaints, such as stomachaches and headaches. Performance at school may decline. Some children may revert to **regressive behavior**—patterns they had outgrown, such as bedwetting, thumb-sucking, or refusal to sleep alone. See Fig. 27-2.

Other signs of a child's anxiety about a change may include nightmares, difficulty falling asleep, and night terrors, as well as fussiness and uncharacteristic emotional neediness. Depression may be evident in children's loss of interest in activities, such as sports, music, or art, that previously engaged them. See Fig. 27-3.

How Parents Can Help. It's up to parents to find ways to help children cope during challenging times of change. The fact that parents are also under stress makes it all the harder. In a crisis, emotional balance is difficult to achieve, and yet is the most useful response. Calm parents who are willing to accept help are best equipped to help children through a crisis.

To give children emotional support in a family crisis, parents should first acknowledge that the crisis exists. Then, they can follow these practical guidelines:

- Be attentive to worries and fears that children express during play.

- Listen when children share worries and fears. Patiently reassure them that they are safe and can depend on parents for comfort and protection.
- Maintain routines and chore expectations. Normalcy gives children stability.
- Provide consistent, steady support throughout the crisis.
- Ask children what they need. Each child's needs may be different.
- If possible, spend extra time with children to offer guidance and nurture them. Offer additional attention and affection, always in ways children welcome or accept.
- Allow children to express anger and frustration. Do *not* be falsely cheerful: "You're lucky! Things could be worse."
- Display patience when children occasionally misbehave.
- Set clear expectations and limits so that children feel secure.
- Seek professional help for children who are unresponsive to offers of comfort and support.

Fig. 27-3. Loss of interest in activities can be a symptom of depression. **At what point should parents seek professional help for their children?**

Family Communication Under Stress

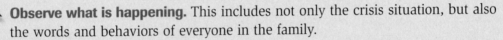

Sometimes a family meeting can help parents and children face a stressful change as a team. To communicate well during a crisis, parents should:

- **Observe what is happening.** This includes not only the crisis situation, but also the words and behaviors of everyone in the family.

- **Ask family members how they feel.** Listen carefully to the responses. Every family member should have an opportunity to feel heard.

- **Answer questions clearly and honestly.** Children deserve the truth, presented in age-appropriate ways.

- **Withhold judgment until all facts are known.** Jumping to conclusions and worrying about things that may not happen can add to the stress unnecessarily.

- **Encourage family members to share opinions and ideas.** It not only helps family members understand each other but also can build a sense of mutual support.

- **Work together as a family.** Cooperate to find solutions.

Time and Attention. One challenge for parents during a stressful change is to remain present for the child. Dealing with a change in practical ways can take hours of a parent's time, and dealing with it emotionally can distract the parent's attention. Some changes, such as a job change or separation, may remove a parent physically for longer periods. Losing part of a parent's time and attention in stressful circumstances cannot always be helped, but it can add to a child's anxiety. Wise parents try to schedule intervals when the child has their full and loving attention.

Effective Communication. When people are stressed, miscommunication can easily occur and make the situation worse. Children need clear, honest information about what is going on. The age-appropriate communication tools you learned in Chapter 21 are all the more important in a crisis. The appropriate level of detail and the best way to present the information will vary with the child's state of development.

- **Infants** can't understand what is going on, but they notice when parents are yelling or tense. They need the security of a parent's calm, loving presence. This is especially true in the case of changes that affect infants directly, such as a new home or new child care arrangements.

- **Toddlers and preschoolers** need brief, straightforward information in simple language that is easy to understand. "Daddy is sick" makes more sense to a young child than a detailed medical description. Toddlers and preschoolers need to feel that whatever is wrong, their parents can handle it. Most of all, they need to know that their parents will be there to comfort and care for them and keep them safe.

- **School-age children and adolescents** may want to know more. Parents can take the cue from the child for how much information to provide. Older children and teens may also be more vocal about their thoughts and feelings. They may want to take a role in helping the family through the crisis. At the same time, they need the opportunity to go on with their lives as much as possible. For example, occasionally getting away with friends gives them a chance to think about something other than what's going on at home.

Getting Outside Help

Sometimes people hesitate to share details of family problems with others. This hesitation can isolate both parents and children, keeping them from getting the support they need.

Ongoing support from relatives, friends, religious groups, or mental health professionals helps parents reassure and support their children. The same support helps children understand what's happening and realize that other people care.

Support is usually just a phone call away. Community service organizations are often listed on the Internet and in the first pages of telephone directories. Phone directories list professional resources under headings such as "Mental Health Services" or "Counselors." Specific assistance is listed by topic, such as "Alcohol Abuse Information and Treatment." Financial assistance is often available for those who cannot afford to pay for professional counseling. See Fig. 27-4.

Fig. 27-4. A professional counselor can help all family members cope with a crisis. **How do families benefit from receiving individual or group counseling?**

Moving

When people move, they often experience a roller coaster of emotions—both sadness over leaving the familiar and excitement about a new environment. Children, in particular, have difficulty leaving the familiar. Because they need security, children may be apprehensive about settling into a new home, making new friends, and attending a new school. Older school-age children and adolescents may grieve the loss of their friends. When the move is initiated by a negative event, such as divorce, death, or job loss, the experience can be even more stressful.

Understanding parents accept and acknowledge children's up-and-down feelings. When parents explain that adjusting to a new place is a gradual process—one that takes time and effort—children feel less immediate pressure to like and accept the changes that come with relocation.

Here are other practical tips parents can use to make moving less stressful for children:

- **Don't announce the move until it's a "sure thing."** Young children have difficulty dealing with uncertainty.
- **If possible, visit the area as a family before the move.** A new school and neighborhood are less mysterious if children can actually see them. If it is not possible to visit, showing the child photographs can be helpful.
- **Involve children in activities in the new neighborhood before the move.** Early, gradual introduction to a new environment helps children feel that not *everything* will be unfamiliar when the move takes place.
- **Invite the child to participate in the moving process.** A young child can pack a small box or suitcase of favorite belongings. Older children can help pack and carry, and can be given a voice in the arrangement or decoration of their rooms. See Fig. 27-5.

Fig. 27-5. Participating in the moving process can help children handle the complicated emotions of a move. **Has your family ever moved? How did you react?**

- **Move at a time that creates the least distress and inconvenience.** Moving during the summer, for example, does not disrupt children's schooling. On the other hand, moving during the school year may allow children to meet others more quickly.
- **Acknowledge the children's feelings and concerns.** Parents can be upbeat and optimistic without denying the elements of grief, loss, and uncertainty involved in the move.
- **Establish routines in the new home as quickly as possible.** Feeling that life is predictable and normal contributes to a child's sense of security.

- **Be positive about a new environment.** Children are often surprised when people in their new neighborhood don't dress or behave exactly like the friends they left behind. Cultural differences may be small or large. Model a spirit of curiosity and adventure in experiencing new food, customs, activities, and friends.

Separation and Divorce

Few life changes are more traumatic—for children or adults—than a parental separation. Some couples use a separation as a breathing time to seek counseling together and try to work out issues between them, in the hope of resuming married life together. If this fails, or if either member of the couple has no hope for saving the marriage, the separation may become formalized with a legal divorce. Children need emotional support at every stage of the process, as the family life they have known ceases to exist and a new pattern of home and relationships begins.

Breaking the News

Separation or divorce is usually very disturbing to the couple's children. To ease children's inevitable fears and concerns about events outside their control, parents can follow these guidelines:

- Tell children, in the presence of all family members, shortly before a parent moves out.
- Reassure children that they did not cause the separation or divorce.
- Answer children's questions honestly and completely. If the parents plan never to get back together, it's best to inform the children rather than leave them with an unrealistic fantasy.
- Be specific about how children's lives will change—residence, school, time with each parent, and so on.
- Assure children that both parents will still love them. Separation or divorce doesn't change either parent's love for a child, even if the parents no longer love each other. See Fig. 27-6.

Fig. 27-6. Children need to know that although some things in their lives will change, they will always be loved by both parents. **What other reassurance do children need?**

Fig. 27-7. Children whose parents are separated or divorced often spend time with each parent on a set schedule. **How can divorced parents ease their children's concerns about such arrangements?**

Custody and Support

Married parents together have physical **custody** of their children—the responsibility for providing a home. After a divorce, custody arrangements differ from one family to the next. In a *shared custody* arrangement, children alternate living with each parent, or parents alternate living in the primary residence with children. Most often, however, children are in a *sole custody* arrangement, in which children live with one parent. In such cases, the other parent usually has *visitation* or *parenting time*—scheduled visits with children. See Fig. 27-7.

Whatever the custody arrangements, both parents are usually legally responsible for meeting the child's material needs. **Child support** consists of regular payments by one parent to the other to help pay the expenses of raising minor children.

Custody, visitation or parenting time, and child support are determined through a legal proceeding, together with a maze of other issues.

For example, who will pay for insurance and college? Who will keep the house? Where will children spend birthdays, holidays, and summer vacations? Divorce laws vary from state to state and can be very complicated. Even when parents agree about the terms of their divorce, it is advisable to engage a lawyer when children are involved. The Internet or the local library can provide information about sources of free legal advice. There are also professional mediators who can help separating couples reach agreement on the best arrangements for themselves and their children.

Helping Children Cope

Children suffer when their parents split up. Parents cannot eliminate their children's pain, but they can ease it. Establishing clear new routines can help restore a sense of security. It's essential that each parent keep commitments and show up for the child when he or she is expected.

Parents should encourage children to maintain ongoing, positive relationships with their non-custodial parents. Parents should also maintain cooperative, civil relationships with their ex-spouses. If there are legal disputes to be settled, they can be handled courteously and in an appropriate time and place.

Divorcing parents should avoid actions that make it even more difficult for children to deal with the divorce. Here are some ways parents can avoid making a child's experience harder than necessary:

- **Never rely on a child for emotional support.** Instead, seek counseling from professionals and encouragement from friends.
- **Do not complain about the other parent to a child.** In most cases, children need to maintain positive relationships with both parents.
- **Do not argue in front of a child.** Children need safety and security, not fear and worry.

- **Never use a child as a messenger.** Talk to the other parent directly or through an attorney. Don't ask the child what happened at the other parent's home.
- **Do not tell a child what to feel.** Parents should *never* label children's feelings as acceptable or unacceptable.

Remarriage and Blended Families

When two adults who have children marry, they form a **blended family** that includes stepparents, stepsiblings, stepgrandparents, and other "step" relatives. A blended family's happiness depends largely on how well the parents support their children's adjustment to this arrangement. See Fig. 27-8.

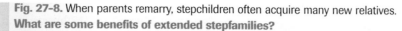

Fig. 27-8. When parents remarry, stepchildren often acquire many new relatives. **What are some benefits of extended stepfamilies?**

Helping Children Adjust

Blended families bring benefits and challenges to the children involved. On the positive side, they have more adults to care for them. Their parents may be happier. They have extra brothers, sisters, and cousins to play with.

On the negative side, children have to share their parent and home with others, who probably do some things differently than the child is used to. A child may no longer be the youngest, the oldest, or the only boy or girl in the family. Children may resent the stepparent for ending their dream that their original parents would get back together. It's not unusual for new stepchildren to be less well-behaved than usual. Successful adjustment takes time, and parents need patience.

Even after the blended family has been together for some time, conflicts can happen despite everyone's best efforts. "You're not my *dad*; you're just my *stepdad*." "Why do I have to get along with *her*? She's my sister only because *you* married her mom." At times like this, parents can help everyone step back and cool off. Sometimes leaving a situation until emotions settle helps everyone behave and think more rationally.

When the family reconvenes, parents can encourage conflicting family members to state views without attacking or blaming others, and to listen to the other's point of view without interruption. Together, the blended family can brainstorm solutions that will satisfy all concerned. Finally, parents can encourage disagreeing family members to share a kind word, a pat, or a hug to show that the conflict has been resolved.

Parent, Stepparent, and Child. If children are older when a parent remarries, they may never relate to their stepparent as they do to the parents they have always known. The children and stepparent don't have the same background of shared experiences. Having some time alone with their original parent, as well as with their stepparent, can be helpful. Parents must balance their special relationship to the children they've had since infancy with a commitment not to show favoritism.

Children may try to challenge the authority of a stepparent. Parents should remain firm in insisting that *both* parents have equal authority in the blended family, and should unite in enforcing the same rules for all children in the family.

Stepsiblings. Sibling rivalry occurs in most families with more than one child, and blended families are no exception. Outings and games that involve the whole family can help. While parents cannot force stepsiblings to be friends, they can insist that the children treat each other with respect. See Fig. 27-9.

Nurturing the New Marriage

Like every change, creating a blended family is a source of stress for the couple who decided to marry. Different parenting styles and expectations can be an added source of tension. The couple should resolve their issues in private and present a united front for the children and stepchildren.

Nurturing their marital relationship is of primary importance for the children as well as themselves. If the new marriage were to dissolve, the children would face yet another crisis. A solid marriage helps give children stability, consistency, and a sense of security.

Fig. 27-10. Parents must be careful not to let problems with finances prevent them from giving their children needed attention. **Why do a family's financial issues affect children as well as their parents?**

Financial Problems

Most couples admit that financial problems are a significant stressor on a marriage. Accumulated debt, unexpected bills, family illness, or job change or loss can cause adults emotional and relationship problems. Financial strain may preoccupy parents to the point that they're unaware that children are worried or upset about the situation. See Fig. 27-10.

While many parents feel that children should not be involved in family financial matters, the fact remains that children are affected by what's happening. Children need to be included, in age-appropriate ways, so they recognize that the family handles crises together and depends on each member for help and support. Here are some tips for parents to help the family cope with financial problems:

- Describe the situation in understandable terms.
- Focus on the family's strengths, such as humor or patience.
- Involve children in brainstorming ways to cut expenses or raise extra income. Treat it as a fun challenge.
- Look for free or inexpensive activities that the family can enjoy together.
- Show appreciation for each family member's contributions.
- Give progress updates at family meetings.

Unemployment

When financial problems arise because a parent loses a job, the stress is compounded. Regardless of the reason the job ended, the unemployed parent may feel a loss of confidence and self-respect. The common social question "What do you do?" can be a source of embarrassment. Health insurance may become an issue for the family if it was provided by the employer.

Modeling CHARACTER

Persevering During Unemployment

Finding a new job may take longer than expected or hoped. The unemployed parent has an opportunity to model *perseverance*—the ability to keep going when things are tough. Instead of giving up in despair, the parent can take positive steps toward a long-term goal. By watching and hearing their unemployed parent talk about looking for a job, children learn to persist in a difficult challenge. They learn by example to:

- Set small, achievable goals as steps toward the larger goal.
- Expect setbacks and bounce back from them.
- Maintain a positive outlook and trust in the final outcome.
- Keep working toward the goal until it is achieved.

Think About It

Describe a situation you have experienced or observed that required perseverance. How did the person keep from getting discouraged? How could that trait be passed on to children?

Looking for work can be a long, frustrating process. In addition to tracking down job leads, the unemployed parent might benefit from taking job training courses or doing volunteer work.

As with other family crises, parents should explain the situation to children calmly and assure them the family will get through this together. Meanwhile, the family can enjoy whatever extra time the situation gives the children and their unemployed parent to be together.

Substance Abuse

Drug and alcohol abuse occur in all kinds of families, regardless of income or family structure. Abuse of illegal or legal drugs or alcohol affects mood and behavior. Over time, a drinker or drug user can develop a mental or physical dependence, making it extremely difficult to stop. Sadly, substance abuse can negatively affect almost every aspect of family life.

When a Parent Abuses Drugs or Alcohol

Parents who abuse alcohol or drugs are often unable to provide for their children's needs. They may lose jobs, become moody and irritable, and create distress in the home. Some children in this situation avoid contact with parents. Some try to assume the role of caregiver to the addicted parent or to other family members.

What can family members do in this situation? First, they should realize what *not* to do. It's best to avoid confronting anyone who is under the influence of drugs or alcohol—calm, rational discussion is not possible. Nagging is not effective. Nor is it useful to make excuses or cover up for the person. He or she needs to experience the consequences of the drug or alcohol problem.

What family members *can* do is take care of themselves and seek help for the addicted person. Support groups and programs for addicts and their families, and treatment programs for addicts, are available in most communities. Searching the phone directory or Internet for "addiction," "alcoholism," or "substance abuse" often yields the names of community resources.

In homes where anyone abuses drugs or alcohol, it's common for families to deny the problem. Talking openly with children about it is healthier. "Mommy acts that way because she is sick" is more comforting to a small child than pretending Mommy's erratic behavior is normal. Older children can learn about addiction. It helps if they can also talk to a trusted adult outside the family or join a support group specifically for children or teens. They need to understand that they did not cause the behavior, they can't control or cure it, and they do not have to take care of the whole family because of it.

THE DEVELOPING BRAIN

Physicians at the Pittsburgh Adolescent Alcohol Research Center used magnetic resonance imaging (MRI) to measure the interior of teens' brains. They compared the brains of teens who were heavy drinkers to those of nondrinkers. The images showed that teens who drank heavily experienced brain shrinkage in the hippocampus, the area responsible for memory and learning.

When Children Use Drugs or Alcohol

Experts say that parents who suspect their children are using alcohol or drugs are usually correct in their assumption. Signs of substance abuse include:

- Uncharacteristic behavior, such as extreme aggression or withdrawal.
- Decline in physical appearance, including unwashed body or clothing.
- Decline in school or recreational performance and involvement.

Because a child's physical and emotional health depends on parents' quick response, parents should never deny, ignore, or minimize warning signs. People who abuse substances as children or teens are more likely to continue to do so into adulthood. In addition, alcohol and drugs can damage the brain, increase depression, and lead to problems with authority figures. Alcohol and drug use is associated with sexual activity and increased suicide risk.

Parents who suspect substance abuse can follow these steps:

- **Investigate.** Gather information to confirm or rule out suspicions. Invading a child's or teen's privacy during this process is justifiable because substance abuse is life-threatening.

- **Choose a good time to talk.** Parents should never discuss the problem when the child is under the influence of a substance.
- **Get help.** A visit to the family physician may be the way to start. He or she can make referrals to other resources. See Fig. 27-11.

Violence in the Home

Family violence, sometimes called *domestic violence*, occurs when a family member uses violent, threatening behaviors to intimidate or control one or more members of the family. Child abuse, discussed in Chapter 2, is a form of family violence.

Family violence can affect all types of people and families. Often, but not always, it is associated with drug or alcohol abuse. The National Institute of Justice and the Centers for Disease Control have estimated that more than a million women and hundreds of thousands of men are the victims of family violence in the United States each year. Most children who are victims of family violence have a mother or father who is also a victim.

Preventing Family Violence

Nonviolent parents create a safe family atmosphere. People who have been taught conflict resolution skills, such as the ones discussed in Chapters 5 and 19, are less likely to become violent. They know that even conflicts involving intense emotions can be settled peacefully.

Family violence can result from inability to cope with stress. Anger and frustration are common responses to stress, making people feel frightened and out of control. To restore and maintain self-control, many people recognize and avoid *personal flashpoints*, situations that are likely to produce negative feelings. They watch themselves for danger signs, such as physical tension and rapid breathing. It's sometimes

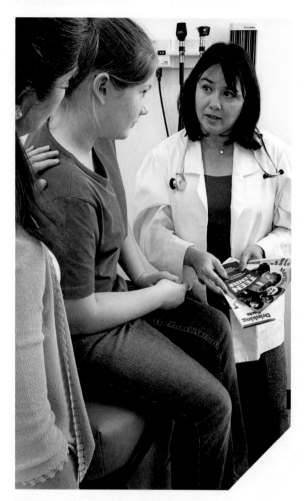

Fig. 27-11. Children with drug and alcohol problems need prompt medical attention. **How might a medical doctor determine whether a person uses drugs or alcohol?**

necessary to walk away from an argument or upsetting situation to regain perspective and self-control.

A parent with difficulty controlling his or her own violent impulses should acknowledge the problem and seek professional help. For the other parent, the first obligation is to protect herself or himself and the children. This means admitting there is a problem and getting help.

Child & Family Services
CAREERS

▶ Family Intervention Specialist

Situations such as family violence, alcohol or drug abuse, mental illness, or trouble with the law can throw a whole family into turmoil. Any of these situations gives rise to a bewildering complex of needs for various family members. A family intervention specialist can help them put the pieces of their lives back together.

Family intervention specialists work in government agencies, schools, hospitals, not-for-profit organizations, or private practices. In addition to providing direct services, such as treatment, counseling, and skills training, family intervention specialists help identify other family needs and make appropriate referrals. They prepare recommendations for medical and psychological treatment, such as hospitalization and short- or long-term therapy. When necessary, they can help family members find alternative living arrangements. Many family intervention specialists are also certified substance abuse counselors.

"I have been a family intervention specialist for seven years with a county agency. In my job, I work with the Department of Juvenile Services to help youth who have recently left the juvenile detention center make a successful transition back home. I love my job because I know I'm making a difference. Whenever one of 'my kids' makes different choices and stays out of the criminal justice system, I know that my years of education, experience, and hard work have been worth it."

CAREER TIPS

- Volunteer at a family shelter.
- Obtain a bachelor's and preferably a master's degree in social services or a related field.
- Get clinical experience in the areas of chemical dependency, family dynamics, family intervention, and child psychology.

Family Violence: Warning Signs

How can an adult determine whether a marriage partner has learned to manage anger and resolve conflict? There are many clues that indicate a person's tendency toward violence:

- Emotionally abusive behavior, such as name-calling or put-downs.
- Quick-tempered responses to small annoyances.
- "In your face," aggressive techniques for handling conflict.

- Threats of violence, even those supposedly made in jest.
- Cruel treatment of family pets or other animals.
- Physically painful treatment, such as pinches, shoves, or grabs, of *anyone* for *any reason*.
- Fascination with lethal weapons, such as guns and knives.

Escaping Violent Relationships

In violent homes, patterns of verbal abuse and insults may translate into physical assaults. If violent behavior goes unchallenged, the attacker often escalates the brutality of the attack.

Violence should *never* be tolerated. In an immediate crisis, an abused person should go somewhere safe, phone 911 or other police emergency number, and remain on the phone with the dispatcher until help arrives. Law enforcement officers can make an immediate arrest if it is clear that an assault has occurred. They can also provide information about family shelters and offer transportation. The reports they file are useful if family members seek court protection from an abusive family member.

Violence Outside the Home

Violence can strike almost anywhere. Parents need to take practical precautions to keep their family safe, while helping children to feel secure rather than fearful most of the time. Striking the balance is not always easy.

School Violence

Although schools are usually safe places, school violence is a reality that many children face. Threats and physical attacks at school can range from bullying to use of knives and guns.

Many schools offer programs to teach students nonviolent ways to handle their anger and settle conflicts. What can parents do to help? They can talk to their children about school rules and personal safety. They can teach them to report threats or weapons to a school official, parent, or the police. Parents can also stay alert for warning signs of problems, become actively involved in their children's schools, and support or start youth programs in their communities.

Gang Violence

Violence is also a common feature of *gangs,* groups of juvenile criminals. Why do gangs appeal to some youth? Some adolescents feel that gangs give them power and respect. Others receive care and attention from gang members that they lack at home. Still others are drawn to the income they receive from committing gang crimes, such as burglary, theft, and drug-dealing.

Today, even quiet neighborhoods may reflect gang activity. Graffiti and other vandalism can detract from the appearance of stores and homes. See Fig. 27-12. Property owners may have to install security systems to prevent burglaries. Parents may need to be especially careful to supervise children so that they don't become the victims of crossfire in gang-related shootings. The fear of very real threats to personal safety can be stressful for children and adults alike.

Parents who educate their children about gangs and the dangers they pose dramatically reduce the likelihood that their children will suffer personal injury. Gang education can be a lifesaver. Some basic guidelines for parents to follow include:

- **Find out about gang activity in your neighborhood.** Schools and law enforcement officials are good sources of information.
- **Identify signs of gang membership.** Learn the manner of dress and favorite haunts of gang members. Caution children against wearing gang-related clothing or visiting known locations where gang members "hang out."

Fig. 27-12. Whether graffiti is the handiwork of violent street gangs or thrill-seeking "taggers," it causes millions of dollars of property damage each year. It also attracts crime and makes people feel unsafe.

Fig. 27-13. When a family's home is destroyed, the loss is much more than a financial one. **What emotional effects might family members feel? Where could they turn for help?**

- **Observe safety practices.** Do not leave young children alone outside the house. Teach older children safe behaviors to practice when they're away from home. Set and enforce curfews for children and teens.
- **Talk with children about concerns, and observe any anxious behaviors.** Encourage children to report any threats made to their safety or any criminal activity they observe. Respond to fears and anxieties that children display about gang activity.

Disasters

No one can predict when a family may be affected by a disaster. Fires, floods, tornadoes, hurricanes, and many other disasters can strike suddenly, affecting one family or thousands. Sometimes those affected suffer only a temporary loss of basic services such as electricity. In more severe cases, families can lose their home, their possessions, and their income. The emotional and physical effects can be overwhelming. See Fig. 27-13.

While the family works to recover from physical effects of the disaster, wise parents also watch their children for symptoms of stress, such as those listed on pages 561-562. As in other crises, it is helpful to talk with children, listen to their feelings, and convey a secure sense that the family will get through the situation together.

Serious Health Concerns

Serious illness or injury can drain a family's emotional and financial resources. Health problems may occur suddenly, giving families little time to plan coping strategies.

Parents should explain the health problem to children in simple terms. Children can benefit from being involved in some way, such as visiting the hospital room or drawing a picture to send to the ill or injured person. A child with a brother or sister in the hospital might take a tour of the pediatric ward. Making the situation seem less mysterious helps in coping with fear.

During a family member's health crisis, all children in the family continue to need attention and care. Parents and adult relatives may need to take turns spending time with the ill or injured person so that someone is always available for other family members. Families can turn to community resources, such as religious organizations, social services, and visiting nurses, for ongoing support during prolonged illness or disabling conditions.

Death

The death of a loved one can be devastating. The first response may be numbness, shock, or denial, especially if the death was unexpected. Grieving can be a roller coaster of emotions, with episodes of anger, guilt, and depression. Mourners may wonder whether the death could have been prevented. Eventually most reach a stage of acceptance. Although they never forget their loved ones, over time the pain of loss lessens and they are able to go on with their lives.

Grief is a normal response to the loss of a loved one. Adults and children need permission to grieve in their own way, at their own pace. They also need permission to laugh and enjoy moments of everyday life without having to look constantly sorrowful. Grieving adults and children can draw support from family members, friends, religious leaders, mental health professionals, and local grief-support groups.

How Children View Death

Death often confuses children. Many don't understand its permanence or reason: "Why can't he come back? Why couldn't doctors fix him?" They might feel insecure or unhappy about the changes death causes within the family. Some invent games about dying or pretend that the death never happened. Older children and adolescents are more likely to think death is unfair and respond with angry outbursts or withdrawal from the family.

When explaining death to a child, parents must be honest. Children should not be allowed to think that their loved one is simply sleeping or will return to them soon. Parents can discuss their religious beliefs with children and comfort them with positive memories of the person they loved.

Coping with children's reactions is a challenge for parents who are also grieving. However, adults who patiently answer questions in terms children can understand, who show extra affection, and who accept occasional emotional outbursts help children move toward acceptance. See Fig. 27-14.

Fig. 27-14. Children need to be allowed to express their grief. **What role can extended family members have in helping children when a loved one dies?**

How Parents Can Help Children Cope with Grief	
Age Group	**Suggestions**
Toddlers and Preschoolers	❑ Maintain regular family routines. ❑ Give extra comfort and assurance. ❑ Avoid unnecessary separations. ❑ Encourage emotional expression through play and interaction.
School-Age Children	❑ Provide structure, reasonable chores, and activities. ❑ Patiently listen and respond to questions and concerns. ❑ Encourage expression of thoughts and feelings. ❑ Gently but firmly limit negative behavior.
Adolescents	❑ Be available if teens wish to share thoughts and feelings. ❑ Urge teens who are reluctant to "open up" to share their feelings with close, stable friends. ❑ Encourage teens to resume physical, recreational, and social activities.

Fig. 27-15. Most families experience the death of a loved one at some time while children are growing up. **Why do children of different ages need different kinds of support from parents?**

Coping with Suicide

While grief is expected at the death of a loved one, additional feelings, such as anger, guilt, and shame, often accompany self-inflicted death. Many people who lose loved ones to suicide can benefit from professional counseling as they struggle to understand and explain their loved one's action.

Parents who must explain a suicide to children should keep explanations simple. Children need to know that they are not to blame—nor should they be encouraged to glamorize the person who took his or her life. In many cases, the person who commits suicide is the victim of serious mental illness, such as depression.

Helping Children Grieve

In most cultures, funerals give family and friends an opportunity to honor a loved one as well as a chance to accept the finality of death.

Many parents wish to spare children the sadness and grief of funerals. However, children then are unable to honor their loved one and say goodbye. Children should be allowed to decide whether they will attend, though experts generally recommend that they do. If children wish to attend, their parents should prepare them by explaining the purpose of the funeral, how long it will last, and what they will see and do.

It is normal for grieving children to show symptoms of stress. Fig. 27-15 suggests practical, developmentally appropriate ways parents can help children who are grieving.

You may notice that these suggestions are similar to those for helping children cope with other sources of stress. Whenever change overwhelms a family, children of all ages need comfort, structure, someone who will listen, and assurance that the parents and family have the strength to pull through the crisis together.

CHAPTER SUMMARY

- One important task of parenting is to help children cope with any stressful family situations that occur.
- When parents use careful communication suited to a child's age, they help children handle crises at their level of understanding.
- Moving isn't typically considered a crisis, but it can still cause stress in children.
- For each crisis that a family faces, parents need to learn and use techniques that make the events manageable for children.
- Parents need not handle situations alone because of the many resources available.

Check Your Facts

1. How should parents handle their own stress-related emotions of denial and guilt?
2. Identify at least three symptoms of a child's stress.
3. What are at least six guidelines for helping children cope with a crisis?
4. Explain at least five ways to help children handle a move.
5. How should a parent tell a child about a divorce that's about to occur?
6. Define custody and child support.
7. In a divorce, what are five "don'ts"?
8. Why should stepparents have equal authority in the family?
9. Identify six ways to help children cope with family financial problems.
10. What should family members do when a parent abuses drugs?
11. What are signs of substance abuse in children and adolescents?
12. How should parents respond to a child's possible substance abuse?
13. How can a parent restore or maintain self-control at stressful times?
14. What is an appropriate immediate response to family violence?
15. What can parents do about gang violence?
16. How do children view death?
17. How can parents help children of different ages cope with death?

Think Critically

1. **Identifying Options.** What can a family do to assimilate well when moving into a different cultural environment?
2. **Recognizing Values.** How can a parent teach a child not to abuse drugs?
3. **Identifying Cause and Effect.** Why does family violence often result from drug and alcohol abuse?
4. **Drawing Conclusions.** What qualities do you think parents need to handle the different challenges in the chapter? Why?

Apply Your Learning

1. **Topics in the News.** Bring in a newspaper article that relates to a topic in the chapter. Summarize the article for a few students. Then work with the group to analyze the situation and evaluate any actions taken by people in the article.

2. **Parental Letter.** Write a letter from a parent to an adolescent who is using drugs. Include your feelings and what you plan to do. Exchange letters with a classmate and write an analysis of the "parent's" handling of the situation.

3. **Communication.** Write the parent's words to a child in these situations: **a)** to an eight-year-old whose other parent is seriously ill; **b)** to a nine-year-old before a divorce; **c)** to a ten-year-old after the parent's job loss.

4. **Response Posters.** Work with a partner to create a poster that illustrates how parents should respond to one situation in the chapter. Present your poster to the class. As other posters are explained, help analyze the ideas and expand on them.

Cross-Curricular Connections

1. **Math.** Find statistics on one of these topics: **a)** divorce; **b)** substance abuse; **c)** family violence; **d)** gangs; **e)** suicide. Summarize what you learned for the class. Discuss what these numbers indicate.

2. **Language Arts.** Learn about one community resource for families facing crisis situations. Write and record a 30-second public service announcement (PSA) that highlights this resource. Ask to run the class PSAs on your school's public address system.

Family & Community Connections

1. **Good Neighbors.** Often neighbors today don't even know each other. Are there any new people in your neighborhood? Talk with your family about what you could do to welcome them and get to know them better. Take action on at least one of your ideas.

2. **Gangs.** Gangs are a problem in many schools and communities. What is being done to prevent gangs and support people affected by gangs in your community and at the state and national levels? Learn about resources and share information with the class. How can parents help children who live close to gang influences?

CHAPTER 28

Child Care and Education Options

CHAPTER OBJECTIVES

- Distinguish between the goals of child care and early childhood education.
- Explain quality and cost considerations when choosing care and education programs for children.
- Describe various options in child care and education programs for children.
- Demonstrate awareness of child care laws and licensing requirements.
- Evaluate a child care or education program.
- Summarize ways for parents to be involved in the program their child attends.

PARENTING TERMS

- learning centers
- licensed
- accredited
- credentials
- play group
- babysitting cooperative
- nanny
- au pair
- family child care
- child care center
- sliding scale
- parent cooperative
- self-care children
- magnet schools
- charter schools

Parents seek child care and education options for many reasons. Working parents need child care during work hours. Young children benefit from opportunities to learn in a group setting, and older children need a quality education. With the wide range of choices available, it's important for parents to plan carefully. By looking closely at all the options, parents are more likely to make a decision that will work best for their family.

Needs for Care and Education

Sooner or later, parents face decisions about getting help to care for children. Both parents may work full time, making child care necessary. Sometimes one parent works while the other parent is in school. Many single parents work because they have no other choice. After a child starts school, working parents may still need to make arrangements for child care after school and on holidays.

Education and social development are additional reasons many parents enroll their children in programs away from home. A stay-at-home parent may feel that the child would benefit from a social setting with other children. Parents may hope a program that teaches young children to listen, take turns, and recognize letters and numbers will prepare their child for kindergarten. Special programs outside the regular school day can enrich an older child's education.

Distinguishing Care from Education

Child care for infants usually focuses on satisfying their physical and emotional needs. Feeding, diapering, cuddling, and napping fill most of the time. As children grow and develop, their needs change. The typical child care provider offers a variety of toys, games, and activities to satisfy these changing needs. When those toys, games, and activities are oriented toward helping the child learn, the program is offering early childhood education.

Child care arrangements and educational programs, while similar in many ways, have different emphases. Child care tends to a child's physical, emotional, and social needs while also offering occasional learning activities. Early childhood education programs mainly focus on a child's intellectual growth while also addressing other needs. Parents choose the emphasis that fits their needs and those of their child. See Fig. 28-1.

Fig. 28-1. Although child care and educational programs have many similarities, their primary goals differ. **Why might it be difficult to distinguish between child care and education?**

Weighing the Choices

When it comes to child care and educational programs for children, parents have many options. Parents need to look closely at themselves, their child, and their situation. The right choice depends on a number of factors, including:

- The child's age, developmental stage, personality, and individual needs.
- The parents' needs, wants, goals, and values.
- Location, convenience, and transportation available.
- Days and hours the program or service is offered.
- Quality and cost.

Investigating Options

Whom can parents trust to take care of their child? Unless they know the caregivers or teachers personally, making the choice isn't easy. This simple step-by-step approach can help parents narrow down their options:

1. **Research.** What experiences have friends and neighbors had with various caregivers or programs? Some communities have a child care referral center that can inform parents about available options. Information about some larger programs may be available on the Internet.
2. **Phone.** Call likely candidates and request information, such as a brochure. Ask a few questions based on the information in this chapter and additional issues of concern. Request references and talk to other parents who have used the facility or caregiver. If any answers are not satisfactory, parents should look for another program.

Fig. 28-2. Parents can learn a lot about a program by visiting and observing it. **What can parents learn in person that they could not find out over the phone?**

3. **Observe.** Quality may be hard to describe, but often "you know it when you see it." Visit a variety of programs, observe carefully, and keep notes. Watch caregivers interact with children. As parents compare and contrast, they will get a clearer sense of what does or doesn't match their values and priorities. See Fig. 28-2.

Evaluating Quality

When researching and comparing options for child care and education, parents need to look for signs that suggest, "This is a quality person or program." Here are some factors to consider.

Philosophy and Goals. Every good program or caregiver is guided by a philosophy and goals. One program may emphasize individual creativity, while another may highlight multicultural awareness. Talking with program directors or individual caregivers can help you identify what they think is important. Observe to evaluate whether their actions match their words.

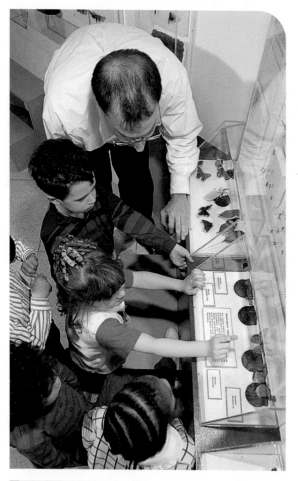

Fig. 28-3. Field trips are an important part of many programs. **How can a child benefit from field trips?**

Routines and Activities. Children find comfort in predictable schedules, with regular times for meals, rest, learning, and play. They learn routines more easily when caregivers provide cues, such as singing a certain song when it's cleanup time. Activities should be well planned, age appropriate, and well supervised by leaders who are relaxed but in control. Group activities need to be balanced with small group fun and solitary play or learning. Caregivers and teachers should patiently guide children while letting them have fun. Field trips can be beneficial when they are well supervised and have a clear purpose. See Fig. 28-3.

Space and Equipment. For group care away from home, the space should be clean, well lit, and visually appealing to children. It should be well organized, with clearly defined areas—often called **learning centers**—for different sorts of activity. Settings with several children need plenty of carefully chosen toys and equipment to avoid conflicts over sharing. Large equipment should be well spaced, giving children enough room to swing and slide without hurting themselves or others. Toys and equipment should follow safety guidelines such as those explained in Chapter 16.

Qualifications. The appropriate qualifications depend on the type of care or program as well as on state requirements. In many states, certain programs must be **licensed**, which means they have written permission from a state agency to operate. Some facilities are also **accredited**, which means they are recognized by a specific organization as meeting high standards of quality. Parents may want caregivers to have a certain level of experience or training, as shown by their **credentials**—evidence, such as degrees or certification, that a person is qualified to perform a specific service.

▶ Child Care Referral Specialist

Child care referral specialists help parents find appropriate child care. They usually begin with an interview, either over the phone or in person, asking the ages of the children, required hours, preferred location, and any special requirements. They discuss different child care options and help parents pinpoint what type of care they prefer.

Specialists also counsel parents on how to evaluate quality child care and why it's important to do so. They determine whether the family is eligible for any assistance with child care expenses. If so, they help them fill out the necessary paperwork. They advise parents on other financial help, such as taking advantage of tax credits.

After gathering information, the specialist searches a database to find licensed providers that match the parents' specific needs and preferences. The specialist then gives the parents contact information for three to five child care providers. Child care referral specialists refer; they do not recommend. In the end, it is up to the parents to choose the option they feel is best.

"Many parents don't even know how or where to begin to look for quality care. They just know they want the best for their child. I can take the guesswork out of the process. When I help them locate child care that meets their needs, I really feel I've done something to make life a little easier for them. That's a good feeling!"

CAREER TIPS

- Take classes in child development, family living, and communication.
- Build computer skills, including word processing, data entry, and database management.
- Volunteer, observe, or work at a child care facility.
- Volunteer or intern at a community child care referral agency.

Managing Costs

When choosing a program, most parents have to consider cost. Fees for full-day child care or early childhood education for a preschooler can range from $4,000 to well over $10,000 a year. Costs of less formal or more personalized arrangements vary widely. By researching and comparing fees, parents can determine which options offer good quality at a cost they can afford. See Fig. 28-4.

Low-income families often have a hard time finding good, affordable child care. Fortunately, they—and families whose children have special needs—may qualify for free or low-cost programs. Families should not rule out a more expensive program they like without first checking to see if financial assistance is available. Some families may be able to adjust priorities in their household budget to allow for a higher-priced program.

Working parents can find out whether their employer offers the option of a *dependent-care flexible spending account*. In this arrangement, money from each paycheck is automatically set aside to be used for child care expenses. The advantage is that money placed in the flexible spending account is not subject to income tax, so it goes further. Parents need to anticipate their annual child care needs closely for these accounts to be cost effective. Money not used by the end of the year is usually not refundable.

Providing for Special Needs

As discussed in Chapter 25, some children have special care or education needs because of physical, emotional, or learning disabilities. Early intervention is especially important for these children. The sooner their special needs are identified and met, the better these children's chances to achieve their full potential. State programs help identify appropriate services and may pay or contribute toward the cost.

Some child care and education programs mix children with and without special needs, in a practice called *inclusion*. Other programs are designed primarily for children with special needs. A parent's choice depends on factors such as the type and severity of their child's disability.

Fig. 28-4. Cost is an important factor in child care decisions. **How can parents determine what they can afford to pay?**

Fig. 28-5. Play groups are popular with stay-at-home parents who want their children to have opportunities for social development. **What might be a disadvantage of play groups?**

Care Arrangements for Young Children

How do parents who are looking for child care choose between in-home care and out-of-home care, or between a school-sponsored center and one run by parents? By looking at each option carefully and considering advantages and disadvantages, parents can choose the best option for their child.

In-Home Care

In-home care is usually the least structured and the most like being home with a parent. Many parents make an informal arrangement with a relative or friend. Grandparents are now the leading providers of child care for pre-schoolers. More than a third take care of their grandchildren at least ten hours a week or keep them overnight without their parents.

Informal arrangements can be convenient, flexible, and low-cost. They can also have drawbacks. For example, a parent may feel uneasy about what the caregiver does nor does not provide—such as too much television and not enough reading—yet feel awkward about raising the issue. The caregiver, too may have misgivings, as when providing child care turns out to be more demanding than expected. To reduce the risk of problems and misunderstandings, the two parties may want to agree in writing on basic issues such as meals, discipline, and activities.

Play Groups. Sometimes friends or neighbors set up an informal **play group** that meets for a few hours a week. Parents take turns watching the children on assigned days. This way all parents get some time to themselves, knowing their child has playmates and supervision. Parents who work full time during the week may be able to find a play group that meets on weekends. See Fig. 28-5.

Babysitting Cooperatives. In a similar but more formal arrangement, parents willing to share child care responsibilities may form a **babysitting cooperative**. When a member of the cooperative needs child care, he or she calls one of the other members on the list. Instead of exchanging money, members "earn" and "spend" hours of child care. Time spent caring for other members' children is credited to the family's account, and time a family's child was in the care of another member is subtracted. Advantages of this arrangement include cost savings and the opportunity for members' children to play together. A downside is that it can be very time-consuming for participants, and there is no guarantee that another parent will always be available to care for the child.

Nannies and Au Pairs. A **nanny** is someone unrelated to the family who takes care of a child or children in the parents' home. Many nannies also do light housekeeping. Often trained professionals, nannies may receive room and board in addition to their salary.

An **au pair** (oh PARE) is a young person from another country who lives with a family and cares for the children. Au pairs also receive room and board plus a small salary.

Families consult with nannies and au pairs to set a schedule tailored to the family's work schedule. Of course, feeding and housing another person plus paying wages can be expensive. Family members also may have trouble adjusting to a new person in their home.

Parents must carefully interview any potential live-in caregivers and check their references and qualifications. An au pair must have working papers and other documentation. All parties should sign a contract specifying duties as well as any benefits, such as insurance and vacation.

Family Child Care Homes

Family child care is an arrangement in which an individual uses his or her own home as a place to provide care for other people's children. The children enjoy personal attention in small groups. As with any child care, quality varies. Some family child care providers have worked in child care centers and plan worthwhile activities for children. Others have less to offer. Parents should visit the home and evaluate the care provided. See Fig. 28-6.

Fig. 28-6. Some people adapt their homes to care for a small number of children. **How can you tell whether the caregivers are skillful and reliable?**

Fig. 28-7. Parents may find a variety of child care centers in different places in their community. **What is one advantage of a child care center compared to other forms of child care?**

Each state sets its own regulations for a family child care home to receive a license. Unlicensed caregivers may violate these laws. Before selecting a family child care home, find out what licensing the home and provider have received.

Most states specify a maximum number of children allowed in family child care at a time, usually five to seven. In addition, most states limit the number of children under age two. Laws and regulations may also set requirements for:

- Criminal background checks.
- CPR training.
- Safety equipment, such as fire extinguishers.
- Written discipline policies.
- Attendance and immunization records.
- Emergency records.
- Healthful foods.
- Age-appropriate toys and games.

Child Care Centers

Many parents choose to entrust their child's care to a **child care center**. With the help of a trained staff, these facilities provide supervised group care and socializing experiences. Large centers often separate children by age, which helps to create an appropriate environment for each age group. Typically the staff provides planned learning activities.

Because of their larger size, child care centers offer some advantages over in-home care. Many parents like their convenient hours and reliability. A center may provide third-shift hours, for example, and it may still be able to operate when employees call in sick. See Fig. 28-7.

Parents should also weigh the drawbacks of center-based care. A shy child may feel lost in group care. Contact with so many children increases the chance of illness. Good programs can be expensive and have long waiting lists.

When visiting and evaluating a child care center, parents should ask about any concerns specific to their situation. In addition, it is helpful to carry and use a checklist similar to the one shown in Fig. 28-8.

Licensing and Accreditation. Child care centers are licensed by the state when they meet minimum standards for health, safety, and staff. The state human services or public health department can give parents information about these minimum standards, which are generally quite detailed.

Many parents want the center they choose to exceed the minimum standards. Accreditation by the National Association for the Education of Young Children (NAEYC) or another accrediting organization is a sign of quality. Parents can learn of accredited programs in their area by calling NAEYC or checking its Web site. Child care centers usually post licensing and accreditation certificates in prominent places.

Fig. 28-8. This checklist is a helpful tool to use when assessing a child care center. **How might this list be adapted when evaluating other types of child care or educational programs?**

Program Evaluation Checklist	
Program	**Health and Safety Practices**
❏ Has a focus and philosophy that appeal to you. ❏ Follows a routine that will help your child feel comfortable. ❏ Offers a variety of interesting, age-appropriate activities. ❏ Schedules time for both active and quiet play. ❏ Provides for group and individual activities. ❏ Uses methods of discipline consistent with your own. ❏ Respects all people. ❏ Is licensed and possibly accredited.	❏ Include policies to minimize the spread of illness. ❏ Specify that toys are to be cleaned and sanitized daily and equipment regularly. ❏ Ensure that children are supervised at all times. ❏ Provide for safe, clutter-free indoor and outdoor play areas. ❏ Include fire extinguishers, smoke detectors, posted emergency numbers and procedures, and other safety features. ❏ Require adults other than parents to have proper authorization and identification to pick up children.
Director	**Environment**
❏ Is approachable and willing to talk with parents. ❏ Exhibits strong leadership within the program. ❏ Is well respected by children, staff, and parents. ❏ Has appropriate credentials and experience.	❏ Is clean, well lighted, comfortable, and appealing to the children. ❏ Provides a variety of toys, books, puzzles, and learning materials in reasonably good condition. ❏ Offers adequate space for activities inside and outside. ❏ Appears to result in generally happy children.
Teachers/Caregivers	**Parents**
❏ Are experienced and educated in child development, first aid, and CPR. ❏ Sincerely enjoy children, greeting them individually and warmly. ❏ Listen and respond to children other than simply with announcements or instructions. ❏ Set appropriate limits for behavior and respond to misbehavior fairly and consistently. ❏ Respond sensitively when a child is afraid, shy, upset, or angry.	❏ Are welcome to visit without advance notice. ❏ Are encouraged to get involved. ❏ Can freely offer suggestions and ideas. ❏ Receive regular reports and communication from teachers or caregivers and the director. ❏ Are respected.

Red Flags Regarding Child Care

Whenever a child is in the care of others, parents should be alert and informed. Watch for these signs that might indicate a problem with a child care facility:

- Parents are not allowed to drop in unannounced.
- Parents are discouraged from becoming involved.
- Crying babies are left unattended.
- Children are out of control.
- The facility has a high staff turnover rate.
- One staff member often takes a child out of sight of other children or adults.
- The child is unusually fearful of going to the facility.
- The child refuses to talk about the day's activities.
- The child has unexplained bruises.

- The child talks about inappropriate actions of adults or other children.
- The child has a noticeable change in behavior, such as nightmares, not eating, or acting strangely.
- The child complains that staff members yell, swear, or act mean.
- Staff members are not willing to discuss parents' concerns.

Child Care Center Staff. Employees are the heart of any program. When evaluating a child care program, parents should learn as much as possible about staff members. What are their credentials and backgrounds? What are their beliefs about children, child development, and guidance? Parents can observe teachers and caregivers, using the checklist on page 592 as a guide. Other parents who are familiar with the center might offer helpful opinions.

Parents should also ask about the staff turnover rate. A low turnover rate, meaning that employees stay with the program a long time, indicates stability and reliability.

Staff-to-Child Ratio. Another gauge of quality is the staff-to-child ratio—that is, the number of caregivers compared to the number of children. State licensing requires a minimum ratio, and some child care centers do better. The younger the children, the higher the ratio of staff members should be. As a general guideline, these staff-to-child ratios are recommended:

- Up to age two—at least one adult for every three children.
- Ages two to three—at least one adult for every four children.
- Ages three to six—at least one adult for every eight children.

Each group needs at least two adults. In case of emergency, one adult can get help while the other stays with the children.

Fig. 28-9. Older adults can have a special place in the lives of children. **How can both young children and senior citizens benefit from time spent together?**

Sponsorship of Centers. Child care centers vary in how they are owned and operated. Sponsorship can affect the philosophy and type of child care program at a given facility. Depending on the community, parents may be able to choose from these options:

- **Not-for-profit centers.** Some centers are run by not-for-profit groups such as religious organizations or the YMCA. Part of their support comes from donations and volunteers. Centers affiliated with a religious community may provide religious instruction.
- **Government-sponsored centers.** Some centers are funded by the government. They may be available only to families whose income falls below a certain level. Fees may be set on a **sliding scale**, a set of rates that vary according to a family's ability to pay.
- **Employer-sponsored centers.** Some companies offer child care as a benefit for their employees. The facility may be on-site or located nearby. Fees are usually low because the employer pays most of the operating costs. If the center is on-site, a nursing mother can use her breaks to feed her child during the day. Some companies don't maintain their own center, but help families of employees pay the cost of outside care.
- **Senior center–sponsored centers.** Some senior centers also house child care centers. Senior citizens are paired with preschool age children for a number of activities. The goal is to establish bonds between the two generations as they interact. See Fig. 28-9.

Parenting Pointers

Tips for Easing Separation

For a young child in child care or an early childhood education program, the hardest part of the day may be the moment the parent leaves. How parents handle the routine can set the tone for the rest of the day. These tips can help make saying goodbye easier:

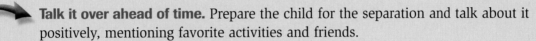

Talk it over ahead of time. Prepare the child for the separation and talk about it positively, mentioning favorite activities and friends.

Avoid a morning rush. Getting everything ready the night before will help make the morning calm and relaxed.

Send along a favorite item. If the child is attached to a blanket or stuffed animal, ask the caregiver if the child can bring it along for reassurance.

Enlist the caregiver's support. Some children adapt better when a caregiver gives extra attention during the moments of separation.

Let the child settle into an activity. Get the child involved in something fun, such as building blocks. A child who is happily engaged is more willing to accept a parent's goodbye.

Be cheerful. Make comments such as, "You get to feed the rabbit today. That sounds like fun."

Announce you are leaving. Slipping away while a child is distracted can result in the child becoming anxious or fearful on discovering that the parent is nowhere to be found.

Be swift and sure. Don't linger for "just a few more minutes."

Establish a brief goodbye routine. Whether it's an affectionate hug or a last wave from the door, repeat the same ritual each day. Children feel secure with routines.

Be reliable. Children leave parents more easily when they are confident of a reunion. Make sure the child is picked up as expected.

- **College- or university-sponsored centers.** Also known as lab centers, these programs are staffed by child development students and their instructors. Because a lab center's purpose is to train teachers of the future and to test new child development theories, children have the advantage of innovative thought.
- **School-sponsored centers.** Some high schools offer on-site child care for staff members and the community. They serve as training laboratories for high school students to learn hands-on child care skills. Fees are usually low. A few schools have child care centers designed to serve the children of teen parents who are attending high school classes.
- **Franchise operations.** These for-profit centers are managed by a central business organization that sets standards and oversees operation. Local businesspersons buy the right to run the center. Thus, franchised centers offer the benefits of both large-scale operation and local responsibility. For some parents, the nationally or regionally known name inspires trust.
- **Privately owned centers.** Some centers are both owned and operated by individuals. Fees at franchised and privately owned centers are usually higher than at other types, as they must cover all operating costs and provide a profit for the owners.
- **Parent cooperatives.** Some parents form a **parent cooperative**, becoming part-owners and administrators of a care center or preschool for their children. Parents hire staff, set program goals, and volunteer several hours a month. Parents who are active in cooperatives enjoy the personal involvement and the advantage of lower costs.

School-Age Child Care

For some children, school doesn't start in the morning until after parents have left for work. Many children get out of school before their parents return home. Parents need to make sure their children are safe during those time gaps, as well as when school is not in session.

Organized Programs

Some schools, religious communities, and community agencies have before- and after-school programs where children can enjoy stories, crafts, sports, recreation, and snacks. They may provide a quiet place for children to do homework. All-day programs may be offered on school holidays and during summer vacations.

As with care for younger children, school-age child care is in short supply. Cost and location are considerations. Publicly funded groups, such as public school systems, often contract the work to a company that manages child care programs. Because the program receives public funding, the cost to the family will typically be lower than for private programs.

Self-Care for "Latchkey" Children

Many children who are old enough can be trusted at home for an hour or two. If parents cannot find other options for before- and after-school care, they may choose to leave a child for a few hours each day without adult supervision. Children who regularly come home to an empty house are often called **self-care children.** Another common term is *latchkey children* because, traditionally, these children wear a house key on a ribbon around their neck.

Fig. 28-10. Parents should realistically assess their children's level of maturity before making a decision about self-care. **What signs of maturity might they look for?**

Local or state law may specify how long, if at all, children of different ages may be left home alone. Other factors for parents to consider include the child's level of maturity, what time of day and for how long the child will be alone, the neighborhood, and the availability of a trusted neighbor in case the child needs help. See Fig. 28-10.

If parents feel children are ready, they can begin preparing them by teaching rules to be followed when they are home alone. These rules, which parents and children should review regularly, can address topics such as:

- **Telephone check-in.** Have children call when they arrive home.
- **Answering the phone.** An answering machine, with a recorded message from the parent, can handle incoming calls.
- **Visitors.** Children should not answer the door or let friends in, unless previously arranged and approved.
- **Activities.** Parents can make it clear that children are expected to do homework or household tasks.
- **Meals and snacks.** Parents can set guidelines ("no snacking after 5:00") and stock the kitchen with healthful foods.
- **Special situations.** Make sure children know what to do if the house key is lost, the electricity goes out, the weather turns severe, or parents don't return home when expected, for example.
- **Emergencies.** Parents should post phone numbers for emergency services and a reliable neighbor or friend, as well as their own work and cell phone numbers. Teach children to call for help and provide a name, address, and description of various emergencies.

Planning for Backup Child Care

No matter how carefully parents choose child care arrangements, things don't always work out as planned. Children and regular caregivers get sick; centers close for weather or holidays. Parents should plan how they will care for a child in these situations.

In some communities, a few child care centers offer short-term emergency care for healthy children, for which parents pay by the day. A local child care referral service should have information about such centers. In addition, some employers make arrangements with a particular provider to provide backup child care for their employees.

Most states do not allow obviously contagious children to enter a child care facility. If no parent, relative, friend, or babysitter can stay home with the child, out-of-home options may be available. A child care center may have a satellite site for mildly ill children, or a community may have a hospital-based program. See Fig. 28-11.

Early Childhood Education

Research shows that amazing development takes place within a child's brain between birth and age three. For this reason, some parents opt for programs that emphasize early childhood education, hoping their children will benefit from more stimulation.

Types of Programs

Early childhood education programs vary in the age of children they target, the skills they teach, and their philosophies of education. They can be large schools or small classes in the teacher's home. Like child care centers, early childhood education programs can have different kinds of public or private sponsorship. Parents should follow the same procedures and criteria to evaluate quality as when seeking quality child care. Options range from programs for infants and toddlers to a variety of preschool, pre-kindergarten, and kindergarten programs.

Head Start Programs. Head Start is a federally funded program for children from birth to age five. To qualify, families must have low incomes, be on public assistance, or have foster children or children with disabilities.

Head Start promotes healthy development in young children to prepare them to succeed in school and later in life. Its child care and education programs are offered in locally run facilities, usually with half-day sessions emphasizing a variety of skill-building activities. In addition, Head Start offers services such as:

- Nutritious meals.
- Medical and dental screenings.
- Immunizations.
- Adult classes in child development, child rearing, health, and nutrition.

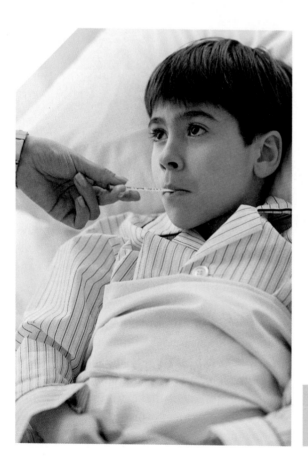

Fig. 28-11. When a child arrives at a care facility for ill children, a health screening is usually done with the parent. **How does this process help the child, the parent, and the care provider?**

Fig. 28-12. Traditional preschools emphasize social development along with learning. **In what ways might playing together at a sand table aid children's development?**

Traditional Preschools. Preschools offer learning experiences for children who are about three to five years old. Half-day sessions are common. Teachers help children learn such skills as naming days of the week, counting to ten, and identifying colors. They also provide opportunities for play and social interaction. See Fig. 28-12.

Montessori Preschools. At a typical Montessori preschool, children handle objects and materials designed for specific educational purposes. Children move among learning centers. In one area they may use beads to add and subtract. In another area they may build with blocks of graduated sizes to get a feel for the concept of volume. Although any school can call itself Montessori, regardless of sponsorship, legitimate programs with trained Montessori teachers can be identified as members of American Montessori Society.

Waldorf Preschools. These independent not-for-profit schools emphasize imagination and creativity. Preschoolers celebrate seasonal holidays of cultures around the world. Stories, myths, and creative arts cultivate children's fantasy. Like Montessori schools, Waldorf schools may continue from pre-kindergarten through grade school or beyond.

Public Pre-kindergarten Programs. In a growing trend, many states offer pre-kindergarten programs run by public school systems and supported by state funds. They are designed primarily for three-, four-, and five-year-olds considered at risk because they meet criteria such as:

- Being from a low-income family.
- Being in the care of a teen mother.
- Having parents with lower levels of education.
- Low birth weight or premature birth.

Pre-kindergarten programs emphasize basic academic skills, such as identifying numbers and letters of the alphabet, in order to prepare children for school. They also stress parental involvement, sometimes including home visits by parent educators.

Kindergarten Programs. Kindergarten classes today are very different from those of 20 years ago. In the past, kindergarten was most children's first opportunity to learn skills such as standing in line, taking turns, washing hands, and putting things away. Today, many of the children entering kindergarten have already spent years in preschool and pre-kindergarten programs. As a result, they have experienced group learning environments and begun to master these skills. Therefore, the focus in most kindergartens is academics. See Fig. 28-13.

Generally, kindergarten classes focus on listening, speaking, reading, writing, and math. Broad areas of science include units on trees, space, or living things. Social studies builds on simple concepts about families, communities, and cultures. The curriculum is enriched with classes such as art, music, and physical education. By the end of the year, many children are reading independently. They may be able to count to 100 and may begin to add and subtract.

Some kindergartens are intense and academic, driven by content and skills. Others are creative and relaxed, aimed at fostering a love of learning. Most programs are a happy medium.

Educational Options for School-Age Children

By the time children reach school age, many parents breathe a huge sigh of relief. However, they still have decisions to make about their children's education. Quality still matters. Children of all ages thrive in settings where curiosity, cooperation, and respect are encouraged.

Fig. 28-13. A recent government report shows that about two-thirds of entering kindergarten children already know the letters of the alphabet. About one-third recognize the letter sound at the beginning of a word. **What do you think children should know before entering kindergarten?**

Fig. 28-14. Charter schools often try innovative approaches to teaching and learning. **How can parents be assured that a charter school is providing a quality education?**

Public Schools

Almost nine out of ten children attend public schools. Most are enrolled in their local district, which offers free education supported by local, state, and federal taxes. Generally, the curriculum meets state requirements. In recent years, many states have begun measuring student performance by proficiency tests to ensure that the school is teaching the basics. Some public school systems offer options such as magnet schools and charter schools.

Magnet Schools. To promote desegregation in the 1970s, some school districts began giving certain schools a distinctive focus—such as science or performing arts—to attract students from all over the district. Many of these **magnet schools** succeed in attracting a diverse group of interested students and families. Because more families may apply than can fit, a magnet school may be competitive and selective, or it may use a lottery system to decide who may attend.

Charter Schools. Some alternative public schools are established by a *charter* (written grant of rights) from the state. Every few years, these **charter schools** must prove that they meet certain performance standards. In return, charter schools get some independence from the rules other public schools must follow. This allows them to try new approaches. Parents may choose charter schools because they usually have smaller class size, individual attention, fresh teaching ideas, or a special focus. Some schools promote a philosophy, such as back-to-the-basics. Others are designed for a particular type of student, such as gifted or at risk. See Fig. 28-14.

Private Schools

Parents may choose a private school for their child. One major difference between public and private schools is funding. Private schools depend on a combination of tuition paid by families, fund-raising by students, and donations from individuals, organizations, and religious institutions.

Private schools that are sponsored by a particular religious organization are often called *parochial* or *sectarian* schools. The largest number of parochial schools are Catholic, but many other faiths operate schools as well. Religion isn't the only reason parents choose these schools. Many parents are attracted by their curriculum, discipline, and traditional values.

Independent private schools are another option. Because they are not sponsored by a funding organization, independent private schools can be very expensive. They typically offer small classes, individual attention, and challenging or enriched curriculum. Some have an excellent reputation.

Homeschooling

Parents may decide they want neither a public nor private school and opt to teach their children at home. In the United States, over one million children are now schooled at home.

Each state has its own laws governing home schooling. Usually parents inform their local school district in writing. They may submit an outline of subjects they will cover and texts they will use. Some states require children to have an assessment or take a standardized test at the end of the year. The results are used to determine whether permission to homeschool will continue.

Homeschooling is a growing trend. Parents who choose it may say they prefer having more control over their child's education, environment, schedule, and curriculum. Children can work at their own pace and are protected from negative elements such as bullies and peer pressure. The flexibility of homeschooling can accommodate a child's special interests or needs.

Homeschooling is not for everyone. Not every parent has the training, time, or patience to be a good teacher. There are costs involved in buying materials. Also, children who are homeschooled may not get to experience organized activities a home cannot easily provide, such as drama programs, sports, and dances. However, parents can become involved in a local homeschooling network, which can help provide such experiences for the children. See Fig. 28-15.

Parental Support and Involvement

Good quality child care and educational facilities offer tremendous advantages. But in the life of a child, nothing takes the place of a caring, supportive, involved parent. Whatever choices they make for their children, parents can show active support by:

• **Easing transitions to a new center or school.** Parents and children can tour the facility ahead of time and meet the instructors.

Fig. 28-15. Homeschooling is a time-consuming option for a parent, but one that many parents find rewarding. **What factors should parents consider in deciding whether or not to homeschool their children?**

- **Communicating frequently with the center or school.** Attend parent-teacher conferences. Read newsletters and notes sent home.
- **Reinforcing program content at home.** Ask the child about events at child care or school. Find "teachable moments" related to what the child is learning.
- **Becoming involved as a volunteer.** Parent volunteers not only provide much-needed support, but gain the opportunity to see the program and their child in action.

Supporting Schoolwork

School-age children need the support of adults, especially parents, to feel good about their achievements. Whatever school the children attend, parents can help promote their academic success by:

- Providing a clear, well-lighted place at home for doing homework.
- Praising their children's efforts and displaying school work.
- Offering homework guidance and a little tutoring, without doing the homework for them.

Providing Enriching Activities

At any age, children benefit from opportunities outside of their regular child care or education schedule. For example, infant-parent classes sponsored by community organizations let parents interact with their baby in activities such as swimming or exercising. These classes stimulate the baby's development as well as parental bonds. See Fig. 28-16.

Museums, parks, zoos, art centers, and many other places offer special-interest short courses for preschool and school-age children, with or without their parents. Many parents enroll their children in organized activities, such as sports, arts programs, youth groups, and day

Fig. 28-16. Even infants can benefit from enriching activities. **How can organized programs help to stimulate a baby's development?**

camps. Children can learn by doing, make friends, and explore a variety of interests.

Pushing a child too hard is a common mistake. Activities that overemphasize competition can be hard on young or sensitive children. Any situation that makes a child feel like a loser is not healthy. In addition, parents must also recognize the difference between involvement and overinvolvement. Some families limit each child to one or two outside activities at a given time. Although educational programs are beneficial, children also need plenty of free, unscheduled time to unwind and be creative.

By choosing quality programs, becoming involved, supporting schoolwork, and providing enriching activities, parents can promote their children's development. It's all part of the care and nurturing that parents provide to help their children develop to their fullest potential.

CHAPTER SUMMARY

- Child care and early childhood education programs have different emphases.
- For the well-being of children, child care and education programs should be selected carefully.
- Child care for children includes in-home care, family child care homes, child care centers, programs for school-age children, and backup care.
- Family child care homes and child care centers are licensed by the state.
- Educational programs of different types are available for children of all ages.
- Parents can support their child's success in whatever program they select.

Check Your Facts

1. How do child care programs and early childhood education compare?
2. What basic considerations are made when parents choose child care and education programs?
3. What are the three recommended steps to take when choosing a program?
4. Describe four factors to examine when choosing a program for children.
5. Is child care affordable? Explain.
6. Describe three types of in-home care.
7. List eight areas of regulation when licensing a family child care home.
8. Why do parents check accreditation?
9. Describe at least four ways a child care center could be sponsored.
10. What determines whether a child is old enough to stay home alone after school?
11. List at least five rules to teach a child who spends time alone at home.
12. Identify six types of early childhood education programs.
13. What is the purpose of Head Start?
14. What is a magnet school?
15. Why do some parents choose to home school their children?
16. List four ways that parents can show support for their child and a program.
17. In what three ways can parents help school-age children succeed academically?
18. What should be considered when involving children in organized activities?

Think Critically

1. **Analyzing Behavior.** Suppose your child is disrespectful, uses foul language, and is having nightmares after three months in child care. What would you do?
2. **Making Predictions.** How do you think a child who has attended a Montessori or Waldorf preschool will adjust to a traditional first grade class? Why?
3. **Analyzing Options.** Which would you prefer for your children: public school, private school, or homeschooling? Why?

Apply Your Learning

1. **Program Assessment.** Visit a child care or child education program in your community. Using the program evaluation checklist in the chapter, assess the facility. In class, describe the program, including both positive and negative qualities.

2. **Laws and Licensing.** Investigate child care laws that cover licensing in your state. Report your findings in class. Discuss whether licensing requirements are reasonable and adequate. What changes, if any, would you make?

3. **Charter Schools.** Check the Internet to find out how charter schools are developed. Then, with a team of students, create a plan for a charter school in your district. What will the purpose of the school be? Write a mission statement that describes this purpose. How will students benefit from attending the school? Write goals that incorporate these benefits. How will the community be involved? Submit your plan to the class for evaluation.

Cross-Curricular Connections

1. **Language Arts.** Suppose you are hiring a nanny to take care of two small children in your home. With a partner, write at least ten questions that you would ask applicants during interviews. Then role-play an interview for the class. Analyze whether you gained the necessary information to hire someone.

2. **Math.** A child care center has six children who are age one, 16 children ages two to three, and 24 children ages three to six. There are seven staff members caring for the children. Evaluate this situation.

Family & Community Connections

1. **School Success.** With your family, think of ways to support school success in your home. Choose several suggestions to try for one month. Then evaluate which ones were most effective. Which ones will you continue?

2. **Support During Illness.** Find out where employed parents in your community can get child care for mildly ill children. Where are such places located? What are the hours, costs, and policies? Which are available on a drop-in basis? Report what you learn. If no such facilities exist, what options do parents have?

Career Guide

When you were a child, did you ever say, "When I grow up, I want to be…."? Perhaps you dreamed of being a dancer, a teacher, or a police officer. Now that your growing years are nearly over, it's time to move from dreaming to planning for a future career. The more time, energy, and thought you put into career decisions, the more likely it is that you will enjoy your work life and be successful on the job.

Fig. CG-1. If you're lucky, you have an interest that could lead to an enjoyable career. **What are some of your interests? What career areas might be related to them?**

Career Planning

A *career* is a series of related jobs in a particular field. You may have more than one career in your lifetime, but that doesn't mean you should leave your career path up to chance. Planning ahead can help you find the field that's right for you. First, examine your interests, abilities, and values. Then figure out what jobs would be a good match. Once you have some ideas, you can explore how to get the training and experience needed to land the job you want.

Taking a Look at Yourself

If you're afraid of animals, you're not likely to become a veterinarian. People wisely choose careers that are a good fit with their personal interests, abilities, and values. Taking a good look at your personal qualities is the first step toward a rewarding career. How do the following relate to you?

- **Interests.** Hobbies, such as sports and drawing, point to personal interests. Could something you do for fun have the potential to become a rewarding career? Some interests can lead to several different careers. For instance, a person who enjoys cooking might attend a culinary school after high school to become a chef. With a degree in education, the same person could become a Family and Consumer Sciences teacher instead. Combining an interest in foods with a talent for writing makes restaurant reviewing a possible option. See Fig. CG-1.

- **Abilities.** Like everyone else, you have certain *aptitudes*—natural talents that you were born with. You also have *skills*—abilities developed through training and practice. You're likely to be most happy in a job that makes use of your aptitudes and skills. To identify your abilities, think about the school subjects you enjoy the most, the skills you've picked up in jobs, and the comments people make about what you do well. Most of all, listen to your own thoughts. A message such as "That was a lot easier than I thought it would be!" might be a clue to a talent you hadn't recognized before.

- **Values.** The career you choose should be consistent with your values. For example, if you value wealth and status, you might be inspired to build a business of your own, that is, to become an *entrepreneur*. If you care deeply about helping others, then social work might be a good choice. Values also affect career choices on a practical level. For instance, someone who feels strongly about making time for family might choose a job with flexible hours.

- **Personality.** Finally, your job should fit your personality. Think about how well you work with others, how much stress you can handle, and what kind of working environment you would like. If you are friendly and outgoing, you might be suited for a sales position. If you enjoy the outdoors, a job as a landscape artist could be among your choices. See Fig. CG-2.

Assessment Tests. School and career counselors, as well as employers, commonly offer *career assessment tests*—tests that reveal a person's interests, skills, and abilities. Some tests measure aptitudes, skills, or knowledge related to a particular subject. Others are personality tests, designed to reveal careers that fit certain personalities and interests. Still others assess what is valued most in a job: independence, recognition, working conditions, and more. These tests can help identify careers that are suitable for you.

If you are interested in taking assessment tests, talk to your school guidance counselor. Your community may also have career specialists, employment agencies, or government job-service offices that provide assessment testing.

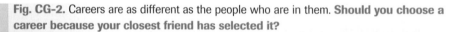

Fig. CG-2. Careers are as different as the people who are in them. **Should you choose a career because your closest friend has selected it?**

Fig. CG-3. Preparing for a career may take a large financial investment. **Why might investing in career education and training pay off in the long run?**

Researching Potential Careers

With a self-assessment done, you should have some careers to consider. One of them might be right for you, but you won't know for sure until you explore a little more. Researching careers provides details about them. What jobs are available in a field? What is the work like? What qualifications does the job require? Is the field growing? To answer all your questions, these sources can help:

- The *Occupational Outlook Handbook* **(OOH).** This publication by the U.S. Bureau of Labor Statistics contains profiles of specific careers. The OOH is available on the Internet and in many libraries.
- **The Occupational Information Network, or O*Net.** This Web site contains a list of occupations sorted into "job families." You can also search for jobs that make use of particular knowledge, skills, or abilities.
- **School guidance offices and career centers.** Consult with the guidance counselor at your high school or, if you are going on to college, with the college's career placement office. Professionals in these offices can direct you to reliable information about fields of interest.
- **Private career counselors and agencies.** The International Association of Counseling Services (IACS) certifies career counseling agencies and provides regional lists of accredited career services.

As you explore each career on your list, think about how well it fits with your aptitudes, skills, interests, values, and personality. Look for the one that fits the best of all.

Making a Career Plan

Narrowing down career options to one may take some time. Once you've decided, you're into the planning stage. How will you get the skills and training needed to qualify for the career you've chosen? A future science teacher would take science courses in school and apply to colleges with good science programs. Getting a college degree and achieving teacher certification are longer-term goals. Taking a summer job as a camp counselor could provide some teaching experiences. As you think about how to reach your career goal, keep these questions in mind:

- **Education and training.** What schools offer the training or education you need?
- **Financial investment.** What will it cost to prepare for this career? How can you find funding? See Fig. CG-3.
- **Time commitment.** Will the career take weeks, months, or years of training or education?
- **Changes in location.** Must you relocate to get training or education? Are jobs in the career available locally or will you need to move?

- **Job opportunities.** How competitive is the field? What skills and experience will make you more appealing to employers?

Consider all these factors carefully when making your career plan. Before you start down any career path, be sure you are willing to see it through to the end. Remember that the career you choose and the steps you take to pursue it will affect your life for many years to come.

Career Preparation

Setting the stage for a satisfying life often means taking some time to prepare for a suitable career. In most cases, two pursuits are critical: education and experience. What you need depends on the career you have in mind.

Education and Training

Many careers call for education beyond high school. You can continue your education in different settings that include the following:

- **Four-year colleges and universities.** At a four-year college or university, you can earn a bachelor's degree, usually in arts or sciences. A bachelor's degree is a requirement for many jobs in such fields as criminal justice, marketing, and information management. Some positions, as in education and science, may require additional schooling beyond a bachelor's degree. See Fig. CG-4.

- **Community and technical colleges.** At these institutions, you earn an associate's degree in two years or less. Programs with this degree prepare you for such careers as veterinary technician, CAD/drafting, paralegal, and medical assistant. An associate's degree can also be a springboard to a four-year degree.

- **Vo-tech centers and trade schools.** Vocational-technical, or vo-tech, centers offer training for specific occupations in such fields as health care and automotive technology. Most offer both daytime and evening classes. Trade schools also provide training in specific fields that include welding, plumbing, computer programming, and graphic design. They may also offer specialized courses not available at other institutions.

- **Military service.** Branches of the armed forces provide education (before and after enlistment) and training in skilled trades. In addition, service personnel can earn money to pay for education after leaving the armed forces.

Fig. CG-4. For many people, college is a first step toward the career they want. **What are some careers that require a college degree?**

Fig. CG-5. Volunteer work is an excellent way to learn about careers and develop skills. **What useful skills might these student volunteers be learning?**

- **Distance learning programs.** Students who cannot attend a traditional college or other institution can pursue an advanced degree through a distance learning program. These programs provide instruction through the mail, videos, or the Internet so students can learn at home.

Work-Based Learning

On-the-job experience is a great way to learn. A part-time job offers this opportunity. You can also participate in *work-based learning*, programs that combine work with study. Many states fund school-to-work programs that give students a chance to develop job skills, gain knowledge, and build confidence.

One form of work-based learning is an apprenticeship, where you learn by doing. Apprentices divide their time between the classroom and the job. Most apprenticeships last for several years and are in skilled trades, such as carpentry. Apprentices earn money while they learn job skills.

Another opportunity for students is an internship. Interns spend a period of time working for a company without pay. In exchange for their labor, interns learn about a career of interest and practice job skills hands-on.

Volunteer Experiences

As treasurer for his school's student senate, one teen improved his bookkeeping skills. Another teen learned patience by helping out at a day care center in her town. These are just two examples of the many skills you can develop as a volunteer. To gain experience working with children and families, for example, you could volunteer at a hospital, child care center, library, or parks and recreation department. See Fig. CG-5.

Does your school offer opportunities for *service learning*? If so, you can use what you learn in the classroom to benefit your community. You may be able to receive academic credit for this type of volunteer work. Such projects as collecting food and clothing for disaster victims may be available through school service clubs like the Key Club. This school club is sometimes an extension of the Kiwanis or Rotary Club, which are community service organizations.

Youth Organizations. Through the United Way, 4-H clubs, and other youth organizations, teens get involved in volunteer work. Many organizations and programs help students develop leadership skills. The United Way, for instance, has youth divisions in various parts of the country. They give high-school students the chance to help out in their communities and to meet other teens interested in community leadership and service.

Another resource for would-be teen volunteers is Youth Service America (YSA). This resource center works with many organizations to provide volunteer opportunities for young Americans ages five to 25. YSA maintains a service called SERVEnet that lists community opportunities by postal (zip) code. SERVEnet is available to both individuals and organizations.

FCCLA. One national organization you might find in your school is Family, Career and Community Leaders of America, or FCCLA. It is open to all middle-school and high-school students who are currently taking, or have taken, courses in Family and Consumer Sciences. FCCLA programs help students develop career skills related to Family and Consumer Sciences. These programs include:

- **Career Connection.** Through this program, students discover their individual strengths, focus their career goals, and learn how to integrate work with personal life.
- **Dynamic Leadership.** This program teaches important leadership skills: modeling good character, problem solving, fostering positive relationships, managing conflicts, team building, and educating peers.
- **Leaders at Work.** This program focuses on developing on-the-job skills related to communication, management, entrepreneurship, and interpersonal relationships.

- **STAR Events.** Students Taking Action with Recognition (STAR) Events help students develop their skills and apply their learning in such areas as "Applied Technology" and "Early Childhood." STAR Events include individualized activities, cooperative activities, and competitions.

Looking For a Job

No matter how well qualified you are, the right job isn't simply going to fall into your lap. Looking for a job requires a focused effort. You have to track down job leads, submit applications, and prepare a résumé that highlights your strengths. Think of a job search as a part-time job, and treat it with the same level of commitment you'd give to any other job.

Come up with a plan to keep your job-search efforts organized. Write down job opportunities you want to pursue and record what you do each day to find a job. Use a small notebook, index cards, or an electronic file for your records. How your records are organized is up to you. You could list entries chronologically (based on what you accomplish each day) or topically (with a section for each job you investigate). See Fig. CG-6.

Finding Job Leads

If you're looking for a job, your first thought may be to check the classified ads in the newspaper. That isn't a bad place to start, but it isn't your only resource, either. For example, if you are looking for a position in a specific industry, you can check the job listings in trade publications devoted to that field. You can also search the Internet or consult an employment agency. Perhaps the most important resource, though, is your personal "network" of friends, relatives, and acquaintances. Any one of these people could be your key to finding a job.

Date	Company Name	Contact Person	Contact Number or E-mail Address	Job Opening
May 25	Jones Mfg.	Maria Lane	555/238-9047	Day Care Provider

Fig. CG-6. A chart like this can help you keep track of your job leads. **What are some other tools you could use to keep your job search well organized?**

The Internet. There are many sites on the Web specifically devoted to jobs. A search for the phrase "job listings" is sure to turn up several. Some sites focus on a particular field, while others are more general. You can search for jobs by title, location, and other criteria. On many sites, you can post your résumé for potential employers to view.

The Internet can also help you look for jobs at a specific company or organization. Visit the company's Web site and look for a link that says something like "Positions Available." This will probably show you a list of job openings at the company. Even if there are no jobs listed, you can still learn more about the company and what it would be like to work there.

Employment Agencies. An *employment agency* is a business that helps employers find qualified candidates for available jobs. Job seekers visit the agency and fill out applications. Employers provide the agency with a list of job openings. Then the agency tries to match workers with jobs.

Public employment agencies, operated by state governments, offer their services at no charge. By contrast, private employment agencies charge a fee to the employer, the job seeker, or both. Some agencies specialize in a particular field, such as technology or health care.

Networking. As the most direct, successful way to job-hunt, *networking* involves using personal and professional contacts to further your career goals. The more people you tell about your job search, the better your chances that someone can be helpful. See Fig. CG-7.

Fig. CG-7. Many jobs are found by word of mouth. **Have any members of your family found jobs this way?**

Could any of the following help you?

- **Teachers and mentors.** Adults who know how your strengths might translate into job skills can provide advice and, if necessary, reference letters.
- **Friends and classmates.** Form a cooperative relationship with other job-seekers. Sharing information on job leads helps all of you.
- **Employers and coworkers.** If you already have a job, your company may post opportunities for advancement within the company. Coworkers may also know of job openings both within and outside your workplace.
- **Organizations.** School organizations and community groups often provide job information. In addition, professional organizations, such as the National Association of

Social Workers (NASW) or the National Association for the Education of Young Children (NAEYC), are usually happy to assist young people who are beginning their careers. Members of these organizations may know of job openings or be able to offer general advice on breaking into the field.

Spend time broadening your network. If one of your contacts helps you get a job interview, be sure to thank that person and follow through. See Fig. CG-8.

Applying for Jobs

Once you find a lead for a job that appeals to you, applying for the position is the next step. In most cases, that means submitting a *résumé*—a brief summary of your career qualifications. Along with your résumé, include a cover letter, explaining how you heard about the job and why you are qualified. Filling out an application form may also be part of the process.

Preparing a Résumé. Since the résumé is often your first contact with an employer, be sure it makes a good impression. It should be concise and accurate, with correct spellings and format. Include your work experiences, skills, education and training, and any personal qualities that will be useful on the job.

Fig. CG-8. It's always thoughtful to thank the person who helps you get a job interview. **How does being courteous to your network contacts benefit you?**

Jay D. Hayes
801 Lincoln Blvd.
Bigtown, NE 68000

Phone: 555/426-5397
Mobile: 555/257-0999
E-mail: jhayes@.......

OBJECTIVE: To obtain a medical assistant position in a clinic setting.

EXPERIENCE: 2005–2007: Stone Pediatric Clinic, Bigtown, NE
Medical Assistant: Responsible for obtaining intake information, taking blood pressure and weight readings, updating computerized records, preparing exam rooms, witnessing and assisting with procedures, and drawing blood.

EDUCATION: Associate Degree—Medical Assistant
Minnesota Technical College, Cold City, MN
May, 2005

SKILLS: Microsoft Office (Word, Excel), medical dictation, phlebotomy, Spanish

REFERENCES: Available upon request

Fig. CG-9. Employers don't usually have time to read long résumés. Even as your job history and educational experiences grow, your résumé should be kept to no more than two pages.

Do not include references unless specifically requested. Fig. CG-9 shows a sample résumé.

Preparing a Cover Letter. With the cover letter, introduce yourself, indicate your interest in the job, display your writing skills, and stress your qualifications. Always include this letter with your résumé. See Fig. CG-10 on page 616.

Filling Out an Application. At some point, you will probably need to fill out a job application. Like résumés, application forms should be completed clearly, accurately, and truthfully. Read instructions carefully before writing, and neatly correct any errors.

You may need to show some form or forms of identification. A driver's license is one possibility.

When you submit an application, have your *references* ready. You'll need the names, addresses, and telephone numbers of two or three people who will speak positively about your personal character and qualifications. A school official, previous employer, clergy member, or long-time adult friend may be a good reference. Avoid listing relatives and friends your own age. Ask permission from people before giving their names.

Interviewing

If your application, résumé, and letter catch an employer's attention, you will probably be asked to come in for an interview. The employer meets with you in person to learn more about you and determine whether you are a good match for the job. The interview can be the deciding factor in whether you will be offered a job. It pays to plan ahead and think about questions that may be asked.

Fig. CG-10. A cover letter introduces an applicant's skills and shows interest in the position. **Would you consider hiring this applicant on the basis of the letter shown here?**

July 18, 2007

Victoria R. Ruling, Practice Manager
Lakeview Pediatrics and Family Practice
111 S. Broadway
High City, MT 59000

Re: Medical Assistant Position, Posting #MA-137

Dear Ms. Ruling:

I am writing in response to your posting on www.midwestmedjobs.com about a medical assistant position at Lakeview Pediatrics and Family Practice. I believe this position to be perfect for someone with my experience, education, and interests.

I believe that I can be an asset to your clinic because of my skills in working with both pediatric patients and parents. In addition, I am eager to learn new skills required by the job. For the past two years, I have worked at a pediatric clinic that serves a multicultural community. I have taken courses in phlebotomy and have learned computerized record-keeping. I am also fluent in both Spanish and English.

A copy of my résumé is enclosed. If you find my qualifications suitable, I would be glad to meet with you for an interview. I am able to travel to Montana on forty-eight hours' notice. I hope to hear from you soon.

Sincerely,

Jay D. Hayes

Enclosure: (1)

Aspects of Industry

Aspect	Related Tasks in Industry
Planning	Decide what to produce or what services to provide; set goals; develop general policies and procedures.
Management	Choose a structure for employees who oversee the work of others; implement methods for operating the business.
Finance	Handle money decisions and procedures; choose and carry out accounting methods.
Technical and Production Skills	Develop skills needed by employees on the job, such as computer skills, machine operation, and teamwork.
Principles of Technology	Understand how technology is used in a specific industry; identify the impact of changing technology on the business; take steps to stay current; analyze new equipment; solve problems with technical or electronic equipment.
Labor and Personnel Issues	Identify worker rights and responsibilities; develop policies that involve labor organizations, cultural sensitivity, and employee concerns.
Community Issues	Develop a positive relationship with the community; provide community support.
Health, Safety, and Environmental Issues	Avoid job-specific health threats; develop employer and employee responsibility for a safe workplace; respect and protect the environment.

Fig. CG-11. In a large industry, your job may be only a small part of the entire picture. **Why might it help you to know how other areas of the company operate?**

Preparing for an Interview

"Be prepared" is a good motto to follow for interviews. Start by writing the date, time, and location of the interview in your job-search notebook, along with the contact person's name. The worst thing you could possibly do is show up on the wrong day! Can you find the place where the interview will be held? If possible, plan your route in advance and figure out how long it takes to get there. On the day of the interview, time your departure so that you arrive about 10 minutes early for the appointment.

Before the interview, do some research to learn about the company. You will make a better impression if you know some basics about what the company does, how large it is, and something about its role in the industry. Having this information will help you ask intelligent questions and show that you are interested.

It also helps to understand how industries function overall. Fig. CG-11 shows different aspects of industry and their main responsibilities. All of these areas impact each other and, thus, the business itself. Understanding the aspects of industry helps you see how a job you would like to have fits into the larger picture.

Finally, as you prepare for your interview, decide what you will wear. Don't underestimate the importance of clothing and personal grooming. You will create a professional impression if your appearance is neat, clean, and appropriate for the workplace. Choose an outfit that is comfortable and fits well. Jeans, T-shirts, athletic shoes, and unconventional garments should not be worn. Avoid flashy jewelry and too many accessories. Good grooming means showering, shaving, and using deodorant. Hair should be clean and combed and nails neatly trimmed. Heavy makeup and strong fragrances should be avoided. See Fig. CG-12.

Practice the Interview. To minimize interview jitters, why not rehearse beforehand? Think about how you will respond to common interview questions. Here are some examples:

- **"Why do you want to work here?"** Display your knowledge about the company and the industry. Show enthusiasm about one or more aspects of the company.

Fig. CG-12. The clothes you choose for an interview aren't likely to be what you wear every day. **How does this young man's clothing contribute to a professional appearance?**

- **"What are your goals?"** Explain how your personal goals relate to the company: "I'd like a job where I can grow professionally as the company grows."
- **"What are your weaknesses?"** Try to shift the focus from your weaknesses to your strengths: "I dislike working under time pressure because I hate cutting corners. I really like to take the time to do the job right."
- **"What can you do for us that others cannot?"** Stay positive. Emphasize your unique combination of skills and experience: "I've taken advanced coursework in production design and have two years of supervisory experience."
- **"What are your salary expectations?"** If a salary range is not stated before the interview, research the current rate for the job in your geographical area. Show that your expectations are reasonable: "If I'm your choice, I'm sure we can reach a reasonable salary figure. Did you have a range in mind?"

Making a Good Impression

Preparing for the interview gives you a head start toward making a good impression. To follow through, keep some basic points of interview etiquette in mind. When you show up for the interview, politely give your name and appointment information to the receptionist and wait patiently until you're called for the interview. Greet the interviewer with a firm, confident handshake as you exchange

Fig. CG-13. A firm handshake gets a job interview going with a good start. **How else can you display professional behavior during an interview?**

introductions, and remember to smile. Then remain standing until you're asked to take a seat. See Fig. CG-13.

During the interview, be polite. Listen without interrupting, and maintain eye contact as much as possible to show that you're paying attention. Sit up straight, with both feet on the floor. Avoid nervous gestures, such as finger-tapping or foot-swinging, and never chew gum.

When you're asked a question, answer thoughtfully and completely. Stay focused on the question and avoid getting sidetracked. If you don't understand a question, ask politely for clarification. Speak at an appropriate volume when asking or responding to questions. Remember to use correct grammar; the way you speak is a sign of your professionalism.

Feel free to ask questions of your own, as well. The interview is not just a chance for the employer to learn more about you: it is also your chance to learn about the company and whether you would like to work there. Consider asking for specifics about the nature of the job, work environment, schedule, and opportunities for advancement. However, avoid asking about pay or benefits unless the interviewer brings up these issues. These topics may be covered at the end of the interview or in a second interview. If not, you can discuss them if you are offered the job.

When you leave, do your best to establish a concrete next step. For example, you might say, "I am definitely excited about this opportunity. When can I expect to hear from you?"

Following Up

After an interview, what could you do to improve your chances of a job offer? First, mail a businesslike thank-you letter within one to two days. A thank-you letter reinforces the positive impressions you've already made. Restate your interest in the job (if you are still interested) and your qualifications. Also, follow up on any requests the potential employer may have made, such as providing references or contact information.

If you've been asked to contact the employer, do so at the requested time. If the company promises to contact you and does not do so, telephone to politely request the status of your application. Attend a second interview, if asked. Record all requests and follow-up actions in your job-search notebook.

Finally, mentally review the interview session. Think about ways you might improve your responses to certain questions or your overall interview style. Make note of key information about the job, such as employer expectations and job responsibilities, as well as any unanswered questions you may have. See Fig. CG-14.

Responding to a Job Offer. Not every interview leads to a job offer—and even if you do receive one, you may not want to accept. Think carefully about what you have learned about the job, considering questions like these:
- Does the work interest you?
- Do you think you will fit in at the company?
- Are the pay and benefits acceptable?
- Will this job be a step toward your long-term career goals?

If you decide to accept an offer, you will receive information about the start date and any orientation or training needed. You may attend follow-up meetings regarding pay, benefits, job expectations, and work schedules.

If you do not want the job, politely thank the company representative for the offer but indicate that you're no longer interested. You do not need to give a reason. If you still aren't sure, you can ask for 24 to 48 hours in which to make your decision. During this period, you can ask the company any questions you still have about the position. Get back to the company with a decision by the promised time.

Success on the Job

Once you start a new job, you'll naturally be anxious to make a good impression. Doing your best work is essential, but being a good employee means more than that. It also means showing maturity and responsibility, working well with others, and displaying ethical behavior.

Fig. CG-14. After an interview, make notes about what you were told. Also, list any questions that have since come to mind. **How could this information be useful?**

Responsible Work Habits

For as long as people have worked for a living, a strong work ethic has contributed to success. A *work ethic* is the level of commitment you devote to doing the best job you can. An employee with a strong work ethic is dependable and willing to give extra. Here are other ways you can show a strong work ethic:

- **Earn your pay.** Complete assigned tasks on time and do the best job you can. Keep your work area neat and organized. Use company resources, such as copiers and postage meters, only for work.
- **Use time responsibly.** Arrive on time and return promptly from breaks and meals. Don't chat extensively or conduct personal business on company time. See Fig. CG-15.

Fig. CG-15. Whether you punch a time clock or keep track of your own hours, punctuality counts with an employer. **In what other ways can you make good use of time on the job?**

- **Respect rules.** Learn and follow your supervisor's rules and company policies. If you have a question, consult an employee handbook or ask your supervisor.
- **Dress appropriately.** Always look clean and neat, and wear clean, unwrinkled clothing that is suitable for your work environment. If you are unsure what to wear, take your cues from the way most coworkers dress.
- **Maintain safety standards.** Be familiar with your job's safety requirements. Learn to operate all equipment safely, and ask for help if you have questions. Immediately report unsafe practices or conditions to your supervisor. See Fig. CG-16.

Fig. CG-16. Safety is a greater concern in some jobs than in others. **What safety measures would be particularly important when working with children?**

- **Be flexible.** Be willing to work with new people, try new methods, and accept extra work in a "crunch."
- **Maintain confidentiality.** Information about the company should stay within the company, unless you are specifically given permission to reveal it.
- **Have a positive attitude.** Try to be patient with coworkers and employers, even when getting along with them is difficult. When faced with a problem, look for solutions instead of excuses.
- **Learn from your mistakes.** If you make a mistake, admit it and accept the consequences of your actions. Make improvements if needed.

Job Skills

No matter what job you choose, certain skills are vital. These include the ability to communicate well, solve problems, and work as a team. Fig. CG-17 summarizes basic abilities that employers are likely to expect of employees.

Communication Skills. An important key to success—in a job and in life—is the ability to communicate effectively. Communication takes several forms.

- **Speaking.** Speak clearly, at an appropriate speed and volume. Express your ideas as clearly and concisely as possible, focusing on your point and avoiding technical terms that could confuse your listener.
- **Listening.** Focus your attention on the speaker. Maintain eye contact and nod or ask questions at appropriate intervals to show that you are paying attention.
- **Reading.** On the job, you may often get information from such written sources as office policies, instruction lists, technical manuals, graphs, reports, and schedules. Read at a reasonable pace, making sure you comprehend the material. If you have trouble, consult the author or a coworker for clarification.
- **Writing.** Memos, business letters, reports, and e-mail are typical types of business writing. All of these communications should be

Basic Workplace Skills	
Type of Skill	**Examples**
Basic Skills	Reading; writing; speaking; listening; mathematics
Thinking Skills	Creative thinking; decision making; problem solving; visualizing; learning; reasoning
Personal Qualities	Responsibility; self-esteem; social skills; self-management; honesty
Resource Management Skills	Time management; money management; using materials; space management; staff management
Interpersonal Skills	Working on teams; teaching others; serving customers; leadership; negotiation; working well with people from diverse backgrounds
Information Skills	Using data; maintaining files; interpreting information; communicating; using computers
Systems Skills	Understanding social, organizational, and technological systems; monitoring and correcting system performance; designing or improving systems
Technology Skills	Selecting equipment and tools; applying technology to specific tasks; maintaining and troubleshooting technology

Fig. CG-17. This table groups workplace skills into several basic categories. **Which skills fit into more than one category?**

Fig. CG-18. Sometimes body language sends unmistakable messages—and sometimes it doesn't. **If you're not sure what someone is thinking, what would you do?**

thorough, well organized, and to the point. Use correct grammar and appropriate formatting. Date each document and clearly indicate who should receive it.

- **Body language.** Nonverbal communication, including posture, gestures, and facial expressions, can "paint a picture" of your thoughts and attitudes. Arms crossed and held tightly across your body may express defiance, while yawning or glancing away is a sign of boredom. Show respect for coworkers by using appropriate body language. See Fig. CG-18.

Math Skills. If you think you won't need math skills in the work world, think again. A department budget, cost analysis, and expense report are just a few examples of math in action. Useful math skills include problem-solving techniques and making calculations on paper, in your head, or on a computer. If you lack math skills, consider taking refresher courses at a school or tutoring center. Some workplaces also provide remedial training in math.

Thinking Skills. The thinking skills admired in the workplace are more complex than a thought that just comes to mind. Valued workers think both critically and creatively. In doing so, they make fair decisions based on sound logic and complete information. They recognize problems and analyze them to identify possible solutions and consequences. They evaluate options in order to choose the best solution. In addition, they apply learning techniques to develop new knowledge and skills for the job.

Management Skills. Management skills are important even when you don't hold a management position. No matter what your job is, you are more effective when you can manage these resources:

- **Time.** Carefully plan and prioritize what you need to accomplish. Prepare and follow schedules to help you meet goals. Avoid such time-wasters as procrastination and disorganization.
- **Space.** Keep your work space organized and avoid holding on to things you no longer need.
- **Materials.** Keep track of the supplies you have and request new ones before you run out. Keep materials organized so you can find them quickly.

- **Staff.** If you are in charge of a team, delegate responsibilities to those who are best able to handle them. Make sure employees are given the authority they need to carry out assigned tasks. Hold regular meetings with your team to keep track of what people are doing and smooth over any conflicts.
- **Money.** Prepare and use budgets to make sure your costs do not exceed the company's ability to pay. Keep track of spending on a project, and make adjustments as needed to stay within the budget.

Teamwork

If you work well with others, you have a valuable workplace skill. Teamwork exists in many work environments. The best teams combine the knowledge and skills of individual members to make the group function better as a whole. Team members divide responsibilities based on who is best qualified for each task.

All members do their share and pitch in to help others who may fall behind. Members stay in touch with team goals. Above all, they treat each other respectfully. See Fig. CG-19.

Respect. The key to teamwork is mutual respect. Team members must be willing to put aside their differences. They work effectively with people of different ages, backgrounds, abilities, and attitudes. Instead of concentrating on differences, they focus on what each team member contributes to the group.

Conflict Resolution. For teams to function well, they must resolve conflicts that arise. To deal with disputes successfully, be willing to consider other views and compromise. Try to work together to find a solution that satisfies everyone. If you cannot reach a solution, seek your supervisor's help. Most of all, avoid personal attacks. Focus on the issues in the conflict, not on the personalities involved.

Fig. CG-19. The old saying "Two heads are better than one" is the principle behind teamwork. **How does this apply to ideas as well as workload?**

Fig. CG-20. In the work world, leadership is a responsibility that comes with certain positions. **How could someone who isn't a designated leader also show those skills?**

Leadership Skills. Often a team works well thanks to an effective team leader. Again, it is not only managers who display leadership skills. In any position, a person might occasionally take charge of a group or simply guide a coworker. Anyone can benefit from learning to lead.

The best leaders communicate well with others. Instead of imposing their own views on everyone, they encourage team members to contribute ideas. They always listen with respect. When a situation calls for it, however, they can make a firm decision. In addition, they delegate tasks effectively to make the most of each team member's skills and abilities. See Fig. CG-20.

Ethics in the Workplace

Suppose you are a manager in a superstore. One day your boss says, "From now on, I want you to make all your workers put in extra hours without listing them on their time sheets. That way it won't cost the company any extra, and we can still meet all our quotas." Should you do what your boss asks? Dilemmas like this require an ethical response. Using *ethics*, you apply guidelines that help you distinguish right from wrong.

Ethical principles are involved in many situations. Deciding whether it's all right to use the office copier for personal business is a minor ethical decision. Deciding whether to "cook the books" to inflate a company's stock value is a major one. When faced with an ethical decision on the job, try asking yourself the following questions:

- Does my decision comply with the law?
- Is my decision fair to all involved?
- Will my decision harm anyone?
- Have I communicated my decision honestly?
- Can I enforce my decision without guilt, embarrassment, or regrets?
- Do I admit and take responsibility for my mistakes?

Work and Personal Life

You've probably already discovered that it can be difficult at times to manage the responsibilities you have at school as well as those in your personal life. Adding a career can complicate schedules even more. To cope with all the demands in life, call upon the skills you've learned. Use your resources and manage your time well. Try to solve problems before they become overwhelming. Ask for help when you need it. If stress enters the picture, remember to take care of your health with nutritious foods and exercise and make time for rest and relaxation. These actions can make all the difference in how you handle everyday pressures, and in turn, your success on the job. See Fig. CG-21.

Fig. CG-21. When work schedules and home responsibilities are both demanding, people often feel pressure to get everything done. **What are some suggestions for coping?**

Leaving a Job

In the ideal world, you leave one job for another that takes you closer to your career goals. Finding a new position before quitting the one you have typically makes a better impression on potential employers.

Maintaining good relations with employers and coworkers is worthwhile. They might become part of your professional network and references for your next job. To leave in good standing, give reasonable notice before you resign. Two weeks is standard. If possible, also help train your replacement.

Leaving a job under less than ideal circumstances is awkward. Although being fired or asked to resign doesn't reflect well, such events need not derail career plans. After all, people who were fired *do* get hired again. Learning from negative experiences shows growth.

What can be said at future interviews after a forced job loss? The best strategy is to acknowledge the problem. Certain workplace policies may have been troubling. Differences with a supervisor may have caused tension. Words should be chosen carefully when describing the situation. One interviewee said, "I felt that some of my supervisor's practices were unfair. I could either accept them or leave." This statement shows an objective view of the situation and takes responsibility for actions. If the person had said, "My boss always thought she was right," what would that have reflected?

When you think about leaving a job, consider the decision carefully. Many jobs are steppingstones toward your career goal. Evaluate a move in terms of how it can take you where you want to go in the world of work.

Fig. CG-22. Training classes teach new information and methods to use on the job. Learning more about how to work with children who have disabilities will help these people be more effective as special education teachers.

Lifelong Learning

During your work life, you may change jobs, or even careers, many times. With each new position, you acquire new skills and possibly refresh some that you haven't used in a while. Even if you stay in the same job all your life, continually expanding your knowledge and skills enables you to keep up with changing times.

Fortunately, there are many ways to continue your education after entering the workforce. One way is to take seminars and training classes at your workplace. Some companies offer these classes so employees can gain knowledge and skills that will help them on the job. For example, workers might take a class to learn about new software or to gain in-depth knowledge about some aspect of the industry. See Fig. CG-22.

Another option is *continuing education*—school courses aimed at working adults. In some cases, employers pay for courses that make workers more effective on the job. Even if you must pay the costs, however, continuing your education may be worthwhile. If you want to advance in your career or gain skills to work in a new field, more education may help you pave the way.

Glossary

A

abstinence Refraining from any form of sexual activity. (Ch. 3)

accredited Recognized by a specific organization as meeting certain high standards of quality. (Ch. 28)

active listening A technique of listening that actively draws people out and acknowledges their feelings. Active listeners try to understand both verbal and nonverbal messages without attempting to judge or correct. (Ch. 21)

adoption A legal process by which people acquire the rights and responsibilities of parenthood for children who are not biologically their own. (Ch. 6, 7)

adoptive parents Persons who accept legal responsibility for children who were not born to them, raising them as their own. (Ch. 1)

advocates Persons who speak up to defend another's welfare and rights. Parents are a child's primary advocates. (Ch. 25)

ambidextrous (am-beh-DEK-struhs) Able to use both hands equally well to perform activities. (Ch. 15)

amniocentesis (am-nee-oh-sen-TEE-suhs) A prenatal test that involves removing a small amount of the amniotic fluid that surrounds the developing fetus. (Ch. 8)

amniotic fluid (am-nee-AH-tik) Fluid that cushions a developing baby from outside pressures. (Ch. 8)

anemia A condition in which there are too few red blood cells in the body. (Ch. 9)

anesthetic (an-ess-THET-ik) A medication that causes loss of sensation. (Ch. 11)

anorexia nervosa An eating disorder that involves an extreme urge to lose weight by self-starvation. (Ch. 18)

anxiety disorder A disorder in which anxiety (worry and fear) becomes so extreme that it interferes with everyday life. (Ch. 18)

Apgar scale A system used to rate an infant's physical condition minutes after delivery to detect any problems that require immediate emergency treatment. (Ch. 11)

articulation The ability to pronounce words clearly. (Ch. 17)

assertiveness Behavior that shows equal respect for oneself and others. (Ch. 19)

attachment behavior Behavior that indicates an infant is beginning to recognize and trust his or her caregivers. Typically occurs between three and six months of age. (Ch. 13)

attention deficit hyperactivity disorder (ADHD) A disorder in which children have trouble controlling their behavior or paying attention. (Ch. 25)

au pair (oh PARE) A young person from another country who lives with a family and cares for their children. Au pairs typically receive room and board plus a small salary. (Ch. 28)

autism A type of pervasive developmental disorder. Children with autism do not communicate well, lack the desire to be held or cuddled, do not respond to affection or engage in imaginative play, and often show repetitive patterns of behavior, interests, and activities. (Ch. 25)

B

baby blues Periods of negative feelings that many new mothers experience in the days and weeks following childbirth. (Ch. 12)

babysitting cooperative A group of parents who share child care responsibilities. Members of the cooperative "earn" and "spend" hours of child care, calling on one another as needed. (Ch. 28)

bilingual Able to speak two languages. (Ch. 17)

biological parents The parents to which a child is born. (Ch. 1)

birth coach A person who helps a woman through the birth process. (Ch. 10)

birth defect An abnormality that is present at or before birth and results in mental or physical disability. (Ch. 8)

birthing center A facility designed specifically to provide a homelike environment for giving birth. May be a special part of a hospital, a separate building affiliated with a hospital, or an independent facility run by a health care provider. (Ch. 10)

birthing room A homelike room, provided in some hospitals, in which a woman can remain before, during, and after giving birth. (Ch. 10)

birth plan A list of preferences concerning birth options, such as whether the woman will receive pain medication. (Ch. 10)

blended family A family formed when a single parent marries. May include each spouse's children from previous marriages, as well as new children of the couple. (Ch. 1, 27)

bonding The process of forming an attachment, or feeling of close connection, between parent and child. (Ch. 11)

breech presentation A situation in which an unborn baby, close to the time of delivery, is positioned with the feet or buttocks closest to the cervix, rather than the normal head-down position. (Ch. 11)

budget A plan for saving and spending money that helps individuals and families meet their financial goals. (Ch. 26)

bulimia nervosa An eating disorder during which bouts of extreme eating are followed by vomiting or taking laxatives to lose what was eaten. (Ch. 18)

bullying Behaviors ranging from verbal taunts, threats, and intimidation to deliberate physical injury. (Ch. 19)

C

caregivers Persons in parenting roles who care for and guide children. (Ch. 1)

centration The ability to focus on only one quality at a time. (Ch. 17)

certified nurse-midwife A professional trained to care for women with low-risk pregnancies and to deliver their babies. (Ch. 9)

cesarean delivery (si-SAIR-ee-in) A procedure in which a baby is delivered through a surgical opening in the mother's abdomen. Sometimes called a *C-section*. (Ch. 11)

character Moral strength to do what is right. Persons with character show qualities such as respect, fairness, trustworthiness, and responsibility through their words and actions. (Ch. 22)

charter schools Alternative public schools established by a charter, or written grant of rights, from the state. In exchange for meeting certain performance standards, they are given some independence from the rules that other public schools must follow. (Ch. 28)

child abuse Intentional or neglectful physical, emotional, or sexual injury to a child. (Ch. 2)

child care center A facility with a trained staff that provides supervised group child care and socializing experiences. (Ch. 28)

child care power of attorney A legal document through which a parent temporarily gives an agent the power to act in his or her place. (Ch. 2)

child neglect Failure to meet a child's basic physical and emotional needs. (Ch. 2)

child support Regular payments made by one parent to the other after a divorce to help pay the expenses of raising children who are minors. (Ch. 27)

chorionic villi sampling (CORE-ee-on-ik VILL-eye) A prenatal test that involves taking a sample of cells from the placenta. (Ch. 8)

chronic Term used to describe an illness that lasts a long time or that frequently recurs. Examples include allergies, asthma, and diabetes. (Ch. 16)

circumcision (sur-kuhm-SIH-zhun) A surgical procedure performed on some newborn males in which part of the foreskin is cut away from the tip of the penis. (Ch. 11)

citizenship A person's membership and participation in a particular group, such as a nation, school, or family. (Ch. 22)

classification A method of organizing information that involves grouping objects by common traits. (Ch. 17)

clique A small, exclusive friendship group that restricts who can join. (Ch. 19)

closed adoption An adoption in which the birth parents remain anonymous and do not have contact with the child after the adoption takes place. (Ch. 6)

cognitive impairments Disabilities that result in significantly below-average intelligence and skills in self-care and communication. (Ch. 25)

colic Discomfort that causes infants to cry for several hours at a stretch with no apparent cause. (Ch. 14)

colostrum (kuh-LAHS-trum) The first breast milk; a yellow fluid that a new mother produces for a few days after delivery. Colostrum is rich in nutrients and helps protect newborns from infection. (Ch. 11, 14)

communication The process of sharing information, thoughts, and feelings. (Ch. 21)

compassion Demonstration of care and concern for another. (Ch. 22)

compromise An agreement in which each person gets some, but not all, of what he or she wants. (Ch. 5)

conception The uniting of male and female reproductive cells after sexual intercourse. (Ch. 7)

concepts General mental categories of objects or ideas. (Ch. 17)

congenital Present at birth but not inherited from parents. (Ch. 25)

conscience (KAHN-shens) An inner sense of right and wrong that prompts good behavior and causes feelings of guilt about bad behavior. (Ch. 22)

consensus An agreement that is acceptable to everyone involved. (Ch. 5)

conservation The principle that an object's physical properties stay the same even when its appearance changes. (Ch. 17)

constructive play A type of play that involves using materials to achieve a specific goal or purpose, such as building a tower with blocks. (Ch. 20)

contraception The use of drugs, devices, or techniques to prevent pregnancy. Also called *birth control*. (Ch. 7)

contraction A tightening of the uterus muscles followed by relaxation of the muscles. (Ch. 11)

conventions Socially accepted standards of behavior. (Ch. 22)

convulsions Strong and involuntary contractions of the muscles; may occur in children who have a high fever. (Ch. 16)

cooperative play A type of play in which children interact and cooperate with one another. (Ch. 19)

CPR Cardiopulmonary resuscitation; a technique used to keep a person's heart and lungs functioning until medical care arrives. (Ch. 16)

cradle cap An oily, yellowish, patchy scalp condition some infants develop. (Ch. 14)

credentials Evidence, such as degrees or certification, that a person is qualified to perform a specific service. (Ch. 28)

crisis A change that causes severe stress and is so overwhelming that one's usual coping mechanisms are not enough. (Ch. 27)

cultural bias Making assumptions, based on one's own culture, to judge and predict people's behavior. (Ch. 19)

culture The customs and traditions of a specific group of people. (Ch. 1)

custody Responsibility for providing a home for children. After a divorce, one parent may have *sole custody* or two parents may have *shared custody*. (Ch. 27)

D

demand feeding The practice of feeding infants whenever they are hungry, rather than keeping a fixed schedule. (Ch. 14)

development A process that includes physical growth as well as progress in skills and abilities. (Ch. 4)

developmental screening A process that medical professionals use to determine whether a child is developing at a normal pace. Often included in routine checkups for children under five years of age. (Ch. 16)

diaper rash A skin irritation caused by contact with stool or urine in the diaper, diaper material, or laundry products. (Ch. 14)

disability Any physical, mental, or emotional condition that limits one or more major life activities to a large extent. (Ch. 25)

discipline Guidance that helps children learn to behave appropriately. It involves teaching and promoting positive behavior and discouraging negative behavior. (Ch. 23)

dominant Term describing the stronger of two genetic traits. If a child receives a dominant gene and a recessive gene for a trait such as eye color, the dominant one will be expressed. (Ch. 7)

dovetail To go back and forth between the steps of two or more different tasks, such as washing dishes and making soup. (Ch. 26)

dramatic play A type of play in which children assume different identities and take part in make-believe events. (Ch. 20)

dyslexia (dis-LEK-see-uh) A type of learning disorder that causes children to have difficulty with such skills as recognizing words, spelling, and decoding letters into sounds. (Ch. 25)

E

early intervention The process of identifying and providing for a child's special needs as soon as possible. (Ch. 25)

ectopic pregnancy Pregnancy in which the fertilized egg implants outside the uterus, usually in the fallopian tube. Also called a *tubal pregnancy*. (Ch. 8)

egocentric Self-centered; not capable of thinking beyond oneself or seeing another person's point of view. (Ch. 18)

emancipated Freed from parental controls and support. Children are usually emancipated when they turn 18 years of age. (Ch. 2)

embryo (EM-bree-oh) The developing baby from the time of implantation into the uterine wall through about the eighth week of pregnancy. (Ch. 8)

emotional development The area of development that involves learning to recognize feelings and express them appropriately. (Ch. 4)

emotional maturity The ability to understand and act on one's emotions at an adult level of development. (Ch. 3)

empathy Awareness of other people's needs and feelings. (Ch. 18, 22)

enuresis (en-you-REE-sis) A medical term for lack of urinary control. (Ch. 15)

environment All the conditions and circumstances affecting a person's daily life. (Ch. 4)

episiotomy (eh-pee-zee-OTT-uh-mee) A surgical cut made to widen the vaginal opening during labor. (Ch. 11)

ethical choice A decision for action based on one's moral values and principles. (Ch. 22)

exploratory play A type of play in which children use their senses to learn about the world around them. (Ch. 20)

extended family A family including relatives other than parents and children. (Ch. 1)

eye-hand coordination The ability to perceive and manipulate objects in space. (Ch. 15)

F

facilitate To aid children's play without giving them specific instructions. (Ch. 20)

fallopian tubes (fuh-LOH-pee-uhn) The two tubes through which eggs pass on their way from an ovary to the uterus. (Ch. 7)

family child care An arrangement in which an individual uses his or her own home as a place to provide care for other people's children. (Ch. 28)

family life cycle A series of seven stages that many families go through, including the individual stage, marriage, childbearing, parenting, launching, middle years, and senior years. (Ch. 1)

family violence Violent, threatening behavior used by a family member to intimidate or control one or more members of the family. Sometimes called *domestic violence*. (Ch. 27)

fetal alcohol disorders Serious problems in an infant resulting from the mother's use of alcohol during pregnancy. (Ch. 9)

fetal monitor A device that allows medical staff to keep track of the fetus's heart rate during labor and watch for signs of stress. (Ch. 11)

fetus (FEE-tuhs) The developing baby from the beginning of the ninth week of pregnancy until birth. (Ch. 8)

first aid Immediate care provided for a serious injury until medical help arrives. (Ch. 16)

flame resistant Treated with chemicals that will self-extinguish if they catch fire. (Ch. 15)

flextime An arrangement in which employers allow employees to chose their own work hours, within certain limits. (Ch. 26)

fontanels (fahn-tuh-NELZ) The areas between the bone plates of a newborn's skull. During birth, they allow the head to change shape as it squeezes through the birth canal; later they allow the head to grow. (Ch. 13)

foster parents Adults who temporarily accept responsibility and provide care for children who would not otherwise have a safe, secure home. (Ch. 1, 7)

G–H

genetic disorders Medical conditions caused by errors in genes or chromosomes. (Ch. 7)

genetics The study of how traits are passed from parent to child through heredity. (Ch. 7)

gifted Demonstrating, or having the potential to demonstrate, an unusually high level of performance in one or more areas. (Ch. 25)

growth spurts Periods during which a child grows quickly. (Ch. 15)

guardian A person appointed by the court to take legal responsibility for a child when the child's parents have died or are unable to provide care. (Ch. 2)

heredity The biological process by which certain traits are transmitted from parents to their children. (Ch. 4, 7)

I

"I" messages Messages that express how someone else's behavior affects you, without labeling the behavior as good or bad or attacking the other person. (Ch. 21)

immunizations Doses of vaccine given by injection (shots) or by mouth to protect infants and children from specific diseases. (Ch. 14)

incidental learning Unplanned learning that stems from other activities. (Ch. 17)

inclusion The educational practice of mixing children with and without special needs in the same classroom. (Ch. 25)

in-family adoption A situation in which a child is adopted by a grandparent or other member(s) of the extended family. (Ch. 6)

infancy The stage of child development from birth to 12 months of age. (Ch. 4)

infant formula A commercially prepared mixture of milk or milk substitute, water, and added nutrients; used to nourish bottle-fed babies. (Ch. 10, 14)

infertile Unable to conceive a child after trying for 12 months. (Ch. 7)

intellectual development The area of development that involves the ways children develop language, solve problems, and remember what they learn. (Ch. 4)

J–K–L

jaundice A fairly common medical problem that occurs when a newborn's liver is not yet able to break down a substance called *bilirubin*, causing the skin to have a yellowish tint. (Ch. 11)

job sharing An arrangement in which two workers share the duties, hours, and pay of one job. (Ch. 26)

labor The process of giving birth. (Ch. 11)

large motor skills Physical skills that use the large muscle groups, such as those in the back, legs, and arms. Also called *gross motor skills*. (Ch. 13, 15)

learning centers Clearly defined areas for different sorts of activities, as in a child care center. (Ch. 28)

learning disorders Disabilities that affect children's ability either to interpret what they see and hear or to link information from different parts of the brain. (Ch. 25)

learning style A preferred method of taking in and processing information. For example, some people learn best by seeing information written down; others by hearing information. (Ch. 17)

licensed Having written permission from a governing body to operate. In many states, certain types of child care programs must be licensed by a state agency. (Ch. 28)

limits Rules that define the boundary between acceptable and unacceptable behavior. (Ch. 23)

lochia (LO-kee-uh) The normal discharge of blood, tissue, and mucus from the vagina following childbirth. (Ch. 12)

logical consequences Results of negative behavior that are imposed by the parent and make sense in relation to the undesirable behavior. (Ch. 24)

low birth weight A weight of less than 5 pounds, 8 ounces at birth; associated with many health risks. (Ch. 6)

M

magnet schools Public schools with a distinctive focus, such as science or the performing arts, designed to attract a diverse group of interested students and families. (Ch. 28)

manual dexterity The ability to manipulate objects with the hands. (Ch. 15)

materialism The belief that money and possessions bring happiness. (Ch. 26)

mediator An impartial third party who provides guidance to help settle a dispute. (Ch. 5)

mentoring Serving as a trusted guide, usually for someone younger or less experienced. Parents, teachers, coaches, or older siblings can mentor children. (Ch. 5)

miscarriage Spontaneous loss of a pregnancy before the twentieth week of prenatal development. (Ch. 6, 8)

moral development The area of development that involves learning to distinguish between right and wrong. (Ch. 4, 22)

motor skills Abilities that depend on the controlled use of muscles. (Ch. 13)

multitask To do two or more things at the same time, such as folding laundry while listening to a radio talk show. (Ch. 26)

N

nanny Someone unrelated to the family who takes care of a child or children in the parents' home. A nanny is often a trained professional and may receive room and board in addition to a salary. (Ch. 28)

natural consequences Results of negative behavior that follow naturally from the behavior, without being imposed by a parent or caregiver. For example, a toy that is left out in the rain will get wet. (Ch. 24)

negativism Opposition; frequently saying no. Toddlers usually go through a period of negativism as a way of expressing their growing independence. (Ch. 18)

negotiation Discussing a conflict in order to reach an acceptable solution. (Ch. 5)

neurons Nerve cells in the brain. They branch and grow into dense, connective networks through which information is transmitted. (Ch. 17)

nonverbal communication A form of communication in which messages are sent with the tone of voice, eye contact, gestures, facial expressions, and body language. (Ch. 21)

nuclear family A family made up of a mother, a father, and one or more children. (Ch. 1)

nurture To provide the type of care that encourages healthy growth and development. (Ch. 2)

nutrient dense Having calories that are packed with plenty of important nutrients. Examples of nutrient-dense foods include fruits, vegetables, whole grains, legumes, lean meats, and low-fat dairy products. (Ch. 9)

O

object permanence The concept that objects continue to exist even when they are out of sight. (Ch. 13)

obstetrician (OB-stuh-TRISH-uhn) A medical doctor who specializes in pregnancy and delivery. (Ch. 9)

open adoption An adoption in which the birth parents can maintain a close relationship with the child and the adoptive family. (Ch. 6)

orthodontist (OR-thuh-DON-tist) A dentist who specializes in straightening and realigning teeth. (Ch. 16)

orthopedic impairments Disabilities that affect any or all parts of a person's skeletal system, including limbs, bones, muscles, and joints. (Ch. 25)

ovaries (OH-vuh-reez) The two oval-shaped female reproductive organs in which ova are produced and stored. (Ch. 7)

ovulation Process in which a mature ovum is released by an ovary. (Ch. 7)

P–Q

parallel play A type of play in which children play side-by-side, observing and imitating each other's movements but not interacting or cooperating. (Ch. 19)

parental leave A parent's paid or unpaid time off the job after the birth or adoption of a child. Sometimes referred to as *maternity leave* for the mother and *paternity leave* for the father. (Ch. 10)

parent cooperative A child care center or preschool owned and administered by the parents of the children who attend. The parents hire staff, set program goals, and volunteer several hours a month. (Ch. 28)

parenting Providing care, support, and guidance that can lead to a child's healthy development. (Ch. 1)

parenting style A general approach to raising children. The three broad parenting styles include authoritarian, authoritative, and permissive. (Ch. 5)

paternity Biological fatherhood. (Ch. 6)

pediatrician (PEE-dee-uh-TRISH-un) A doctor who specializes in the treatment of infants, children, and adolescents. (Ch. 10)

peer pressure Social pressure to conform or behave in certain ways in order to be accepted by peers. (Ch. 19)

peers People who are about the same age. (Ch. 19)

pervasive developmental disorders A group of disorders that involve delays in the development of social skills and communication skills. (Ch. 25)

physical development The area of development that involves growth in size and weight, along with increasing ability to control and coordinate body movements. (Ch. 4)

pincer grasp The ability to take hold of small objects between thumb and forefinger. (Ch. 13)

placenta (pluh-SENT-uh) Tissue that is attached to the uterine wall, contains a rich network of blood vessels, and is connected to the developing baby by the umbilical cord. (Ch. 8)

play group An informal child care arrangement organized by friends or neighbors. A group of children play together for a few hours each week, and parents take turns watching the children on assigned days. (Ch. 28)

positive guidance Another name for discipline; guidance that helps children learn to behave appropriately. (Ch. 23)

positive reinforcement A response to a desired behavior that makes the behavior likely to be repeated. (Ch. 23)

postpartum depression A mood disorder that sometimes occurs within a year after giving birth. It is marked by negative feelings strong enough to interfere with daily life for an extended period of time. (Ch. 12)

potential The ability to reach a certain level of achievement. (Ch. 2)

preeclampsia (pree-uh-CLAMP-see-uh) A disorder affecting 5 to 10 percent of pregnant women that involves high blood pressure, protein in the urine, and fluid retention. Also called *toxemia* or *pregnancy-induced hypertension*. (Ch. 9)

prejudice A negative opinion that is not based on fact or experience. (Ch. 19)

premature birth The birth of a baby before the thirty-seventh week of pregnancy. (Ch. 6, 8)

prenatal care Health care given during pregnancy. (Ch. 6, 9)

prenatal development The process by which a baby-to-be grows inside the mother. (Ch. 8)

prepared childbirth An approach to giving birth in which the expectant parents understand and take an active role in the birth process. (Ch. 10)

preschoolers Children who are three, four, or five years of age. (Ch. 4)

prioritize To set priorities, such as ranking activities, by deciding what you consider most important. (Ch. 5, 26)

proactive Taking actions to prevent problems before they arise. (Ch. 5)

puberty The stage of physical development when sexual reproduction first becomes possible. (Ch. 4, 15)

puréed Blended into a smooth consistency. (Ch. 14)

R

recessive Term describing the weaker of two genetic traits. Recessive traits are expressed in a child only if the gene for that trait is inherited from both the father and the mother. (Ch. 7)

redirection Distracting a child from an activity in order to prevent negative behavior. (Ch. 23)

reflexes Automatic responses to stimulation. (Ch. 13)

regressive behavior Patterns of behavior that children had previously outgrown, such as bedwetting, thumb-sucking, or refusal to sleep alone, which may reemerge during a family crisis. (Ch. 27)

repetitive play A type of play that involves performing an activity over and over. Repetitive play helps infants learn about cause and effect. (Ch. 20)

resource Anything that can be used to meet a need or to help achieve a goal. (Ch. 5)

restitution The act of paying back a loss in some way, as when a child returns or replaces a stolen item or repays with cash. (Ch. 24)

reversibility The principle that something which has been changed (such as water that has been poured into a differently shaped container) can be changed back to its original state. (Ch. 17)

Rh factor A protein found in the blood of some people. If the blood has this factor, the person has a positive blood type; if not, the person has a negative blood type. (Ch. 9)

role conflicts Clashes that occur when one role, such as employee, negatively affects another role, such as parent. (Ch. 26)

rooming-in The practice of allowing a newborn baby to be cared for in the mother's room rather than in the hospital nursery. (Ch. 11)

S

self-assessment The process of examining one's personal qualities, goals, and plans. (Ch. 3)

self-care children Children who are regularly left at home without adult supervision for a few hours, such as after school. Also called *latchkey children*. (Ch. 28)

self-discipline The ability to manage one's own behavior. (Ch. 23)

self-esteem Positive feelings about oneself. (Ch. 3, 13, 18)

self-image The way you view yourself. Also called *self-concept*. (Ch. 18)

semi-open adoption An adoption in which the birth parents can monitor the child's progress by receiving pictures and letters through the adoption agency or a mediator. (Ch. 6)

sensorimotor period According to Piaget, the first major period of intellectual development, from birth to about age two, when infants and toddlers use their senses and movement to explore and learn about their surroundings. (Ch. 13)

separation anxiety A stress that infants or toddlers feel when separated from familiar people, usually parents. (Ch. 18)

seriation A method of organizing information that involves arranging objects in order by size or number. (Ch. 17)

sexually transmitted diseases (STDs) Infections that are spread through sexual contact. Also called *sexually transmitted infections (STIs)*. (Ch. 3)

shock A dangerous drop in blood flow caused by serious injury. (Ch. 16)

sibling rivalry Competition between brothers and sisters. (Ch. 19)

single-parent family A family made up of one parent and that parent's children. (Ch. 1)

sliding scale A set of rates that vary according to a family's ability to pay. (Ch. 28)

small motor skills Physical skills that involve the small muscle groups, such as those in the fingers, wrists, and ankles. Also called *fine motor skills*. (Ch. 13, 15)

social development The area of development that involves learning to relate to other people. (Ch. 4)

socialization The process of teaching children how to get along well in society. (Ch. 19)

sperm The male reproductive cells. (Ch. 7)

sphincter muscles (SFINK-tuhr) The muscles in the bowel and bladder regions that regulate elimination. (Ch. 15)

stepparent A parent gained when one of a child's original parents remarries. (Ch. 1)

stereotype A fixed, oversimplified mental image of a group of people. (Ch. 19)

stillbirth The death of a fetus (unborn baby) after the twentieth week of pregnancy. (Ch. 6, 8)

stranger anxiety A stage occurring between six and ten months of age during which infants fear unfamiliar people. (Ch. 13)

sudden infant death syndrome (SIDS) The death of a baby under one year old with no known cause. (Ch. 14)

symbolic play A type of play in which common objects become symbols for whatever children imagine. (Ch. 20)

synapses Connections between neurons. (Ch. 17)

T

telecommute To work from home while staying in touch with a central office using technology such as telephones, computers, and fax machines. (Ch. 26)

temperament The general way in which an individual reacts to the world. (Ch. 13)

temper tantrum A fit of anger accompanied by crying, screaming, hitting, or kicking; common in toddlers. (Ch. 18)

termination of parental rights A court order that permanently severs all rights, powers, privileges, immunities, duties, and obligations between parent and child. May be issued when parents neglect their legal responsibility of caring for their children. (Ch. 2)

testes (TES-teez) The two oval-shaped male reproductive organs that produce and store sperm. (Ch. 7)

theory A set of ideas based on observations and analysis. (Ch. 4)

toddlers One- and two-year-old children. (Ch. 4)

transition A phase in which the woman's contractions intensify toward the end of the first stage of labor. (Ch. 11)

trimesters Three-month time periods into which a pregnancy is divided. (Ch. 8)

U–V

ultrasound imaging A process that uses sound waves to create video and still images of a fetus inside the uterus. (Ch. 8)

umbilical cord (uhm-BILL-ih-kuhl) Cord that connects the developing baby to the placenta. (Ch. 8)

uterus (YOO-tuh-russ) The female reproductive organ, located near the ovaries, in which an unborn baby develops; the womb. (Ch. 7)

vaccines Preparations containing a small amount of a dead or weakened disease germ. They allow the body to form defenses against the germ without getting sick. (Ch. 14)

values Strongly held beliefs and ideas about what is important. (Ch. 1, 22)

vernix (VUR-niks) A greasy white material covering the skin of newborns. (Ch. 11)

W–X–Y–Z

weaning The gradual process of replacing bottle-feeding or breast-feeding with drinking from a cup. (Ch. 14)

wellness An approach to life that emphasizes taking positive steps toward overall good health. (Ch. 16)

WIC program A government program designed to help pregnant women, new mothers, infants, and children who are at risk for poor nutrition due to low income or other factors. (Ch. 6)

work ethic The belief that work is valuable and beneficial. (Ch. 22, 26)

zygote (ZIE-goat) The earliest stage of human prenatal development. (Ch. 8)

Credits

Ann's Portrait Designs/
Ann Garvin 17TR, 627
Arnold & Brown 78
Articulate Graphics/Joel &
Sharon Harris 148, 149, 170T
Roger B. Bean 589, 599
Keith Berry 586
Bokelberg, 48
Circle Design/Carol Spengle
150, 168, 171, 233
Ken Clubb 348, 349BL, 349BR,
349TL, 349TR
Corbis 10TM, 69, 76, 77, 146,
157, 163, 174, 236, 262,
268TR, 269, 282, 293, 325,
338, 350, 471, 484, 499,
528, 561, 566, 598, 608, 611,
620, 623
Jim Arbogast 128
G. Baden/Zefa 314TL
Paul Barton 11T, 29, 66, 70,
212, 275, 314BR, 316,
440-441, 506, 610, 626
Peter Barton 105
Joe Bator 562
Bettmann, 85, 86, 89B
Ed Bock 17BR, 75, 414, 444,
585, 591
S. Borges/Zefa 602
Gary Braesch 383
Cameron 235
Cats & Withoos/Zefa 213
Marco Cauz 60
Steve Chen 38
Joyce Choo 342
L. Clark 36
Bryan Cotton 127
Jim Craigmyle 91

Darama 447
Howard Davies 28
Leslie & Mark Degner
12BC, 371
Dex Images 344
DiMaggio/Kalish 343
George Disaris 8TL, 159, 558
Laura Dwight 265B, 268BR
Tim Dwight 362
Paul Edmonson 621T
Randy Faris 71, 498
Jon Feingersh 40, 625/Zefa
Owen Franken 230
Patrik Giardino 218, 391
Rob Goldman 292
Rick Gomez 306
Cal Gwynn 238
H&S Produktion 510
Blaine Harrington 9BR, 240
Elizabeth Hathon 320
Lindsay Hebberd 273
John Henley 554
Julian Hirschowitz 424, 550
Walter Hodges 265T
Ted Horowitz 277
Hurewitz Creative 407
A. Inden/Zefa 291, 571
JDC/502
JFPI Studios 13TR, 403
JLP/Sylvia Torres 118
Alan Jakubek 309
Sean Justice 15BL, 480
Tracy Kahn, 221T
U. Kaiser & Kate Mitchell/
Zefa 15BR, 481, 490
Ronnie Kaufman 112, 442
Michael Kellar 17TL, 186,
569, 588
Layne Kennedy 231
Sharie Kennedy/Zefa 492
Robert Landau 37
Lester Lefkowitz 226
Rob Lewine 14BR, 106,
200, 474

Lightscapes Photography,
Inc. 395
Don Mason 217, 264,
268TC, 313TL
Tom & DeeAnn McCarthy
35, 44, 99, 462, 493
Will & Demi McIntyre 396
Mika/Zefa 576
Raoul Minsart 545
Paul Morris 246
Roy Morsch 507, 544
Mug Shots 16BR, 222, 542
L. Nelson/Zefa 621B
Gabe Palmer 10BL, 68, 89T,
108, 182, 241, 511 (Zefa),
522, 533, 574
Jose Luis Pelaez, Inc. 14BC,
47, 65, 72, 134, 136, 187,
208, 244, 250, 260-261,
285, 456, 552, 553, 609,
614, 624
Bryan F. Peterson 501
Mark Peterson 130, 256
PictureNet 56
Javier Pierini 58
Michael Pole 16TR, 526
Steve Prezant 129, 272, 344
David Raymer 177
Rob & Sas 500, 568
H. Armstrong Roberts 31
Norbert Schaefer 247,
300, 404
George Shelley 380
Ariel Skelley 5, 6, 7BL,
13TL, 30, 33, 84, 104,
116, 142-143, 192, 214,
223, 249, 307T, 374, 400,
417, 433, 436, 485, 531,
534, 535, 543, 546, 590
Steve Starr 73
Tom Stewart 12TM, 59,
90, 111B, 239, 255, 365,
393, 434
Ted Streshinsky 88

Dann Tardif-LWA 9TL, 97, 451, 467, 478, 606
Larry Williams 121, 397
Bob Winsett, 386
David Woods 15BC, 364, 491
Jennie Woodcock 290
Jeff Zaruba 53
Custom Medical Stock Photo 67
Tim Fuller 7BR, 8TR, 10TR, 11B, 12TL&TR, 12BL&BR, 14TL&BL, 16BL, 102, 107, 109, 110, 111T, 114, 115, 117, 119, 120, 132, 135, 137, 138, 147, 155, 158, 161, 162, 166, 206, 215, 220, 228, 229, 254, 274, 280, 284, 286, 295, 297, 299, 304, 308, 311, 313BR, 315, 318TR, 321, 323, 328, 330, 331, 335, 336, 337, 340, 341, 345, 347T, 356, 358, 360, 363, 366, 367, 378, 382, 385, 387, 388, 390, 392, 394, 408, 410, 411, 412, 413, 418, 422, 425, 428, 431, 436T, 448, 449, 450, 452, 453, 454, 463, 465, 488, 489, 538, 540, 541, 548, 549, 551, 565, 567, 570, 573, 575, 578, 582, 584
Dana White Productions 375, 457, 587
Getty Images
Adamsmith 518
Mark Andersen 555
Bruce Ayres 15T, 512, 564
Barros & Barros 523
Jon Bradley 419
Keith Brofsky 516
Nancy Brown 593
David Buffington 482
Tess Codrington 472
Stewart Cohen 613B
Comstock 22-23, 301
Jim Cummins 257, 409
Mel Curtis 8BC, 191
Ann Elliott Cutting 318BL
Donna Day 322

Ghislan & Marie David de Lossy 196
Digital Vision 10BR, 16TC, 17BL, 46, 160, 184, 271, 529, 619
Wayne Eastep 427
Eyewire 7TL, 32, 94
Garry Gay 24
Bob Goldman 185
Mark Hall 505
David W. Hamilton 49
Rusty Hill 198
Walter Hodges 39
Lucille Khornak 57
Michael Krasowitz 8TL, 188
Claudia Kunin 193
Kathi Lamm 4BR, 26
Ken Lax 618
Alan Levenson 601
Niki Mareschai 270
Ericka McConnell 203
Lawrence Migdale 14TR, 475
Rosanne Olson 508
Jose Luis Pelaez, Inc. 368
Barbara Penovar 201, 523
Plush Studios 339
PhotoDisc Collection 62, 221B, 597, 600
Tosca Radigonda 406
Stephanie Rausser 93, 251
Tamara Reynolds 416
Pascal Rondeau 504
Rubberball 496
Stephen Simpson 80
John Slater 190
Steve Satushek 4BL, 51
SW Productions 95, 486
Arthur Tilley 7TR, 34, 41, 83
Thinkstock 460
Tom Tracy 351
Roger Tully 211
Paul Vozdic 13B, 429
Wide Group 468
Ross Whitaker 509
David Woolley 513
Yellow Dog Productions 55
David Young-Wolff 607

Masterfile
Matt Brazier 10TL, 294
Rolf Bruderer 216
Wayne Eardley 175
Kathleen Finlay 332
Rick Gomez 560
Grace/Zefa 415
Michael Kellar 8, BR124, 172
Horst Herget 139
A. Inden/Zefa 9TR, 253
Chad Johnston 248
Michael Mahovitch 369
Tim Mantoani 455
Alison Barnes Martin 268TL, BL
Ray Ooms 298
Tim Pannell 289
Rommel 126
David Schmidt 252
George Shelley 152
Ariel Skelley 354-355, 426
Wei Yen 287
Larry Williams 144
Kevin May 594
PhotoEdit/Tony Freeman 194
PhotoResearchers, Inc. 524
Alex Bartel 170BR
BSIP 179
John Cole 437
A.I. DuPont Institute 521
John Giannicchi 169
Pascal Goetgheluck 151
Richard Hutchings 520
Ruth Jenkinson/Midirs 9BL, 210
Lawrence Migdale 16TL, 532
Hank Morgan 131
Jim Reed 577
Lauren Shear 530
Stanford News Service/Linda A. Cicero 87B
StockFood/Eising 50, 156, 199
Jeff Stoecker 133
USDA 133

Index